D0397515

ON THE BORDER
WITH CROOK

JOHN G. BOURKE
CAPTAIN, THIRD CAVALRY, U.S.A.

A
BISON
BOOK

UNIVERSITY OF NEBRASKA PRESS · LINCOLN

TO FRANCIS PARKMAN,

*whose learned and graceful pen has illustrated the History,
Traditions, Wonders and Resources of the Great West, this
volume,—descriptive of the trials and tribulations, hopes and
fears of brave officers and enlisted men of the regular Army,
who did so much to conquer and develop the empire beyond the
Missouri,—is affectionately inscribed by his admirer and friend,*

JOHN G. BOURKE

Omaha, Nebraska,
August 12, 1891

International Standard Book Number 0–8032–5741–4

Library of Congress Catalog Card Number 74–155699

First Bison Book printing: September 1971

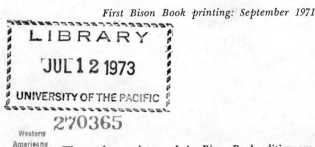
The preface and text of the Bison Book edition are reproduced
from the 1891 edition, published by Charles Scribner's Sons.

Manufactured in the United States of America

PREFACE.

THERE is an old saw in the army which teaches that you can never know a man until after having made a scout with him in bad weather. All the good qualities and bad in the human make-up force their way to the surface under the stimulus of privation and danger, and it not infrequently happens that the comrade who at the military post was most popular, by reason of charm of manner and geniality, returns from this trial sadly lowered in the estimation of his fellows, and that he who in the garrison was most retiring, self-composed, and least anxious to make a display of glittering uniform, has swept all before him by the evidence he has given of fortitude, equanimity, courage, coolness, and good judgment under circumstances of danger and distress. But, whether the maxim be true or false, it is hardly too much for me to claim a hearing while I recall all that I know of a man with whom for more than fifteen years, it was my fortune to be intimately associated in all the changing vicissitudes which constituted service on the "border" of yesterday, which has vanished never to return.

It is not my purpose to write a biography of my late friend and commander—such a task I leave for others to whom it may be more congenial; speaking for myself, I am compelled to say that it is always difficult for me to peruse biography of any kind, especially military, and that which I do not care to read I do not care to ask others to read. In the present volume, there will be found collected descriptions of the regions in which the major portion of General Crook's Indian work was carried on; the people, both red and white, with whom he was brought into contact ; the difficulties with which he had to contend, and the manner in which he overcame them ; and a short sketch of the principles guiding him in his justly famous intercourse with the various tribes—from British America to Mexico, from the Missouri River to the Pacific Ocean—subjugated by him and afterwards placed under his charge.

A military service of nearly forty consecutive years—all of which, excepting the portion spent in the civil war, had been face to face with the most difficult problems of the Indian question, and with the fiercest and most astute of all the tribes of savages encountered by the Caucasian in his conquering advance across the continent—made General Crook in every way worthy of the eulogy pronounced upon him by the grizzled old veteran, General William T. Sherman, upon hearing of his death, that he was the greatest Indian-fighter and manager the army of the United States ever had.

In all the campaigns which made the name of George Crook a beacon of hope to the settler and a terror to the tribes in hostility, as well as in all the efforts which he so successfully made for the elevation of the red man in the path of civilization and which showed that Crook was not a brutal soldier with no instincts save those for slaughter, but possessed of wonderful tenderness and commiseration for the vanquished as well as a most intelligent appreciation of the needs and capabilities of the aborigines, I was by his side, a member of his military staff, and thus obtained an insight into the charms and powers of a character which equalled that of any of the noble sons of whom our country is so justly proud.

CONTENTS.

ON THE BORDER WITH CROOK

CHAPTER I.

OLD CAMP GRANT ON THE RIO SAN PEDRO—DAILY ROUTINE OF LIFE—ARCHITECTURE OF THE GILA—SOLDIERS AS LABORERS—THE MESCAL AND ITS USES—DRINK AND GAMBLING—RATTLESNAKE BITES AND THE GOLONDRINA WEED—SODA LAKE AND THE DEATH VALLEY—FELMER AND HIS RANCH.

DANTE ALIGHIERI, it has always seemed to me, made the mistake of his life in dying when he did in the picturesque capital of the Exarchate five hundred and fifty years ago. Had he held on to this mortal coil until after Uncle Sam had perfected the "Gadsden Purchase," he would have found full scope for his genius in the description of a region in which not only purgatory and hell, but heaven likewise, had combined to produce a bewildering kaleidoscope of all that was wonderful, weird, terrible, and awe-inspiring, with not a little that was beautiful and romantic.

The vast region in the southwest corner of the United States, known on the maps as the Territories of Arizona and New Mexico, may, with perfect frankness, be claimed as the wonder-land of the northern part of America, with the exception, perhaps, of the Republic of Mexico, of which it was once a fragment, and to which, ethnographically, it has never ceased to belong.

In no other section can there be found such extensive areas of desert crossed in every direction by the most asperous mountains, whose profound cañons are the wonder of the world, whose parched flanks are matted with the thorny and leafless vegetation of the tropics, and whose lofty summits are black with the foliage of pines whose graceful branches bend in the welcome breezes from the temperate zone. Here one stumbles at almost every step upon the traces of former populations, of whom so little is known, or sees repeated from peak to peak the signal smokes of the fierce Apaches, whose hostility to the white man dates back to the time of Cortés.

I will begin my narrative by a brief reference to the condition of affairs in Arizona prior to the arrival of General Crook, as by no other means can the arduous nature of the work he accomplished be understood and appreciated. It was a cold and cheerless day—March 10, 1870—when our little troop, "F" of the Third Cavalry, than which a better never bore guidon, marched down the vertical-walled cañon of the Santa Catalina, crossed the insignificant sand-bed of the San Pedro, and came front into line on the parade-ground of Old Camp Grant, at the mouth of the Aravaypa. The sun was shining brightly, and where there was shelter to be found in the foliage of mesquite or cottonwood, there was the merry chatter of birds ; but in the open spaces the fierce breath of the norther, laden with dust and discomfort, made the new-comers imagine that an old-fashioned home winter had pursued them into foreign latitudes. A few military formalities hastily concluded, a few words of kindly greeting between ourselves and the members of the First Cavalry whom we met there, and ranks were broken, horses led to the stables, and men filed off to quarters. We had become part and parcel of the garrison of Old Camp Grant, the memory of which is still fragrant as that of the most forlorn parody upon a military garrison in that most woe-begone of military departments, Arizona.

Of our march over from the Rio Grande it is not worth while to speak ; as the reader advances in this book he will find references to other military movements which may compensate for the omission, even when it is admitted that our line of travel from Fort Craig lay through a region but little known to people in the East, and but seldom described. For those who may be sufficiently interested to follow our course, I will say that we started from Craig, marched to the tumble-down village of "Paraje de San Cristobal," at the head of the "Jornada del Muerto" (The Day's Journey of the Dead Man), which is the Sahara of New Mexico, then across to the long-since abandoned camp at what was called Fort MacRae, where we forded the river to the west, and then kept along the eastern rim of the timber-clad Mimbres Mountains, through Cow Springs to Fort Cummings, and thence due west to Camp Bowie, situated in the " Apache Pass" of the Chiricahua Mountains in Southeastern Arizona, a total distance of some one hundred and seventy miles as we marched.

There were stretches of country picturesque to look upon and capable of cultivation, especially with irrigation ; and other expanses not a bit more fertile than so many brick-yards, where all was desolation, the home of the cactus and the coyote.   Arizona was in those days separated from " God's country " by a space of more than fifteen hundred miles, without a railroad, and the officer or soldier who once got out there rarely returned for years.

Our battalion slowly crawled from camp to camp, with no incident to break the dull monotony beyond the ever-recurring signal smokes of the Apaches, to show that our progress was duly watched from the peaks on each flank ; or the occasional breaking down of some of the wagons and the accompanying despair of the quartermaster, with whose afflictions I sympathized sincerely, as that quartermaster was myself.

I used to think that there never had been such a wagon-train, and that there never could again be assembled by the Government mules of whose achievements more could be written—whose necks seemed to be ever slipping through their collars, and whose heels never remained on *terra firma* while there was anything in sight at which to kick.   Increasing years and added experience have made me more conservative, and I am now free to admit that there have been other mules as thoroughly saturated with depravity as "Blinky Jim," the lop-eared dun " wheeler" in the water-wagon team ; other artists whose attainments in profanity would put the blush upon the expletives which waked the echoes of the mirage-haunted San Simon, and other drivers who could get as quickly, unmistakably, emphatically, and undeniably drunk as Mullan, who was down on the official papers as the driver of the leading ambulance, but, instead of driving, was generally driven.

There would be very little use in attempting to describe Old Fort Grant, Arizona, partly because there was really no fort to describe, and partly because few of my readers would be sufficiently interested in the matter to follow me to the end. It was, as I have already said, recognized from the tide-waters of the Hudson to those of the Columbia as the most thoroughly God-forsaken post of all those supposed to be included in the annual Congressional appropriations. Beauty of situation or of construction it had none ; its site was the supposed junction of the sand-bed of the Aravaypa with the sand-bed of the San Pedro, which complacently figured on the topographical charts of the time as creek and river respectively, but generally were dry as a lime-burner's hat excepting during the "rainy season." Let the reader figure to himself a rectangle whose four sides were the row of officers' "quarters," the adjutant's office, post bakery, and guard house, the commissary and quartermaster's storehouses, and the men's quarters and sutler's store, and the "plan," if there was any "plan," can be at once understood. Back of the quartermaster's and commissary storehouses, some little distance, were the blacksmith's forge, the butcher's "corral," and the cavalry stables, while in the rear of the men's quarters, on the banks of the San Pedro, and not far from the traces of the ruins of a prehistoric village or pueblo of stone, was the loose, sandy spot upon which the bucking "bronco" horses were broken to the saddle. Such squealing and struggling and biting and kicking, and rolling in the dust and getting up again, only to introduce some entirely original combination of a hop, skip, and jump, and a double back somersault, never could be seen outside of a herd of California "broncos." The animal was first thrown, blindfolded, and then the bridle and saddle were put on, the latter girthed so tightly that the horse's eyes would start from their sockets. Then, armed with a pair of spurs of the diameter of a soup-plate and a mesquite club big enough to fell an ox, the Mexican "vaquero" would get into the saddle, the blinds would be cast off, and the circus begin. There would be one moment of sweet doubt as to what the "bronco" was going to do, and now and then there would be aroused expectancy that a really mild-mannered steed had been sent to the post by some mistake of the quartermaster's department. But this doubt never lasted very long ; the genuine "bronco" can always be known from the spurious one by the fact that when he makes up his mind to "buck" he sets out upon his work without delay, and with a vim that means business. If there were many horses arriving in a " bunch," there would be lots of fun and no little danger and excitement. The men would mount, and amid the encouraging comments of the on-lookers begin the task of subjugation. The bronco, as I have said, or should have said, nearly always looked around and up at his rider with an expression of countenance that was really benignant, and then he would roach his back, get his four feet bunched together, and await developments. These always came in a way productive of the best results ; if the rider foolishly listened to the suggestions of his critics, he would almost always mistake this temporary paroxysm of docility for fear or lack of spirit.

And then would come the counsel, inspired by the Evil One himself : " Arrah, thin, shtick yer sphurs int' him, Moriarty."

This was just the kind of advice that best suited the " bronco's " feelings, because no sooner would the rowels strike his flanks than the air would seem to be filled with a mass of mane and tail rapidly revolving, and of hoofs flying out in defiance of all the laws of gravity, while a descendant of the kings of Ireland, describing a parabolic orbit through space, would shoot like a meteor into the sand, and plough it up with his chin and the usual elocutionary effects to be looked for under such circumstances.

Yes, those were happy, happy days—for the " broncos " and the by-standers.

There were three kinds of quarters at Old Camp Grant, and he who was reckless enough to make a choice of one passed the rest of his existence while at the post in growling at the better luck of the comrades who had selected either one of the others.

There was the adobe house, built originally for the kitchens of the post at the date of its first establishment, some time in 1857 ; there were the " jacal " sheds, built of upright logs, chinked with mud and roofed with smaller branches and more mud ; and the tents, long since " condemned " and forgotten by the quartermaster to whom they had originally been invoiced. Each and all of these examples of the Renaissance style of architecture, as it found expression in the valley of the Gila, was provided with a " ramada " in front, which, at a small expenditure of labor in erecting a few additional upright saplings and cross-pieces, and a covering of cottonwood foliage, secured a modicum of shelter from the fierce shafts of a sun which shone not to warm and enlighten, but to enervate and kill.

The occupants of the ragged tentage found solace in the pure air which merrily tossed the flaps and flies, even if it brought with it rather more than a fair share of heat and alkali dust from the deserts of Sonora. Furthermore, there were few insects to bother, a pleasing contrast to the fate of those living in the houses, which were veritable museums of entomology, with the choicest specimens of centipedes, scorpions, "vinagrones," and, occasionally, tarantulas, which the Southwest could produce.

On the other hand, the denizens of the adobe and the "jacal outfits" became inured to insect pests and felicitated themselves as best they could upon being free from the merciless glare of the sun and wind, which latter, with its hot breath, seemed to take delight in peeling the skin from the necks and faces of all upon whom it could exert its nefarious powers. My assignment was to one of the rooms in the adobe house, an apartment some four-teen by nine feet in area, by seven and a half or eight in height. There was not enough furniture to occasion any anxiety in case of fire : nothing but a single cot, one rocking-chair—visitors, when they came, generally sat on the side of the cot—a trunk, a shelf of books, a small pine wash-stand, over which hung a mirror of greenish hue, sold to me by the post trader with the assurance that it was French plate. I found out afterward that the trader could not always be relied upon, but I'll speak of him at another time. There were two window-curtains, both of chintz ; one concealed the dust and fly specks on the only window, and the other covered the row of pegs upon which hung sabre, forage cap, and uniform.

In that part of Arizona fires were needed only at intervals, and, as a consequence, the fireplaces were of insignificant dimensions, although they were placed, in the American fashion, on the side of the rooms, and not, as among the Mexicans, in the corners. There was one important article of furniture connected with the fireplace of which I must make mention—the long iron poker with which, on occasion, I was wont to stir up the embers, and also to stir up the Mexican boy Esperidion, to whom, in the wilder freaks of my imagination, I was in the habit of alluding as my "valet."

The quartermaster had recently received permission to expend "a reasonable amount " of paint upon the officers' quarters, pro-vided the same could be done "by the labor of the troops."

This "labor of the troops" was a great thing. It made the poor wretch who enlisted under the vague notion that his admiring country needed his services to quell hostile Indians, suddenly find himself a brevet architect, carrying a hod and doing odd jobs of plastering and kalsomining. It was an idea which never fully commended itself to my mind, and I have always thought that the Government might have been better served had such work, and all other not strictly military and necessary for the proper police and cleanliness of the posts, been assigned to civilians just as soon as representatives of the different trades could be attracted to the frontier. It would have cost a little more in the beginning, but it would have had the effect of helping to settle up our waste land on the frontier, and that, I believe, was the principal reason why we had a standing army at all.

The soldier felt discontented because no mention had been made in the recruiting officer's posters, or in the contract of enlistment, that he was to do such work, and he not unusually solved the problem by "skipping out" the first pay-day that found him with enough money ahead to risk the venture. It goes without saying that the work was never any too well done, and in the present case there seemed to be more paint scattered round about my room than would have given it another coat. But the floor was of rammed earth and not to be spoiled, and the general effect was certainly in the line of improvement. Colonel Dubois, our commanding officer, at least thought so, and warmly congratulated me upon the snug look of everything, and added a very acceptable present of a picture—one of Prang's framed chromos, a view of the Hudson near the mouth of Esopus Creek —which gave a luxurious finish to the whole business. Later on, after I had added an Apache bow and quiver, with its complement of arrows, one or two of the bright, cheery Navajo rugs, a row of bottles filled with select specimens of tarantulas, spiders, scorpions, rattlesnakes, and others of the fauna of the country, and hung upon the walls a suit of armor which had belonged to some Spanish foot-soldier of the sixteenth century, there was a sybaritic suggestiveness which made all that has been related of the splendors of Solomon and Sardanapalus seem commonplace.

Of that suit of armor I should like to say a word : it was found by Surgeon Steyer, of the army, enclosing the bones of a man, in the arid country between the waters of the Rio Grande and the

Pecos, in the extreme southwestern corner of the State of Texas, more than twenty years ago. Various conjectures were advanced and all sorts of theories advocated as to its exact age, some people thinking that it belonged originally to Coronado's expedition, which entered New Mexico in 1541. My personal belief is that it belonged to the expedition of Don Antonio Espejo, or that of Don Juan de Oñate, both of whom came into New Mexico about the same date—1581–1592—and travelled down the Concho to its confluence with the Rio Grande, which would have been just on the line where the skeleton in armor was discovered. There is no authentic report to show that Coronado swung so far to the south ; his line of operations took in the country farther to the north and east, and there are the best of reasons for believing that he was the first white man to enter the fertile valley of the Platte, not far from Plum Creek, Nebraska.

But, be that as it may, the suit of armor—breast and back plates, gorget and helmet—nicely painted and varnished, and with every tiny brass button duly cleaned and polished with acid and ashes, added not a little to the looks of a den which without them would have been much more dismal.

For such of my readers as may not be up in these matters, I may say that iron armor was abandoned very soon after the Conquest, as the Spaniards found the heat of these dry regions too great to admit of their wearing anything so heavy ; and they also found that the light cotton-batting "escaupiles" of the Aztecs served every purpose as a protection against the arrows of the naked savages by whom they were now surrounded.

There was not much to do in the post itself, although there was a sufficiency of good, healthy exercise to be counted upon at all times outside of it. I may be pardoned for dwelling upon trivial matters such as were those entering into the sum total of our lives in the post, but, under the hope that it and all in the remotest degree like it have disappeared from the face of the earth never to return, I will say a few words.

In the first place, Camp Grant was a hot-bed of the worst kind of fever and ague, the disease which made many portions of Southern Arizona almost uninhabitable during the summer and fall months of the year. There was nothing whatever to do except scout after hostile Apaches, who were very bold and kept the garrison fully occupied. What with sickness, heat, bad water, flies, sand-storms, and utter isolation, life would have been dreary and dismal were it not for the novelty which helped out the determination to make the best of everything. First of all, there was the vegetation, different from anything to be seen east of the Missouri : the statuesque " pitahayas," with luscious fruit ; the massive biznagas, whose juice is made into very palatable candy by the Mexicans ; the bear's grass, or palmilla ; the Spanish bayonet, the palo verde, the various varieties of cactus, principal among them being the nopal, or plate, and the cholla, or nodular, which possesses the decidedly objectionable quality of separating upon the slightest provocation, and sticking to whatever may be nearest ; the mesquite, with palatable gum and nourishing beans ; the mescal, beautiful to look upon and grateful to the Apaches, of whom it is the main food-supply ; the scrub oak, the juniper, cottonwood, ash, sycamore, and, lastly, the pine growing on the higher points of the environing mountains, were all noted, examined, and studied, so far as opportunity would admit.

And so with the animal life : the deer, of the strange variety called " the mule " ; the coyotes, badgers, pole-cats, rabbits, gophers—but not the prairie-dog, which, for some reason never understood by me, does not cross into Arizona ; or, to be more accurate, does just cross over the New Mexican boundary at Fort Bowie in the southeast, and at Tom Keam's ranch in the Moqui country in the extreme northeast.

Strangest of all was the uncouth, horrible " escorpion," or " Gila monster," which here found its favorite habitat and attained its greatest dimensions. We used to have them not less than three feet long, black, venomous, and deadly, if half the stories told were true. The Mexicans time and time again asserted that the escorpion would kill chickens, and that it would eject a poisonous venom upon them, but, in my own experience, I have to say that the old hen which we tied in front of one for a whole day was not molested, and that no harm of any sort came to her beyond being scared out of a year's growth. Scientists were wont to ridicule the idea of the Gila monster being venomous, upon what ground I do not now remember, beyond the fact that it was a lizard, and all lizards were harmless. But I believe it is now well established that the monster is not to be handled with impunity.

although, like many other animals, it may lie torpid and inoffen-
sive for weeks, and even months, at a time.   It is a noteworthy fact
that the Gila monster is the only reptile on earth to-day that exactly fills the description of the basilisk or cockatrice of mediæval
fable, which, being familiar to the first-comers among the Castilians, could hardly have added much to its popularity among them.

It may not be amiss to say of the vegetation that the mescal
was to the aborigines of that region much what the palm is to
the nomads of Syria.   Baked in ovens of hot stone covered with
earth, it supplied a sweet, delicious, and nutritive food ; its juice
could be fermented into an alcoholic drink very acceptable to
the palate, even if it threw into the shade the best record ever
made by "Jersey lightning" as a stimulant.   Tear out one of
the thorns and the adhering filament, and you had a very fair
article of needle and thread ; if a lance staff was needed, the sapling mescal stood ready at hand to be so utilized ; the stalk, cut
into sections of proper length, and provided with strings of sinew,
became the Apache fiddle—I do not care to be interrupted by
questions as to the quality of the music emitted by these fiddles,
as I am now trying to give my readers some notion of the eco-
nomic value of the several plants of the Territory, and am not
ready to enter into a disquisition upon melody and such matters,
in which, perhaps, the poor little Apache fiddle would cut but a
slim figure—and in various other ways this strange, thorny-
leafed plant seemed anxious to show its friendship for man.   And
I for one am not at all surprised that the Aztecs reverenced it as
one of their gods, under the name of Quetzalcoatl.*

The "mesquite" is a member of the acacia family, and from
its bark annually, each October, exudes a gum equal to the best
Arabic that ever descended the Nile from Khartoum.   There are
three varieties of the plant, two of them edible and one not.
One of the edible kinds—the "tornillo," or screw—grows luxu-
riantly in the hot, sandy valley of the Colorado, and forms the
main vegetable food of the Mojave Indians ; the other, with pods
shaped much like those of the string-bean of our own markets,
is equally good, and has a sweet and pleasantly acidulated taste.
The squaws take these beans, put them in mortars, and pound
them into meal, of which bread is made, in shape and size and

---

* Quetzalcoatl is identified with the maguey in Kingsborough, vol. vi., 107.

weight not unlike the elongated projectiles of the three-inch rifled cannon.

Alarcon, who ascended the Colorado River in 1541, describes such bread as in use among the tribes along its banks ; .and Cabeza de Vaca and his wretched companions, sole survivors of the doomed expedition of Panfilo de Narvaez, which went to pieces near the mouth of the Suwanee River, in Florida, found this bread in use among the natives along the western part of their line of march, after they had succeeded in escaping from the Indians who had made them slaves, and had, in the guise of medicine-men, tramped across the continent until they struck the Spanish settlements near Culiacan, on the Pacific coast, in 1536.   But Vaca calls it " mizquiquiz." Castaneda relates that in his day (1541) the people of Sonora (which then included Arizona) made a bread of the mesquite, shaping it like a cheese ; it had the property of keeping for a whole year.

There was so little hunting in the immediate vicinity of the post, and so much danger attending the visits of small parties to the higher hills a few miles off, in which deer, and even bear, were to be encountered, that nothing in that line was attempted except when on scout ; all our recreation had to be sought within the limits of the garrison, and evolved from our own personal resources.   The deficiency of hunting did not imply that there was any lack of shooting about the post ; all that any one could desire could be had for the asking, and that, too, without moving from under the " ramadas " back of the quarters.   Many and many a good line shot we used to make at the coyotes and skunks which with the going down of the sun made their appearance in the garbage piles in the ravines to the north of us.

There was considerable to be done in the ordinary troop duties, which began at reveille with the " stables," lasting half an hour, after which the horses and mules not needed for the current tasks of the day were sent out to seek such nibbles of pasturage as they might find under the shade of the mesquite.   A strong guard, mounted and fully armed, accompanied the herd, and a number of horses, saddled but loosely cinched, remained behind under the grooming-sheds, ready to be pushed out after any raiding party of Apaches which might take a notion to sneak up and stampede the herd at pasture.

Guard mounting took place either before or after breakfast, according to season, and then followed the routine of the day : inspecting the men's mess at breakfast, dinner, and supper; a small amount of drill, afternoon stables, dress or undress parade at retreat or sundown, and such other occupation as might suggest itself in the usual visit to the herd to see that the pasturage selected was good, and that the guards were vigilant ; some absorption in the recording of the proceedings of garrison courts-martial and boards of survey, and then general *ennui*, unless the individual possessed enough force to make work for himself.

This, however, was more often the case than many of my readers would imagine, and I can certify to no inconsiderable amount of reading and study of Spanish language and literature, of mineralogy, of botany, of history, of constitutional or of international law, and of the belles-lettres, by officers of the army with whom I became acquainted at Old Camp Grant ; Fort Craig, New Mexico, and other dismal holes—more than I have ever known among gentlemen of leisure anywhere else.   It was no easy matter to study with ink drying into gum almost as soon as dipped out by the pen, and paper cracking at the edges when folded or bent.

The newspapers of the day were eagerly perused—when they came ; but those from San Francisco were always from ten to fifteen days old, those from New York about five to six weeks, and other cities any intermediate age you please.   The mail at first came every second Tuesday, but this was increased soon to a weekly service, and on occasion, when chance visitors reported some happening of importance, the commanding officer would send a courier party to Tucson with instructions to the postmaster there to deliver.

The temptations to drink and to gamble were indeed great, and those who yielded and fell by the way-side numbered many of the most promising youngsters in the army.   Many a brilliant and noble fellow has succumbed to the *ennui* and gone down, wrecking a life full of promise for himself and the service.   It was hard for a man to study night and day with the thermometer rarely under the nineties even in winter at noon, and often climbing up to and over the 120 notch on the Fahrenheit scale before the meridian of days between April 1st and October 15th ; it was hard to organize riding or hunting parties when all the horses had just returned worn out by some rough scouting in the Pinal or Sierra Ancha. There in the trader's store was a pleasant, cool room, with a minimum of flies, the latest papers, perfect quiet, genial companionship, cool water in "ollas" swinging from the rafters, and covered by boards upon which, in a thin layer of soil, grew a picturesque mantle of green barley, and, on a table conveniently near, cans of lemon-sugar, tumblers and spoons, and one or two packs of cards. My readers must not expect me to mention ice or fruits. I am not describing Delmonico's; I am writing of Old Camp Grant, and I am painting the old hole in the most rosy colors I can employ. Ice was unheard of, and no matter how high the mercury climbed or how stifling might be the sirocco from Sonora, the best we could do was to cool water by evaporation in "ollas" of earthenware, manufactured by the Papago Indians living at the ruined mission of San Xavier, above Tucson.

To revert to the matter of drinking and gambling. There is scarcely any of either at the present day in the regular army. Many things have combined to bring about such a desirable change, the principal, in my opinion, being the railroads which have penetrated and transformed the great American continent, placing comforts and luxuries within reach of officers and men, and absorbing more of their pay as well as bringing them within touch of civilization and its attendant restraints. Of the two vices, drunkenness was by all odds the preferable one. For a drunkard, one can have some pity, because he is his own worst enemy, and, at the worst, there is hope for his regeneration, while there is absolutely none for the gambler, who lives upon the misfortunes and lack of shrewdness of his comrades. There are many who believe, or affect to believe, in gaming for the excitement of the thing and not for the money involved. There may be such a thing, but I do not credit its existence. However, the greatest danger in gambling lay in the waste of time rather than in the loss of money, which loss rarely amounted to very great sums, although officers could not well afford to lose anything.

I well remember one great game, played by a party of my friends—but at Fort Laramie, Wyoming, and not in Arizona—which illustrates this better than I can describe. It was an all-night game—ten cents to come in and a quarter limit—and there was no small amount of engineering skill shown before the first call for reveille separated the party. "Fellows," said one of the quartette, in speaking of it some days afterward, "I tell you it was a struggle of the giants, and when the smoke of battle cleared away, I found I'd lost two dollars and seventy-five cents."

As it presents itself to my recollection now, our life wasn't so very monotonous ; there was always something going on to interest and instruct, even if it didn't amuse or enliven.

" Corporal Dile's har-r-r-se 's bit by a ratthler 'n th' aff hind leg "; and, of course, everybody turns out and gets down to the stables as fast as possible, each with his own prescription, which are one and all discarded for the great Mexican panacea of a poultice of the "golondrina" weed. Several times I have seen this used, successfully and unsuccessfully, and I do not believe in its vaunted efficacy by any means.

" Oscar Hutton 's bin kicked 'n th' jaw by a mewel." Hutton was one of the post guides, a very good and brave man. His jaw was hopelessly crushed by a blow from the lightning hoofs of a miserable " bronco " mule, and poor Hutton never recovered from the shock. He died not long after, and, in my opinion, quite as much from chagrin at being outwitted as from the injury inflicted.

Hutton had had a wonderful experience in the meanest parts of our great country—and be it known that Uncle Sam can hold his own with any prince or potentate on God's footstool in the matter of mean desert land. All over the great interior basin west of the Rockies Hutton had wandered in the employ of the United States with some of the Government surveying parties. Now he was at the mouth of the Virgin, where there is a salt mine with slabs two and three feet thick, as clear as crystal ; next he was a wanderer in the dreaded " Death Valley," below the sea-level, where there is no sign of animal life save the quickly darting lizard, or the vagrant duck whose flesh is bitter from the water of " soda " lakes, which offer to the wanderer all the comforts of a Chinese laundry, but not one of those of a home. At that time I only knew of these dismal places from the relation of Hutton, to which I listened open-mouthed, but since then I have had some personal acquaintance, and can aver that in naught did he overlap the truth. The ground is covered for miles with pure baking-soda—I decline to specify what brand, as I am not writing this as an advertisement, and my readers can consult individual preference if they feel so disposed—which rises in a cloud of dry, irritating dust above the horse's houghs, and if agitated by the hot winds, excoriates the eyes, throat, nostrils, and ears of the unfortunate who may find himself there. Now and then one discerns in the dim distance such a deceiving body of water as the "Soda Lake," which tastes like soapsuds, and nourishes no living thing save the worthless ducks spoken of, whose flesh is uneatable except to save one from starvation.

Hutton had seen so much hardship that it was natural to expect him to be meek and modest in his ideas and demeanor, but he was, on the contrary, decidedly vain and conceited, and upon such a small matter that it ought not really to count against him. He had six toes on each foot, a fact to which he adverted with pride. "Bee gosh," he would say, "there hain't ennuther man 'n th' hull dog-goned outfit 's got ez menny toes 's me."

Then there was the excitement at Felmer's ranch, three miles above the post. Felmer was the post blacksmith, and lived in a little ranch in the fertile "bottom" of the San Pedro, where he raised a "patch" of barley and garden-truck for sale to the garrison. He was a Russian or a Polynesian or a Turk or a Theosophist or something—he had lived in so many portions of the world's surface that I never could keep track of him. I distinctly remember that he was born in Germany, had lived in Russia or in the German provinces close to Poland, and had thence travelled everywhere. He had married an Apache squaw, and from her learned the language of her people. She was now dead, but Joe was quite proud of his ability to cope with all the Apaches in Arizona, and in being a match for them in every wile. One hot day—all the days were comfortably warm, but this was a "scorcher"—there was a sale of condemned Government stock, and Joe bought a mule, which the auctioneer facetiously suggested should be called "Lazarus," he had so many sores all over his body. But Joe bought him, perfectly indifferent to the scoffs and sneers of the by-standers. "Don't you think the Apaches may get him?" I ventured to inquire. "That's jest what I'm keeping him fur; *bait*—unnerstan'? 'N Apache 'll come down 'n my alfalfy field 'n git thet mewel, 'n fust thing you know thar 'll be a joke on *somebody*."

Felmer was a first-class shot, and we naturally supposed that the joke would be on the deluded savage who might sneak down to ride away with such a crow-bait, and would become the mark for an unerring rifle. But it was not so to be. The wretched quadruped had his shoes pulled off, and was then turned loose in alfalfa and young barley, to his evident enjoyment and benefit. Some time had passed, and we had almost forgotten to twit Felmer about his bargain. It's a very thin joke that cannot be made to last five or six weeks in such a secluded spot as Old Camp Grant, and, for that reason, at least a month must have elapsed when, one bright Sunday afternoon, Felmer was rudely aroused from his siesta by the noise of guns and the voices of his Mexican herders crying: "Apaches! Apaches!" And there they were, sure enough, and on top of that sick, broken-down cast-off of the quartermaster's department—three of them, each as big as the side of a house, and poor Joe so dazed that for several minutes he couldn't fire a shot.

The two bucks in front were kicking their heels into the mule's ribs, and the man in rear had passed a hair lariat under the mule's tail, and was sawing away for dear life. And the mule? Well, the mule wasn't idle by any means, but putting in his best licks in getting over the ground, jumping "arroyos" and rocks, charging into and over nopals and chollas and mesquite, and fast leaving behind him the valley of the San Pedro, and getting into the foot-hills of the Pinaleno Range.

CHAPTER II.

WE had all sorts of visitors from the adjacent country. The first I remember was a squaw whose nose had been cut off by a brutal and jealous husband. The woman was not at all bad looking, and there was not a man at the post who did not feel sorry for the unfortunate who, for some dereliction, real or imagined, had been so savagely disfigured.

This shocking mode of punishment, in which, by the way, the Apache resembled some of the nations of antiquity, prevailed in full vigor until after General Crook had subjected this fierce tribe to law and discipline, and the first, or, at least, among the very first, regulations he laid down for their guidance was that the women of the tribe must be treated just as kindly as the men, and each and every infraction of the rule was threatened with the severest punishment the whole military force could inflict. Since then the practice has wholly died out among both the Apaches and the Hualpais.

Then there came an old withered crone, leading a woman somewhat younger, but still shrivelled with the life of care and drudgery which falls to the lot of the Apache matron, and a third member of this interesting party, a boy ten or twelve years old, who was suffering from the bite of a rattlesnake, which had caused his right leg to shrink and decay. The medicine-men of their band had sung vigorously and applied such medicine as they thought best suited to the case, but it proved to be beyond their skill, and they had advised this journey to Camp Grant, to see what the white man's medicine could do for the sufferer.

Still another interesting picture framed in my memory is that of the bent old dotard who wished to surrender on account of frankly confessed impotency to remain longer on the war-path. Battles were for young men only ; as people grew older they got more sense, and all should live as brothers. This world was large enough for everybody, and there should be enough to eat for the Indians and the white men, too. There were men whose hearts were hard and who would not listen to reason ; they wished to fight, but as for himself, his legs could not climb the mountains any longer, and the thorns were bad when they scratched his skin. His heart was good, and so long as this stone which he placed on the ground should last he wanted to let the Great Father know that he meant to be his friend. Had his brother, the post commander, any tobacco ?

Many an hour did I sit by the side of our friend and brother, watching him chip out arrow-heads from fragments of beer bottles, or admiring the dexterity with which he rubbed two sticks together to produce flame. Matches were his greatest treasure, and he was never tired begging for them, and as soon as obtained, he would wrap them up carefully in a piece of buckskin to screen from the weather. But we never gave him reason to suspect that our generosity was running away with our judgment. We were careful not to give him any after we found out that he could make fire so speedily and in a manner so strange, and which we were never tired of seeing.

These members of the tribe were all kept as prisoners, more to prevent communication with the enemy than from any suspected intention of attempting an escape. They were perfectly contented, were well fed, had no more to do than was absolutely good for them in the way of exercise, and except that they had to sleep under the eyes of the sentinels at night, were as free as any one else in the garrison. Once or twice Indian couriers came over from Camp Apache—or Thomas, as it was then called—in the Sierra Blanca. Those whom I first saw were almost naked, their only clothing being a muslin loin-cloth, a pair of pointed-toed moccasins, and a hat of hawk feathers. They had no arms but lances and bows and arrows. One of them bore a small round shield of raw-hide decked with eagle plumage , another had a pretty fiddle made of a joint of the bamboo-like stalk of the century plant, and a third had a pack of monte cards, cut out of dried pony skin and painted to represent rudely the figures in the four suits.

Their lank, long black hair, held back from the eyes by bands of red flannel ; their superb chests, expanded by constant exercise in the lofty mountains, and their strongly muscled legs confirmed all that I had already learned of their powers of endurance from the half-breed Mexicans and the tame Apaches at the post—people like Manuel Duran, Nicolas, and Francisco, who were what were then known as tame Apaches, and who had never lived with the others in the hills, but belonged to a section which had made peace with the whites many years previously and had never broken it ; or escaped captives like José Maria, José de Leon, Victor Ruiz, or Antonio Besias, who had been torn away from their homes in Sonora at an early age, and had lived so long with the savages that they had become thoroughly conversant with all their ideas and customs as well as their language. Nearly all that class of interpreters and guides are now dead. Each had a wonderful history, well worthy of recital, but I cannot allow myself to be tempted into a more extended reference to any of them at this moment.

The fact that the post trader had just received a stock of *new* goods meant two things—it meant that he had made a mistake in his order and received a consignment different from the *old* goods which he had hitherto taken so much pride in keeping upon his shelves, and it meant that the paymaster was about to pay us a visit, and leave a share of Uncle Sam's money in the country.

There were two assistants in the store, Paul and Speedy.

Paul was getting along in years, but Speedy was young and bright. Paul had at one period in his life possessed some intelligence and a fair education, but whiskey, cards, and tobacco had long ago blunted what faculties he could claim, and left him a poor hulk, working for his board and drinks at such odd jobs as there were to do about the premises. He had been taught the trade of cabinet-making in Strassburg, and when in good humor, and not too drunk, would join and polish, carve and inlay boxes, made of the wood of the mesquite, madroño, manzanita, ash, and walnut, which would delight the eyes of the most critical.

Speedy was the most active man about the post. He was one

of our best runners, and by all odds the best swimmer in the cool, deep pools which the San Pedro formed where it came up out of the sands a short distance below the officers' quarters, and where we often bathed in the early evening hours, with some one of the party on guard, because the lurking Apaches were always a standing menace in that part of Arizona.

I do not know what has become of Speedy. He was an exceptionally good man in many ways, and if not well educated, made up in native intelligence what others more fortunate get from books. From a Yankee father he inherited the Maine shrewdness in money matters and a keenness in seeing the best points in a bargain. A Spanish mother endowed him with a fund of gentle politeness and good manners.

When he came to bid me good-by and tell me that he had opened a "Monte Pio," or pawnbroker's shop, in Tucson, I ventured to give him a little good advice.

"You must be careful of your money, Speedy. Pawnbroking is a risky business. You'll be likely to have a great deal of unsalable stuff left on your hands, and it don't look to me as if five per cent. was enough interest to charge. The laws of New York, I believe, allow one to charge twenty per cent. per annum."

"Cap., what's per annum?"

"Why, every year, of course."

"Oh, but you see mine is five per cent. a week."

Speedy was the only man I ever knew who had really seen a ghost. As he described it to us, it had much the appearance of a "human," and was mounted on a pretty good specimen of a Sonora plug, and was arrayed in a suit of white canvas, with white helmet, green veil, blue goggles, and red side whiskers. It didn't say a word to my friend, but gave him a decidedly cold stare, which was all that Speedy cared to wait for before he broke for the brush. A hundred yards or so in rear there was a train of pack mules, laden with cot frames, bath-tubs, hat boxes, and other trumpery, which may or may not have had something to do with the ghost in advance. Speedy and his mule were too agitated to stop to ask questions, and continued on into Hermosillo.

Information received about this time from Sonora reported that an English "lud" was "roughing it" in and about the Yaqui country, and it is just possible that he could have given much information about the apparition had it been demanded ; but Speedy persisted in his belief that he had had a " call " from the other world, and was sorely depressed for several weeks.

Speedy rendered valuable help in our self-imposed task of digging in the "ruins" alongside of our quarters—vestiges of an occupancy by a pre-historic race, allied to the Pueblos of the Rio Grande or to the Pimas and Papagoes.

Broken pottery, painted and unpainted, a flint knife or two, some arrow-heads, three or four stone hatchets, and more of the same sort, were our sole reward for much hard work. The great question which wrought us up to fever heat was, Who were these inhabitants ? Felmer promptly decided that they were Phœnicians—upon what grounds I do not know, and it is very doubtful if Felmer knew either—but Oscar Hutton " 'lowed they mout 'a' bin some o' them Egyptian niggers as built the pyramids in th' Bible."

The paymaster had come and gone ; the soldiers had spent their last dollar ; the last " pay-day drunk " had been rounded up and was now on his way to the guard-house, muttering a maudlin defiance to Erin's foes ; the sun was shining with scorching heat down upon the bed of pebbles which formed the parade-ground ; the flag hung limp and listless from the pudgy staff ; the horses were out on herd ; the scarlet-shouldered blackbirds, the cardinals, the sinsontes, and the jays had sought the deepest shadows ; there was no sound to drown the insistent buzz of the aggravating flies or the voice of the Recorder of the Garrison Court just assembled, which was trying Privates A. and B. and C. and D. and others, names and rank now forgotten, for having " then and there," " on or about," and " at or near " the post of Camp Grant, Arizona, committed sundry and divers crimes against the law and regulations—when, straight across the parade, with the swiftness of a frightened deer, there ran a half or three-quarters naked Mexican, straight to the door of the " comandante's " quarters.

He was almost barefooted, the shoes he had on being in splinters. His trousers had been scratched so by the thorns and briars that only rags were now pendent from his waist. His hat had been dropped in his terrified flight from some unexplained danger, which the wan face, almost concealed by matted locks, and the shirt covered with blood still flowing

freely from a wound in the chest, conclusively showed to have
been an Apache ambuscade.

With faltering voice and in broken accents the sufferer explained that he was one of a party of more than thirty Mexicans coming up from Tucson to work on the ranch of Kennedy
and Israel, who lived about a mile from our post down the San
Pedro.   There were a number of women and several children
with the train, and not a soul had the slightest suspicion of
danger, when suddenly, on the head of the slope leading up
to the long "mesa" just this side of the Cañon del Oro, they
had found themselves surrounded on three sides by a party of
Apaches, whose strength was variously put at from thirty to fifty
warriors.

The Americans and Mexicans made the best fight possible,
and succeeded in keeping back the savages until the women and
children had reached a place of comparative safety; but both
Kennedy and Israel were killed, and a number of others killed
or wounded, our informant being one of the latter, with a severe
cut in the left breast, where a bullet had ploughed round his
ribs without doing very serious damage.   The Apaches fell to
plundering the wagons, which were loaded with the general
supplies that ranchmen were in those days compelled to keep in
stock, for feeding the numbers of employees whom they had to
retain to cultivate their fields, as well as to guard them, and the
Mexicans, seeing this, made off as fast as their legs could carry
them, under the guidance of such of their party as were familiar
with the trails leading across the Santa Catalina range to the
San Pedro and Camp Grant.   One of these trails ran by way of
Apache Springs at the northern extremity of the range, and was
easy of travel, so that most of the people were safe, but we were
strongly urged to lose no time in getting round by the longer
road, along which the Apaches were believed to have pursued a
few men.

The Mexican, Domingo, had seen Sergeants Warfield and
Mott, two old veterans, on his way through the post, and they,
without waiting for orders, had the herd run in and saddles got
out in anticipation of what their experience taught them was
sure to come.   Every man who could be put on horseback was
mounted at once, without regard to his company or regiment,
and in less than twenty minutes the first detachment was crossing

the San Pedro and entering the long defile known as the Santa
Catalina Cañon—not very well equipped for a prolonged campaign, perhaps, as some of the men had no water in canteens and
others had only a handful of crackers for rations, but that made
no difference. Our business was to rescue women and children
surrounded by savages, and to do it with the least delay possible.
At least, that was the way Colonel Dubois reasoned on the
subject, and we had only our duty to do—obey orders.

A second detachment would follow after us, with a wagon
containing water in kegs, rations for ten days, medical supplies,
blankets, and every other essential for making such a scout as
might become necessary.

Forward! was the word, and every heel struck flank and every
horse pressed upon the bit. Do our best, we couldn't make very
rapid progress through the cañon, which for its total length of
twelve miles was heavy with shifting sand.

Wherever there was a stretch of hard pan, no matter how
short, we got the best time out of it that was possible. The distance seemed interminable, but we pressed on, passing the Four-
mile Walnut, on past the Cottonwood, slipping along without a
word under the lofty walls which screened us from the rays of the
sun, although the afternoon was still young. But in much less
time than we had a right to expect we had reached the end of the
bad road, and halted for a minute to have all loose cinches re-
tightened and everything made ready for rapid travelling on to
the Cañon del Oro.

In front of us stretched a broken, hilly country, bounded on
the east and west by the Tortolita and the Sierra Santa Catalina
respectively. The summer was upon us, but the glories of the
springtime had not yet faded from the face of the desert, which
still displayed the splendors of millions of golden crocuses, with
countless odorless verbenas of varied tints, and acres upon acres
of nutritious grasses, at which our horses nibbled every time we
halted for a moment. The cañon of the Santa Catalina for more
than four miles of its length is no wider than an ordinary street
in a city, and is enclosed by walls rising one thousand feet above
the trail. Wherever a foothold could be found, there the thorny-
branched giant cactus stood sentinel, or the prickly plates of the
nopal matted the face of the escarpment. High up on the wall
of the cañon, one of the most prominent of the pitahayas or

giant cacti had been transfixed by the true aim of an Apache arrow, buried up to the feathers.

For the beauties or eccentricities of nature we had no eyes. All that we cared to know was how long it would take to put us where the train had been ambushed and destroyed. So, on we pushed, taking a very brisk gait, and covering the ground with rapidity.

The sun was going down in a blaze of scarlet and gold behind the Tortolita Range, the Cañon del Oro was yet several miles away, and still no signs of the party of which we were in such anxious search. "They must have been nearer the Cañon del Oro than the Mexican thought," was the general idea, for we had by this time gained the long mesa upon which we had been led to believe we should see the ruins of the wagons.

We were now moving at a fast walk, in line, with carbines at an "advance," and everything ready for a fight to begin on either flank or in front, as the case might be ; but there was no enemy in sight. We deployed as skirmishers, so as to cover as much ground as possible, and pick up any dead body that might be lying behind the mesquite or the palo verde which lined the road. A sense of gloom spread over the little command, which had been hoping against hope to find the survivors alive and the savages still at bay. But, though the coyote yelped to the moon, and flocks of quail whirred through the air when raised from their seclusion in the bushes, and funereal crows, perched upon the tops of the pitahayas, croaked dismal salutations, there was no sound of the human voices we longed to hear.

But don't be too sure. Is that a coyote's cry or the wail of a fellow-creature in distress ? A coyote, of course. Yes, it is, and no, it isn't. Every one had his own belief, and would tolerate no dissent. "Hel-lup! Hel-lup! My God, hel-lup !" "This way, Mott! Keep the rest of the men back there on the road." In less than ten seconds we had reached a small arroyo, not very deep, running parallel to the road and not twenty yards from it, and there, weak and faint and covered with his own blood, was our poor, unfortunate friend, Kennedy. He was in the full possession of his faculties and able to recognize every one whom he knew and to tell a coherent story. As to the first part of the attack, he concurred with Domingo, but he furnished the additional information that as soon as the Apaches saw that the greater number of the party had withdrawn with the women and children, of whom there were more than thirty all told, they made a bold charge to sweep down the little rear-guard which had taken its stand behind the wagons. Kennedy was sure that the Apaches had suffered severely, and told me where to look for the body of the warrior who had killed his partner, Israel. Israel had received a death-wound in the head which brought him to his knees, but before he gave up the ghost his rifle, already in position at his shoulder, was discharged and killed the tall, muscular young savage who appeared to be leading the attack.

Kennedy kept up the unequal fight as long as he could, in spite of the loss of the thumb of his left hand, shot off at the first volley ; but when the Mexicans at each side of him fell, he drew his knife, cut the harness of the "wheeler" mule nearest him, sprang into the saddle, and charged right through the Apaches advancing a second time. His boldness disconcerted their aim, but they managed to plant an arrow in his breast and another in the ribs of his mule, which needed no further urging to break into a mad gallop over every rock and thorn in its front. Kennedy could not hold the bridle with his left hand, and the pain in his lung was excruciating—"Jes' like 's if I'd swallowed a coal o' fire, boys," he managed to gasp, half inarticulately. But he had run the mule several hundreds of yards, and was beginning to have a faint hope of escaping, when a bullet from his pursuers struck its hind-quarters and pained and frightened it so much that it bucked him over its head and plunged off to one side among the cactus and mesquite, to be seen no more. Kennedy, by great effort, reached the little arroyo in which we found him, and where he had lain, dreading each sound and expecting each moment to hear the Apaches coming to torture him to death. His fears were unfounded. As it turned out, fortunately for all concerned, the Apaches could not resist the temptation to plunder, and at once began the work of breaking open and pilfering every box and bundle the wagons contained, forgetting all about the Mexicans who had made their escape to the foot-hills, and Kennedy, who lay so very, very near them.

Half a dozen good men were left under command of a sergeant to take care of Kennedy, while the rest hurried forward to see what was to be seen farther to the front.

It was a ghastly sight, one which in its details I should like to spare my readers. There were the hot embers of the new wagons, the scattered fragments of broken boxes, barrels, and packages of all sorts ; copper shells, arrows, bows, one or two broken rifles, torn and burned clothing. There lay all that was mortal of poor Israel, stripped of clothing, a small piece cut from the crown of the head, but thrown back upon the corpse—the Apaches do not care much for scalping—his heart cut out, but also thrown back near the corpse, which had been dragged to the fire of the burning wagons and had been partly consumed ; a lance wound in the back, one or two arrow wounds—they may have been lance wounds, too, but were more likely arrow wounds, the arrows which made them having been burned out ; there were plenty of arrows lying around—a severe contusion under the left eye, where he had been hit perhaps with the stock of a rifle or carbine, and the death wound from ear to ear, through which the brain had oozed.

The face was as calm and resolute in death as Israel had been in life. He belonged to a class of frontiersmen of which few representatives now remain—the same class to which belonged men like Pete Kitchen, the Duncans, of the San Pedro ; Darrel Duppa and Jack Townsend, of the Agua Fria ; men whose lives were a romance of adventure and danger, unwritten because they never frequented the towns, where the tenderfoot correspondent would be more likely to fall in with some border Munchausen, whose tales of privation and peril would be in the direct ratio of the correspondent's receptivity and credulity.

It was now too dark to do anything more, so we brought up Kennedy, who seemed in such good spirits that we were certain he would pull through, as we could not realize that he had been hit by an arrow at all, but tried to console him with the notion that the small round hole in his chest, from which little if any blood had flown, had been made by a buck-shot or something like it. But Kennedy knew better. "No, boys," he said sadly, shaking his head, "it's all up with me. I'm a goner. I know it was an arrow, 'cause I broke the feather end off. I'm goin' to die."

Sentinels were posted behind the bushes, and the whole command sat down to keep silent watch for the coming of the morrow. The Apaches might double back—there was no knowing what they might do—and it was best to be on our guard. The old rule of the frontier, as I learned it from men like Joe Felmer, Oscar Hutton, and Manuel Duran, amounted to this :

" When you see Apache 'sign,' be *keerful;* 'n' when you don' see nary sign, be *more* keerful."

The stars shone out in their grandest effulgence, and the feeble rays of the moon were no added help to vision. There is only one region in the whole world, Arizona, where the full majesty can be comprehended of that text of Holy Writ which teaches : " The Heavens declare the glory of God, and the firmament showeth His handiwork." Midnight had almost come, when the rumble of wheels, the rattle of harness, and the cracking of whips heralded the approach of wagons and ambulance and the second detachment of cavalry. They brought orders from Colonel Dubois to return to the post as soon as the animals had had enough rest, and then as fast as possible, to enable all to start in pursuit of the Apaches, whose trail had been " cut " a mile or two above Felmer's, showing that they had crossed the Santa Catalina Range, and were making for the precipitous country close to the head of the Aravaypa.

The coming day found our party astir and hard at work. First, we hunted up the body of the Apache who had shot Israel. Lieutenant George Bacon, First Cavalry, found it on a shelf of rock, in a ravine not a hundred yards from where the white enemy lay, shot, as Israel was, through the head. We did not disturb it, but as much cannot be averred of the hungry and expectant coyotes and the raw-necked buzzards, which had already begun to draw near.

The trail of the savages led straight toward the Santa Catalina, and a hurried examination disclosed a very curious fact, which later on was of great importance to the troops in pursuit. There had been a case of patent medicine in the wagons, and the Apaches had drunk the contents of the bottles, under the impression that they contained whiskey. The result was that, as the signs showed, there were several of the Indians seriously incapacitated from alcoholic stimulant of some kind, which had served as the menstruum for the drugs of the nostrum. They had staggered from cactus to cactus, falling into mesquite, in contempt of the thorns on the branches, and had lain sprawled at full length in the sand, oblivious of the danger incurred. It would have been a curious experience for the raiders could we have arrived twenty-four hours sooner.

Fully an hour was consumed in getting the horses and mules

down to the water in the Cañon del Oro, and in making a cup of coffee, for which there was the water brought along in the kegs in the wagons. Everything and everybody was all right, excepting Kennedy, who was beginning to act and talk strangely; first exhilarated and then excited, petulant and despondent. His sufferings were beginning to tell upon him, and he manifested a strange aversion to being put in the same vehicle with a dead man. We made the best arrangement possible for the comfort of our wounded friend, for whom it seemed that the ambulance would be the proper place. But the jolting and the upright position he was compelled to take proved too much for him, and he begged to be allowed to recline at full length in one of the wagons.

His request was granted at once; only, as it happened, he was lifted into the wagon in which the stiff, stark corpse of Israel was glaring stonily at the sky. A canvas 'paulin was stretched over the corpse, half a dozen blankets spread out to make as soft a couch as could be expected, and then Kennedy was lifted in, and the homeward march resumed with rapid gait. Animals and men were equally anxious to leave far in the rear a scene of such horror, and without whip or spur we rolled rapidly over the gravelly "mesa," until we got to the head of the Santa Catalina Cañon, and even there we progressed satisfactorily, as, notwithstanding the deep sand, it was all down grade into the post.

In crossing the San Pedro, the wagon in which Kennedy was riding gave a lurch, throwing him to one side; to keep himself from being bumped against the side, he grasped the first thing within reach, and this happened to be the cold, clammy ankle of the corpse. One low moan, or, rather, a groan, was all that showed Kennedy's consciousness of the undesirable companionship of his ride. The incident didn't really make very much difference, however, as his last hours were fast drawing near, and Death had already summoned him. He breathed his last in the post hospital before midnight. An autopsy revealed the presence of a piece of headless arrow, four or five inches long, lodged in the left lung.

The funeral ceremonies did not take much time. There was no lumber in that section of country for making coffins. Packing boxes, cracker boxes, anything that could be utilized, were made to serve the purpose, and generally none were used. The whole garrison turned out. A few words from the Book of Common Prayer—"Man that is born of woman," etc.; a few clods of earth rattling down; then a layer of heavy rocks and spiny cactus, to keep the coyotes from digging up the bones; more earth; and all was over, excepting the getting ready for the pursuit.

This was to be prosecuted by Lieutenant Howard B. Cushing, an officer of wonderful experience in Indian warfare, who with his troop, "F" of the Third Cavalry, had killed more savages of the Apache tribe than any other officer or troop of the United States Army has done before or since. During the latter days of the preceding fall, 1869, he had struck a crushing blow at the courage of the Apaches infesting the country close to the Guadalupe Range in southwestern Texas, and had killed and wounded many of the adults, and captured a number of children and a herd of ponies.

But Lieutenant Franklin Yeaton, a brave and exceedingly able officer, just out of West Point, was fatally wounded on our side, and the more Cushing brooded over the matter, the hotter flamed his anger, until he could stand it no longer, but resolved to slip back across country and try his luck over again. He had hauled Yeaton and the rest of the wounded for four marches on rudely improvised "travois" across the snow, which lay unusually deep that winter, until he found a sheltered camping-place near the Peñasco, a branch of the Pecos, where he left his impedimenta under a strong guard, and with the freshest horses and men turned back, rightly surmising that the hostiles would have given up following him, and would be gathered in their ruined camp, bewailing the loss of kindred.

He had guessed rightly, and at the earliest sign of morning in the east was once again leading his men to the attack upon the Apaches, who, not knowing what to make of such an utterly unexpected onslaught, fled in abject terror, leaving many dead on the ground behind them.

All this did not exactly compensate for the loss of Yeaton, but it served to let out some of Cushing's superfluous wrath, and keep him from exploding.

Cushing belonged to a family which won deserved renown during the War of the Rebellion. One brother blew up the ram *Albemarle;* another died most heroically at his post of duty on the battle-field of Gettysburg ; there was still another in the navy who died in service, I do not remember where ; and the one of whom I am speaking, who was soon to die at the hands of the Apaches, and deserves more than a passing word.

He was about five feet seven in height, spare, sinewy, active as a cat ; slightly stoop-shouldered, sandy complexioned, keen gray or bluish-gray eyes, which looked you through when he spoke and gave a slight hint of the determination, coolness, and energy which had made his name famous all over the southwestern border.   There is an alley named after him in Tucson, and there is, or was, when last I saw it, a tumble-down, worm-eaten board to mark his grave, and that was all to show where the great American nation had deposited the remains of one of its bravest.

But I am anticipating altogether too much, and should be getting ready to follow the trail of the marauders.   Cushing didn't seem to be in any particular hurry about starting, and I soon learned that he intended taking his ease about it, as he wanted to let the Indians be thrown off their guard completely and imagine that the whites were not following their trail.   Let them once suspect that a party was in pursuit, and they would surely break up their trail and scatter like quail, and no one then could hope to do anything with them.

Every hoof was carefully looked at, and every shoe tacked on tight ; a few extra shoes for the fore-feet were taken along in the pack train, with fifteen days' rations of coffee, hard tack, and bacon, and one hundred rounds of ammunition.

All that could be extracted from the Mexicans in the way of information was pondered over, and submitted to the consideration of Felmer and Manuel Duran, the guides who were to conduct the column.   Some of the Mexican men were composed and fully recovered from the effects of their terrible experience, and those who were wounded were doing well ; but the women still trembled at the mere name of an Apache, and several of them did nothing but tell their beads in gratitude to Heaven for the miracle of their escape.

In Arizona, New Mexico, and southwestern Texas it has been remarked that one has to ascend the bed of a stream in order to get water.   This rule is especially true of the Aravaypa.   There is not a drop, as a usual thing, at its mouth, but if you ascend the cañon five or six miles, the current trickles above the sand, and a mile or two more will bring you to a stream of very respectable dimensions, flowing over rocky boulders of good size, between towering walls which screen from the sun, and amid scenery which is picturesque, romantic, and awe-inspiring. The raiders left the cañon of the Aravaypa at its most precipitous part, not far from the gypsum out-crop, and made a straight shoot for the mouth of the San Carlos. This, however, was only a blind, and inside of three miles there was no trail left, certainly not going in the direction of Mount Turnbull.

Manuel Duran was not at all worried ; he was an Apache himself, and none of the tricks of the trade had the slightest effect upon his equanimity. He looked over the ground carefully. Ah ! here is a stone which has been overturned in its place, and here some one has cut that branch of mesquite ; and here—look ! we have it, the shod-hoof track of one of Israel's mules ! There is nothing the matter at all. The Apaches have merely scattered and turned, and instead of going toward the junction of the Gila and the San Carlos, have bent to the west and started straight for the mouth of the San Pedro, going down by the head of Deer Creek, and over to the Rock Creek, which rises in the "Dos Narices" Mountain, not twelve miles from Grant itself. Patient search, watching every blade of grass, every stone or bush, and marching constantly, took the command to the mouth of the San Pedro, across the Gila, up to the head of the Disappointment Creek, in the Mescal Mountains, and over into the foot-hills of the Pinal—and not into the foot-hills merely, but right across the range at its highest point.

The Apaches were evidently a trifle nervous, and wanted to make as big a circuit as possible to bewilder pursuers ; but all their dodges were vain. From the top of the Pinal a smoke was detected rising in the valley to the north and east, and shortly afterward the evidence that a party of squaws and children, laden with steamed mescal, had joined the raiders, and no doubt were to remain with them until they got home, if they were not already home.

Cushing would hardly wait till the sun had hidden behind the Superstition Mountains or the Matitzal before he gave the order to move on. Manuel was more prudent, and not inclined to risk anything by undue haste.

He would wait all night before he would risk disappointment in an attack upon an enemy whom he had followed so far.   Manuel wouldn't allow any of the Americans to come near while he made his preparations for peeping over the crest of the "divide." Tying a large wisp of palmilla or bear's grass about his head, he crawled or wriggled on hands and knees to the position giving the best view down the valley, and made all the observations desired.

The night was long and cold and dark, and the men had been at least an hour in position overlooking the smouldering fires of the enemy, and ready to begin the attack the moment that it should be light enough to see one's hand in front of him, when an accidental occurrence precipitated an engagement.

One of the old men—one of the party of mescal gatherers who had joined the returning war-party—felt cold and arose from his couch to stir the embers into a blaze.   The light played fitfully upon his sharp features and gaunt form, disclosing every muscle.

To get some additional fuel, he advanced toward the spot where Cushing crouched down awaiting the favorable moment for giving the signal to fire.   The savage suspects something, peers ahead a little, and is satisfied that there is danger close by.   He turns to escape, crying out that the Americans have come, and awakening all in the camp.

The soldiers raised a terrific yell and poured in a volley which laid low a number of the Apaches ; the latter scarcely tried to fight in the place where they stood, as the light of the fire made their presence perfectly plain to the attacking party.   So their first idea was to seek a shelter in the rocks from which to pick off the advancing skirmishers.   In this they were unsuccessful, and death and ruin rained down upon them.   They made the best fight they could, but they could do nothing. Manuel saw something curious rushing past him in the gloom. He brought rifle to shoulder and fired, and, as it turned out, killed two at one shot—a great strong warrior, and the little boy of five or six years old whom he had seized, and was trying to hurry to a place of safety, perched upon his shoulders.

It was a ghastly spectacle, a field of blood won with but slight loss to ourselves.   But I do not care to dilate upon the scene, as it is my intention to give only a meagre outline description of what Arizona was like prior to the assignment of General Crook to the command.   The captured women and boys stated they were a band of Pinals who had just returned from a raid down into Sonora before making the attack upon the wagons of Kennedy and Israel. Some of their bravest warriors were along, and they would have made a determined fight had they not all been more or less under the influence of the stuff they had swallowed out of the bottles captured with the train. Many had been very drunk, and all had been sickened, and were not in condition to look out for surprise as they ordinarily did. They had thought that by doubling across the country from point to point, any Americans who might try to follow would surely be put off the scent ; they did not know that there were Apaches with the soldiers.

CHAPTER III.

OF the return march very little need be said. The story would become too long, and there would be needless repetition if an attempt were to be made to describe each scout in detail. There are others to come of much more importance, and covering the same region, so that the reader will lose nothing by the omission.

There was the usual amount of rough mountain climbing, wearing out shoes and patience and nerve strength all at one and the same time ; there was the usual deprivation of water to be expected in the arid wastes of southern Arizona, where springs are few and far between ; there were the usual tricks for getting along without much to drink, such as putting a pebble or twig in the mouth to induce a more copious flow of saliva ; and when camp was made and the water was found to be not all that it might be, there were other tricks for cleaning it, or, at least, causing a deposition of the earthy matter held in suspension, by cutting up a few plates of the nopal and letting them remain in the kettle for a short time, until their mucilaginous juice had precipitated everything. But a still better plan was to improve the good springs, which was a labor of love with officers and men, and many a fine water hole in Arizona has been the scene of much hard work in digging out, building up with cracker boxes or something to hold the water and keep it from soaking into the earth.

Camp Grant was reached at last, and the prisoners turned over to the care of the guard, and Lieutenant Cushing, his first duty in the Territory accomplished with so much credit to himself and his men, made ready to start out on another and a longer trip just as soon as the signal should be given by the post commander.

Our troop was peculiarly situated. It had a second mount of ponies, captured from the Apaches against whom Cushing had done such good service in southwestern Texas. Orders came down in due time from San Francisco to turn them in and have them sold by the quartermaster; but until these orders came— and owing to the slowness of mail communications in those days, they did not come for several months—we had the advantage of being able to do nearly twice as much work as troops less fortunately placed.

The humdrum life of any post in Arizona in those days was enough to drive one crazy. The heat in most of them became simply unendurable, although here the great dryness of the atmosphere proved a benefit. Had the air been humid, very few of our garrison would now be alive to tell of temperatures of one hundred and twenty and over, and of days during the whole twenty-four hours of which the thermometer did not register below the one hundred notch.

There was a story current that the heat had one time become so excessive that two thermometers had to be strapped together to let the mercury have room to climb. That was before my arrival, and is something for which I do not care to vouch. I give the story as it was given to me by my friend, Jack Long, of whom I am soon to speak.

In every description of Arizona that I have ever seen, and I claim to be familiar with most if not all that has appeared in print, there occurs the story of the soldier who came back to Fort Yuma after his blankets, finding the next world too cold to suit him. I make reference to the story because many worthy people would find it hard to believe that a man had been in Arizona who did not tell this story in his first chapter, but it has grown to be such a mouldy military chestnut that I may be pardoned for omitting it.

There were all kinds of methods of killing the hours. One that interested everybody for a while was the battles which we stirred up between the nests of red and black ants, which could

be found in plenty and of great size close to the post. I have
seen the nests in question three or four feet high, and not less
than six feet long, crowded with industrious population. The
way to start the battle was to make a hole in each nest and
insert cans which had lately been emptied of peaches or other
sweets.

These would soon fill with the battalions of the two colors,
and could then be poured into a basin, where the combat *à
outrance* never failed to begin at once. The red ants were
much the braver, and one of that color would tackle two, and
even three, of the black. If the rumpus lasted for any length of
time, queens would appear, as if to superintend what was going
on. At least, that was our impression when we saw the large-
bodied, yellow-plush insects sallying from the depths of the
nests.

We had not been back in the post a week before we had something to talk about. A Mexican who was doing some work for
the Government came up to confer with the commanding officer
as to details. He left the adjutant's office before mid-day, and
had not gone one thousand yards—less, indeed, than rifle-shot—
from the door, when an Apache, lurking in ambush behind a
clump of palmilla, pierced him through and through with a
lance, and left him dead, weltering in his own blood. To attempt
pursuit was worse than useless, and all we could do was to bury
the victim.

It was this peculiarity of the Apaches that made them such a
terror to all who came in contact with them, and had compelled
the King of Spain to maintain a force of four thousand dragoons
to keep in check a tribe of naked savages, who scorned to wear
any protection against the bullets of the Castilians, who would
not fight when pursued, but scattered like their own crested
mountain quail, and then hovered on the flanks of the whites,
and were far more formidable when dispersed than when they
were moving in compact bodies. This was simply the best military policy for the Apaches to adopt—wear out the enemy by
vexatious tactics, and by having the pursuit degenerate into a
will-o'-th'-wisp chase. The Apaches could find food on every hill-
side, and the water-holes, springs, and flowing streams far up in
the mountains were perfectly well known to them.

The Caucasian troops, of whatever nationality, would wander

about, half-crazed with thirst, and maddened by the heat of the day or chilled by the cold winds of night in the mountains, and unable to tell which plants were of value as food and which were not.

The Apache was in no sense a coward. He knew his business, and played his cards to suit himself. He never lost a shot, and never lost a warrior in a fight where a brisk run across the nearest ridge would save his life and exhaust the heavily clad soldier who endeavored to catch him. Apaches in groups of two and three, and even individual Apaches, were wont to steal in close to the military posts and ranchos, and hide behind some sheltering rock, or upon the summit of some conveniently situated hill, and there remain for days, scanning the movements of the Americans below, and waiting for a chance to stampede a herd, or kill a herder or two, or "jump" a wagon-train.

They knew how to disguise themselves so thoroughly that one might almost step upon a warrior thus occupied before he could detect his presence. Stripped naked, with head and shoulders wrapped up in a bundle of yucca shoots or "sacaton" grass, and with body rubbed over with the clay or sand along which it wriggled as sinuously and as venomously as the rattler itself, the Apache could and did approach to within ear-shot of the whites, and even entered the enclosures of the military camps, as at Grant and Crittenden, where we on several occasions discovered his foot-prints alongside the "ollas," or water-jars.

On such occasions he preferred to employ his lance or bow, because these made no sound, and half or even a whole day might elapse before the stiffened and bloody corpse of the herder or wagoner would be found, and the presence of Indians in the vicinity become known. At least twenty such examples could be given from my own knowledge, occurring at Prescott, Tucson, Camp Grant, Camp Crittenden, Tres Alamos, Florence, Williamson's Valley, and elsewhere. They were regarded as the natural features of the country, and every settler rather expected them as a matter of course. Well did Torquemada, the Spanish writer (A.D. 1709), deplore the inability of the Spaniards to make headway against this tribe of naked savages.

Californians old enough to remember the days when San Francisco had a Mining Stock Exchange, may recall the names of

Lent and Harpending, who were two of the most prominent of the members. An expedition, equipped at the expense of these gentlemen, made its way into Arizona to examine the mining "prospects" discovered in the vicinity of Fort Bowie. They had to come overland, of course, as there were no railroads, and wagons had to be taken from Los Angeles, the terminal point of steamer navigation, unless people preferred to keep on down to San Diego, and then cross the desert, via Fort Yuma, and on up the dusty valley of the Gila River to Tucson or Florence. The party of which I am now speaking was under the command of two gentlemen, one named Gatchell and the other Curtis, from the Comstock Mines in Nevada, and had reached and passed the picturesque little adobe town of Florence, on the Gila, and was progressing finely on the road toward Tucson, when "Cocheis," the bold leader of the Chiricahuas, on his march up from Sonora to trade stolen horses and have a talk with the Pinals, swooped down upon them. It was the old, old Arizona story. No one suspected danger, because there had been no signs of Indians on the trip since leaving the villages of the peaceful Pimas, on the Gila, near Maricopa Wells.

It was a perfect duplication of the Kennedy-Israel affair, almost to the slightest details. Mr. Curtis received a bad wound in the lungs. Mr. Gatchell was also wounded, but how severely I cannot remember, for the very good reason that there was so much of that kind of thing going on during the period of my stay at Camp Grant that it is really impossible to avoid mixing up some of the minor details of the different incidents so closely resembling one another.

When this party reached the post of Camp Grant they could easily have demanded the first prize at a tramp show ; they were not clothed in rags—they were not clothed in anything. When they escaped from the wagon-train they were wearing nothing but underclothing, on account of the excessive heat of the day ; when they got into Camp Grant most of the underwear had disappeared, torn off by the cactus, palo verde, mesquite, mescal, and other thorny vegetation run against in their flight. Their feet evidenced the rough, stony nature of the ground over which they had tramped and bumped, and thorns stuck in their legs, feet, and arms. There was not much done for these poor wretches, all of whom seemed to be gentlemen of education and refinement. We shared the misery of the post with them, which was about all we could pretend to do. Vacant rooms were found for them in the Israel ranch, and there they stayed for a few days, just long enough for every one to catch the fever.

Before we start out in pursuit of the attacking Apaches, let me relate the story told all over southern Arizona about the spot where this Gatchell-Curtis train had been surprised. It was known as the scene of the ambuscade of the Miller-Tappan detail, and frontier tale-tellers used to while away the sultry hours immediately after the setting of the sun in relating how the soldiers under Carroll had been ambushed and scattered by the onslaught of the Apaches, their commander, Lieutenant Carroll, killed at the first fire. One of the survivors became separated from his comrades in their headlong flight into Camp Grant. What became of him was never fully known, but he had been seen to fall wounded in the head or face, and the soldiers and Mexicans seemed to be of but one opinion as to the direction in which he had strayed ; so there was no difficulty in getting a band of expert trailers to go out with the troops from the camp, and after burying the dead, make search for the missing man. His foot-prints were plainly discernible for quite a distance in the hard sand and gravel, until they led to a spring or "water-hole," where one could plainly read the "sign" that the wounded man had stopped, knelt down, drunk, washed his wound, torn off a small piece of his blouse, perhaps as a bandage, and written his name on a rock in his own blood.

So far, so good ; the Mexicans who had been in the searching party did not object to telling that much, but anything beyond was told by a shrug of the shoulders and a " Quien sabe ? "

One day it happened that José Maria was in a communicative mood, and I induced him to relate what he knew. His story amounted to just this : After leaving the " water-hole," the wounded man had wandered aimlessly in different directions, and soon began to stagger from bush to bush ; his strength was nearly gone, and with frequency he had taken a seat on the hard gravel under such shade as the mesquites afforded.

After a while other tracks came in on the trail alongside of those of the man—they were the tracks of an enormous mountain lion ! The beast had run up and down along the trail for a short distance, and then bounded on in the direction taken by the wanderer. The last few bounds measured twenty-two feet, and then there were signs of a struggle, and of SOMETHING having been dragged off through the chapparal and over the rocks, and that was all.

Our men were ready for the scout, and so were those of the detachment of " K " Troop, First Cavalry, who were to form part of our expedition—a gallant troop and a fine regiment.

The quarters were all in bustle and confusion, and even at their best would have looked primitive and uncouth. They were made of unhewn logs set upright into the ground and chinked with mud, and roofed in the same early English style, with the addition of a ceiling of old pieces of canvas to keep the centipedes from dropping down.

On the walls were a couple of banjos, and there were intimations that the service of the troop had been of a decidedly active nature, in the spoils of Apache villages clustered against the cottonwood saplings. There were lances with tips of obsidian, and others armed with the blades of old cavalry sabres ; quivers of coyote and mountain lion skin filled with arrows, said by the Mexican guides to be poisonous ; and other relics of aboriginal ownership in raw-hide playing-cards, shields, and one or two of the century-plant fiddles.

The gloom of the long sleeping room was relieved by the bright colors of a few Navajo blankets, and there hung from the rafters large earthenware jars, called " ollas," the manufacture of the peaceful Papagoes, in which gallons of water cooled by rapid evaporation.

There were no tin wash-basins, but a good substitute was found in the pretty Apache baskets, woven so tightly of grasses and roots that water could no more leak through them than it could through the better sort of the Navajo blankets. A half a dozen, maybe more, of the newspaper illustrations and cartoons of the day were pasted in spots where they would be most effective, and over in the coolest corner was the wicker cage of a pet mocking-bird. There were other pets by this time in the Apache children captured in the skirmishes already had with the natives. The two oldest of the lot—" Sunday " and " Dandy Jim "—were never given any dinner until they had each first shot an arrow into the neck of an olive-bottle inserted into one of the adobe walls of the quartermaster's corral. The ease with which these youngsters not over nine or ten years old did this used to surprise me, but it seemed to make them regard the Americans as a very peculiar people for demanding such a slight task.

Out on the trail again, down the San Pedro and over the Gila, but keeping well to the west until we neared the Mineral Creek country ; then up across the lofty Pinal Range, on whose summits the cool breezes were fragrant with the balsamic odors of the tall, straight pines, over into the beautiful little nook known as Mason's Valley, in which there was refreshing grass for the animals and a trickling stream of pure water to slake their thirst. Then back to the eastward until we struck the waters of the Pinal Creek, and had followed it down to the " Wheat Fields," and still no signs of Indians. The rainy season had set in, and every track was obliterated almost as soon as made.

One night we bivouacked at a spot not far from where the mining town of Globe now stands, and at a ledge of rocks which run across the valley of Pinal Creek, but part for a few feet to permit the feeble current to flow through. The sky was comparatively clear, a few clouds only flitting across the zenith. Back of us, hanging like a shroud over the tops of the Pinal, were heavy, black masses, from whose pendulous edges flashed the lightning, and from whose cavernous depths roared and growled the thunder.

" That looks very much like a cloud-burst coming," said Cushing ; " better be on the safe side, anyhow." So he gave orders to move all the bedding and all the supplies of the pack-train higher up the side of the hill. The latter part of the order was obeyed first, and almost if not quite all the ammunition, bacon, coffee, and sugar had been carried out of reach of possible danger, and most of the blankets and carbines had been shifted— everything, in fact, but the hard tack—when we noticed that the volume of water in the creek had unaccountably increased, and the next moment came the warning cry : " Look out ! Here she comes ! " A solid wall of water—I do not care to say how many feet high—was rushing down the cañon, sweeping all before it, and crushing a path for itself over the line along which our blankets had been spread so short a time previously.

The water didn't make very much noise. There was no sound

but a SISH ! That meant more than my pen can say. All that
we had carried to the higher slopes of the cañon side was saved.
All that we had not been able to move was swept away, but there
was nothing of value to any one excepting a mule belonging to
one of the guides, which was drowned, and a lot of harness or
rigging from the pack-train, which, with the hard tack, found a
watery grave.

Cushing, too, would have been swept off in the current had he
not been seized in the strong grasp of Sergeant Warfield and
" Big Dan Miller," two of the most powerful men in the troop.
The rain soaked through us all night, and we had to make the
best of it until dawn, when we discovered to our great surprise
and satisfaction that the stream, which had been gorged between
the rocks at our camp, widened below, and this had allowed the
current to expand and to slacken, dropping here and there in the
valley most of the plunder which was of consequence to us, especially the hard bread.

All this meant an exasperating delay of twenty-four hours to
dry our blankets upon the rocks, and to spread out our sodden
food, and save as much of it as we could from mildew.

From there we made a detour over to Pinto Creek, where I
may inform those of my readers who take an interest in such
things, there are one or two exceptionally well-preserved cliff-
dwellings, which we examined with much curiosity.

Not far from there we came upon the corn-fields of a band of
Apaches, and destroyed them, eating as many of the roasting ears
as we could, and feeding the rest to our stock.

Such were the military instructions of twenty and twenty-five
years ago. As soldiers we had to obey, even if we could feel that
these orders must have been issued under a misconception of the
Indian character. The more the savage is attached to the soil by
the ties of a remunerative husbandry, the more is he weaned
from the evil impulses which idleness engenders. This proposition seems just as clear as that two and two make four, but some
people learn quickly, and others learn slowly, and preachers,
school-teachers, and military people most slowly of all.

Our presence was discovered by the Apache look-outs before
we were able to effect a surprise, or, to be candid, we stumbled in
upon the nook, or series of nooks, in which this planting was
going on, and beyond exchanging a few shots and wounding, as

we learned afterward, a couple of the young men, did not do much at that moment ; but we did catch two squaws, from whom some information was extracted.

They agreed to lead us to where there was another " rancheria " a few miles off, in another cañon over toward Tonto Creek. We found the enemy, sure enough, but in such an inaccessible position, up among lofty hills covered with a dense jungle of scrub oak, that we could do nothing beyond firing shots in reply to those directed against us, and were so unfortunate as to lose our prisoners, who darted like jack-rabbits into the brush, and were out of sight in a flash. Why did we not catch them again ? Oh, well, that is something that no one could do but the gentle reader. The gentle reader generally is able to do more than the actors on the ground, and he may as well be allowed a monopoly in the present case.

We growled and grumbled a good deal at our hard luck, and made our way to the Mesquite Springs, where the ranch of Archie Mac Intosh has since been erected, and there went into camp for the night. Early the next morning we crossed the Salt River and ascended the Tonto Creek for a short distance, passing through a fertile valley, once well settled by a tribe whose stone houses now in ruins dotted the course of the stream, and whose pottery, stone axes, and other vestiges, in a condition more or less perfect, could be picked up in any quantity. We turned back, recrossed the Salt or Salado, and made a long march into the higher parts of the Sierra Apache, striking a fresh trail, and following it energetically until we had run it into the camp of a scouting party of the First Cavalry, from Camp MacDowell, under Colonel George B. Sanford, who had had a fight with these same Indians the previous day, and killed or captured most of them.

Sanford and his command treated us most kindly, and made us feel at home with them. They did not have much to offer beyond bacon and beans ; but a generous, hospitable gentleman can offer these in a way that will make them taste like canvas-back and terrapin. When we left Sanford, we kept on in the direction of the Sombrero Butte and the mouth of Cherry Creek, to the east, and then headed for the extreme sources of the San Carlos River, a trifle to the south.

Here we had the good luck to come upon a village of Apaches, who abandoned all they possessed and fled to the rocks as soon as our rapid advance was announced in the shrill cries of their vedettes perched upon the higher peaks.

In this place the "medicine-men" had been engaged in some of their rites, and had drawn upon the ground half-completed figures of circles, crosses, and other lines which we had no time to examine. We looked through the village, whose "jacales" were of unusually large size, and while interested in this work the enemy began to gather in the higher hills, ready to pick off all who might become exposed to their aim. They had soon crawled down within very close proximity, and showed great daring in coming up to us. I may be pardoned for describing in something of detail what happened to the little party which stood with me looking down, or trying to look down, into a low valley or collection of swales beneath us. Absolutely nothing could be seen but the red clay soil, tufted here and there with the Spanish bayonet or the tremulous yucca. So well satisfied were we all that no Apaches were in the valley that I had already given the order to dismount and descend the steep flanks of the hill to the lower ground, but had hardly done so before there was a puff, a noise, and a tzit !—all at once, from the nearest clump of sacaton or yucca, not more than a hundred yards in front. The bullet whizzed ominously between our heads and struck my horse in the neck, ploughing a deep but not dangerous wound.

Our horses, being fresh "broncos," became disturbed, and it was all we could do to keep them from breaking away. When we had quieted them a little, we saw two of the Apaches—stark naked, their heads bound up with yucca, and their bodies red with the clay along which they had crawled in order to fire the shot—scampering for their lives down the valley.

We got down the hill, leading our horses, and then took after the fugitives, all the time yelling to those of our comrades whom we could see in advance to head the Indians off. One of the savages, who seemed to be the younger of the two, doubled up a side ravine, but the other, either because he was run down or because he thought he could inflict some damage upon us and then escape, remained hidden behind a large mesquite. Our men made the grievous mistake of supposing that the Indian's gun was not loaded. Only one gun had been seen in the possession of the two whom we had pursued, and this having been discharged, we were certain that the savage had not had time to reload it.

It is quite likely that each of the pair had had a rifle, and that the young boy, previous to running up the cañon to the left, had given his weapon to his elder, who had probably left his own on the ground after once firing it.

Be this as it may, we were greeted with another shot, which killed the blacksmith of "K" Troop, First Cavalry, and right behind the shot came the big Indian himself, using his rifle as a shillelah, beating Corporal Costello over the head with it and knocking him senseless, and then turning upon Sergeant Harrington and a soldier of the First Cavalry named Wolf, dealing each a blow on the skull, which would have ended them had not his strength begun to ebb away with his life-blood, now flowing freely from the death-wound through the body which we had succeeded in inflicting.

One horse laid up, three men knocked out, and another man killed was a pretty steep price to pay for the killing of this one Indian, but we consoled ourselves with the thought that the Apaches had met with a great loss in the death of so valiant a warrior. We had had other losses on that day, and the hostiles had left other dead ; our pack-train was beginning to show signs of wear and tear from the fatigue of climbing up and down these stony, brush-covered, arid mountain-sides. One of the mules had broken its neck or broken its back by slipping off a steep trail, and all needed some rest and recuperation.

From every peak now curled the ominous signal smoke of the enemy, and no further surprises would be possible. Not all of the smokes were to be taken as signals; many of them might be signs of death, as the Apaches at that time adhered to the old custom of abandoning a village and setting it on fire the moment one of their number died, and as soon as this smoke was seen the adjacent villages would send up answers of sympathy.

Cushing thought that, under all the circumstances, it would be good policy to move over to some eligible position where we could hold our own against any concentration the enemy might be tempted to make against us, and there stay until the excitement occasioned by our presence in the country had abated.

The spring near the eastern base of the Pinal Mountains, where the "killing" of the early spring had taken place, suggested itself, and thither we marched as fast as our animals could make the trip. But we had counted without our host; the waters were so polluted with dead bodies, there were so many skulls in the spring itself, that no animal, much less man, would imbibe of the fluid. The ground was strewn with bones—ribs and arms and vertebræ—dragged about by the coyotes, and the smell was so vile that, tired as all were, no one felt any emotion but one of delight when Cushing gave the order to move on.

The Apaches had been there to bury their kinsfolk and bewail their loss, and in token of grief and rage had set fire to all the grass for several miles, and consequently it was to the direct benefit of all our command, two-footed or four-footed, to keep moving until we might find a better site for a bivouac.

We did not halt until we had struck the San Carlos, some thirty-five miles to the east, and about twelve or fourteen miles above its junction with the Gila. Here we made camp, intending to remain several days. A rope was stretched from one to the other of two stout sycamores, and to this each horse and mule was attached by its halter. Pickets were thrown out upon the neighboring eminences, and a detail from the old guard was promptly working at bringing in water and wood for the campfires. The grooming began, and ended almost as soon as the welcome cry of "Supper!" resounded. The coffee was boiling hot; the same could be said of the bacon; the hard tack had mildewed a little during the wet weather to which it had been exposed, but there was enough roasted mescal from the Indian villages to eke out our supplies.

The hoofs and back of every animal had been examined and cared for, and then blankets were spread out and all hands made ready to turn in. There were no tents, as no shelter was needed, but each veteran was wise enough to scratch a little semicircle in the ground around his head, to turn the rain should any fall during the night, and to erect a wind-brake to screen him from the chill breezes which sometimes blew about midnight.

Although there was not much danger of a night-attack from the Apaches, who almost invariably made their onset with the first twinkle of the coming dawn in the east, yet a careful watch was always kept, to frustrate their favorite game of crawling on hands and feet up to the horses, and sending an arrow into the herd or the sentinel, as might happen to be most convenient.

Not far from this camp I saw, for the first time, a fight between a tarantula and a "tarantula hawk." Manuel Duran had always insisted that the gray tarantula could whip the black one, and that there was something that flew about in the evening that could and would make the quarrelsome gray tarantula seek safety in abject flight. It was what we used to call in my school-boy days "the devil's darning-needle" which made its appearance, and seemed to worry the great spider very much. The tarantula stood up on its hind legs, and did its best to ward off impending fate, but it was no use. The "hawk" hit the tarantula in the back and apparently paralyzed him, and then seemed to be pulling at one of the hind legs. I have since been informed that there is some kind of a fluid injected into the back of the tarantula which acts as a stupefier, and at the same time the "hawk" deposits its eggs there, which, hatching, feed upon the spider. For all this I cannot vouch, as I did not care to venture too near those venomous reptiles and insects of that region, at least not until after I had acquired more confidence from greater familiarity with them.

We saw no more Indian "sign" on that trip, which had not been, however, devoid of all incident.

And no sooner had we arrived at Camp Grant than we were out again, this time guided by an Apache squaw, who had come into the post during our absence, and given to the commanding officer a very consistent story of ill-treatment at the hands of her people. She said that her husband was dead, killed in a fight with the troops, and that she and her baby had not been treated with the kindness which they had a right to expect. I do not remember in what this ill-treatment consisted, but most likely none of the brothers of the deceased had offered to marry the widow and care for her and her little one, as is the general custom, in which the Apaches resemble the Hebrews of ancient times. If the troops would follow her, she would guide them into a very bad country, where there was a "rancheria" which could be attacked and destroyed very readily.

So back we went, this time on foot, carrying our rations on our backs, crossing the Piñaleno to the south of the Aravaypa, and ascending until we reached the pine forest upon its summit; then down into the valley at the extreme head of the Aravaypa, and over into the broken country on the other side of the Gabilan, or Hawk Cañon.

Everything had happened exactly as the squaw had predicted it would, and she showed that she was familiar with the slightest details of the topography, and thus increased our confidence in what we had to expect to such an extent that she was put in the lead, and we followed on closely, obeying all her directions and instructions. Our men refrained from whistling, from talking —almost, I might say, from breathing—because she insisted upon such perfect silence while on the march. There were few instructions given, and these were passed from mouth to mouth in whispers. No one dared strike a match, lest the flash should alarm some of the enemy's pickets. We had no pack-train, and that great source of noise—the shouting of packers to straying mules—was done away with. All our rations were on our own backs, and with the exception of one led mule, loaded with a couple of thousand rounds of extra ammunition, we had absolutely nothing to impede the most rapid march. We walked slowly over the high mountains, and down into deep ravines, passing through a country which seemed well adapted for the home of Indians. There were groves of acorn-bearing oaks, a considerable amount of mescal, Spanish bayonet, some mesquite, and a plenty of grasses whose seeds could be gathered by the squaws in their long, conical baskets, and then ground between two oblong, half-round stones into a meal which would make a pretty good mush.

It was very dark and quite chilly as dawn drew nigh, and every one was shivering with cold and hunger and general nervous excitement. The squaw whispered that we were close upon the site of the "rancheria," which was in a little grassy amphitheatre a short distance in front. Slowly we drew nearer and nearer to the doomed village, and traversed the smooth, open place whereon the young bucks had been playing their great game of "mushka," in which they roll a hoop and then throw lance staves to fall to the ground as the hoop ceases to roll. Very near this was a slippery-faced rock—either slate or basalt, the darkness did not permit a close examination—down which the children had been sliding to the grass, and, just within biscuit-throw, the "jacales" of saplings and branches.

Two of our party crawled up to the village, which preserved an ominous silence. There were no barking dogs, no signs of fire, no wail of babes to testify to the presence of human or animal

life—in one word, the Apaches had taken the alarm and abandoned their habitation. But they did not leave us shivering long
in doubt as to where they had gone, but at once opened from the
peaks with rifles, and at the first fire wounded two of our men.
It was entirely too dark for them to do much harm, and utterly
beyond our power to do anything against them. Their position
was an impregnable one on the crest of the surrounding ridges,
and protected by a heavy natural *cheval de frise* of the scrub oak
and other thorny vegetation of the region.

Cushing ordered the command to fall back on the trail and
take up position on the hill in the pass overlooking the site of
the "rancheria." This we did without difficulty and without
loss. The Apaches continued their firing, and would have made
us pay dear for our rashness in coming into their home had not
our withdrawal been covered by a heavy fog, which screened the
flanks of the mountains until quite a late hour in the morning,
something very unusual in Arizona, which is remarkably free
from mists at all seasons.

Indignation converged upon the wretched squaw who had induced us to come into what had all the appearance of a set ambuscade. The men had bound her securely, and a rope was now
brought out—a lariat—and cries were heard on all sides to "hang
her, hang her!" It is easy to see now that she may have been
perfectly innocent in her intentions, and that it was not through
collusion with the people in the village, but rather on account of
her running away from them, that the Apaches had been on the
look-out for an advance from the nearest military post; but on
that cold, frosty morning, when all were cross and tired and
vexed with disappointment, it looked rather ominous for the
woman for a few minutes.

She was given the benefit of the doubt, and to do the men
justice, they were more desirous of scaring than of killing her
for her supposed treachery. She stuck to her story ; she was
dissatisfied with her people on account of bad treatment, and
wanted to lead us to a surprise of their home. She did not pretend to say how it came about that they were ready for us, but
said that some of their young men out hunting, or squaws out
cutting and burning mescal, might have seen us coming up the
mountain, or "cut" our trail the night previous, and given the
alarm. She would stay with us as long as we chose to remain in

those hills, but her opinion was that nothing could now be done with the people of that " rancheria," because the whole country would be alarmed with signal smokes, and every mountain would have a picket on the look-out for us. Better return to the camp and wait until everything had quieted down, and then slip out again.

There was still a good deal of growling going on, and not all of the men were satisfied with her talk. They shot angry glances at her, and freely expressed their desire to do her bodily harm, which threats she could perfectly understand without needing the slightest knowledge of our language. To keep her from slipping off as the two other squaws had done a fortnight previously, she was wrapped from head to feet with rope, so that it was all she could do to breathe, much less think of escaping. Another rope fastened her to a palo verde close to the little fire at which our coffee was made, and alongside whose flickering embers the sentinel paced as night began to draw its curtains near. She lay like a log, making not the slightest noise or movement, but to all appearances perfectly reconciled to the situation, and, after a while, fell off into a profound sleep.

We had what was known as "a running guard," which means that every man in the camp takes his turn at the duty of sentinel during the night. This made the men on post have about half to three-quarters of an hour's duty each. Each of those posted near the prisoner gave a careful look at her as he began to pace up and down near her, and each found that she was sleeping calmly and soundly, until about eleven o'clock, or maybe a few minutes nearer midnight, a recruit, who had just taken his turn on post, felt his elbows pinioned fast behind him and his carbine almost wrenched from his grasp. He was very muscular, and made a good fight to retain his weapon and use it, but it fell to the ground, and the naked woman plunged down the side of the hill straight through the chapparal into the darkness profound.

Bang ! bang ! sounded his carbine just as soon as he could pick it up from the ground where it lay, and bang ! bang ! sounded others, as men half-asleep awakened to the belief that there was a night attack. This firing promptly ceased upon Cushing's orders. There was not the slightest possible use in wasting ammunition, and in besides running the risk of hitting some of our own people. The squaw had escaped, and that was enough. There lay her clothing, and the cocoon-like bundle of rope which had bound her. She had wriggled out of her fastenings, and sprung upon the sentinel, who was no doubt the least vigilant of all whom she had observed, and had tried to snatch his weapon from him and thus prevent an alarm being given until she had reached the bottom of the hill. All the clothing she had on at the moment when she made her rush upon the sentinel was an old and threadbare cavalry cape which hardly covered her shoulders.

Cold and damp and weary, we started on our homeward trip, feeling as spiritless as a brood of half-drowned chickens. Even the Irish had become glum, and could see nothing ridiculous in our mishap—a very bad sign.

"Blessed are they that expect nothing." We didn't expect and we didn't receive any mercy from our comrades upon getting back to the mess, and the sharp tongue of raillery lost none of its power when the squaw came in close upon our heels, saying that she could not leave her baby, that her breast cried for it. She had told the truth. If we did not believe her story, we could kill her, but let her see her baby again. Her desire was gratified, and no harm came to her. The ordinary stagnation of the post had been interrupted during our absence by the advent of an addition to the little circle of captives, and there was much curiosity to get a good look at the little black-eyed mite which lay cuddled up in the arms of its dusky mother.

I have purposely withheld mention of the only lady who shared the life of Camp Grant with us—Mrs. Dodds, the wife of Doctor Dodds, our post surgeon, or one of them, because we had two medical officers. She was of a very sweet, gentle disposition, and never once murmured or complained, but exerted herself to make the life of her husband as comfortable as possible.

Their quarters had a very cosey look, and one would find it hard to believe that those comfortable chairs were nothing but barrels sawed out to shape and cushioned and covered with chintz. That lounge was merely a few packing boxes concealed under blankets and mattresses. Everything else in the apartment was on the same scale and made of corresponding materials. There was a manifest determination to do much with little, and much had been done.

Mrs. Dodds wore her honors as the belle of the garrison with

becoming graciousness and humility. She received in the kind-
est spirit the efforts made by all of the rougher sex to render her
stay among them pleasant and, if possible, interesting. Not a
day passed that did not find her the recipient of some token of
regard. It might not always be the most appropriate sort of a
thing, but that really made very little difference. She accepted
everything and tried to look as if each gift had been the one for
which she had been longing during her whole life. She had a rattlesnake belt, made from one of the biggest and most vicious reptiles ever seen in the vicinity. She had Apache baskets, war-clubs,
playing-cards, flutes, fiddles, and enough truck of the same kind
to load an army-wagon. The largest Gila monsters would have
been laid at her feet had she not distinctly and emphatically
drawn the line at Gila monsters. Tarantulas and centipedes, if
properly bottled, were not objectionable, but the Gila monster
was more than she could stand, and she so informed intending
donors. She has been dead a number of years, but it is hardly
likely that she ever forgot until she drew her last breath the
days and weeks and months of her existence at Camp Grant.

Our own stay at the delightful summer resort had come to an
end. Orders received from department headquarters transferred
our troop to Tucson, as being a more central location and nearer
supplies. Lieutenant Cushing was ordered to take the field and
keep it until further orders, which meant that he was to be free
to roam as he pleased over any and all sections of the territory
infested by the Apaches, and to do the best he could against them.

To a soldier of Cushing's temperament this meant a great deal,
and it is needless to say that no better selection for such a duty
could have been made.

We were packed up and out of the post in such quick time that
I do not remember whether it was twelve hours or twenty-four.
To be sure, we did not have an immense amount of plunder to
pack. None the less did we work briskly to carry out orders and
get away in the shortest time possible.

We had to leave one of our men in the hospital ; he had accidentally shot himself in the leg, and was now convalescing from
the amputation. But the rest were in the saddle and out on the
road through the Santa Catalina Cañon before you could say
Jack Robinson.

And not altogether without regret. There was a bright side

to the old rookery, which shone all the more lustrously now that we were saying farewell.

We had never felt lonesome by any means. There was always something going on, always something to do, always something to see.

The sunrises were gorgeous to look upon at the hour for morning stables, when a golden and rosy flush bathèd the purple peaks of the Pinaleño, and at eventide there were great banks of crimson and purple and golden clouds in the western horizon which no painter would have dared depict upon canvas.

There were opportunities for learning something about mineralogy in the "wash" of the cañons, botany on the hill-sides, and insect life and reptile life everywhere. Spanish could be picked up from Mexican guides and packers, and much that was quaint and interesting in savage life learned from an observation of the manners of the captives—representatives of that race which the Americans have so frequently fought, so generally mismanaged, and so completely failed to understand.

There was much rough work under the hardest of conditions, and the best school for learning how to care for men and animals in presence of a sleepless enemy, which no amount of "book l'arnin'" could supply.

The distance from Old Camp Grant to Tucson, Arizona, over the wagon-road, was fifty-five measured miles. The first half of the journey, the first day's march—as far as the Cañon del Oro —has already been described. From the gloomy walls of the shady cañon, in which tradition says gold was found in abundance in the earliest days of occupation by the Caucasians, the wagons rolled rapidly over the Eight-mile Mesa, over some slightly hilly and sandy country, until after passing the Riito, when Tucson came in sight and the road became firmer. All the way, on both sides of the road, and as far as eye could reach, we had in sight the stately mescal, loaded with lovely velvety flowers ; the white-plumed Spanish bayonet, the sickly green palo verde, without a leaf ; the cholla, the nopal, the mesquite, whose "beans" were rapidly ripening in the sultry sun, and the majestic "pitahaya," or candelabrum cactus, whose ruby fruit had long since been raided upon and carried off by flocks of bright-winged humming-birds, than which no fairer or more alert can be seen this side of Brazil. The "pitahaya" attains a great height in the vicinity of Grant, Tucson, and MacDowell, and one which we measured by its shadow was not far from fifty-five to sixty feet above the ground.

On this march the curious rider could see much to be remembered all the days of his life. Piles of loose stones heaped up by loving hands proclaimed where the Apaches had murdered their white enemies. The projection of a rude cross of mescal or Spanish bayonet stalks was evidence that the victim was a Mexican, and a son of Holy Mother Church. Its absence was no index of religious belief, but simply of the nationality being American.

Of the weird, blood-chilling tales that were narrated as each of these was passed I shall insert only one. It was the story, briefly told, of two young men whose train had been attacked, whose comrades had been put to flight, and who stood their ground resolutely until the arrows and bullets of the foe had ended the struggle. When found, one of the bodies was pierced with sixteen wounds, the other with fourteen.

On the left flank, or eastern side, the view was hemmed in for the whole distance by the lofty, pine-clad Sierra Santa Catalina ; but to the north one could catch glimpses of the summit of the black Pinal ; to the west there was a view over the low-lying Tortolita clear to the dim, azure outlines which, in the neighborhood of the Gila Bend, preserved in commemorative mesa-top the grim features of Montezuma, as Mexican myth fondly averred.

A little this side was the site of the " Casa Grande," the old pile of adobe, which has been quite as curious a ruin in the contemplation of the irrepressible Yankee of modern days as it was to Coronado and his followers when they approached it under the name of " Chichilticale " more than three centuries and a half ago.

Still nearer was the " Picacho," marking the line of the Great Southern Mail road ; at its base the ranch of Charlie Shibell, where the stages changed teams and travellers stopped to take supper, the scene of as many encounters with the Apaches as any other spot in the whole Southwest. Follow along a little more to the left, and there comes the Santa Teresa Range, just back of Tucson, and credited by rumors as reliable as any ever brought by contraband during the war with being the repository of fabulous wealth in the precious metals ; but no one has yet had the Aladdin's lamp to rub and summon the obedient genii who would disclose the secret of its location.

Far off to the south rises the glistening cone of the Baboquivari, the sacred mountain in the centre of the country of the gentle Papagoes, and on the east, as we get down nearer to the Riito, the more massive outlines of the Santa Rita peak overshadowing the town of Tucson, and the white, glaring roof of the beautiful mission ruin of San Xavier del Bac.

Within this space marched the columns of the Coronado expedition, armed to the teeth in all the panoply of grim war, and bent on destruction and conquest ; and here, too, plodded meek friar and learned priest, the sons of Francis or of Loyola, armed with the irresistible weapons of the Cross, the Rosary, and the Sacred Text, and likewise bent upon destruction and conquest —the destruction of idols and the conquest of souls.

These were no ordinary mortals, whom the imagination may depict as droning over breviary or mumbling over beads. They were men who had, in several cases at least, been eminent in civil pursuits before the whispers of conscience bade them listen to the Divine command, " Give up all and follow Me." Eusebio Kino was professor of mathematics in the University of Ingoldstadt, and had already made a reputation among the scholars of Europe, when he relinquished his titles and position to become a member of the order of Jesuits and seek a place in their missionary ranks on the wildest of frontiers, where he, with his companions, preached the word of God to tribes whose names even were unknown in the Court of Madrid.

Of these men and their labors, if space allow, we may have something to learn a chapter or two farther on. Just now I find that all my powers of persuasion must be exerted to convince the readers who are still with me that the sand " wash " in which we are floundering is in truth a river, or rather a little river—the "Riito"—the largest confluent of the Santa Cruz. Could you only arrange to be with me, you unbelieving Thomases, when the deluging rains of the summer solstice rush madly down the rugged face of the Santa Catalina and swell this dry sand-bed to the dimensions of a young Missouri, all tales would be more easy for you to swallow.

But here we are. That fringe of emerald green in the " bottom" is the barley land surrounding Tucson; those gently waving cottonwoods outline the shrivelled course of the Santa Cruz; those trees with the dark, waxy-green foliage are the pomegranates behind Juan Fernandez's corral. There is the massive wall of the church of San Antonio now; we see streets and houses, singly or in clusters, buried in shade or unsheltered from the vertical glare of the most merciless of suns. Here are pigs staked out to wallow in congenial mire—that is one of the charming customs of the Spanish Southwest; and these—ah, yes, these are dogs, unchained and running amuck after the heels of the horses, another most charming custom of the country.

Here are "burros" browsing upon tin cans—still another institution of the country—and here are the hens and chickens, and the houses of mud, of one story, flat, cheerless, and monotonous were it not for the crimson "rastras" of chile which, like mediæval banners, are flung to the outer wall. And women, young and old, wrapped up in "rebosos" and "tapalos," which conceal all the countenance but the left eye; and men enfolded in cheap poll-parrotty blankets of cotton, busy in leaning against the door-posts and holding up the weight of "sombreros," as large in diameter as cart-wheels and surrounded by snakes of silver bullion weighing almost as much as the wearers.

The horses are moving rapidly down the narrow street without prick of spur. The wagons are creaking merrily, pulled by energetic mules, whose efforts need not the urging of rifle-cracking whip in the hands of skilful drivers. It is only because the drivers are glad to get to Tucson that they explode the long, deadly black snakes, with which they can cut a welt out of the flank or brush a fly from the belly of any animal in their team. All the men are whistling or have broken out in glad carol. Each heart is gay, for we have at last reached Tucson, the commercial *entrepôt* of Arizona and the remoter Southwest—Tucson, the Mecca of the dragoon, the Naples of the desert, which one was to see and die; Tucson, whose alkali pits yielded water sweeter than Well of Zemzem, whose maidens were more charming, whose society was more hospitable, merchants more progressive, magazines better stocked, climate more dreamy, than any town from Santa Fé to Los Angeles; from Hermosillo, in Sonora, to the gloomy chasm of the Grand Cañon—with one exception only: its great rival, the thoroughly American town of Prescott, in the bosom of the pine forests, amid the granite crags of the foot-hills of the Mogollon.

Camp Lowell, as the military post was styled, was located on the eastern edge of the town itself. In more recent years it has been moved seven or eight miles out to where the Riito is a flowing stream. We took up position close to the quartermaster's corral, erected such tents as could be obtained, and did much solid work in the construction of "ramadas" and other conveniences of branches. As a matter of comfort, all the unmarried officers boarded in the town, of which I shall endeavor to give a succinct but perfectly fair description as it impressed itself upon me during the months of our sojourn in the intervals between scouts against the enemy, who kept our hands full.

My eyes and ears were open to the strange scenes and sounds which met them on every side. Tucson was as foreign a town as if it were in Hayti instead of within our own boundaries. The language, dress, funeral processions, religious ceremonies, feasts, dances, games, joys, perils, griefs, and tribulations of its population were something not to be looked for in the region east of the Missouri River. I noted them all as well as I knew how, kept my own counsel, and give now the *résumé* of my notes of the time.

The "Shoo Fly" restaurant, which offered the comforts of a home to the weary wayfarer in Tucson, Arizona, circa 1869, was named on the principle of "*lucus à non lucendo*"—the flies wouldn't shoo worth a cent. Like the poor, they remained always with us. But though they might bedim the legend, "All meals payable in advance," they could not destroy the spirit of the legend, which was the principle upon which our most charming of landladies, Mrs. Wallen, did business.

Mrs. Wallen deserves more than the hasty reference she is receiving in these pages. She was a most attentive and well-meaning soul, understood the mysteries, or some of the mysteries, of the culinary art, was anxious to please, had never seen better days, and did not so much as pretend to have seen any, not even through a telescope.

She was not a widow, as the proprieties demanded under the circumstances—all landladies that I've ever read or heard of have been widows—but the circumstance that there was a male attached to the name of Wallen did not cut much of a figure in the case, as it was a well-understood fact that Mrs. Wallen was a woman of nerve and bound to have her own way in all things. Consequently, the bifurcated shadow which flitted about in the corral feeding the chickens, or made its appearance from time to time in the kitchen among the tomato peelings, did not make a very lasting impression upon either the regulars or the "mealers," the two classes of patrons upon whose dollars our good hostess depended for the support of her establishment.

One line only will be needed to lay before the reader the interior view of the "Shoo Fly." It was a long, narrow, low-ceiled room of adobe, whose walls were washed in a neutral yellowish tint, whose floor was of rammed earth and ceiling of white muslin. Place here and there, in convenient positions, eight or ten tables of different sizes; cover them with cheap cloths, cheap china and glass—I use the term "cheap" in regard to quality only, and not in regard to the price, which had been dear enough, as everything was in those days of freighting with mule and "bull" teams from Leavenworth and Kit Carson. Place in the centre of each table a lead castor with the obsolete yellow glass bottles; put one large, cheap mirror on the wall facing the main entrance, and not far from it a wooden clock, which probably served some mysterious purpose other than time-keeping, because it was never wound up. Have pine benches, and home-made chairs, with raw-hide bottoms fastened with strings of the same material to the framework. Make the place look decidedly neat and clean, notwithstanding the flies and the hot alkali dust which penetrated upon the slightest excuse. Bring in two bright, pleasant-mannered Mexican boys, whose dark complexions were well set off by neat white cotton jackets and loose white cotton trousers, with sometimes a colored sash about the waist. Give each of these young men a fly-flapper as a badge of office, and the "Shoo Fly" is open for the reception of guests.

Napkins designated the seats of the regular boarders. "Mealers" were not entitled to such distinction and never seemed to expect it. There was no bill of fare. None was needed. Boarders always knew what they were going to get—same old thing. There never was any change during all the time of my acquaintance with the establishment, which, after all is said and done, certainly contrived to secure for its patrons all that the limited market facilities of the day afforded. Beef was not always easy to procure, but there was no lack of bacon, chicken, mutton, and kid meat. Potatoes ranked as luxuries of the first class, and never sold for less than ten cents a pound, and often could not be had for love or money. The soil of Arizona south of the Gila did not seem to suit their growth, but now that the Apaches have for nearly twenty years been docile in northern Arizona, and left its people free from terror and anxiety, they have succeeded in raising the finest "Murphies" in the world in the damp lava soil of the swales upon the summit of the great Mogollon Plateau.

There was plenty of "jerked" beef, savory and palatable enough in stews and hashes ; eggs, and the sweet, toothsome black "frijoles" of Mexico ; tomatoes equal to those of any part of our country, and lettuce always crisp, dainty, and delicious. For fresh fruit, our main reliance was upon the "burro" trains coming up from the charming oasis of Hermosillo, the capital of Sonora—a veritable garden of the Hesperides, in which Nature was most lavish with her gifts of honey-juiced oranges, sweet limes, lemons, edible quinces, and luscious apricots ; but the apple, the plum, and the cherry were unknown to us, and the strawberry only occasionally seen.

Very frequently the presence of Apaches along the road would cause a panic in trains coming up from the south, and then there would be a fruit famine, during which our sole reliance would be upon the mainstay of boarding-house prosperity— stewed peaches and prunes. There were two other articles of food which could be relied upon with reasonable certainty—the red beet, which in the "alkali" lands attains a great size, and the black fig of Mexico, which, packed in ceroons of cow's hide, often was carried about for sale.

Chile colorado entered into the composition of every dish, and great, velvety-skinned, delicately flavored onions as large as dinner plates ended the list—that is to say, the regular list. On some special occasion there would be honey brought in from the Tia Juana Ranch in Lower California, three or four hundred miles westward, and dried shrimps from the harbor of Guaymas. In the harbor of Guaymas there are oysters, too, and they are not bad, although small and a trifle coppery to the taste of those who try them for the first time. Why we never had any of them was, I suppose, on account of the difficulty of getting them through

in good condition without ice, so we had to be content with the
canned article, which was never any too good. From the Rio
Grande in the neighborhood of El Paso there came the "pasas,"
or half-dried grape, in whose praise too much could not be said.

The tables were of pine, of the simplest possible construction.
All were bad enough, but some were a trifle more rickety than
others. The one which wobbled the least was placed close to the
north side of the banqueting-hall, where the windows gave the
best "view."

Around this Belshazzarian board assembled people of such consideration as Governor Safford, Lieutenant-Governor Bashford,
Chief-Justice John Titus, Attorney-General MacCaffrey, the genial Joe Wasson, Tom Ewing, and several others. I was on a
number of occasions honored with a seat among them, and enjoyed at one and the same moment their conversation and the
"view" of which I have spoken.

There was a foreground of old tin tomato cans, and a middle
distance of chicken feathers and chile peppers, with a couple of
"burros" in the dim perspective, and the requisite flitting of
lights and shadows in the foliage of one stunted mesquite-bush,
which sheltered from the vertical rays of the sun the crouching
form of old Juanita, who was energetically pounding between
smooth stones the week's washing of the household, and supplying in the gaudy stripes of her bright "serape" the amount of
color which old-school critics used to maintain was indispensable
to every landscape.

Juanita was old and discreet, but her thoughts were not altogether on the world to come. Her face was ordinarily plastered
with flour-paste, the cosmetic of the Southwest. Why this attention to her toilet, the wisest failed to tell. Often did I assure
her that nothing could improve her complexion—a statement not
to be controverted—and never did she fail to rebuke me with her
most bewitching smile, and the words, "Ah! Don Juan, you're
such a flatterer."

The gentlemen whose names I have just given are nearly all
dead or so well advanced in years and dignity that what I have
to say now will not sound like flattery. They had each and all
travelled over a great deal of the earth's surface, and several of
them were scholars of ripe learning. I was much younger then
than I am now, and of course the attainments of men so much

older than myself made a deep impression upon me, but even to this day I would place the names of Titus and Bashford in the list of scholars of erudition whom I have known, and very high up in the list, too.

The remainder of the patrons seemed to be about evenly divided between the cynical grumblers who, having paid their score with regularity, arrogated to themselves the right to asperse the viands; and the eulogists who, owing to temporary financial embarrassments, were unable to produce receipts, and sought to appease their not by any means too hard-hearted landlady by the most fulsome adulation of the table and its belongings.

Like the brokers of Wall Street who are bulls to-day and bears to-morrow, it not infrequently happened among the "Shoo Fly's" patrons that the most obdurate growler of last week changed front and assumed position as the Advocatus Diaboli of this.

But, take them for all in all, they were a good-hearted, whole-souled lot of men, who had roughed it and smoothed it in all parts of the world, who had basked in the smiles of Fortune and had not winced at her frown; a trifle too quick on the trigger, perhaps, some of them, to be perfectly well qualified to act as Sunday-school superintendents, yet generous to the comrade in distress and polite to all who came near them. The Western man —the Pacific Sloper especially—is much more urbane and courteous under such circumstances than his neighbor who has grown up on the banks of the Delaware or Hudson. There was bitter rivalry between Mrs. Wallen and Mr. Neugass, the proprietor of the "Palace"—a rivalry which diffused itself among their respective adherents.

I make the statement simply to preserve the record of the times, that the patrons of the "Shoo Fly" never let go an opportunity to insinuate that the people to be met at the "Palace" were, to a large extent, composed of the "*nouveaux riches.*" There was not the slightest foundation for this, as I can testify, because I afterward sat at Neugass's tables, when Mrs. Wallen had retired from business and gone into California, and can recall no difference at all in the character of the guests.

Tucson enjoyed the singular felicity of not possessing anything in the shape of a hotel. Travellers coming to town, and not provided with letters which would secure them the hospitality of private houses, craved the privilege of "making down" their blankets in the most convenient corral, and slept till early morn, undisturbed save by the barking of dogs, which never ceased all through the night, or the crowing of loud-voiced chanticleers, which began ere yet the dawn had signalled with its first rosy flush from the peak of the Santa Rita. It was the customary thing for wagon trains to halt and go into camp in the middle of the plaza in front of the cathedral church of San Antonio, and after the oxen or mules had been tied to the wheels, the drivers would calmly proceed to stretch out tired limbs in the beautiful moonlight.

I never could see the advantage of such a state of affairs, and felt that it belittled the importance of the town, which really did a very large business with the surrounding country for hundreds of miles. There are always two and even three different ways of looking at the same proposition, and to Bob Crandall and Vet Mowry this manner of camping "*à la belle étoile*" was the one thing "to which they pointed with pride." It was proof of the glorious climate enjoyed by Tucson. Where else in the whole world, sir, could a man camp out night after night all the year round ? Was it in Senegambia ? No, sir. In Nova Zembla ? No, sir. In Hong Kong ? No, sir. In Ireland ?—but by this time one could cut off the button, if necessary, and break away.

So there were only three places in which people could get acquainted with one another—in the "Shoo Fly" or "Palace" restaurants ; in the gambling resorts, which never closed, night or day, Sunday or Monday ; and at the post-office, in the long line of Mexicans and Americans slowly approaching the little square window to ask for letters.

For the convenience of my readers and myself, I will take the liberty of presenting some of my dead and gone friends in the "Shoo Fly," where we can have seats upon which to rest, and tables upon which to place our elbows, if we so desire.

But first a word or two more about Tucson itself.

It was in those days the capital of the Territory of Arizona, and the place of residence of most of the Federal officials. Its geographical situation was on the right bank of the pretty little stream called the Santa Cruz, a mile or more above where it ran into the sands. In round figures, it was on the 32d degree of north latitude, and not far from the 112th degree west from

Greenwich. The valley of the Santa Cruz, although not much over a mile and a half wide, is wonderfully fertile, and will yield bountifully of all cereals, as well as of the fruits of the south temperate or north tropical climes, and could easily have supported a much larger population, but on account of the bitter and unrelenting hostilities waged by the Apaches, not more than 3,200 souls could be claimed, although enthusiasts often deluded themselves into a belief in much higher figures, owing to the almost constant presence of trains of wagons hauled by patient oxen or quick-moving mules, or "carretas" drawn by the philosophical donkey or "burro" from Sonora. The great prairie-schooners all the way from the Missouri River made a very imposing appearance, as, linked two, and even three, together, they rolled along with their heavy burdens, to unload at the warehouses of the great merchants, Lord & Williams, Tully, Ochoa & De Long, the Zeckendorfs, Fish & Collingwood, Leopoldo Carrillo, or other of the men of those days whose transactions ran each year into the hundreds of thousands of dollars.

Streets and pavements there were none; lamps were unheard of; drainage was not deemed necessary, and water, when not bought from the old Mexican who hauled it in barrels in a dilapidated cart from the cool spring on the bishop's farm, was obtained from wells, which were good and sweet in the first months of their career, but generally became so impregnated with "alkali" that they had to be abandoned; and as lumber was worth twenty-five cents a foot, and therefore too costly to be used in covering them, they were left to dry up of their own accord, and remain a menace to the lives and limbs of belated pedestrians. There was no hint in history or tradition of a sweeping of the streets, which were every bit as filthy as those of New York.

The age of the garbage piles was distinctly defined by geological strata. In the lowest portion of all one could often find arrow-heads and stone axes, indicative of a pre-Columbian origin; super-imposed conformably over these, as the geologists used to say, were skins of chile colorado, great pieces of rusty spurs, and other reliquiæ of the "Conquistadores," while high above all, stray cards, tomato cans, beer bottles, and similar evidences of a higher and nobler civilization told just how long the Anglo-Saxon had called the territory his own.

This filthy condition of the streets gave rise to a weird system

of topographical designation. " You want to find the Governor's ?
Wa'al, podner, jest keep right down this yere street past the Pal-
ace s'loon, till yer gets ter the second manure-pile on yer right;
then keep to yer left past the post-office, 'n' yer'll see a dead burro
in th' middle of th' road, 'n' a mesquite tree 'n yer lef', near a
Mexican ' tendajon ' (small store), 'n' jes' beyond that 's the
Gov.'s outfit. Can't miss it. Look out fur th' dawg down ter
Muñoz's corral; he 's a salviated son ov a gun. "

It took some time for the ears of the "tenderfoot" just out
from the States to become habituated to the chronology of that
portion of our vast domain. One rarely heard months, days, or
weeks mentioned. The narrator of a story had a far more convenient method of referring back to dates in which his auditory
might be interested. "Jes' about th' time Pete Kitchen's ranch
was jumped "—which wasn't very satisfactory, as Pete Kitchen's
ranch was always getting "jumped." "Th' night afore th' Maricopa stage war tuck in." "A week or two arter Winters made
his last ' killin' ' in th' Dragoons." "Th' last fight down to th'
Picach." "Th' year th' Injuns run off Tully, Ochoa 'n' DeLong
bull teams."

Or, under other aspects of the daily life of the place, there
would be such references as, "Th' night after Duffield drawed his
gun on Jedge Titus "—a rather uncertain reference, since Duffield
was always " drawin' his gun " on somebody. "Th' time of th'
feast (*i.e.*, of Saint Augustine, the patron saint of the town),
when Bob Crandall broke th' ' Chusas ' game fur six hundred
dollars," and other expressions of similar tenor, which replaced
the recollections of " mowing time," and " harvest," and "sheep-
shearing " of older communities.

Another strain upon the unduly excitable brain lay in the impossibility of learning exactly how many miles it was to a given
point. It wasn't " fifty miles," or " sixty miles," or "just a trifle
beyond the Cienaga, and that 's twenty-five miles," but rather,
" Jes' on th' rise of the mesa as you git to th' place whar Saman-
iego's train stood off th' Apaches;" or, " A little yan way from
whar they took in Colonel Stone's stage ;" or, "Jes' whar th' big
' killin' ' tuk place on th' long mesa," and much more of the
same sort.

There were watches and clocks in the town, and some Americans went through the motions of consulting them at intervals.

So far as influence upon the community went, they might just as well have been in the bottom of the Red Sea. The divisions of the day were regulated and determined by the bells which periodically clanged in front of the cathedral church. When they rang out their wild peal for early Mass, the little world by the Santa Cruz rubbed its eyes, threw off the slight covering of the night, and made ready for the labors of the day. The alarm clock of the Gringo might have been sounding for two hours earlier, but not one man, woman, or child would have paid the slightest attention to the cursed invention of Satan. When the Angelus tolled at meridian, all made ready for the noon-day meal and the postprandial siesta ; and when the hour of vespers sounded, adobes dropped from the palsied hands of listless workmen, and docile Papagoes, wrapping themselves in their pieces of "manta" or old "rebosos," turned their faces southward, mindful of the curfew signal learned from the early missionaries.

They were a singular people, the Papagoes ; honest, laborious, docile, sober, and pure—not an improper character among them. Only one white man had ever been allowed to marry into the tribe —Buckskin Aleck Stevens, of Cambridge, Mass., and that had to be a marriage with bell, book, and candle and every formality to protect the bride.

I do not know anything about the Papagoes of to-day, and am prepared to hear that they have sadly degenerated. The Americans have had twenty years in which to corrupt them, and the intimacy can hardly have been to the advantage of the red man.

CHAPTER IV.

"SEE yar, muchacho, move roun' lively now, 'n' git me a Jinny Lin' steak." It was a strong, hearty voice which sounded in my ears from the table just behind me in the "Shoo Fly," and made me mechanically turn about, almost as much perplexed as was the waiter-boy, Miguel, by the strange request.

"Would you have any objection, sir, to letting me know what you mean by a Jenny Lind steak?"

"A Jinny Lin' steak, mee son, 's a steak cut from off a hoss's upper lip. I makes it a rule allers to git what I orders; 'n' ez far 's I kin see, I'll get a Jinny Lin' steak anyhow in this yere outfit, so I'm kinder takin' time by the fetlock, 'n' orderin' jes' what I want. My name's Jack Long; what mout your'n be?"

It was apparent, at half a glance, that Jack Long was not "in sassiety," unless it might be a "sassiety" decidedly addicted to tobacco, given to the use of flannel instead of "b'iled" shirts, never without six-shooter on hip, and indulging in profanity by the wholesale.

A better acquaintance with old Jack showed that, like the chestnut, his roughest part was on the outside. Courage, tenderness, truth, and other manly attributes peered out from under roughness of garb and speech. He was one of Gray's "gems of purest ray serene," born in "the dark, unfathomed caves" of frontier isolation.

Jack Long had not always been "Jack" Long. Once, way

back in the early fifties, he and his "podners" had struck it rich on some "placer" diggings which they had preëmpted on the Yuba, and in less than no time my friend was heralded to the mountain communities as "Jedge" Long. This title had never been sought, and, in justice to the recipient, it should be made known that he discarded it at once, and would none of it. The title "Jedge" on the frontier does not always imply respect, and Jack would tolerate nothing ambiguous.

He was bound to be a gentleman or nothing. Before the week was half over he was arrayed, not exactly like Solomon, but much more conspicuously, in the whitest of "b'iled" shirts, in the bosom of which glistened the most brilliant diamond cluster pin that money could procure from Sacramento. On the warty red fingers of his right hand sparkled its mate, and pendent from his waist a liberal handful of the old-fashioned seals and keys of the time attracted attention to the ponderous gold chain encircling his neck, and securing the biggest specimen of a watch known to fact or fiction since the days of Captain Cuttle.

Carelessly strolling up to the bar of the "Quartz Rock," the "Hanging Wall," or the "Golden West," he would say, in the cheeriest way :

"Gents, what'll yer all hev ? It's mine this time, barkeep." And, spurning the change obsequiously tendered by the officiating genius of the gilded slaughter-house of morality, Jack would push back the twenty-dollar gold piece with which he usually began his evenings with "the boys," and ask, in a tone of injured pride : "Is there any use in insultin' a man when he wants to treat his friends ?" And barkeeper and all in the den would voice the sentiment that a "gent" who was as liberal with his double eagles as Colonel Long was a gent indeed, and a man anybody could afford to tie to.

It was the local paper which gave Jack his military title, and alluded to the growing demand that the colonel should accept the nomination for Congress. And to Congress he would have gone, too, had not fickle Fortune turned her back upon her whilom favorite.

Jack had the bad luck to fall in love and to be married—not for the first time, as he had had previous experience in the same direction, his first wife being the youngest daughter of the great Indian chief "Cut-Mouth John," of the Rogue River tribe, who ran away from Jack and took to the mountains when her people went on the war-path. The then wife was a white woman from Missouri, and, from all I can learn, a very good mate for Jack, excepting that prosperity turned her head and made her very extravagant. So long as Jack's mine was panning out freely Jack didn't mind much what she spent, but when it petered, and economy became necessary, dissensions soon arose between them, and it was agreed that they were not compatible.

"If you don't like me," said Mrs. Long one day, "give me a divorce and one-half of what you have, and I'll leave you."

"'Nuff sed," was Jack's reply, "'n' here goes."

The sum total in the Long exchequer was not quite $200. Of this, Jack laid to one side a double eagle, for a purpose soon to be explained. The remainder was divided into two even piles, one of which was handed over to his spouse. The doors of the wardrobe stood open, disclosing all of Jack's regal raiment. He seized a pair of trousers, tore them leg from leg, and then served in much the same way every coat, waistcoat, or undergarment he owned. One pile of remnants was assigned to the stupefied woman, who ten minutes previously had been demanding a separation.

Before another ten had passed her own choicest treasures had shared the same fate, and her ex-liege lord was devoting his attention to breaking the cooking stove, with its superstructure of pots and pans and kettles, into two little hillocks of battered fragments; and no sooner through with that than at work sawing the tables and chairs in half and knocking the solitary mirror into smithereens.

"Thar yer are," said Jack. "Ye 'v' got half th' money, 'n' yer kin now tek yer pick o' what's left."

The stage had come along on its way down to Sacramento, and Jack hailed the driver. "Mrs. Long's goin' down th' road a bit ter see some o' her kin, 'n' ter get a breath o' fresh air. Tek her ez fur ez this 'll pay fur, 'n' then *she*'ll tell whar else she wants ter go."

And that was Jack Long's divorce and the reason why he left the mining regions of California and wandered far and near, beginning the battle of life anew as packer and prospector, and drifting down into the drainage of the Gila and into the "Shoo Fly" restaurant, where we have just met him.

There shall be many other opportunities of meeting and conversing with old Jack before the campaigning against the Apaches is half through, so we need not urge him to remain now that he has finished his meal and is ready to sally forth. We return heartily the very cheery greeting tendered by the gentleman who enters the dining-room in his place. It is ex-Marshal Duffield, a very peculiar sort of a man, who stands credited in public opinion with having killed thirteen persons. How much of this is truth and how much is pure gossip, as meaningless as the chatter of the "pechotas" which gather along the walls of the corral every evening the moment the grain of the horses is dealt out to them, I cannot say ; but if the reader desire to learn of a unique character in our frontier history he will kindly permit me to tell something of the only man in the Territory of Arizona, and I may say of New Mexico and western Texas as well, who dared wear a plug hat. There was nothing so obnoxious in the sight of people living along the border as the black silk tile. The ordinary man assuming such an addition to his attire would have done so at the risk of his life, but Duffield was no ordinary individual. He wore clothes to suit himself, and woe to the man who might fancy otherwise.

Who Duffield was before coming out to Arizona I never could learn to my own satisfaction. Indeed, I do not remember ever having any but the most languid interest in that part of his career, because he kept us so fully occupied in keeping track of his escapades in Arizona that there was very little time left for investigations into his earlier movements. Yet I do recall the whispered story that he had been one of President Lincoln's discoveries, and that the reason for his appointment lay in the courage Duffield had displayed in the New York riots during the war. It seems—and I tell the tale with many misgivings, as my memory does not retain all the circumstances—that Duffield was passing along one of the streets in which the rioters were having things their own way, and there he saw a poor devil of a colored man fleeing from some drunken pursuers, who were bent on hanging him to the nearest lamp-post. Duffield allowed the black man to pass him, and then, as the mob approached on a hot scent, he levelled his pistol—his constant companion—and blew out the brains of the one in advance, and, as the story goes, hit two others, as fast as he could draw bead on them, for I must

take care to let my readers know that my friend was one of the
crack shots of America, and was wont while he lived in Tucson
to drive a ten-penny nail into an adobe wall every day before he
would go into the house to eat his evening meal. At the present
moment he was living at the "Shoo Fly," and was one of the
most highly respected members of the mess that gathered there.
He stood not less than six feet three in his stockings, was extremely broad-shouldered, powerful, muscular, and finely knit;
dark complexion, black hair, eyes keen as briars and black as jet,
fists as big as any two fists to be seen in the course of a day; dis-
putatious, somewhat quarrelsome, but not without very amiable
qualities. His bravery, at least, was never called in question. He
was no longer United States marshal, but was holding the position
of Mail Inspector, and the manner in which he discharged his
delicate and dangerous duties was always commendable and very
often amusing.

"You see, it 's jest like this," he once remarked to the postmaster of one of the smallest stations in his jurisdiction, and in
speaking the inspector's voice did not show the slightest sign of
anger or excitement—"you see, the postmaster-general is growling at me because there is so much thieving going on along this
line, so that I'm gittin' kind o' tired 'n' must git th' whole bizz off
mee mind ; 'n' ez I 've looked into the whole thing and feel satisfied that you're the thief, I think you'd better be pilin' out o'
here without any more nonsense."

The postmaster was gone inside of twelve hours, and there was
no more stealing on that line while Duffield held his position.
Either the rest of the twelve dollars per annum postmasters were
an extremely honest set, or else they were scared by the mere presence of Duffield. He used to be very fond of showing his powerful muscle, and would often seize one of the heavy oak chairs in
the "Congress Hall" bar-room in one hand, and lift it out at
arm's length ; or take some of the people who stood near him and
lift them up, catching hold of the feet only.

How well I remember the excitement which arose in Tucson
the day that "Waco Bill" arrived in town with a wagon train on
its way to Los Angeles. Mr. "Waco Bill" was a "tough" in the
truest sense of the term, and being from half to three-quarters
full of the worst liquor to be found in Tucson—and I hope I am
violating no confidence when I say that some of the vilest coffin

varnish on the mundane sphere was to be found there by those who tried diligently—was anxious to meet and subdue this Duffield, of whom such exaggerated praise was sounding in his ears.

"Whar's Duffer?" he cried, or hiccoughed, as he approached the little group of which Duffield was the central figure. "I want Duffer (*hic*); he's my meat. Whoop!"

The words had hardly left his mouth before something shot out from Duffield's right shoulder. It was that awful fist, which could, upon emergency, have felled an ox, and down went our Texan sprawling upon the ground. No sooner had he touched Mother Earth than, true to his Texan instincts, his hand sought his revolver, and partly drew it out of holster. Duffield retained his preternatural calmness, and did not raise his voice above a whisper the whole time that his drunken opponent was hurling all kinds of anathemas at him ; but now he saw that something must be done. In Arizona it was not customary to pull a pistol upon a man ; that was regarded as an act both unchristian-like and wasteful of time—Arizonanas nearly always shot out of the pocket without drawing their weapons at all, and into Mr. "Waco Bill's" groin went the sure bullet of the man who, local wits used to say, wore crape upon his hat in memory of his departed virtues.

The bullet struck, and Duffield bent over with a most Chesterfieldian bow and wave of the hand : "My name's Duffield, sir," he said, "and them 'ere's mee visitin' card."

If there was one man in the world who despised another it was Chief-Justice John Titus in his scorn for the ex-marshal, which found open expression on every occasion. Titus was a gentleman of the old school, educated in the City of Brotherly Love, and anxious to put down the least semblance of lawlessness and disorder ; yet here was an officer of the Government whose quarrels were notorious and of every-day occurrence.

Persuasion, kindly remonstrance, earnest warning were alike ineffectual, and in time the relations between the two men became of the most formal, not to say rancorous, character. Judge Titus at last made up his mind that the very first excuse for so doing he would have Duffield hauled up for carrying deadly weapons, and an occasion arose much sooner than he imagined.

There was a "baile" given that same week, and Duffield was present with many others. People usually went on a peace footing to these assemblies—that is to say, all the heavy armament was left at home, and nothing taken along but a few Derringers, which would come handy in case of accident.

There were some five or six of us—all friends of Duffield—sitting in a little back room away from the long saloon in which the dance was going on, and we had Duffield in such good humor that he consented to produce some if not all of the weapons with which he was loaded. He drew them from the arm-holes of his waistcoat, from his boot-legs, from his hip-pockets, from the back of his neck, and there they all were—eleven lethal weapons, mostly small Derringers, with one knife. Comment was useless; for my own part, I did not feel called upon to criticise my friend's eccentricities or amiable weaknesses, whatever they might be, so I kept my mouth shut, and the others followed my example. I suppose that on a war-footing nothing less than a couple of Gatling guns would have served to round out the armament to be brought into play.

Whether it was a true alarm or a false one I couldn't tell, but the next day Judge Titus imagined that a movement of Duffield's hand was intended to bring to bear upon himself a portion of the Duffield ordnance, and he had the old man arrested and brought before him on the charge of carrying concealed deadly weapons.

The court-room was packed with a very orderly crowd, listening attentively to a long exordium from the lips of the judge upon the enormity and the uselessness of carrying concealed deadly weapons. The judge forgot that men would carry arms so long as danger real or imaginary encompassed them, and that the opinions prevailing upon that subject in older communities could not be expected to obtain in the wilder regions.

In Arizona, the reader should know, all the officers of the law were Americans. In New Mexico, on the contrary, they were almost without exception Mexicans, and the legal practice was entirely different from our own, as were the usages and customs of various kinds. For example, one could go before one of those Rio Grande alcaldes in Socorro, San Antonio, or Sabinal, and wear just what clothes he pleased, or not wear any if he didn't please; it would be all right. He might wear a hat, or go in his shirt sleeves, or go barefoot, or roll himself a cigarrito, and it would be all right. But let him dare enter with spurs, and the ushers would throw him out, and it was a matter of great good luck if he did not find himself in the calaboose to boot, for contempt of court.

"Call the first witness ; call Charles O. Brown."

Mr. Charles O. Brown, under oath, stated his name, residence, and occupation, and was then directed to show to the judge and jury how the prisoner—Duffield—had drawn his revolver the day previous.

"Well, jedge, the way he drawed her was jest this." And suiting the action to the word, Mr. Charles O. Brown, the main witness for the prosecution, drew a six-shooter, fully cocked, from the holster on his hip. There was a ripple of laughter in the courtroom, as every one saw at once the absurdity of trying to hold one man responsible for the misdemeanor of which a whole community was guilty, and in a few minutes the matter was *nolle prossed*.

I will end up the career of the marshal in this chapter, as we shall have no further cause to introduce him in these pages. His courage was soon put to the severest sort of a test when a party of desperadoes from Sonora, who had been plundering in their own country until driven across the line, began their operations in Arizona. At the dead of night they entered Duffield's house, and made a most desperate assault upon him while asleep in his bed. By some sort of luck the blow aimed with a hatchet failed to hit him on head or neck—probably his assailants were too drunk to see what they were doing—and chopped out a frightful gash in the shoulder, which would have killed the general run of men. Duffield, as has been shown, was a giant in strength, and awakened by the pain, and at once realizing what had happened, he sprang from his couch and grappled with the nearest of the gang of burglars, choked him, and proceeded to use him as a weapon with which to sweep out of the premises the rest of the party, who, seeing that the household had been alarmed, made good their escape.

Duffield was too much exhausted from loss of blood to retain his hold upon the rascal whom he had first seized, so that Justice did not succeed in laying her hands upon any of the band. When Duffield recovered sufficiently to be able to reappear on the streets, he did not seem to be the same man. He no longer took pleasure in rows, but acted like one who had had enough of battles, and was willing to live at peace with his fellow-men.

Unfortunately, if one acquire the reputation of being " a bad man " on the frontier, it will stick to him for a generation after he has sown his wild oats, and is trying to bring about a rotation of crops.

Duffield was killed at Tombstone ten years since, not far from the Contention Mine, by a young man named Holmes, who had taken up a claim in which Duffield asserted an interest. The moment he saw Duffield approaching he levelled a shot-gun upon him, and warned him not to move a foot, and upon Duffield's still advancing a few paces he filled him full of buckshot, and the coroner's jury, without leaving their seats, returned a verdict of justifiable homicide, because the old, old Duffield, who was " on the shoot," was still remembered, and the new man, who had turned over a new leaf and was trying to lead a new life, was still a stranger in the land.

Peace to his ashes !

There were military as well as non-military men in Tucson, and although the following incident did not occur under my personal observation, and was one of those stories that " leak out," I tell it as filling in a gap in the description of life as it was in Arizona twenty and twenty-five years ago. All the persons concerned were boarders at the " Shoo Fly," and all are now dead, or out of service years and years ago.

The first was the old field officer whom, for want of a better name, every one called " Old Uncle Billy N——." He had met with a grievous misfortune, and lost one of his eyes, but bore his trouble with stoicism and without complaint. During a brief visit to Boston, he had arranged with an oculist and optician to have made for him three glass eyes. " But I don't clearly understand what you want with so many," said the Boston man.

"Well, I'll tell you," replied the son of Mars. " You see, I want one for use when I'm sober, one when I'm drunk, and one when I'm p—— d—— drunk."

The glass eyes were soon ready to meet the varying conditions of the colonel's life, and gave the old man the liveliest satisfaction. Not long after his return to the bracing climate of Tucson he made the round of the gaming-tables at the Feast of Saint Augustine, which was then in full blast, and happened to "copper" the ace, when he should have bet " straight," and bet on the queen when that fickle lady was refusing the smile of her countenance to all her admirers. It was a gloomy day for the colonel when he awaked to find himself almost without a dollar, and no paymaster to be expected from San Francisco for a couple of months. A brilliant thought struck him ; he would economize by sending back to Boston two of his stock of glass eyes, which he did not really need, as the " sober " and "tolerably drunk " ones had never been used, and ought to fetch something of a price at second-hand.

The Boston dealer, however, curtly refused to negotiate a sale, saying that he did not do business in that way, and, as if to add insult to injury, enclosed the two eyes in a loose sheet of paper, which was inscribed with a pathetic story about "The Drunkard Saved." It took at least a dozen rounds of drinks before the colonel could drown his wrath, and satisfy the inquiries of condoling friends who had learned of the brutal treatment to which he had been subjected.

A great friend of the colonel's was Al. Garrett, who in stature was his elder's antithesis, being as short and wiry as the colonel was large and heavy. Garrett was an extremely good-hearted youngster, and one of the best horsemen in the whole army. His admirers used to claim that he could ride anything with four legs to it, from a tarantula to a megatherium. Semig, the third of the trio, was a Viennese, a very cultivated man, a graduate in medicine, an excellent musician, a graceful dancer, well versed in modern languages, and well educated in every respect. He was the post surgeon at Camp Crittenden, sixty miles to the south of Tucson, but was temporarily at the latter place.

He and Garrett and Uncle Billy were making the best of their way home from supper at the " Shoo Fly " late one evening, and had started to cut across lots after passing the " Plaza."

There were no fences, no covers—nothing at all to prevent pedestrians from falling into some one of the innumerable abandoned wells which were to be met with in every block, and it need surprise no one to be told that in the heat of argument about some trivial matter the worthy medical officer, who was walking in the middle, fell down plump some fifteen or twenty feet, landing in a more or less bruised condition upon a pile of adobes and pieces of rock at the bottom.

Garrett and his elderly companion lurched against each other and continued the discussion, oblivious of the withdrawal of their companion, who from his station at the bottom of the pit, like another Joseph, was bawling for his heartless brothers to return and take him out. After his voice failed he bethought him of his revolver, which he drew from hip, and with which he blazed away, attracting the attention of a party of Mexicans returning from a dance, who too hastily concluded that Semig was a "Gringo" spoiling for a fight, whereupon they gave him their best services in rolling down upon him great pieces of adobe, which imparted renewed vigor to Semig's vocalization and finally awakened the Mexicans to a suspicion of the true state of the case.

The poor doctor never heard the last of his mishap, and very likely was glad to receive the order which transferred him to the Modoc War, wherein he received the wounds of which he afterward died. He showed wonderful coolness in the Lava Beds, and even after the Indians had wounded him in the shoulder and he had been ordered off the field, he refused to leave the wounded under fire until a second shot broke his leg and knocked him senseless.

Associated with Semig in my recollection is the name of young Sherwood, a First Lieutenant in the Twenty-first Infantry, who met his death in the same campaign. He was a man of the best impulses, bright, brave, and generous, and a general favorite.

This rather undersized gentleman coming down the street is a man with a history—perhaps it might be perfectly correct to say with two or three histories. He is Don Estevan Ochoa, one of the most enterprising merchants, as he is admitted to be one of the coolest and bravest men, in all the southwestern country. He has a handsome face, a keen black eye, a quick, business-like air, with very polished and courteous manners.

During the war the Southern leaders thought they would establish a chain of posts across the continent from Texas to California, and one of their first movements was to send a brigade of Texans to occupy Tucson. The commanding general—Turner by name—sent for Don Estevan and told him that he had been informed that he was an outspoken sympathizer with the cause of the Union, but he hoped that Ochoa would see that the Union was a thing of the past, and reconcile himself to the new state of affairs, and take the oath to the Confederacy, and thus relieve the new commander from the disagreeable responsibility of confiscating his property and setting him adrift outside his lines.

Don Estevan never hesitated a moment. He was not that kind of a man. His reply was perfectly courteous, as I am told all the talk on the part of the Confederate officer had been. Ochoa owed all he had in the world to the Government of the United States, and it would be impossible for him to take an oath of fidelity to any hostile power or party. When would General Turner wish him to leave ?

He was allowed to select one of his many horses, and to take a pair of saddle-bags filled with such clothing and food as he could get together on short notice, and then, with a rifle and twenty rounds of ammunition, was led outside the lines and started for the Rio Grande. How he ever made his way across those two hundred and fifty miles of desert and mountains which intervened between the town of Tucson and the Union outposts nearer to the Rio Grande, I do not know—nobody knows. The country was infested by the Apaches, and no one of those upon whom he turned his back expected to hear of his getting through alive. But he did succeed, and here he is, a proof of devotion to the cause of the nation for which it would be hard to find a parallel. When the Union troops reoccupied Tucson Don Estevan resumed business and was soon wealthy again, in spite of the tribute levied by the raiding Apaches, who once ran off every head of draught oxen the firm of Tully, Ochoa & De Long possessed, and never stopped until they had crossed the Rio Salado, or Salt River, where they killed and "jerked" the meat on the slope of that high mesa which to this day bears the name of "Jerked Beef Butte."

Another important factor in the formative period of Arizona's growth is this figure walking briskly by, clad in the cassock of an ecclesiastic. It is Bishop Salpointe, a man of learning, great administrative capacity, and devoted to the interests of his people. He preaches little, but practises much. In many ways unknown to his flock he is busy with plans for their spiritual and worldly advancement, and the work he accomplishes in establishing schools, both in Tucson and in the Papago village of San Xavier, is something which should not soon be forgotten by the people benefited. He is very poor. All that one can see in his house is a crucifix and a volume of precious manuscript notes upon the

Apaches and Papagoes. He seems to be always cheerful. His poverty he freely shares with his flock, and I have often thought that if he ever had any wealth he would share that too.

This one whom we meet upon the street as we leave to visit one of the gambling saloons is Pete Kitchen. We shall be in luck if he invite us to visit him at his "ranch," which has all the airs of a feudal castle in the days of chivalry. Peter Kitchen has probably had more contests with Indians than any other settler in America. He comes from the same stock which sent out from the lovely vales and swales in the Tennessee Mountains the contingent of riflemen who were to cut such a conspicuous figure at the battle of New Orleans, and Peter finds just as steady employment for his trusty rifle as ever was essential in the Delta.

Approaching Pete Kitchen's ranch, one finds himself in a fertile valley, with a small hillock near one extremity. Upon the summit of this has been built the house from which no effort of the Apaches has ever succeeded in driving our friend. There is a sentinel posted on the roof, there is another out in the "cienaga" with the stock, and the men ploughing in the bottom are obliged to carry rifles, cocked and loaded, swung to the plough handle. Every man and boy is armed with one or two revolvers on hip. There are revolvers and rifles and shotguns along the walls and in every corner. Everything speaks of a land of warfare and bloodshed. The title of "Dark and Bloody Ground" never fairly belonged to Kentucky. Kentucky never was anything except a Sunday-school convention in comparison with Arizona, every mile of whose surface could tell its tale of horror were the stones and gravel, the sage-brush and mescal, the mesquite and the yucca, only endowed with speech for one brief hour.

Within the hospitable walls of the Kitchen home the traveller was made to feel perfectly at ease. If food were not already on the fire, some of the women set about the preparation of the savory and spicy stews for which the Mexicans are deservedly famous, and others kneaded the dough and patted into shape the paper-like tortillas with which to eat the juicy frijoles or dip up the tempting chile colorado. There were women carding, spinning, sewing—doing the thousand and one duties of domestic life in a great ranch, which had its own blacksmith, saddler, and wagonmaker, and all other officials needed to keep the machinery running smoothly.

Between Pete Kitchen and the Apaches a ceaseless war was waged, with the advantages not all on the side of Kitchen. His employees were killed and wounded, his stock driven away, his pigs filled with arrows, making the suffering quadrupeds look like perambulating pin-cushions—everything that could be thought of to drive him away; but there he stayed, unconquered and unconquerable.

Men like Estevan Ochoa and Pete Kitchen merit a volume by themselves. Arizona and New Mexico were full of such people, not all as determined and resolute as Pete; not all, nor nearly all, so patriotic and self-denying as Don Estevan, but all with histories full of romance and excitement. Few of them yet remain, and their deeds of heroism will soon be forgotten, or, worse luck yet, some of the people who never dreamed of going down there until they could do so in a Pullman car will be setting themselves up as heroes, and having their puny biographies written for the benefit of the coming generations.

Strangest recollection of all that I have of those persons is the quietness of their manner and the low tone in which they usually spoke to their neighbors. They were quiet in dress, in speech, and in conduct—a marked difference from the more thoroughly dramatized border characters of later days.

CHAPTER V.

IT has been shown that Tucson had no hotels. She did not need any at the time of which I am writing, as her floating population found all the ease and comfort it desired in the flare and glare of the gambling hells, which were bright with the lustre of smoking oil lamps and gay with the varicolored raiment of moving crowds, and the music of harp and Pan's pipes. In them could be found nearly every man in the town at some hour of the day or night, and many used them as the Romans did their "Thermæ"—as a place of residence.

All nationalities, all races were represented, and nearly all conditions of life. There were cadaverous-faced Americans, and Americans whose faces were plump; men in shirt sleeves, and men who wore their coats as they would have done in other places; there were Mexicans wrapped in the red, yellow, and black striped cheap "serapes," smoking the inevitable cigarrito, made on the spot by rolling a pinch of tobacco in a piece of corn shuck; and there were other Mexicans more thoroughly Americanized, who were clad in the garb of the people of the North. Of Chinese and negroes there were only a few—they had not yet made acquaintance to any extent with that section of our country; but their place was occupied by civilized Indians, Opatas, Yaquis, and others, who had come up with "bull" teams and pack trains from Sonora. The best of order prevailed, there being no noise save the hum of conversation or the click of the chips on the different tables. Tobacco smoke ascended from cigarritos, pipes, and the vilest of cigars, filling all the rooms with the foulest of odors. The bright light from the lamps did not equal the steely glint in the eyes of the "bankers," who ceaselessly and imperturbably dealt out the cards from faro boxes, or set in motion the balls in roulette.

There used to be in great favor among the Mexicans, and the Americans, too, for that matter, a modification of roulette called "chusas," which never failed to draw a cluster of earnest players, who would remain by the tables until the first suggestion of daylight. High above the squeak of Pan's pipes or the plinkety-plink-plunk of the harps sounded the voice of the "banker:" "Make yer little bets, gents; make yer little bets; all's set, the game's made, 'n' th' ball's a-rollin'." Blue chips, red chips, white chips would be stacked high upon cards or numbers, as the case might be, but all eventually seemed to gravitate into the maw of the bank, and when, for any reason, the "game" flagged in energy, there would be a tap upon the bell by the dealer's side, and "drinks all round" be ordered at the expense of the house.

It was a curious exhibit of one of the saddest passions of human nature, and a curious jumble of types which would never press against each other elsewhere. Over by the faro bank, in the corner, stood Bob Crandall, a faithful wooer of the fickle goddess Chance. He was one of the handsomest men in the Southwest, and really endowed with many fine qualities; he had drifted away from the restraints of home life years ago, and was then in Tucson making such a livelihood as he could pick up as a gambler, wasting brain and attainments which, if better applied, would have been a credit to himself and his country.

The beautiful diamond glistening upon Bob Crandall's breast had a romantic history. I give it as I remember it:

During the months that Maximilian remained in Mexico there was a French brigade stationed at the two towns of Hermosillo and Magdalena, in Sonora. Desertions were not rare, and, naturally enough, the fugitives made their way when they could across the boundary into the United States, which maintained a by no means dubious attitude in regard to the foreign occupation.

One of these deserters approached Crandall on the street, and asked him for assistance to enable him to get to San Francisco. He had a stone which he believed was of great value, which was part of the plunder coming to him when he and some comrades had looted the hacienda of an affluent Mexican planter. He would sell this for four hundred francs—eighty dollars.

Crandall was no judge of gems, but there was something so

brilliant about the bauble offered to him that he closed the bargain and paid over the sum demanded by the stranger, who took his departure and was seen no more. Four or five years afterward Crandall was making some purchases in a jewellery store in San Francisco, when the owner, happening to see the diamond he was wearing, inquired whether he would be willing to sell it, and offered fifteen hundred dollars cash for the gem which had been so lightly regarded. Nothing further was ever learned of its early ownership, and it is likely enough that its seizure was only one incident among scores that might be related of the French occupation—not seizures by the foreigners altogether, but those made also by the bandits with whom the western side of the republic swarmed for a time.

There was one poor wretch who could always be seen about the tables ; he never played, never talked to any one, and seemed to take no particular interest in anything or anybody. What his name was no one knew or cared ; all treated him kindly, and anything he wished for was supplied by the charity or the generosity of the frequenters of the gaming-tables. He was a trifle "off," but perfectly harmless ; he had lost all the brain he ever had through fright in an Apache ambuscade, and had never recovered his right mind. The party to which he belonged had been attacked not far from Davidson's Springs, but he was one of those who had escaped, or at least he thought he had until he heard the "swish" and felt the pull of the noose of a lariat which a young Apache hiding behind a sage-brush had dexterously thrown across his shoulders. The Mexican drew his ever-ready knife, slashed the raw-hide rope in two, and away he flew on the road to Tucson, never ceasing to spur his mule until both of them arrived, trembling, covered with dust and lather, and scared out of their wits, and half-dead, within sight of the green cotton-woods on the banks of the Santa Cruz.

Then one was always sure to meet men like old Jack Dunn, who had wandered about in all parts of the world, and has since done such excellent work as a scout against the Chiricahua Apaches. I think that Jack is living yet, but am not certain. If he is, it will pay some enterprising journalist to hunt him up and get a few of his stories out of him ; they'll make the best kind of reading for people who care to hear of the wildest days on the wildest of frontiers. And there were others—men who have passed away, men like James Toole, one of the first mayors of Tucson, who dropped in, much as I myself did, to see what was to be seen. Opposed as I am to gambling, no matter what protean guise it may assume, I should do the gamblers of Tucson the justice to say that they were as progressive an element as the town had. They always had plank floors, where every other place was content with the bare earth rammed hard, or with the curious mixture of river sand, bullock's blood, and cactus juice which hardened like cement and was used by some of the more opulent. But with the exception of the large wholesale firms, and there were not over half a dozen of them all told, the house of the governor, and a few— a very few—private residences of people like the Carillos, Sam Hughes, Hiram Stevens, and Aldrich, who desired comfort, there were no wooden floors to be seen in that country.

The gaming establishments were also well supplied with the latest newspapers from San Francisco, Sacramento, and New York, and to these all who entered, whether they played or not, were heartily welcome. Sometimes, but not very often, there would be served up about midnight a very acceptable lunch of "frijoles," coffee, or chocolate, "chile con carne," "enchiladas," and other dishes, all hot and savory, and all thoroughly Mexican. The flare of the lamps was undimmed, the plinkety-plunk of the harps was unchecked, and the voice of the dealer was abroad in the land from the setting of the sun until the rising of the same, and until that tired luminary had again sunk to rest behind the purple caps of the Santa Teresa, and had again risen rejuvenated to gladden a reawakened earth with his brightest beams. Sunday or Monday, night or day, it made no difference—the game went on ; one dealer taking the place of another with the regularity, the precision, and the stolidity of a sentinel.

" Isn't it ra-a-a-ther late for you to be open ? " asked the tenderfoot arrival from the East, as he descended from the El Paso stage about four o'clock one morning, and dragged himself to the bar to get something to wash the dust out of his throat.

" Wa-a-al, it *is* kinder late fur th' night afore last," genially replied the bartender ; " but 's jest 'n th' shank o' th' evenin' fur t'-night."

It was often a matter of astonishment to me that there were so few troubles and rows in the gambling establishments of Tucson. They did occur from time to time, just as they might happen anywhere else, but not with sufficient frequency to make a feature of the life of the place.

Once what threatened to open up as a most serious affair had a very ridiculous termination. A wild-eyed youth, thoroughly saturated with "sheep-herder's delight" and other choice vintages of the country, made his appearance in the bar of "Congress Hall," and announcing himself as "Slap-Jack Billy, the Pride of the Pan-handle," went on to inform a doubting world that he could whip his weight in "b'ar-meat"—

> "Fur ber-lud's mee color,
>   I kerries mee corfin on mee back,
>   'N' th' hummin' o' pistol-balls, bee jingo,
>   Is me-e-e-u-u-sic in mee ears." (Blank, blank, blank.)

Thump! sounded the brawny fist of "Shorty" Henderson, and down went Ajax struck by the offended lightning. When he came to, the "Pride of the Pan-handle" had something of a job in rubbing down the lump about as big as a goose-egg which had suddenly and spontaneously grown under his left jaw; but he bore no malice and so expressed himself.

"Podners (blank, blank, blank), this 'ere's the most sociablest crowd I ever struck; let's all hev a drink."

If the reader do not care for such scenes, he can find others perhaps more to his liking in the various amusements which, under one pretext or another, extracted all the loose change of the town. The first, in popular estimation, were the "maromas," or tight-rope walkers and general acrobats, who performed many feats well deserving of the praise lavished upon them by the audience. Ever since the days of Cortés the Mexicans have been noted for gymnastic dexterity; it is a matter of history that Cortés, upon returning to Europe, took with him several of the artists in this line, whose agility and cunning surprised those who saw them perform in Spain and Italy.

There were trained dogs and men who knew how to make a barrel roll up or down an inclined plane. All these received a due share of the homage of their fellow-citizens, but nothing to compare to the enthusiasm which greeted the advent of the genuine "teatro." That was *the* time when all Tucson turned out to do honor to the wearers of the buskin. If there was a man, woman, or child in the old pueblo who wasn't seated on one of the cottonwood saplings which, braced upon other saplings, did duty as benches in the corral near the quartermaster's, it was because that man, woman, or child was sick, or in jail. It is astonishing how much enjoyment can be gotten out of life when people set about the task in dead earnest.

There were gross violations of all the possibilities, of all the congruities, of all the unities in the play, "Elena y Jorge," presented to an appreciative public the first evening I saw the Mexican strolling heavy-tragedy company in its glory. But what cared we ? The scene was lighted by bon-fires, by great torches of wood, and by the row of smoking foot-lights running along the front of the little stage.

The admission was regulated according to a peculiar plan : for Mexicans it was fifty cents, but for Americans, one dollar, because the Americans had more money. Another unique feature was the concentration of all the small boys in the first row, closest to the actors, and the clowns who were constantly running about, falling head over heels over the youngsters, and in other ways managing to keep the audience in the best of humor during the rather long intervals between the acts.

The old ladies who sat bunched up on the seats a little farther in rear seemed to be more deeply moved by the trials of the heroine than the men or boys, who continued placidly to puff cigarettes or munch sweet quinces, as their ages and tastes dictated. It was a most harrowing, sanguinary play. The plot needs very few words. Elena, young, beautiful, rich, patriotic ; old uncle, miser, traitor, mercenary, anxious to sell lovely heiress to French officer for gold ; French officer, coward, liar, poltroon, steeped in every crime known to man, anxious to wed lovely heiress for her money alone ; Jorge, young, beautiful, brave, conscientious, an expert in the art of war, in love with heiress for her own sweet sake, but kept from her side by the wicked uncle and his own desire to drive the last cursed despot from the fair land of his fathers.

(Dirge, by the orchestra ; cries of " Muere !" (*i.e.*, May he die ! or, Let him die !) from the semi-circle of boys, who ceased work upon their quinces " for this occasion only.")

I despised that French officer, and couldn't for the life of me understand how any nation, no matter how depraved, could afford to keep such a creature upon its military rolls. I don't think I ever heard any one utter in the same space of time more thoroughly villainous sentiments than did that man, and I was compelled, as a matter of principle, to join with the "muchachos" in their chorus of " Muere !"

As for Doña Elena, the way she let that miserable old uncle see that his schemes were understood, and that never, never, would she consent to become the bride of a traitor and an invader, was enough to make Sarah Bernhardt turn green with envy.

And Jorge—well, Jorge was not idle. There he was all the time, concealed behind a barrel or some other very inadequate cover, listening to every word uttered by the wicked old uncle, the mercenary French officer, and the dauntless Helen. He was continually on the go, jumping out from his concealment, taking the hand of his adored one, telling her his love, but always interrupted by the sudden return of the avuncular villain or the foe of his bleeding country. It is all over at last ; the curtain rings down, and the baffled Gaul has been put to flight ; the guards are dragging the wretched uncle off to the calaboose, and Jorge and his best girl entwine themselves in each other's arms amid thunders of applause.

Then the payazo, or clown, comes to the front, waving the red, white, and green colors of the Mexican republic, and chanting a song in which the doings of the invaders are held up to obloquy and derision.

Everybody would be very hungry by this time, and the old crones who made a living by selling hot suppers to theatre-goers reaped their harvest. The wrinkled dames whose faces had been all tears only a moment ago over the woes of Elena were calm, happy, and voracious. Plate after plate of steaming hot " enchiladas " would disappear down their throats, washed down by cups of boiling coffee or chocolate ; or perhaps appetite demanded "tamales" and "tortillas," with plates of "frijoles " and " chile con carne."

" Enchiladas" and "tamales " are dishes of Aztec origin, much in vogue on the south side of the Rio Grande and Gila. The former may be described as corn batter cakes, dipped in a stew of red chile, with tomato, cheese, and onions chopped fine.

" Tamales " are chopped meat—beef, pork, or chicken, or a mixture of all three—combined with corn-meal and rolled up in husks and boiled or baked. Practically, they are croquettes.

These dishes are delicious, and merit an introduction to American tables. No one can deny that when a Mexican agrees to furnish a hot supper, the hot supper will be forthcoming. What caloric cannot be supplied by fuel is derived from chile, red pepper, with white pepper, green, and a trifle of black, merely to show that the cook has no prejudices on account of color.

The banquet may not have been any too grand, out in the open air, but the gratitude of the bright-eyed, sweet-voiced young señoritas who shared it made it taste delicious. Tucson etiquette in some things was ridiculously strict, and the occasions when young ladies could go, even in parties, with representatives of the opposite sex were few and far between—and all the more appreciated when they did come.

If ever there was created a disagreeable feature upon the fair face of nature, it was the Spanish dueña. All that were to be met in those days in southern Arizona seemed to be possessed of an unaccountable aversion to the mounted service. No flattery would put them in good humor, no cajolery would blind them, intimidation was thrown away. There they would sit, keeping strict, dragon-like watch over the dear little creatures who responded to the names of Anita, Victoria, Concepcion, Guadalupe, or Mercedes, and preventing conversation upon any subject excepting the weather, in which we became so expert that it is a wonder the science of meteorology hasn't made greater advances than it has during the past two decades.

The bull fight did not get farther west than El Paso. Tucson never had one that I have heard of, and very little in the way of out-door "sport" beyond chicken fights, which were often savage and bloody. The rapture with which the feminine heart welcomed the news that a "baile" was to be given in Tucson equalled the pleasure of the ladies of Murray Hill or Beacon Street upon the corresponding occasions in their localities. To be sure, the ceremony of the Tucson affairs was of the meagrest. The rooms were wanting in splendor, perhaps in comfort—but the music was on hand, and so were the ladies, young and old, and their cavaliers, and all hands would manage to have the best sort of a time. The ball-room was one long apartment, with earthen floor, having around its sides low benches, and upon its walls a few cheap mirrors and half a dozen candles stuck to the adobe by melted tallow, a bit of moist clay, or else held in tin sconces, from which they emitted the sickliest light upon the heads and forms of the highly colored saints whose pictures were to be seen in the most eligible places. If the weather happened to be chilly enough in the winter season, a petty fire would be allowed to blaze in one of the corners, but, as a general thing, this was not essential.

The summer climate of Tucson is sultry, and the heat will often run up as high as 120° Fahr.; the fall months are dangerous from malaria, and the springs disagreeable from sand storms, but the winters are incomparable. Neither Italy nor Spain can compare with southern Arizona in balminess of winter climate, and I know of no place in the whole world superior to Tucson as a sanitarium for nervous and pulmonary diseases, from November to March, when the patient can avoid the malaria-breeding fall months and the disagreeable sand storms of the early spring.

The nights in Tucson during the greater part of the year are so cool that blankets are agreeable covering for sleepers. There are times in Tucson, as during the summer of 1870, when for more than a week the thermometer never indicates lower than 98° by day or night. And there are localities, like forts or camps —as they were then styled—Grant, MacDowell, Mojave, Yuma, Beale's Springs, Verde, and Date Creek, where this rule of excessive and prolonged heat never seemed to break. The winter nights of Tucson are cold and bracing, but it is a dry cold, without the slightest suggestion of humidity, and rarely does the temperature fall much below the freezing-point.

The moment you passed the threshold of the ball-room in Tucson you had broken over your head an egg-shell filled either with cologne of the most dubious reputation or else with finely cut gold and silver paper. This custom, preserved in this out-of-the-way place, dates back to the "Carnestolends" or Shrove-Tuesday pranks of Spain and Portugal, when the egg was really broken over the head of the unfortunate wight and the pasty mass covered over with flour.

Once within the ball-room there was no need of being presented to any one. The etiquette of the Spaniards is very elastic, and is based upon common sense. Every man who is good enough to be invited to enter the house of a Mexican gentleman is good enough to enter into conversation with all the company he may meet there.

Our American etiquette is based upon the etiquette of the

English. Ever since King James, the mild-mannered lunatic, sold his orders of nobility to any cad who possessed the necessary six thousand pounds to pay for an entrance into good society, the aristocracy of England has been going down-hill, and what passes with it for manners is the code of the promoted plutocrat, whose ideas would find no place with the Spaniards, who believe in " *sangre azul* " or nothing. There was very little conversation between the ladies and the gentlemen, because the ladies preferred to cluster together and discuss the neighbors who hadn't been able to come, or explain the details of dresses just made or to be made.

Gentlemen invited whom they pleased to dance, and in the intervals between the figures there might be some very weak attempt at conversation, but that was all, except the marching of the gentle female up to the counter and buying her a handkerchief full of raisins or candies, which she carefully wrapped up and carried home with her, in accordance with a custom which obtained among the Aztecs and also among their Spanish conquerors, and really had a strong foothold in good old England itself, from which latter island it did not disappear until A.D. 1765.

While the language of conversation was entirely Spanish, the figures were called off in English, or what passed for English in those days in Arizona : " Ally man let 'n' all shassay ; " " Bal'nce t' yer podners 'n' all han's roun'; " " Dozydozy-chaat 'n' swing."

What lovely times we used to have ! What enchanting music from the Pan's pipes, the flute, the harp, the bass-drum, and the bull-fiddle all going at once ! How lovely the young ladies were ! How bright the rooms were with their greasy lamps or their candles flickering from the walls ! It can hardly be possible that twenty years and more have passed away, yet there are the figures in the almanac which cannot lie.

After the " baile " was over, the rule was for the younger participants to take the music and march along the streets to the houses of the young ladies who had been prevented from attending, and there, under the window, or, rather, in front of the window—because all the houses were of one story, and a man could not get under the windows unless he crawled on hands and knees —pour forth their souls in a serenade.

The Spanish serenader, to judge him by his songs, is a curious blending of woe and despair, paying court to a damsel whose heart is colder than the crystalline ice that forms in the mountains. The worst of it all is, the young woman, whose charms of person are equalled by the charms of her mind, does not seem to care a rush what becomes of the despairing songster, who threatens to go away forever, to sail on unknown seas, to face the nameless perils of the desert, if his suit be not at once recognized by at least one frosty smile. But at the first indication of relenting on the part of the adored one, the suitor suddenly recollects that he cannot possibly stand the fervor of her glance, which rivals the splendor of the sun, and, accordingly, he begs her not to look upon him with those beautiful orbs, as he has concluded to depart forever and sing his woes in distant lands. Having discharged this sad duty at the windows of Doña Anita Fulana, the serenaders solemnly progress to the lattice of Doña Mercedes de Zutana, and there repeat the same heart-rending tale of disappointed affection.

It was always the same round of music, taken in the same series—"La Paloma," "Golondrina," and the rest. I made a collection of some twenty of these ditties or madrigals, and was impressed with the poetic fervor and the absolute lack of common sense shown in them all, which is the best evidence that as love songs they will bear comparison with any that have ever been written. The music in many cases was excellent, although the execution was with very primitive instruments. I do not remember a single instance where the fair one made the least sign of approval or pleasure on account of such serenades, and I suppose that the Mexican idea is that she should not, because if there is a polite creature in the world it is the Mexican woman, no matter of what degree.

The most tender strains evoked no response, and the young man, or men, as the case might be, could have held on until morning and sung himself or themselves into pneumonia for all the young lady seemed to care.

> "No me mires con esos tus ojos,
>   (Fluke-fluky-fluke ; plink, planky-plink.)
> "Mas hermosos que el sol en el cielo,
>   (Plinky-plink ; plinky-plink.)
> "Que me mires de dicha y consuelo,
>   (Fluky-fluky-fluke ; plink-plink.)
> "Que me mata ! que me mata ! tu mirar."
>   (Plinky-plink, fluky-fluke ; plinky-plink ; fluke-fluke.)

But it is morning now, and the bells are clanging for first mass, and we had better home and to bed. Did we so desire we could enter the church, but as there is much to be said in regard to the different feasts, which occurred at different seasons and most acceptably divided the year, we can leave that duty unfulfilled for the present and give a few brief sentences to the christenings and funerals, which were celebrated under our observation.

The Mexicans used to attach a great deal of importance to the naming of their children, and when the day for the christening had arrived, invitations scattered far and near brought together all the relatives and friends of the family, who most lavishly eulogized the youngster, and then partook of a hearty collation, which was the main feature of the entertainment.

Funerals, especially of children, were generally without coffins, owing to the great scarcity of lumber, and nearly always with music at the head of the procession, which slowly wended its way to the church to the measure of plaintive melody.

Birthdays were not observed, but in their stead were kept the days of the saints of the same name. For example, all the young girls named Anita would observe Saint Ann's day, without regard to the date of their own birth, and so with the Guadalupes and Francescas and others.

I should not omit to state that there were whole blocks of houses in Tucson which did not have a single nail in them, but had been constructed entirely of adobes, with all parts of the wooden framework held together by strips of raw-hide.

Yet in these comfortless abodes, which did not possess ten dollars' worth of furniture, one met with charming courtesy from old and young. "Ah ! happy the eyes that gaze upon thee," was the form of salutation to friends who had been absent for a space —" Dichosos los ojos que ven a V." "Go thou with God," was the gentle mode of saying farewell, to which the American guest would respond, as he shifted the revolvers on his hip and adjusted the quid of tobacco in his mouth : " Wa-al, I reckon I'll git." But the Mexican would arrange the folds of his serape, bow most politely, and say : " Ladies, I throw myself at your feet "—" À los pies de VV., señoritas."

Thus far there has been no mention of that great lever of public opinion—the newspaper. There was one of which I will now say a word, and a few months later, in the spring of 1870, the town saw a second established, of which a word shall be said in its turn. The *Weekly Arizonian* was a great public journal, an organ of public opinion, managed by Mr. P. W. Dooner, a very able editor.

It was the custom in those days to order the acts and resolutions of Congress to be published in the press of the remoter Territories, thus enabling the settlers on the frontier to keep abreast of legislation, especially such as more immediately affected their interests. Ordinarily the management of the paper went no farther than the supervision of the publication of such acts, bills, etc.; and the amount of outside information finding an outlet in the scattered settlements of Arizona and New Mexico was extremely small, and by no means recent. With a few exceptions, all the journals of those days were printed either in Spanish alone, or half in Spanish and half in English, the exceptions being sheets like the *Miner*, of Prescott, Arizona, which from the outset maintained the principle that our southwestern territories should be thoroughly Americanized, and that by no surer method could this be effected than by a thoroughly American press. Mr. John H. Marion was the enunciator of this seemingly simple and common-sense proposition, and although the *Miner* has long since passed into other hands, he has, in the columns of the *Courier*, owned and edited by him, advocated and championed it to the present day.

There may have been other matter in the *Weekly Arizonian* besides the copies of legislative and executive documents referred to, but if so I never was fortunate enough to see it, excepting possibly once, on the occasion of my first visit to the town, when I saw announced in bold black and white that "Colonel" Bourke was paying a brief visit to his friend, Señor So-and-so. If there is one weak spot in the armor of a recently-graduated lieutenant, it is the desire to be called colonel before he dies, and here was the ambition of my youth gratified almost before the first lustre had faded from my shoulder-straps. It would serve no good purpose to tell how many hundred copies of that week's issue found their way into the earliest outgoing mail, addressed to friends back in the States. I may be pardoned for alluding to the reckless profanity of the stage-driver upon observing the great bulk of the load his poor horses were to carry. The stage-drivers were an exceptionally profane set, and this one, Frank Francis, was an adept in the business. He has long since gone to his reward in the skies, killed, if I have not made a great mistake, by the Apaches in Sonora, in 1881. He was a good, "square" man, as I can aver from an acquaintance and friendship cemented in later days, when I had to take many and many a lonesome and dangerous ride with him in various sections and on various routes in that then savage-infested region. It was Frank's boast that no "Injuns" should ever get either him or the mail under his care. "All you've got to do with 'n Injun 's to be smarter nor he is. Now, f'r instance, 'n Injun 'll allers lie in wait 'longside the road, tryin' to ketch th' mail. Wa'al, I never don' go 'long no derned road, savey? I jest cut right 'cross lots, 'n' dern my skin ef all th' Injuns this side o' Bitter Creek kin tell whar to lay fur *me*." This and similar bits of wisdom often served to soothe the frightened fancy of the weary "tenderfoot" making his first trip into that wild region, especially if the trip was to be by night, as it generally was.

Whipping up his team, Frank would take a shoot off to one side or the other of the road, and never return to it until the faint tinge of light in the east, or the gladsome crow of chanticleer announced that the dawn was at hand and Tucson in sight. How long they had both been in coming! How the chilling air of night had depressed the spirits and lengthened the hours into eternities! How grand the sky was with its masses of worlds peeping out from depths of blue, unsounded by the telescopes of less favored climes! How often, as the stars rose behind some distant hill-top, did they appear to the fancy as the signal lights of distant Apache raiding parties, and freeze the blood, already coagulated, by suddenly coming upon the gaunt, blackened frame of some dead giant cactus stretching out its warning arms behind a sharp turn in the line of travel!

To this feeling of disquietude the yelping of the coyote added no new horrors; the nervous system was already strained to its utmost tension, and any and all sounds not immediately along the trail were a pleasant relief. They gave something of which to think and a little of which to talk besides the ever-present topic of "Injuns, Injuns." But far different was the sensation as the morning drew near, and fluttering coveys of quail rose with a whirr from their concealment under the mesquite, or pink-eared jack-rabbits scurried from under the horses' feet. Then it was that driver and passenger alike, scared from a fretful doze, would nervously grasp the ever-ready rifle or revolver, and look in vain for the flight of arrows or await the lance-thrust of skulking foes.

Through it all, however, Frank remained the same kind, entertaining host; he always seemed to consider it part of his duties to entertain each one who travelled with him, and there was no lack of conversation, such as it was. "Never knowed Six-toed Petey Donaldson? Wa'al, I sw'ar! Look like enough to be Petey's own brother. Thought mebbe you mout 'a' bin comin' out ter administer on th' estate. Not thet Petey hed enny t' leave, but then it's kind o' consolin' t' a feller to know thet his relatives hev come out ter see about him. How did Petey die? Injuns. Th' Apaches got him jest this side o' the Senneky (Cienaga); we'll see it jest 's soon 's we rise th' hill yander." By the time that the buckboard drew up in front of the post-office, what with cold and hunger and thirst and terror, and bumping over rocks and against giant cactus, and every other kind of cactus, and having had one or two runaways when the animals had struck against the adhering thorns of the pestiferous "cholla," the traveller was always in a suitable frame of mind to invite Frank to "take suthin'," and Frank was too much of a gentleman to think of refusing.

"Now, lemme give yer good advice, podner," Frank would say in his most gracious way, " 'n' doan't drink none o' this yere 'Merican whiskey; it 's no good. Jes' stick to mescal; *that 's* the stuff. Yer see, the alkali water 'n' sand hereabouts 'll combine with mescal, but they p'isens a man when he tries to mix 'em with whiskey, 'specially this yere Kansas whiskey " (the "tenderfoot" had most likely just come over from Kansas); " 'n' ef he doan' get killed deader nor a door-nail, why, his system's all chock full o' p'isen, 'n' there you are."

The establishment of the rival paper, the *Citizen*, was the signal for a war of words, waxing in bitterness from week to week, and ceasing only with the death of the *Arizonian*, which took place not long after. One of the editors of the *Citizen* was Joe Wasson, a very capable journalist, with whom I was afterward associated intimately in the Black Hills and Yellowstone country during the troubles with the Sioux and Cheyennes. He was a well-informed man, who had travelled much and seen life in many phases. He was conscientious in his ideas of duty, and full of the energy and "snap" supposed to be typically American. He approached every duty with the alertness and earnestness of a Scotch terrier. The telegraph was still unknown to Arizona, and for that reason the *Citizen* contained an unusually large amount of editorial matter upon affairs purely local. Almost the very first columns of the paper demanded the sweeping away of garbage-piles, the lighting of the streets by night, the establishment of schools, and the imposition of a tax upon the gin-mills and gambling-saloons.

Devout Mexicans crossed themselves as they passed this fanatic, whom nothing would seem to satisfy but the subversion of every ancient institution. Even the more progressive among the Americans realized that Joe was going a trifle too far, and felt that it was time to put the brakes upon a visionary theorist whose war-cry was "Reform!" But no remonstrance availed, and editorial succeeded editorial, each more pungent and aggressive than its predecessors. What was that dead burro doing on the main street? Why did not the town authorities remove it?

"Valgame! What is the matter with the man? and why does he make such a fuss over Pablo Martinez's dead burro, which has been there for more than two months and nobody bothering about it? Why, it was only last week that Ramon Romualdo and I were talking about it, and we both agreed that it ought to be removed some time very soon. Bah! I will light another cigarette. These Americans make me sick—always in a hurry, as if the devil were after them."

In the face of such antagonism as this the feeble light of the *Arizonian* flickered out, and that great luminary was, after the lapse of a few years, succeeded by the *Star*, whose editor and owner arrived in the Territory in the latter part of the year 1873, after the Apaches had been subdued and placed upon reservations.

CHAPTER VI.

THE Feast of San Juan brought out some very curious customs. The Mexican gallants, mounted on the fieriest steeds they could procure, would call at the homes of their "dulcineas," place the ladies on the saddle in front, and ride up and down the streets, while disappointed rivals threw fire-crackers under the horses' feet. There would be not a little superb equestrianism displayed ; the secret of the whole performance seeming to consist in the nearness one could attain to breaking his neck without doing so.

There is another sport of the Mexicans which has almost if not quite died out in the vicinity of Tucson, but is still maintained in full vigor on the Rio Grande : running the chicken—"correr el gallo." In this fascinating sport, as it looked to be for the horsemen, there is or was an old hen buried to the neck in the sand, and made the target for each rushing rider as he swoops down and endeavors to seize the crouching fowl. If he succeed, he has to ride off at the fastest kind of a run to avoid the pursuit of his comrades, who follow and endeavor to wrest the prize from his hands, and the result, of course, is that the poor hen is pulled to pieces.

Nothing would give me greater pleasure than to describe for the benefit of my readers the scenes presenting themselves during the "Funccion of San Agostin" in Tucson, or that of San Francisco in the Mexican town of Madalena, a hundred and twenty-five miles, more or less, to the south ; the music, the dancing, the gambling, the raffles, the drinking of all sorts of beverages strange to the palate of the American of the North ; the dishes, hot and cold, of the Mexican cuisine, the trading going on in all kinds of truck brought from remote parts of the country, the religious ceremonial brilliant with lights and sweet with music and redolent with incense.

For one solid week these "funcciones lasted," and during the whole time, from early morn till dewy eve, the thump, thump of the drum, the plinky, plink, plink of the harp, and the fluky-fluke of the flute accented the shuffling feet of the unwearied dancers. These and events like them deserve a volume by themselves. I hope that what has already been written may be taken as a series of views, but not the complete series of those upon which we looked from day to day. No perfect picture of early times in Arizona and New Mexico could be delineated upon my narrow canvas; the sight was distracted by strange scenes, the ears by strange sounds, many of each horrible beyond the wildest dreams. There was the ever-dreadful Apache on the one hand to terrify and torment, and the beautiful ruin of San Xavier on the other to bewilder and amaze.

Of all the mission churches within the present limits of the United States, stretching in the long line from San Antonio, Texas, to the presidio of San Francisco, and embracing such examples as San Gabriel, outside of Los Angeles, and the mission of San Diego, there is not one superior, and there are few equal, to San Xavier del Bac, the church of the Papago Indians, nine miles above Tucson, on the Santa Cruz. It needs to be seen to be appreciated, as no literal description, certainly none of which I am capable, can do justice to its merits and beauty. What I have written here is an epitome of the experience and knowledge acquired during years of service there and of familiarity with its people and the conditions in which they lived.

My readers should bear in mind that during the whole period of our stay in or near Tucson we were on the go constantly, moving from point to point, scouting after an enemy who had no rival on the continent in coolness, daring, and subtlety. To save repetition, I will say that the country covered by our movements comprehended the region between the Rio Azul in New Mexico, on the east, to Camp MacDowell, on the west; and from Camp Apache, on the north, to the Mexican pueblos of Santa Cruz and Madalena, far to the south. Of all this I wish to say the least possible, my intention being to give a clear picture of Arizona as it was before the arrival of General Crook, and not to enter into unnecessary details, in which undue reference must necessarily be had to my own experiences.

But I do wish to say that we were for a number of weeks accompanied by Governor Safford, at the head of a contingent of Mexican volunteers, who did very good service in the mountains on the international boundary, the Huachuca, and others. We made camp one night within rifle-shot of what has since been the flourishing, and is now the decayed, mining town of Tombstone. On still another evening, one of our Mexican guides—old Victor Ruiz, one of the best men that ever lived on the border—said that he was anxious to ascertain whether or not his grandfather's memory was at fault in the description given of an abandoned silver mine, which Ruiz was certain could not be very far from where we were sitting. Naturally enough, we all volunteered to go with him in his search, and in less than ten minutes we had reached the spot where, under a mass of earth and stone, was hidden the shaft of which our guide had spoken.

The stories that have always circulated in Arizona about the fabulous wealth of her mineral leads as known to the Spaniards have been of such a character as to turn the brain of the most conservative. The Plancha de la Plata, where a lump of virgin silver weighing over two thousand pounds was exhumed ; the " Thorn Mine," or the " Lost Cabin Mine," in the Tonto Basin ; the " Salero," where the padre in charge, wishing to entertain his bishop in proper style, and finding that he had no salt-cellars ready, ordered certain of the Indians to dig out enough ore to make a solid silver basin, which was placed in all its crudity before the superior—all these were ringing in our ears, and made our task of moving the rocks and débris a very light one.

Disappointment attended our discovery ; the assays of the ore forwarded to San Francisco were not such as to stimulate the work of development ; the rock was not worth more than seventeen dollars a ton, which in those years would not half pay the cost of reduction of silver.

We were among the very first to come upon the rich ledges of copper which have since furnished the mainstay to the prosperity of the town of Clifton, on the border of New Mexico, and we knocked off pieces of pure metal, and brought them back to

Tucson to show to the people there, on returning from our scouts
in the upper Gila.

On one occasion the Apaches ran off the herd of sheep belonging to Tully, Ochoa & DeLong, which were grazing in the foot-hills
of the Santa Teresa not two miles from town.   The young Mexican who was on duty as "pastor" kept his ears open for the
tinkle of the bell, and every now and then would rouse himself
from his doze to look around the mesquite under which he sat,
to ascertain that his flock was all right.   Gradually, the heat of
the day became more and more oppressive, and the poor boy, still
hearing the tintinnabulation, was in a delightful day-dream,
thinking of his supper, perhaps, when he half-opened his eyes,
and saw leering at him a full-grown Apache, who had all the
while been gently shaking the bell taken an hour or two before
from the neck of the wether which, with the rest of the flock, was
a good long distance out of sight behind the hills, near the
"Punta del Agua."   The boy, frightened out of his wits, screamed
lustily, and the Apache, delighted by his terror, flung the bell
at his head, and then set off at a run to gain the hills where
his comrades were.   The alarm soon reached town, and the
sheep were recovered before midnight, and by dawn the next
day were back on their old pasturage, excepting the foot-sore
and the weary, too weak to travel.

Our scouting had its share of incidents grave, gay, melancholy, ludicrous; men killed and wounded; Apaches ditto; and
the usual amount of hard climbing by day, or marching by night
upon trails which sometimes led us upon the enemy, and very
often did not.

There was one very good man, Moore, if I remember his name
correctly, who died of the "fever"—malaria—and was carried
from the "Grassy Plain" into old Camp Goodwin, on the Gila,
near the Warm Spring.   No sooner had we arrived at Goodwin
than one of the men—soldier or civilian employee, I do not know
now—attempted to commit suicide, driven to despair by the utter
isolation of his position; and two of our own company—Sergeant John Mott and one other, both excellent men—dropped
down, broken up with the "fever," which would yield to nothing
but the most heroic treatment with quinine.

In a skirmish with the Apaches near the head of Deer Creek,

one of our men, named Shire, was struck by a rifle ball in the knee-cap, the ball ranging downward, and lodging in the lower leg near the ankle bone. We were sore distressed. There was no doctor with the little command, a criminal neglect for which Cushing was not responsible, and there was no guide, as Manuel Duran, who generally went out with us, was lying in Tucson seriously ill. No one was hurt badly enough to excite apprehension excepting Shire, whose wound was not bleeding at all, the hemorrhage being on the inside.

Sergeant Warfield, Cushing, and I stayed up all night talking over the situation, and doing so in a low tone, lest Shire should suspect that we had not been telling the truth when we persuaded him to believe that he had been hit by a glancing bullet, which had benumbed the whole leg but had not inflicted a very serious wound.

Our Mexican packers were called into consultation, and the result was that by four in the morning, as soon as a cup of coffee could be made, I was on my way over to the Aravaypa Cañon at the head of a small detachment in charge of the wounded man, who was firmly strapped to his saddle. We got along very well so long as we were on the high hills and mountains, where the horse of the sufferer could be led, and he himself supported by friendly hands on each side. To get down into the chasm of the Aravaypa was a horse of altogether a different color. The trail was extremely steep, stony, and slippery, and the soldier, heroic as he was, could not repress a groan as his horse jarred him by slipping under his weight on the wretched path. At the foot of the descent it was evident that something else in the way of transportation would have to be provided, as the man's strength was failing rapidly and he could no longer sit up.

Lieutenant Cushing's orders were for me to leave the party just as soon as I thought I could do so safely, and then ride as fast as the trail would permit to Camp Grant, and there get all the aid possible. It seemed to me that there could be no better time for hurrying to the post than the present, which found the detachment at a point where it could defend itself from the attack of any roving party of the enemy, and supplied with grass for the animals and fuel and water for the men.

Shire had fainted as I mounted and started with one of the

men, Corporal Harrington, for the post, some twelve miles away. We did not have much more of the cañon to bother us, and made good speed all the way down the Aravaypa and into the post, where I hurriedly explained the situation and had an ambulance start up the cañon with blankets and other comforts, while in the post itself everything was made ready for the amputation in the hospital, which all knew to be a foregone conclusion, and a mounted party was sent to Tucson to summon Dr. Durant to assist in the operation.

Having done all this, I started back up the cañon and came upon my own detachment slowly making its way down. In another hour the ambulance had rolled up to the door of the hospital, and the wounded man was on a cot under the influence of anæsthetics. The amputation was made at the upper third of the thigh, and resulted happily, and the patient in due time recovered, although he had a close call for his life.

The winter of 1870 and the spring of 1871 saw no let up in the amount of scouting which was conducted against the Apaches. The enemy resorted to a system of tactics which had often been tried in the past and always with success. A number of simultaneous attacks were made at points widely separated, thus confusing both troops and settlers, spreading a vague sense of fear over all the territory infested, and imposing upon the soldiery an exceptional amount of work of the hardest conceivable kind.

Attacks were made in southern Arizona upon the stage stations at the San Pedro, and the Cienaga, as well as the one near the Picacho, and upon the ranchos in the Barbacomori valley, and in the San Pedro, near Tres Alamos. Then came the news of a fight at Pete Kitchen's, and finally, growing bolder, the enemy drove off a herd of cattle from Tucson itself, some of them beeves, and others work-oxen belonging to a wagon-train from Texas. Lastly came the killing of the stage mail-rider, between the town and the Mission church of San Xavier, and the massacre of the party of Mexicans going down to Sonora, which occurred not far from the Sonoita.

One of the members of this last party was a beautiful young Mexican lady—Doña Trinidad Aguirre—who belonged to a very respectable family in the Mexican Republic, and was on her way back from a visit to relatives in Tucson.

That one so young, so beautiful and bright, should have been snatched away by a most cruel death at the hands of savages, aroused the people of all the country south of the Gila, and nothing was talked of, nothing was thought of, but vengeance upon the Apaches.

Cushing all this time had kept our troop moving without respite. There were fights, and ambuscades, and attacks upon "rancherias," and night-marches without number, several resulting in the greatest success. I am not going to waste any space upon these, because there is much of the same sort to come, and I am afraid of tiring out the patience of my readers before reaching portions of this book where there are to be found descriptions of very spirited engagements.

The trail of the raiders upon the ranch at the "Cienaga" (now called "Pantano" by the Southern Pacific Railroad people) took down into the "Mestinez," or Mustang Mountains, so called from the fact that a herd of wild ponies were to be found there or not far off. They did not number more than sixty all told when I last saw them in 1870, and were in all probability the last herd of wild horses within the limits of the United States. In this range, called also the "Whetstone" Mountains, because there exists a deposit or ledge of the rock known as "novaculite" or whetstone of the finest quality, we came upon the half calcined bones of two men burned to death by the Apaches; and after marching out into the open valley of the San Pedro, and crossing a broad expanse covered with yucca and sage-brush, we came to a secluded spot close to the San José range, where the savages had been tearing up the letters contained in one of Uncle Sam's mail-bags, parts of which lay scattered about.

When the work-oxen of the Texans were run off, the Apaches took them over the steepest, highest and rockiest part of the Sierra Santa Catalina, where one would not believe that a bird would dare to fly. We followed closely, guided by Manuel Duran and others, but progress was difficult and slow, on account of the nature of the trail. As we picked our way, foot by foot, we could discern the faintest sort of a mark, showing that a trail had run across there and had lately been used by the Apaches. But all the good done by that hard march was the getting back of the meat of the stock which the Apaches killed just the moment they reached the cañons under the Trumbull Peak. Two or three of the oxen were still alive, but so nearly run to death that we killed them as an act of mercy.

Three of our party were hurt in the mêlée, and we scored three hits, one a beautiful shot by Manuel, who killed his man the moment he exposed himself to his aim, and two wounded, how seriously we could not tell, as by the time we had made our way to the top of the rocks the enemy had gone with their wounded, leaving only two pools of blood to show where the bullets had taken effect.

The trail leading to the place where the Apaches had taken refuge was so narrow that one of our pack-mules lost his footing and fell down the precipice, landing upon the top of a tree below and staying there for a full minute, when the branches broke under him and let him have another fall, breaking his back and making it necessary to blow his brains out as soon as the action was over and we could take time to breathe.

Then followed the fearful scene of bloodshed known as the "Camp Grant Massacre," which can only be referred to—a full description would require a volume of its own. A small party of Apaches had presented themselves at Camp Grant, and made known to the commanding officer that they and their friends up in the Aravaypa Cañon were willing and anxious to make peace and to stay near the post, provided they could get food and clothing. They were told to return with their whole tribe, which they soon did, and there is no good reason for supposing that the greater portion of them were not honest in their professions and purposes. The blame of what was to follow could not be laid at the doors of the local military authorities, who exerted themselves in every way to convey information of what had happened to the Department headquarters, then at Los Angeles. As previously stated, there was no mode of communication in Arizona save the stage, which took five days to make the trip from Tucson to Los Angeles, and as many more for a return trip, there being no telegraph in existence.

Weeks and weeks were frittered away in making reports which should have reached headquarters at once and should have been acted upon without the delay of a second. The story was circulated and generally believed, that the first report was returned to the officer sending it, with instructions to return it to Department headquarters "properly briefed," that is, with a synopsis of its contents properly written on the outer flap of the communication when folded. There was no effort made, as there should have been made, to separate the peaceably disposed Indians from those who still preferred to remain out on the warpath, and as a direct consequence of this neglect ensued one of the worst blots in the history of American civilization, the "Camp Grant Massacre."

A party of more than one hundred Papago Indians, from the village of San Xavier, led by a small detachment of whites and half-breed Mexicans from Tucson, took up the trail of one of the parties of raiders which had lately attacked the settlers and the peaceable Indians in the valley of the Santa Cruz. What followed is matter of history. The pursuing party claimed that the trails led straight to the place occupied by the Apaches who had surrendered at Camp Grant, and it is likely that this is so, since one of the main trails leading to the country of the Aravaypa and Gila bands passed under the Sierra Pinaleno, near the point in question. It was claimed further that a horse belonging to Don Leopoldo Carrillo was found in the possession of one of the young boys coming out of the village, and that some of the clothing of Doña Trinidad Aguirre was also found.

These stories may be true, and they may be after-thoughts to cover up and extenuate the ferocity of the massacre which spared neither age nor sex in its wrath, but filled the valley of the Aravaypa with dead and dying. The incident, one of the saddest and most terrible in our annals, is one over which I would gladly draw a veil. To my mind it indicated the weak spot in all our dealings with the aborigines, a defective point never repaired and never likely to be. According to our system of settling up the public lands, there are no such things as colonies properly so called. Each settler is free to go where he pleases, to take up such area as the law permits, and to protect himself as best he can. The army has always been too small to afford all the protection the frontier needed, and affairs have been permitted to drift along in a happy-go-lucky sort of a way indicative rather of a sublime faith in divine providence than of common sense and good judgment.

The settlers, in all sections of the West, have been representative of the best elements of the older States from which they set forth, but it is a well-known fact that among them have been a fair, possibly more than a fair, share of the reckless, the idle and the dissolute. On the other hand, among the savages, there have been as many young bloods anxious to win renown in battle as there have been old wise-heads desirous of preserving the best feeling with the new neighbors. The worst members of the two races are brought into contact, and the usual results follow ; trouble springs up, and it is not the bad who suffer, but the peaceably disposed on each side.

On the 5th day of May, 1871, Lieutenant Howard B. Cushing, Third Cavalry, with several civilians and three soldiers, was killed by the Chiricahua Apaches, under their famous chief " Cocheis," at the Bear Springs, in the Whetstone Mountains, about thirty-five miles from Tucson and about the same distance to the east of old Camp Crittenden. Cushing's whole force numbered twenty-two men, the larger part of whom were led into an ambuscade in the cañon containing the spring. The fight was a desperate one, and fought with courage and great skill on both sides. Our forces were surrounded before a shot had been fired ; and it was while Cushing was endeavoring to lead his men back that he received the wounds which killed him. Had it not been for the courage and good judgment displayed by Sergeant John Mott, who had seen a great amount of service against the Apaches, not one of the command would have escaped alive out of the cañon.

Mott was in command of the rear-guard, and, in coming up to the assistance of Lieutenant Cushing, detected the Apaches moving behind a low range of hills to gain Cushing's rear. He sent word ahead, and that induced Lieutenant Cushing to fall back.

After Cushing dropped, the Apaches made a determined charge and came upon our men hand to hand. The little detachment could save only those horses and mules which were ridden at the moment the enemy made the attack, because the men who had dismounted to fight on foot were unable to remount, such was the impetuosity of the rush made by the Chiricahuas. There were enough animals to "ride and tie," and Mott, by keeping up on the backbone of the hills running along the Barbacomori Valley, was enabled to reach Camp Crittenden without being surrounded or ambuscaded.

Inside of forty-eight hours there were three troops of cavalry *en route* to Crittenden, and in pursuit of the Apaches, but no good could be effected. Major William J. Ross, at that time in command of Camp Crittenden, was most energetic in getting word to the various military commands in the southern part of the country, as well as in extending every aid and kindness to the wounded brought in by Mott.

When the combined force had arrived at Bear Spring, there was to be seen every evidence of a most bloody struggle. The bodies of Lieutenant Cushing and comrades lay where they had fallen, stripped of clothing, which the Apaches always carried off from their victims. In all parts of the narrow little cañon were the carcasses of ponies and horses half-eaten by the coyotes and buzzards ; broken saddles, saddle-bags, canteens with bullet-holes in them, pieces of harness and shreds of clothing scattered about, charred to a crisp in the flames which the savages had ignited in the grass to conceal their line of retreat.

Of how many Apaches had been killed, there was not the remotest suggestion to be obtained. That there had been a heavy loss among the Indians could be suspected from the signs of bodies having been dragged to certain points, and there, apparently, put on pony-back.

The Chiricahuas seemed to have ascended the cañon until they had attained the crest of the range in a fringe of pine timber ; but no sooner did they pass over into the northern foot-hills than they broke in every direction, and did not re-unite until near our boundary line with Mexico, where their trail was struck and followed for several days by Major Gerald Russell of the Third Cavalry. They never halted until they had regained the depths of the Sierra Madre, their chosen haunt, and towards which Russell followed them so long as his broken-down animals could travel.

Of the distinguished services rendered to Arizona by Lieutenant Cushing, a book might well be written. It is not intended to disparage anybody when I say that he had performed herculean and more notable work, perhaps, than had been performed by any other officer of corresponding rank either before or since. Southern Arizona owed much to the gallant officers who wore out strength and freely risked life and limb in her defence—men of the stamp of Devin, C. C. Carr, Sanford, Gerald Russell, Winters, Harris, Almy, Carroll, McCleave, Kelly, and many others. They were all good men and true ; but if there were any choice among them I am sure that the verdict, if left to those soldiers themselves, would be in favor of Cushing.

Standing on the summit of the Whetstone Range, which has no great height, one can see the places, or the hills overlooking them, where several other officers met their death at the hands of the same foe. To the west is Davidson's Cañon, where the Apaches ambushed and killed Lieutenant Reid T. Stewart and Corporal Black ; on the north, the cone of Trumbull overlooks the San Carlos Agency, where the brave Almy fell ; to the northwest are the Tortolita hills, near which Miller and Tappan were killed in ambuscade, as already narrated ; and to the east are the Chiricahua Mountains, in whose bosom rests Fort Bowie with its grewsome graveyard filled with such inscriptions as "Killed by the Apaches," "Met his death at the hands of the Apaches," "Died of wounds inflicted by Apache Indians," and at times "Tortured and killed by Apaches." One visit to that cemetery was warranted to furnish the most callous with nightmares for a month.

CHAPTER VII.

WHEN General Crook received orders to go out to Arizona and assume command of that savage-infested Department, he at once obeyed the order, and reached his new post of duty without baggage and without fuss.

All the baggage he had would not make as much compass as a Remington type-writer. The only thing with him which could in any sense be classed as superfluous was a shotgun, but without this or a rifle he never travelled anywhere.

He came, as I say, without the slightest pomp or parade, and without any one in San Francisco, except his immediate superiors, knowing of his departure, and without a soul in Tucson, not even the driver of the stage which had carried him and his baggage, knowing of his arrival. There were no railroads, there were no telegraphs in Arizona, and Crook was the last man in the world to seek notoriety had they existed. His whole idea of life was to do each duty well, and to let his work speak for itself.

He arrived in the morning, went up to the residence of his old friend, Governor Safford, with whom he lunched, and before sundown every officer within the limits of what was then called the southern district of Arizona was under summons to report to him ; that is, if the orders had not reached them they were on the way.

From each he soon extracted all he knew about the country, the lines of travel, the trails across the various mountains, the fords where any were required for the streams, the nature of the soil, especially its products, such as grasses, character of the climate, the condition of the pack-mules, and all pertaining to them, and every other item of interest a commander could possibly want to have determined. But in reply not one word, not one glance, not one hint, as to what he was going to do or what he would like to do.

This was the point in Crook's character which made the strongest impression upon every one coming in contact with him —his ability to learn all that his informant had to supply, without yielding in return the slightest suggestion of his own plans and purposes. He refused himself to no one, no matter how humble, but was possessed of a certain dignity which repressed any approach to undue familiarity. He was singularly averse to the least semblance of notoriety, and was as retiring as a girl. He never consulted with any one; made his own plans after the most studious deliberation, and kept them to himself with a taciturnity which at times must have been exasperating to his subordinates. Although taciturn, reticent, and secretive, moroseness formed no part of his nature, which was genial and sunny. He took great delight in conversation, especially in that wherein he did not have to join if indisposed.

He was always interested in the career and progress of the young officers under him, and glad to listen to their plans and learn their aspirations. No man can say that in him the subaltern did not have the brightest of exemplars, since Crook was a man who never indulged in stimulant of any kind—not so much as tea or coffee—never used tobacco, was never heard to employ a profane or obscene word, and was ever and always an officer to do, and do without pomp or ceremony, all that was required of him, and much more.

No officer could claim that he was ever ordered to do a duty when the Department commander was present, which the latter would not in person lead. No officer of the same rank, at least in our service, issued so few orders. According to his creed, officers did not need to be devilled with orders and instructions and memoranda ; all that they required was to obtain an insight into what was desired of them, and there was no better way to inculcate this than by personal example.

Therefore, whenever there was a trouble of any magnitude under Crook's jurisdiction he started at once to the point nearest the skirmish line, and stayed there so long as the danger existed ; but he did it all so quietly, and with so little parade, that half the time no one would suspect that there was any hostility threatened until after the whole matter had blown over or been stamped out, and the General back at his headquarters.

This aversion to display was carried to an extreme ; he never liked to put on uniform when it could be avoided ; never allowed an orderly to follow him about a post, and in every manner possible manifested a nature of unusual modesty, and totally devoid of affectation. He had one great passion—hunting, or better say, hunting and fishing. Often he would stray away for days with no companion but his dog and the horse or mule he rode, and remain absent until a full load of game—deer, wild turkey, quail, or whatever it might happen to be—rewarded his energy and patience. From this practice he diverged slightly as he grew older, yielding to the expostulations of his staff, who impressed upon him that it was nothing but the merest prudence to be accompanied by an Indian guide, who could in case of necessity break back for the command or the post according to circumstances.

In personal appearance General Crook was manly and strong ; he was a little over six feet in height, straight as a lance, broad and square-shouldered, full-chested, and with an elasticity and sinewiness of limb which betrayed the latent muscular power gained by years of constant exercise in the hills and mountains of the remoter West.

In his more youthful days, soon after being graduated from the Military Academy, he was assigned to duty with one of the companies of the Fourth Infantry, then serving in the Oregon Territory. It was the period of the gold-mining craze on the Pacific coast, and prices were simply prohibitory for all the comforts of life. Crook took a mule, a frying-pan, a bag of salt and one of flour, a rifle and shotgun, and sallied out into the wilderness. By his energy and skill he kept the mess fully supplied with every kind of wild meat—venison, quail, duck, and others—and at the end of the first month, after paying all the expenses on account of ammunition, was enabled from the funds realized by selling the surplus meat to miners and others, to declare a dividend of respectable proportions, to the great delight of his messmates.

His love for hunting and fishing, which received its greatest impetus in those days of his service in Oregon and Northern California, increased rather than diminished as the years passed by. He became not only an exceptionally good shot, but acquired a familiarity with the habits of wild animals possessed by but few naturalists. Little by little he was induced to read upon the subject, until the views of the most eminent ornithologists and naturalists were known to him, and from this followed in due sequence a development of his taste for taxidermy, which enabled him to pass many a lonesome hour in the congenial task of preserving and mounting his constantly increasing collection of birds and pelts.

There were few, if any, of the birds or beasts of the Rocky Mountains and the country west of them to the waters of the Pacific, which had not at some time furnished tribute to General Crook's collection. In the pursuit of the wilder animals he cared nothing for fatigue, hunger, or the perils of the cliffs, or those of being seized in the jaws of an angry bear or mountain lion.

He used to take great, and, in my opinion, reprehensible risks in his encounters with grizzlies and brown bears, many of whose pelts decorated his quarters. Many times I can recall in Arizona, Wyoming, and Montana, where he had left the command, taking with him only one Indian guide as a companion, and had struck out to one flank or the other, following some " sign," until an hour or two later a slender signal smoke warned the pack-train that he had a prize of bear-meat or venison waiting for the arrival of the animals which were to carry it back to camp.

Such constant exercise toughened muscle and sinew to the rigidity of steel and the elasticity of rubber, while association with the natives enabled him constantly to learn their habits and ideas, and in time to become almost one of themselves.

If night overtook him at a distance from camp, he would picket his animal to a bush convenient to the best grass, take out his heavy hunting-knife and cut down a pile of the smaller branches of the pine, cedar, or sage-brush, as the case might be, and with them make a couch upon which, wrapped in his overcoat and saddle-blanket, he would sleep composedly till the rise of the morning star, when he would light his fire, broil a slice of venison, give his horse some water, saddle up and be off to look for the trail of his people.

His senses became highly educated ; his keen, blue-gray eyes would detect in a second and at a wonderful distance the slightest movement across the horizon ; the slightest sound aroused his curiosity, the faintest odor awakened his suspicions. He noted the smallest depression in the sand, the least deflection in the twigs or branches; no stone could be moved from its position in the trail without appealing at once to his perceptions. He became skilled in the language of "signs" and trails, and so perfectly conversant with all that is concealed in the great book of Nature that, in the mountains at least, he might readily take rank as being fully as much an Indian as the Indian himself.

There never was an officer in our military service so completely in accord with all the ideas, views, and opinions of the savages whom he had to fight or control as was General Crook. In time of campaign this knowledge placed him, as it were, in the secret councils of the enemy; in time of peace it enabled him all the more completely to appreciate the doubts and misgivings of the Indians at the outset of a new life, and to devise plans by which they could all the more readily be brought to see that civilization was something which all could embrace without danger of extinction.

But while General Crook was admitted, even by the Indians, to be more of an Indian than the Indian himself, it must in no wise be understood that he ever occupied any other relation than that of the older and more experienced brother who was always ready to hold out a helping hand to the younger just learning to walk and to climb. Crook never ceased to be a gentleman. Much as he might live among savages, he never lost the right to claim for himself the best that civilization and enlightenment had to bestow. He kept up with the current of thought on the more important questions of the day, although never a student in the stricter meaning of the term. His manners were always extremely courteous, and without a trace of the austerity with which small minds seek to hedge themselves in from the approach of inferiors or strangers. His voice was always low, his conversation easy, and his general bearing one of quiet dignity.

He reminded me more of Daniel Boone than any other character, with this difference, that Crook, as might be expected, had the advantages of the better education of his day and generation. But he certainly recalled Boone in many particulars; there was the same perfect indifference to peril of any kind, the same coolness, an equal fertility of resources, the same inner knowledge of the wiles and tricks of the enemy, the same modesty and disinclination to parade as a hero or a great military genius, or to obtrude upon public notice the deeds performed in obedience to the promptings of duty.

Such was Arizona, and such was General George Crook when he was assigned to the task of freeing her from the yoke of the shrewdest and most ferocious of all the tribes encountered by the white man within the present limits of the United States.

A condensed account of the Apaches themselves would seem not to be out of place at this point, since it will enable the reader all the more readily to comprehend the exact nature of the operations undertaken against them, and what difficulties, if any, were to be encountered in their subjugation and in their elevation to a higher plane of civilization.

With a stupidity strictly consistent with the whole history of our contact with the aborigines, the people of the United States have maintained a bitter and an unrelenting warfare against a people whose name was unknown to them.   The Apache is not the Apache ; the name " Apache " does not occur in the language of the " Tinneh," by which name, or some of its variants as " Inde," " Dinde," or something similar, our Indian prefers to designate himself " The Man ; " he knows nothing, or did not know anything until after being put upon the Reservations, of the new-fangled title " Apache," which has come down to us from the Mexicans, who borrowed it from the Maricopas and others, in whose language it occurs with the signification of " enemy."

It was through the country of the tribes to the south that the Spaniards first were brought face to face with the " Tinneh " of Arizona, and it was from these Maricopas and others that the name was learned of the desperate fighters who lived in the higher ranges with the deer, the elk, the bear, and the coyote.

And as the Spaniards have always insisted upon the use of a name which the Apaches have as persistently repudiated ; and as the Americans have followed blindly in the footsteps of the Castilian, we must accept the inevitable and describe this tribe under the name of the Apaches of Arizona, although it is much like invading England by way of Ireland, and writing of the Anglo-Saxons under the Celtic designation of the " Sassenach."

The Apache is the southernmost member of the great Tinneh family, which stretches across the circumpolar portion of the

American Continent, from the shores of the Pacific to the western line of Hudson's Bay. In the frozen habitat of their hyperborean ancestors, the Tinneh, as all accounts agree, are perfectly good-natured, lively, and not at all hard to get along with.

But once forced out from the northern limits of the lake region of British America—the Great Slave, the Great Bear, and others —whether by over-population, failure of food, or other cause, the Tinneh appears upon the stage as a conqueror, and as a diplomatist of the first class; he shows an unusual astuteness even for an Indian, and a daring which secures for him at once and forever an ascendency over all the tribes within reach of him. This remark will apply with equal force to the Rogue Rivers of Oregon, the Umpquas of northern California, the Hoopas of the same State, and the Navajoes and Apaches of New Mexico, Chihuahua and Sonora, all of whom are members of this great Tinneh family.

In the Apache the Spaniard, whether as soldier or priest, found a foe whom no artifice could terrify into submission, whom no eloquence could wean from the superstitions of his ancestors. Indifferent to the bullets of the arquebuses in the hands of soldiers in armor clad, serenely insensible to the arguments of the friars and priests who claimed spiritual dominion over all other tribes, the naked Apache, with no weapons save his bow and arrows, lance, war-club, knife and shield, roamed over a vast empire, the lord of the soil—fiercer than the fiercest of tigers, wilder than the wild coyote he called his brother.

For years I have collected the data and have contemplated the project of writing the history of this people, based not only upon the accounts transmitted to us from the Spaniards and their descendants, the Mexicans, but upon the Apache's own story as conserved in his myths and traditions; but I have lacked both the leisure and the inclination to put the project into execution. It would require a man with the even-handed sense of justice possessed by a Guizot, and the keen, critical, analytical powers of a Gibbon, to deal fairly with a question in which the ferocity of the savage Red-man has been more than equalled by the ferocity of the Christian Caucasian; in which the occasional treachery of the aborigines has found its best excuse in the unvarying Punic faith of the Caucasian invader; in which promises on each side have been made only to deceive and to be broken; in which the red hand of war has rested most heavily upon shrieking mother and wailing babe.

If from this history the Caucasian can extract any cause of self-laudation I am glad of it : speaking as a censor who has read the evidence with as much impartiality as could be expected from one who started in with the sincere conviction that the only good Indian was a dead Indian, and that the only use to make of him was that of a fertilizer, and who, from studying the documents in the case, and listening little by little to the savage's own story, has arrived at the conclusion that perhaps Pope Paul III. was right when he solemnly declared that the natives of the New World had souls and must be treated as human beings, and admitted to the sacraments when found ready to receive them, I feel it to be my duty to say that the Apache has found himself in the very best of company when he committed any atrocity, it matters not how vile, and that his complete history, if it could be written by himself, would not be any special cause of self-complacency to such white men as believe in a just God, who will visit the sins of parents upon their children even to the third and the fourth generation.

We have become so thoroughly Pecksniffian in our self-laudation, in our exaltation of our own virtues, that we have become grounded in the error of imagining that the American savage is more cruel in his war customs than other nations of the earth have been ; this, as I have already intimated, is a misconception, and statistics, for such as care to dig them out, will prove that I am right. The Assyrians cut their conquered foes limb from limb ; the Israelites spared neither parent nor child ; the Romans crucified head downward the gladiators who revolted under Spartacus ; even in the civilized England of the past century, the wretch convicted of treason was executed under circumstances of cruelty which would have been too much for the nerves of the fiercest of the Apaches or Sioux. Instances in support of what I here assert crop up all over the page of history ; the trouble is not to discover them, but to keep them from blinding the memory to matters more pleasant to remember. Certainly, the American aborigine is not indebted to his pale-faced brother, no matter of what nation or race he may be, for lessons in tenderness and humanity.

Premising the few remarks which I will allow myself to make

upon this subject, by stating that the territory over which the
Apache roamed a conqueror, or a bold and scarcely resisted raider,
comprehended the whole of the present Territories of Arizona and
New Mexico, one half of the State of Texas—the half west of San
Antonio—and the Mexican states of Sonora and Chihuahua, with
frequent raids which extended as far as Durango, Jalisco, and
even on occasion the environs of Zacatecas, I can readily make
the reader understand that an area greater than that of the whole
German Empire and France combined was laid prostrate under
the heel of a foe as subtle, as swift, as deadly, and as uncertain as
the rattle-snake or the mountain lion whose homes he shared.

From the moment the Castilian landed on the coast of the
present Mexican Republic, there was no such thing thought of
as justice for the American Indian until the authorities of the
Church took the matter in hand, and compelled an outward regard
for the rights which even animals have conceded to them.

Christopher Columbus, whom some very worthy people are
thinking of having elevated to the dignity of a saint, made use of
bloodhounds for running down the inhabitants of Hispaniola.

The expedition of D'Ayllon to the coast of Chicora, now known
as South Carolina, repaid the kind reception accorded by the
natives by the basest treachery; two ship-loads of the unfortu-
nates enticed on board were carried off to work in the mines of
the invaders.

Girolamo Benzoni, one of the earliest authors, describes the
very delightful way the Spaniards had of making slaves of all
the savages they could capture, and branding them with a red-
hot iron on the hip or cheek, so that their new owners could
recognize them the more readily.

Cabeza de Vaca and his wretched companions carried no arms,
but met with nothing but an ovation from the simple-minded
and grateful natives, whose ailments they endeavored to cure by
prayer and the sign of the cross.

Yet, Vaca tells us, that as they drew near the settlements of
their own countrymen they found the whole country in a tumult,
due to the efforts the Castilians were making to enslave the popu-
lace, and drive them by fire and sword to the plantations newly
established.   Humboldt is authority for the statement that the
Apaches resolved upon a war of extermination upon the Spaniards, when they learned that all their people taken captive by the

king's forces had been driven off, to die a lingering death upon the sugar plantations of Cuba or in the mines of Guanaxuato.

Drawing nearer to our own days, we read the fact set down in the clearest and coldest black and white, that the state governments of Sonora and Chihuahua had offered and paid rewards of three hundred dollars for each scalp of an Apache that should be presented at certain designated headquarters, and we read without a tremor of horror that individuals, clad in the human form—men like the Englishman Johnson, or the Irishman Glanton—entered into contracts with the governor of Chihuahua to do such bloody work.

Johnson was "a man of honor." He kept his word faithfully, and invited a large band of the Apaches in to see him and have a feast at the old Santa Rita mine in New Mexico—I have been on the spot and seen the exact site—and while they were eating bread and meat, suddenly opened upon them with a light field-piece loaded to the muzzle with nails, bullets, and scrap-iron, and filled the court-yard with dead.

Johnson, I say, was "a gentleman," and abided by the terms of his contract; but Glanton was a blackguard, and set out to kill anything and everything in human form, whether Indian or Mexican. His first "victory" was gained over a band of Apaches with whom he set about arranging a peace in northern Chihuahua, not far from El Paso. The bleeding scalps were torn from the heads of the slain, and carried in triumph to the city of Chihuahua, outside of whose limits the "conquerors" were met by a procession of the governor, all the leading state dignitaries and the clergy, and escorted back to the city limits, where—as we are told by Ruxton, the English officer who travelled across Chihuahua on horse-back in 1835–1837—the scalps were nailed with frantic joy to the portals of the grand cathedral, for whose erection the silver mines had been taxed so outrageously.

Glanton, having had his appetite for blood excited, passed westward across Arizona until he reached the Colorado River, near where Fort Yuma now stands. There he attempted to cross to the California or western bank, but the Yuma Indians, who had learned of his pleasant eccentricities of killing every one, without distinction of age, sex, or race, who happened to be out on the trail alone, let Glanton and his comrades get a few yards into the river, and then opened on them from an ambush in the reeds and killed the last one.

And then there have been "Pinole Treaties," in which the Apaches have been invited to sit down and eat repasts seasoned with the exhilarating strychnine. So that, take it for all in all, the honors have been easy so far as treachery, brutality, cruelty, and lust have been concerned. The one great difference has been that the Apache could not read or write and hand down to posterity the story of his wrongs as he, and he alone, knew them.

When the Americans entered the territory occupied or infested by the Apaches, all accounts agree that the Apaches were friendly. The statements of Bartlett, the commissioner appointed to run the new boundary line between the United States and Mexico, are explicit upon this point. Indeed, one of the principal chiefs of the Apaches was anxious to aid the new-comers in advancing farther to the south, and in occupying more of the territory of the Mexicans than was ceded by the Gadsden purchase. One of Bartlett's teamsters—a Mexican teamster named Jesus Vasquez —causelessly and in the coldest blood drew bead upon a prominent Apache warrior and shot him through the head. The Apaches did nothing beyond laying the whole matter before the new commissioner, whose decision they awaited hopefully. Bartlett thought that the sum of thirty dollars, deducted from the teamster's pay in monthly instalments, was about all that the young man's life was worth. The Apaches failed to concur in this estimate, and took to the war-path ; and, to quote the words of Bartlett, in less than forty-eight hours had the whole country for hundreds of miles in every direction on fire, and all the settlers that were not killed fleeing for their lives to the towns on the Rio Grande. A better understanding was reached a few years after, through the exertions of officers of the stamp of Ewell, who were bold in war but tender in peace, and who obtained great influence over a simple race which could respect men whose word was not written in sand.

At the outbreak of the war of the Rebellion, affairs in Arizona and New Mexico became greatly tangled. The troops were withdrawn, and the Apaches got the notion into their heads that the country was to be left to them and their long-time enemies, the Mexicans, to fight for the mastery.

Rafael Pumpelly, who at that time was living in Arizona, gives a vivid but horrifying description of the chaotic condition in which affairs were left by the sudden withdrawal of the troops, leaving the mines, which, in each case, were provided with stores or warehouses filled with goods, a prey to the Apaches who swarmed down from the mountains and the Mexican bandits who poured in from Sonora.

There was scarcely any choice between them, and occasionally it happened, when the mining superintendent had an unusual streak of good luck, that he would have them both to fight at once, as in Pumpelly's own case.

Not very long previous to this, Arizona had received a most liberal contingent of the toughs and scalawags banished from San Francisco by the efforts of its Vigilance Committee, and until these last had shot each other to death, or until they had been poisoned by Tucson whiskey or been killed by the Apaches, Arizona's chalice was filled to the brim, and the most mendacious real-estate boomer would have been unable to recommend her as a suitable place for an investment of capital.

It is among the possibilities that the Apaches could have been kept in a state of friendliness toward the Americans during these troublous days, had it not been for one of those accidents which will occur to disturb the most harmonious relations, and destroy the effect of years of good work. The Chiricahua Apaches, living close to what is now Fort Bowie, were especially well behaved, and old-timers have often told me that the great chief, Cocheis, had the wood contract for supplying the "station" of the Southern Overland Mail Company at that point with fuel. The Pinals and the other bands still raided upon the villages of northern Mexico; in fact, some of the Apaches have made their home in the Sierra Madre, in Mexico; and until General Crook in person led a small expedition down there, and pulled the last one of them out, it was always understood that there was the habitat and the abiding place of a very respectable contingent—so far as numbers were concerned—of the tribe.

A party of the Pinal Apaches had engaged in trade with a party of Mexicans close to Fort Bowie—and it should be understood that there was both trade and war with the Castilian, and, worst of all, what was stolen from one Mexican found ready sale to another, the plunder from Sonora finding its way into the hands of the settlers in Chihuahua, or, if taken up into our country, selling without trouble to the Mexicans living along the Rio Grande —and during the trade had drunk more whiskey, or mescal, than was good for them ; that is to say, they had drunk more than one drop, and had then stolen or led away with them a little boy, the child of an Irish father and a Mexican mother, whom the Mexicans demanded back.

The commanding officer, a lieutenant of no great experience, sent for the brother of Cocheis, and demanded the return of the babe ; the reply was made, and, in the light of years elapsed, the reply is known to have been truthful, that the Chiricahuas knew nothing of the kidnapped youngster and therefore could not restore him. The upshot of the affair was that Cocheis's brother was killed "while resisting arrest." In Broadway, if a man "resist arrest," he is in danger of having his head cracked by a policeman's club ; but in the remoter West, he is in great good luck, sometimes, if he don't find himself riddled with bullets.

It is an excellent method of impressing an Indian with the dignity of being arrested ; but the cost of the treatment is generally too great to make it one that can fairly be recommended for continuous use. In the present instance, Cocheis, who had also been arrested, but had cut his way out of the back of the tent in which he was confined, went on the war-path, and for the next ten years made Arizona and New Mexico—at least the southern half of them—and the northern portions of Sonora and Chihuahua, about the liveliest places on God's footstool.

The account, if put down by a Treasury expert, would read something like this :

DR.

"The United States to Cocheis,
" For one brother, killed ' while resisting arrest.' "

CR.

" By ten thousand (10,000) men, women, and children killed, wounded, or tortured to death, scared out of their senses or driven out of the country, their wagon and pack-trains run off and destroyed, ranchos ruined, and all industrial development stopped."

If any man thinks that I am drawing a fancy sketch, let him write to John H. Marion, Pete Kitchen, or any other old pioneer

whose residence in either Arizona or New Mexico has been sufficiently long to include the major portion of the time that the
whole force of the Apache nation was in hostilities.

I have said that the exertions of the missionaries of the Roman
Catholic Church, ordinarily so successful with the aborigines of
our Continent, were nugatory with the Apaches of Arizona; I
repeat this, at the same time taking care to say that unremitting
effort was maintained to open up communication with the various
bands nearest to the pueblos which, from the year 1580, or there-
about, had been brought more or less completely under the sway
of the Franciscans.

With some of these pueblos, as at Picuris, the Apaches had
intermarried, and with others still, as at Pecos, they carried on
constant trade, and thus afforded the necessary loop-hole for
the entrance of zealous missionaries. The word of God was
preached to them, and in several instances bands were coaxed to
abandon their nomadic and predatory life, and settle down in
permanent villages. The pages of writers, like John Gilmary
Shea, fairly glow with the recital of the deeds of heroism performed in this work; and it must be admitted that perceptible
traces of it are still to be found among the Navajo branch of
the Apache family, which had acquired the peach and the apricot, the sheep and the goat, the cow, the donkey and the horse,
either from the Franciscans direct, or else from the pueblo
refugees who took shelter with them in 1680 at the time of the
Great Rebellion, in which the pueblos of New Mexico arose *en
masse* and threw off the yoke of Spain and the Church, all for
twelve years of freedom, and the Moquis threw it off forever.
Arizona—the Apache portion of it—remained a sealed book to the
friars, and even the Jesuits, in the full tide of their career as
successful winners of souls, were held at arm's length.

There is one point in the mental make-up of the Apache
especially worthy of attention, and that is the quickness with
which he seizes upon the salient features of a strategetical combination, and derives from them all that can possibly be made to
inure to his own advantage. For generations before the invasion
by the Castilians—that is to say, by the handful of Spaniards,
and the colony of Tlascaltec natives and mulattoes, whom Espejo
and Onate led into the valley of the Rio Grande between 1580
and 1590—the Apache had been the unrelenting foe of the

Pueblo tribes; but the moment that the latter determined to throw off the galling yoke which had been placed upon their necks, the Apache became their warm friend, and received the fugitives in the recesses of the mountains, where he could bid defiance to the world. Therefore, we can always depend upon finding in the records of the settlements in the Rio Grande valley, and in Sonora and Chihuahua, that every revolt or attempted revolt, of the Pueblos or sedentary tribes meant a corresponding increase in the intensity of the hostilities prosecuted by the Apache nomads.

In the revolts of 1680, as well as those of 1745 and 1750, the Apache swept the country far to the south. The great revolt of the Pueblos was the one of 1680, during which they succeeded in driving the governor and the surviving Spanish colonists from Santa Fé down to the present town of Juarez (formerly El Paso del Norte), several hundred miles nearer Mexico. At that place Otermin made a stand, but it was fully twelve years before the Spanish power was re-established through the efforts of Vargas and Cruzate. The other two attempts at insurrection failed miserably, the second being merely a local one among the Papagoes of Arizona. It may be stated, in round terms, that from the year 1700 until they were expelled from the territory of Mexico, the exertions of the representatives of the Spanish power in "New Spain" were mainly in the direction of reducing the naked Apache, who drove them into a frenzy of rage and despair by his uniform success.

The Tarahumaris, living in the Sierra Madre south of the present international boundary, were also for a time a thorn in the side of the European; but they submitted finally to the instructions of the missionaries who penetrated into their country, and who, on one occasion at least, brought them in from the war-path before they had fired a shot.

The first reference to the Apaches by name is in the account of Espejo's expedition—1581—where they will be found described as the "Apichi," and from that time down the Spaniards vie with each other in enumerating the crimes and the atrocities of which these fierce Tinneh have been guilty. Torquemada grows eloquent and styles them the Pharaohs ("Faraones") who have persecuted the chosen people of Israel (meaning the settlers on the Rio Grande).

Yet all the while that this black cloud hung over the fair face of nature—raiding, killing, robbing, carrying women and children into captivity—Jesuit and Franciscan vied with each other in schemes for getting these savages under their control.

Father Eusebio Kino, of whom I have already spoken, formulated a plan in or about 1710 for establishing, or re-establishing, a mission in the villages of the Moquis, from which the Franciscans had been driven in the great revolt and to which they had never permanently returned. Questions of ecclesiastical jurisdiction seem to have had something to do with delaying the execution of the plan, which was really one for the spiritual and temporal conquest of the Apache, by moving out against him from all sides, and which would doubtless have met with good results had not Kino died at the mission of Madalena a few months after. Father Sotomayor, another Jesuit, one of Kino's companions, advanced from the " Pimeria," or country of the Pimas, in which Tucson has since grown up, to and across the Salt River on the north, in an unsuccessful attempt to begin negotiations with the Apaches.

The overthrow of the Spanish power afforded another opportunity to the Apache to play his cards for all they were worth ; and for fully fifty years he was undisputed master of Northwestern Mexico—the disturbed condition of public affairs south of the Rio Grande, the war between the United States and the Mexican Republic, and our own Civil War, being additional factors in the equation from which the Apache reaped the fullest possible benefit.

It is difficult to give a fair description of the personal appearance of the Apaches, because there is no uniform type to which reference can be made ; both in physique and in facial lineaments there seem to be two distinct classes among them. Many of the tribes are scarcely above medium size, although they look to be still smaller from their great girth of chest and width of shoulders. Many others are tall, well-made, and straight as arrows. There are long-headed men, with fine brows, aquiline noses, well-chiselled lips and chins, and flashing eyes ; and there are others with the flat occiput, flat nose, open nostrils, thin, everted lips, and projecting chins.

One general rule may be laid down : the Apache, to whichever type he may belong, is strongly built, straight, sinewy, well-muscled, extremely strong in the lower limbs, provided with a round barrel chest, showing good lung power, keen, intelligent-looking eyes, good head, and a mouth showing determination, decision, and cruelty. He can be made a firm friend, but no mercy need be expected from him as an enemy.

He is a good talker, can argue well from his own standpoint, cannot be hoodwinked by sophistry or plausible stories, keeps his word very faithfully, and is extremely honest in protecting property or anything placed under his care. No instance can be adduced of an Apache sentinel having stolen any of the government or other property he was appointed to guard. The Chiricahua and other Apache scouts, who were enlisted to carry on General Crook's campaign against "Geronimo," remained for nearly one week at Fort Bowie, and during that time made numbers of purchases from the post-trader, Mr. Sydney R. De Long. These were all on credit, as the scouts were about leaving with the gallant and lamented Crawford on the expedition which led to his death. Some months after, as I wished to learn something definite in regard to the honesty of this much-maligned people, I went to Mr. De Long and asked him to tell me what percentage of bad debts he had found among the Apaches. He examined his books, and said slowly : "They have bought seventeen hundred and eighty dollars' worth, and they have paid me back every single cent."

"And what percentage of bad debts do you find among your white customers ? "

A cynical smile and a pitying glance were all the reply vouchsafed.

Around his own camp-fire the Apache is talkative, witty, fond of telling stories, and indulging in much harmless raillery. He is kind to children, and I have yet to see the first Indian child struck for any cause by either parent or relative. The children are well provided with games of different kinds, and the buck-skin doll-babies for the little girls are often very artistic in make-up. The boys have fiddles, flutes, and many sorts of diversion, but at a very early age are given bows and arrows, and amuse themselves as best they can with hunting for birds and small animals. They have sham-fights, wrestling matches, foot-races, games of shinny and "muskha," the last really a series of lance-throws along the ground, teaching the youngster steadiness of aim and keeping every muscle fully exercised. They learn at a very early age the names and attributes of all the animals and plants about them ; the whole natural kingdom, in fact, is understood as far as their range of knowledge in such matters extends. They are inured to great fatigue and suffering, to deprivation of water, and to going without food for long periods.

Unlike the Indians of the Plains, east of the Rocky Mountains, they rarely become good horsemen, trusting rather to their own muscles for advancing upon or escaping from an enemy in the mountainous and desert country with which they, the Apaches, are so perfectly familiar. Horses, mules, and donkeys, when captured, were rarely held longer than the time when they were needed to be eaten ; the Apache preferred the meat of these animals to that of the cow, sheep, or goat, although all the last-named were eaten. Pork and fish were objects of the deepest repugnance to both men and women ; within the past twenty years—since the Apaches have been enrolled as scouts and police at the agencies—this aversion to bacon at least has been to a great extent overcome ; but no Apache would touch fish until Geronimo and the men with him were incarcerated at Fort Pickens, Florida, when they were persuaded to eat the pompano and other delicious fishes to be found in Pensacola Bay.

When we first became apprised of this peculiarity of the Apache appetite, we derived all the benefit from it that we could in driving away the small boys who used to hang around our mess-canvas in the hope of getting a handful of sugar, or a piece of cracker, of which all hands, young and old, were passionately fond. All we had to do was to set a can of salmon or lobster in the middle of the canvas, and the sight of that alone would drive away the bravest Apache boy that ever lived ; he would regard as uncanny the mortals who would eat such vile stuff. They could not understand what was the meaning of the red-garmented Mephistophelian figure on the can of devilled ham, and called that dish " Chidin-bitzi " (ghost meat), because they fancied a resemblance to their delineations of their gods or spirits or ghosts.

The expertness of the Apache in all that relates to tracking either man or beast over the rocky heights, or across the interminable sandy wastes of the region in which he makes his home, has been an occasion of astonishment to all Caucasians who have had the slightest acquaintance with him.   He will follow through grass, over sand or rock, or through the chapparal of scrub oak, up and down the flanks of the steepest ridges, traces so faint that to the keenest-eyed American they do not appear at all.

Conversely, he is fiendishly dexterous in the skill with which he conceals his own line of march when a pursuing enemy is to be thrown off the track.   No serpent can surpass him in cunning ; he will dodge and twist and bend in all directions, boxing the compass, doubling like a fox, scattering his party the moment a piece of rocky ground is reached over which it would, under the best circumstances, be difficult to follow.   Instead of moving in file, his party will here break into skirmishing order, covering a broad space and diverging at the most unexpected moment from the primitive direction, and not perhaps reuniting for miles. Pursuit is retarded and very frequently baffled.   The pursuers must hold on to the trail, or all is lost.   There must be no guess-work.   Following a trail is like being on a ship : so long as one is on shipboard, he is all right ; but if he once go overboard, he is all wrong.   So with a trail : to be a mile away from it is fully as bad as being fifty, if it be not found again.   In the meantime the Apache raiders, who know full well that the pursuit must slacken for a while, have reunited at some designated hill, or near some spring or water " tank," and are pushing across the high mountains as fast as legs harder than leather can carry them.   If there be squaws with the party, they carry all plunder on their backs in long, conical baskets of their own make, unless they have made a haul of ponies, in which case they sometimes ride, and at all times use the animals to pack.

At the summit of each ridge, concealed behind rocks or trees, a few picked men, generally not more than two or three, will remain waiting for the approach of pursuit; when the tired cavalry draw near, and begin, dismounted, the ascent of the mountain, there are always good chances for the Apaches to let them have half a dozen well-aimed shots—just enough to check the onward movement, and compel them to halt and close up, and, while all this is going on, the Apache rear-guard, whether in the saddle or on foot, is up and away, as hard to catch as the timid quail huddling in the mesquite.

Or it may so happen the Apache prefers, for reasons best known to himself, to await the coming of night, when he will sneak in upon the herd and stampede it, and set the soldiery on foot, or drive a few arrows against the sentinels, if he can discern where they may be moving in the gloom.

All sorts of signals are made for the information of other parties of Apaches. At times, it is an inscription or pictograph incised in the smooth bark of a sycamore ; at others, a tracing upon a smooth-faced rock under a ledge which will protect it from the elements ; or it may be a knot tied in the tall sacaton or in the filaments of the yucca ; or one or more stones placed in the crotch of a limb, or a sapling laid against another tree, or a piece of buckskin carelessly laid over a branch. All these, placed as agreed upon, afford signals to members of their own band, and only Apaches or savages with perceptions as keen would detect their presence.

When information of some important happening is to be communicated to a distance and at once, and the party is situated upon the summit of a mountain chain or in other secure position, a fire is lighted of the cones of the resinous pine, and the smoke is instantaneously making its way far above the tracery of the foliage. A similar method is employed when they desire to apprise kinsfolk of the death of relatives ; in the latter case the brush " jacal " of the deceased — the whole village, in fact—is set on fire and reduced to ashes.

The Apache was a hard foe to subdue, not because he was full of wiles and tricks and experienced in all that pertains to the art of war, but because he had so few artificial wants and depended almost absolutely upon what his great mother—Nature—stood ready to supply. Starting out upon the war-path, he wore scarcely any clothing save a pair of buckskin moccasins reaching to mid-thigh and held to the waist by a string of the same material ; a piece of muslin encircling the loins and dangling down behind about to the calves of the legs, a war-hat of buckskin surmounted by hawk and eagle plumage, a rifle (the necessary ammunition in belt) or a bow, with the quiver filled with arrows reputed to be poisonous, a blanket thrown over the shoulders, a watertight wicker jug to serve as a canteen, and perhaps a small amount of " jerked " meat, or else of " pinole " or parched corn-meal.

That is all, excepting his sacred relics and " medicine," for now is the time when the Apache is going to risk no failure by neglecting the precaution needed to get all his ghosts and gods on his side. He will have sacred cords of buckskin and shells, sacred sashes ornamented with the figures of the powers invoked to secure him success; possibly, if he be very opulent, he may have bought from a "medicine man" a sacred shirt, which differs from the sash merely in being bigger and in having more figures; and a perfect menagerie of amulets and talismans and relics of all kinds, medicine arrows, pieces of crystal, petrified wood, little bags of the sacred meal called "hoddentin," fragments of wood which has been struck by lightning, and any and all kinds of trash which his fancy or his fears have taught him are endowed with power over the future and the supernatural. Like the Roman he is not content with paying respect to his own gods; he adopts those of all the enemies who yield to his power. In many and many an instance I have seen dangling from the neck, belt or wrist of an Apache warrior the cross, the medals, the *Agnus Dei* or the rosary of the Mexican victims whom his rifle or arrow had deprived of life.

To his captives the Apache was cruel, brutal, merciless; if of full age, he wasted no time with them, unless on those rare occasions when he wanted to extract some information about what his pursuers were doing or contemplated doing, in which case death might be deferred for a few brief hours. Where the captive was of tender years, unable to get along without a mother's care, it was promptly put out of its misery by having its brains dashed against a convenient rock or tree; but where it happened that the raiders had secured boys or girls sufficiently old to withstand the hardships of the new life, they were accepted into the hand and treated as kindly as if Apache to the manner-born.

It was often a matter of interest to me to note the great amount of real, earnest, affectionate good-will that had grown up between the Mexican captives and the other members of the tribe; there were not a few of these captives who, upon finding a chance, made their escape back to their own people, but in nearly all cases they have admitted to me that their life among the savages was one of great kindness, after they had learned enough of the language to understand and be understood.

Many of these captives have risen to positions of influence among the Apaches. There are men and women like "Severi-ano," "Concepcion," "Antonio," "Jesus Maria," "Victor,"

"Francesca," "Maria," and others I could name, who have amassed property and gained influence among the people who led them into slavery.

A brief account of the more prominent of foods entering into the dietary of the Apache may not be out of place, as it will serve to emphasize my remarks concerning his ability to practically snap his fingers at any attempts to reduce him to starvation by the ordinary methods. The same remarks, in a minor degree, apply to all our wilder tribes. Our Government had never been able to starve any of them until it had them placed on a reservation. The Apache was not so well provided with meat as he might have been, because the general area of Arizona was so arid and barren that it could not be classed as a game country ; nevertheless, in the higher elevations of the Sierra Mogollon and the San Francisco, there were to be found plenty of deer, some elk, and, in places like the Grand Cañon of the Colorado, the Cañon of the Rio Salado, and others, there were some Rocky Mountain sheep ; down on the plains or deserts, called in the Spanish idiom "playas" or "beaches," there were quite large herds of antelope, and bears were encountered in all the high and rocky places.

Wild turkeys flock in the timbered ranges, while on the lower levels, in the thickets of sage-brush and mesquite, quail are numerous enough to feed Moses and all the Israelites were they to come back to life again. The jack-rabbit is caught by being "rounded up," and the field-rat adds something to the meat supply. The latter used to be caught in a very peculiar way. The rat burrowed under a mesquite or other bush, and cast up in a mound all the earth excavated from the spot selected for its dwelling ; and down through this cut or bored five or six entrances, so that any intruder, such as a snake, would be unable to bar the retreat of the inmates, who could seek safety through some channel other than the one seized upon by the invader.

The Apache was perfectly well acquainted with all this, and laid his plans accordingly. Three or four boys would surround each habitation, and, while one took station at the main entrance and laid the curved end of his "rat-stick" across its mouth, the others devoted themselves to prodding down with their sticks into the other channels. The rats, of course, seeing one hole undisturbed, would dart up that, and, when each had reached the opening, he would rest for a moment, with his body just half out, while he scanned the horizon to see where the enemy was. That was the supreme moment for both rat and Apache, and, with scarcely any percentage of errors worth mentioning, the Apache was nearly always successful. He would quickly and powerfully draw the stick towards him and break the back of the poor rodent, and in another second have it dangling from his belt. One gash of the knife would eviscerate the little animal, and then it was thrown upon a bed of hot coals, which speedily burned off all the hair and cooked it as well.

The above completed the list of meats of which use was made, unless we include the horses, cows, oxen, donkeys, sheep, and mules driven off from Mexicans and Americans, which were all eaten as great delicacies. Some few of the meats prepared by the Apache cooks are palatable, and I especially remember their method of baking a deer's head surrounded and covered by hot embers. They roast a side of venison to perfection over a bed of embers, and broil liver and steak in a savory manner; but their *bonne bouche*, when they can get it, is an unborn fawn, which they believe to be far more delicious than mule meat.

The mainstay of the Apache larder was always the mescal, or agave—the American aloe—a species of the so-called century plant. This was cut down by the squaws and baked in "mescal-pits," made for all the world like a clam-bake. There would be first laid down a course of stones, then one of wet grass, if procurable, then the mescal, then another covering of grass, and lastly one of earth. All over Arizona old "mescal-pits" are to be found, as the plant was always cooked as close as possible to the spot where it was cut, thus saving the women unnecessary labor.

Three days are required to bake mescal properly, and, when done, it has a taste very much like that of old-fashioned molasses candy, although its first effects are those of all the aloe family. The central stalk is the best portion, as the broad, thorny leaves, although yielding a sweet mass, are so filled with filament that it is impossible to chew them, and they must be sucked.

The fruit of the Spanish bayonet, when dried, has a very pleasant taste, not unlike that of a fig. It can also be eaten in the raw or pulpy state, but will then, so the Apaches tell me, often bring on fever.

Of the bread made from mesquite beans, as of the use made of the fruit of the giant cactus, mention has already been made in the beginning of this work. Sweet acorns are also used freely.

The "nopal," or Indian fig, supplies a fruit which is very good, and is much liked by the squaws and children, but it is so covered with a beard of spines, that until I had seen some of the squaws gathering it, I could not see how it could be so generally employed as an article of food. They would take in one hand a small wooden fork made for the purpose, and with that seize the fruit of the plant ; with the other hand, a brush made of the stiff filaments of the sacaton was passed rapidly over the spines, knocking them all off much sooner than it has taken to write this paragraph on the typewriter. It requires no time at all to fill a basket with them, and either fresh or dried they are good food.

The seeds of the sunflower are parched and ground up with corn-meal or mesquite beans to make a rich cake.

There are several varieties of seed-bearing grasses of importance to the Apache. The squaws show considerable dexterity in collecting these ; they place their conical baskets under the tops of the stalks, draw these down until they incline over the baskets, and then hit them a rap with a small stick, which causes all the seed to fall into the receptacle provided.

In damp, elevated swales the wild potatoes grow plentifully. These are eaten by both Apaches and Navajoes, who use with them a pinch of clay to correct acridity. A small black walnut is eaten, and so is a wild cherry. The wild strawberry is too rare to be noticed in this treatise, but is known to the Apaches. Corn was planted in small areas by the Sierra Blanca band whenever undisturbed by the scouting parties of their enemies. After General Crook had conquered the whole nation and placed the various bands upon reservations, he insisted upon careful attention being paid to the planting of either corn or barley, and immense quantities of each were raised and sold to the United States Government for the use of its horses and mules. Of this a full description will follow in due time.

The Apaches have a very strict code of etiquette, as well as morals, viewed from their own standpoint. It is considered very impolite for a stranger to ask an Apache his name, and an Apache will never give it, but will allow the friend at his side to reply for him ; the names of the dead are never referred to, and it is an insult to speak of them by name. Yet, after a good long while has elapsed, the name of a warrior killed in battle or distinguished in any way may be conferred upon his grandchild or some other relative.

No Apache, no matter what his standing may be in society, will speak to or of his mother-in-law—a courtesy which the old lady reciprocates. One of the funniest incidents I can remember was seeing a very desperate Chiricahua Apache, named "Ka-e-tennay," who was regarded as one of the boldest and bravest men in the whole nation, trying to avoid running face to face against his mother-in-law ; he hung on to stones, from which had he fallen he would have been dashed to pieces or certainly broken several of his limbs. There are times at the Agencies when Indians have to be counted for rations—even then the rule is not relaxed. The mother-in-law will take a seat with her son-in-law and the rest of the family ; but a few paces removed, and with her back turned to them all ; references to her are by signs only—she is never mentioned otherwise.

When an Apache young man begins to feel the first promptings of love for any particular young damsel, he makes known the depth and sincerity of his affection by presenting the young woman with a calico skirt, cut and sewed by his own fair fingers. The Apache men are good sewers, and the Navajo men do all the knitting for their tribe, and the same may be said of the men of the Zunis.

Only ill-bred Americans or Europeans, who have never had any "raising," would think of speaking of the Bear, the Snake, the Lightning or the Mule, without employing the reverential prefix "Ostin," meaning "Old Man," and equivalent to the Roman title "Senator." But you can't teach politeness to Americans, and the Apache knows it and wastes no time or vain regrets on the defects of their training.

"You must stop talking about bear," said a chief to me one night at the camp-fire, " or we 'll not have a good hunt."

In the same manner no good will come from talking about owls, whose hooting, especially if on top of a " jacal," or in the branches of a tree under which people are seated or sleeping, means certain death. I have known of one case where our bravest scouts ran away from a place where an owl had perched and begun its lugubrious ditty, and at another time the scouts, as we were about entering the main range of the Sierra Madre, made a great fuss and would not be pacified until one of the whites of our command had released a little owl which he had captured. This same superstition obtained with equal force among the Romans, and, indeed, there are few if any spots in the world, where the owl has not been regarded as the messenger of death or misfortune.

When an Apache starts out on the war-path for the first four times, he will refrain from letting water touch his lips ; he will suck it through a small reed or cane which he carries for the purpose. Similarly, he will not scratch his head with the naked fingers, but resorts to a small wooden scratcher carried with the drinking-tube. Traces of these two superstitions can also be found in other parts of the globe. There are all kinds of superstitions upon every conceivable kind of subject, but there are too many of them to be told *in extenso* in a book treating of military campaigning.

As might be inferred, the "medicine men" wield an amount of influence which cannot be understood by civilized people who have not been brought into intimate relations with the aborigines in a wild state. The study of the religious life and thought of our savage tribes has always been to me of the greatest interest and of supreme importance ; nothing has been so neglected by the Americans as an examination into the mental processes by which an Indian arrives at his conclusions, the omens, auguries, hopes and fears by which he is controlled and led to one extreme or the other in all he does, or a study of the leaders who keep him under control from the cradle to the grave. Certainly, if we are in earnest in our protestations of a desire to elevate and enlighten the aborigine—which I for one most sincerely doubt— then we cannot begin too soon to investigate all that pertains to him mentally as well as physically. Looking at the subject in the strictest and most completely practical light, we should save millions of dollars in expenditure, and many valuable lives, and not be making ourselves a holy show and a laughing-stock for the rest of the world by massing troops and munitions of war from the four corners of the country every time an Indian medicine man or spirit doctor announces that he can raise the dead. Until we provide something better, the savage will rely upon his own religious practices to help him through all difficulties, and his medicine man will be called upon to furnish the singing, drumming and dancing that may be requisite to cure the sick or avert disease of any kind.

The "cures" of the medicine men are effected generally by incantations, the sprinkling of hoddentin or sacred powder, sweatbaths, and at times by suction of the arm, back or shoulder in which pain may have taken up its abode. If they fail, as they very often do, then they cast about and pretty soon have indicated some poor old crone as the maleficent obstacle to the success of their ministrations, and the miserable hag is very soon burnt or stoned to death.

The influence quietly exerted upon tribal councils by the women of the Apache and Navajo tribes has been noted by many observers.

I will curtail my remarks upon the manners and customs of the Apaches at this point, as there will necessarily be many other allusions to them before this narrative shall be completed. One thing more is all I care to say. The endurance of their warriors while on raids was something which extorted expressions of wonder from all white men who ever had anything to do with their subjugation. Seventy-five miles a day was nothing at all unusual for them to march when pursued, their tactics being to make three or four such marches, in the certainty of being able to wear out or throw off the track the most energetic and the most intelligent opponents.

Their vision is so keen that they can discern movements of troops or the approach of wagon-trains for a distance of thirty miles, and so inured are they to the torrid heats of the burning sands of Arizona south of the Gila and Northern Mexico, that they seem to care nothing for temperatures under which the American soldier droops and dies. The Apache, as a matter of fact, would strip himself of everything and travel naked, which the civilized man would not do; but the amount of clothing retained by the soldiers was too small to be considered a very important factor.

If necessary, the Apache will go without water for as long a time almost as a camel. A small stone or a twig inserted in the mouth will cause a more abundant flow of saliva and assuage his thirst. He travels with fewer "impedimenta" than any other tribe of men in the world, not even excepting the Australians, but sometimes he allows himself the luxury or comfort of a pack of cards, imitated from those of the Mexicans, and made out of horse-hide, or a set of the small painted sticks with which to play the game of " Tze-chis," or, on occasions when an unusually large number of Apaches happen to be travelling together, some one of the party will be loaded with the hoops and poles of the " mushka ; " for, be it known, that the Apache, like savages everywhere, and not a few civilized men, too, for that matter, is so addicted to gambling that he will play away the little he owns of clothing and all else he possesses in the world.

Perhaps no instance could afford a better idea of the degree of ruggedness the Apaches attain than the one coming under my personal observation in the post hospital of Fort Bowie, in 1886, where one of our Apache scouts was under treatment for a gunshot wound in the thigh. The moment Mr. Charles Lummis and myself approached the bedside of the young man, he asked for a " tobacco-shmoke," which he received in the form of a bunch of cigarettes. One of these he placed in his mouth, and, drawing a match, coolly proceeded to strike a light on his foot, which, in its horny, callous appearance, closely resembled the back of a mud tortoise.

CHAPTER VIII.

HOW it all came about I never knew; no one ever knew. There were no railroads and no telegraphs in those days, and there were no messages flashed across the country telling just what was going to be done and when and how. But be all that as it may, before any officer or man knew what had happened, and while the good people in Tucson were still asking each other whether the new commander had a "policy" or not—he had not, but that's neither here nor there—we were out on the road, five full companies of cavalry, and a command of scouts and trailers gathered together from the best available sources, and the campaign had begun.

Rumors had reached Tucson—from what source no one could tell—that the Government would not permit Crook to carry on offensive operations against the Apaches, and there were officers in the Department, some even in our own command, who were inclined to lend an ear to them. They were enthusiasts, however, who based their views upon the fact that "Loco" and "Victorio," prominent chiefs of the Warm Springs band over in New Mexico, had been ever since September of the year 1869, a period of not quite two years, encamped within sight of old Fort Craig, New Mexico, on the Rio Grande, waiting to hear from the Great Father in regard to having a Reservation established for them where they and their children could live at peace.

The more conservative sadly shook their heads. They *knew* that there had not been time for the various documents and reports in the case to make the round of the various bureaus in

Washington, and lead to the formulation of any scheme in the premises. It used to take from four to six months for such a simple thing as a requisition for rations or clothing to produce any effect, and, of course, it would seem that the caring for a large body would consume still longer time for deliberation. But, no matter what Washington officialism might do or not do, General Crook was not the man to delay at his end of the line. We were on our way to Fort Bowie, in the eastern section of Arizona, leaving Tucson at six o'clock in the morning of July 11, 1871, and filing out on the mail road where the heat before ten o'clock attained 110° Fahrenheit in the shade, as we learned from the party left behind in Tucson to bring up the mail.

As it happened, Crook's first movement was stopped ; but not until it had almost ended and been, what it was intended to be, a "practice march" of the best kind, in which officers and men could get acquainted with each other and with the country in which at a later moment they should have to work in earnest. Our line of travel lay due east one hundred and ten miles to old Fort Bowie, thence north through the mountains to Camp Apache, thence across an unmapped region over and at the base of the great Mogollon range to Camp Verde and Prescott on the west. In all, some six hundred and seventy-five miles were travelled, and most of it being in the presence of a tireless enemy, made it the best kind of a school of instruction. The first man up in the morning, the first to be saddled, the first ready for the road, was our indefatigable commander, who, in a suit of canvas, and seated upon a good strong mule, with his rifle carried across the pommel of his saddle, led the way.

With the exception of Colonel Guy V. Henry, Captain W. W. Robinson of the Seventh Cavalry, and myself, none of the officers of that scout are left in the army. Major Ross, our capable quartermaster, is still alive and is now a citizen of Tucson. Crook, Stanwood, Smith, Meinhold, Mullan, and Brent are dead, and Henry has had such a close call for his life (at the Rosebud, June 17, 1876) that I am almost tempted to include him in the list.

The detachment of scouts made a curious ethnographical collection. There were Navajoes, Apaches, Opatas, Yaquis, Pueblos, Mexicans, Americans, and half-breeds of any tribe one could name. It was an *omnium gatherum*—the best that could be

summoned together at the time ; some were good, and others
were good for nothing.   They were a fair sample of the social
driftwood of the Southwest, and several of them had been concerned in every revolution or counter-revolution in northwestern
Mexico since the day that Maximilian landed.   Manuel Duran,
the old Apache, whom by this time I knew very intimately,
couldn't quite make it all out.   He had never seen so many
troops together before without something being in the wind, and
what it meant he set about unravelling.   He approached, the
morning we arrived at Sulphur Springs, and in the most confidential manner asked me to ride off to one side of the road with
him, which I, of course, did.

"You are a friend of the new Comandante," he said, "and I
am a friend of yours.   You must tell me *all*."

"But, Manuel, I do not fully understand what you are driving
at."

"Ah, mi teniente, you cannot fool me.   I am too old ; I know
all about such things."

"But, tell me, Manuel, what is this great mystery you wish
to know?"

Manuel's right eyelid dropped just a trifle, just enough to be
called a wink, and he pointed with his thumb at General Crook
in advance.   His voice sank to a whisper, but it was still perfectly clear and plain, as he asked : " When is the new Comandante going to pronounce ?"

I didn't explode nor roll out of the saddle, although it was
with the greatest difficulty I kept from doing either ; but the
idea of General Crook, with five companies of cavalry and one
of scouts, revolting against the general Government and issuing a "pronunciamiento," was too much for my gravity, and I
yelled.   Often in succeeding years I have thought of that talk
with poor Manuel, and never without a chuckle.

We learned to know each other, we learned to know Crook, we
learned to know the scouts and guides, and tell which of them
were to be relied upon, and which were not worth their salt ; we
learned to know a great deal about packers, pack-mules and packing, which to my great surprise I found to be a science and such
a science that as great a soldier as General Crook had not thought
it beneath his genius to study it ; and, applying the principles
of military discipline to the organization of trains, make them

as nearly perfect as they ever have been or can be in our army history. Last, but not least, we learned the country—the general direction of the rivers, mountains, passes, where was to be found the best grazing, where the most fuel, where the securest shelter. Some of the command had had a little experience of the same kind previously, but now we were all in attendance at a perambulating academy, and had to answer such questions as the general commanding might wish to propound on the spot.

Side scouts were kept out constantly, and each officer, upon his return, was made to tell all he had learned of the topography and of Indian " sign." There was a great plenty of the latter, but none of it very fresh ; in the dim distance, on the blue mountain-tops, we could discern at frequent intervals the smoke sent up in signals by the Apaches ; often, we were at a loss to tell whether it was smoke or the swift-whirling " trebillon " of dust, carrying off in its uncanny embrace the spirit of some mighty chief. While we slowly marched over " playas " of sand, without one drop of water for miles, we were tantalized by the sight of cool, pellucid lakelets from which issued water whose gurgle and ripple could almost be heard, but the illusion dissipated as we drew nearer and saw that the mirage-fiend had been mocking our thirst with spectral waters.

Our commanding general showed himself to be a man who took the deepest interest in everything we had to tell, whether it was of peccaries chased off on one side of the road, of quail flushed in great numbers, of the swift-walking, long-tailed road-runner— the " paisano " or " chapparal cock," of which the Mexicans relate that it will imprison the deadly rattler by constructing around its sleeping coils a fence of cactus spines ; of tarantulas and centipedes and snakes—possibly, some of the snake-stories of Arizona may have been a trifle exaggerated, but then we had no fish, and a man must have something upon which to let his imagination have full swing ; of badgers run to their holes ; of coyotes raced to death ; of jackass-rabbits surrounded and captured; and all the lore of plant and animal life in which the Mexican border is so rich. Nothing was too insignificant to be noted, nothing too trivial to be treasured up in our memories; such was the lesson taught during our moments of conversation with General Crook. The guides and trailers soon found that although they who had been born and brought up in that vast region could tell

Crook much, they could never tell him anything twice, while as for reading signs on the trail there was none of them his superior.

At times we would march for miles through a country in which grew only the white-plumed yucca with trembling, serrated leaves; again, mescal would fill the hillsides so thickly that one could almost imagine that it had been planted purposely; or we passed along between masses of the dust-laden, ghostly sage-brush, or close to the foul-smelling joints of the "hediondilla." The floral wealth of Arizona astonished us the moment we had gained the higher elevations of the Mogollon and the other ranges. Arizona will hold a high place in any list that may be prepared in this connection; there are as many as twenty and thirty different varieties of very lovely flowers and blossoms to be plucked within a stone's-throw of one's saddle after reaching camp of an evening,—phloxes, marguerites, chrysanthemums, verbenas, golden-rod, sumach, columbines, delicate ferns, forget-me-nots, and many others for which my very limited knowledge of botany furnishes no name. The flowers of Arizona are delightful in color, but they yield no perfume, probably on account of the great dryness of the atmosphere.

As for grasses one has only to say what kind he wants, and lo! it is at his feet—from the coarse sacaton which is deadly to animals except when it is very green and tender; the dainty mesquite, the bunch, and the white and black grama, succulent and nutritious. But I am speaking of the situations where we would make camp, because, as already stated, there are miles and miles of land purely desert, and clothed only with thorny cacti and others of that ilk. I must say, too, that the wild grasses of Arizona always seemed to me to have but slight root in the soil, and my observation is that the presence of herds of cattle soon tears them up and leaves the land bare.

If the marching over the deserts had its unpleasant features, certainly the compensation offered by the camping places in the cañons, by limpid streams of rippling water, close to the grateful foliage of cottonwood, sycamore, ash, or walnut; or, in the mountains, the pine and juniper, and sheltered from the sun by walls of solid granite, porphyry or basalt, was a most delightful antithesis, and one well worthy of the sacrifices undergone to attain it. Strong pickets were invariably posted, as no risks could be run in that region; we were fortunate to have just enough evidence of the close proximity of the Apaches to stimulate all to keep both eyes open.

"F" troop of the Third Cavalry, to which I belonged, had the misfortune to give the alarm to a large band of Chiricahua Apaches coming down the Sulphur Springs Valley from Sonora, with a herd of ponies or cattle ; we did not have the remotest idea that there were Indians in the country, not having seen the faintest sign, when all of a sudden at the close of a night march, very near where the new post of Camp Grant has since been erected on the flank of the noble Sierra Bonita or Mount Graham, we came upon their fires with the freshly slaughtered beeves undivided, and the blood still warm ; but our advance had alarmed the enemy, and they had moved off, scattering as they departed.

Similarly, Robinson I think it was, came so close upon the heels of a party of raiders that they dropped a herd of fifteen or twenty "burros" with which they had just come up from the Mexican border. Our pack-trains ran in upon a band of seven bears in the Aravaypa cañon which scared the mules almost out of their senses, but the packers soon laid five of the ursines low and wounded the other two which, however, escaped over the rough, dangerous rocks.

There were sections of country passed over which fairly reeked with the baleful malaria, like the junction of the San Carlos and the Gila. There were others along which for miles and miles could be seen nothing but lava, either in solid waves, or worse yet, in "nigger-head" lumps of all sizes. There were mountain ranges with flanks hidden under a solid matting of the scrub-oak, and others upon whose summits grew dense forests of graceful pines, whose branches, redolent with balsamic odors, screened from the too fierce glow of the noonday sun. There were broad stretches of desert, where the slightest movement raised clouds of dust which would almost stifle both men and beasts ; and gloomy ravines and startling cañons, in whose depths flowed waters as swift and clear and cool as any that have ever rippled along the pages of poetry.

Camp Apache was reached after a march and scout of all the intermediate country and a complete familiarization with the course of all the streams passed over *en route*. Nature had been more than liberal in her apportionment of attractions at this point, and there are truly few fairer scenes in the length and breadth of our territory. The post, still in the rawest possible state and not half-constructed, was situated upon a gently sloping mesa, surrounded by higher hills running back to the plateaux which formed the first line of the Mogollon range. Grass was to be had in plenty, while, as for timber, the flanks of every eleva- tion, as well as the summits of the mountains themselves, were covered with lofty pine, cedar, and oak, with a sprinkling of the "madroño," or mountain mahogany.

Two branches of the Sierra Blanca River unite almost in front of the camp, and supply all the water needed for any purpose, besides being stocked fairly well with trout, a fish which is rare in other sections of the Territory. Hunting was very good. and the sportsman could find, with very slight trouble, deer, bear, elk, and other varieties of four-footed animals, with wild turkey and quail in abundance. In the vicinity of this lovely site lived a large number of the Apaches, under chiefs who were peaceably disposed towards the whites—men like the old Miguel, Eski- tistsla, Pedro, Pitone, Alchise, and others, who expressed them- selves as friendly, and showed by their actions the sincerity of their avowals. They planted small farms with corn, gathered the wild seeds, hunted, and were happy as savages are when unmolested. Colonel John Green, of the First Cavalry, was in command, with two troops of his own regiment and two compa- nies of the Twenty-third Infantry. Good feeling existed between the military and the Indians, and the latter seemed anxious to put themselves in "the white man's road."

General Crook had several interviews with Miguel and the others who came in to see him, and to them he explained his views. To my surprise he didn't have any "policy," in which respect he differed from every other man I have met, as all seem to have "policies" about the management of Indians, and the less they know the more "policy" they seem to keep in stock. Crook's talk was very plain ; a child could have understood every word he said. He told the circle of listening Indians that he had not come to make war, but to avoid it if possible. Peace was the best condition in which to live, and he hoped that those who were around him would see that peace was not only prefera- ble, but essential, and not for themselves alone, but for the rest of their people as well. The white people were crowding in all over the Western country, and soon it would be impossible for any one to live upon game ; it would be driven away or killed off. Far better for every one to make up his mind to plant and to raise horses, cows, and sheep, and make his living in that way ; his animals would thrive and increase while he slept, and in less than no time the Apache would be wealthier than the Mexican. So long as the Apache behaved himself he should receive the fullest* protection from the troops, and no white man should be allowed to do him harm ; but so long as any fragment of the tribe kept out on the war-path, it would be impossible to afford all the protection to the well-disposed that they were entitled to receive, as bad men could say that it was not easy to discriminate between those who were good and those who were bad.   Therefore, he wished to ascertain for himself just who were disposed to remain at peace permanently and who preferred to continue in hostility. He had no desire to punish any man or woman for any acts of the past.   He would blot them all out and begin over again.   It was no use to try to explain how the war with the whites had begun.   All that he cared to say was, that it must end, and end at once.   He would send out to all the bands still in the mountains, and tell them just the same thing.   He did not intend to tell one story to one band and another to another ; but to all the same words, and it would be well for all to listen with both ears. If every one came in without necessitating a resort to bloodshed he should be very glad ; but, if any refused, then he should expect the good men to aid him in running down the bad ones. That was the way the white people did ; if there were bad men in a certain neighborhood, all the law-abiding citizens turned out to assist the officers of the law in arresting and punishing those who would not behave themselves.   He hoped that the Apaches would see that it was their duty to do the same.   He hoped to be able to find work for them all.   It was by work, and by work only, that they could hope to advance and become rich.

He wanted them always to tell him the exact truth, as he should never say anything to them which was not true ; and he hoped that as they became better acquainted, they would always feel that his word could be relied on.   He would do all in his power for them, but would never make them a promise he could not carry out.   There was no good in such a manner of doing, and bad feeling often grew up between good friends through misunderstandings in regard to promises not kept.   He would make no such promises ; and as the way in which they might remember a thing might happen to be different from the way in which he remembered it, he would do all he could to prevent misunderstandings, by having every word he said to them put down in black and white on paper, of which, if they so desired, they could keep a copy. When men were afraid to put their words on paper, it looked as if they did not mean half what they said. He wanted to treat the Apache just the same as he would treat any other man—as a man. He did not believe in one kind of treatment for the white and another for the Indian. All should fare alike ; but so long as the Indian remained ignorant of our laws and language it was for his own good that the troops remained with him, and he must keep within the limits of the Reservations set apart for him. He hoped the time would soon come when the children of the Apaches would be going to school, learning all the white men had to teach to their own children, and all of them, young or old, free to travel as they pleased all over the country, able to work anywhere, and not in fear of the white men or the white men of them. Finally, he repeated his urgent request that every effort should be made to spread these views among all the others who might still be out in the mountains, and to convince them that the safest and best course for all to adopt was that of peace with all mankind. After a reasonable time had been given for all to come in, he intended to start out in person and see to it that the last man returned to the Reservations or died in the mountains.

To all this the Apaches listened with deep attention, at intervals expressing approbation after their manner by heavy grunts and the utterance of the monosyllable "Inju" (good).

The Apaches living in the vicinity of Camp Apache are of purer Tinneh blood than those bands which occupied the western crest of the long Mogollon plateau, or the summits of the lofty Matitzal. The latter have very appreciably intermixed with the conquered people of the same stock as the Mojaves and Yumas of the Colorado valley, and the consequence is that the two languages are, in many cases, spoken interchangeably, and not a few of the chiefs and head men possess two names—one in the Apache, the other in the Mojave tongue.

After leaving Camp Apache, the command was greatly reduced by the departure of three of the companies in as many directions;

one of these—Guy V. Henry's—ran in on a party of hostile Apaches and exchanged shots, killing one warrior whose body fell into our hands. The course of those who were to accompany General Crook was nearly due west, along the rim of what is called the Mogollon Mountain or plateau, a range of very large size and great elevation, covered on its summits with a forest of large pine-trees. It is a strange upheaval, a strange freak of nature, a mountain canted up on one side ; one rides along the edge and looks down two and three thousand feet into what is termed the " Tonto Basin," a weird scene of grandeur and rugged beauty. The " Basin " is a basin only in the sense that it is all lower than the ranges enclosing it—the Mogollon, the Matitzal and the Sierra Ancha—but its whole triangular area is so cut up by ravines, arroyos, small stream beds and hills of very good height, that it may safely be pronounced one of the roughest spots on the globe. It is plentifully watered by the affluents of the Rio Verde and its East Fork, and by the Tonto and the Little Tonto; since the subjugation of the Apaches it has produced abundantly of peaches and strawberries, and potatoes have done wonderfully on the summit of the Mogollon itself in the sheltered swales in the pine forest. At the date of our march all this section of Arizona was still unmapped, and we had to depend upon Apache guides to conduct us until within sight of the Matitzal range, four or five days out from Camp Apache.

The most singular thing to note about the Mogollon was the fact that the streams which flowed upon its surface in almost every case made their way to the north and east into Shevlon's Fork, even where they had their origin in springs almost upon the crest itself. One exception is the spring named after General Crook (General's Springs), which he discovered, and near which he had such a narrow escape from being killed by Apaches—that makes into the East Fork of the Verde. It is an awe-inspiring sensation to be able to sit or stand upon the edge of such a precipice and look down upon a broad expanse mantled with juicy grasses, the paradise of live stock. There is no finer grazing section anywhere than the Tonto Basin, and cattle, sheep, and horses all now do well in it. It is from its ruggedness eminently suited for the purpose, and in this respect differs from the Sulphur Springs valley which has been occupied by cattlemen to the exclusion of the farmer, despite the fact that all along its length

one can find water by digging a few feet beneath the surface.
Such land as the Sulphur Springs valley would be more profitably
employed in the cultivation of the grape and cereals than as a
range for a few thousand head of cattle as is now the case.

The Tonto Basin was well supplied with deer and other wild
animals, as well as with mescal, Spanish bayonet, acorn-bearing
oak, walnuts, and other favorite foods of the Apaches, while the
higher levels of the Mogollon and the other ranges were at one
and the same time pleasant abiding-places during the heats of
summer, and ramparts of protection against the sudden incursion
of an enemy. I have already spoken of the wealth of flowers to
be seen in these high places ; I can only add that throughout
our march across the Mogollon range—some eleven days in time—
we saw spread out before us a carpet of colors which would rival
the best examples of the looms of Turkey or Persia.

Approaching the western edge of the plateau, we entered the
country occupied by the Tonto Apaches, the fiercest band of this
wild and apparently incorrigible family. We were riding along
in a very lovely stretch of pine forest one sunny afternoon, admiring the wealth of timber which would one day be made tributary
to the world's commerce, looking down upon the ever-varying
colors of the wild flowers which spangled the ground for leagues
(because in these forests upon the summits of all of Arizona's great
mountain ranges there is never any underbrush, as is the case in
countries where there is a greater amount of humidity in the
atmosphere), and ever and anon exchanging expressions of pleasure and wonder at the vista spread out beneath us in the immense
Basin to the left and front, bounded by the lofty ridges of the
Sierra Ancha and the Matitzal ; each one was talking pleasantly
to his neighbor, and as it happened the road we were pursuing—
to call it road where human being had never before passed—was
so even and clear that we were riding five and six abreast, General
Crook, Lieutenant Ross, Captain Brent, Mr. Thomas Moore, and
myself a short distance in advance of the cavalry, and the pack-
train whose tinkling bells sounded lazily among the trees—and
were all delighted to be able to go into camp in such a romantic
spot—when " whiz ! whiz ! " sounded the arrows of a small party
of Tontos who had been watching our advance and determined to
try the effects of a brisk attack, not knowing that we were
merely the advance of a larger command.

The Apaches could not, in so dense a forest, see any distance ahead; but did not hesitate to do the best they could to stampede us, and consequently attacked boldly with arrows which made no noise to arouse the suspicions of the white men in rear. The arrows were discharged with such force that one of them entered a pine-tree as far as the feathers, and another not quite so far, but still too far to allow of its extraction. There was a trifle of excitement until we could get our bearings and see just what was the matter, and in the mean time every man had found his tree without waiting for any command. The Apaches—of the Tonto band—did not number more than fifteen or twenty at most and were already in retreat, as they saw the companies coming up at a brisk trot, the commanders having noticed the confusion in the advance. Two of the Apaches were cut off from their comrades, and as we supposed were certain to fall into our hands as prisoners. This would have been exactly what General Crook desired, because he could then have the means of opening communication with the band in question, which had refused to respond to any and all overtures for the cessation of hostilities.

There they stood; almost entirely concealed behind great boulders on the very edge of the precipice, their bows drawn to a semicircle, eyes gleaming with a snaky black fire, long unkempt hair flowing down over their shoulders, bodies almost completely naked, faces streaked with the juice of the baked mescal and the blood of the deer or antelope—a most repulsive picture and yet one in which there was not the slightest suggestion of cowardice. They seemed to know their doom, but not to fear it in the slightest degree. The tinkling of the pack-train bells showed that all our command had arrived, and then the Apaches, realizing that it was useless to delay further, fired their arrows more in bravado than with the hope of inflicting injury, as our men were all well covered by the trees, and then over the precipice they went, as we supposed, to certain death and destruction. We were all so horrified at the sight, that for a moment or more it did not occur to any one to look over the crest, but when we did it was seen that the two savages were rapidly following down the merest thread of a trail outlined in the vertical face of the basalt, and jumping from rock to rock like mountain sheep. General Crook drew bead, aimed quickly and fired; the arm of one of the fugitives hung limp by his side, and the red stream gushing out showed that he had been badly hurt; but he did not relax his speed a particle, but kept up with his comrade in a headlong dash down the precipice, and escaped into the scrub-oak on the lower flanks although the evening air resounded with the noise of carbines reverberating from peak to peak.   It was so hard to believe that any human beings could escape down such a terrible place, that every one was rather in expectation of seeing the Apaches dashed to pieces, and for that reason no one could do his best shooting.

At this time we had neither the detachment of scouts with which we had left Tucson—they had been discharged at Camp Apache the moment that General Crook received word that the authorities in Washington were about to make the trial of sending commissioners to treat with the Apaches—nor the small party of five Apaches who had conducted us out from Camp Apache until we had reached the centre of the Mogollon ; and, as the country was unmapped and unknown, we had to depend upon ourselves for reaching Camp Verde, which no one in the party had ever visited.

We had reached the eastern extremity of the plateau, and could see the Bradshaw and other ranges to the west and south, and the sky-piercing cone of the San Francisco to the northwest, but were afraid to trust ourselves in the dark and forbidding mass of brakes and cañons of great depth which filled the country immediately in our front.   It was the vicinity of the Fossil Creek cañon, some fifteen hundred to two thousand feet deep, which we deemed it best to avoid, although had we known it we might have crossed in safety by an excellent, although precipitous, trail.   Our only guide was Archie MacIntosh, who belonged up in the Hudson's Bay Company's territory, and was totally unacquainted with Arizona, but a wonderful man in any country.   He and General Crook and Tom Moore conferred together, and concluded it was best to strike due north and head all the cañons spoken of.   This we did, but the result was no improvement, as we got into the Clear Creek cañon, which is one of the deepest and most beautiful to look upon in all the Southwest, but one very hard upon all who must descend and ascend.   When we descended we found plenty of cold, clear water, and the banks of the stream lined with the wild hop, which loaded the atmosphere with a heavy perfume of lupulin.

Still heading due north, we struck the cañon of Beaver Creek, and were compelled to march along its vertical walls of basalt, unable to reach the water in the tiny, entrancing rivulet below, but at last ran in upon the wagon-road from the Little Colorado to Camp Verde. We were getting rapidly down from the summit of the Mogollon, and entering a country exactly similar to that of the major portion of Southern Arizona. There was the same vegetation of yucca, mescal, nopal, Spanish bayonet, giant cactus, palo verde, hediondilla, mesquite, and sage-brush, laden with the dust of summer, but there was also a considerable sprinkling of the cedar, scrub-pine, scrub-oak, madroño, or mountain mahogany, and some little mulberry.

Near this trail there are to be seen several archæological curiosities worthy of a visit from the students of any part of the world. There is the wonderful "Montezuma's Well," a lakelet of eighty or ninety feet in depth, situated in the centre of a subsidence of rock, in which is a cave once inhabited by a prehistoric people, while around the circumference of the pool itself are the cliff-dwellings, of which so many examples are to be encountered in the vicinity. One of these cliff-dwellings, in excellent preservation when I last visited it, is the six-story house of stone on the Beaver Creek, which issues from the cave at Montezuma's Wells, and flows into the Verde River, near the post of the same name. We came upon the trails of scouting parties descending the Mogollon, and learned soon after that they had been made by the commands of Lieutenants Crawford and Morton, both of whom had been doing excellent and arduous work against the hostile bands during the previous summer.

I have already remarked that during this practice march all the members of our command learned General Crook, but of far greater consequence than that was the fact that he learned his officers and men. He was the most untiring and indefatigable man I ever met; and, whether climbing up or down the rugged face of some rocky cañon, facing sun or rain, never appeared to be in the slightest degree distressed or annoyed. No matter what happened in the camp, or on the march, he knew it; he was always awake and on his feet the moment the cook of the pack-train was aroused to prepare the morning meal, which was frequently as early as two o'clock, and remained on his feet during the remainder of the day. I am unable to explain exactly how he did it, but I can assure my readers that Crook learned, while on that march, the name of every plant, animal, and mineral passed near the trail, as well as the uses to which the natives put them, each and all ; likewise the habits of the birds, reptiles, and animals, and the course and general character of all the streams, little or big.   The Indians evinced an awe for him from the first moment of their meeting ; they did not seem to understand how it was that a white man could so quickly absorb all that they had to teach.

In the character of General Crook there appeared a very remarkable tenderness for all those for whose care he in any manner became responsible ; this tenderness manifested itself in a way peculiar to himself, and, as usual with him, was never made the occasion or excuse for parade.   He was at all times anxious to secure for his men while on campaign all the necessaries of life, and to do that he knew from his very wide experience that there was nothing to compare to a thoroughly organized and well-equipped pack-train, which could follow a command by night or by day, and into every locality, no matter how rocky, how thickly wooded, or how hopelessly desert.   He made the study of pack-trains the great study of his life, and had always the satisfaction of knowing that the trains in the department under his control were in such admirable condition, that the moment trouble was threatened in other sections, his pack-trains were selected as being best suited for the most arduous work.   He found the nucleus ready to hand in the system of pack-transportation which the exigencies of the mining communities on the Pacific coast had caused to be brought up from Chili, Peru, and the western States of the Mexican Republic.

The fault with these trains was that they were run as money-making concerns, and the men, as well as the animals belonging to them, were in nearly every case employed as temporary make-shifts, and as soon as the emergency had ended were discharged. The idea upon which Crook worked, and which he successfully carried out, was to select trains under the pack-masters who had enjoyed the widest experience, and were by nature best adapted to the important duties they would be called upon to perform. Those who were too much addicted to alcoholic stimulants, or were for other cause unsuited, were as opportunity presented replaced by better material.   As with the men, so with the animals ; the ill-assorted collections of bony giants and undersized Sonora "rats," whose withers were always a mass of sores and whose hoofs were always broken and out of sorts, were as speedily as possible sold off or transferred to other uses, and in their places we saw trains of animals which in weight, size and build, were of the type which experience had shown to be most appropriate.

The "aparejos," or pack-cushions, formerly issued by the quartermaster's department, had been burlesques, and killed more mules than they helped in carrying their loads. Crook insisted upon having each mule provided with an "aparejo" made especially for him, saying that it was just as ridiculous to expect a mule to carry a burden with an ill-fitting "aparejo" as it would be to expect a soldier to march comfortably with a knapsack which did not fit squarely to his back and shoulders. Every article used in these pack-trains had to be of the best materials, for the very excellent reason that while out on scout, it was impossible to replace anything broken, and a column might be embarrassed by the failure of a train to arrive with ammunition or rations—therefore, on the score of economy, it was better to have all the very best make in the first place.

According to the nomenclature then in vogue in pack-trains, there were to be placed upon each mule in due order of sequence a small cloth extending from the withers to the loins, and called from the office it was intended to perform, the "suadera," or sweat-cloth. Then came, according to the needs of the case, two or three saddle blankets, then the "aparejo" itself—a large mattress, we may say, stuffed with hay or straw—weighing between fifty-five and sixty-five pounds, and of such dimensions, as to receive and distribute to best advantage all over the mule's back the burden to be carried which was known by the Spanish term of "cargo." Over the "aparego," the "corona," and over that the "suvrinhammer," and then the load or "cargo" evenly divided so as to balance on the two sides. In practice, the "corona" is not now used, except to cover the "aparejo" after reaching camp, but there was a time way back in Andalusia and in the Chilean Andes when the heart of the "arriero" or muleteer, or "packer," as he is called in the dreadfully prosy language of the quartermaster's department, took the greatest delight in devising the pattern, quaint or horrible, but always gaudy and in the gayest of colors, which should decorate and protect his favorite mules. I do not know how true it is, but "Chileno John" and others told me that the main service expected of the "corona" was to enable the "arriero" who couldn't read or write to tell just where his own "aparejos" were, but of this I am unable to say anything positively.

The philological outrage which I have written phonetically as "suvrin-hammer" would set devout Mohammedans crazy were they to know of its existence; it is a base corruption of the old Hispano-Moresque term "sobre-en-jalma,"—over the jalma,—the Arabic word for pack-saddle, which has wandered far away, far from the date-palms of the Sahara, and the rippling fountains of Granada, to gladden the hearts and break the tongues of Cape Cod Yankees in the Gila Valley. In the same boat with it is the Zuni word "Tinka" for the flux to be used in working silver; it is a travelled word, and first saw the light in the gloomy mountain ranges of far-off Thibet, where it was pronounced "Tincal" or "Atincal," and meant borax; thence, it made its way with caravans to and through Arabia and Spain to the Spanish settlements in the land of the West. Everything about a pack-train was Spanish or Arabic in origin, as I have taken care to apprise my readers in another work, but it may be proper to repeat here that the first, as it was the largest organized pack-train in history, was that of fifteen thousand mules which Isabella the Catholic called into the service of the Crown of Castile and Leon at the time she established the city of Santa Fé in the "Vega," and began in good earnest the siege of Granada.

One could pick up not a little good Spanish in a pack-train in the times of which I speak—twenty-one years ago—and there were many expressions in general use which preserved all the flavor of other lands and other ideas. Thus the train itself was generally known as the "atajo;" the pack-master was called the "patron;" his principal assistant, whose functions were to attend to everything pertaining to. the loads, was styled "cargador;" the cook was designated the "cencero," from the fact that he rode the bell-mare, usually a white animal, from the superstition prevailing among Spanish packers that mules liked the color white better than any other.

Packers were always careful not to let any stray colts in among the mules, because they would set the mules crazy. This idea is not an absurd one, as I can testify from my personal observation. The mules are so anxious to play with young colts that they will do nothing else ; and, being stronger than the youngster, will often injure it by crowding up against it.   The old mules of a train know their business perfectly well.   They need no one to show them where their place is when the evening's "feed" is to be apportioned on the canvas, and in every way deport themselves as sedate, prim, well-behaved members of society, from whom all vestiges of the frivolities of youth have been eradicated. They never wander far from the sound of the bell, and give no trouble to the packers "on herd."

But a far different story must be told of the inexperienced, skittish young mule, fresh from the blue grass of Missouri or Nebraska.   He is the source of more profanity than he is worth, and were it not that the Recording Angel understands the aggravation in the case, he would have his hands full in entering all the "cuss words" to which the green pack-mule has given rise. He will not mind the bell, will wander away from his comrades on herd, and in sundry and divers ways demonstrates the perversity of his nature.   To contravene his maliciousness, it is necessary to mark him in such a manner that every packer will see at a glance that he is a new arrival, and thereupon set to work to drive him back to his proper place in his own herd.   The most certain, as it is the most convenient way to effect this, is by neatly roaching his mane and shaving his tail so that nothing is left but a pencil or tassel of hair at the extreme end.   He is now known as a "shave-tail," and everybody can recognize him at first sight.   His sedate and well-trained comrade is called a "bell-sharp." ·

These terms, in frontier sarcasm, have been transferred to officers of the army, who, in the parlance of the packers, are known as "bell-sharps" and "shave-tails" respectively; the former being the old captain or field-officer of many "fogies," who knows too much to be wasting his energies in needless excursions about the country, and the latter, the youngster fresh from his studies on the Hudson, who fondly imagines he knows it all, and is not above having people know that he does.   He is a "shave-tail"— all elegance of uniform, spick-span new, well groomed, and without sense enough to come in for "feed" when the bell rings. On the plains these two classes of very excellent gentlemen used to be termed "coffee-coolers" and "goslings."

There are few more animated sights than a pack-train at the

moment of feeding and grooming the mules. The care shown equals almost that given to the average baby, and the dumb animals seem to respond to all attentions. General Crook kept himself posted as to what was done to every mule, and, as a result, had the satisfaction of seeing his trains carrying a net average of three hundred and twenty pounds to the mule, while a pamphlet issued by the Government had explicitly stated that the highest average should not exceed one hundred and seventy-five. So that, viewed in the most sordid light, the care which General Crook bestowed upon his trains yielded wonderful results. Not a day passed that General Crook did not pass from one to two hours in personal inspection of the workings of his trains, and he has often since told me that he felt then the great responsibility of having his transportation in the most perfect order, because so much was to be demanded of it.

The packers themselves were an interesting study, drawn as they were from the four corners of the earth, although the major portion, as was to be expected, was of Spanish-American origin. Not an evening passed on this trip across the mountains of the Mogollon Range that Crook did not quietly take a seat close to the camp-fire of some of the packers, and listen intently to their "reminiscences" of early mining days in California or "up on the Frazer in British Columbia." "Hank 'n Yank," Tom Moore, Jim O'Neill, Charlie Hopkins, Jack Long, Long Jim Cook, and others, were "forty-niners," and well able to discuss the most exciting times known to the new Pactolus, with its accompanying trying days of the vigilance committee and other episodes of equal interest. These were "men" in the truest sense of the term; they had faced all perils, endured all privations, and conquered in a manly way, which is the one unfailing test of greatness in human nature. Some of the narratives were mirth-provoking beyond my powers of repetition, and for General Crook they formed an unfailing source of quiet amusement whenever a chance offered to listen to them as told by the packers.

One of our men—I have forgotten to mention him sooner— was Johnnie Hart, a very quiet and reserved person, with a great amount of force, to be shown when needed. There was little of either the United States or Mexico over which he had not wandered as a mining "prospector," delving for metals, precious or non-precious. Bad luck overtook him in Sonora just about when that country was the scene of the liveliest kind of a time between the French and the native Mexicans, and while the hostile factions of the Gandaras and the Pesquieras were doing their best to destroy what little the rapacity of the Gallic invaders left intact. Johnnie was rudely awakened one night by a loud rapping at the door of the hut in which he had taken shelter, and learned, to his great surprise, that he was needed as a "voluntario," which meant, as nearly as he could understand, that he was to put on handcuffs and march with the squad to division headquarters, and there be assigned to a company. In vain he explained, or thought he was explaining, that he was an American citizen and not subject to conscription. All the satisfaction he got was to be told that every morning and evening he was to cheer "for our noble Constitution and for General Pesquiera."

After all, it was not such a very hard life. The marches were short, and the country well filled with chickens, eggs, and goats. What more could a soldier want ? So, our friend did not complain, and went about his few duties with cheerfulness, and was making rapid progress in the shibboleth of " Long live our noble Constitution and General Pesquiera,"—when, one evening, the first sergeant of his company hit him a violent slap on the side of the head, and said : " You idiot, do you not know enough to cheer for General Gandara ?" And then it was that poor Johnnie learned for the first time—he had been absent for several days on a foraging expedition and had just returned—that the general commanding had sold out the whole division to General Gandara the previous day for a dollar and six bits a head.

This was the last straw. Johnnie Hart was willing to fight, and it made very little difference to him on which side ; but he could not put up with such a sudden swinging of the pendulum, and as he expressed it, "made up his mind to skip the hull outfit 'n punch the breeze fur Maz'tlan."

All the packers were sociable, and inclined to be friendly to every one. The Spaniards, like "Chileno John," José de Leon, Lauriano Gomez, and others, were never more happy—work completed—than in explaining their language to such Americans as evinced a desire to learn it. Gomez was well posted in Spanish literature, especially poetry, and would often recite for us with much animation and expression the verses of his native tongue. He preferred the madrigals and love ditties of all kinds ; and was never more pleased than when he had organized a quartette and had begun to awaken the echoes of the grand old cañons or forests with the deliciously plaintive notes of "La Golondrina," "Adios de Guaymas," or other songs in minor key, decidedly nasalized. I may say that at a later date I have listened to a recitation by a packer named Hale, of Espronceda's lines—"The Bandit Chief" —in a very creditable style in the balsam-breathing forests of the Sierra Madre.

The experiences of old Sam Wisser, in the more remote portions of Sonora and Sinaloa, never failed to "bring down the house," when related in his homely Pennsylvania-German brogue. I will condense the story for the benefit of those who may care to listen. Sam's previous business had been "prospecting" for mines, and, in pursuit of his calling, he had travelled far and near, generally so intent upon the search for wealth at a distance that he failed to secure any of that which often lay at his feet. Equipped with the traditional pack-mule, pick, spade, frying-pan, and blankets, he started out on his mission having as a companion a man who did not pretend to be much of a "prospector," but was travelling for his health, or what was left of it. They had not reached the Eldorado of their hopes ; but were far down in Sinaloa when the comrade died, and it became Sam's sad duty to administer upon the "estate." The mule wasn't worth much and was indeed almost as badly worn out as its defunct master. The dead man's clothing was buried with him, and his revolver went a good ways in paying the expenses of interment. There remained nothing but a very modest-looking valise nearly filled with bottles, pill-boxes, and pots of various medicinal preparations warranted to cure all the ills that flesh is heir to. An ordinary man would have thrown all this away as so much rubbish, but our friend was a genius—he carefully examined each and every package, and learned exactly what they were all worth according to the advertisements. Nothing escaped his scrutiny, from the picture of the wretch "before taking," to that of the rubicund, aldermanic, smiling athlete "after taking six bottles." All the testimonials from shining lights of pulpit and bar were read through from date to signature, and the result of it all was that Sam came to the very logical conclusion that if he had in his possession panaceas for all ailments, why should he not practise the healing art ? The next morning dawned upon a new Esculapius, and lighted up the legend

"Medico" tacked upon the frame of the door of Sam's hovel. It made no difference to the budding practitioner what the disorder was; he had the appropriate remedy at hand, and was most liberal in the amount of dosing to be given to his patients, which went far to increase their confidence in a man who seemed so willing to give them the full worth of their money. The only trouble was that Sam never gave the same dose twice to the same patient; this was because he had no memorandum books, and could not keep in mind all the circumstances of each case. The man who had Croton-oil pills in the morning received a tablespoonful of somebody's "Siberian Solvent" at night, and there was such a crowd that poor Sam was kept much more busy than he at first supposed he should be, because the people were not disposed to let go by an opportunity of ridding themselves of all infirmities, when the same could be eradicated by a physician who accepted in payment anything from a two-bit-piece to a string of chile colorado. Sam's practice was not confined to any one locality. It reached from the southern end of the Mexican State of Sinaloa to the international boundary. Sam, in other words, had become a travelling doctor—he kept travelling—but as his mule had had a good rest and some feed in the beginning of its master's new career, the pursuers were never able to quite catch up with the Gringo quack whose nostrums were depopulating the country.

From the valley of the Verde to the town of Prescott, according to the steep roads and trails connecting them in 1871, was something over fifty-five miles, the first part of the journey extremely rough and precipitous, the latter half within sight of hills clad with graceful pines and cooled by the breezes from the higher ranges. The country was well grassed; there was a very pleasing absence of the cactus vegetation to be seen farther to the south, adobe houses were replaced by comfortable-looking dwellings and barns of plank or stone; the water in the wells was cold and pure, and the lofty peaks, the San Francisco and the Black Range and the Bradshaw, were for months in the year buried in snow.

CHAPTER IX.

THE PICTURESQUE TOWN OF PRESCOTT—THE APACHES ACTIVE
NEAR PRESCOTT—"TOMMY" BYRNE AND THE HUALPAIS
—THIEVING INDIAN AGENTS—THE MOJAVES, PI-UTES AND
AVA-SUPAIS—THE TRAVELS OF FATHERS ESCALANTE AND
GARCES—THE GODS OF THE HUALPAIS—THE LORING MAS-
SACRE—HOW PHIL DWYER DIED AND WAS BURIED—THE
INDIAN MURDERERS AT CAMP DATE CREEK PLAN TO KILL
CROOK—MASON JUMPS THE RENEGADES AT THE "MUCHOS
CAÑONES"—DELT-CHE AND CHA-LIPUN GIVE TROUBLE—
THE KILLING OF BOB WHITNEY.

A FEW words should be spoken in praise of a community
which of all those on the southwestern frontier preserved
the distinction of being thoroughly American. Prescott was not
merely picturesque in location and dainty in appearance, with
all its houses neatly painted and surrounded with paling fences
and supplied with windows after the American style—it was a
village transplanted bodily from the centre of the Delaware, the
Mohawk, or the Connecticut valley. Its inhabitants were Americans; American men had brought American wives out with them
from their old homes in the far East, and these American wives
had not forgotten the lessons of elegance and thrift learned in
childhood. Everything about the houses recalled the scenes
familiar to the dweller in the country near Pittsburgh or other
busy community. The houses were built in American style; the
doors were American doors and fastened with American bolts and
locks, opened by American knobs, and not closed by letting
a heavy cottonwood log fall against them.

The furniture was the neat cottage furniture with which all
must be familiar who have ever had the privilege of entering an
American country home; there were carpets, mirrors, rocking-
chairs, tables, lamps, and all other appurtenances, just as one
might expect to find them in any part of our country excepting

Arizona and New Mexico. There were American books, American newspapers, American magazines—the last intelligently read. The language was American, and nothing else—the man who hoped to acquire a correct knowledge of Castilian in Prescott would surely be disappointed. Not even so much as a Spanish advertisement could be found in the columns of *The Miner*, in which, week after week, John H. Marion fought out the battle of "America for the Americans." The stores were American stores, selling nothing but American goods. In one word, the transition from Tucson to Prescott was as sudden and as radical as that between Madrid and Manchester.

In one respect only was there the slightest resemblance : in Prescott, as in Tucson, the gambling saloons were never closed· Sunday or Monday, night or morning, the "game" went, and the voice of the "dealer" was heard in the land. Prescott was essentially a mining town deriving its business from the wants of the various "claims" on the Agua Fria, the Big Bug and Lynx Creek on the east, and others in the west as far as Cerbat and Mineral Park. There was an air of comfort about it which indicated intelligence and refinement rather than wealth which its people did not as yet enjoy.

At this time, in obedience to orders received from the Secretary of War, I was assigned to duty as aide-de-camp, and in that position had the best possible opportunity for becoming acquainted with the country, the Indians and white people in it, and to absorb a knowledge of all that was to be done and that was done. General Crook's first move was to bring the department headquarters to Prescott; they had been for a long while at Los Angeles, California, some five hundred miles across the desert, to the west, and in the complete absence of railroad and telegraph facilities they might just as well have been in Alaska. His next duty was to perfect the knowledge already gained of the enormous area placed under his charge, and this necessitated an incredible amount of travelling on mule-back, in ambulance and buckboard, over roads, or rather trails, which eclipsed any of the horrors portrayed by the pencil of Doré. There was great danger in all this, but Crook travelled without escort, except on very special occasions, as he did not wish to break down his men by overwork.

The Apaches had been fully as active in the neighborhood of

Prescott as they had been in that of Tucson, and to this day such names as "The Burnt Ranch"—a point four miles to the north-west of the town—commemorate attacks and massacres by the aborigines. The mail-rider had several times been "corraled" at the Point of Rocks, very close to the town, and all of this portion of Arizona had groaned under the depredations not of the Apaches alone but of the Navajos, Hualpais, and Apache-Mojaves, and now and then of the Sevinches, a small band of thieves of Pi-Ute stock, living in the Grand Cañon of the Colorado on the northern boundary of the territory. I have still preserved as relics of those days copies of *The Miner* of Prescott and of *The Citizen* of Tucson, in every column of which are to be found references to Indian depredations.

There should still be in Washington a copy of the petition forwarded by the inhabitants pleading for more adequate protection, in which are given the names of over four hundred American citizens killed in encounters with the savages within an extremely limited period—two or three years—and the dates and localities of the occurrences.

Fort Whipple, the name of the military post within one mile of the town, was a ramshackle, tumble-down palisade of unbarked pine logs hewn from the adjacent slopes; it was supposed to "command" something, exactly what, I do not remember, as it was so dilapidated that every time the wind rose we were afraid that the palisade was doomed. The quarters for both officers and men were also log houses, with the exception of one single-room shanty on the apex of the hill nearest to town, which was constructed of unseasoned, unpainted pine planks, and which served as General Crook's "Headquarters," and, at night, as the place wherein he stretched his limbs in slumber. He foresaw that the negotiations which Mr. Vincent Collyer had been commissioned to carry on with the roving bands of the Apaches would result in naught, because the distrust of the savages for the white man, and all he said and did, had become so confirmed that it would take more than one or two pleasant talks full of glowing promises to eradicate it. Therefore, General Crook felt that it would be prudent for him to keep himself in the best physical trim, to be the better able to undergo the fatigues of the campaigns which were sure to come, and come very soon.

The Apaches are not the only tribe in Arizona; there are several others, which have in the past been a source of trouble to the settlers and of expense to the authorities. One of these was the Hualpais, whose place of abode was in the Grand Cañon, and who were both brave and crafty in war ; they were then at Camp Beale Springs in northwestern Arizona, forty-five miles from the Colorado River, and under the care of an officer long since dead—Captain Thomas Byrne, Twelfth Infantry, who was a genius in his way. "Old Tommy," as he was affectionately called by every one in the service or out of it, had a "deludherin' tongue," which he used freely in the cause of peace, knowing as he did that if this small tribe of resolute people should ever return to the war-path, it would take half a dozen regiments to dislodge them from the dizzy cliffs of the "Music," the "Sunup," the "Wickyty-wizz," and the "Diamond."

So Tommy relied solely upon his native eloquence, seconded by the scantiest allowance of rations from the subsistence stores of the camp. He acquired an ascendancy over the minds of the chiefs and head men—"Sharum," "Levy-Levy," "Sequonya," "Enyacue-yusa," "Ahcula-watta," "Colorow," and "Hualpai Charlie"—which was little short of miraculous. He was an old bachelor, but seemed to have a warm spot in his heart for all the little naked and half-naked youngsters in and around his camp, to whom he gave most liberally of the indigestible candy and sweet cakes of the trader's store.

The squaws were allowed all the hard-tack they could eat, but only on the most solemn occasions could they gratify their taste for castor oil—the condition of the medical supplies would not warrant the issue of all they demanded. I have read that certain of the tribes of Africa use castor oil in cooking, but I know of no other tribe of American Indians so greedy for this medicine. But taste is at best something which cannot be explained or accounted for; I recall that the trader at the San Carlos Agency once made a bad investment of money in buying cheap candies ; they were nearly all hoarhound and peppermint, which the Apaches would not buy or accept as a gift.

Tommy had succeeded in impressing upon the minds of his savage wards the importance of letting him know the moment anything like an outbreak, no matter how slight it might be, should be threatened. There was to be no fighting, no firing of guns and pistols, and no seeking redress for injuries excepting through the commanding officer, who was the court of last appeal. One day "Hualpai Charlie" came running in like an antelope, all out of breath, his eyes blazing with excitement: "Cappy Byrne—get yo' sogy—heap quick. White man over da Min'nul Pa'k, all bloke out." An investigation was made, and developed the cause of "Charlie's" apprehensions: the recently established mining town of "Mineral Park" in the Cerbat range had "struck it rich," and was celebrating the event in appropriate style; bands of miners, more or less sober, were staggering about in the one street, painting the town red. There was the usual amount of shooting at themselves and at the few lamps in the two saloons, and "Charlie," who had not yet learned that one of the inalienable rights of the Caucasian is to make a fool of himself now and then, took fright, and ran in the whole fourteen miles to communicate the first advices of the "outbreak" to his commanding officer and friend.

Captain Byrne was most conscientious in all his dealings with these wild, suspicious people, and gained their affection to an extent not to be credited in these days, when there seems to be a recurrence to the ante-bellum theory that the only good Indian —be it buck, squaw, or puling babe—is the dead one. I have seen the old man coax sulking warriors back into good humor, and persuade them that the best thing in the world for them all was the good-will of the Great Father. "Come now, Sharum," I have heard him say, "shure phat is de matther wid yiz? Have yiz ivir axed me for anythin' that oi didn't *promise* it to yiz?"

Poor Tommy was cut off too soon in life to redeem all his pledges, and I fear that there is still a balance of unpaid promises, comprehending mouth organs, hoop skirts, velocipedes, anything that struck the fancy of a chief and for which he made instant demand upon his military patron. To carry matters forward a little, I wish to say that Tommy remained the "frind," as he pronounced the term, of the Hualpais to the very last, and even after he had been superseded by the civil agent, or acting agent, he remained at the post respected and regarded by all the tribe as their brother and adviser.

Like a flash of lightning out of a clear sky, the Hualpais went on the war-path, and fired into the agency buildings before leaving for their old strongholds in the Cañon of the Colorado. No one knew why they had so suddenly shown this treacherous nature, and the territorial press (there was a telegraph line in operation by this time) was filled with gloomy forebodings on account of the "well-known treachery of the Indian character." Tommy Byrne realized full well how much it would cost Uncle Sam in blood and treasure if this outbreak were not stopped in its incipiency, and without waiting for his spirited little horse to be saddled—he was a superb rider—threw himself across its back and took out into the hills after the fugitives. When the Hualpais saw the cloud of dust coming out on the road, they blazed into it, but the kind Providence, which is said to look out for the Irish under all circumstances, took pity on the brave old man, and spared him even after he had dashed up—his horse white with foam—to the knot of chiefs who stood on the brow of a lava mesa.

At first the Hualpais were sullen, but soon they melted enough to tell the story of their grievances, and especially the grievance they had against Captain Byrne himself. The new agent had been robbing them in the most bare-faced manner, and in their ignorance they imagined that it was Tommy Byrne's duty to regulate all affairs at his camp. They did not want to hurt him, and would let him go safely back, but for them there was nothing but the war-path and plenty of it.

Tommy said gently, "Come back with me, and I'll see that you are righted." Back they went, following after the one, un-armed man. Straight to the beef scales went the now thoroughly aroused officer, and in less time than it takes to relate, he had detected the manner in which false weights had been secured by a tampering with the poise. A two-year-old Texas steer, which, horns and all, would not weigh eight hundred pounds, would mark seventeen hundred, and other things in the same ratio. Nearly the whole amount of the salt and flour supply had been sold to the miners in the Cerbat range, and the poor Hualpais, who had been such valiant and efficient allies, had been swindled out of everything but their breath, and but a small part of that was left.

Tommy seized upon the agency and took charge; the Hual-pais were perfectly satisfied, but the agent left that night for California and never came back. A great hubbub was raised about the matter, but nothing came of it, and a bitter war was averted by the prompt, decisive action of a plain, unlettered officer, who had no ideas about managing savages beyond treating them with kindness and justice.

General Crook not only saw to the condition of the Hualpais, but of their relatives, the Mojaves, on the river, and kept them both in good temper towards the whites ; not only this, but more than this—he sent up among the Pi-Utes of Nevada and Southern Utah and explained the situation to them and secured the promise of a contingent of one hundred of their warriors for service against the Apaches, should the latter decline to listen to the propositions of the commissioner sent to treat with them.   When hostilities did break out, the Pi-Utes sent down the promised auxiliaries, under their chief, "Captain Tom," and, like the Hualpais, they rendered faithful service.

What has become of the Pi-Utes I cannot say, but of the Hualpais I am sorry to have to relate that the moment hostilities ended, the Great Father began to ignore and neglect them, until finally their condition became so deplorable that certain fashionable ladies of New York, who were doing a great deal of good unknown to the world at large, sent money to General Crook to be used in keeping them from starving to death.

Liquor is freely given to the women, who have become fearfully demoralized, and I can assert of my own knowledge that five years since several photographers made large sales along the Atlantic and Pacific railroad of the pictures of nude women of this once dreaded band, which had committed no other offence than that of trusting in the faith of the Government of the United States.

In the desolate, romantic country of the Hualpais and their brothers, the Ava-Supais, amid the Cyclopean monoliths which line the cañons of Cataract Creek, the Little Colorado, the Grand Cañon or the Diamond, one may sit and listen, as I have often listened, to the simple tales and myths of a wild, untutored race. There are stories to be heard of the prowess of "Mustamho" and "Matyavela," of "Pathrax-sapa" and "Pathrax-carrawee," of the goddess "Cuathenya," and a multiplicity of deities—animal and human—which have served to beguile the time after the day's march had ended and night was at hand.   All the elements of nature are actual, visible entities for these simple children— the stars are possessed of the same powers as man, all the chief animals have the faculty of speech, and the coyote is the one who is man's good friend and has brought him the great boon of fire. The gods of the Hualpais are different in name though not in functions or peculiarities from those of the Apaches and Navajos, but are almost identical with those of the Mojaves.

As with the Apaches, so with the Hualpais, the "medicine men" wield an unknown and an immeasurable influence, and claim power over the forces of nature, which is from time to time renewed by rubbing the body against certain sacred stones not far from Beale Springs. The Hualpai medicine men also indulge in a sacred intoxication by breaking up the leaves, twigs, and root of the stramonium or "jimson weed," and making a beverage which, when drunk, induces an exhilaration, in the course of which the drunkard utters prophecies.

While the colonies along the Atlantic coast were formulating their grievances against the English crown and preparing to throw off all allegiance to the throne of Great Britain, two priests of the Roman Catholic Church were engaged in exploring these desolate wilds, and in making an effort to win the Hualpais and their brothers to Christianity.

Father Escalante started out from Santa Fé, New Mexico, in the year 1776, and travelling northwest through Utah finally reached the Great Salt Lake, which he designated as the Lake of the Timpanagos. This name is perfectly intelligible to those who happen to know of the existence down to the present day of the band of Utes called the Timpanoags, who inhabit the cañons close to the present city of Salt Lake. Travelling on foot southward, Escalante passed down through Utah and crossed the Grand Cañon of the Colorado, either at what is now known as Lee's Ferry, or the mouth of the Kanab Wash, or the mouth of the Diamond; thence east through the Moqui and the Zuni villages back to Santa Fé. Escalante expected to be joined near the Grand Cañon by Father Garces, who had travelled from the mission of San Gabriel, near Los Angeles, and crossed the Colorado in the country inhabited by the Mojaves; but, although each performed the part assigned to him, the proposed meeting did not take place.

It is impossible to avoid reference to these matters, which will obtrude themselves upon the mind of any one travelling through Arizona. There is an ever-present suggestion of the past and unknown, that has a fascination all its own for those who yield to it. Thus, at Bowers' Ranch on the Agua Fria, eighteen miles northeast from Prescott, one sits down to his supper in a room which once formed part of a prehistoric dwelling; and the same thing may be said of Wales Arnold's, over near Montezuma's Wells, where many of the stones used in the masonry came from the pueblo ruins close at hand.

Having visited the northern line of his department, General Crook gave all his attention to the question of supplies; everything consumed in the department, at that date, had to be freighted at great expense from San Francisco, first by steamship around Cape San Lucas to the mouth of the Rio Colorado, then up the river in small steamers as far as Ehrenburg and Fort Mojave, and the remainder of the distance—two hundred miles— by heavy teams. To a very considerable extent, these supplies were distributed from post to post by pack-trains, a proceeding which evoked the liveliest remonstrances from the contractors interested in the business of hauling freight, but their complaints availed them nothing. Crook foresaw the demands that the near future would surely make upon his pack-trains, which he could by no surer method keep in the highest discipline and efficiency than by having them constantly on the move from post to post carrying supplies. The mules became hardened, the packers made more skilful in the use of all the "hitches"—the "Diamond" and others—constituting the mysteries of their calling, and the detachments sent along as escorts were constantly learning something new about the country as well as how to care for themselves and animals.

Sixty-two miles from Prescott to the southwest lay the sickly and dismal post of Camp Date creek, on the creek of the same name. Here were congregated about one thousand of the band known as the Apache-Yumas, with a sprinkling of Apache-Mojaves, tribes allied to the Mojaves on the Colorado, and to the Hualpais, but differing from them in disposition, as the Date Creek people were not all anxious for peace, but would now and then send small parties of their young men to raid and steal from the puny settlements like Wickenburg. The culmination of the series was the "Loring" or "Wickenburg" massacre, so-called from the talented young scientist, Loring, a member of the Wheeler surveying expedition, who, with his companions— a stage-load—was brutally murdered not far from Wickenburg;

of the party only two escaped, one a woman named Shephard, and the other a man named Kruger, both badly wounded.

General Crook was soon satisfied that this terrible outrage had been committed by a portion of the irreconcilable element at the Date Creek Agency, but how to single them out as individuals and inflict the punishment their crime deserved, without entailing disaster upon well-meaning men, women, and babies who had not been implicated, was for a long while a most serious problem. There were many of the tribe satisfied to cultivate peaceful relations with the whites, but none so favorably disposed as to impart the smallest particle of information in regard to the murder, as it was no part of their purpose to surrender any of their relatives for punishment.

It would take too much time to narrate in detail the "patient search and vigil long" attending the ferreting out of the individuals concerned in the Loring massacre; it was a matter of days and weeks and months, but Crook knew that he had the right clew, and, although many times baffled, he returned to the scent with renewed energy and determination. The culprits, who included in their ranks, or at least among their sympathizers, some very influential men of the tribe, had also begun, on their side, to suspect that all was not right; one of them, I understood, escaped to Southern California, and there found work in some of the Mexican settlements, which he could do readily as he spoke Spanish fluently, and once having donned the raiment of civilization, there would be nothing whatever to distinguish him from the average of people about him.

Word reached General Crook, through the Hualpais, that when next he visited Camp Date Creek, he was to be murdered with all those who might accompany him. He was warned to be on the look-out, and told that the plan of the conspirators was this : They would appear in front of the house in which he should take up his quarters, and say that they had come for a talk upon some tribal matter of importance ; when the General made his appearance, the Indians were to sit down in a semicircle in front of the door, each with his carbine hidden under his blanket, or carelessly exposed on his lap. The conversation was to be decidedly harmonious, and there was to be nothing said that was not perfectly agreeable to the whites. After the "talk" had progressed a few minutes, the leading conspirator would remark that they would all be the better for a little smoke, and as soon as the tobacco was handed out to them, the chief conspirator was to take some and begin rolling a cigarette. (The Indians of the southwest do not ordinarily use the pipe.) When the first puff was taken from the cigarette, the man next to the chief was to suddenly level his weapon and kill General Crook, the others at the very same moment taking the lives of the whites closest to them. The whole tribe would then be made to break away from the reserve and take to the inaccessible cliffs and cañons at the head of the Santa Maria fork of the Bill Williams. The plan would have succeeded perfectly, had it not been for the warning received, and also for the fact that the expected visit had to be made much sooner than was anticipated, and thus prevented all the gang from getting together.

Captain Philip Dwyer, Fifth Cavalry, the officer in command of the camp, suddenly died, and this took me down post-haste to assume command. Dwyer was a very brave, handsome, and intelligent soldier, much beloved by all his comrades. He was the only officer left at Date Creek—all the others and most of the garrison were absent on detached service of one kind and another —and there was no one to look after the dead man but Mr. Wilbur Hugus, the post trader, and myself. The surroundings were most dismal and squalid ; all the furniture in the room in which the corpse lay was two or three plain wooden chairs, the bed occupied as described, and a pine table upon which stood a candlestick, with the candle melted and burned in the socket. Dwyer had been "ailing" for several days, but no one could tell exactly what was the matter with him ; and, of course, no one suspected that one so strong and athletic could be in danger of death.

One of the enlisted men of his company, a bright young trumpeter, was sitting up with him, and about the hour of midnight, Dwyer became a trifle uneasy and asked : "Can you sing that new song, 'Put me under the daisies'?"

"Oh, yes, Captain," replied the trumpeter ; "I have often sung it, and will gladly sing it now."

So he began to sing, very sweetly, the ditty, which seemed to calm the nervousness of his superior officer. But the candle had burned down in the socket, and when the young soldier went to replace it, he could find neither candle nor match, and he saw in the flickering light and shadow that the face of the Captain was strangely set, and of a ghastly purplish hue. The trumpeter ran swiftly to the nearest house to get another light, and to call for help, but upon returning found the Captain dead.

Many strange sights have I seen, but none that produced a stranger or more pathetic appeal to my emotions than the funeral of Phil Dwyer; we got together just as good an apology for a coffin as that timberless country would furnish, and then wrapped our dead friend in his regimentals, and all hands were then ready to start for the cemetery.

At the head marched Mr. Hugus, Doctor Williams (the Indian agent), myself, and Lieutenant Hay, of the Twenty-third Infantry, who arrived at the post early in the morning; then came the troop of cavalry, dismounted, and all the civilians living in and around the camp; and lastly every Indian—man, woman, or child—able to walk or toddle, for all of them, young or old, good or bad, loved Phil Dwyer. The soldiers and civilians formed in one line at the head of the grave, and the Apache-Yumas in two long lines at right angles to them, and on each side. The few short, expressive, and tender sentences of the burial service were read, then the bugles sang taps, and three volleys were fired across the hills, the clods rattled down on the breast of the dead, and the ceremony was over.

As soon as General Crook learned of the death of Dwyer, he hurried to Date Creek, now left without any officer of its proper garrison, and informed the Indians that he intended having a talk with them on the morrow, at a place designated by himself. The conspirators thought that their scheme could be carried out without trouble, especially since they saw no signs of suspicion on the part of the whites. General Crook came to the place appointed, without any escort of troops, but carelessly strolling forward were a dozen or more of the packers, who had been engaged in all kinds of mêlées since the days of early California mining. Each of these was armed to the teeth, and every revolver was on the full cock, and every knife ready for instant use. The talk was very agreeable, and not an unpleasant word had been uttered on either side, when all of a sudden the Indian in the centre asked for a little tobacco, and, when it was handed to him, began rolling a cigarette; before the first puff of smoke had rolled away from his lips one of the warriors alongside of him levelled his carbine full at General Crook, and fired. Lieutenant

Ross, aide-de-camp to the General, was waiting for the movement, and struck the arm of the murderer so that the bullet was deflected upwards, and the life of the General was saved. The scrimmage became a perfect Kilkenny fight in another second or two, and every man made for the man nearest to him, the Indian who had given the signal being grasped in the vise-like grip of Hank Hewitt, with whom he struggled vainly. Hewitt was a man of great power and able to master most men other than professional athletes or prize-fighters; the Indian was not going to submit so long as life lasted, and struggled, bit, and kicked to free himself, but all in vain, as Hank had caught him from the back of the head, and the red man was at a total disadvantage. Hewitt started to drag his captive to the guard-house, but changed his mind, and seizing the Apache-Mojave by both ears pulled his head down violently against the rocks, and either broke his skull or brought on concussion of the brain, as the Indian died that night in the guard-house.

Others of the party were killed and wounded, and still others, with the ferocity of tigers, fought their way out through our feeble lines, and made their way to the point of rendezvous at the head of the Santa Maria. Word was at once sent to them by members of their own tribe that they must come in and surrender at once, or else the whole party must expect to be punished for what was originally the crime of a few. No answer was received, and their punishment was arranged for; they were led to suppose that the advance was to be made from Date Creek, but, after letting them alone for several weeks—just long enough to allay to some extent their suspicions—Crook pushed out a column of the Fifth Cavalry under command of Colonel Julius W. Mason, and by forced marches under the guidance of a strong detachment of Hualpai scouts, the encampment of the hostiles was located just where the Hualpais said it would be, at the "Muchos Cañones," a point where five cañons united to form the Santa Maria; and there the troops and the scouts attacked suddenly and with spirit, and in less than no time everything was in our hands, and the enemy had to record a loss of more than forty. It was a terrible blow, struck at the beginning of winter and upon a band which had causelessly slaughtered a stageful of our best people, not as an act of war, which would have been excusable, but as an act of highway robbery, by sneaking off the reservation where the

Government was allowing them rations and clothing in quantity sufficient to eke out their own supplies of wild food.   This action of the "Muchos Cañones" had a very beneficial effect upon the campaign which began against the Apaches in the Tonto Basin a few weeks later.   It humbled the pride of those of the Apache-Yumas who had never been in earnest in their professions of peace, and strengthened the hands of the chiefs like "Jam-aspi," "Ochacama," "Hoch-a-chi-waca," "Quaca-thew-ya," and "Tom," who were sincerely anxious to accept the new condition of things.   There was a third element in this tribe, led by a chief of ability, "Chimahuevi-Sal," which did not want to fight, if fighting could be avoided, but did not care much for the new white neighbors whom they saw crowding in upon them. "Chimahuevi-Sal" made his escape from the reservation with about one hundred and fifty of his followers, intending to go down on the south side of the Mexican line and find an asylum among the Cocopahs.   They were pursued and brought back without bloodshed by Captain James Burns, a brave and humane officer of the Fifth Cavalry, who died sixteen years ago worn out by the hard work demanded in Arizona.

It does not seem just, at first sight, to deny to Indians the right to domicile themselves in another country if they so desire, and if a peaceful life can be assured them; but, in the end, it will be found that constant visiting will spring up between the people living in the old home and the new, and all sorts of complications are sure to result.   The Apache-Mojaves and the Apache-Tontos, living in the Tonto Basin, misapprehending the reasons for the cessation of scouting against them, had become emboldened to make a series of annoying and destructive attacks upon the ranchos in the Agua Fria Valley, upon those near Wickenburg, and those near what is now the prosperous town of Phœnix, in the Salt River Valley.   Their chiefs "Delt-che" (The Red Ant) and "Cha-lipun" (The Buckskin-colored Hat) were brave, bold, able, and enterprising, and rightfully regarded as among the worst enemies the white men ever had.   The own-ers of two of the ranchos attacked were very peculiar persons. One of them, Townsend, of the Dripping Springs in the Middle Agua Fria, was supposed to be a half-breed Cherokee from the Indian Nation; he certainly had all the looks—the snapping black eyes, the coal-black, long, lank hair, and the swarthy skin—

of the full-blooded aborigine, with all the cunning, shrewdness, contempt for privation and danger, and ability to read "sign," that distinguish the red men.   It was his wont at the appearance of the new moon, when raiding parties of Apaches might be expected, to leave his house, make a wide circuit in the mountains and return, hoping to be able to "cut" the trail of some prowlers ; if he did, he would carefully secrete himself in the rocks on the high hills overlooking his home, and wait until the Apaches would make some movement to let him discover where they were and what they intended doing.

He was a dead shot, cunning as a snake, wily and brave, and modest at the same time, and the general belief was that he had sent twenty-seven Apaches to the Happy Hunting Grounds. Townsend and Boggs, his next-door neighbor who lived a mile or two from him, had made up their minds that they would "farm" in the fertile bottom lands of the Agua Fria ; the Apaches had made up their minds that they should not ; hence it goes without saying that neither Townsend nor Boggs, nor any of their hired men, ever felt really lonesome in the seclusion of their lovely valley.   The sequel to this story is the sequel to all such stories about early Arizona : the Apaches "got him" at last, and my friend Townsend has long been sleeping his last sleep under the shadow of a huge bowlder within a hundred yards of his home at the "Dripping Springs."

The antipodes of Townsend's rancho, as its proprietor was the antipodes of Townsend himself, was the "station" of Darrel Duppa at the "sink" of the same Agua Fria, some fifty miles below.   Darrel Duppa was one of the queerest specimens of humanity, as his ranch was one of the queerest examples to be found in Arizona, and I might add in New Mexico and Sonora as well.   There was nothing superfluous about Duppa in the way of flesh, neither was there anything about the "station" that could be regarded as superfluous, either in furniture or ornament. Duppa was credited with being the wild, harum-scarum son of an English family of respectability, his father having occupied a position in the diplomatic or consular service of Great Britain, and the son having been born in Marseilles.   Rumor had it that Duppa spoke several languages—French, Spanish, Italian, German—that he understood the classics, and that, when sober, he used faultless English.   I can certify to his employment of excellent French and Spanish, and what had to my ears the sound of pretty good Italian, and I know too that he was hospitable to a fault, and not afraid of man or devil. Three bullet wounds, received in three different fights with the Apaches, attested his grit, although they might not be accepted as equally conclusive evidence of good judgment. The site of his "location" was in the midst of the most uncompromising piece of desert in a region which boasts of possessing more desert land than any other territory in the Union. The surrounding hills and mesas yielded a perennial crop of cactus, and little of anything else.

The dwelling itself was nothing but a "ramada," a term which has already been defined as a roof of branches ; the walls were of rough, unplastered wattle work, of the thorny branches of the ironwood, no thicker than a man's finger, which were lashed by thongs of raw-hide to horizontal slats of cottonwood ; the floor of the bare earth, of course—that almost went without saying in those days—and the furniture rather too simple and meagre even for Carthusians. As I recall the place to mind, there appears the long, unpainted table of pine, which served for meals or gambling, or the rare occasions when any one took into his head the notion to write a letter. This room constituted the ranch in its entirety. Along the sides were scattered piles of blankets, which about midnight were spread out as couches for tired laborers or travellers. At one extremity, a meagre array of Dutch ovens, flat-irons, and frying-pans revealed the "kitchen," presided over by a hirsute, husky-voiced gnome, half Vulcan, half Centaur, who, immersed for most of the day in the mysteries of the larder, at stated intervals broke the stillness with the hoarse command : "Hash pile ! Come a' runnin' !" There is hardly any use to describe the rifles, pistols, belts of ammunition, saddles, spurs, and whips, which lined the walls, and covered the joists and cross-beams ; they were just as much part and parcel of the establishment as the dogs and ponies were. To keep out the sand-laden wind, which blew fiercely down from the north when it wasn't blowing down with equal fierceness from the south, or the west, or the east, strips of canvas or gunny-sacking were tacked on the inner side of the cactus branches.

My first visit to this Elysium was made about midnight, and I remember that the meal served up was unique if not absolutely paralyzing on the score of originality. There was a great plenty of Mexican figs in raw-hide sacks, fairly good tea, which had the one great merit of hotness, and lots and lots of whiskey; but there was no bread, as the supply of flour had run short, and, on account of the appearance of Apaches during the past few days, it had not been considered wise to send a party over to Phœnix for a replenishment. A wounded Mexican, lying down in one corner, was proof that the story was well founded. All the light in the ranch was afforded by a single stable lantern, by the flickering flames from the cook's fire, and the glinting stars. In our saddle-bags we had several slices of bacon and some biscuits, so we did not fare half so badly as we might have done. What caused me most wonder was why Duppa had ever concluded to live in such a forlorn spot; the best answer I could get to my queries was that the Apaches had attacked him at the moment he was approaching the banks of the Agua Fria at this point, and after he had repulsed them he thought he would stay there merely to let them know he could do it. This explanation was satisfactory to every one else, and I had to accept it.

We should, before going farther, cast a retrospective glance upon the southern part of the territory, where the Apaches were doing some energetic work in be-devilling the settlers; there were raids upon Montgomery's at "Tres Alamos," the "Cienaga," and other places not very remote from Tucson, and the Chiricahuas apparently had come up from Sonora bent upon a mission of destruction. They paid particular attention to the country about Fort Bowie and the San Simon, and had several brushes with Captain Gerald Russell's Troop "K" of the Third Cavalry. While watering his horses in the narrow, high, rock-walled defile in the Dragoon Mountains, known on the frontier at that time as "Cocheis's Stronghold," Russell was unexpectedly assailed by Cocheis and his band, the first intimation of the presence of the Chiricahuas being the firing of the shot, which, striking the guide, Bob Whitney, in the head, splashed his brains out upon Russell's face. Poor Bob Whitney was an unusually handsome fellow, of great courage and extended service against the Apaches; he had been wounded scores of times, I came near saying, but to be exact, he had been wounded at least half a dozen times by both bullets and arrows. He and Maria Jilda Grijalva, an escaped Mexican prisoner, who knew every foot of the southern

Apache country, had been guides for the commands of Winters and Russell, and had seen about as much hard work as men care to see in a whole generation.

So far as the army was concerned, the most distressing of all these skirmishes and ambuscades was that in which Lieutenant Reid T. Steward lost his life in company with Corporal Black, of his regiment, the Fifth Cavalry. They were ambushed near the spring in the Davidson Cañon, twenty-five or thirty miles from Tucson, and both were killed at the same moment.

CHAPTER X.

CROOK BEGINS HIS CAMPAIGN—THE WINTER MARCH ACROSS
THE MOGOLLON PLATEAU—THE GREAT PINE BELT—BOBBY-
DOKLINNY, THE MEDICINE MAN—COOLEY AND HIS APACHE
WIFE—THE APACHE CHIEF ESQUINOSQUIZN—THE APACHE
GUIDE NANAAJE—THE FEAST OF DEAD-MULE MEAT—THE
FIGHT IN THE CAVE IN THE SALT RIVER CAÑON—THE
DEATH-CHANT—THE CHARGE—THE DYING MEDICINE MAN
—THE SCENE IN THE CAVE.

SO long as the representative of the Government, Mr. Vincent
Collyer, remained in Arizona ; so long as there flickered
the feeblest ray of light and hope that hostilities might be averted
and peace secured, Crook persisted in keeping his troops ready
to defend the exposed ranchos and settlements as fully as possible, but no offensive movements were permitted, lest the Apaches
should have reason to believe that our people meant treachery,
and were cloaking military operations under the mask of peace
negotiations. These conferences, or attempts at conferences,
came to naught, and at last, about the date of the attack made
upon General Crook and his party at Camp Date Creek, orders
were received to drive the Apaches upon the reservations assigned
them and to keep them there.

The time fixed by General Crook for the beginning of his
campaign against the Apaches had been the 15th of November,
1872—a date which would have marked the beginning of winter
and made the retreat of the different bands to the higher elevations of the mountain ranges a source of great discomfort, not
to say of suffering to them, as their almost total want of clothing
would cause them to feel the fullest effects of the colder temperature, and also there would be increased danger of detection by
the troops, to whose eyes, or those of the Indian scouts accompanying them, all smokes from camp-fires would be visible.

The incident just related as happening at Camp Date Creek

precipitated matters somewhat, but not to a very appreciable extent, since Mason's attack upon the bands of Apache-Mojaves and Apache-Yumas in the "Muchos Cañones" did not take place until the last days of the month of September, and those bands having but slender relations with the other portions of the Apache family over in the Tonto Basin, the latter would not be too much on their guard. Crook started out from his headquarters at Fort Whipple on the day set, and marched as fast as his animals would carry him by way of Camp Verde and the Colorado Chiquito to Camp Apache, a distance, as the roads and trails then measured, of about two hundred and fifty miles. Upon the summit of the Colorado plateau, which in places attains an elevation of more than ten thousand feet, the cold was intense, and we found every spring and creek frozen solid, thus making the task of watering our stock one of great difficulty.

Our line of march led through the immense pine forests, and to the right of the lofty snow-mantled peak of San Francisco, one of the most beautiful mountains in America. It seems to have been, at some period not very remote, a focus of volcanic disturbance, pouring out lava in inconceivable quantities, covering the earth for one hundred miles square, and to a depth in places of five hundred feet. This depth can be ascertained by any geologist who will take the trail out from the station of Ash Fork, on the present Atlantic and Pacific Railroad, and go north-northeast, to the Cataract Cañon, to the village of the Ava-Supais. In beginning the descent towards the Cataract Cañon, at the "Black Tanks," the enormous depth of the "flow" can be seen at a glance. What was the "forest primeval" at that time on the Mogollon has since been raided by the rapacious forces of commerce, and at one point—Flagstaff, favorably located in the timber belt—has since been established the great Ayers-Riordan saw and planing mill, equipped with every modern appliance for the destruction of the old giants whose heads had nodded in the breezes of centuries. Man's inhumanity to man is an awful thing. His inhumanity to God's beautiful trees is scarcely inferior to it. Trees are nearly human ; they used to console man with their oracles, and I must confess my regret that the Christian dispensation has so changed the opinions of the world that the soughing of the evening wind through their branches is no longer a message of hope or a solace to sorrow. Reflection tells me that without the use of this great belt of timber the construction of the railroad from El Paso to the City of Mexico would have been attended with increased expense and enhanced difficulty—perhaps postponed for a generation—but, for all that, I cannot repress a sentiment of regret that the demands of civilization have caused the denudation of so many square miles of our forests in all parts of the timbered West.

Our camp was aroused every morning at two o'clock, and we were out on the road by four, making long marches and not halting until late in the afternoon. Camp Apache was reached by the time expected, and the work of getting together a force of scouts begun at once. One of the first young men to respond to the call for scouts to enlist in the work of ferreting out and subjugating the hostiles was "Na-kay-do-klunni," called afterwards by the soldiers "Bobby Doklinny." I have still in my possession, among other papers, the scrap of manuscript upon which is traced in lead pencil the name of this Apache, whom I enrolled among the very first at Camp Apache on this occasion. The work of enlistment was afterwards turned over to Lieutenant Alexander O. Brodie, of the First Cavalry, as I was obliged to leave with General Crook for the south. "Bobby," to adopt the soldiers' name, became in his maturity a great "medicine man" among his people, and began a dance in which he used to raise the spirits of his ancestors. Of course, he scared the people of the United States out of their senses, and instead of offering him a bonus for all the ghosts he could bring back to life, the troops were hurried hither and thither, and there was an "outbreak," as is always bound to be the case under such circumstances. "Bobby Doklinny" was killed, and with him a number of his tribe, while on our side there was grief for the death of brave officers and gallant men.

One of the white men met at Camp Apache was Corydon E. Cooley, who had married a woman of the Sierra Blanca band, and had acquired a very decided influence over them. Cooley's efforts were consistently in the direction of bringing about a better understanding between the two races, and so far as "Pedro's" and "Miguel's" people were concerned, his exertions bore good fruit. But it is of Mrs. Cooley I wish to speak at this moment. She was, and I hope still is, because I trust that she is still alive, a woman of extraordinary character, anxious to advance and to have her children receive all the benefits of education. She tried hard to learn, and was ever on the alert to imitate the housekeeping of the few ladies who followed their husbands down to Camp Apache, all of whom took a great and womanly interest in the advancement of their swarthy sister. On my way back from the snake dance of the Moquis I once dined at Cooley's ranch in company with Mr. Peter Moran, the artist, and can assure my readers that the little home we entered was as clean as homes generally are, and that the dinner served was as good as any to be obtained in Delmonico's.

For those readers who care to learn of such things I insert a brief description of "Cooley's Ranch" as we found it in that year, 1881, of course many years after the Apaches had been subdued. The ranch was on the summit of the Mogollon plateau, at its eastern extremity, near the head of Show Low Creek, one of the affluents of the Shevlons Fork of the Colorado Chiquito. The contour of the plateau is here a charming series of gentle hills and dales, the hills carpeted with juicy black "grama," and spangled with flowers growing at the feet of graceful pines and majestic oaks ; and the dales, watered by babbling brooks flowing through fields of ripening corn and potatoes. In the centre of a small but exquisitely beautiful park, studded with pine trees without undergrowth, stood the frame house and the outbuildings of the ranch we were seeking. Cooley was well provided with every creature comfort to be looked for in the most prosperous farming community in the older States. His fields and garden patches were yielding bountifully of corn, pumpkins, cucumbers, wheat, peas, beans, cabbage, potatoes, barley, oats, strawberries, gooseberries, horse-radish, and musk-melons. He had set out an orchard of apple, crab, dwarf pear, peach, apricot, quince, plum, and cherry trees, and could supply any reasonable demand for butter, cream, milk, eggs, or fresh meat from his poultry yard or herd of cows and drove of sheep. There was an ice-house well filled, two deep wells, and several springs of pure water. The house was comfortably furnished, lumber being plenty and at hand from the saw-mill running on the property.

Four decidedly pretty gipsy-like little girls assisted their mother in gracefully doing the honors to the strangers, and conducted us to a table upon which smoked a perfectly cooked meal of Irish stew of mutton, home-made bread, boiled and stewed mushrooms—plucked since our arrival—fresh home-made butter, buttermilk, peas and beans from the garden, and aromatic coffee. The table itself was neatly spread, and everything was well served. If one Apache woman can teach herself all this, it does not seem to be hoping for too much when I express the belief that in a few years others may be encouraged to imitate her example. I have inherited from General Crook a strong belief in this phase of the Indian problem. Let the main work be done with the young women, in teaching them how to cook, and what to cook, and how to become good housekeepers, and the work will be more than half finished. In all tribes the influence of the women, although silent, is most potent. Upon the squaws falls the most grievous part of the burden of war, and if they can be made to taste the luxuries of civilized life, and to regard them as necessaries, the idea of resuming hostilities will year by year be combated with more vigor. It was upon this principle that the work of missionary effort was carried on among the Canadian tribes, and we see how, after one or two generations of women had been educated, all trouble disappeared, and the best of feeling between the two races was developed and maintained for all time.

From Camp Apache to old Camp Grant was by the trail a trifle over one hundred miles, but over a country so cut up with cañons, and so rocky, that the distance seemed very much greater. The cañon of the Prieto or Black River, the passage of the Apache range, the descent of the Aravaypa, were all considered and with justice to be specially severe upon the muscles and nerves of travellers, not only because of depth and steepness, but also because the trail was filled with loose stones which rolled from under the careless tread, and wrenched the feet and ankles of the unwary.

Of the general character of the approaches to old Camp Grant, enough has already been written in the earlier chapters. I wish to add that the marches were still exceptionally long and severe, as General Crook was determined to arrive on time, as promised to the chiefs who were expecting him. On account of getting entangled in the cañons back of the Picacho San Carlos, it took us more than twenty-four hours to pass over the distance between the Black River and the mouth of the San Carlos, the start being made at six o'clock one day, and ending at eight o'clock the next morning, a total of twenty-six hours of marching and climbing. Every one in the command was pretty well tired out, and glad to throw himself down with head on saddle, just as soon as horses and mules could be lariated on grass and pickets established, but General Crook took his shot-gun and followed up the Gila a mile or two, and got a fine mess of reed birds for our breakfast. It was this insensibility to fatigue, coupled with a contempt for danger, or rather with a skill in evading all traps that might be set for him, which won for Crook the admiration of all who served with him ; there was no private soldier, no packer, no teamster, who could " down the ole man " in any work, or outlast him on a march or a climb over the rugged peaks of Arizona ; they knew that, and they also knew that in the hour of danger Crook would be found on the skirmish line, and not in the telegraph office.

At old Camp Grant, the operations of the campaign began in earnest ; in two or three days the troops at that post were ready to move out under command of Major Brown, of the Fifth Cavalry, and the general plan of the campaign unfolded itself. It was to make a clean sweep of the Tonto Basin, the region in which the hostiles had always been so successful in eluding and defying the troops, and this sweep was to be made by a number of converging columns, each able to look out for itself, each provided with a force of Indian scouts, each followed by a pack-train with all needful supplies, and each led by officers physically able to go almost anywhere. After the centre of the Basin had been reached, if there should be no decisive action in the meantime, these commands were to turn back and break out in different directions, scouring the country, so that no nook or corner should be left unexamined. The posts were stripped of the last available officer and man, the expectation being that, by closely pursuing the enemy, but little leisure would be left him for making raids upon our settlements, either military or civil, and that the constant movements of the various detachments would always bring some within helping distance of beleaguered stations.

General Crook kept at the front, moving from point to point, along the whole periphery, and exercising complete personal supervision of the details, but leaving the movements from each post under the control of the officers selected for the work.

Major George M. Randall, Twenty-third Infantry, managed affairs at Camp Apache, having under him as chief of scouts, Mr. C. E. Cooley, of whom mention has just been made. Major George F. Price, Fifth Cavalry, commanded from Date Creek. Major Alexander MacGregor, First Cavalry, had the superintendence of the troops to move out from Fort Whipple; Colonel Julius W. Mason, Fifth Cavalry, of those to work down from Camp Hualpai, while those of the post of Camp MacDowell were commanded by Captain James Burns, Fifth Cavalry. Colonel C. C. C. Carr, First Cavalry, led those from Verde. All these officers were experienced, and of great discretion and good judgment. Each and all did excellent work and struck blow after blow upon the savages.

Before starting out, General Crook's instructions were communicated to both Indian scouts and soldiers at Camp Grant; as they were of the same tenor as those already given at other posts, I have not thought it necessary to repeat them for each post. Briefly, they directed that the Indians should be induced to surrender in all cases where possible; where they preferred to fight, they were to get all the fighting they wanted, and in one good dose instead of in a number of petty engagements, but in either case were to be hunted down until the last one in hostility had been killed or captured. Every effort should be made to avoid the killing of women and children. Prisoners of either sex should be guarded from ill-treatment of any kind. When prisoners could be induced to enlist as scouts, they should be so enlisted, because the wilder the Apache was, the more he was likely to know of the wiles and stratagems of those still out in the mountains, their hiding-places and intentions. No excuse was to be accepted for leaving a trail; if horses played out, the enemy must be followed on foot, and no sacrifice should be left untried to make the campaign short, sharp, and decisive.

Lieutenant and Brevet Major William J. Ross, Twenty-first Infantry, and myself were attached to the command of Major Brown, to operate from Camp Grant, through the Mescal, Pinal, Superstition, and Matitzal ranges, over to Camp MacDowell and there receive further instructions. Before leaving the post, I had to record a very singular affair which goes to show how thoroughly self-satisfied and stupid officialism can always become if properly encouraged. There was a Roman Catholic priest dining at our

mess—Father Antonio Jouvenceau—who had been sent out from
Tucson to try and establish a mission among the bands living in
the vicinity of Camp Apache.   There wasn't anything in the
shape of supplies in the country outside of the army stores, and
of these the missionary desired permission to buy enough to keep
himself alive until he could make other arrangements, or become
accustomed to the wild food of such friends as he might make
among the savages.   Every request he made was refused on the
ground that there was no precedent.   I know that there was "no
precedent" for doing anything to bring savages to a condition of
peace, but I have never ceased to regret that there was not, because
I feel sure that had the slightest encouragement been given to
Father Antonio or to a handful of men like him, the wildest of
the Apaches might have been induced to listen to reason, and
there would have been no such expensive wars.   A missionary
could not well be expected to load himself down with supplies
and carry them on his own back while he was hunting favorable
specimens of the Indians upon whom to make an impression.
There were numbers of Mexican prisoners among the Apaches
who retained enough respect for the religion of their childhood
to be from first acquaintance the firm and devoted friends of the
new-comer, and once set on a good basis in the Apache villages,
the rest would have been easy.   This, however, is merely conjecture on my part.

The new recruits from among the Apaches were under the
command of a chief responding to the name of "Esquinosquizn,"
meaning "Bocon" or Big Mouth.   He was crafty, cruel, daring,
and ambitious; he indulged whenever he could in the intoxicant
"Tizwin," made of fermented corn and really nothing but a
sour beer which will not intoxicate unless the drinker subject
himself, as the Apache does, to a preliminary fast of from two to
four days.   This indulgence led to his death at San Carlos some
months later.   The *personnel* of Brown's command was excellent;
it represented soldiers of considerable experience and inured to
all the climatic variations to be expected in Arizona, and nowhere
else in greater degree.   There were two companies of the Fifth
Cavalry, and a detachment of thirty Apache scouts, that being
as many as could be apportioned to each command in the initial
stages of the campaign.   Captain Alfred B. Taylor, Lieutenant
Jacob Almy, Lieutenant William J. Ross, and myself constituted

the commissioned list, until, at a point in the Superstition Mountains, we were joined by Captain James Burns and First Lieutenant Earl D. Thomas, Fifth Cavalry, with Company G of that regiment, and a large body—not quite one hundred—of Pima Indians. In addition to the above we had Archie MacIntosh, Joe Felmer, and Antonio Besias as guides and interpreters to take charge of the scouts. Mr. James Dailey, a civilian volunteer, was also with the command. The pack train carried along rations for thirty days, and there was no lack of flour, bacon, beans, coffee, with a little chile colorado for the packers, and a small quantity of dried peaches and chocolate, of which many persons in that country made use in preference to coffee. We were all cut down to the lowest notch in the matter of clothing, a deprivation of which no one complained, since the loss was not severely felt amid such surroundings.

It was now that the great amount of information which General Crook had personally absorbed in regard to Arizona came of the best service. He had been in constant conference with the Apache scouts and interpreters concerning all that was to be done and all that was positively known of the whereabouts of the hostiles; especially did he desire to find the "rancheria" of the chief "Chuntz," who had recently murdered in cold blood, at Camp Grant, a Mexican boy too young to have been a cause of rancor to any one. It may be said in one word that the smallest details of this expedition were arranged by General Crook in person before we started down the San Pedro. He had learned from "Esquinosquizn" of the site of the rancheria supposed to be occupied by "Deltchay" in the lofty range called the "Four Peaks" or the "Matitzal," the latter by the Indians and the former by the Americans, on account of there being the distinctive feature of four peaks of great elevation overlooking the country for hundreds of miles in all directions. One of the most important duties confided to our force was the destruction of this rancheria if we could find it. These points were not generally known at the time we left Grant, neither was it known that one of our Apache guides, "Nantaje," christened "Joe" by the soldiers, had been raised in that very stronghold, and deputed to conduct us to it. First, we were to look up "Chuntz," if we could, and wipe him out, and then do our best to clean up the stronghold of "Deltchay."

I will avoid details of this march because it followed quite closely the line of the first and second scouts made by Lieutenant Cushing, the preceding year, which have been already outlined. We followed down the dusty bottom of the San Pedro, through a jungle of mesquite and sage brush, which always seem to grow on land which with irrigation will yield bountifully of wheat, and crossed over to the feeble streamlet marked on the maps as Deer Creek. We crossed the Gila at a point where the Mescal and Pinal ranges seemed to come together, but the country was so broken that it was hard to tell to which range the hills belonged. The trails were rough, and the rocks were largely granites, porphyry, and pudding stones, often of rare beauty. There was an abundance of mescal, cholla cactus, manzanita, Spanish bayonet, pitahaya, and scrub oak so long as we remained in the foothills, but upon gaining the higher levels of the Pinal range, we found first juniper, and then pine of good dimensions and in great quantity. The scenery upon the summit of the Pinal was exhilarating and picturesque, but the winds were bitter and the ground deep with snow, so that we made no complaint when the line of march led us to a camp on the northwest extremity, where we found water trickling down the flanks of the range into a beautiful narrow cañon, whose steep walls hid us from the prying gaze of the enemy's spies, and also protected from the wind ; the slopes were green with juicy grama grass, and dotted with oaks which gracefully arranged themselves in clusters of twos and threes, giving grateful shade to men and animals. Far above us waved the branches of tall pines and cedars, and at their feet could be seen the banks of snow, but in our own position the weather was rather that of the south temperate or the northern part of the torrid zone.

This rapid change of climate made scouting in Arizona very trying. During this campaign we were often obliged to leave the warm valleys in the morning and climb to the higher altitudes and go into bivouac upon summits where the snow was hip deep, as on the Matitzal, the Mogollon plateau, and the Sierra Ancha. To add to the discomfort, the pine was so thoroughly soaked through with snow and rain that it would not burn, and unless cedar could be found, the command was in bad luck. Our Apache scouts, under MacIntosh, Felmer, and Besias, were kept from twelve to twenty-four hours in advance of the main body, but always in communication, the intention being to make use of them to determine the whereabouts of the hostiles, but to let the soldiers do the work of cleaning them out. It was difficult to restrain the scouts, who were too fond of war to let slip any good excuse for a fight, and consequently MacIntosh had two or three skirmishes of no great consequence, but which showed that his scouts could be depended upon both as trailers and as a fighting force. In one of these, the village or "rancheria" of "Chuntz," consisting of twelve "jacales," was destroyed with a very full winter stock of food, but only one of the party was wounded, and all escaped, going in the direction of the Cañon of the Rio Salado or Salt River. The advance of the scouts had been discovered by a squaw, who gave the alarm and enabled the whole party to escape.

A day or two after this, the scouts' again struck the trail of the enemy, and had a sharp brush with them, killing several and capturing three. The Apaches had been making ready to plant during the coming spring, had dug irrigating ditches, and had also accumulated a great store of all kinds of provisions suited to their needs, among others a full supply of baked mescal, as well as of the various seeds of grass, sunflower, and the beans of mesquite which form so important a part of their food. As well as could be determined, this was on or near the head of the little stream marked on the maps as Raccoon Creek, on the south slope of the Sierra Ancha. Close by was a prehistoric ruin, whose wall of rubble stone was still three feet high. On the other (the south) side of the Salt River we passed under a well-preserved cliff-dwelling in the cañon of Pinto Creek, a place which I have since examined carefully, digging out sandals of the "palmilla" fibre, dried mescal, corn husks and other foods, and some small pieces of textile fabrics, with one or two axes and hammers of stone, arrows, and the usual débris to be expected in such cases. We worked our way over into the edge of the Superstition Mountains. There was very little to do, and it was evident that whether through fear of our own and the other commands which must have been seen, or from a desire to concentrate during the cold weather, the Apaches had nearly all abandoned that section of country, and sought refuge somewhere else.

The Apache scouts, however, insisted that we were to find a "heap" of Indians "poco tiempo" (very soon). By their advice, most of our officers and men had provided themselves with moccasins which would make no noise in clambering over the rocks or down the slippery trails where rolling stones might arouse the sleeping enemy. The Apaches, I noticed, stuffed their moccasins with dry hay, and it was also apparent that they knew all the minute points about making themselves comfortable with small means. Just as soon as they reached camp, those who were not posted as pickets or detailed to go off on side scouts in small parties of five and six, would devote their attention to getting their bed ready for the night; the grass in the vicinity would be plucked in handfuls, and spread out over the smoothed surface upon which two or three of the scouts purposed sleeping together; a semicircle of good-sized pieces of rock made a wind break, and then one or two blankets would be spread out, and upon that the three would recline, huddling close together, each wrapped up in his own blanket. Whenever fires were allowed, the Apaches would kindle small ones, and lie down close to them with feet towards the flame. According to the theory of the Indian, the white man makes so great a conflagration that, besides alarming the whole country, he makes it so hot that no one can draw near, whereas the Apache, with better sense, contents himself with a small collection of embers, over which he can if necessary crouch and keep warm.

The fine condition of our pack-trains awakened continued interest, and evoked constant praise; the mules had followed us over some of the worst trails in Arizona, and were still as fresh as when they left Grant, and all in condition for the most arduous service with the exception of two, one of which ate, or was supposed to have eaten, of the insect known as the "Compra mucho" or the "Niña de la Tierra," which is extremely poisonous to those animals which swallow it in the grass to which it clings. This mule died. Another was bitten on the lip by a rattlesnake, and though by the prompt application of a poultice of the weed called the "golondrina" we managed to save its life for a few days, it too died. On Christmas Day we were joined by Captain James Burns, Fifth Cavalry, with Lieutenant Earl D. Thomas, of the same regiment, and a command consisting of forty enlisted men of Company G, and a body of not quite one hundred Pima Indians. They had been out from MacDowell for six days, and had crossed over the highest point of the Matitzal

range, and had destroyed a "rancheria," killing six and capturing two ; one, a squaw, sent in to MacDowell, and the other, a
small but very bright and active boy, whom the men had promptly
adopted, and upon whom had been bestowed the name "Mike"
Burns, which he has retained to this day. This boy, then not
more than six or seven years old, was already an expert in the
use of the bow and arrow, and, what suited Captain Burns much
better, he could knock down quail with stones, and add much to
the pleasures of a very meagre mess, as no shooting was allowed.
During the past twenty years, Mike Burns has, through the
interposition of General Crook, been sent to Carlisle, and there
received the rudiments of an education ; we have met at the San
Carlos Agency, and talked over old times, and I have learned
what was not then known, that in Burns's fight with the band on
the summit of the Four Peaks, seven of the latter were killed,
and the men and women who escaped, under the leadership of
Mike's own father, hurried to the stronghold in the cañon of the
Salt River, where they were all killed by our command a few days
later. On the evening of the 27th of December, 1872, we were
bivouacked in a narrow cañon called the Cottonwood Creek,
flowing into the Salado at the eastern base of the Matitzal, when
Major Brown announced to his officers that the object for which
General Crook had sent out this particular detachment was almost
attained ; that he had been in conference with "Nantaje," one
of our Apache scouts, who had been brought up in the cave in
the cañon of the Salt River, and that he had expressed a desire
to lead us there, provided we made up our minds to make the
journey before day-dawn, as the position of the enemy was such
that if we should be discovered on the trail, not one of our party
would return alive. The Apaches are familiar with the stars,
and "Nantaje" had said that if we were to go, he wanted to start
out with the first appearance above the eastern horizon of a certain star with which he was acquainted.

Brown gave orders that every officer and man who was not in
the best condition for making a severe march and climb over
rugged mountains, should stay with the pack-trains and be on
the watch for any prowling band of the enemy. First, there was
made a pile of the *aparejos* and supplies which could serve in
emergency as a breastwork for those to remain behind ; then a
picket line was stretched, to which the mules and horses could be

tied, and kept under shelter from fire ; and lastly, every officer and man looked carefully to his weapons and ammunition, for we were to start out on foot and climb through the rough promontory of the Matitzal into the Salt River Cañon, and on to the place in which we were to come upon the cave inhabited by the hostiles of whom we were in search. Every belt was filled with cartridges, and twenty extra were laid away in the blanket which each wore slung across his shoulders, and in which were placed the meagre allowance of bread, bacon, and coffee taken as provision, with the canteen of water. The Apache scouts had asked the privilege of cooking and eating the mule which had died during the morning, and as the sky had clouded and the light of small fires could not well be seen, Major Brown consented, and they stuffed themselves to their hearts' content, in a meal which had not a few points of resemblance to the "Festins à manger tout," mentioned by Father Lafitau, Parkman, and other writers. Before eight o'clock, we were on our way, "Nantaje" in the van, and all marching briskly towards the summit of the high mesas which enclosed the cañon.

The night became extremely cold, and we were only too glad of the opportunity of pushing ahead with vigor, and regretted very much to hear the whispered command to halt and lie down until the last of the rear-guard could be heard from. The Apache scouts in front had detected lights in advance, and assured Major Brown that they must be from the fires of the Indians of whom we were in quest. While they went ahead to search and determine exactly what was the matter, the rest of us were compelled to lie prone to the ground, so as to afford the least chance to the enemy to detect any signs of life among us ; no one spoke beyond a whisper, and even when the cold compelled any of the party to cough, it was done with the head wrapped up closely in a blanket or cape. "Nantaje," "Bocon," and others were occupied with the examination of the track into which the first-named had stepped, as he and Brown were walking ahead ; it seemed to the Indian to be the footprint of a man, but when all had nestled down close to the earth, covered heads over with blankets, and struck a match, it proved to be the track of a great bear, which closely resembles that of a human being. Within a few moments, Felmer, Archie, and the others, sent on to discover the cause of the fires seen ahead, returned with the intelligence that the

Apaches had just been raiding upon the white and Pima Indian settlements in the valley of the Gila, and had driven off fifteen horses and mules, which, being barefoot and sore from climbing the rocky trail up the face of the mountain, had been abandoned in a little nook where there was a slight amount of grass and a little water. Worst news of all, there had been four large "wickyups" in the same place which had just been vacated, and whether on account of discovering our approach or not it was hard to say.

We were becoming rather nervous by this time, as we still had in mind what "Nantaje" had said the previous evening about killing the last of the enemy, or being compelled to fight our own way back. "Nantaje" was thoroughly composed, and smiled when some of the party insinuated a doubt about the existence of any large "rancheria" in the neighborhood. "Wait and see," was all the reply he would vouchsafe.

By advice of "Nantaje," Major Brown ordered Lieutenant William J. Ross to proceed forward on the trail with twelve or fifteen of the best shots among the soldiers, and such of the packers as had obtained permission to accompany the command. "Nantaje" led them down the slippery, rocky, dangerous trail in the wall of the gloomy cañon, which in the cold gray light of the slowly creeping dawn, and under the gloom of our surroundings, made us think of the Valley of the Shadow of Death. "They ought to be very near here," said Major Brown. "Good Heavens! what is all that?" It was a noise equal to that of a full battery of six-pounders going off at once. Brown knew that something of the greatest consequence had happened, and he wasn't the man to wait for the arrival of messengers; he ordered me to take command of the first forty men in the advance, without waiting to see whether they were white or red, soldiers or packers, and go down the side of the cañon on the run, until I had joined Ross, and taken up a position as close to the enemy as it was possible for me to get without bringing on a fight; meantime, he would gather up all the rest of the command, and follow me as fast as he could, and relieve me. There was no trouble at all in getting down that cañon; the difficulty was to hold on to the trail; had any man lost his footing, he would not have stopped until he had struck the current of the Salado, hundreds of feet below. In spite of everything, we clambered down, and by great good luck broke no necks. As we turned a sudden angle in the wall, we saw the condition of affairs most completely. The precipice forming that side of the cañon was hundreds of feet in height, but at a point some four or five hundred feet below the crest had fallen back in a shelf upon which was a cave of no great depth. In front of the cave great blocks of stone furnished a natural rampart behind which the garrison could bid defiance to the assaults of almost any enemy; in this eyrie, the band of " Nanni-chaddi " felt a security such as only the eagle or the vulture can feel in the seclusion of the ice-covered dizzy pinnacles of the Andes; from the shelf upon which they lived these savages, who seem to me to have been the last of the cliff-dwellers within our borders, had on several occasions watched the commands of Sanford and Carr struggling to make their way up the stream in the cañon below. The existence of one, or perhaps two, rancherias somewhere within this gloomy cañon had long been suspected, but never demonstrated until the present moment. When we joined Ross we heard his story told in few words : he and his small band of twelve had followed Felmer and MacIntosh down the face of the cliff until they had reached the small open space in front of the cave ; there they saw within a very few yards of them the party of raiders just returned from the Gila settlements, who had left at pasture the band of fifteen ponies which we had seen. These warriors were dancing, either to keep themselves warm or as a portion of some religious ceremonial, as is generally the case with the tribes in the southwest. Close by them crouched half a dozen squaws, aroused from slumber to prepare food for the hungry braves. The flames of the fire, small as it was, reflected back from the high walls, gave a weird illumination to the features of the circle, and enabled the whites to take better aim upon their unsuspecting victims. Ross and " Nantaje " consulted in whispers, and immediately it was decided that each man should with the least noise possible cock his piece and aim at one of the group without reference to what his next-door neighbor might be doing. Had not the Apaches been interested in their own singing, they might surely have heard the low whisper: ready ! aim ! fire ! but it would have been too late ; the die was cast, and their hour had come.

The fearful noise which we had heard, reverberating from peak to peak and from crag to crag, was the volley poured in by Ross and his comrades, which had sent six souls to their last account, and sounded the death-knell of a powerful band. The surprise and terror of the savages were so complete that they thought only of the safety which the interior of the cave afforded, and as a consequence, when my party arrived on the scene, although there were a number of arrows thrown at us as we descended the path and rounded the angle, yet no attempt was made at a counter-assault, and before the Apaches could recover from their astonishment the two parties united, numbering more than fifty, nearer sixty, men, had secured position within thirty yards of one flank of the cave, and within forty yards of the other, and each man posted behind rocks in such a manner that he might just as well be in a rifle pit. My instructions were not to make any fight, but to keep the Apaches occupied, in case they tried to break out of the trap, and to order all men to shelter themselves to the utmost. Major Brown was down with the remainder of the command almost before a shot could be exchanged with the enemy, although there were two more killed either a moment before his arrival or very soon after. One of these was a Pima, one of our own allies, who persisted in disregarding orders, and exposed himself to the enemy's fire, and was shot through the body and died before he ever knew what had struck him. The other was one of the Apaches who had sneaked down along our right flank, and was making his way out to try to open up communication with another village and get its people to attack us in rear. He counted without his host, and died a victim to his own carelessness ; he had climbed to the top of a high rock some distance down the cañon, and there fancied himself safe from our shots, and turned to give a yell of defiance. His figure outlined against the sky was an excellent mark, and there was an excellent shot among us to take full advantage of it. Blacksmith John Cahill had his rifle in position like a flash, and shot the Indian through the body. At the time of the fight, we did not know that the savage had been killed, although Cahill insisted that he had shot him as described, and as those nearest him believed. The corpse could not be found in the rocks before we left, and therefore was not counted, but the squaws at San Carlos have long since told me that their relative was killed there, and that his remains were found after we had left the neighborhood.

Brown's first work was to see that the whole line was impregnable to assault from the beleaguered garrison of the cave, and then he directed his interpreters to summon all to an unconditional surrender. The only answer was a shriek of hatred and defiance, threats of what we had to expect, yells of exultation at the thought that not one of us should ever see the light of another day, but should furnish a banquet for the crows and buzzards, and some scattering shots fired in pure bravado. Brown again summoned all to surrender, and when jeers were once more his sole response, he called upon the Apaches to allow their women and children to come out, and assured them kind treatment. To this the answer was the same as before, the jeers and taunts of the garrison assuring our people that they were in dead earnest in saying that they intended to fight till they died. For some moments the Apaches resorted to the old tactics of enticing some of our unwary soldiers to expose themselves above the wall of rocks behind which Major Brown ordered all to crouch ; a hat or a war bonnet would be set up on the end of a bow, and held in such a way as to make-believe that there was a warrior behind it, and induce some one proud of his marksmanship to " lay " for the red man and brother, who would, in his turn, be "laying" for the white man in some coign of vantage close to where his squaw was holding the head-gear. But such tricks were entirely too transparent to deceive many, and after a short time the Apaches themselves grew tired of them, and began to try new methods. They seemed to be abundantly provided with arrows and lances, and of the former they made no saving, but would send them flying high in air in the hope that upon coming back to earth they might hit those of our rearguard who were not taking such good care of themselves as were their brothers at the front on the skirmish line.

There was a lull of a few minutes ; each side was measuring its own strength and that of its opponent. It was apparent that any attempt to escalade without ladders would result in the loss of more than half our command ; the great rock wall in front of the cave was not an inch less than ten feet in height at its lowest point, and smooth as the palm of the hand ; it would be madness to attempt to climb it, because the moment the assailants reached the top, the lances of the invested force could push them back to the ground wounded to death. Three or four of our picked shots were posted in eligible positions overlooking the places where the Apaches had been seen to expose themselves ; this, in the hope that any recurrence of such fool-hardiness would afford an opportunity for the sharpshooters to show their skill. Of the main body, one-half was in reserve fifty yards behind the skirmish line—to call it such where the whole business was a skirmish line—with carbines loaded and cocked, and a handful of cartridges on the clean rocks in front, and every man on the lookout to prevent the escape of a single warrior, should any be fortunate enough to sneak or break through the first line. The men on the first line had orders to fire as rapidly as they chose, directing aim against the roof of the cave, with the view to having the bullets glance down among the Apache men, who had massed immediately back of the rock rampart.

This plan worked admirably, and, so far as we could judge, our shots were telling upon the Apaches, and irritating them to that degree that they no longer sought shelter, but boldly faced our fire and returned it with energy, the weapons of the men being reloaded by the women, who shared their dangers. A wail from a squaw, and the feeble cry of a little babe, were proof that the missiles of death were not seeking men alone. Brown ordered our fire to cease, and for the last time summoned the Apaches to surrender, or to let their women and children come out unmo-lested. On their side, the Apaches also ceased all hostile demon-stration, and it seemed to some of us Americans that they must be making ready to yield, and were discussing the matter among themselves. Our Indian guides and interpreters raised the cry, "Look out ! There goes the death song; they are going to charge !" It was a weird chant, one not at all easy to describe; half wail and half exultation—the frenzy of despair and the wild cry for revenge. Now the petulant, querulous treble of the squaws kept time with the shuffling feet, and again the deeper growl of the savage bull-dogs, who represented manhood in that cave, was flung back from the cold pitiless brown of the cliffs.

"Look out ! Here they come !" Over the rampart, guided by one impulse, moving as if they were all part of the one body, jumped and ran twenty of the warriors—superb-looking fellows all of them ; each carried upon his back a quiver filled with the long reed arrows of the tribe, each held in his hand a bow and a rifle, the latter at full cock. Half of the party stood upon the rampart, which gave them some chance to sight our men behind the smaller rocks in front, and blazed away for all they were worth—they were trying to make a demonstration to engage our attention, while the other part suddenly slipped down and around our right flank, and out through the rocks which had so effectively sheltered the retreat of the one who had so nearly succeeded in getting away earlier in the morning. Their motives were divined, and the move was frustrated; our men rushed to the attack like furies, each seeming to be anxious to engage the enemy at close quarters. Six or seven of the enemy were killed in a space not twenty-five feet square, and the rest driven back within the cave, more or less wounded.

Although there was a fearful din from the yells, groans, wails of the squaws within the fortress, and the re-echoing of volleys from the walls of the cañon, our command behaved admirably, and obeyed its orders to the letter. The second line never budged from its place, and well it was that it had stayed just there. One of the charging party, seeing that so much attention was converged upon our right, had slipped down unnoticed from the rampart, and made his way to the space between our two lines, and had sprung to the top of a huge boulder, and there had begun his war-whoop, as a token of encouragement to those still behind. I imagine that he was not aware of our second line, and thought that once in our rear, ensconced in a convenient nook in the rocks, he could keep us busy by picking us off at his leisure. His chant was never finished; it was at once his song of glory and his death song; he had broken through our line of fire only to meet a far more cruel death. Twenty carbines were gleaming in the sunlight just flushing the cliffs; forty eyes were sighting along the barrels. The Apache looked into the eyes of his enemies, and in not one did he see the slightest sign of mercy; he tried to say something; what it was we never could tell. "No! No! soldados!" in broken Spanish, was all we could make out before the resounding volley had released another soul from its earthly casket, and let the bleeding corpse fall to the ground as limp as a wet moccasin. He was really a handsome warrior; tall, well-proportioned, finely muscled, and with a bold, manly countenance; "shot to death" was the verdict of all who paused to look upon him, but that didn't half express the state of the case; I have never seen a man more thoroughly shot to pieces than was this one; every bullet seemed to have struck, and not less than eight or ten had inflicted mortal wounds.

The savages in the cave, with death now staring them in the face, did not seem to lose their courage—or, shall we say despair? They resumed their chant, and sang with vigor and boldness, until Brown determined that the battle or siege must end. Our two lines were now massed in one, and every officer and man told to get ready a package of cartridges; then as fast as the breech-block of the carbine could be opened and lowered, we were to fire into the mouth of the cave, hoping to inflict the greatest damage by glancing bullets, and then charge in by the entrance on our right flank, back of the rock rampart which had served as the means of exit for the hostiles when they made their attack. The din and tumult increased twenty-fold beyond the last time; lead poured in by the bucketful, but, strangely enough, there was a lull for a moment or two, and without orders. A little Apache boy, not over four years old, if so old, ran out from within the cave, and stood, with thumb in mouth, looking in speechless wonder and indignation at the belching barrels. He was not in much danger, because all the carbines were aiming upwards at the roof, nevertheless a bullet—whether from our lines direct, or hurled down from the rocky ceiling—struck the youngster on the skull, and ploughed a path for itself around to the back of his neck, leaving a welt as big as one's finger. The youngster was knocked off his feet, and added the tribute of his howls to the roars and echoes of the conflict. "Nantaje" sprang like a deer to where the boy lay, and grasped him by one arm, and ran with him behind a great stone. Our men spontaneously ceased firing for one minute to cheer "Nantaje" and the "kid;" the fight was then resumed with greater vigor. The Apaches did not relax their fire, but, from the increasing groans of the women, we knew that our shots were telling either upon the women in the cave, or upon their relatives among the men for whom they were sorrowing.

It was exactly like fighting with wild animals in a trap: the Apaches had made up their minds to die if relief did not reach them from some of the other "rancherias" supposed to be close by. Ever since early morning nothing had been seen of Burns and Thomas, and the men of Company G. With a detachment of Pima guides, they had been sent off to follow the trail of the fifteen ponies found at day-dawn; Brown was under the impression that the raiding party belonging to the cave might have split into two or three parties, and that some of the latter ones might be trapped and ambuscaded while ascending the mountain. This was before Ross and "Nantaje" and Felmer had discovered the cave and forced the fight. This part of our forces had marched a long distance down the mountain, and was returning to rejoin us, when the roar of the carbines apprised them that the worst kind of a fight was going on, and that their help would be needed badly; they came back on the double, and as soon as they reached the summit of the precipice were halted to let the men get their breath. It was a most fortunate thing that they did so, and at that particular spot. Burns and several others went to the crest and leaned over to see what all the frightful hubbub was about. They saw the conflict going on beneath them, and in spite of the smoke could make out that the Apaches were nestling up close to the rock rampart, so as to avoid as much as possible the projectiles which were raining down from the roof of their eyrie home.

It didn't take Burns five seconds to decide what should be done; he had two of his men harnessed with the suspenders of their comrades, and made them lean well over the precipice, while the harness was used to hold them in place; these men were to fire with their revolvers at the enemy beneath, and for a volley or so they did very effective work, but their Irish blood got the better of their reason, and in their excitement they began to throw their revolvers at the enemy; this kind of ammunition was rather too costly, but it suggested a novel method of annihilating the enemy. Burns ordered his men to get together and roll several of the huge boulders, which covered the surface of the mountain, and drop them over on the unsuspecting foe. The noise was frightful; the destruction sickening. Our volleys were still directed against the inner faces of the cave and the roof, and the Apaches seemed to realize that their only safety lay in crouching close to the great stone heap in front; but even this precarious shelter was now taken away; the air was filled with the bounding, plunging fragments of stone, breaking into thousands of pieces, with other thousands behind, crashing down with the momentum gained in a descent of hundreds of feet. No human voice could be heard in such a cyclone of wrath; the volume of dust was so dense that no eye could pierce it, but over on our left it seemed that for some reason we could still discern several figures guarding that extremity of the enemy's line—the old "Medicine Man," who, decked in all the panoply of his office, with feathers on head, decorated shirt on back, and all the sacred insignia known to his people, had defied the approach of death, and kept his place, firing coolly at everything that moved on our side that he could see, his rifle reloaded and handed back by his assistants—either squaws or young men—it was impossible to tell which, as only the arms could be noted in the air. Major Brown signalled up to Burns to stop pouring down his boulders, and at the same time our men were directed to cease firing, and to make ready to charge ; the fire of the Apaches had ceased, and their chant of defiance was hushed. There was a feeling in the command as if we were about to rush through the gates of a cemetery, and that we should find a ghastly spectacle within, but, at the same time, it might be that the Apaches had retreated to some recesses in the innermost depths of the cavern, unknown to us, and be prepared to assail all who ventured to cross the wall in front.

Precisely at noon we advanced, Corporal Hanlon, of Company G, Fifth Cavalry, being the first man to surmount the parapet. I hope that my readers will be satisfied with the meagrest description of the awful sight that met our eyes : there were men and women dead or writhing in the agonies of death, and with them several babies, killed by our glancing bullets, or by the storm of rocks and stones that had descended from above. While one portion of the command worked at extricating the bodies from beneath the pile of débris, another stood guard with cocked revolvers or carbines, ready to blow out the brains of the first wounded savage who might in his desperation attempt to kill one of our people. But this precaution was entirely useless. All idea of resistance had been completely knocked out of the heads of the survivors, of whom, to our astonishment, there were over thirty.

How any of the garrison had ever escaped such a storm of missiles was at first a mystery to us, as the cave was scarcely a cave at all, but rather a cliff dwelling, and of no extended depth. However, there were many large slabs of flat thin stone within the enclosure, either left there by Nature or carried in by the squaws, to be employed in various domestic purposes. Behind and under these many of the squaws had crept, and others had piled up the dead to screen themselves and their children from the fury of our assault. Thirty-five, if I remember aright, were still living, but in the number are included all who were still breathing; many were already dying, and nearly one-half were dead before we started out of that dreadful place. None of the warriors were conscious except one old man, who serenely awaited the last summons; he had received five or six wounds, and was practically dead when we sprang over the entrance wall. There was a general sentiment of sorrow for the old "Medicine Man" who had stood up so fiercely on the left of the Apache line; we found his still warm corpse, crushed out of all semblance to humanity, beneath a huge mass of rock, which had also extinguished at one fell stroke the light of the life of the squaw and the young man who had remained by his side. The amount of plunder and supplies of all kinds was extremely great, and the band inhabiting these cliffs must have lived with some comfort. There was a great amount of food—roasted mescal, seeds of all kinds, jerked mule or pony meat, and all else that these savages were wont to store for the winter; bows and arrows in any quantity, lances, war clubs, guns of various kinds, with ammunition fixed and loose; a perfect stronghold well supplied. So much of the mescal and other food as our scouts wished to pack off on their own backs was allowed them, and everything else was given to the flames. No attempt was made to bury the dead, who, with the exception of our own Pima, were left where they fell.

Brown was anxious to get back out of the cañon, as the captive squaws told him that there was another "rancheria" in the Superstition Mountains on the south side of the cañon, and it was probable that the Indians belonging to it would come up just as soon as they heard the news of the fight, and attack our column in rear as it tried to make its way back to the top of the precipice. The men who were found dancing by Ross had, just that moment, returned from a raid upon the Pima villages and the outskirts of Florence, in the Gila valley, where they had been successful in getting the ponies we recovered, as well as in killing some of the whites and friendly Indians living there. We had not wiped out all the band belonging to the cave; there were six or seven of the young women who had escaped and made their way down to the foot of the precipice, and on into the current of the Salado; they

would be sure to push on to the other "rancheria," of which we
had been told. How they came to escape was this : at the very
first streak of light, or perhaps a short time before, they had been
sent—six young girls and an old woman—to examine a great
" mescal pit " down in the cañon, and determine whether the food
was yet ready for use. The Apaches always preferred to let their
mescal cook for three days, and at the end of that time would pull
out a plug made of the stalk of the plant, which should always be
put into the " pit " or oven, and if the end of that plug is cooked,
the whole mass is cooked. We had smelt the savory odors arising
from the " pit " as we climbed down the face of the cliff, early in
the day. John de Laet describes a mescal heap, or a furnace of
earth covered with hot rocks, upon which the Chichimecs (the
name by which the Spaniards in early times designated all the
wild tribes in the northern part of their dominions in North
America) placed their corn-paste or venison, then other hot
rocks, and finally earth again. This mode of cooking, he says,
was imitated by the Spaniards in New Mexico. (*Lib.* 7, *cap.* 3.)
The Apache-Mojave squaws at the San Carlos Agency still periodically mourn for the death of seventy-six of their people in this
cave, and when I was last among them, they told a strange story
of how one man escaped from our scrutiny, after we had gained
possession of the stronghold.

He had been badly wounded by a bullet in the calf of the left
leg, in the very beginning of the fight, and had lain down behind
one of the great slabs of stone which were resting against the walls ;
as the fight grew hotter and hotter, other wounded Indians sought
shelter close to the same spot, and after a while the corpses of the
slain were piled up there as a sort of a breastwork. When we
removed the dead, it never occurred to any of us to look behind the
stone slabs, and to this fact the Indian owed his salvation. He
could hear the scouts talking, and he knew that we were going to
make a rapid march to reunite with our pack-train and with other
scouting parties. He waited until after we had started out on
the trail, and then made for himself a support for his injured
limb out of a broken lance-staff, and a pair of crutches out of two
others. He crawled or climbed up the wall of the cañon, and
then made his way along the trail to the Tonto Creek, to meet
and to turn back a large band of his tribe who were coming down
to join " Nanni-chaddi. " He saved them from Major Brown,

but it was a case of jumping out of the frying-pan into the fire. They took refuge on the summit of "Turret Butte," a place deemed second only to the Salt River cave in impregnability, and supposed to be endowed with peculiar "medicine" qualities, which would prevent an enemy from gaining possession of it. But here they were surprised by the command of Major George M. Randall, Twenty-third Infantry, and completely wiped out, as will be told on another page.

We got away from the cañon with eighteen captives, women and children, some of them badly wounded ; we might have saved a larger percentage of the whole number found living in the cave at the moment of assault, but we were not provided with medical supplies, bandages, or anything for the care of the sick and wounded. This one item will show how thoroughly out of the world the Department of Arizona was at that time ; it was difficult to get medical officers out there, and the resulting condition of affairs was such an injustice to both officers and men that General Crook left no stone unturned until he had rectified it. The captives were seated upon the Pima ponies left back upon the top of the mountain ; these animals were almost played out ; their feet had been knocked to pieces coming up the rocky pathway, during the darkness of night ; and the cholla cactus still sticking in their legs, showed that they had been driven with such speed, and in such darkness, that they had been unable to pick their way. But they were better than nothing, and were kept in use for the rest of that day. Runners were despatched across the hills to the pack-train, and were told to conduct it to a small spring, well known to our guides, high up on the nose of the Matitzal, where we were all to unite and go into camp.

It was a rest and refreshment sorely needed, after the scrambling, slipping, and sliding over and down loose rocks which had been dignified with the name of marching, during the preceding two days. Our captives were the recipients of every attention that we could give, and appeared to be improving rapidly, and to have regained the good spirits which are normally theirs. Mounted couriers were sent in advance to Camp MacDowell, to let it be known that we were coming in with wounded, and the next morning, early, we set out for that post, following down the course of what was known as Sycamore Creek to the Verde River, which latter we crossed in front of the post.

CHAPTER XI.

THE wounded squaws were forwarded to old Camp Grant,
just as soon as able to travel, and our command remained
for several days in the camp, until joined by other detachments,
when we returned to the Superstition range, this time in considerable strength, the whole force consisting of the companies of
Adams, Montgomery, Hamilton, Taylor, Burns, and Almy—all of
the Fifth Cavalry, with the following additional officers : Lieutenants Rockwell, Schuyler, and Keyes, of the Fifth ; Ross, of the
Twenty-third Infantry ; Bourke, of the Third Cavalry ; and Mr.
James Daily, General Crook's brother-in-law, as volunteer. The
guides, as before, were MacIntosh, Felmer, and Besias, with thirty
Apache scouts, under the leadership of "Esquinosquizn." This
march was simply a repetition of the former ; there was the same
careful attention to details—no fires allowed except when the
light could not be discerned by the lynx-eyed enemy ; no shouting, singing, whistling, lighting of matches, or anything else
which might attract attention. There was the same amount of
night-marching, side scouting to either flank or in advance, the
same careful scrutiny of the minutest sign on the trail. The
presence of the Indian scouts saved the white soldiers a great
deal of extra fatigue, for the performance of which the Apaches
were better qualified. It was one of the fundamental principles
upon which General Crook conducted all his operations, to enlist
as many of the Indians as could be induced to serve as scouts,

because by this means he not only subtracted a considerable element from those in hostility and received hostages, as it were, for the better behavior of his scouts' kinsmen, but he removed from the shoulders of his men an immense amount of arduous and disagreeable work, and kept them fresh for any emergency that might arise. The Apaches were kept constantly out on the flanks, under the white guides, and swept the country of all hostile bands. The white troops followed upon the heels of the Indians, but at a short distance in the rear, as the native scouts were better acquainted with all the tricks of their calling, and familiar with every square acre of the territory. The longer we knew the Apache scouts, the better we liked them. They were wilder and more suspicious than the Pimas and Maricopas, but far more reliable, and endowed with a greater amount of courage and daring. I have never known an officer whose experience entitled his opinion to the slightest consideration, who did not believe as I do on this subject. On this scout Captain Hamilton was compelled to send back his Maricopas as worthless; this was before he joined Brown at MacDowell.

All savages have to undergo certain ceremonies of lustration after returning from the war-path where any of the enemy have been killed. With the Apaches these are baths in the sweat-lodge, accompanied with singing and other rites. With the Pimas and Maricopas these ceremonies are more elaborate, and necessitate a seclusion from the rest of the tribe for many days, fasting, bathing, and singing. The Apache "bunches" all his religious duties at these times, and defers his bathing until he gets home, but the Pima and Maricopa are more punctilious, and resort to the rites of religion the moment a single one, either of their own numbers or of the enemy, has been laid low. For this reason Brown started out from MacDowell with Apaches only.

It was noticed with some concern by all his friends that old Jack Long was beginning to break; the fatigue and exertion which the more juvenile members of the expedition looked upon as normal to the occasion, the night marches, the exposure to the cold and wind and rain and snow, the climbing up and down steep precipices, the excitement, the going without food or water for long periods, were telling visibly upon the representative of an older generation. Hank 'n Yank, Chenoweth, Frank Monach, and Joe Felmer "'lowed th' ole man was off his feed," but it was, in truth, only the summons sent him by Dame Nature that he had overdrawn his account, and was to be in the future bankrupt in health and strength. There was an unaccountable irritability about Jack, a fretfulness at the end of each day's climbing, which spoke more than words could of enfeebled strength and nervous prostration. He found fault with his cook, formerly his pride and boast. "Be-gosh," he remarked one evening, "seems t' me yer a-burnin' everything; next I know, ye 'll be a-burnin' water." There were sarcastic references to the lack of "horse sense" shown by certain unnamed "shave-tail leftenants" in the command—shafts which rebounded unnoticed from the armor of Schuyler and myself, but which did not make us feel any too comfortable while the old veteran was around. Day by day, meal after meal, his cook grew worse, or poor Jack grew no better. Nothing spread upon the canvas would tempt Jack's appetite; he blamed it all on the culinary artist, never dreaming that he alone was at fault, and that his digestion was a thing of the past, and beyond the skill of cook or condiment to revive.

"He ain't a pastry cook," growled Jack, "nor yet a hasty cook, nor a tasty cook, but fur a dog-goned nasty cook, I'll back 'm agin th' hull Pacific Slope." When he heard some of the packers inveighing against Tucson whiskey, Jack's rage rose beyond bounds. "Many a time 'n oft," he said, "Arizona whiskey 's bin plenty good enough fur th' likes o' me; it 's good 's a hoss liniment, 'n it 's good 's a beverage, 'n I've tried it both ways, 'n I know; 'n thet 's more 'n kin be said for this yere dude whiskey they gits in Dilmonico's." There wasn't a drop of stimulant as such, with the whole command, that I knew of, but in my own blankets there was a pint flask filled with rather better stuff than was ordinarily to be obtained, which I had been keeping in case of snake bites or other accidents. It occurred to me to present a good drink of this to Jack, but as I did not like to do this with so many standing around the fire, I approached the blankets upon which Jack was reclining, and asked: "See here, Jack, I want you to try this water; there's something very peculiar about it."

"Thet 's allers th' way with these yere shave-tail leftenants they 's gittin' in th' army now-a-days; allers complainin' about su'thin; water! Lor'! yer orter bin with me when I was minin' up on th' Frazer. Then ye'd a' known what water was * * * Water, be-gosh! why, Major, I'll never forget yer's long's I live"—and in the exuberance of his gratitude, the old man brevetted me two or three grades.

From that on Jack and I were sworn friends; he never levelled the shafts of his sarcasm either at me or my faithful mule, "Malaria." "Malaria" had been born a first-class mule, but a fairy godmother, or some other mysterious cause, had carried the good mule away, and left in its place a lop-eared, mangy specimen, which enjoyed the proud distinction of being considered, without dissent, the meanest mule in the whole Department of Arizona. Not many weeks after that poor old Jack died; he was in camp with one of the commands on the San Carlos, and broke down entirely; in his delirium he saw the beautiful green pastures of the Other Side, shaded by branching oaks; he heard the rippling of pellucid waters, and listened to the gladsome song of merry birds. "Fellers," he said, "it is beautiful over thar; the grass is so green, and the water so cool; I am tired of marchin', 'n I reckon I'll cross over 'n go in camp"—so poor old Jack crossed over to come back no more.

All through the Superstition Mountains, we worked as carefully as we had worked in the more northern portion on our trip to MacDowell, but we met with less success than we had anticipated; on the morning of the 15th of January, after a toilsome night-climb over rough mesas and mountains, we succeeded in crawling upon a small rancheria ere the first rays of the sun had surmounted the eastern horizon; but the occupants were too smart for us and escaped, leaving three dead in our hands and thirteen captives—women and children; we also captured the old chief of the band, who, like his people, seemed to be extremely poor. Three days later we heard loud shouting from a high mountain to the left of the trail we were following. Thinking at first that it was from some hostile parties, Major Brown sent out a detachment of the scouts to run them off. In about half an hour or less a young boy not more than eight years old came down to see the commanding officer, who had halted the column until he could learn what was wanted. The youngster was very much agitated, and trembled violently; he said that he had been sent down to say that his people did not want any more war, but were desirous of making peace. He was given something to eat and tobacco to smoke, and afterwards one of the pack-mules was led up and its "cargo" unloaded so that the cook might give the ambassador a good stomachful of beans always kept cooked in a train. The Apache was very grateful, and after talking with the scouts was much more at his ease. He was presented with an old blouse by one of the officers, and then Major Brown told him that he was too young to represent anybody, but not too young to see for himself that we did not want to harm any people who were willing to behave themselves. He could return in safety to his own people up on the hill, and tell them that they need not be afraid to send in any one they wished to talk for them, but to send in some grown persons. The boy darted up the flanks of the mountain with the agility of a jack rabbit, and was soon lost to view in the undergrowth of scrub oak ; by the time we had ascended the next steep grade there was more shouting, and this time the boy returned with a wrinkled squaw, who was at once ordered back—after the usual feed—one of our people going with her to tell the men of the band that we were not women or babies, and that we could talk business with men only.

This summons brought back a very decrepit antique, who supported his palsied limbs upon one of the long walking-canes so much in use among the Apaches. He too was the recipient of every kindness, but was told firmly that the time for fooling had long since gone by, and that to-day was a much better time for surrendering than to-morrow ; our command would not harm them if they wanted to make peace, but the country was full of scouting parties and at any moment one of these was likely to run in upon them and kill a great many ; the best thing, the safest thing, for them to do was to surrender at once and come with us into Camp Grant. The old chief replied that it was not possible for him to surrender just then and there, because his band had scattered upon learning of our approach, but if we would march straight for Grant he would send out for all his people, gather them together, and catch up with us at the junction of the Gila and San Pedro, and then accompany us to Camp Grant or other point to be agreed upon.

We moved slowly across the mountains, getting to the place of meeting on the day assigned, but there were no Indians, and we all felt that we had been outwitted. The scouts however said,

" Wait and see ! " and sure enough, that evening, the old chief and a small party of his men arrived and had another talk and smoke with Major Brown, who told them that the only thing to do was to see General Crook whose word would determine all questions. Every man in the column was anxious to get back, and long before reveille most of them were up and ready for the word for breakfast and for boots and saddles. There was a feeling that so far as the country south of the Salt River was concerned, the campaign was over ; and though we saw no men, women, or children other than those captured by us on the way, all felt that the surrender would surely take place as agreed upon.

When we started up the dusty valley of the San Pedro not one of the strangers had arrived, but as we drew nigh to the site of the post, it seemed as if from behind clusters of sage brush, giant cactus, palo verde or mesquite, along the trail, first one, then another, then a third Apache would silently join the column with at most the greeting of " Siquisn " (My brother). When we reported to Crook again at the post, whither he had returned from MacDowell, there were one hundred and ten people with us, and the whole business done so quietly that not one-half the command ever knew whether any Apaches had joined us or not. With these Indians General Crook had a long and satisfactory talk, and twenty-six of them enlisted as scouts. From this point I was sent by General Crook to accompany Major Brown in a visit to the celebrated chief of the Chiricahua Apaches, " Cocheis," of which visit I will speak at length later on.

We rejoined the command at the foot of Mount Graham, where General Crook had established the new post of Camp Grant. It offered many inducements which could not well be disregarded in that arid section ; the Graham Mountain, or Sierra Bonita as known to the Mexicans, is well timbered with pine and cedar; has an abundance of pure and cold water, and succulent pasturage; there is excellent building-stone and adobe clay within reach, and nothing that could reasonably be expected is lacking. There were twelve or thirteen companies of cavalry concentrated at the new camp, and all or nearly all these were, within a few days, on the march for the Tonto Basin, to give it another overhauling.

I do not wish to describe the remainder of the campaign in detail ; it offered few features not already presented to my readers; it was rather more unpleasant than the first part, on account of being to a greater extent amid the higher elevations of the Sierra Ancha and the Matitzal and Mogollon, to which the hostiles had retreated for safety. There was deeper snow and much more of it, more climbing and greater heights to attain, severer cold and more discomfort from being unable to find dry fuel. There was still another source of discomfort which should not be overlooked. At that time the peculiar disease known as the epizoötic made its appearance in the United States, and reached Arizona, crippling the resources of the Department in horses and mules; we had to abandon our animals, and take our rations and blankets upon our own backs, and do the best we could. In a very few weeks the good results became manifest, and the enemy showed signs of weakening. The best element in this campaign was the fact that on so many different occasions the Apaches were caught in the very act of raiding, plundering, and killing, and followed up with such fearful retribution. Crook had his forces so disposed that no matter what the Apaches might do or not do, the troops were after them at once, and, guided as we were by scouts from among their own people, escape was impossible. For example, a large band struck the settlements near the town of Wickenburg, and there surprised a small party of young men, named Taylor, recently arrived from England or Wales. All in the party fell victims to the merciless aim of the assailants, who tied two of them to cactus, and proceeded deliberately to fill them with arrows. One of the poor wretches rolled and writhed in agony, breaking off the feathered ends of the arrows, but each time he turned his body, exposing a space not yet wounded, the Apaches shot in another barb. The Indians then robbed the ranchos, stole or killed all the cattle and horses, and struck out across the ragged edge of the great Bradshaw Mountain, then over into the Tonto Basin. Having twenty-four hours the start of the troops, they felt safe in their expedition, but they were followed by Wesendorf, of the First Cavalry; by Rice, of the Twenty-third Infantry; by Almy, Watts, and myself; by Woodson, of the Fifth; and lastly by Randall, of the Twenty-third, who was successful in running them to earth in the stronghold on the summit of Turret Butte, where they fancied that no enemy would dare follow.

Randall made his men crawl up the face of the mountain on

hands and feet, to avoid all danger of making noise by the rattling of stones, and shortly after midnight had the satisfaction
of seeing the glimmer of fires amid the rocks scattered about on
the summit. He waited patiently until dawn, and then led the
charge, the Apaches being so panic-stricken that numbers of the
warriors jumped down the precipice and were dashed to death.
This and the action in the cave in the Salt River Cañon were
the two affairs which broke the spirit of the Apache nation ; they
resembled each other in catching raiders just in from attacks
upon the white settlements or those of friendly tribes, in surprising bands in strongholds which for generations had been invested
with the attribute of impregnability, and in inflicting great loss
with comparatively small waste of blood to ourselves.

In singling out these two incidents I, of course, do not wish
in the slightest degree to seem to disparage the gallant work performed by the other officers engaged, each and all of whom are
entitled to as much credit as either Randall or Brown for earnest,
intelligent service, gallantry in trying situations, and cheerful
acceptance of the most annoying discomforts. No army in the
world ever accomplished more with the same resources than did
the little brigade which solved the Apache problem under Crook
in the early seventies. There were no supplies of food beyond
the simplest components of the ration and an occasional can of
some such luxury as tomatoes or peaches ; no Pullman cars to
transport officers in ease and comfort to the scene of hostilities ; no
telegraph to herald to the world the achievements of each day.
There was the satisfaction of duty well performed, and of knowing
that a fierce, indomitable people who had been a scourge in the history of two great nations had been humbled, made to sue for peace,
and adopt to a very considerable extent the ways of civilization.

The old settlers in both northern and southern Arizona still
speak in terms of cordial appreciation of the services of officers
like Hall, Taylor, Burns, Almy, Thomas, Rockwell, Price, Park-
hurst, Michler, Adam, Woodson, Hamilton, Babcock, Schuyler,
and Watts, all of the Fifth Cavalry ; Ross, Reilley, Sherwood,
Theller and Major Miles, of the Twenty-first Infantry ; Gar-
vey, Bomus, Carr, Grant, Bernard, Brodie, Vail, Wessendorf,
McGregor, Hein, Winters, Harris, Sanford, and others, of the
First Cavalry ; Randall, Manning, Rice, and others, of the
Twenty-third Infantry ; Gerald Russell, Morton, Crawford,

ford, Cushing, Cradlebaugh, of the Third Cavalry ; Byrne, of the Twelfth Infantry, and many others who during this campaign, or immediately preceding it, had rendered themselves conspicuous by most efficient service.   The army of the United States has no reason to be ashamed of the men who wore its uniform during the dark and troubled period of Arizona's history ; they were grand men ; they had their faults as many other people have, but they never flinched from danger or privation.   I do not mean to say that I have given a complete list ; it is probable that many very distinguished names have been omitted, for which I apologise now by saying that I am not writing a history, but rather a series of reminiscences of those old border days.   I would not intentionally fail in paying tribute to any brave and deserving comrade, but find it beyond my power to enumerate all.

There was one class of officers who were entitled to all the praise they received and much more besides, and that class was the surgeons, who never flagged in their attentions to sick and wounded, whether soldier or officer, American, Mexican, or Apache captive, by night or by day.   Among these the names of Stirling, Porter, Matthews, Girard, O'Brien, Warren E. Day, Steiger, Charles Smart, and Calvin Dewitt will naturally present themselves to the mind of any one familiar with the work then going on, and with them should be associated those of the guides, both red and white, to whose fidelity, courage, and skill we owed so much.

The names of Mason McCoy, Edward Clark, Archie MacIntosh, Al Spears, C. E. Cooley, Joe Felmer, Al Seiber, Dan O'Leary, Lew Elliott, Antonio Besias, Jose De Leon, Maria Jilda Grijalba, Victor Ruiz, Manuel Duran, Frank Cahill, Willard Rice, Oscar Hutton, Bob Whitney, John B. Townsend, Tom Moore, Jim O'Neal, Jack Long, Hank 'n Yank (Hewitt and Bartlett), Frank Monach, Harry Hawes, Charlie Hopkins, and many other scouts, guides, and packers of that onerous, dangerous, and crushing campaign, should be inscribed on the brightest page in the annals of Arizona, and locked up in her archives that future generations might do them honor.   The great value of the services rendered by the Apache scouts " Alchesay," " Jim," " Elsatsoosn," " Machol," " Blanquet," " Chiquito," " Kelsay," " Kasoha," " Nantaje," " Nannasaddi," was fittingly acknowledged by General Crook in the orders issued at the time of the surrender of the Apaches, which took place soon after.

Many enlisted men rendered service of a most important and efficient character, which was also acknowledged at the same time and by the same medium ; but, on account of lack of space, it is impossible for me to mention them all ; conspicuous in the list are the names of Buford, Turpin, Von Medern, Allen, Barrett, Heineman, Stanley, Orr, Lanahan, Stauffer, Hyde, and Hooker.

In the first week of April, a deputation from the hostile bands reached Camp Verde, and expressed a desire to make peace ; they were told to return for the head chiefs, with whom General Crook would talk at that point. Signal fires were at once set on all the hills, scouts sent to all places where they would be likely to meet with any of the detachments in the Tonto Basin or the Mogollon, and all possible measures taken to prevent any further hostilities, until it should be seen whether or not the enemy were in earnest in professions of peace.

Lieutenant Jacob Almy, Fifth Cavalry, with whose command I was on duty, scoured the northwest portion of the Tonto Basin, and met with about the same experiences as the other detachments ; but I wish to tell that at one of our camping-places, on the upper Verde, we found a ruined building of limestone, laid in adobe, which had once been of two or three stories in height, the corner still standing being not less than twenty-five feet above the ground, with portions of rafters of cottonwood, badly decayed, still in place. It was the opinion of both Almy and myself, after a careful examination, that it was of Spanish and not of Indian origin, and that it had served as a depot for some of the early expeditions entering this country ; it would have been in the line of advance of Coronado upon Cibola, and I then thought and still think that it was most probably connected with his great expedition which passed across Arizona in 1541. All this is conjecture, but not a very violent one ; Coronado is known to have gone to " Chichilticale," supposed to have been the " Casa Grande " on the Gila ; if so, his safest, easiest, best supplied, and most natural line of march would have been up the valley of the Verde near the head of which this ruin stands.

Another incident was the death of one of our packers, Presiliano Monje, a very amiable man, who had made friends of all our party. He had caught a bad cold in the deep snows on the summit of the Matitzal Range, and this developed into an attack of pneumonia ; there was no medical officer with our small command, and all we could do was based upon ignorance and inexperience, no matter how much we might desire to help him. Almy hoped that upon descending from the high lands into the warm valley of the Verde, the change would be beneficial to our patient; but he was either too far gone or too weak to respond, and the only thing left for us to do was to go into bivouac and try the effect of rest and quiet. For two days we had carried Monje in a chair made of mescal stalks strapped to the saddle, but he was by this time entirely too weak to sit up, and we were all apprehensive of the worst. It was a trifle after midnight, on the morning of the 23d of March, 1873, that "the change" came, and we saw that it was a matter of minutes only until we should have a death in our camp; he died before dawn and was buried immediately after sunrise, under the shadow of a graceful cottonwood, alongside of two pretty springs whose babbling waters flowed in unison with the music of the birds. In Monje's honor we named the cañon "Dead Man's Cañon," and as such it is known to this day.

At Camp Verde we found assembled nearly all of Crook's command, and a dirtier, greasier, more uncouth-looking set of officers and men it would be hard to encounter anywhere. Dust, soot, rain, and grime had made their impress upon the canvas suits which each had donned, and with hair uncut for months and beards growing with straggling growth all over the face, there was not one of the party who would venture to pose as an Adonis ; but all were happy, because the campaign had resulted in the unconditional surrender of the Apaches and we were now to see the reward of our hard work. On the 6th of April, 1873, the Apache-Mojave chief "Cha-lipun" (called "Charley Pan" by the Americans), with over three hundred of his followers, made his unconditional submission to General Crook ; they represented twenty-three hundred of the hostiles.

General Crook sat on the porch of Colonel Coppinger's quarters and told the interpreters that he was ready to hear what the Indians had to say, but he did not wish too much talk. "Cha-lipun" said that he had come in, as the representative of all the Apaches, to say that they wanted to surrender because General Crook had "too many cartridges of copper" ("demasiadas cartuchos de cobre"). They had never been afraid of the Amer-

icans alone, but now that their own people were fighting against
them they did not know what to do ; they could not go to sleep
at night, because they feared to be surrounded before daybreak ;
they could not hunt—the noise of their guns would attract the
troops ; they could not cook mescal or anything else, because the
flame and smoke would draw down the soldiers; they could not
live in the valleys—there were too many soldiers ; they had retreated to the mountain tops, thinking to hide in the snow until
the soldiers went home, but the scouts found them out and the
soldiers followed them.   They wanted to make peace, and to be
at terms of good-will with the whites.

Crook took "Cha-lipun" by the hand, and told him that, if he
would promise to live at peace and stop killing people, he would
be the best friend he ever had.   Not one of the Apaches had
been killed except through his own folly ; they had refused to
listen to the messengers sent out asking them to come in ; and
consequently there had been nothing else to do but to go out
and kill them until they changed their minds.   It was of no use to
talk about who began this war ; there were bad men among all
peoples ; there were bad Mexicans, as there were bad Americans
and bad Apaches ; our duty was to end wars and establish peace,
and not to talk about what was past and gone.   The Apaches must
make this peace not for a day or a week, but for all time ; not
with the Americans alone, but with the Mexicans as well ; and
not alone with the Americans and Mexicans, but with all the
other Indian tribes.   They must not take upon themselves the
redress of grievances, but report to the military officer upon their
reservation, who would see that their wrongs were righted.   They
should remain upon the reservation, and not leave without written passes ; whenever the commanding officer wished to ascertain
the presence of themselves or any of the bands upon the reservation, they should appear at the place appointed to be counted.
So long as any bad Indians remained out in the mountains, the
reservation Indians should wear tags attached to the neck, or in
some other conspicuous place, upon which tags should be inscribed
their number, letter of band, and other means of identification.
They should not cut off the noses of their wives when they
became jealous of them.   They should not be told anything that
was not exactly true.   They should be fully protected in all respects while on the reservation.   They should be treated exactly

as white men were treated ; there should be no unjust punishments. They must work like white men ; a market would be found for all they could raise, and the money should be paid to themselves and not to middlemen. They should begin work immediately ; idleness was the source of all evils, and work was the only cure. They should preserve order among themselves ; for this purpose a number would be enlisted as scouts, and made to do duty in keeping the peace ; they should arrest and confine all drunkards, thieves, and other offenders.

CHAPTER XII.

THERE was no time lost in putting the Apaches to work. As soon as the rest of the band had come in, which was in less than a week, the Apaches were compelled to begin getting out an irrigating ditch, under the superintendence of Colonel Julius W. Mason, Fifth Cavalry, an officer of much previous experience in engineering. Their reservation was established some miles above the post, and the immediate charge of the savages was intrusted to Lieutenant Walter S. Schuyler, Fifth Cavalry, who manifested a wonderful aptitude for the delicate duties of his extra-military position. There were absolutely no tools on hand belonging to the Indian Bureau, and for that matter no medicines, and only the scantiest supplies, but Crook was determined that work should be begun without the delay of a day. He wanted to get the savages interested in something else besides tales of the war-path, and to make them feel as soon as possible the pride of ownership, in which he was a firm believer.

According to his idea, the moment an Indian began to see the fruits of his industry rising above the ground, and knew that there was a ready cash market awaiting him for all he had to sell, he would see that " peace hath her victories no less renowned than war." He had been going on the war-path, killing and rob-bing the whites, not so much because his forefathers had been doing it before him, but because it was the road to wealth, to fame, to prominence and distinction in the tribe. Make the

Apache or any other Indian see that the moment he went on the war-path two white men would go out also ; and make him see that patient industry produces wealth, fame, and distinction of a much more permanent and a securer kind than those derived from a state of war, and the Indian would acquiesce gladly in the change. But neither red man nor white would submit peaceably to any change in his mode of life which was not apparently to his advantage.

The way the great irrigating ditch at Camp Verde was dug was this. All the Apaches were made to camp along the line of the proposed canal, each band under its own chiefs. Everything in the shape of a tool which could be found at the military post of Camp Verde or in those of Whipple and Hualpai was sent down to Mason. There were quantities of old and worn-out spades, shovels, picks, hatchets, axes, hammers, files, rasps, and camp kettles awaiting the action of an inspector prior to being thrown away and dropped from the returns as " worn out in service." With these and with sticks hardened in the fire, the Apaches dug a ditch five miles long, and of an average cross-section of four feet wide by three deep, although there were places where the width of the upper line was more than five feet, and that of the bottom four, with a depth of more than five. The men did the excavating ; the women carried off the earth in the conical baskets which they make of wicker-work. As soon as the ditch was ready, General Crook took some of the chiefs up to his headquarters at Fort Whipple, and there had them meet deputations from all the other tribes living within the territory of Arizona, with whom they had been at war—the Pimas, Papagoes, Maricopas, Yumas, Cocopahs, Hualpais, Mojaves, Chimahuevis—and with them peace was also formally made.

Mason and Schuyler labored assiduously with the Apaches, and soon had not less than fifty-seven acres of land planted with melons and other garden truck, of which the Indians are fond, and every preparation made for planting corn and barley on a large scale. A large water-wheel was constructed out of packing-boxes, and at a cost to the Government, including all labor and material, of not quite thirty-six dollars. The prospects of the Apaches looked especially bright, and there was hope that they might soon be self-sustaining ; but it was not to be. A " ring " of Federal officials, contractors, and others was formed in Tucson, which exerted great influence in the national capital, and succeeded in securing the issue of peremptory orders that the Apaches should leave at once for the mouth of the sickly San Carlos, there to be herded with the other tribes. It was an outrageous proceeding, one for which I should still blush had I not long since gotten over blushing for anything that the United States Government did in Indian matters. The Apaches had been very happy at the Verde, and seemed perfectly satisfied with their new surroundings. There had been some sickness, occasioned by their using too freely the highly concentrated foods of civilization, to which they had never been accustomed ; but, aside from that, they themselves said that their general condition had never been so good.

The move did not take place until the winter following, when the Indians flatly refused to follow the special agent sent out by the Indian Bureau, not being acquainted with him, but did consent to go with Lieutenant George O. Eaton, Fifth Cavalry, who has long since resigned from the army, and is now, I think, Surveyor-General of Montana. At Fort Apache the Indians were placed under the charge of Major George M. Randall, Twenty-third Infantry, assisted by Lieutenant Rice, of the same regiment. This portion of the Apache tribe is of unusual intelligence, and the progress made was exceptionally rapid. Another large body had been congregated at the mouth of the San Carlos, representing those formerly at old Camp Grant, to which, as we have seen, were added the Apache-Mojaves from the Verde. The Apache-Mojave and the Apache-Yuma belonged to one stock, and the Apache or Tinneh to another. They speak different languages, and although their habits of life are almost identical, there is sufficient divergence to admit of the entrance of the usual jealousies and bickerings bound to arise when two strange, illiterate tribes are brought in enforced contact.

The strong hand and patient will of Major J. B. Babcock ruled the situation at this point ; he was the man for the place, and performed his duties in a manner remarkable for its delicate appreciation of the nature of the Indians, tact in allaying their suspicions, gentle firmness in bringing them to see that the new way was the better, the only way. The path of the military officers was not strewn with roses ; the Apaches showed a willingness to conform to the new order of things, but at times failed to apprehend all that was required of them, at others showed an inclination to backslide.

Crook's plan was laid down in one line in his instructions to officers in charge of reservations : " Treat them as children in *ignorance*, not in *innocence*." His great principle of life was, " The greatest of these is charity." He did not believe, and he did not teach, that an Indian could slough off the old skin in a week or a month ; he knew and he indicated that there might be expected a return of the desire for the old wild life, with its absolute freedom from all restraint, its old familiar food, and all its attendant joys, such as they were. To conquer this as much as possible, he wanted to let the Indians at times cut and roast mescal, gather grass seeds and other diet of that kind, and, where it could be done without risk, go out on hunts after antelope and deer. It could not be expected that all the tribe should wish to accept the manner of life of the whites ; there would surely be many who would prefer the old order of things, and who would work covertly for its restitution. Such men were to be singled out, watched, and their schemes nipped in the bud.

There were outbreaks, attempted outbreaks, and rumors of outbreaks at Verde, Apache, and at the San Carlos, with all the attendant excitement and worry. At or near the Verde, in the " Red Rock country," and in the difficult brakes of the "Hell" and " Rattlesnake" cañons issuing out of the San Francisco Peak, some of the Apache-Mojaves who had slipped back from the party so peremptorily ordered to the San Carlos had secreted themselves and begun to give trouble. They were taken in hand by Schuyler, Seiber, and, at a later date, by Captain Charles King, the last-named being dangerously wounded by them at the " Sunset Pass." At the San Carlos Agency there were disputes of various kinds springing up among the tribes, and worse than that a very acrimonious condition of feeling between the two men who claimed to represent the Interior Department. As a sequel to this, my dear friend and former commanding officer, Lieutenant Jacob Almy, lost his life.

Notwithstanding the chastisement inflicted upon the Apaches, some of the minor chiefs, who had still a record to make, preferred to seclude themselves in the cañons and cliffs, and defy the powers of the general government. It was a source of pride to know that they were talked about by the squaws and children upon the reserve, as men whom the whites had not been able to capture or reduce. Towards these men, Crook was patient to a wonderful degree, thinking that reason would assert itself after a time, and that, either of their own motion, or through the persuasion of friends, they would find their way into the agencies.

The ostensible reason for the absence of these men was their objection to the system of "tagging" in use at the agencies, which General Crook had introduced for the better protection of the Indians, as well as to enable the commanding officers to tell at a moment's notice just where each and every one of the males capable of bearing arms was to be found. These tags were of various shapes, but all small and convenient in size; there were crosses, crescents, circles, diamonds, squares, triangles, etc., each specifying a particular band, and each with the number of its owner punched upon it. If a scouting party found Apaches away from the vicinity of the agencies, they would make them give an account of themselves, and if the pass shown did not correspond with the tags worn, then there was room for suspicion that the tags had been obtained from some of the Agency Indians in gambling—in the games of "Con Quien," "Tze-chis," "Mush-ka"—to which the Apaches were passionately addicted, and in which they would play away the clothes on their backs when they had any. Word was sent to the Indians of whom I am writing to come in and avoid trouble, and influences of all kinds were brought to bear upon the squaws with them—there were only a few—to leave the mountains, and return to their relatives at the San Carlos. The principal chiefs were gradually made to see that they were responsible for this condition of affairs, and that they should compel these outlaws to obey the orders which had been issued for the control of the whole tribe. So long as they killed no one the troops and Apache scouts would not be sent out against them; they should be given ample opportunity for deciding; but it might be well for them to decide quickly, as in case of trouble arising at San Carlos, the whole tribe would be held responsible for the acts of these few. One of them was named "Chuntz," another "Chaundezi," and another "Clibicli;" there were more in the party, but the other names have temporarily escaped my memory. The meaning of the first word I do not know; the second means "Long Ear," and is the Apache term for mule; the third I do not know, but it has something to do with horse, the first syllable meaning horse, and the whole word, I believe, means "the horse that is tied." They lived in the cañon of the Gila, and would often slip in by night to see their relatives at the agency.

One night there was an awful time at San Carlos ; a train of wagons laden with supplies for Camp Apache had halted there, and some of the teamsters let the Apaches, among whom were the bad lot under Chuntz, have a great deal of vile whiskey. All hands got gloriously drunk, and when the teamsters refused to let their red-skinned friends have any more of the poisonous stuff the Apaches killed them. If it could only happen so that every man who sold whiskey to an Indian should be killed before sundown, it would be one of the most glorious things for the far western country. In the present case, innocent people were hurt, as they always are ; and General Crook informed the chiefs that he looked to them to put a prompt termination to such excesses, and that if they did not he would take a hand himself. With that he returned to headquarters. The chiefs sent out spies, definitely placed the outlaws, who had been in the habit of changing their lodging or hiding spots with great frequency, and then arranged for their capture and delivery to the military authorities. They were surprised, summoned to surrender, refused, and attempted to fight, but were all killed ; and as the Apaches knew no other mode of proving that they had killed them, and as they could not carry in the whole body of each one, they cut off the heads and brought them to San Carlos, in a sack, and dumped them out on the little parade in front of the commanding officer's tent.

The Apaches of Arizona were now a conquered tribe, and, as Crook well expressed the situation in a General Order, his troops had terminated a campaign which had lasted from the days of Cortés. The view entertained of the work performed in Arizona by those in authority may be summed up in the orders issued by General Schofield, at that date in command of the Military Division of the Pacific :

[*General Orders No. 7.*]

HEADQUARTERS MILITARY DIVISION OF THE PACIFIC,
SAN FRANCISCO, CAL., April 28, 1873.

To Brevet Major-General George Crook, commanding the Department of Arizona, and to his gallant troops, for the extraordinary service they have rendered in the late campaign against the Apache Indians, the Division Commander extends his thanks and his congratulations upon their brilliant successes. They have merited the gratitude of the nation.

By order of MAJOR-GENERAL SCHOFIELD.

(Signed) J. C. KELTON,
Assistant Adjutant-General.

Randall and Babcock persevered in their work, and soon a change had appeared in the demeanor of the wild Apaches ; at San Carlos there grew up a village of neatly made brush huts, arranged in rectilinear streets, carefully swept each morning, while the huts themselves were clean as pie-crust, the men and women no longer sleeping on the bare ground, but in bunks made of saplings, and elevated a foot or more above the floor ; on these, blankets were neatly piled. The scouts retained in service as a police force were quietly given to understand that they must be models of cleanliness and good order as well as of obedience to law. The squaws were encouraged to pay attention to dress, and especially to keep their hair clean and brushed. No abuse of a squaw was allowed, no matter what the excuse might be. One of the most prominent men of the Hualpai tribe—"Qui-ua-than-yeva"—was sentenced to a year's imprisonment because he persisted in cutting off the nose of one of his wives. This fearful custom finally yielded, and there are now many people in the Apache tribe itself who have never seen a poor woman thus disfigured and humiliated.

Crook's promise to provide a ready cash market for everything the Apaches could raise was nobly kept. To begin with, the enlistment of a force of scouts who were paid the same salary as white soldiers, and at the same periods with them, introduced among the Apaches a small, but efficient, working capital. Unaccustomed to money, the men, after receiving their first pay, spent much of it foolishly for candy and other trivial things. Nothing was said about that ; they were to be made to understand that the money paid them was their own to spend or to save as they pleased, and to supply as much enjoyment as they could extract from it. But, immediately after pay-day, General Crook went among the Apaches on the several reservations and made inquiries of each one of the principal chiefs what results had come to their wives and families from this new source of wealth. He explained that money could be made to grow just as an acorn would grow into the oak; that by spending it foolishly, the Apaches treated it just as they did the acorn which they trod under foot; but by investing their money in California horses and sheep, they would be gaining more money all the time they slept, and by the time their children had attained maturity the hills would be dotted with herds of horses and flocks of sheep. Then they would be rich like the white men ; then they could travel about and see the world ; then they would not be dependent upon the Great Father for supplies, but would have for themselves and their families all the food they could eat, and would have much to sell.

The Apaches did send into Southern California and bought horses and sheep as suggested, and they would now be self-supporting had the good management of General Crook not been ruthlessly sacrificed and destroyed.   Why it is that the Apache, living as he does on a reservation offering all proper facilities for the purpose, is not raising his own meat, is one of the conundrums which cannot be answered by any one of common sense.   The influences against it are too strong : once let the Indian be made self-supporting, and what will become of the gentle contractor ?

Some slight advance has been made in this direction during the past twenty years, but it has been ridiculously slight in comparison with what it should have been.   In an examination which General Crook made into the matter in 1884 it was found that there were several herds of cattle among the Indians, one herd that I saw numbering 384 head.   It was cared for and herded in proper manner ; and surely if the Apaches can do that much in one, or two, or a dozen cases, they can do it in all with anything like proper encouragement.   The proper encouragement of which I speak is "the ready cash market" promised by General Crook, and by means of which he effected so much.

In every band of aborigines, as in every community of whites, or of blacks, or of Chinese, there are to be found men and women who are desirous of improving the condition of themselves and families ; and alongside of them are others who care for nothing but their daily bread, and are not particularly careful how they get that so that they get it.   There should be a weeding out of the progressive from the non-progressive element, and by no manner of means can it be done so effectually as by buying from the industrious all that they can sell to the Government for the support of their own people. There should be inserted in every appropriation bill for the support of the army or of the Indians the provision that anything and everything called for under a contract for supplies, which the Indians on a reservation or in the vicinity of a military post can supply, for the use of the troops or for the consumption of the tribe, under treaty stipulations, shall be bought of the individual Indians raising it and at a cash price not less than the price at which the contract has been awarded. For example, because it is necessary to elucidate the simplest propositions in regard to the Indians, if the chief "A" has, by industry and thrift, gathered together a herd of one hundred cattle, all of the increase that he may wish to sell should be bought from him ; he will at once comprehend that work has its own reward, and a very prompt and satisfactory one. He has his original numbers, and he has a snug sum of money too ; he buys more cattle, he sees that he is becoming a person of increased importance, not only in the eyes of his own people but in that of the white men too ; he encourages his sons and all his relatives to do the same as he has done, confident that their toil will not go unrewarded.

Our method has been somewhat different from that. Just as soon as a few of the more progressive people begin to accumulate a trifle of property, to raise sheep, to cultivate patches of soil and raise scanty crops, the agent sends in the usual glowing report of the occurrence, and to the mind of the average man and woman in the East it looks as if all the tribe were on the highway to prosperity, and the first thing that Congress does is to curtail the appropriations. Next, we hear of " disaffection," the tribe is reported as " surly and threatening," and we are told that the " Indians are killing their cattle." But, whether they go to war or quietly starve on the reservation effects no change in the system ; all supplies are bought of a contractor as before, and the red man is no better off, or scarcely any better off, after twenty years of peace, than he was when he surrendered. The amount of beef contracted for during the present year—1891—for the Apaches at Camp Apache and San Carlos, according to the *Southwestern Stockman* (Wilcox, Arizona), was not quite two million pounds, divided as follows : eight hundred thousand pounds for the Indians at San Carlos, on the contract of John H. Norton, and an additional five hundred thousand pounds for the same people on the contract of the Chiricahua Cattle Company; and five hundred thousand pounds for the Indians at Fort Apache, on the contract of John H. Norton. Both of the above contracting parties are known to me as reliable and trustworthy; I am not finding fault with them for getting a good, fat contract; but I do find fault with a system which keeps the Indian a savage, and does not stimulate him to work for his own support.

At one time an epidemic of scarlet fever broke out among the children on the Apache reservation, and numbers were carried off. Indians are prone to sacrifice property at the time of death of relations, and, under the advice of their "Medicine Men," slaughtered altogether nearly two thousand sheep, which they had purchased with their own money or which represented the increase from the original flock. Crook bought from the Apaches all the hay they would cut, and had the Quartermaster pay cash for it; every pound of hay, every stick of wood, and no small portion of the corn used by the military at Camp Apache and San Carlos were purchased from the Apaches as individuals, and not from contractors or from tribes. The contractors had been in the habit of employing the Apaches to do this work for them, paying a reduced scale of remuneration and often in store goods, so that by the Crook method the Indian received from two to three times as much as under the former system, and this to the great advantage of Arizona, because the Indian belongs to the Territory of Arizona, and will stay there and buy what he needs from her people, but the contractor has gone out to make money, remains until he accomplishes his object, and then returns to some congenial spot where his money will do most good for himself. Of the contractors who made money in Arizona twenty years ago not one remained there : all went into San Francisco or some other large city, there to enjoy their accumulations. I am introducing this subject now because it will save repetition, and will explain to the average reader why it was that the man who did so much to reduce to submission the worst tribes this country has ever known, and who thought of nothing but the performance of duty and the establishment of a permanent and honorable peace, based—to quote his own language—"upon an exact and even-handed justice to red men and to white alike," should have been made the target for the malevolence and the rancor of every man in the slightest degree interested in the perpetuation of the contract system and in keeping the aborigine in bondage.

To sum up in one paragraph, General Crook believed that the American Indian was a human being, gifted with the same god-like apprehension as the white man, and like him inspired by noble impulses, ambition for progress and advancement, but subject to the same infirmities, beset with the same or even greater temptations, struggling under the disadvantages of an inherited ignorance, which had the double effect of making him doubt his own powers in the struggle for the new life and suspicious of the truthfulness and honesty of the advocates of all innovations. The American savage has grown up as a member of a tribe, or rather of a clan within a tribe ; all his actions have been made to conform to the opinions of his fellows as enunciated in the clan councils or in those of the tribe.

It is idle to talk of de-tribalizing the Indian until we are ready to assure him that his new life is the better one. By the Crook method of dealing with the savage he was, at the outset, de-tribalized without knowing it ; he was individualized and made the better able to enter into the civilization of the Caucasian, which is an individualized civilization. As a scout, the Apache was enlisted as an individual ; he was made responsible individually for all that he did or did not. He was paid as an individual. If he cut grass, he, and not his tribe or clan, got the money ; if he split fuel, the same rule obtained ; and so with every grain of corn or barley which he planted. If he did wrong, he was hunted down as an individual until the scouts got him and put him in the guard-house. If his friends did wrong, the troops did not rush down upon him and his family and chastise them for the wrongs of others ; he was asked to aid in the work of ferreting out and apprehending the delinquent ; and after he had been brought in a jury of the Apaches themselves deliberated upon the case and never failed in judgment, except on the side of severity.

There were two cases of chance-medley coming under my own observation, in both of which the punishment awarded by the Apache juries was much more severe than would have been given by a white jury. In the first case, the man supposed to have done the killing was sentenced to ten years' hard labor ; in the other, to three. A white culprit was at the same time sentenced in Tucson for almost the same offence to one year's confinement in jail. Indians take to trials by jury as naturally as ducks take to water. Trial by jury is not a system of civilized people; it is the survival of the old trial by clan, the rudimentary justice known to all tribes in the most savage state.

General Crook believed that the Indian should be made self-supporting, not by preaching at him the merits of labor and the grandeur of toiling in the sun, but by making him see that every drop of honest sweat meant a penny in his pocket. It was idle to expect that the Indian should understand how to work intelligently in the very beginning; he represented centuries of one kind of life, and the Caucasian the slow evolution of centuries under different conditions and in directions diametrically opposite. The two races could not, naturally, understand each other perfectly, and therefore to prevent mistakes and the doing of very grievous injustice to the inferior, it was the duty and to the interest of the superior race to examine into and understand the mental workings of the inferior.

The American Indian, born free as the eagle, would not tolerate restraint, would not brook injustice; therefore, the restraint imposed must be manifestly for his benefit, and the government to which he was subjected must be eminently one of kindness, mercy, and absolute justice, without necessarily degenerating into weakness. The American Indian despises a liar. The American Indian is the most generous of mortals : at all his dances and feasts the widow and the orphan are the first to be remembered. Therefore, when he meets with an agent who is " on the make," that agent's influence goes below zero at once; and when he enters the trader's store and finds that he is charged three dollars and a half for a miserable wool hat, which, during his last trip to Washington, Albuquerque, Omaha, or Santa Fé, as the case may be, he has seen offered for a quarter, he feels that there is something wrong, and he does not like it any too well. For that reason Crook believed that the Indians should be encouraged to do their own trading and to set up their own stores. He was not shaken in this conviction when he found agents interested in the stores on the reservations, a fact well understood by the Apaches as well as by himself. It was a very touching matter at the San Carlos, a few years ago, to see the then agent counting the proceeds of the weekly sales made by his son-in-law—the Indian trader.

At the date of the reduction of the Apaches, the success of the Government schools was not clearly established, so that the subject of Indian instruction was not then discussed except theoretically. General Crook was always a firm believer in the education of the American Indian ; not in the education of a handful of boys and girls sent to remote localities, and there inoculated with new ideas and deprived of the old ones upon which they would have to depend for getting a livelihood ; but in the education of the younger generation as a generation. Had the people of the United States taken the young generation of Sioux and Cheyennes in 1866, and educated them in accordance with the terms of the treaty, there would not have been any trouble since. The children should not be torn away from the parents to whom they are a joy and a consolation, just as truly as they are to white parents ; they should be educated within the limits of the reservation so that the old folks from time to time could get to see them and note their progress. As they advanced in years, the better qualified could be sent on to Carlisle and Hampton, and places of that grade. The training of the Indian boy or girl should be largely industrial, but as much as possible in the line of previous acquirement and future application. Thus, the Navajos, who have made such advances as weavers and knitters, might well be instructed in that line of progress, as might the Zunis, Moquis, and other Pueblos.

After the Indian had returned to his reservation, it was the duty of the Government to provide him with work in his trade, whatever it might be, to the exclusion of the agency hanger-on. Why should boys be trained as carpenters and painters, and then see such work done by white men at the agency, while they were forced to remain idle ? This complaint was made by one of the boys at San Carlos. Why should Apache, Sioux, or Cheyenne children who have exerted themselves to learn our language, be left unemployed, while the work of interpretation is done, and never done any too well, at the agencies by white men ? Does it not seem a matter of justice and common sense to fill all such positions, as fast as the same can be done without injustice to faithful incumbents under the present system, by young men trained in our ideas and affiliated to our ways ? Let all watchmen and guardians of public stores—all the policemen on the reserves —be natives; let all hauling of supplies be done by the Indians themselves, and let them be paid the full contract rate if they are able to haul no more than a portion of the supplies intended for their use.

Some of these ideas have already been adopted, in part, by the Indian Bureau, and with such success that there is more than a reasonable expectancy that the full series might be considered and adopted with the best results.   Instruct the young women in the rudiments of housekeeping, as already outlined.   Provide the reservations with saw-mills and grist-mills, and let the Indians saw their own planks and grind their own meal and flour. This plan has been urged by the Apaches so persistently during recent years that it would seem not unreasonable to make the experiment on some of the reservations.   Encourage them to raise chickens and to sell eggs; it is an industry for which they are well fitted, and the profits though small would still be profits, and one drop more in the rivulet of gain to wean them from idleness, ignorance, and the war-path.   Let any man who desires to leave his reservation and hunt for work, do so; give him a pass; if he abuses the privilege by getting drunk or begging, do not give him another.   I have known many Indians who have worked away from their own people and always with the most decided benefit.   They did not always return, but when they did they did not believe in the prophecies of the "Medicine Men," or listen to the boasts of those who still long for the war-path.

The notion that the American Indian will not work is a fallacious one; he will work just as the white man will—when it is to his advantage to do so.   The adobes in the military post of Fort Wingate, New Mexico, were all made by Navajo Indians, the brothers of the Apaches.   The same tribe did no small amount of work on the grading of the Atlantic and Pacific Railroad where it passes across their country.   The American Indian is a slave to drink where he can get it, and he is rarely without a supply from white sources; he is a slave to the passion of gaming; and he is a slave to his superstitions, which make the "Medicine Men" the power they are in tribal affairs as well as in those relating more strictly to the clan and family.   These are the three stumbling-blocks in the pathway of the Indian's advancement;

how to remove them is a most serious problem.   The Indian is not the only one in our country who stumbles from the same cause ; we must learn to be patient with him, but merciless toward all malefactors caught selling intoxicating liquors to red men living in the tribal relation.   Gambling and superstition will be eradicated in time by the same modifying influences which have wrought changes among the Caucasian nations ; education will afford additional modes of killing time, and be the means of exposing the puerility of the pretensions of the prophets.

CHAPTER XIII.

IN the fall and winter of 1874, General Crook made a final tour of examination of his department and the Indian tribes therein. He found a most satisfactory condition of affairs on the Apache reservation, with the Indians working and in the best of spirits. On this trip he included the villages of the Moquis living in houses of rock on perpendicular mesas of sandstone, surrounded by dunes or "medanos" of sand, on the northern side of the Colorado Chiquito. The Apaches who had come in from the war-path had admitted that a great part of the arms and ammunition coming into their hands had been obtained in trade with the Moquis, who in turn had purchased from the Mormons or Utes. Crook passed some eight or ten days among the Moquis during the season when the peaches were lusciously ripe and being gathered by the squaws and children. These peach orchards, with their flocks of sheep and goats, are evidences of the earnest work among these Moquis of the Franciscan friars during the last years of the sixteenth and the earlier ones of the seventeenth centuries. Crook let the Moquis know that he did not intend to punish them for what might have been the fault of their ignorance, but he wished to impress upon them that in future they must in no manner aid or abet tribes in hostility to the Government of the United States. This advice the chiefs accepted in very good part, and I do not believe that they have since been guilty of any misdemeanor of the same nature.

Of this trip among the Moquis, and of the Moquis themselves, volumes might be written. There is no tribe of aborigines on the face of the earth, there is no region in the world, better deserving of examination and description than the Moquis and the country they inhabit. It is unaccountable to me that so many of our own countrymen seem desirous of taking a flying trip to Europe when at their feet, as it were, lies a land as full of wonders as any depicted in the fairy tales of childhood. Here, at the village of Hualpi, on the middle mesa, is where I saw the repulsive rite of the Snake Dance, in which the chief "Medicine Men" prance about among women and children, holding live and venomous rattlesnakes in their mouths. Here, one sees the "Painted Desert," with its fantastic coloring of all varieties of marls and ochreous earths, equalling the tints so lavishly scattered about in the Cañon of the Yellowstone. Here, one begins his journey through the petrified forests, wherein are to be seen the trunks of giant trees, over one hundred feet long, turned into precious jasper, carnelian, and banded agate. Here, one is within stone's throw of the Grand Cañon of the Colorado and the equally deep lateral cañons of the Cataract and the Colorado Chiquito, on whose edge he may stand in perfect security and gaze upon the rushing torrent of the mighty Colorado, over a mile beneath. Here is the great Cohonino Forest, through which one may ride for five days without finding a drop of water except during the rainy season. Truly, it is a wonderland, and in the Grand Cañon one can think of nothing but the Abomination of Desolation.

There is a trail descending the Cataract Cañon so narrow and dangerous that pack trains rarely get to the bottom without accidents. When I went down there with General Crook, we could hear the tinkling of the pack-train bell far up in the cliffs above us, while the mules looked like mice, then like rats, then like jack-rabbits, and finally like dogs in size. One of our mules was pushed off the trail by another mule crowding up against it, and was hurled over the precipice and dashed into a pulp on the rocks a thousand feet below. There is no place in the world at present so accessible, and at the same time so full of the most romantic interest, as are the territories

of Arizona and New Mexico : the railroad companies have been
derelict in presenting their attractions to the travelling public,
else I am sure that numbers of tourists would long since have
made explorations and written narratives of the wonders to be
seen.

General Crook did not limit his attentions to the improvement
of the Indians alone.   There was a wide field of usefulness open
to him in other directions, and he occupied it and made it his
own.   He broke up every one of the old sickly posts, which had
been hotbeds of fever and pestilence, and transferred the garrisons to elevated situations like Camp Grant, whose beautiful
situation has been alluded to in a previous chapter.   He connected every post in the department with every other post by
first-class roads over which wagons and ambulances of all kinds
could journey without being dashed to pieces.   In several cases,
roads were already in existence, but he devoted so much care to
reducing the length and to perfecting the carriage-way that they
became entirely new pathways, as in the case of the new road
between Camps Whipple and Verde.   The quarters occupied by
officers and men were made habitable by repairs or replaced by
new and convenient houses.   The best possible attention was
given to the important matter of providing good, pure, cool
water at every camp.   The military telegraph line was built from
San Diego, California, to Fort Yuma, California, thence to
Maricopa Wells, Arizona, where it bifurcated, one line going on
to Prescott and Fort Whipple, the other continuing eastward to
Tucson, and thence to San Carlos and Camp Apache, or rather to
the crossing of the Gila River, fifteen miles from San Carlos.

For this work, the most important ever undertaken in Arizona
up to that time, Congress appropriated something like the sum
of fifty-seven thousand dollars, upon motion of Hon. Richard C.
McCormick, then Delegate ; the work of construction was superintended by General James J. Dana, Chief Quartermaster of the
Department of Arizona, who managed the matter with such care
and economy that the cost was some ten or eleven thousand dollars less than the appropriation.   The citizens of Arizona living
nearest the line supplied all the poles required at the lowest
possible charge.   When it is understood that the total length of
wire stretched was over seven hundred miles, the price paid (less
than forty-seven thousand dollars) will show that there was very

little room for excessive profit for anybody in a country where all transportation was by wagon or on the backs of mules across burning deserts and over lofty mountains. The great task of building this line was carried out successfully by Major George F. Price, Fifth Cavalry, since dead, and by Lieutenant John F. Trout, Twenty-third Infantry.

One of the first messages transmitted over the wire from Prescott to Camp Apache was sent by an Apache Indian, to apprise his family that he and the rest of the detachment with him would reach home on a certain day. To use a Hibernicism, the wire to Apache did not go to Apache, but stopped at Grant, at the time of which I am writing. General Crook sent a message to the commanding officer at Camp Grant, directing him to use every endeavor to have the message sent by the Apache reach its destination, carrying it with the official dispatches forwarded by courier to Camp Apache. The family and friends of the scout were surprised and bewildered at receiving a communication sent over the white man's talking wire (Pesh-bi-yalti), of which they had lately been hearing so much; but on the day appointed they all put on their thickest coats of face paint, and donned their best bibs and tuckers, and sallied out on foot and horseback to meet the incoming party, who were soon descried descending the flank of an adjacent steep mountain. That was a great day for Arizona; it impressed upon the minds of the savages the fact that the white man's arts were superior to those which their own "Medicine Men" pretended to possess, and made them see that it would be a good thing for their own interests to remain our friends.

The Apaches made frequent use of the wire. A most amusing thing occurred at Crook's headquarters, when the Apache chief "Pitone," who had just come up from a mission of peace to the Yumas, on the Colorado, and who had a grievance against "Pascual," the chief of the latter tribe, had the operator, Mr. Strauchon, inform "Pascual" that if he did not do a certain thing which he had promised to do, the Apaches would go on the war-path, and fairly wipe the ground with the Yumas. There couldn't have been a quainter antithesis of the elements of savagery and enlightenment than the presence of that chief in the telegraph office on such a mission. The Apaches learned after a while how to stop the communication by telegraph, which they did very adroitly by pulling down the wire, cutting it in two, and tying the ends together with a rubber band, completely breaking the circuit. The linemen would have to keep their eyes open to detect just where such breaks existed.

General Crook held that it was the height of folly for the troops of the United States to attempt to carry on an offensive campaign against an enemy whose habits and usages were a mystery to them, and whose territory was a sealed book. Therefore, he directed that each scouting party should map out its own trail, and send the result on to the headquarters, to be incorporated in the general map of the territory which was to be made by the engineer officers in San Francisco. Arizona was previously unknown, and much of its area had never been mapped. He encouraged his officers by every means in his power to acquire a knowledge of the rites and ceremonies, the ideas and feelings, of the Indians under their charge; he believed, as did the late General P. H. Sheridan, that the greater part of our troubles with the aborigines arose from our ignorance of their character and wants, their aspirations, doubts, and fears. It was much easier and very much cheaper to stifle and prevent an outbreak than it was to suppress one which had gained complete headway. These opinions would not be worthy of note had not Crook and his friend and superior, Sheridan, been officers of the American army; the English—in Canada, in New Zealand, in Australia, in India—have found out the truth of this statement; the French have been led to perceive it in their relations with the nomadic tribes of Algeria; and the Spaniards, to a less extent perhaps, have practised the same thing in America. But to Americans generally, the aborigine is a nonentity except when he is upon the war-path. The moment he concludes to live at peace with the whites, that moment all his troubles begin. Never was there a truer remark than that made by Crook: "The American Indian commands respect for his rights only so long as he inspires terror for his rifle." Finally Crook was anxious to obtain for Arizona, and set out in the different military posts, such fruits and vines as might be best adapted to the climate. This project was never carried out, as the orders transferring the General to another department arrived, and prevented, but it is worth while to know that several of the springs in northern Arizona were planted with water-cress by Mrs. Crook, the General's wife, who had followed him to Arizona, and remained there until his transfer to another field.

Only two clouds, neither bigger than a man's hand, but each fraught with mischief to the territory and the whole country, appeared above Arizona's horizon—the Indian ring and the Chiricahuas. The Indian ring was getting in its work, and had already been remarkably successful in some of its manipulations of contracts. The Indian Agent, Dr. Williams, in charge of the Apache-Yumas and Apache-Mojaves, had refused to receive certain sugar on account of the presence of great boulders in each sack. Peremptory orders for the immediate receipt of the sugar were received in due time from Washington. Williams placed one of these immense lumps of stone on a table in his office, labelled "Sample of sugar received at this agency under contract of ———." Williams was a very honest, high-minded gentleman, and deserved something better than to be hounded into an insane asylum, which fate he suffered. I will concede, to save argument, that an official who really desires to treat Indians fairly and honestly must be out of his head, but this form of lunacy is harmless, and does not call for such rigorous measures.

The case of the Chiricahua Apaches was a peculiar one : they had been specially exempted from General Crook's jurisdiction, and in his plans for the reduction of the other bands in hostility they had not been considered. General O. O. Howard had gone out on a special mission to see the great chief "Cocheis," and, at great personal discomfort and no little personal risk, had effected his purpose. They were congregated at the "Stronghold," in the Dragoon Mountains, at the same spot where they had had a fight with Gerald Russell a few months previously. Their chief, "Cocheis," was no doubt sincere in his determination to leave the war-path for good, and to eat the bread of peace. Such, at least, was the opinion I formed when I went in to see him, as a member of Major Brown's party, in the month of February, 1873.

"Cocheis" was a tall, stately, finely built Indian, who seemed to be rather past middle life, but still full of power and vigor, both physical and mental. He received us urbanely, and showed us every attention possible. I remember, and it shows what a deep impression trivial circumstances will sometimes make, that his right hand was badly burned in two circular holes, and that he explained to me that they had been made by his younger wife, who was jealous of the older and had bitten him, and that the wounds had been burned out with a kind of "moxa" with which the savages of this continent are familiar. Trouble arose on account of this treaty from a combination of causes of no consequence when taken singly, but of great importance in the aggregate. The separation of the tribe into two sections, and giving one kind of treatment to one and another to another, had a very bad effect : some of the Chiricahuas called their brethren at the San Carlos " squaws," because they had to work ; on their side, a great many of the Apaches at the San Carlos and Camp Apache, feeling that the Chiricahuas deserved a whipping fully as much as they did, were extremely rancorous towards them, and never tired of inventing stories to the disparagement of their rivals or an exaggeration of what was truth. There were no troops stationed on the Chiricahua reservation to keep the unruly young bucks in order, or protect the honest and well-meaning savages from the rapacity of the white vultures who flocked around them, selling vile whiskey in open day. All the troubles of the Chiricahuas can be traced to this sale of intoxicating fluids to them by worthless white men.

Complaints came up without cease from the people of Sonora, of raids alleged to have been made upon their exposed hamlets nearest the Sierra Madre ; Governor Pesquiera and General Crook were in correspondence upon this subject, but nothing could be done by the latter because the Chiricahuas were not under his jurisdiction. How much of this raiding was fairly attributable to the Chiricahuas who had come in upon the reservation assigned them in the Dragoon Mountains, and how much was chargeable to the account of small parties which still clung to the old fastnesses in the main range of the Sierra Madre will never be known; but the fact that the Chiricahuas were not under military surveillance while all the other bands were, gave point to the insinuations and emphasis to the stories circulated to their disparagement.

Shortly after the Apaches had been put upon the various reservations assigned them, it occurred to the people of Tucson that they were spending a great deal of money for the trials, re-trials, and maintenance of murderers who killed whom they pleased, passed their days pleasantly enough in jail, were defended by shrewd " Jack lawyers," as they were called, and under one pre-

text or another escaped scot free.   There had never been a judi-
cial execution in the territory, and, under the technicalities of
law, there did not appear much chance of any being recorded for
at least a generation.   It needed no argument to make plain to the
dullest comprehension that that sort of thing would do good to no
one ; that it would end in perpetuating a bad name for the town ;
and destroy all hope of its becoming prosperous and populous
with the advent of the railroads of which mention was now frequently made.   The more the matter was talked over, the more
did it seem that something must be done to free Tucson from the
stigma of being the refuge of murderers of every degree.

One of the best citizens of the place, a Mexican gentleman
named Fernandez, I think, who kept a *monte pio*, or pawnbroker's shop, in the centre of the town not a block from the
post-office, was found dead in his bed one morning, and alongside of him his wife and baby, all three with skulls crushed by
the blow of bludgeons or some heavy instrument.   All persons—
Mexicans and Americans—joined in the hunt for the assassins,
who were at last run to the ground, and proved to be three Mexicans, members of a gang of bandits who had terrorized the
northern portions of Sonora for many years.   They were tracked
by a most curious chain of circumstances, the clue being given
by a very intelligent Mexican, and after being run down one of
their number confessed the whole affair, and showed where the
stolen jewellery had been buried under a mesquite bush, in plain
sight of, and close to, the house of the Governor.   I have already
written a description of this incident, and do not care to reproduce it here, on account of lack of space, but may say that the
determination to lynch them was at once formed and carried into
effect, under the superintendence of the most prominent citizens,
on the " Plaza " in front of the cathedral.   There was another
murderer confined in the jail for killing a Mexican "to see him
wriggle."   This wretch, an American tramp, was led out to his
death along with the others, and in less than ten minutes four
human forms were writhing on the hastily constructed gallows.
Whatever censure might be levelled against this high-handed
proceeding on the score of illegality was rebutted by the citizens
on the ground of necessity and the evident improvement of the
public morals which followed, apparently as a sequence of these
drastic methods.

Greater authority was conferred upon the worthy Teutonic apothecary who had been acting as probate judge, or rather much of the authority which he had been exercising was confirmed, and the day of evil-doers began to be a hard and dismal one. The old judge was ordinarily a pharmacist, and did not pretend to know anything of law, but his character for probity and honesty was so well established that the people, who were tired of lawyers, voted to put in place a man who would deal out justice, regardless of personal consequences. The blind goddess had no worthier representative than this frontier Hippocrates, in whose august presence the most hardened delinquents trembled. Blackstone and Coke and Littleton and Kent were not often quoted in the dingy halls of justice where the " Jedge " sat, flanked and backed by shelves of bottles bearing the cabalistic legends, " Syr. Zarzæ Comp.," "Tinc. Op. Camphor," "Syr. Simpl.," and others equally inspiring, and faced by the small row of books, frequently consulted in the knottier and more important cases, which bore the titles " Materia Medica," " Household Medicine," and others of the same tenor. Testimony was never required unless it would serve to convict, and then only a small quantity was needed, because the man who entered within the portals of this abode of Esculapius and of Justice left all hope behind. Every criminal arraigned before this tribunal was already convicted ; there remained only the formality of passing sentence, and of determining just how many weeks to affix as the punishment in the " shane gang." An adjustment of his spectacles, an examination of the " Materia Medica," and the Judge was ready for business. Pointing his long finger at the criminal, he would thunder : "Tu eres vagabundo " (thou art a tramp), and then proceed to sentence the delinquent on his face to the chain-gang for one week, or two, or three, as the conditions of his physiognomy demanded.

" Jedge, isn't thet a r-a-a-ther tough dose to give t' a poor fellow what knowed your grandfadder ? " asked one American prisoner who had received an especially gratifying assurance of the Judge's opinion of his moral turpitude.

" Ha ! you knowed my grandfaddy ; vere abouts, mine frient, you know him ? " queried the legal functionary.

" Wa'al, Jedge, it's jest like this. Th' las' time I seed the ole gent was on th' Isthmus o' Panama ; he war a-swingin' by his tail from th' limbs of a cocoanut tree, a-gatherin' o' cocoanuts, 'n——"

" Dare ; dat vill do, mine frient, dat vill do. I gifs you an-
odder two viks mit der shane-gang fur gontembt ov goort ; how
you like dat ? "

Many sly jokes were cracked at the old judge's expense, and
many side-splitting stories narrated of his eccentricities and curious legal interpretations ; but it was noticed that the supply of
tramps was steadily diminishing, and the town improving in
every essential. If the Judge ever made a mistake on the side of
mercy I never happened to hear of it, although I do not attempt to
say that he may not, at some time in his legal career, have shown
tenderness unrecorded. He certainly did heroic work for the
advancement of the best interests of Tucson and a good part of
southern Arizona.

The orders of the War Department transferring General Crook
to the command of the Department of the Platte arrived in the
middle of March, and by the 25th of that month, 1875, he, with
his personal staff, had started for the new post of duty. A banquet and reception were tendered by the citizens of Prescott and
northern Arizona, which were attended by the best people of that
section. The names of the Butlers, Bashfords, Marions, Heads,
Brooks, Marks, Bowers, Buffums, Hendersons, Bigelows, Rich-
ards, and others having charge of the ceremonies, showed how
thoroughly Americanized that part of Arizona had become.
Hundreds walked or rode out to the " Burnt Ranch " to say the
last farewell, or listen to the few heartfelt words of kindness
with which General Kautz, the new commander, wished Crook
godspeed and good luck in his new field of labor. Crook bade
farewell to the people for whom he had done so much, and whom
he always held so warmly in his heart ; he looked for the last
time, it might be, upon the snowy peak of the San Francisco,
and then headed westward, leaving behind him the Wonderland
of the Southwest, with its fathomless cañons, its dizzy crags, its
snow-mantled sierras, its vast deserts, its blooming oases—its
vast array of all the contradictions possible in topography. The
self-lacerating Mexican *penitente*, and the self-asserting American
prospector, were to fade from the sight, perhaps from the memory ;
but the acts of kindness received and exchanged between man
and man of whatever rank and whatever condition of life were to
last until memory itself should depart.

The journey from Whipple or Prescott to Los Angeles was in

those days over five hundred miles in length, and took at least eleven days under the most favorable conditions; it obliged one to pass through the territory of the Hualpais and the Mojaves, to cross the Colorado River at the fort of the same name, and drive across the extreme southern point of Nevada, and then into California in the country of the Chimahuevis; to drag along over the weary expanse of the "Soda Lake," where for seven miles the wheels of the wagons cut their way into the purest baking soda, and the eyes grew weak with gazing out upon a snowy area of dazzling whiteness, the extreme end of the celebrated "Death Valley." After reaching San Bernardino, the aspect changed completely: the country became a fairyland, filled with grapes and figs and oranges, merry with the music of birds, bright with the bloom of flowers. Lowing herds and buzzing bees attested that this was indeed a land of milk and honey, beautiful to the eye, gladsome to every sense. The railroad had not yet reached Los Angeles, so that to get to San Francisco, travellers who did not care to wait for the weekly steamer were obliged to secure seats in the "Telegraph" stage line. This ran to Bakersfield in the San Joaquin Valley, the then terminus of the Southern Pacific Railroad, and through some of the country where the Franciscans had wrought such wonderful results among the savages whom they had induced to live in the "Missions." In due course of time Crook arrived at Omaha, Nebraska, his new headquarters, where the citizens tendered him a banquet and reception, as had those of the California metropolis—San Francisco.

CHAPTER XIV.

THE new command stretched from the Missouri River to the western shores of the Great Salt Lake, and included the growing State of Nebraska and the promising territories of Wyoming, Utah, and part of Idaho. The Indian tribes with which more or less trouble was to be expected were : the Bannocks and Shoshones, in Idaho and western Wyoming; the Utes, in Utah and western Wyoming; the Sioux, Cheyennes, and Arapahoes, in Dakota and Nebraska ; the Otoes, Poncas, Omahas, Winnebagoes, and Pawnees, in various sections of Nebraska. The last five bands were perfectly peaceful, and the only trouble they would occasion would be on account of the raids made upon them by the hostiles and their counter-raids to steal ponies. The Pawnees had formerly been the active and daring foe of the white men, but were now disposed to go out, whenever needed, to attack the Sioux or Dakotas. The Utes, Bannocks, and Shoshones claimed to be friendly, as did the Arapahoes, but the hostile feelings of the Cheyennes and Sioux were scarcely concealed, and on several occasions manifested in no equivocal manner. The Utes, Bannocks, and Shoshones were "mountain" Indians, but were well supplied with stock ; they often made incursions into the territory of the "plains" tribes, their enemies, of whom the most powerful were the Sioux and Cheyennes, whose numbers ran into the thousands.

There was much smouldering discontent among the Sioux and Cheyennes, based upon our failure to observe the stipulations of the treaty made in 1867, which guaranteed to them an immense strip of country, extending, either as a reservation or a hunting ground, clear to the Big Horn Mountains. By that treaty they had been promised one school for every thirty children, but no schools had yet been established under it. Reports of the fabulous richness of the gold mines in the Black Hills had excited the cupidity of the whites and the distrust of the red men. The latter knew only too well, that the moment any mineral should be found, no matter of what character, their reservation would be cut down ; and they were resolved to prevent this, unless a most liberal price should be paid for the property. The Sioux had insisted upon the abandonment of the chain of posts situated along the line of the Big Horn, and had carried their point ; but, in 1874, after the murder of Lieutenant Robertson, or Robinson, of the Fourteenth Infantry, while in charge of a wood-chopping party on Laramie Peak, and their subsequent refusal to let their agent fly the American flag over the agency, General John E. Smith, Fourteenth Infantry, at the head of a strong force, marched over to the White Earth country and established what have since been designated as Camps Sheridan and Robinson at the agencies of the great chiefs " Spotted Tail " and " Red Cloud " respectively. In 1874, General Custer made an examination of the Black Hills, and reported finding gold " from the grass roots down." In the winter of that year a large party of miners, without waiting for the consent of the Indians to be obtained, settled on the waters of Frenchman, or French, Creek, built a stockade, and began to work with rockers. These miners were driven about from point to point by detachments of troops, but succeeded in maintaining a foothold until the next year. One of the commands sent to look them up and drive them out was the company of the Third Cavalry commanded by Brevet Lieutenant-Colonel Guy V. Henry, which was caught in a blizzard and nearly destroyed. In the early months of 1875, a large expedition, well equipped, was sent to explore and map the Black Hills and the adjacent country. The main object was the determination of the auriferous character of the ledges and the value of the country as a mining district ; the duty of examination into these features devolved upon the geologists and engineers sent out by the Department of the Interior, namely, Messrs. Janney, McGillicuddy, Newton, Brown, and Tuttle. The military escort, consisting of six full companies of the Second and Third Cavalry, two pieces of artillery, and several companies of the Ninth and Fourteenth Infantry to guard supply trains, was employed in furnishing the requisite protection to the geologists, and in obtaining such additional information in regard to the topography of the country, the best lines for wagon roads, and sites for such posts as might be necessary in the future. This was under the command of Colonel R. I. Dodge, of the Twenty-third Infantry, and made a very complete search over the whole of the hills, mapping the streams and the trend of the ranges, and opening up one of the most picturesque regions on the face of the globe.

It was never a matter of surprise to me that the Cheyennes, whose corn-fields were once upon the Belle Fourche, the stream which runs around the hills on the north side, should have become frenzied by the report that these lovely valleys were to be taken from them whether they would or no.   In the summer of 1876 the Government sent a commission, of which Senator William B. Allison, of Iowa, was chairman, and the late Major-General Alfred H. Terry, a member, to negotiate with the Sioux for the cession of the Black Hills, but neither Sioux nor Cheyennes were in the humor to negotiate.   There appeared to be a very large element among the Indians which would sooner have war than peace ; all sorts of failures to observe previous agreements were brought up, and the advocates of peace were outnumbered.   One day it looked very much as if a general *mêlée* was about to be precipitated.   The hostile element, led by "Little Big Man," shrieked for war, and "Little Big Man" himself was haranguing his followers that that was as good a moment as any to begin shooting.   The courage and coolness of two excellent officers, Egan and Crawford, the former of the Second, the latter of the Third Cavalry, kept the savages from getting too near the Commissioners : their commands formed line, and with carbines at an "advance" remained perfectly motionless, ready to charge in upon the Indians should the latter begin an attack.   Egan has often told me that he was apprehensive lest the accidental discharge of a carbine or a rifle on one side or the other should precipitate a conflict in which much blood would surely be shed. Egan has been many years dead—worn out in service—and poor Crawford was killed by Mexican irregular troops at the moment that he had surprised and destroyed the village of the Chiricahua Apache chief "Geronimo," in the depths of the Sierra Madre,

Mexico. Much of our trouble with these tribes could have been averted, had we shown what would appear to them as a spirit of justice and fair dealing in this negotiation. It is hard to make the average savage comprehend why it is that as soon as his reservation is found to amount to anything he must leave and give up to the white man. Why should not Indians be permitted to hold mining or any other kind of land? The whites could mine on shares or on a royalty, and the Indians would soon become workers in the bowels of the earth. The right to own and work mines was conceded to the Indians by the Crown of Spain, and the result was beneficial to both races. In 1551, the Spanish Crown directed that "Nadie los impidiese que pudiesem tomar minas de Oro, i Plata i beneficiarlas como hacian los Castellanos."—*Herrera, Decade, VIII., lib. 8, cap. 12, p. 159.* The policy of the American people has been to vagabondize the Indian, and throttle every ambition he may have for his own elevation; and we need not hug the delusion that the savage has been any too anxious for work, unless stimulated, encouraged, and made to see that it meant his immediate benefit and advancement.

During the closing hours of the year 1875 the miners kept going into the Black Hills, and the Indians kept annoying all wagon-trains and small parties found on the roads. There were some killed and others wounded and a number of wagons destroyed, but hostilities did not reach a dangerous state, and were confined almost entirely to the country claimed by the Indians as their own. It was evident, however, to the most obtuse that a very serious state of affairs would develop with the coming of grass in the spring. The Indians were buying all the arms, ammunition, knives, and other munitions of war from the traders and every one else who would sell to them. On our side the posts were filled with supplies, garrisons changed to admit of the concentration of the largest possible numbers on most threatened localities, and the efficient pack-trains which had rendered so valuable a service during the campaign in Arizona were brought up from the south and congregated at Cheyenne, Wyoming. The policy of the Government must have seemed to the Indians extremely vacillating. During the summer of 1876 instructions of a positive character were sent to General Crook, directing the expulsion from the Black Hills of all unauthorized persons there assembled. General Crook went across country to the stockade erected on French Creek, Dakota, and there had an interview with the miners, who promised to leave the country, first having properly recorded their claims, and await the action of Congress in regard to the opening of that region to settlement. As winter approached another tone was assumed in our dealings with the Sioux and Cheyennes : word was sent to the different bands living at a distance from the agencies that they must come in to be enrolled or inspected ; some obeyed the summons, some quietly disregarded it, and one band—a small one, under "Sitting Bull"—flatly refused compliance. The Indians did not seem to understand that any one had a right to control their movements so long as they remained within the metes and bounds assigned them by treaty.

Neither "Crazy Horse" nor "Sitting Bull" paid any attention to the summons; and when early in the summer (1875) a message reached them, directing them to come in to Red Cloud Agency to confer with the Black Hills Commission, this is the reply which Louis Richaud, the half-breed messenger, received : "Are you the Great God that made me, or was it the Great God that made me who sent you ? If He asks me to come see him, I will go, but the Big Chief of the white men must come see me. I will not go to the reservation. I have no land to sell. There is plenty of game here for us. We have enough ammunition. We don't want any white men here." "Sitting Bull" delivered the above in his haughtiest manner, but "Crazy Horse" had nothing to say. "Crazy Horse" was the general, the fighter ; "Sitting Bull" was a "Medicine Man" and a fine talker, and rarely let pass an opportunity for saying something. He was, in that one respect, very much like old "Shunca luta," at Red Cloud, who was always on his feet in council or conference.

Upon the recommendation of Inspector Watkins of the Indian Bureau, made in the winter of 1875, the War Department was instructed to take in hand the small band of five hundred Sioux supposed to be lurking in the country bounded by the Big Horn Mountains, the Tongue and the Yellowstone rivers. The inspector expressed the opinion that a regiment of cavalry was all that was needed to make a quick winter campaign and strike a heavy and decisive blow. This opinion was not, however, borne out by the facts. The number of Indians out in that country was absolutely unknown to our people, and all guesses as to their strength were wildly conjectural. The country in which the coming operations were to be carried on was as different as different could be from the rugged ranges, the broken mesas, and the arid deserts of Arizona. Topographically, it might be styled a great undulating plain, rolling like the waves of ocean—a sea of grass, over which still roamed great herds of buffalo, and antelope by the hundred. It is far better watered than either New Mexico or Arizona, and has a vegetation of an entirely different type. There is considerable cactus of the plate variety in certain places, but the general rule is that the face of nature is covered with bunch and buffalo grass, with a straggling growth of timber along the water courses—cottonwood, ash, willow, and now and then a little oak. On the summits of the buttes there is pine timber in some quantity, and upon the higher elevations of the ranges like the Big Horn the pine, fir, and other coniferæ grow very dense ; but at the height of eleven thousand feet all timber ceases and the peaks project perfectly bald and tower upwards toward the sky, enveloped in clouds and nearly all the year round wrapped in snow. Coal is to be found in wonderful abundance and of excellent quality, and it is now asserted that the State of Wyoming is better supplied with carbon than is the State of Pennsylvania. Coal oil is also found in the Rattlesnake basin, but has not yet been made commercially profitable.

Montana, situated to the north of Wyoming, is perhaps a trifle colder in winter, but both are cold enough ; although, strange to say, few if any of the settlers suffer from the effects of the severe reduction of temperature—at least few of those whose business does not compel them to face the blizzards. Stage-drivers, stockmen, settlers living on isolated ranchos, were the principal sufferers. Both Wyoming and Montana were fortunate in securing a fine class of population at the outset, men and women who would stand by the new country until after all the scapegraces, scoundrels, and cutthroats who had flocked in with the advent of the railroads had died off, most of them with their boots on. The Union Pacific Railroad crossed the Territory from east to west, making the transportation of supplies a matter of comparative ease, and keeping the various posts within touch of civilization. South of the North Platte River the country was held by the troops of the United States, and was pretty well understood and fairly well mapped; north of that stream was a *terra incognita*, of which no accurate charts existed, and of which extremely little information could be obtained. Every half-breed at Red Cloud or Spotted Tail Agency who could be secured was employed as a scout, and placed under the command of Colonel Thaddeus H. Stanton, of the Pay Department, who was announced as Chief of Scouts.

The Sioux and Cheyennes whom we were soon to face were "horse" Indians, who marched and fought on horseback; they kept together in large bodies, and attacked by charging and attempting to stampede the herds of the troops. They were well armed with the newest patterns of magazine arms, and were reported to be possessed of an abundance of metallic cartridges. Their formidable numbers, estimated by many authorities at as many as fifty thousand for the entire nation, had given them an overweening confidence in themselves and a contempt for the small bodies of troops that could be thrown out against them, and it was generally believed by those pretending to know that we should have all the fighting we wanted. These were the points upon which the pessimists most strongly insisted. The cloud certainly looked black enough to satisfy any one, but there was a silver lining to it which was not perceptible at first inspection. If a single one of these large villages could be surprised and destroyed in the depth of winter, the resulting loss of property would be so great that the enemy would suffer for years; their exposure to the bitter cold of the blizzards would break down any spirit, no matter how brave; their ponies would be so weak that they could not escape from an energetic pursuit, and the advantages would seem to be on the side of the troops.

Crook took up his quarters in Cheyenne for a few days to push forward the preparations for the departure of the column of cavalry which was to compose the major part of the contemplated expedition. Cheyenne was then wild with excitement concerning the Indian war, which all the old frontiersmen felt was approaching, and the settlement of the Black Hills, in which gold in unheard-of sums was alleged to be hidden. No story was too wild, too absurd, to be swallowed with eagerness and published as a fact in the papers of the town. Along the streets were camped long trains of wagons loading for the Black Hills; every store advertised a supply of goods suited to the Black Hills' trade ; the hotels were crowded with men on their way to the new El Dorado ; even the stage-drivers, boot-blacks, and bell-boys could talk nothing but Black Hills—Black Hills. So great was the demand for teams to haul goods to the Black Hills that it was difficult to obtain the necessary number to carry the rations and ammunition needed for Crook's column. Due north of Cheyenne, and ninety miles from it, lay old Fort Laramie, since abandoned ; ninety-five miles to the northwest of Laramie lay Fort Fetterman, the point of departure for the expedition. To reach Fort Laramie we had to cross several small but useful streamlets—the Lodge Pole, Horse, and Chug—which course down from the higher elevations and are lost in the current of the North Platte and Laramie rivers.

The country was well adapted for the grazing of cattle, and several good ranchos were already established ; at " Portuguese " Phillip's, at the head of the Chug, and at F. M. Phillips's, at the mouth of the same picturesque stream, the traveller was always sure of hospitable, kind treatment. The march of improvement has caused these ranchos to disappear, and their owners, for all I know to the contrary, have been dead for many years, but their memory will be cherished by numbers of belated wayfarers, in the army and out of it, who were the recipients of their kind attentions. The road leading out of Cheyenne through Fort Laramie to the Black Hills was thronged with pedestrians and mounted men, with wagons and without—all *en route* to the hills which their fancy pictured as stuffed with the precious metals. Not all were intent upon mining or other hard work : there was more than a fair contingent of gamblers and people of that kind, who relieved Cheyenne and Denver and Omaha of much uneasiness by their departure from those older cities to grow up with the newer settlements in the Indian Pactolus. There were other roads leading to the Black Hills from points on the Missouri River, and from Sidney and North Platte, Nebraska, but they offered no such inducements as the one from Cheyenne, because it crossed the North Platte River by a free Government bridge, constructed under the superintendence of Captain William S. Stanton, of the Corps of Engineers. By taking this route all dangers and delays by ferry were eliminated.

Much might be written about old Fort Laramie. It would

require a volume of itself to describe all that could be learned regarding it from the days when the hardy French traders from Saint Louis, under Jules La Ramie, began trading with the Sioux and Cheyennes and Arapahoes, until the Government of the United States determined to establish one of its most important garrisons to protect the overland travel to the gold-fields of California. Many an old and decrepit officer, now on the retired list, will revert in fancy to the days when he was young and athletic, and Fort Laramie was the centre of all the business, and fashion, and gossip, and mentality of the North Platte country ; the cynic may say that there wasn't much, and he may be right, but it represented the best that there was to be had.

Beyond Fort Laramie,. separated by ninety-five miles of most unpromising country, lies the post of Fort Fetterman, on the right bank of the North Platte. Boulders of gneiss, greenstone, porphyry, and other rocks from the Laramie Peak lined the bottoms and sides of the different dry arroyos passed on the march. Not all the ravines were dry ; in a few there was a good supply of water, and the whole distance out from Fort Laramie presented no serious objections on that score. In the " Twin Springs," "Horse-shoe" Creek, "Cave" Springs, "Elk Horn" Creek, "Lake Bonté," "Wagon Hound," "Bed-tick," and "Whiskey Gulch" a supply, greater or less in quantity, dependent upon season, could generally be found. Much of the soil was a gypsiferous red clay ; in all the gulches and ravines were to be seen stunted pine and cedar. The scenery was extremely monotonous, destitute of herbage, except buffalo grass and sage brush. An occasional buffalo head, bleaching in the sun, gave a still more ghastly tone to the landscape. Every few minutes a prairie dog projected his head above the entrance of his domicile and barked at our cortege passing by. Among the officers and soldiers of the garrison at Fort Fetterman, as well as among those who were reporting for duty with the expedition, the topics of conversation were invariably the probable strength and position of the enemy, the ability of horses and men to bear the extreme cold to which they were sure to be subjected, and other matters of a kindred nature which were certain to suggest themselves.

There, for example, was the story, accepted without question, that the Sioux had originally shown a very friendly spirit toward the Americans passing across their country to California, until on one occasion a man offered grievous wrong to one of the young squaws, and that same evening the wagon-train with which he was travelling was surrounded by a band of determined warriors, who quietly expressed a desire to have an interview with the criminal. The Americans gave him up, and the Sioux skinned him alive; hence the name of "Raw Hide Creek," the place where this incident occurred.

Another interesting story was that of the escape of one of the corporals of Teddy Egan's company of the Second Cavalry from the hands of a party of Sioux raiders on Laramie Peak; several of the corporal's comrades were killed in their blankets, as the attack was made in the early hours of morning, but the corporal sprang out in his bare feet and escaped down to the ranchos on the La Bonté, but his feet were so filled with fine cactus thorns and cut up with sharp stones that he was for months unable to walk.

"Black Coal," one of the chiefs of the Arapahoes, came in to see General Crook while at Fetterman, and told him that his tribe had information that the hostiles were encamped on the lower Powder, below old Fort Reno, some one hundred and fifty miles from Fetterman. Telegraphic advices were received from Fort Laramie to the effect that three hundred lodges of northern Sioux had just come in at Red Cloud Agency; and the additional information that the supplies of the Indian Bureau at that agency were running short, and that no replenishment was possible until Congress should make another appropriation.

This news was both good and bad, bitter and sweet; we should have a smaller number of Sioux to drive back to the reservation; but, on the other hand, if supplies were not soon provided, all the Indians would surely take to the Black Hills and Big Horn country, where an abundance of game of all kinds was still to be found. The mercury still remained down in the bottom of the bulb, and the ground was covered deep with snow. In Wyoming the air is so dry that a thermometer marking zero, or even ten degrees below that point on the Fahrenheit scale, does not indicate any serious discomfort; the air is bracing, and the cold winters seem to have a beneficial effect upon the general health of the inhabitants. We have no sturdier, healthier people in our country than the settlers in Wyoming and Montana.

Winter campaigning was an entirely different matter; even

the savages hibernated during the cold months, and sought the shelter of friendly cliffs and buttes, at whose feet they could pitch their tepees of buffalo or elk skin, and watch their ponies grazing upon the pasturage. The ponies of the Indians, the mares and foals especially, fare poorly during this season; they have no protection from the keen northern blasts, but must huddle together in ravines and "draws," or "coulées," as the French half-breeds call them, until the worst is over. They become very thin and weak, and can hardly haul the "travois" upon which the family supplies must be packed. Then is assuredly the time to strike, provided always that the soldiers be not caught and frozen to death by some furious storm while on the march, or after being wounded. Crook wanted to have our animals kept in the best condition, at least in a condition somewhat better than that of the Indian ponies. He knew that the amount of grass to be depended upon would be very limited: much of the country would be burned over by the Indians to prepare for the new growth; much would lie under deep snow, and not be accessible to our horses; much would be deadened by wind and storm; so that the most prudent course would be to move out from Fetterman with a wagon-train loaded with grain, which could be fed in small quantities to supplement the pasturage that might be found, and would keep our mules and horses in strength and health. A depot would be established at some convenient point, and from that scouts and explorations into all sections of the surrounding country could be made by light, swift-moving columns. Officers and men were informed that so long as with the wagon-train they would be allowed plenty of warm bedding and a minimum supply of "A" and "dog" tents, but upon starting out for any movement across country they would have to do without anything but the clothing upon their backs. Particular attention was bestowed upon this subject of clothing; and when I say that the mercury frequently congeals in the bulb, and that the spirit thermometers at Fort Fred Steele, Wyoming, that winter registered as low as 61° below, Fahrenheit, the necessity of precaution will be apparent. The most elastic interpretation was given to the word "uniform," so as to permit individual taste and experience to have full play in the selection of the garments which were to protect from bitter cold and fierce wind.

Thinking that such particulars may be of interest to a portion of my readers, I will say a few words in regard to the clothing worn by different members of the expedition. For cavalry, great care was demanded to protect feet, knees, wrists, and ears ; the foot soldier can stamp his feet or slap his hands and ears, but the mounted man must hold his reins and sit up straight in the saddle. Commencing with the feet, first a pair of close-fitting lamb's-wool socks was put on, then one of the same size as those worn by women, so as to come over the knees. Indian moccasins of buckskin, reaching well up the leg, were generally preferred to boots, being warmer and lighter ; cork soles were used with them, and an overboot of buffalo hide, made with the hairy side inward and extending up nearly the whole length of the leg, and opening down the side and fastened by buckles something after the style of the breeches worn by Mexican "vaqueros." These overboots were soled, heeled, and boxed with leather, well tanned. Some officers preferred to wear the leggings separate, and to use the overshoe supplied by the Quartermaster's Department. By this method, one could disrobe more readily after reaching camp and be free to move about in the performance of duty while the sun might be shining ; but it was open to the objection that, on account of the clumsy make of the shoes, it was almost impossible to get into the stirrups with them.

All people of experience concurred in denouncing as pernicious the practice of wearing tight shoes, or the use of any article of raiment which would induce too copious a flow of perspiration, the great danger being that there would be more likelihood of having the feet, or any other part of the body in which the circulation might be impeded, frozen during spells of intense cold ; or of having the same sad experience where there would be a sudden checking of the perspiration, which would almost certainly result in acute pneumonia. For underwear, individual preferences were consulted, the general idea being to have at least two kinds of material used, principally merino and perforated buckskin ; over these was placed a heavy blue flannel shirt, made double-breasted, and then a blouse, made also double-breasted, of Mission or Minnesota blanket, with large buttons, or a coat of Norway kid lined with heavy flannel. When the blizzards blew nothing in the world would keep out the cold but an overcoat of buffalo or bearskin or beaver, although for many the overcoats made in Saint Paul of canvas, lined with the heaviest blanket, and strapped and belted tight about the waist, were pronounced sufficient. The head was protected by a cap of cloth, with fur border to pull down over the ears ; a fur collar enclosed the neck and screened the mouth and nose from the keen blasts ; and the hands were covered by woollen gloves and over-gauntlets of beaver or musk-rat fur. For rainy or snowy weather most of the command had two india-rubber ponchos sewed together, which covered both rider and horse. This was found very cumbersome and was generally discarded, but at night it was decidedly valuable for the exclusion of dampness from either ground or sky. Our bedding while with the wagon-trains was ample, and there was no complaint from either officers or men. Everybody adhered to the one style ; buffalo robes were conceded to be the most suitable covering. First, there would be spread down upon the ground the strip of canvas in which the blankets or robes were to be rolled for the march ; then the india-rubber ponchos spoken of ; then, for those who had them, a mattress made of chopped cork, of a total thickness of one inch, sewed in transverse layers so as to admit of being rolled more compactly ; lastly, the buffalo robes and the blankets or cotton comforters, according to preference. The old wise-heads provided themselves with bags of buffalo robe, in which to insert the feet, and with small canvas cylinders, extending across the bed and not more than eight inches in diameter, which became a safe receptacle for extra underwear, socks, handkerchiefs, and any papers that it might be necessary to carry along. In all cases, where a man has the choice of making a winter campaign or staying at home, I would advise him to remember *Punch's* advice to those who were thinking of getting married.

General Crook had had much previous experience in his campaign against the Pi-Utes and Snakes of Idaho and northern Nevada in 1866–7, during which time his pack-trains had been obliged to break their way through snow girth deep, and his whole command had been able to make but thirty-three miles in twelve days—a campaign of which little has been written, but which deserves a glorious page in American history as resulting in the complete subjugation of a fierce and crafty tribe, and in being the means of securing safety to the miners of Nevada while they developed ledges which soon afterwards poured into the national treasury four hundred millions of dollars in dividends and wages.

On the 1st of March, 1876, after a heavy fall of snow the previous night, and in the face of a cold wind, but with the sun shining brightly down upon us, we left Fetterman for the Powder River and Big Horn. Officers and men were in the best of spirits, and horses champed eagerly upon the bit as if pleased with the idea of a journey. We had ten full companies of cavalry, equally divided between the Second and Third Regiments, and two companies of the Fourth Infantry. The troops were under the immediate command of Colonel Joseph J. Reynolds, of the Third Cavalry, Brevet Major-General. His staff officers were Lieutenants Morton and Drew, both of the Third Cavalry, acting as adjutant and quartermaster, respectively.

General Reynolds divided his forces into battalions of two companies each, one pack-train being attached to each of the mounted battalions, the infantry remaining with the wagons.

These battalions were composed as follows : " M " and " E," Third Cavalry, under Captain Anson Mills ; " A " and " D," Third Cavalry, under Captain William Hawley ; " I " and " K," Second Cavalry, under Major H. E. Noyes ; " A " and " B," Second, under Major T. B. Dewees ; " F," Third Cavalry, and " E," Second, under Colonel Alex. Moore, of the Third Cavalry ; " C " and " I," Fourth Infantry, under Major E. M. Coates, of the same regiment. Assistant Surgeon C. E. Munn was medical officer, assisted by A. A. Surgeon Ridgeley and by Hospital Steward Bryan. The subordinate officers in command of companies, or attached to them, were Captains Egan and Peale, of the Second Cavalry, and Ferris, of the Fourth Infantry ; Lieutenants Robinson, Rawolle, Pearson, Sibley, Hall, of the Second Cavalry, and Paul, J. B. Johnson, Lawson, Robinson, and Reynolds, of the Third Cavalry ; Mason, of the Fourth Infantry.

There were eighty-six mule-wagons loaded with forage, and three or four ambulances carrying as much as they safely could of the same. The pack-train, in five divisions of eighty mules each, was under the supervision of Mr. Thomas Moore, Chief of Transportation, and was assigned as follows : MacAuliffe, to the 1st Battalion ; Closter, to the 2d ; Foster, to the 3d ; Young, to the 4th ; De Laney, to the 5th.

The advance of the column was led by Colonel Thaddeus H.

Stanton and the band of half-breed scouts recruited at the Red Cloud and Spotted Tail agencies. General Crook marched with these nearly all the time, and I was so much interested in learning all that was possible about the northwest country, and the Indians and the half-breeds inhabiting it, that I devoted all the time I could to conversing with them. Frank Gruard, a native of the Sandwich Islands, was for some years a mail-rider in northern Montana, and was there captured by the forces of "Crazy Horse"; his dark skin and general appearance gave his captors the impression that Frank was a native Indian whom they had recaptured from the whites; consequently, they did not kill him, but kept him a prisoner until he could recover what they believed to be his native language—the Sioux. Frank remained several years in the household of the great chief "Crazy Horse," whom he knew very well, as well as his medicine man—the since renowned "Sitting Bull." Gruard was one of the most remarkable woodsmen I have ever met; no Indian could surpass him in his intimate acquaintance with all that pertained to the topography, animal life, and other particulars of the great region between the head of the Piney, the first affluent of the Powder on the west, up to and beyond the Yellowstone on the north; no question could be asked him that he could not answer at once and correctly. His bravery and fidelity were never questioned; he never flinched under fire, and never growled at privation. Louis Richaud, Baptiste Pourrier ("Big Bat"), Baptiste Garnier ("Little Bat"), Louis Changrau, Speed Stagner, Ben Clarke, and others were men of excellent record as scouts, and all rendered efficient service during the entire expedition. There was one representative of the public press— Mr. Robert E. Strahorn, of the *Rocky Mountain News*, who remained throughout the entire campaign, winter and summer, until the last of the hostiles had surrendered.

CHAPTER XV.

MOVING INTO THE BIG HORN COUNTRY IN WINTER—THE
HERD STAMPEDED—A NIGHT ATTACK—"JEFF'S" OOZING
COURAGE—THE GRAVE-YARD AT OLD FORT RENO—IN A
MONTANA BLIZZARD—THE MERCURY FROZEN IN THE
BULB—KILLING BUFFALO—INDIAN GRAVES—HOW CROOK
LOOKED WHILE ON THIS CAMPAIGN—FINDING A DEAD
INDIAN'S ARM—INDIAN PICTURES.

THE march from Fort Fetterman to old Fort Reno, a distance of ninety miles, led us through a country of which
the less said the better; it is suited for grazing and may appeal to the eyes of a cow-boy, but for the ordinary observer, especially during the winter season, it presents nothing to charm
any sense; the landscape is monotonous and uninviting, and the
vision is bounded by swell after swell of rolling prairie, yellow
with a thick growth of winter-killed buffalo or bunch grass, with
a liberal sprinkling of that most uninteresting of all vegetation
—the sage-brush. The water is uniformly and consistently bad
—being both brackish and alkaline, and when it freezes into ice
the ice is nearly always rotten and dangerous, for a passage at
least by mounted troops or wagons. Wood is not to be had for
the first fifty miles, and has to be carried along in wagons for
commands of any size. Across this charming expanse the wind
howled and did its best to freeze us all to death, but we were
too well prepared.

The first night out from Fetterman the presence of hostile
Indians was indicated by the wounding of our herder, shot
in the lungs, and by the stampeding of our herd of cattle—forty-
five head—which were not, however, run off by the attacking
party, but headed for the post and could not be turned and
brought back. There was very little to record of this part of
the march : a night attack or two, the firing by our pickets at
anything and everything which looked like a man, the killing of

several buffaloes by the guides in front—old bulls which would pull all the teeth out of one's head were they to be chewed ; better success with antelope, whose meat was tender and palatable ; the sight of a column of dust in the remote distance, occasioned, probably, by the movement of an Indian village, and the flashing of looking-glass signals by hostiles on our right flank, made the sum total of events worthy of insertion in the journals kept at the time.   Lodge-pole trails and pony tracks increased in numbers, and a signal smoke curled upwards from one of the distant buttes in our front.   On our left, the snow-clad masses of the "Big Horn" range rose slowly above the horizon, and on the right the sullen, inhospitable outline of the "Pumpkin Buttes."   General Crook ordered that the greatest care should be taken in the manner of posting sentinels, and in enjoining vigilance upon them ; he directed that no attempt should be made to catch any of the small parties of the enemy's videttes, which began to show themselves and to retreat when followed ; he explained that all they wanted was to entice us into a pursuit which could have no effect beyond breaking down twenty or thirty of our horses each time.

We were out of camp, and following the old Montana road by daylight of the 5th of March, 1876, going down the "Dry Fork" of the Powder.   There was no delay on any account, and affairs began to move like clock-work.   The scenery was dreary ; the weather bitter cold ; the bluffs on either side bare and sombre prominences of yellow clay, slate, and sandstone.   The leaden sky overhead promised no respite from the storm of cold snow and wind beating into our faces from the northwest.   A stranger would not have suspected at first glance that the command passing along the defile of this miserable little sand-bed had any connection with the military organization of the United States ; shrouded from head to foot in huge wrappings of wool and fur, what small amount of uniform officers or men wore was almost entirely concealed from sight ; but a keener inspection would have convinced the observer that it was an expedition of soldiers, and good ones at that.   The promptness, ease, and lack of noise with which all evolutions were performed, the compactness of the columns, the good condition of arms and horses, and the care displayed in looking after the trains, betokened the discipline of veteran soldiery.

That evening a party of picked scouts, under Frank Gruard, was sent to scour the country in our front and on our right flank; there was no need of examining the country on the left, as the Big Horn range was so close, and there was no likelihood of the savages going up on its cold flanks to live during winter while such better and more comfortable localities were at hand in the river and creek bottoms. The sun was just descending behind the summits of the Big Horn, having emerged from behind a bank of leaden clouds long enough to assure us that he was still in existence, and Major Coates was putting his pickets in position and giving them their final instructions, when a bold attack was made by a small detachment of the Sioux; their advance was detected as they were creeping upon us through a grove of cottonwoods close to camp, and although there was a brisk interchange of leaden compliments, no damage was done to our people beyond the wounding slightly of Corporal Slavey, of Coates's company. Crook ordered a large force to march promptly to the other side of camp, thinking that the enemy was merely making a "bluff" on one extremity, but would select a few bold warriors to rush through at the other end, and, by waving blankets, shrieking, firing guns, and all other tricks of that sort, stampede our stock and set us afoot. The entire command kept under arms for half an hour and was then withdrawn. From this on we had the companies formed each morning at daybreak, ready for the attack which might come at any moment. The early hour set for breaking camp no doubt operated to frustrate plans of doing damage to the column entertained by wandering bodies of the Sioux and Cheyennes.

Colonel Stanton was accompanied by a colored cook, Mr. Jefferson Clark, a faithful henchman who had followed the fortunes of his chief for many years. Jeff wasn't a bad cook, and he was, according to his own story, one of the most bloodthirsty enemies the Sioux ever had; it was a matter of difficulty to restrain him from leaving the command and wandering out alone in quest of aboriginal blood. This night-attack seemed to freeze all the fight out of Jeff, and he never again expressed the remotest desire to shoot anything, not even a jack-rabbit. But the soldiers had no end of fun with him, and many and many a trick was played, and many and many a lie told, to make his hair stiffen, and his eyes to glaze in terror.

When we reached the "Crazy Woman's Fork" of the Powder River, camp was established, with an abundance of excellent water and any amount of dry cottonwood fuel; but grass was not very plentiful, although there had been a steady improvement in that respect ever since leaving the South Cheyenne. We had that day passed through the ruins of old Fort Reno, one of the military cantonments abandoned by the Government at the demand of the Sioux in 1867. Nothing remained except a few chimneys, a part of the bake-house, and some fragments of the adobe walls of the quarters or offices. The grave-yard had a half dozen or a dozen of broken, dilapidated head-boards to mark the last resting-places of brave soldiers who had fallen in desperate wars with savage tribes that civilization might extend her boundaries. Our wagon-train was sent back under escort of the infantry to Fort Reno, there to await our return.

All the officers were summoned to hear from General Crook's own lips what he wanted them to do. He said that we should now leave our wagons behind and strike out with the pack-trains; all superfluous baggage must be left in camp; every officer and every soldier should be allowed the clothes on his back and no more; for bedding each soldier could carry along one buffalo robe or two blankets; to economize transportation, company officers should mess with their men, and staff officers or those "unattached" with the pack-trains; officers to have the same amount of bedding as the men; each man could take one piece of shelter tent, and each officer one piece of canvas, or every two officers one tent fly. We were to start out on a trip to last fifteen days unless the enemy should be sooner found, and were to take along half rations of bacon, hard tack, coffee, and sugar.

About seven o'clock on the night of March 7, 1876, by the light of a three-quarters moon, we began our march to the north and west, and made thirty-five miles. At first the country had the undulating contour of that near old Fort Reno, but the prairie "swells" were soon superseded by bluffs of bolder and bolder outline until, as we approached the summit of the "divide" where "Clear Fork" heads, we found ourselves in a region deserving the title mountainous. In the bright light of the moon and stars, our column of cavalry wound up the steep hill-sides like an enormous snake, whose scales were glittering revolvers and carbines. The view was certainly very exhilarating, backed as it was by the majestic landscape of moonlight on the Big Horn Mountains. Cynthia's silvery beams never lit up a mass of mountain crests more worthy of delineation upon an artist's canvas. Above the frozen apex of " Cloud Peak " the evening star cast its declining rays. Other prominences rivalling this one in altitude thrust themselves out against the midnight sky. Exclamations of admiration and surprise were extorted from the most stolid as the horses rapidly passed from bluff to bluff, pausing at times to give every one an opportunity to study some of Nature's noble handiwork.

But at last even the gorgeous vista failed to alleviate the cold and pain in benumbed limbs, or to dispel the drowsiness which Morpheus was placing upon exhausted eyelids. With no small degree of satisfaction we noticed the signal which at five o'clock in the morning of March 8th bade us make camp on the Clear Fork of the Powder. The site was dreary enough ; scarcely any timber in sight, plenty of water, but frozen solid, and only a bare picking of grass for our tired animals. However, what we most needed was sleep, and that we sought as soon as horses had been unsaddled and mules unpacked. Wrapped up in our heavy overcoats and furs we threw ourselves on the bleak and frozen ground, and were soon deep in slumber. After lying down in the bright, calm, and cheerful moonlight, we were awakened about eight o'clock by a bitter, pelting storm of snow which blew in our teeth whichever way we turned, and almost extinguished the petty fires near which the cooks were trying to arrange breakfast, if we may dignify by such a lofty title the frozen bacon, frozen beans, and frozen coffee which constituted the repast. It is no part of a soldier's business to repine, but if there are circumstances to justify complaint they are the absence of warmth and good food after a wearisome night march and during the prevalence of a cold winter storm. After coffee had been swallowed General Crook moved the command down the " Clear Fork " five miles, to a pleasant cove where we remained all the rest of that day. Our situation was not enviable. It is true we experienced nothing we could call privation or hardship, but we had to endure much positive discomfort. The storm continued all day, the wind blowing with keenness and at intervals with much power. Being without tents, there was nothing to do but grin and bear it. Some of our people stretched blankets to the branches of trees, others found a questionable shelter under the bluffs, one or two constructed nondescript habitations of twigs and grass, while General Crook and Colonel Stanton seized upon the abandoned den of a family of beavers which a sudden change in the bed of the stream had deprived of their home. To obtain water for men and animals holes were cut in the ice, which was by actual measurement eighteen inches thick, clear in color and vitreous in texture. We hugged the fires as closely as we dared, ashes and cinders being cast into our faces with every turn in the hurricane. The narrow thread of the stream, with its opaque and glassy surface of ice, covered with snow, here drifted into petty hillocks, here again carried away before the gale, looked the picture of all that could be imagined cheerless and drear. We tried hard to find pleasure in watching the trouble of our fellow-soldiers obliged for any reason to attempt a crossing of the treacherous surface. Commencing with an air of boldness and confidence—with some, even of indifference—a few steps forward would serve to intimidate the unfortunate wight, doubly timid now that he saw himself the butt of all gibes and jeers. Now one foot slips, now another, but still he struggles manfully on, and has almost gained the opposite bank, when— slap! bang! both feet go from under him, and a dint in the solid ice commemorates his inglorious fall. In watching such episodes we tried to dispel the wearisomeness of the day. Every one welcomed the advent of night, which enabled us to seek such rest as could be found, and, clad as we were last night, in the garments of the day, officers and men huddled close together to keep from freezing to death. Each officer and man had placed one of his blankets upon his horse, and, seeing that there was a grave necessity of doing something to prevent loss of life, General Crook ordered that as many blankets as could be spared from the pack-trains should be spread over the sleepers.

It snowed fiercely all night, and was still snowing and blustering savagely when we were aroused in the morning; but we pushed out over a high ridge which we took to be part of the chain laid down on the map as the "Wolf" or "Panther" mountains. The storm continued all day, and the fierce north wind still blew in our teeth, making us imagine old Boreas to be in league with the Indians to prevent our occupancy of the country. Mustaches and beards coated with pendent icicles several inches long and bodies swathed in raiment of furs and hides made this expedition of cavalry resemble a long column of Santa Clauses on their way to the polar regions to lay in a new supply of Christmas gifts. We saw some very fresh buffalo manure and also some new Indian sign. Scouts were pushed ahead to scour the country while the command went into bivouac in a secluded ravine which afforded a sufficiency of water, cottonwood fuel, and good grass, and sheltered us from the observation of roving Indians, although the prevailing inclement weather rendered it highly improbable that many hunters or spies would be far away from their villages. The temperature became lower and lower, and the regular indications upon our thermometer after sundown were − 6° and − 10° of the Fahrenheit scale. Men and animals had not yet suffered owing to the good fortune in always finding ravines in which to bivouac, and where the vertical clay banks screened from the howling winds. The snow continued all through the night of the 9th and the day of the 10th of March, but we succeeded in making pretty good marches, following down the course of Prairie Dog Creek for twenty-two miles in the teeth of a blast which was laden with minute crystals of snow frozen to the sharpness of razors and cutting the skin wherever it touched. Prairie Dog Creek at first flows through a narrow gorge, but this widens into a flat valley filled with the burrows of the dainty little animals which give the stream its name and which could be seen in numbers during every lull in the storm running around in the snow to and from their holes and making tracks in every direction. Before seeing this I had been under the impression that the prairie dog hibernated.

While the severity of the weather had had but slight effect upon the command directly, the slippery trail, frozen like glass, imposed an unusual amount of hard labor upon both human and equine members, and it was only by the greatest exertion that serious accidents were averted in the crossing of the little ravines which intersected the trail every two or three hundred yards. One of the corporals of " D " Company, Third Cavalry, was internally injured, to what extent could not be told at the moment, by his horse falling upon him while walking by his side. A " travois " was made of two long saplings and a blanket, in which the sufferer was dragged along behind a mule. The detachment of guides, sent out several nights previously, returned this evening, reporting having found a recently abandoned village of sixty "tepis," and every indication of long habitancy. The Indians belonging thereto had plenty of meat—buffalo, deer, and elk— some of which was left behind upon departure. A young puppy, strangled to death, was found hanging to a tree. This is one of the greatest delicacies of every well-regulated Sioux feast—choked pup. It also figures in their sacrifices, especially all those in any manner connected with war. The guides had brought back with them a supply of venison, which was roasted on the embers and pronounced delicious by hungry palates. The storm abated during the night, and there were glimpses of the moon behind fleeting clouds, but the cold became much more intense, and we began to suffer. The next morning our thermometer failed to register. It did not mark below — 22° Fahrenheit, and the mercury had passed down into the bulb and congealed into a solid button, showing that at least — 39° had been reached. The wind, however, had gone down, for which we were all thankful. The sun shone out bright and clear, the frost on the grass glistened like diamonds, and our poor horses were coated with ice and snow.

We marched north eight or nine miles down the Tongue River, which had to be crossed six times on the ice. This was a fine stream, between thirty and forty yards wide, its banks thickly fringed with box-elder, cottonwood, and willow. Grama grass was abundant in the foot-hills close by, and in all respects except cold this was the finest camp yet made. The main command halted and bivouacked at this point, to enable the guides to explore to the west, to the Rosebud, and beyond. On the night of March 11th we had a lovely moonlight, but the cold was still hard to bear, and the mercury was again congealed. Fortunately no one was frozen, for which fact some credit is due to the precautions taken in the matter of clothing, and to the great care manifested by our medical officer, Surgeon Munn. The exemption of the command from frost-bite was not more remarkable than the total absence of all ailments of a pneumonitic type; thus far, there had not been a single instance of pneumonia, influenza, or even simple cold. I have no hesitancy in saying that the climate of Wyoming or Montana is better suited for invalids suffering from lung disorders, not of an aggravated nature, than is that of Florida; I have some personal acquaintance with the two sections, and the above is my deliberate conviction.

Despite the hyperborean temperature, the genial good-humor and cheerfulness of the whole command was remarkable and deserving of honorable mention. Nothing tries the spirit and temper of the old veteran, not to mention the young recruit, as does campaigning under unusual climatic vicissitudes, at a time when no trace of the enemy is to be seen. To march into battle with banners flying, drums beating, and the pulse throbbing high with the promptings of honorable ambition and enthusiasm, in unison with the roar of artillery, does not call for half the nerve and determination that must be daily exercised to pursue mile after mile in such terrible weather, over rugged mountains and through unknown cañons, a foe whose habits of warfare are repugnant to every principle of humanity, and whose presence can be determined solely by the flash of the rifle which lays some poor sentry low, or the whoop and yell which stampede our stock from the grazing-grounds. The life of a soldier, in time of war, has scarcely a compensating feature ; but he ordinarily expects palatable food whenever obtainable, and good warm quarters during the winter season. In campaigning against Indians, if anxious to gain success, he must lay aside every idea of good food and comfortable lodgings, and make up his mind to undergo with cheerfulness privations from which other soldiers would shrink back dismayed. His sole object should be to strike the enemy and to strike him hard, and this accomplished should be full compensation for all privations undergone. With all its disadvantages this system of Indian warfare is a grand school for the cavalrymen of the future, teaching them fortitude, vigilance, self-reliance, and dexterity, besides that instruction in handling, marching, feeding, and fighting troops which no school can impart in text-books.

This manner of theorizing upon the subject answered excellently well, except at breakfast, when it strained the nervous system immensely to admit that soldiers should under any circumstances be sent out on winter campaigns in this latitude. Our cook had first to chop with an axe the bacon which over night had frozen hard as marble ; frequently the hatchet or axe was broken in the contest. Then if he had made any "soft bread," that is, bread made of flour and baked in a frying-pan, he had to place that before a strong fire for several minutes to thaw it so it could be eaten, and all the forks, spoons, and knives had to be run through hot water or hot ashes to prevent them from taking the skin off the tongue. The same rule had to be observed with the bits when our horses were bridled. I have seen loaves of bread divided into two zones—the one nearer the blazing fire soft and eatable, the other still frozen hard as flint and cold as charity. The same thing was to be noticed in the pans of beans and other food served up for consumption.

For several days we had similar experiences which need not be repeated. Our line of march still continued northward, going down the Tongue River, whose valley for a long distance narrowed to a little gorge bordered by bluffs of red and yellow sandstone, between one hundred and fifty and two hundred feet high—in some places much higher—well fringed with scrub pine and juniper. Coal measures of a quality not definitely determined cropped out in all parts of the country. By this time we were pretty far advanced across the borders of the Territory of Montana, and in a region well grassed with grama and the "black sage," a plant almost as nutritious as oats. The land in the stream bottoms seemed to be adapted for cultivation. Again the scouts crossed over to the Rosebud, finding no signs of the hostiles, but bringing back the meat of two buffalo bulls which they had killed. This was a welcome addition to the food of men without fresh meat of any kind; our efforts to coax some of the fish in the stream to bite did not meet with success; the weather was too cold for them to come out of the deep pools in which they were passing the winter. The ice was not far from two feet in thickness, and the trout were torpid. The scouts could not explain why they had not been able to place the villages of the hostiles, and some of our people were beginning to believe that there were none out from the reservations, and that all had gone in upon hearing that the troops had moved out after them; in this view neither Frank Gruard, "Big Bat," nor the others of the older heads concurred.

"We'll find them pretty soon" was all that Frank would say. As we approached the Yellowstone we came upon abandoned villages, with the frame-work of branches upon which the squaws had been drying meat; one or two, or it may have been three, of these villages had been palisaded as a protection against the incursions of the Absaroka or Crows of Montana, who raided upon the villages of the Sioux when the latter were not raiding upon theirs. Cottonwood by the hundreds of cords lay scattered about the villages, felled by the Sioux as a food for their ponies, which derive a small amount of nourishment from the inner bark. There were Indian graves in numbers : the corpse, wrapped in its best blankets and buffalo robes, was placed upon a scaffold in the branches of trees, and there allowed to dry and to decay. The cottonwood trees here attained a great size : four, five, and six feet in diameter ; and all the conditions for making good camps were satisfied : the water was excellent, after the ice had been broken ; a great sufficiency of succulent grass was to be found in the nooks sheltered from the wind ; and as for wood, there was more than we could properly use in a generation. One of the cooks, by mistake, made a fire at the foot of a great hollow cottonwood stump; in a few moments the combustible interior was a mass of flame, which hissed and roared through that strange chimney until it had reached an apparent height of a hundred feet above the astonished packers seated at its base. Buffalo could be seen every day, and the meat appeared at every meal to the satisfaction of all, notwithstanding its stringiness and exceeding toughness, because we could hit nothing but the old bulls. A party of scouts was sent on in front to examine the country as far as the valley of the Yellowstone, the bluffs on whose northern bank were in plain sight.

There was a great and unexpected mildness of temperature for one or two days, and the thermometer indicated for several hours as high as 20° above zero, very warm in comparison with what we had had. General Crook and the half-breeds adopted a plan of making themselves comfortable which was generally imitated by their comrades. As soon as possible after coming into camp, they would sweep clear of snow the piece of ground upon which they intended making down their blankets for the night ; a fire would next be built and allowed to burn fiercely for an hour, or as much longer as possible. When the embers had been brushed away and the canvas and blankets spread out, the warmth under the sleeper was astonishingly comfortable. Our pack-mules, too, showed an amazing amount of intelligence. I have alluded to the great trouble and danger experienced in getting them and our horses across the different "draws" or "coulées" impeding the march. The pack-mules, of their own motion, decided that they would get down without being a source of solicitude to those in charge of them ; nothing was more amusing than to see some old patriarch of the train approach the glassy ramp leading to the bottom of the ravine, adjust his hind feet close together and slide in triumph with his load secure on his back. This came near raising a terrible row among the packers, who, in the absence of other topics of conversation, began to dispute concerning the amount of sense or "savey" exhibited by their respective pets. One cold afternoon it looked as if the enthusiastic champions of the respective claims of "Pinto Jim" and "Keno" would draw their knives on each other, but the affair quieted down without bloodshed. Only one mule had been injured during this kind of marching and sliding—one broke its back while descending an icy ravine leading to the "Clear Fork" of the Powder.

Not many moments were lost after getting into bivouac before all would be in what sailors call "ship shape." Companies would take the positions assigned them, mounted vedettes would be at once thrown out on the nearest commanding hills, horses unsaddled and led to the grazing-grounds, mules unpacked and driven after, and wood and water collected in quantities for the cooks, whose enormous pots of beans and coffee would exhale a most tempting aroma. After eating dinner or supper, as you please, soldiers, packers, and officers would gather around the fires, and in groups discuss the happenings of the day and the probabilities of the future. The Spaniards have a proverb which may be translated—"A man with a good dinner inside of him looks upon the world through rosy spectacles" :

> "Barriga llena,
> Corazon contento."

There was less doubt expressed of our catching Indians ; the evidences of their presence were too tangible to admit of any ambiguity, and all felt now that we should run in upon a party of considerable size unless they had all withdrawn to the north of the Yellowstone. These opinions were confirmed by the return of Frank Gruard with a fine young mule which had been left behind by the Sioux in one of the many villages occupied by them along this stream-bed ; the animal was in fine condition, and its abandonment was very good proof of the abundance of stock with which the savages must be blessed.

This is how General Crook appeared on this occasion, as I find recorded in my notes : boots, of Government pattern, number 7 ; trousers, of brown corduroy, badly burned at the ends ; shirt, of brown, heavy woollen ; blouse, of the old army style ; hat, a brown Kossuth of felt, ventilated at top. An old army overcoat, lined with red flannel, and provided with a high collar made of the skin of a wolf shot by the general himself, completed his costume, excepting a leather belt with forty or fifty copper cartridges, held to the shoulders by two leather straps. His horse and saddle were alike good, and with his rifle were well cared for.

The General in height was about six feet—even, perhaps, a trifle taller ; weight, one hundred and seventy pounds ; build, spare and straight ; limbs, long and sinewy ; complexion, nervo-sanguine ; hair, light-brown ; cheeks, ruddy, without being florid ; features, delicately and firmly chiselled ; eyes, blue-gray ; nose, a pronounced Roman and quite large ; mouth, mild but firm, and showing with the chin much resolution and tenacity of purpose.

As we halted for the night, a small covey of pin-tailed grouse flew across the trail. Crook, with seven shots of his rifle, laid six of them low, all but one hit in neck or head. This shooting was very good, considering the rapidity with which it had to be done, and also the fact that the shooter's hands were numb from a long march in the saddle and in the cold. These birds figured in an appetizing stew at our next breakfast. We remained in bivouac for a day at the mouth of a little stream which we took to be Pumpkin Creek, but were not certain, the maps being unreliable ; here was another abandoned village of the Sioux in which we came across a ghastly token of human habitancy, in the half-decomposed arm of an Indian, amputated at the elbow-joint, two fingers missing, and five buckshot fired into it. The guides conjectured that it was part of the anatomy of a Crow warrior who had been caught by the Sioux in some raid upon their herds and cut limb from limb.

The forest of cottonwoods at this place was very dense, and the trees of enormous size. Upon the inner bark of a number, the Sioux had delineated in colors many scenes which were not comprehensible to us. There were acres of fuel lying around us, and we made liberal use of the cottonwood ashes to boil a pot of hominy with corn from the pack train. Half a dozen old buffaloes were seen close to camp during the day, one of which animals was shot by General Crook. When our guides returned from the Yellowstone, they brought with them the carcasses of six deer, five white-tailed and one black-tailed, which were most acceptable to the soldiers. All the trails seen by this reconnoitring party had led over towards the Powder River, none being found in the open valley of the Yellowstone. The Sioux and Cheyennes would naturally prefer to make their winter habitations in the deeper and therefore warmer cañons of the Rosebud, Tongue, and Powder, where the winds could not reach them and their stock. The country hereabouts was extremely rough, and the bluffs were in many places not less than seven hundred and fifty feet in height above the surface of the stream. It had again become cold and stormy, and snow was falling, with gusts of wind from the north. The mercury during the night indicated 10° below zero, but the sky with the coquetry of a witch had resumed its toilet of blue pinned with golden stars. Our course led north and east to look for some of the trails of recent date ; the valleys of the creeks seemed to be adapted for agriculture, and our horses did very well on the rich herbage of the lower foothills. The mountains between the Tongue and the Powder, and those between the Tongue and the Rosebud as well, are covered with forests of pine and juniper, and the country resembles in not a little the beautiful Black Hills of Dakota.

This was the 16th of March, and we had not proceeded many miles before our advance, under Colonel Stanton, had sighted and pursued two young bucks who had been out hunting for game, and, seeing our column advancing, had stationed themselves upon the summit of a ridge, and were watching our movements. Crook ordered the command to halt and bivouac at that point on the creek which we had reached. Coffee was made for all hands, and then the purposes of the general commanding made themselves known. He wanted the young Indians to think that we were a column making its way down towards the Yellowstone with no intention of following their trail ; then, with the setting of the sun, or a trifle sooner, we were to start out and march all night in the hope of striking the band to which the young men belonged, and which must be over on the Powder as there was no water nearer in quantity sufficient for ponies and families. The day had been very blustering and chilly, with snow clouds lowering over us.

CHAPTER XVI.

GENERAL CROOK directed General J. J. Reynolds, Third Cavalry, to take six companies of cavalry, and, with the half-breed scouts, make a forced march along the trail of the hunters, and see just what he could find. If the trail led to a village, Reynolds should attack ; if not, the two portions of the command were to unite on the Powder at or near a point designated. Crook was very kindly disposed towards General Reynolds, and wanted to give him every chance to make a brilliant reputation for himself and retrieve the past. Reynolds had been in some kind of trouble in the Department of Texas, of which he had been the commander, and as a consequence of this trouble, whatever it was, had been relieved of the command and ordered to rejoin his regiment. We were out on the trail by half-past five in the afternoon, and marched rapidly up a steep ravine, which must have been either Otter or Pumpkin Creek, and about half-past two in the morning of March 17, 1876, were able to discern through the darkness the bluffs on the eastern side of the Big Powder ; the night was very cold, the wind blew keenly and without intermission, and there were flurries of snow which searched out the tender spots left in our faces.

It was of course impossible to learn much of the configuration and character of the country in such darkness and under such circumstances, but we could see that it was largely of the kind called in Arizona " rolling mesa," and that the northern exposure of the hills was plentifully covered with pine and juniper, while grass was in ample quantity, and generally of the best quality of grama. Stanton led the advance, having Frank Gruard and one or two assistants trailing in the front. The work was excellently well done, quite as good as the best I had ever seen done by the Apaches. Stanton, Mr. Robert E. Strahorn, Hospital Steward Bryan, and myself made a small party and kept together; we were the only white men along not connected with the reservations.

This march bore grievously upon the horses; there were so many little ravines and gullies, dozens of them not more than three or four feet in depth, which gashed the face of nature and intersected the course we were pursuing in so many and such unexpected places, that we were constantly halting to allow of an examination being made to determine the most suitable places for crossing, without running the risk of breaking our own or our horses' necks. The ground was just as slippery as glass, and so uneven that when on foot we were continually falling, and when on horseback were in dread of being thrown and of having our horses fall upon us, as had already happened in one case on the trip. To stagger and slip, wrenching fetlocks and pasterns, was a strain to which no animals could be subjected for much time without receiving grave injuries. Our horses seemed to enter into the spirit of the occasion, and when the trail was at all decent would press forward on the bit without touch of spur. When Frank Gruard had sighted the bluffs of the Powder, the command halted in a deep ravine, while Frank and a picked detail went out in front some distance to reconnoitre. The intense cold had made the horses impatient, and they were champing on the bits and pawing the ground with their hoofs in a manner calculated to arouse the attention of an enemy, should one happen to be in the vicinity. They were suffering greatly for water; the ice king had set his seal upon all the streams during the past week, and the thickness of the covering seen was from two and a half to three feet. This thirst made them all the more restless and nervous. While we halted in this ravine, many of the men lay down to sleep, much to the alarm of the officers, who, in fear that they would not awaken again, began to shake and kick them back to wakefulness.

By looking up at the "Dipper" we could see that we were travelling almost due east, and when our scouts returned they brought the important information that the two Indians whom we had been following had been members of a hunting party of forty, mounted, whose trail we were now upon. Frank led off at a smart pace, and we moved as fast as we could in rear; the mists and clouds of night were breaking, and a faint sign in the east told the glad news that dawn was coming. Directly in front of us and at a very short distance away, a dense column of smoke betrayed the existence of a village of considerable size, and we were making all due preparations to attack it when, for the second time, Frank returned with the information that the smoke came from one of the burning coal-measures of which Montana and Wyoming were full. Our disappointment was merely temporary; we had not begun fairly to growl at our luck before Frank returned in a most gleeful mood, announcing that the village had been sighted, and that it was a big one at the base of the high cliffs upon which we were standing.

The plan of battle was after this manner: Reynolds had three battalions, commanded respectively by Moore, Mills, and Noyes. Noyes's battalion was to make the first move, Egan's company, with its revolvers, charging in upon the village, and Noyes cutting out and driving off the enemy's herd of ponies. Mills was to move in rear of Noyes, and, after the village had been charged, move into and take possession of it, occupy the plum thicket surrounding it, and destroy all the "tepis" and plunder of all kinds. These battalions were to descend into the valley of the Powder through a ravine on our right flank, while Moore with his two companies was to move to the left and take up a position upon the hills overlooking the village, and receive the flying Indians with a shower of lead when they started to flee from their lodges, and attempted to get positions in the brakes or bluffs to annoy Egan.

Noyes led off with his own and Egan's companies, and Frank Gruard, "Big Bat," and others of the scouts showing the path down the ravine; the descent was a work of herculean difficulty for some of the party, as the horses slipped and stumbled over the icy ground, or pressed through the underbrush and fallen rocks and timber. At length we reached the narrow valley of the Powder, and all hands were impatient to begin the charge at once. This, Major Noyes would not allow; he sent Gruard, "Big Bat," and "Little Bat" to the front to look at the ground and report whether or not it was gashed by any ravines which would render

the advance of cavalry difficult. Their report was favorable,
nothing being seen to occasion fear that a mounted force could
not approach quite close to the lodges. It was a critical moment,
as Frank indicated where the Indian boys were getting ready to
drive the herds of ponies down to water, which meant that the
village would soon be fully aroused. At last we were off, a small
band of forty-seven all told, including the brave "Teddy" Egan
himself, Mr. Strahorn, the representative of the *Rocky Mountain News*, a man who displayed plenty of pluck during the
entire campaign, Hospital Steward Bryan, and myself. We moved
out from the gulch in column of twos, Egan at the head; but
upon entering the main valley the command "Left front into
line" was given, and the little company formed a beautiful line
in less time than it takes to narrate it. We moved at a fast
walk, and as soon as the command "Charge" should be given,
we were to quicken the gait to a trot, but not move faster on
account of the weak condition of our stock. When the end of
the village was reached we were to charge at full gallop down
through the lines of "tepis," firing our revolvers at everything
in sight; but if unable to storm the village, we were to wheel
about and charge back. Just as we approached the edge of the
village we came upon a ravine some ten feet in depth and of a varying width, the average being not less than fifty. We got down this
deliberately, and at the bottom and behind a stump saw a young
boy about fifteen years old driving his ponies. He was not ten
feet off. The youngster wrapped his blanket about him and stood
like a statue of bronze, waiting for the fatal bullet; his features
were as immobile as if cut in stone. The American Indian
knows how to die with as much stoicism as the East Indian. I
levelled my pistol. "Don't shoot," said Egan, "we must make
no noise." We were up on the bench upon which the village
stood, and the war-whoop of the youngster was ringing wildly in
the winter air, awakening the echoes of the bald-faced bluffs.
The lodges were not arranged in any order, but placed where
each could secure the greatest amount of protection from the configuration of the coves and nooks amid the rocks. The ponies
close to the village trotted off slowly to the right and left as we
drew near; the dogs barked and howled and scurried out of sight;
a squaw raised the door of her lodge, and seeing the enemy yelled
with all her strength, but as yet there had been not one shot fired.

We had emerged from the clump of cottonwoods and the thick undergrowth of plum bushes immediately alongside of the nearest "tepis," when the report of the first Winchester and the zipp of the first bullet notified us that the fun had begun.

The enemy started out from their lodges, running for the rocky bluffs overlooking the valley, there to take position, but turning to let us have the benefit of a shot every moment or so. We could not see much at which to fire, the "tepis" intervening, but we kept on our way through the village, satisfied that the flight of the hostiles would be intercepted by Moore from his place upon the hills. The Indians did not shoot at our men, they knew a trick worth two of that: they fired deliberately at our horses, with the intention of wounding some of them and rendering the whole line unmanageable. The first shot struck the horse of the troop blacksmith in the intestines, and made him rear and plunge and fall over backwards. That meant that both horse and man were *hors du combat* until the latter could extricate himself, or be extricated from under the dying, terrified animal. The second bullet struck the horse of Steward Bryan in the head, and knocked out both his eyes; as his steed stiffened in death, Bryan, who was riding next to me, called out, "There is something the matter with my horse!" The third missile was aimed at "Teddy" Egan, but missed him and cut the bridle of my old plug as clean as if it had been a piece of tissue paper. From that on the fire became a volley, although the people of the village were retreating to a place of safety for their women and children.

The herd of ponies had been "cut out," and they were now afoot unless they could manage to recapture them. Two or three boys made an attempt to sneak around on our right flank and run the herd back up among the high bluffs, where they would be practically safe from our hands. This was frustrated by Egan, who covered the line of approach with his fire, and had the herd driven slightly to our rear. The advantages, however, were altogether on the side of the Sioux and Cheyennes, as our promised support did not arrive as soon as expected, and the fire had begun to tell upon us; we had had three men wounded, one in the lower part of the lungs, one in the elbow-joint, and one in the collar-bone or upper part of the chest; six horses had been killed and three wounded, one of the latter being Egan's own, which had been hit in the neck. The men wounded were not the men on the wounded horses, so that at this early stage of the skirmish we had one-fourth of our strength disabled. We held on to the village as far as the centre, but the Indians, seeing how feeble was our force, rallied, and made a bold attempt to surround and cut us off. At this moment private Schneider was killed. Egan was obliged to dismount the company and take shelter in the plum copse along the border of the ice-locked channel of the Powder, and there defend himself to the best of his ability until the arrival of the promised reënforcements.

Noyes had moved up promptly in our rear and driven off the herd of ponies, which was afterwards found to number over seven hundred; had he charged in echelon on our left, he would have swept the village, and affairs would have had a very different ending, but he complied with his instructions, and did his part as directed by his commander. In the work of securing the herd of ponies, he was assisted by the half-breed scouts.

Colonel Stanton and Lieutenant Sibley, hearing the constant and heavy firing in front, moved up without orders, leading a small party of the scouts, and opened an effective fire on our left. Half an hour had passed, and Moore had not been heard from; the Indians under the fire from Stanton and Sibley on our left, and Egan's own fire, had retired to the rocks on the other side of the "tepis," whence they kept plugging away at any one who made himself visible. They were in the very place where it was expected that Moore was to catch them, but not a shot was heard for many minutes; and when they were it was no help to us, but a detriment and a danger, as the battalion upon which we relied so much had occupied an entirely different place—one from which the fight could not be seen at all, and from which the bullets dropped into Egan's lines.

Mills advanced on foot, passing by Egan's left, but not joining him, pushed out from among the lodges the scattering parties still lurking there, and held the undergrowth on the far side; after posting his men advantageously, he detailed a strong party to burn and destroy the village. Egan established his men on the right, and sent a party to aid in the work of demolition and destruction. It was then found that a great many of our people had been severely hurt by the intense cold. In order to make the charge as effective as possible, we had disrobed and thrown to one side, upon entering the village, all the heavy or cumbrous wraps with which we could dispense. The disagreeable consequence was that many men had feet and fingers, ears and noses frozen, among them being Lieutenant Hall and myself. Hall had had much previous experience in the polar climate of these northwestern mountains, and showed me how to treat myself to prevent permanent disability.

He found an air-hole in the ice, into which we thrust feet and hands, after which we rubbed them with an old piece of gunnysack, the roughest thing we could find, to restore circulation. Steward Bryan, who seemed to be full of resources and forethought, had carried along with him a bottle of tincture of iodine for just such emergencies ; this he applied liberally to our feet and to all the other frozen limbs, and thus averted several cases of amputation. While Steward Bryan was engaged in his work of mercy, attending to the wounded and the frozen, Mills's and Egan's detachments were busy setting fire to the lodges, of elk and buffalo hide and canvas, which numbered over one hundred.

For the information of readers who may never have seen such lodges or "tepis," as they are called in the language of the frontier, I will say that they are large tents, supported upon a conical frame-work of fir or ash poles about twenty feet long, spread out at the bottom so as to give an interior space with a diameter of from eighteen to twenty-five feet. This is the average size, but in each large village, like the present one, was to be found one or more very commodious lodges intended for the use of the "council" or for the ceremonies of the "medicine" bands ; there were likewise smaller ones appropriated to the use of the sick or of women living in seclusion. In the present case, the lodges would not burn, or, to speak more explicitly, they exploded as soon as the flames and heat had a chance to act upon the great quantities of powder in kegs and canisters with which they were all supplied. When these loose kegs exploded the lodge-poles, as thick as a man's wrist and not less than eighteen feet long, would go sailing like sky-rockets up into the air and descend to smash all obstacles in their way. It was a great wonder to me that some of our party did not receive serious injuries from this cause.

In one of the lodges was found a wounded squaw, who stated that she had been struck in the thigh in the very beginning of the fight as her husband was firing out from the entrance to the lodge. She stated that this was the band of "Crazy Horse," who had with him a force of the Minneconjou Sioux, but that the forty new canvas lodges clustered together at the extremity by which we had entered belonged to some Cheyennes who had recently arrived from the "Red Cloud" Agency. Two lodges of Sioux had arrived from the same agency two days previously with the intention of trading with the Minneconjoux.

What with the cold threatening to freeze us, the explosions of the lodges sending the poles whirling through the air, and the leaden attentions which the enemy was once more sending in with deadly aim, our situation was by no means agreeable, and I may claim that the notes jotted down in my journal from which this narrative is condensed were taken under peculiar embarrassments. "Crazy Horse's" village was bountifully provided with all that a savage could desire, and much besides that a white man would not disdain to class among the comforts of life.

There was no great quantity of baled furs, which, no doubt, had been sent in to some of the posts or agencies to be traded off for the ammunition on hand, but there were many loose robes of buffalo, elk, bear, and beaver; many of these skins were of extra fine quality. Some of the buffalo robes were wondrously embroidered with porcupine quills and elaborately decorated with painted symbolism. One immense elk skin was found as large as two and a half army blankets; it was nicely tanned and elaborately ornamented. The couches in all the lodges were made of these valuable furs and peltries. Every squaw and every buck was provided with a good-sized valise of tanned buffalo, deer, elk, or pony hide, gaudily painted, and filled with fine clothes, those of the squaws being heavily embroidered with bead-work. Each family had similar trunks for carrying kitchen utensils and the various kinds of herbs that the plains' tribes prized so highly. There were war-bonnets, strikingly beautiful in appearance, formed of a head-band of red cloth or of beaver fur, from which depended another piece of red cloth which reached to the ground when the wearer was mounted, and covered him and the pony he rode. There was a crown of eagle feathers, and similar plumage was affixed to the tail-piece. Bells, ribbons, and other gew-gaws were also attached and occasionally I have noticed a pair of buffalo horns, shaved down fine, surmounting the head. Altogether, these feather head-dresses of the tribes in the Missouri drainage were the most impressive and elegant thing to be seen on the border. They represented an investment of considerable money, and were highly treasured by the proud possessors. They were not only the *indicia* of wealth, but from the manner in which the feathers were placed and nicked, the style of the ornamentation, and other minute points readily recognizable by the other members of the tribe, all the achievements of the wearer were recorded. One could tell at a glance whether he had ever stolen ponies, killed men, women, or children, been wounded, counted "coup," or in any other manner demonstrated that his deeds of heroism were worthy of being chanted in the dances and around the camp-fires. In each lodge there were knives and forks, spoons, tin cups, platters, mess-pans, frying-pans, pots and kettles of divers shapes, axes, hatchets, hunting-knives, water-kegs, blankets, pillows, and every conceivable kind of truck in great profusion. Of the weight of dried and fresh buffalo meat and venison no adequate idea can be given ; in three or four lodges I estimated that there were not less than one thousand pounds. As for ammunition, there was enough for a regiment ; besides powder, there was pig-lead with the moulds for casting, metallic cartridges, and percussion caps. One hundred and fifty saddles were given to the flames.

Mills and Egan were doing excellent work in the village itself ; the herd of ponies was in Noyes's hands, and why we should not have held our place there, and if necessary fortified and sent word to Crook to come across the trail and join us, is one of those things that no man can explain. We had lost three killed, and had another man wounded mortally. General Reynolds concluded suddenly to withdraw from the village, and the movement was carried out so precipitately that we practically abandoned the victory to the savages. There were over seven hundred ponies, over one hundred and fifty saddles, tons upon tons of meat, hundreds of blankets and robes, and a very appreciable addition to our own stock of ammunition in our hands, and the enemy driven into the hills, while we had Crook and his four companies to depend upon as a reserve, and yet we fell back at such a rate that our dead were left in the hands of the Indians, and, as was whispered among the men, one of our poor soldiers fell alive into the enemy's hands and was cut limb from limb. I do not state this fact of my own knowledge, and I can only say that I believe it to be true. We pushed up the Powder as fast as our weary horses could be made to move, and never halted until after we had reached the mouth of Lodge Pole Creek, where we awaited the arrival of General Crook.

The bivouac at the mouth of the Lodge Pole was especially dreary and forlorn; the men nicknamed it "Camp Inhospitality": there was a sufficiency of water—or ice—enough wood, but very little grass for the animals. There was nothing to eat; not even for the wounded men, of whom we had six, who received from Surgeon Munn and his valuable assistant, Steward Bryan, and Doctor Ridgeley all the care which it was possible to give. Here and there would be found a soldier, or officer, or scout who had carried a handful of cracker-crumbs in his saddle-bags, another who had had the good sense to pick up a piece of buffalo meat in the village, or a third who could produce a spoonful of coffee. With these a miserable apology was made for supper, which was not ready until very late; because the rear-guard of scouts and a handful of soldiers—which, under Colonel Stanton, Frank Gruard, "Big Bat," and others, had rounded up and driven off the herd of ponies—did not join until some time after sundown. A small slice of buffalo meat, roasted in the ashes, went around among five or six; and a cup of coffee would be sipped like the pipe of peace at an Indian council.

The men, being very tired with the long marching, climbing, and fighting of the past two days, were put on a "running guard" to give each the smallest amount possible of work and the greatest of sleep. No guard was set over the herd, and no attempt was made to protect it, and in consequence of this great neglect the Indians, who followed us during the night, had not the slightest trouble in recovering nearly all that originally belonged to them. Even when the loss was discovered and the fact reported that the raiders were still in sight, going over a low bluff down the valley, no attention was paid, and no attempt made to pursue and regain the mainstay of Indian hostility. The cold and exposure had begun to wear out both horses and men, and Doctor Munn had now all he could do in looking after the numerous cases of frost-bite reported in the command; my recollection is that there were sixty-six men whose noses, feet, or fingers were more or less imperilled by the effects of the cold. Added to these were two cases of inflammatory rheumatism, which were almost as serious as those of the wounded men.

Crook reached camp about noon of the 18th of March, and it goes without saying that his presence was equal to that of a thousand men. He expressed his gratification upon hearing of our successful finding of "Crazy Horse's" village, as that chief was justly regarded as the boldest, bravest, and most skilful warrior in the whole Sioux nation; but he could not conceal his disappointment and chagrin when he learned that our dead and wounded had been needlessly abandoned to the enemy, and that with such ample supplies of meat and furs at hand our men had been made to suffer from hunger and cold, with the additional fatigue of a long march which could have been avoided by sending word to him. Crook, with a detachment from the four companies left with him, had come on a short distance in advance of Hawley's and Dewees's battalions, and run in upon the rear-guard of the Cheyennes and Sioux who had stampeded so many of the ponies from Reynolds's bivouac; the General took sight at one of the Indians wearing a war-bonnet and dropped him out of the saddle; the Indian's comrades seized him and took off through the broken country, but the pony, saddle, buffalo robe, blanket, and bonnet of the dead man fell into our hands, together with nearly a hundred of the ponies; which were driven along to our forlorn camp at the confluence of the Lodge Pole and the Powder.

There was nothing for Crook to do but abandon the expedition, and return to the forts, and reorganize for a summer campaign. We had no beef, as our herd had been run off on account of the failure to guard it; we were out of supplies, although we had destroyed enough to last a regiment for a couple of months; we were encumbered with sick, wounded, and cripples with frozen limbs, because we had not had sense enough to save the furs and robes in the village; and the enemy was thoroughly aroused, and would be on the *qui vive* for all that we did. To old Fort Reno, by way of the valley of the Powder, was not quite ninety miles. The march was uneventful, and there was nothing to note beyond the storms of snow and wind, which lasted, with some spasmodic intermissions, throughout the journey. The wind blew from the south, and there was a softening of the ground, which aggravated the disagreeable features by adding mud to our other troubles.

The Indians hung round our camps every night, occasionally firing a shot at our fires, but more anxious to steal back their ponies than to fight. To remove all excuse for their presence Crook ordered that the throats of the captured ponies be cut, and this was done on two different nights : first, some fifty being knocked in the head with axes, or having their throats cut with the sharp knives of the scouts, and again, another " bunch " of fifty being shot before sun-down. The throat-cutting was determined upon when the enemy began firing in upon camp, and was the only means of killing the ponies without danger to our own people. It was pathetic to hear the dismal trumpeting (I can find no other word to express my meaning) of the dying creatures, as the breath of life rushed through severed wind-pipes. The Indians in the bluffs recognized the cry, and were aware of what we were doing, because with one yell of defiance and a parting volley, they left us alone for the rest of the night.

Steaks were cut from the slaughtered ponies and broiled in the ashes by the scouts ; many of the officers and soldiers imitated their example. Prejudice to one side, the meat is sweet and nourishing, not inferior to much of the stringy beef that used to find its way to our markets.

Doctor Munn, Doctor Ridgeley, and Steward Bryan were kept fully occupied in tending to the patients under their charge, and were more than pleased when the wagon-train was reached, and " travois" and saddles could be exchanged for ambulances and wagons.

Our reception by our comrades back at the wagon-train— Coates, Ferris, and Mason—was most cordial and soldier-like. The most gratifying proof of their joy at our return was found in the good warm supper of coffee, bacon, and beans prepared for every one of our columns, commissioned and enlisted. The ice in the Powder proved very treacherous, as all "alkali" ice will ; it was not half so thick as it had been found on the Tongue, where it had ranged from two to three feet. General Crook distributed the troops to the various military posts, and returned to his headquarters in Omaha. The conduct of certain officers was the subject of an investigation by a general court-martial, but it is not my purpose to overcrowd my pages with such matters, which can be readily looked up by readers interested in them. On our way down to Cheyenne, we encountered squads upon squads of adventurers, trudging on foot or riding in wagons to the Black Hills. At "Portuguese Phillip's" ranche, sixty-eight of these travellers had sat down to supper in one day; while at Fagan's, nearer Cheyenne, during the snow-storm of March 26th and 27th, two hundred and fifty had slept in the kitchens, stables, and out-houses.

CHAPTER XVII.

THE lack of coöperation by the troops in the Department of Dakota had been severely felt ; such coöperation had been promised and confidently expected. It needed no profoundly technical military mind to see that with two or three strong columns in the field seeking out the hostiles, each column able to hold its own against the enemy, the chances of escape for the Sioux and Cheyennes would be materially lessened, and those of success for the operations of either column, or both, perceptibly increased. But, with the exception of a telegram from General Custer, then at Fort Lincoln, dated February 27th, making inquiry as to the time fixed for the departure of the column under Reynolds—which question was answered by wire the same day— nothing had been heard of any column from the Missouri River camps going out after the Indians whom the authorities wished to have driven into the reservations.

With the opening of spring the phases of the problem presented greater complexity. The recalcitrant Indians were satisfied of their ability not only to elude pursuit but to present a bold front to the troops, and to whip them on the field of their choice. They had whipped us—so at least it seemed to them—on the 17th of March ; why could they not do the same on any other day—the 17th of May, or the 17th of August ? Crook determined to wait for the new grass, without which it would be impossible to campaign far away from the line of supplies, and to let the ground

become thoroughly dry from the early thaws, before he resumed the offensive. This would give to such columns as might
be designated in the north as coöperating forces opportunity to get into the field ; as it would also afford the restless
young element on the several reservations chance to deliberate
between the policy of peace and war, between remaining quiet
at the agencies, or starting out on a career of depredation and
bloodshed.

Each day came news, stoutly denied by the agents, that there
were parties slipping away to recruit the forces of the hostiles ;
it was only prudent to know in advance exactly how many there
would be in our front, and have them in our front instead of
imperilling our rear by starting out with a leaven of discontent
which might do grievous harm to the ranchos and settlements
near the Union Pacific Railroad. That the main body of the
Sioux and Cheyennes was " ugly " no longer admitted of doubt.
Hostilities were not limited to grumbling and growling, to surly
looks and ungracious acts, to mere threats against the agents or
some isolated ranchos ; they became active and venomous, especially along the lines of travel leading to the disputed territory—
the " Black Hills."   Attacks upon trains were a daily—an hourly
—occurrence.   In one of these the son-in-law of " Red Cloud "
was killed.   To defend these travellers there was no better method
than by carrying the war into Africa, and, by means of swift-
moving columns, come upon the villages of the hostiles and
destroy them, giving no time to the young men for amusements.

Three of the infantry companies from Fort Omaha and Fort
Bridger were detailed to guard the road between Fort Laramie
and Custer City ; each company went into an entrenched camp
with rifle-pits dug, and all preparations made for withstanding
a siege until help should arrive.   Trains could make their way
from one to the other of these fortified camps with much less danger than before their establishment, while there were two companies of cavalry, under officers of great experience, to patrol from
Buffalo Gap, at the entrance to the hills, and the North Platte.
These officers were Captain Russell, who had seen much service in
Arizona and New Mexico against the Apaches, and " Teddy "
Egan, of the Second Cavalry, who had led the charge into the
village of " Crazy Horse " on St. Patrick's Day.   Both of these
officers and their troops did all that Crook expected of them, and

that was a great deal. The same praise belongs to the little detachments of infantry, who rendered yeoman service. Egan was fortunate enough to come up just in the nick of time, as a train was surrounded and fired upon by six hundred warriors ; he led the charge, and the Indians took to flight.

There were attacks all along the line : eastward in Nebraska, the Sioux became very bold, and raided the horse and cattle ranchos in the Loup Valley ; they were pursued by Lieutenant Charles Heyl, Twenty-third Infantry, with a small detail of men mounted upon mules from the quartermaster's corral, and compelled to stand and fight, dropping their plunder, having one of their number killed, but killing one of our best men—Corporal Dougherty. In Wyoming, they raided the Chug, and there killed one of the old settlers—Huntoon—and ran off thirty-two horses. Lieutenant Allison, Second Cavalry, took the trail, and would have run his prey down had it not been for a blinding snow-storm which suddenly arose and obliterated the tracks of the marauders ; sufficient was learned, however, to satisfy Allison that the raiders were straight from the Red Cloud Agency. When the body of Huntoon was found, it had eleven wounds— three from arrows. The same or similar tales came in from all points of the compass—from the villages of the friendly Shoshones and Bannocks in the Wind River Mountains to the scattered homes on the Lodge Pole and the Frenchman.

A large number of the enlisted men belonging to the companies at Fort D. A. Russell (near Cheyenne, Wyoming) deserted, alleging as a reason that they did not care to serve under officers who would abandon their dead and dying to the foe. Every available man of the mounted service in the Department of the Platte was called into requisition for this campaign ; the posts which had been garrisoned by them were occupied by infantry companies sent from Omaha, Salt Lake, and elsewhere. The point of concentration was Fort Fetterman, and the date set as early as practicable after the first day of May. Two other strong columns were also to take the field—one under General John Gibbon, consisting of the troops from the Montana camps ; the other, under General Alfred H. Terry, to start from Fort Lincoln, and to comprise every man available from the posts in the eastern portion of the Department of Dakota. While the different detachments were marching to the point of rendezvous, Crook hurried to Fort

Laramie, and thence eastward to the Red Cloud Agency to hold a conference with the chiefs.

It was during trips like this—while rolling over the endless plains of Wyoming, now rivalling the emerald in their vernal splendors—that General Crook was at his best: a clear-headed thinker, a fluent conversationalist, and a most pleasant companion. He expressed himself freely in regard to the coming campaign, but said that while the Sioux and Cheyennes were a brave and bold people, from the very nature of the case they would never stand punishment as the Apaches had done. The tribes of the plains had accumulated much property in ponies and other things, and the loss of that would be felt most deeply. Crook hoped to sound the chiefs at the Red Cloud Agency, and learn about where each stood on the question of peace or hostility ; he also hoped to be able to enlist a small contingent of scouts for service with the troops. General Crook was unable to find the agent who was absent, but in his place he explained to the agency clerk what he wanted. The latter did all he could to prevent any of the chiefs from coming to see General Crook ; nevertheless, "Sitting Bull of the South," "Rocky Bear," and "Three Bears," prominent in the tribe, came over to the office of the military commander, Major Jordan, of the Ninth Infantry, and there met Crook, who had with him Colonel Stanton, Colonel Jordan, Frank Gruard, and myself. These men spoke in most favorable terms of the propositions laid down by General Crook, and old "Sitting Bull" (who, although bearing the same name, was as good as *the* "Sitting Bull" was bad) assured General Crook that even if no other chief in the tribe assisted, he would gather together thirty-five or forty of his young men and go with the soldiers to help drive the hostiles back to their reservations.

Although frustrated by the machinations of underlings of the Indian Bureau at that particular time, all these men kept the word then given, and appeared in the campaign undertaken later on in the fall. "Sitting Bull" was too feeble to go out in person, but sent some of his best young men ; and "Three Bears" and "Rocky Bear" went as they promised they would, and were among the bravest and most active of all the command, red or white. When Agent Hastings returned there seemed to be a great change in the feelings of the Indians, and it was evident

that he had done his best to set them against the idea of helping
in the campaign. He expressed himself to the effect that while
he would not forbid any Indian from going, he would not recommend any such movement. General Crook said that at the
council where General Grant had decided that the northern Sioux
should go upon their reservations or be whipped, there were present, Secretary Chandler, Assistant Secretary Cowan, Commissioner Smith, and Secretary Belknap. The chiefs were, "Red
Cloud," "Old Man afraid of his Horses," "Blue Horse," "American Horse," "Little Wound," "Sitting Bull of the South," and
"Rocky Bear." With Agent Hastings were, Inspector Vandever,
and one of the contractors for Indian supplies, and Mr. R. E.
Strahorn. The contractor to whom reference is here made was
afterwards—in the month of November, 1878—convicted by a
Wyoming court, for frauds at this time, at this Red Cloud
Agency, and sent to the penitentiary for two years. Nothing
came of this part of the conference; the Indians, acting under
bad advice, as we learned afterwards, declined to entertain any
proposition of enlisting their people as scouts, and were then
told by General Crook that if they were not willing to do their
part in maintaining order among their own people and in their
own country, he would telegraph for the Crows, and Bannocks,
and Shoshones to send down the bands they had asked permission to send.

The Sioux appeared very much better off than any of the tribes
I had seen until that time. All of the men wore loose trousers
of dark blue cloth; moccasins of buck or buffalo skin covered
with bead work; and were wrapped in Mackinaw blankets, dark
blue or black in color, closely enveloping the frame; some of
these blankets were variegated by a transverse band of bright
red cloth worked over with beads, while underneath appeared
dark woollen shirts. Strings of beads, shells, and brass rings encircled each neck. The hair was worn long but plain, the median
line painted with vermilion or red ochre. Their faces were not
marked with paint of any kind, an unusual thing with Indians
in those days.

Smoking was done with beautiful pipes of the reddish ochreous
stone called "Catlinite," brought from the quarries on the Missouri. The bowls were prolonged to allow the nicotine to flow
downwards, and were decorated with inlaid silver, speaking highly

of the industrial capabilities of our aborigines. The stem was a long reed or handle of ash, perforated and beautifully ornamented with feathers and porcupine quills. Each smoker would take three or four whiffs, and then pass the pipe to the neighbor on his left.

General Crook was grievously disappointed at the turn affairs had taken, but he said nothing and kept his own counsel. Had he obtained three or four hundred warriors from Red Cloud and Spotted Tail the hostile element would have been reduced to that extent, and the danger to the feeble and poorly protected settlements along the Union Pacific lessened in the same ratio, leaving out of consideration any possible value these young men might be as scouts and trailers, familiar with all the haunts and devices of the hostiles. Be it remembered that while these efforts were going on, the hay scales at the Red Cloud Agency had been burned, and the government herds run off from both Red Cloud and Spotted Tail Agencies.

We left the Red Cloud Agency at four o'clock in the morning, and began the ascent of the Valley of the "White Earth" creek. After going several miles, on looking back we saw a great cloud of signal smoke puff up from the bluffs back of the Indian villages, but just what sort of a signal it was no one in our party knew. As it happened, we had a strong force, and instead of the usual escort of ten men or less, with which General Crook travelled from one post or agency to another, we had no less than sixty-five men all told, made up of Crook's own escort, the escort of Paymaster Stanton, returning from the pay trip. Colonel Ludington, Inspector General of the Department of the Platte, was also present with his escort, returning from a tour of inspection of the troops and camps along the northern border. A dozen or more of the ranchers and others living in the country had improved the opportunity to get to the railroad with perfect safety, and thus we were a formidable body. At the head of the White Earth we halted alongside of a pretty spring to eat some lunch, and there were passed by the mail-rider, a man named Clark, who exchanged the compliments of the day, and then drove on toward the post which he was never to reach. He was ambuscaded and killed by the band of Sioux who had planned to assassinate Crook but were deterred by our unexpectedly large force, and, rather than go without killing something, slaughtered the poor mail-rider, and drove off his horses. That was the meaning of the smoke puff at Red Cloud ; it was, as we learned long afterwards, the signal to the conspirators that Crook and his party were leaving the post.

We passed through Laramie and on to Fetterman as fast as horses and mules could draw us. Not all the troops had yet reached Fetterman, the condition of the road from Medicine Bow being fearfully bad. Crook, after some difficulty, had a cable ferry established, in working order. The first day sixty thousand pounds of stores were carried across the river ; the second, one hundred thousand pounds, besides soldiers by solid companies. Every wagon and nearly every mule and horse had to be carried over in the same manner, because the animals would not approach the swift current of the swollen Platte ; here they showed more sense than the men in charge of them, and seemed to know instinctively that the current of the river was too strong to be breasted by man or horse. One of the teamsters, Dill, fell into the river, and was swept down before the eyes of scores of terrified spectators and drowned. The current had the velocity of a mill-race, and the depth was found to vary from ten to twelve feet close to the shore. Frank Gruard was sent across the North Platte with a small party of scouts and soldiers to examine into the condition of the road, and while out on this duty came very near being cut off by a reconnoitring band of the enemy.

General Crook assumed command in General Orders, No. 1, May 28, 1876. Colonel William B. Royall, Third Cavalry, was assigned to the command of the fifteen companies of cavalry forming part of the expedition, having under him Colonel Alexander W. Evans, commanding the ten companies of the Third Cavalry, and Major H. E. Noyes, commanding the five of the Second Cavalry.

Five companies of the Ninth and Fourth Infantry were placed under the command of Colonel Alexander Chambers, of the Fourth Infantry ; Captain Nickerson and Lieutenant Bourke were announced as Aides-de-Camp ; Captain George M. Randall, Twenty-third Infantry, as Chief of Scouts ; Captain William Stanton as Chief Engineer Officer ; Captain John V. Furey as Chief Quartermaster ; First Lieutenant John W. Bubb as Commissary of Subsistence ; Assistant Surgeon Albert

Hartsuff as Medical Director. The companies starting out on this expedition and the officers connected with them were as follows : Company "A," Third Cavalry, Lieutenant Charles Morton ; Company " B," Third Cavalry, Captain Meinhold, Lieutenant Simpson ; Company " C," Third Cavalry, Captain Van Vliet, Lieutenant Von Leuttewitz ; Company " D," Third Cavalry, Captain Guy V. Henry, Lieutenant W. W. Robinson ; Company "E," Third Cavalry, Captain Sutorius ; Company "F," Third Cavalry, Lieutenant B. Reynolds ; Company " G," Third Cavalry, Lieutenant Emmet Crawford ; Company "I," Third Cavalry, Captain Andrews, Lieutenants A. D. King and Foster ; Company " L," Third Cavalry, Captain P. D. Vroom, Lieutenant Chase ; Company " M," Third Cavalry, Captain Anson Mills and Lieutenants A. C. Paul and Schwatka ; Company "A," Second Cavalry, Captain Dewees, Lieutenant Peirson ; Company " B," Second Cavalry, Lieutenant Rawolle ; Company " E," Second Cavalry, Captain Wells, Lieutenant Sibley ; Company "I," Second Cavalry, Captain H. E. Noyes ; Company "G," Second Cavalry, Lieutenants Swigert and Huntington ; Company " C," Ninth Infantry, Captain Sam Munson, Lieutenant T. H. Capron ; Company " H," Ninth Infantry, Captain A. S. Burt, Lieutenant E. B. Robertson ; Company " G," Ninth Infantry, Captain T. B. Burroughs, Lieutenant W. L. Carpenter ; Company " D," Fourth Infantry, Captain A. B. Cain, Lieutenant H. Seton ; Company " F," Fourth Infantry, Captain Gerard Luhn.

Assistant surgeons : Patzki, Stevens, and Powell.

Chief of pack trains : Mr. Thomas Moore.

Chief of wagon trains : Mr. Charles Russell.

Guides : Frank Gruard, Louis Richaud, Baptiste Pourrier (" Big Bat").

The press of the country was represented by Joseph Wasson, of the *Press*, Philadelphia, *Tribune*, New York, and *Alta California*, of San Francisco, California ; Robert E. Strahorn, of the *Tribune*, Chicago, *Rocky Mountain News*, Denver, Colorado, *Sun*, Cheyenne, Wyoming, and *Republican*, Omaha, Nebraska ; John F. Finerty, *Times*, Chicago ; T. B. MacMillan, *Inter-Ocean*, Chicago ; R. B. Davenport, *Herald*, New York.

Our camp on the north side of the North Platte presented a picturesque appearance, with its long rows of shelter tents arranged symmetrically in a meadow bounded on three sides by the stream ; the herds of animals grazing or running about ; the trains of wagons and mules passing from point to point, united to form a picture of animation and spirit. We had a train of one hundred and three six-mule wagons, besides one of hundreds of pack-mules ; and the work of ferriage became too great for mortal strength, and the ferrymen were almost exhausted both by their legitimate duties and by those of mending and splicing the boat and the cable which were leaking or snapping several times a day.

May 29, 1876, saw the column moving out from its camp in front of Fort Fetterman ; the long black line of mounted men stretched for more than a mile with nothing to break the sombreness of color save the flashing of the sun's rays back from carbines and bridles. An undulating streak of white told where the wagons were already under way, and a puff of dust just in front indicated the line of march of the infantry battalion. As we were moving along the same road described in the campaign of the winter, no further mention is necessary until after passing old Fort Reno. Meinhold, with two companies, was sent on in advance to reconnoitre the country, and report the state of the road as well as any signs of the proximity of large bands of the enemy. Van Vliet was instructed to push ahead, and keep a look-out for the Crow and Shoshone scouts who had promised to join the command at or near Reno. In spite of the fact that summer was already with us, a heavy snow-storm attacked the column on June 1st, at the time of our coming in sight of the Big Horn Mountains. The day was miserably cold, water froze in the camp-kettles, and there was much discomfort owing to the keen wind blowing down from the frozen crests of the Big Horn. From Reno, Gruard, Richaud, and "Big Bat" were sent to see what had become of the Crows, and lead them back to our command on the line of march.

Before he left Frank gave an account, from the story told him by the Sioux who had participated in it, of the massacre near this place of the force of officers and men enticed out from old Fort Kearney. In this sad affair we lost three officers—Fetterman, Brown, and Grummond—and seventy-five enlisted, with three civilians, names unknown. The Sioux admitted to Frank that they had suffered to the extent of one hundred and eighty-five, killed and wounded. I mention this story here at the place where we heard it from Frank's lips, although we afterwards marched over the very spot where the massacre occurred.

We broke camp at a very early hour, the infantry being out on the road by four o'clock each morning, the cavalry remaining for some time later to let the animals have the benefit of the grass freshened by the frost of the night previous. We were getting quite close to Cloud Peak, the loftiest point in the Big Horn range ; its massy dome towered high in the sky, white with a mantle of snow ; here and there a streak of darkness betrayed the attempts of the tall pine trees on the summit to penetrate to the open air above them. Heavy belts of forest covered the sides of the range below the snow line, and extended along the skirts of the foot-hills well out into the plains below. The singing of meadow-larks, and the chirping of thousands of grasshoppers, enlivened the morning air ; and save these no sound broke the stillness, except the rumbling of wagons slowly creeping along the road. The dismal snow-storm of which so much complaint had been made was rapidly superseded by most charming weather : a serene atmosphere, balmy breeze, and cloudless sky were the assurances that summer had come at last, and, as if anxious to repair past negligence, was about to favor us with all its charms. The country in which we now were was a great grassy plain covered with herbage just heading into seed. There was no timber except upon the spurs of the Big Horn, which loomed up on our left covered with heavy masses of pine, fir, oak, and juniper. From the innumerable seams and gashes in the flanks of this noble range issue the feeders of the Tongue and Powder, each insignificant in itself, but so well distributed that the country is as well adapted for pasturage as any in the world. The bluffs are full of coal of varying qualities, from lignite to a good commercial article ; one of the men of the command brought in a curious specimen of this lignite, which at one end was coal and at the other was silicified. Buffalo tracks and Indian signs were becoming frequent.

Clear Creek, upon which we made camp, was a beautiful stream—fifty feet wide, two feet deep ; current rapid and as much as eight miles an hour ; water icy-cold from the melting of the snow-banks on the Big Horn ; bottom of gravel ; banks gently sloping ; approaches good. Grass was excellent, but fuel rather scarce in the immediate vicinity of the road. Birds, antelope, and fish began to figure on the mess canvas ; the fish, a variety of sucker, very palatable, were secured by shooting a bullet under them and stunning them, so that they rose to the surface, and were then seized. Trout were not yet found ; they appear in the greatest quantity in the waters of Tongue River, the next stream beyond to the west. There is a variety of tortoise in the waters of these mountains which is most toothsome, and to my uncultivated taste fully as good as the Maryland terrapin.

Here we were visited by messengers from a party of Montana miners who were travelling across country from the Black Hills back to the Yellowstone ; the party numbered sixty-five, and had to use every precaution to prevent stampede and surprise ; every night they dug rifle-pits, and surrounded themselves with rocks, palisades, or anything else that could be made to resist a charge from the Sioux, whose trails were becoming very thick and plenty. There were many pony, but few lodge-pole, tracks, a sure indication that the men were slipping out from Red Cloud and Spotted Tail agencies and uniting with the hostiles, but leaving their families at home, under the protection of the reservations. It always seemed to me that that little party of Montana miners displayed more true grit, more common sense, and more intelligence in their desperate march through a scarcely known country filled with hostile Indians than almost any similar party which I can now recall ; they were prepared for every emergency, and did excellent service under Crook at the Rosebud ; but before reaching their objective point, I am sorry to say, many of their number fell victims to a relentless and wily foe.

To prevent any stampede of our stock which might be attempted, our method of establishing pickets became especially rigid : in addition to the mounted vedettes encircling bivouac, and occupying commanding buttes and bluffs, solid companies were thrown out a mile or two in advance and kept mounted, with the purpose of holding in check all parties of the enemy which might attempt to rush down upon the herds and frighten them off by waving blankets, yelling, firing guns, or other tricks in which the savages were adepts. One platoon kept saddled ready for instant work ; the others were allowed to loosen the cinches, but not to unsaddle. Eight miles from the ruins of old Fort Kearney, to the east, we passed Lake De Smet, named after the zealous missionary, Father De Smet, whose noble life was devoted to the advancement of the Sioux, Pawnees, Arapahoes, Crows, Blackfeet, Cheyennes, Cœurs d'Alenes, and Nez Percés, and whose silent ministrations refute the calumny that the American Indian is not responsive to efforts for his improvement. The view of this body of water, from the roadside, is very beautiful ; in length, it is nearly three miles ; in width, not quite a mile. The water is clear and cold, but alkaline and disagreeable to the taste. Game and ducks in great numbers resort to this lake, probably on account of the mineral contained in its waters, and a variety of pickerel is said to be abundant. Buffalo were seen near this bivouac—at old Fort Kearney—and elk meat was brought into camp with beaver, antelope, pin-tailed grouse, and sickle-billed curlew.

Our camp on Prairie Dog Creek, at its junction with the Tongue River, was memorable from being the scene of the killing of the first buffalo found within shooting distance of the column. Mosquitoes became troublesome near the water courses. Prairie-dog villages lined the trail in all places where the sandy soil admitted of easy digging. The last hour or two of this march was very unpleasant. The heat of the sun became almost unbearable. Dense masses of clouds moved sluggishly up from the west and north, while light flaky feathers of vapor flitted across the sky, coquetting with the breeze, now obscuring the sun, now revealing his rays. Low, rumbling thunder sullenly boomed across the horizon, and with the first flash of lightning changed into an almost continuous roar. The nearest peaks of the Big Horn were hid from our gaze. The heavy arch of clouds supported itself upon the crests of the bluffs enclosing the valley of our camp. It was a pretty picture ; the parks of wagons and pack-mules, the bright rows of tentage, and the moving animals and men gave enough animation to relieve the otherwise too sombre view of the elements at war. Six buffaloes were killed this day.

On the 7th of June we buried the soldier of Meinhold's company who had accidentally wounded himself with his own revolver while chopping wood. Besides the escort prescribed by the regulations, the funeral cortege was swollen by additions from all the companies of the expedition, the pack-train, wagoners, officers, and others, reaching an aggregate of over six hundred.

Colonel Guy V. Henry, Third Cavalry, read in a very feeling manner the burial service from the "Book of Common Prayer," the cavalry trumpets sounded "taps," a handful of earth was thrown down upon the remains, the grave was rapidly filled up, and the companies at quick step returned to their tents. There was no labored panegyric delivered over the body of Tiernan, but the kind reminiscences of his comrades were equivalent to an eulogy of which an archbishop might have been proud. Soldiers are the freest from care of any set of men on earth; the grave had not closed on their comrade before they were discussing other incidents of the day, and had forgotten the sad rites of sepulture in which they had just participated. To be more charitable, we were seeing so much that was novel and interesting that it was impossible to chain the mind down to one train of thought. Captain Noyes had wandered off during the storm of the night previous, and remained out of camp all night hunting for good trout pools. A herd of buffaloes had trotted down close to our bivouac, and many of our command had been unable to resist the temptation to go out and have a shot; we knocked over half a dozen or more of the old bulls, and brought the meat back for the use of the messes.

The conversation ran upon the difficulty experienced by the pioneer party under Captain Andrews, Third Cavalry, in smoothing and straightening the road during the marches of the past two or three days. General Crook had been successful in finding the nests and the eggs of some rare birds, the white-ringed blackbird, the Missouri skylark, and the crow of this region. He had all his life been an enthusiastic collector of specimens in natural history, especially in all that relates to nests and eggs, and had been an appreciative observer of the valuable work done on the frontier in that direction by Captain Charles Bendire, of the First Cavalry.

During the 8th of June there was some excitement among us, owing to the interchange of conversation between our pickets and a party of Indians late the previous night. It could not be determined at the moment whether the language used was Sioux or Crow, or both, but there was a series of calls and questions which our men did not fully understand; one query was to the effect that ours might be a Crow camp. A pony was found outside our lines, evidently left by the visitors. Despatches were received by General Crook notifying him that all able-bodied male Indians had left the Red Cloud Agency, and that the Fifth Cavalry had been ordered up from Kansas to take post in our rear; also that the Shoshones had sent one hundred and twenty of their warriors to help him, and that we should look for their arrival almost any day. They were marching across the mountains from their reservation in the Wind River range, in the heart of the Rockies.

June 9, 1876, the monotony of camp life was agreeably broken by an attack upon our lines made in a most energetic manner by the Sioux and Cheyennes. We had reached a most picturesque and charming camp on the beautiful Tongue River, and had thrown out our pickets upon the hill tops, when suddenly the pickets began to show signs of uneasiness, and to first walk and then trot their horses around in a circle, a warning that they had seen something dangerous. The Indians did not wait for a moment, but moved up in good style, driving in our pickets and taking position in the rocks, from which they rained down a severe fire which did no great damage but was extremely annoying while it lasted. We had only two men wounded, one in the leg, another in the arm, both by glancing bullets, and neither wound dangerous, and three horses and two mules wounded, most of which died. The attacking party had made the mistake of aiming at the tents, which at the moment were unoccupied; but bullets ripped through the canvas, split the ridge poles, smashed the pipes of the Sibley stoves, and imbedded themselves in the tail-boards of the wagons. Burt, Munson, and Burroughs were ordered out with their rifles, and Mills was ordered to take his own company of the Third Cavalry and those of Sutorius, Andrews, and Lawson, from Royall's command, and go across the Tongue and drive the enemy, which they did. The infantry held the buttes on our right until after sundown.

This attack was only a bluff on the part of "Crazy Horse" to keep his word to Crook that he would begin to fight the latter just as soon as he touched the waters of the Tongue River; we had scoffed at the message at first, believing it to have been an invention of some of the agency half-breeds, but there were many who now believed in its authenticity. Every one was glad the attack had been made; if it did nothing else, it proved that we were not going to have our marching for nothing ; it kept vedettes and guards on the alert and camp in condition for fight at a moment's notice. Grass becoming scarce on Tongue River Crook moved his command to the confluence of the two forks of Goose Creek, which is the largest affluent of the Tongue ; the distance was a trifle over seventeen miles, and during the march a hail-storm of great severity visited us and continued its pestiferous attentions for some time after tents had been erected. The situation at the new camp had many advantages : excellent pasturage was secured from the slopes of the hills ; water flowed in the greatest profusion—clear, sweet, and icy cold, murmuring gently in the channels on each side ; fire-wood in sufficiency could be gathered along the banks; the view of the mountains was beautiful and exhilarating, and the climate serene and bracing. Goose Creek was twenty-five yards wide, with a uniform depth of three feet, but greatly swollen by recent rains and the melting of the snow-banks up in the mountains.

We had to settle down and await the return of Frank Gruard, Louis Richaud, and "Big Bat," concerning whose safety not a few of the command began to express misgivings, notwithstanding they were all experienced frontiersmen, able to look out for their own safety under almost any contingencies. The more sanguine held to the view that the Crows had retired farther into their own country on account of the assembling of great bands of their enemies—the Sioux and Cheyennes—and that our emissaries had to travel much farther than they had first contemplated. But they had been separated from us for ten or twelve days, and it was becoming a matter of grave concern what to do about them.

In a bivouac of that kind the great object of life is to kill time. Drilling and guard duty occupy very few minutes, reading and writing become irksome, and conversation narrowly escapes the imputation of rank stupidity. We had enjoyed several pony races, but the best plugs for that sort of work—Major Burt's white and Lieutenant Robertson's bay—had both been shot during the skirmish of the 9th of the month, the former fatally, and we no longer enjoyed the pleasure of seeing races in which the stakes were nothing but a can of corn or a haunch of venison on each side, but which attracted as large and as deeply interested crowds as many more pretentious affairs within the

limits of civilization. The sending in of the mail every week or
ten days excited a ripple of concern, and the packages of letters
made up to be forwarded showed that our soldiers were men of
intelligence and not absolutely severed from home ties. The
packages were wrapped very tightly, first in waxed cloth and
then in oiled muslin, the official communications of most importance being tied to the courier's person, the others packed on a
led mule. At sundown the courier, Harrison, who had undertaken this dangerous business, set out on his return to Fort
Fetterman, accompanied by a non-commissioned officer whose
time had expired. They were to ride only by night, and never
follow the road too closely; by hiding in little coves high up in
the hills during the day they could most easily escape detection
by prowling bands of Indians coming out from the agencies, but
at best it was taking their lives in their hands.

The packers organized a foot-race, and bets as high as five
and ten thousand dollars were freely waged. These were of
the class known in Arizona as "jawbone," and in Wyoming as
"wind"; the largest amount of cash that I saw change hands
was twenty-five cents. Rattlesnakes began to emerge from their
winter seclusion, and to appear again in society; Lieutenant
Lemly found an immense one coiled up in his blankets, and
waked the echoes with his yells for help. The weather had assumed a most charming phase; the gently undulating prairie
upon whose bosom camp reposed was decked with the greenest
and most nutritive grasses; our animals lazily nibbled along
the hill skirts or slept in the genial light of the sun. In the
shade of the box-elder and willows along the stream beds the
song of the sweet-voiced meadow lark was heard all day. At
rare moments the chirping of grasshoppers might be distinguished in the herbage; in front of our line of tents a cook was
burning or browning coffee—it was just as often one as the
other—an idle recruit watching the process with a semi-attentive
stupefaction. The report of a carbine, aimed and fired by one
exasperated teamster at another attracted general notice; the
assailant was at once put in confinement and a languid discussion
of the merits or supposed merits of the case undulated from
tent to tent. Parties of whist-players devoted themselves to
their favorite game; other players eked out a share of diversion
with home-made checker-boards. Those who felt disposed to

test their skill as anglers were fairly rewarded ; the trout began
to bite languidly at first and with exasperating deliberation, but
making up for it all later on, when a good mess could be hooked
in a few minutes.   Noyes and Wells and Randall were the trout
maniacs, but they had many followers in their gentle lunacy,
which, before the hot weather had ended, spread throughout the
whole command.   Mills and his men were more inclined to go
up in the higher altitudes and hunt for bear ; they brought in a
good-sized "cinnamon," which was some time afterwards followed by other specimens of the bruin family ; elk and deer and
buffaloes, the last chiefly the meat of old bulls driven out of the
herds to the northwest, gave relish and variety to the ordinary
rations and additional topics for conversation.

General Crook was an enthusiastic hunter and fisher, and never
failed to return with some tribute exacted from the beasts of the
hills or the swimmers of the pools ; but he frequently joined
Burt and Carpenter in their search for rare birds and butterflies,
with which the rolling plains at the base of the Big Horn were
filled.   We caught one very fine specimen of the prairie owl,
which seemed wonderfully tame, and comported itself with rare
dignity ; the name of "Sitting Bull" was conferred unanimously,
and borne so long as the bird honored camp with its presence.
Lieutenant Foster made numbers of interesting sketches of the
scenery of the Big Horn and the hills nearest the Goose Creek ;
one of the packers, a man with decided artistic abilities, named
Stanley, was busy at every spare moment sketching groups of
teamsters, scouts, animals, and wagons, with delicacy of execution and excellent effect.   Captain Stanton, our engineer officer,
took his altitudes daily and noted the positions of the stars.
Newspapers were read to pieces, and such books as had found
their way with the command were passed from hand to hand and
read eagerly.   Mr. Wasson and I made an arrangement to peruse
each day either one of Shakespeare's plays or an essay by Macau-
lay, and to discuss them together.   The discovery of the first mess
of luscious strawberries occasioned more excitement than any of
the news received in the journals of the time, and an alarm on
the picket line from the accidental discharge of a carbine or rifle
would bring out all the conversational strength of young and old.

It was whispered that one of our teamsters was a woman, and
no other than "Calamity Jane," a character famed in border

story ; she had donned the raiment of the alleged rougher sex, and was skinning mules with the best of them. She was eccentric and wayward rather than bad, and had adopted male attire more to aid her in getting a living than for any improper purpose. "Jane" was as rough and burly as any of her messmates, and it is doubtful if her sex would ever have been discovered had not the wagon-master noted that she didn't cuss her mules with the enthusiasm to be expected from a graduate of Patrick & Saulsbury's Black Hills Stage Line, as she had represented herself to be. The Montana miners whom we had found near old Fort Reno began to "prospect" the gulches, but met with slight success.

During the afternoon of June 14th Frank Gruard and Louis Richaud returned, bringing with them an old Crow chief ; they reported having been obliged to travel as far as old Fort Smith, on the Big Horn, and that they had there seen a large village of Crows, numbering more than two hundred lodges. While preparing a cup of coffee the smoke from their little fire was discovered by the Crow scouts, and all the young warriors of the village, mistaking them for a small band of Sioux raiders, charged across the river and attacked them, nearly killing both Frank and Bat before mutual recognition was made and satisfactory greetings exchanged. The Crows were at first reluctant to send any of their men to aid in the war against the Sioux, alleging that they were compelled to get meat for their women and children, and the buffaloes were now close to them in great herds ; we might stay out too long ; the enemy was so close to the Crows that reprisals might be attempted, and many of the Crow women, children, and old men would fall beneath the bullet and the lance. But at last they consented to send a detachment of one hundred and seventy-five of their best men to see Crook and talk the matter over. Frank led them to our deserted camp on the Tongue River, upon seeing which they became alarmed, and supposed that we must have had a defeat from the Sioux and been compelled to abandon the country ; only sixteen followed further ; of these Frank and Louis took the old chief and rode as rapidly as possible to our camp on the Goose, leaving Bat to jog along with fifteen others and join at leisure.

General Crook ordered a hot meal of coffee, sugar, biscuits, butter, venison, and stewed dried apples to be set before the guest and guides, and then had a long talk with the former through the "sign language," the curious medium of correspondence between all the tribes east of the Rocky Mountains, from the Saskatchewan to the Pecos. This language is ideagraphic and not literal in its elements, and has strong resemblance to the figure speech of deaf mutes. Every word, every idea to be conveyed, has its characteristic symbol; the rapidity of transmission is almost telegraphic; and, as will be demonstrated later on, every possible topic finds adequate expression. The old chief explained to Frank that the troops from Montana (Gibbon's command) were encamped on the left bank of the Yellowstone, opposite the mouth of the Rosebud, unable to cross; the hostile Sioux were watching the troops from the other side. An attempt made by Gibbon to throw his troops across had resulted in the drowning of one company's horses in the flood; the Sioux had also, in some unexplained way, succeeded in running off the ponies belonging to the thirty Crow scouts attached to Gibbon's command.

The main body of the hostile Sioux and Cheyennes was encamped on the Tongue, near the mouth of Otter Creek, and between that and the Yellowstone. The Crows had heard that a large band of Shoshones had started out to join Crook, and should soon be with him at his present camp. It was a small detachment of Crow scouts that had alarmed our pickets by yelling some ten nights previously. As soon as the meal and the conversation were ended Crook sent the old chief back with Louis Richaud and Major Burt, who from previous service among the Crows was well acquainted with many of them, to halt the main body and induce them to enter our camp. Burt was entirely successful in his mission, and before dusk he was with us again, this time riding at the head of a long retinue of savage retainers, whose grotesque head-dresses, variegated garments, wild little ponies, and war-like accoutrements made a quaint and curious spectacle.

While the main column halted just inside our camp, the three chiefs—"Old Crow," "Medicine Crow," and "Good Heart"—were presented to General Crook, and made the recipients of some little attentions in the way of food. Our newly-arrived allies bivouacked in our midst, sending their herd of ponies out to graze alongside of our own horses. The entire band numbered one hundred and seventy-six, as near as we could ascertain; each had two ponies. The first thing they did was to erect the war-lodges of saplings, covered over with blankets or pieces of canvas; fires were next built, and a feast prepared of the supplies of coffee, sugar, and hard-tack dealt out by the commissary; these are the prime luxuries of an Indian's life. A curious crowd of lookers-on—officers, soldiers, teamsters, and packers—congregated around the little squads of Crows, watching with eager attention their every movement. The Indians seemed proud of the distinguished position they occupied in popular estimation, and were soon on terms of easy familiarity with the soldiers, some of whom could talk a sentence or two of Crow, and others were expert to a slight extent in the sign language.

In stature, complexion, dress, and general demeanor a marked contrast was observable between our friends and the Sioux Indians, a contrast decidedly to the advantage of the former. The Absaroka or Crow Indians, perhaps as a consequence of their residence among the elevated banks and cool, fresh mountain ranges between the Big Horn River and the Yellowstone, are somewhat fairer than the other tribes about them; they are all above medium height, not a few being quite tall, and many have a noble expression of countenance. Their dress consisted of a shirt of flannel, cotton, or buckskin; breech-clout; leggings of blanket; moccasins of deer, elk, or buffalo hide; coat of bright-colored blanket, made with loose sleeves and hood; and a head-dress fashioned in divers shapes, but most frequently formed from an old black army hat, with the top cut out and sides bound round with feathers, fur, and scarlet cloth. Their arms were all breech-loaders, throwing cartridges of calibre .50 with an occasional .45. Lances, medicine-poles, and tomahawks figured in the procession. The tomahawks, made of long knives inserted in shafts or handles of wood and horn, were murderous weapons. Accompanying these Indians were a few little boys, whose business was to hold horses and other unimportant work while their elders conducted the dangerous operations of the campaign.

At "retreat" all the battalion commanders and staff officers assembled in front of the tent of the commanding general, and listened to his terse instructions regarding the approaching march. We were to cut loose from our wagons, each officer and soldier carrying four days' rations of hard bread, coffee, and bacon in saddle-pockets, and one hundred rounds of ammunition in belts or pouches; one blanket to each person. The wagons

were to be parked and left behind in a defensible position on the
Tongue or Goose, and under the protection of the men unable
for any reason to join in the forward movement ; all the infantrymen who could ride and who so desired were to be mounted on
mules from the pack-trains with saddles from the wagons or
from the cavalry companies which could spare them.   If successful in attacking a village, the supplies of dried meat and other
food were to be saved, and we should then, in place of returning
immediately to our train, push on to make a combination with
either Terry or Gibbon, as the case might be.

Scarcely had this brief conference been ended when a long line
of glittering lances and brightly polished weapons of fire announced the anxiously expected advent of our other allies, the
Shoshones or Snakes, who, to the number of eighty-six, galloped
rapidly up to headquarters and came left front into line in
splendid style.   No trained warriors of civilized armies ever executed the movement more prettily.   Exclamations of wonder
and praise greeted the barbaric array of these fierce warriors,
warmly welcomed by their former enemies but at present strong
friends—the Crows.   General Crook moved out to review their
line of battle, resplendent in all the fantastic adornment of
feathers, beads, brass buttons, bells, scarlet cloth, and flashing
lances.   The Shoshones were not slow to perceive the favorable
impression made, and when the order came for them to file off by
the right moved with the precision of clock-work and the pride
of veterans.

A grand council was the next feature of the evening's entertainment.   Around a huge fire of crackling boughs the officers
of the command arranged themselves in two rows, the interest
and curiosity depicted upon their countenances acting as a foil
to the stolidity and imperturbable calmness of the Indians
squatted upon the ground on the other side.   The breezes blowing the smoke aside would occasionally enable the flames to
bring out in bold and sudden relief the intense blackness of the
night, the sepulchral whiteness of the tents and wagon-sheets,
the blue coats of officers and soldiers (who thronged among the
wagons behind their superiors), the red, white, yellow, and black
beaded blankets of the savages, whose aquiline features and glittering eyes had become still more aquiline and still more glittering, and the small group in the centre of the circle composed of

General Crook and his staff, the interpreters—Frank Gruard and "Big Bat" and Louis—and the Indian chiefs. One quadrant was reserved for the Shoshones, another for the Crows. Each tribe selected one spokesman, who repeated to his people the words of the General as they were made known by the interpreters. Ejaculations of "Ugh! ugh!" were the only signs of approval, but it was easy enough to see that nothing was lost that was addressed to them. Pipes of the same kind as those the Sioux have were kept in industrious circulation. The remarks made by General Crook were almost identical with those addressed to the Crows alone earlier in the evening; the Indians asked the privilege of scouting in their own way, which was conceded.

An adjournment was ordered at between ten and eleven o'clock to allow such of our allies as so desired to seek much-needed rest. The Shoshones had ridden sixty miles, and night was far advanced. The erroneousness of this assumption was disclosed very speedily. A long series of monotonous howls, shrieks, groans, and nasal yells, emphasized by a perfectly ear-piercing succession of thumps upon drums improvised from "par-fleche" (tanned buffalo skin), attracted nearly all the soldiers and many of the officers not on duty to the allied camp. Peeping into the different lodges was very much like peeping through the key-hole of Hades.

Crouched around little fires not affording as much light as an ordinary tallow candle, the swarthy figures of the naked and half-naked Indians were visible, moving and chanting in unison with some leader. No words were distinguishable; the ceremony partook of the nature of an abominable incantation, and as far as I could judge had a semi-religious character. One of the Indians, mounted on a pony and stripped almost naked, passed along from lodge to lodge, stopping in front of each and calling upon the Great Spirit (so our interpreter said) to send them plenty of scalps, a big Sioux village, and lots of ponies. The inmates would respond with, if possible, increased vehemence, and the old saying about making night hideous was emphatically suggested. With this wild requiem ringing in his ears one of our soldiers, a patient in hospital, Private William Nelson, Company "L," Third Cavalry, breathed his last. The herd of beef cattle, now reduced to six, became scared by the din and broke madly for the hills. All night the rain pattered down.

Among our Crows were said to be some very distinguished warriors ; one of these pointed out to me had performed during the preceding winter the daring feat of stealing in alone upon a Sioux village and getting a fine pony, which he tied loosely to a stake outside ; then he crept back, lifted up the flap of one of the lodges, and called gently to the sleepers, who, unsuspecting, answered the grunt, which awakened them, and thus betrayed just where the men were lying ; the Crow took aim coolly and blew the head off of one of the Sioux, slipped down through the village, untied and mounted his pony, and was away like the wind before the astonished enemy could tell from the screaming and jabbering squaws what was the matter.

All through the next day, June 15, 1876, camp was a bee-hive of busy preparation. Colonel Chambers had succeeded in finding one hundred and seventy-five infantrymen who could ride, or were anxious to try, so as to see the whole trip through in proper shape. These were mounted upon mules from the wagon and pack trains, and the first hour's experience with the reluctant Rosinantes equalled the best exhibition ever given by Barnum. Tom Moore organized a small detachment of packers who had had any amount of experience ; two of them—Young and Delaney—had been with the English in India, in the wars with the Sikhs and Rohillas, and knew as much as most people do about campaigning and all its hardships and dangers. The medical staff was kept busy examining men unfit to go to the front, but it was remarkable that the men ordered to remain behind did so under protest. The wagons were parked in a great corral, itself a sort of fortification against which the Sioux would not heedlessly rush. Within this corral racks made of willow branches supported loads of wild meat, drying in the sun : deer and antelope venison, buffalo, elk, and grizzly-bear meat, the last two killed by a hunting party from the pack-train the previous day.

The preparations which our savage allies were making were no less noticeable : in both Snake and Crow camps could be seen squads of young warriors looking after their rifles, which, by the way, among the Shoshones, I forgot to mention, were of the latest model—calibre .45—and kept with scrupulous care in regular gun-racks. Some were sharpening lances or adorning them with feathers and paint ; others were making "coup" sticks, which are long willow branches about twelve feet from end to end, stripped of leaves and bark, and having each some distinctive mark, in the way of feathers, bells, fur, paint, or bright-colored cloth or flannel. These serve a singular purpose : the great object of the Shoshones, Crows, Cheyennes, and Dakotas in making war is to set the enemy afoot. This done, his destruction is rendered more easy if not more certain. Ponies are also the wealth of the conquerors ; hence, in dividing the spoil, each man claims the animals first struck by his " coup " stick.

With the Snakes were three white men—Cosgrove, Yarnell, and Eckles—all Texans ; and one French-Canadian half-breed, named Luisant. Cosgrove, the leading spirit, was, during the Rebellion, a captain in the 32d Texas Cavalry, C. S. A., and showed he had not forgotten the lessons of the war by the appearance of discipline and good order evinced by his command, who, in this respect, were somewhat ahead of the Crows. We were informed that on the march over from Wind River, the Snakes, during one afternoon, killed one hundred and seventy-five buffaloes on the eastern slope of the Owl Creek Mountains. In the early hours of the afternoon the Crows had a foot-race, for twenty cartridges a side ; the running was quite good for the distance of one hundred and fifty yards.

At sunset we buried Private Nelson, who had died the previous night. The funeral cortege was decidedly imposing, because, as on all former occasions of the same nature, all officers and men not engaged on other duty made it a point to be present at the grave of every dead comrade ; the noise of the parting volleys brought our savages up on a gallop, persuaded that the Sioux were making a demonstration against some part of our lines ; they dashed up to the side of the grave, and there they sat motionless upon their ponies, feathers nodding in the breeze, and lances gleaming in the sun. Some of them wore as many as four rings in each ear, the entire cartilage being perforated from apex to base.

CHAPTER XVIII.

ON the 16th of June, by five o'clock in the morning, our
whole command had broken camp and was on its way westward; we crossed Tongue River, finding a swift stream, rather
muddy from recent rains, with a current twenty-five yards wide,
and four feet deep; the bottom of hard-pan, but the banks on
one side muddy and slippery.

The valley, as we saw it from the bluffs amid which we
marched, presented a most beautiful appearance—green with
juicy grasses, and dark with the foliage of cottonwood and willow.
Its sinuosities encircled many park-like areas of meadow, bounded
on the land side by bluffs of drift. The Indians at first marched
on the flank, but soon passed the column and took the lead, the
"medicine men" in front; one of the head "medicine men" of
the Crows kept up a piteous chant, reciting the cruelties of their
enemies and stimulating the young men to deeds of martial
valor. In every possible way these savages reminded me of the
descriptions I had read of the Bedouins.

Our course turned gradually to the northwest, and led us
across several of the tributaries of the Tongue, or "Deje-ajie" as
the Crows called it, each of these of good dimensions, and carrying
the unusual flow due to the rapid melting of snow in the higher
elevations. The fine grass seen close to the Tongue disappeared,
and the country was rather more barren, with many prairie-
dog villages. The soil was made up of sandstones, with a great
amount of both clay and lime, shales and lignite, the latter burnt
out. Some of the sandstone had been filled with pyrites, which
had decomposed and left it in a vesicular state. There were a

great many scrub pines in the recesses of the bluffs. The cause for the sudden disappearance of the grass was soon apparent : the scouts ran in upon a herd of buffaloes whose cast-off bulls had been the principal factor in our meat supply for more than a week ; the trails ran in every direction, and the grass had been nipped off more closely than if cut by a scythe. There was much more cactus than we had seen for some time, and a reappearance of the sage-brush common nearer to Fort Fetterman.

In the afternoon, messengers from our extreme advance came as fast as ponies would carry them, with the information that we were upon the trail of a very great village of the enemy. The cavalry dismounted and unsaddled, seeking the shelter of all the ravines to await the results of the examination to be made by a picked detail from the Crows and Shoshones. The remaining Indians joined in a wild, strange war-dance, the younger warriors becoming almost frenzied before the exercises terminated. The young men who had been sent out to spy the land rejoined us on a full run ; from the tops of the hills they yelled like wolves, the conventional signal among the plains tribes that the enemy has been sighted. Excitement, among the Indians at least, was at fever heat ; many of the younger members of the party re-echoed the ululation of the incoming scouts ; many others spurred out to meet them and escort them in with becoming honors. The old chiefs held their bridles while they dismounted, and the less prominent warriors deferentially formed in a circle to listen to their narrative. It did not convey much information to my mind, unaccustomed to the indications so familiar to them. It simply amounted to this, that the buffaloes were in very large herds directly ahead of us, and were running away from a Sioux hunting party.

Knowing the unfaltering accuracy of an Indian's judgment in matters of this kind, General Crook told the chiefs to arrange their plan of march according to their own ideas. On occasions like this, as I was told by our scouts and others, the young men of the Assiniboines and Northern Sioux were required to hold in each hand a piece of buffalo chip as a sign that they were tell-ing the truth ; nothing of that kind occurred on the occasion in question. While the above was going on, the Indians were charging about on their hardy little ponies, to put them out of breath, so that, when they regained their wind, they would not fail to sustain a whole day's battle. A little herb is carried along, to be given to the ponies in such emergencies, but what virtues are attributed to this medicine I was unable to ascertain. Much solemnity is attached to the medicine arrows of the " medicine men," who seem to possess the power of arbitrarily stopping a march at almost any moment. As I kept with them, I had opportunity to observe all that they did, except when every one was directed to keep well to the rear, as happened upon approaching a tree—juniper or cedar—in the fork of whose lower branches there was a buffalo head, before which the principal " medicine man " and his assistant halted and smoked from their long pipes.

Noon had passed, and the march was resumed to gain the Rosebud, one of the tributaries of the Yellowstone, marking the ultimate western limit of our campaign during the previous winter. We moved along over an elevated, undulating, grassy table-land. Without possessing any very marked beauty, there was a certain picturesqueness in the country which was really pleasing. Every few rods a petty rivulet coursed down the hill-sides to pay its tribute to the Tongue ; there was no timber, except an occasional small cottonwood or willow, to be seen along the banks of these little water-courses, but wild roses by the thousand laid their delicate beauties at our feet ; a species of phlox, daintily blue in tint, was there also in great profusion, while in the bushes multitudes of joyous-voiced singing-birds piped their welcome as the troops filed by. Yet this lovely country was abandoned to the domination of the thriftless savage, the buffalo, and the rattlesnake ; we could see the last-named winding along through the tall grass, rattling defiance as they sneaked away. Buffalo spotted the landscape in every direction, in squads of ten and twelve and "bunches" of sixty and seventy. These were not old bulls banished from the society of their mates, to be attacked and devoured by coyotes, but fine fat cows with calves ambling close behind them. One young bull calf trotted down close to the column, his eyes beaming with curiosity and wonder. He was allowed to approach within a few feet, when our prosaic Crow guides took his life as the penalty of his temerity. Thirty buffaloes were killed that afternoon, and the choice pieces— hump, tenderloin, tongue, heart, and rib steaks—packed upon our horses. The flesh was roasted in the ashes, a pinch of salt sprinkled over it, and a very savory and juicy addition made to our scanty supplies. The Indians ate the buffalo liver raw, sometimes sprinkling a pinch of gall upon it; the warm raw liver alone is not bad for a hungry man, tasting very much like a raw oyster. The entrails are also much in favor with the aborigines; they are cleaned, wound round a ramrod, or something akin to it if a ramrod be not available, and held in the hot ashes until cooked through; they make a palatable dish; the buffalo has an intestine shaped like an apple, which is filled with chyle, and is the *bonne bouche* of the savages when prepared in the same manner as the other intestines, excepting that the contents are left untouched.

While riding alongside of one of our Crow scouts I noticed tears flowing down his cheeks, and very soon he started a wail or chant of the most lugubrious tone; I respected his grief until he had wept to his heart's content, and then ventured to ask the cause of such deep distress; he answered that his uncle had been killed a number of years before by the Sioux, and he was crying for him now and wishing that he might come back to life to get some of the ponies of the Sioux and Cheyennes. Two minutes after having discharged the sad duty of wailing for his dead relative, the young Crow was as lively as any one else in the column.

We bivouacked on the extreme head-waters of the Rosebud, which was at that point a feeble rivulet of snow water, sweet and palatable enough when the muddy ooze was not stirred up from the bottom. Wood was found in plenty for the slight wants of the command, which made small fires for a few moments to boil coffee, while the animals, pretty well tired out by the day's rough march of nearly forty miles, rolled and rolled again in the matted bunches of succulent pasturage growing at their feet. Our lines were formed in hollow square, animals inside, and each man sleeping with his saddle for a pillow and with arms by his side. Pickets were posted on the bluffs near camp, and, after making what collation we could, sleep was sought at the same moment the black clouds above us had begun to patter down rain. A party of scouts returned late at night, reporting having come across a small gulch in which was a still burning fire of a band of Sioux hunters, who in the precipitancy of their flight had left behind a blanket of India-rubber. We came near having a casualty in the accidental discharge of the revolver of

Mr. John F. Finerty, the bullet burning the saddle and break-ing it, but, fortunately, doing no damage to the rider. By day-light of the next day, June 17, 1876, we were marching down the Rosebud.

The Crow scouts with whom I was had gone but a short dis-tance when shots were heard down the valley to the north, followed by the ululation proclaiming from the hill-tops that the enemy was in force and that we were in for a fight. Shot after shot followed on the left, and by the time that two of the Crows reached us, one of them severely wounded and both crying, "Sioux! Sioux!" it was plain that something out of the com-mon was to be expected. There was a strong line of pickets out on the hills on that flank, and this was immediately strengthened by a respectable force of skirmishers to cover the cavalry horses, which were down at the bottom of the amphitheatre through which the Rosebud at that point ran. The Shoshones promptly took position in the hills to the left, and alongside of them were the companies of the Fourth Infantry, under Major A. B. Cain, and one or two of the cavalry companies, dismounted.

The Sioux advanced boldly and in overwhelming force, cover-ing the hills to the north, and seemingly confident that our com-mand would prove an easy prey. In one word, the battle of the Rosebud was a trap, and "Crazy Horse," the leader in command here as at the Custer massacre a week later, was satisfied he was going to have everything his own way. He stated afterwards, when he had surrendered to General Crook at the agency, that he had no less than six thousand five hundred men in the fight, and that the first attack was made with fifteen hundred, the others being concealed behind the bluffs and hills. His plan of battle was either to lead detachments in pursuit of his people, and turning quickly cut them to pieces in detail, or draw the whole of Crook's forces down into the cañon of the Rosebud, where escape would have been impossible, as it formed a verita-ble *cul de sac*, the vertical walls hemming in the sides, the front being closed by a dam and abatis of broken timber which gave a depth of ten feet of water and mud, the rear, of course, to be shut off by thousands of yelling, murderous Sioux and Chey-ennes. That was the Sioux programme as learned that day, or afterwards at the agencies from the surrendered hostiles in the spring of the following year.

While this attack was going on on our left and front, a determined demonstration was made by a large body of the enemy on
our right and rear, to repel which Colonel Royall, Third Cavalry,
was sent with a number of companies, mounted, to charge and
drive back. I will restrict my observations to what I saw, as the
battle of the Rosebud has been several times described in books
and any number of times in the correspondence sent from the
command to the journals of those years. The Sioux and
Cheyennes, the latter especially, were extremely bold and fierce,
and showed a disposition to come up and have it out hand to
hand; in all this they were gratified by our troops, both red and
white, who were fully as anxious to meet them face to face and
see which were the better men. At that part of the line the
enemy were disconcerted at a very early hour by the deadly fire
of the infantry with their long rifles. As the hostiles advanced
at a full run, they saw nothing in their front, and imagined that
it would be an easy thing for them to sweep down through the
long ravine leading to the amphitheatre, where they could see
numbers of our cavalry horses clumped together. They advanced in excellent style, yelling and whooping, and glad of the
opportunity of wiping us off the face of the earth. When Cain's
men and the detachments of the Second Cavalry which were
lying down behind a low range of knolls rose up and delivered a
withering fire at less than a hundred and fifty yards, the Sioux
turned and fled as fast as " quirt " and heel could persuade their
ponies to get out of there.

But, in their turn, they re-formed behind a low range not
much over three hundred yards distant, and from that position
kept up an annoying fire upon our men and horses. Becoming
bolder, probably on account of re-enforcements, they again
charged, this time upon a weak spot in our lines a little to
Cain's left ; this second advance was gallantly met by a counter-
charge of the Shoshones, who, under their chief " Luishaw,"
took the Sioux and Cheyennes in flank and scattered them before them. I went in with this charge, and was enabled to
see how such things were conducted by the American savages,
fighting according to their own notions. There was a headlong
rush for about two hundred yards, which drove the enemy back
in confusion ; then was a sudden halt, and very many of the
Shoshones jumped down from their ponies and began firing from

the ground ; the others who remained mounted threw themselves alongside of their horses' necks, so that there would be few good marks presented to the aim of the enemy. Then, in response to some signal or cry which, of course, I did not understand, we were off again, this time for good, and right into the midst of the hostiles, who had been halted by a steep hill directly in their front. Why we did not kill more of them than we did was because they were dressed so like our own Crows that even our Shoshones were afraid of mistakes, and in the confusion many of the Sioux and Cheyennes made their way down the face of the bluffs unharmed.

From this high point there could be seen on Crook's right and rear a force of cavalry, some mounted, others dismounted, apparently in the clutches of the enemy ; that is to say, a body of hostiles was engaging attention in front and at the same time a large mass, numbering not less than five hundred, was getting ready to pounce upon the rear and flank of the unsuspecting Americans. I should not forget to say that while the Shoshones were charging the enemy on one flank, the Crows, led by Major George M. Randall, were briskly attacking them on the other ; the latter movement had been ordered by Crook in person and executed in such a bold and decisive manner as to convince the enemy that, no matter what their numbers were, our troops and scouts were anxious to come to hand-to-hand encounters with them. This was really the turning-point of the Rosebud fight for a number of reasons : the main attack had been met and broken, and we had gained a key-point enabling the holder to survey the whole field and realize the strength and intentions of the enemy. The loss of the Sioux at this place was considerable both in warriors and ponies ; we were at one moment close enough to them to hit them with clubs or " coup " sticks, and to inflict considerable damage, but not strong enough to keep them from getting away with their dead and wounded. A number of our own men were also hurt, some of them quite seriously. I may mention a young trumpeter—Elmer A. Snow, of Company M, Third Cavalry—who went in on the charge with the Shoshones, one of the few white men with them ; he displayed noticeable gallantry, and was desperately wounded in both arms, which were crippled for life ; his escape from the midst of the enemy was a remarkable thing.

I did not learn until nightfall that at the same time they made the charge just spoken of; the enemy had also rushed down through a ravine on our left and rear, reaching the spring alongside of which I had been seated with General Crook at the moment the first shots were heard, and where I had jotted down the first lines of the notes from which the above condensed account of the fight has been taken. At that spring they came upon a young Shoshone boy, not yet attained to years of manhood, and shot him through the back and killed him, taking his scalp from the nape of the neck to the forehead, leaving his entire skull ghastly and white. It was the boy's first battle, and when the skirmishing began in earnest he asked permission of his chief to go back to the spring and decorate himself with face-paint, which was already plastered over one cheek, and his medicine song was half done, when he received the fatal shot.

Crook sent orders for all troops to fall back until the line should be complete; some of the detachments had ventured out too far, and our extended line was too weak to withstand a determined attack in force. Burt and Burroughs were sent with their companies of the Ninth Infantry to drive back the force which was congregating in the rear of Royall's command, which was the body of troops seen from the hill crest almost surrounded by the foe. Tom Moore with his sharpshooters from the pack-train, and several of the Montana miners who had kept along with the troops for the sake of a row of some kind with the natives, were ordered to get into a shelf of rocks four hundred yards out on our front and pick off as many of the hostile chiefs as possible and also to make the best impression upon the flanks of any charging parties which might attempt to pass on either side of that promontory. Moore worried the Indians so much that they tried to cut off him and his insignificant band. It was one of the ridiculous episodes of the day to watch those well-meaning young warriors charging at full speed across the open space commanded by Moore's position; not a shot was fired, and beyond taking an extra chew of tobacco, I do not remember that any of the party did anything to show that he cared a continental whether the enemy came or stayed. When those deadly rifles, sighted by men who had no idea what the word " nerves " meant, belched their storm of lead in among the braves and their ponies, it did not take more than seven seconds for the former to conclude that home, sweet home was a good enough place for them.

While the infantry were moving down to close the gap on Royall's right, and Tom Moore was amusing himself in the rocks, Crook ordered Mills with five companies to move out on our right and make a demonstration down stream, intending to get ready for a forward movement with the whole command. Mills moved out promptly, the enemy falling back on all sides and keeping just out of fair range. I went with Mills, having returned from seeing how Tom Moore was getting along, and can recall how deeply impressed we all were by what we then took to be trails made by buffaloes going down stream, but which we afterwards learned had been made by the thousands of ponies belonging to the immense force of the enemy here assembled. We descended into a measly-looking place : a cañon with straight walls of sandstone, having on projecting knobs an occasional scrub pine or cedar ; it was the locality where the savages had planned to entrap the troops, or a large part of them, and wipe them out by closing in upon their rear. At the head of that column rode two men who have since made their mark in far different spheres : John F. Finerty, who has represented one of the Illinois districts in Congress; and Frederick Schwatka, noted as a bold and successful Arctic explorer.

Crook recalled our party from the cañon before we had gone too far, but not before Mills had detected the massing of forces to cut him off. Our return was by another route, across the high hills and rocky places, which would enable us to hold our own against any numbers until assistance came. Crook next ordered an advance of our whole line, and the Sioux fell back and left us in undisputed possession of the field. Our total loss was fifty-seven, killed or wounded—some of the latter only slightly. The heaviest punishment had been inflicted upon the Third Cavalry, in Royall's column, that regiment meeting with a total loss of nine killed and fifteen wounded, while the Second Cavalry had two wounded, and the Fourth Infantry three wounded. In addition to this were the killed and wounded among the scouts, and a number of wounds which the men cared for themselves, as they saw that the medical staff was taxed to the utmost. One of our worst wounded was Colonel Guy V. Henry, Third Cavalry, who was at first believed to have lost both eyes and to have been marked for death ; but, thanks to good nursing, a wiry frame, and strong vitality, he has since recovered vision and some part of his former physical powers. The officers who served on Crook's staff that day had close calls, and among others Bubb and Nickerson came very near falling into the hands of the enemy. Colonel Royall's staff officers, Lemly and Foster, were greatly exposed, as were Henry. Vroom, Reynolds, and others of that part of the command. General Crook's horse was shot from under him, and there were few, if any, officers or soldiers, facing the strength of the Sioux and Cheyennes at the Rosebud, who did not have some incident of a personal nature by which to impress the affair upon their memories for the rest of their lives.

The enemy's loss was never known. Our scouts got thirteen scalps, but the warriors, the moment they were badly wounded, would ride back from the line or be led away by comrades, so that we then believed that their total loss was much more severe. The behavior of Shoshones and Crows was excellent. The chief of the Shoshones appeared to great advantage, mounted on a fiery pony, he himself naked to the waist and wearing one of the gorgeous head-dresses of eagle feathers sweeping far along the ground behind his pony's tail. The Crow chief, " Medicine Crow," looked like a devil in his war-bonnet of feathers, fur, and buffalo horns.

We had pursued the enemy for seven miles, and had held the field of battle, without the slightest resistance on the side of the Sioux and Cheyennes. It had been a field of their own choosing, and the attack had been intended as a surprise and, if possible, to lead into an ambuscade also ; but in all they had been frustrated and driven off, and did not attempt to return or to annoy us during the night. As we had nothing but the clothing each wore and the remains of the four days' rations with which we had started, we had no other resource but to make our way back to the wagon trains with the wounded. That night was an unquiet and busy time for everybody. The Shoshones caterwauled and lamented the death of the young warrior whose life had been ended and whose bare skull still gleamed from the side of the spring where he fell. About midnight they buried him, along with our own dead, for whose sepulture a deep trench was dug in the bank of the Rosebud near the water line, the bodies laid in a row, covered with stones, mud, and earth packed down, and a great fire kindled on top and allowed to burn all night. When we broke camp the next morning the entire command marched over the graves, so as to obliterate every trace and prevent prowling savages from exhuming the corpses and scalping them.

A rough shelter of boughs and branches had been erected for the wounded, and our medical officers, Hartsuff, Patzki, and Stevens, labored all night, assisted by Lieutenant Schwatka, who had taken a course of lectures at Bellevue Hospital, New York. The Shoshones crept out during the night and cut to pieces the two Sioux bodies within reach; this was in revenge for their own dead, and because the enemy had cut one of our men to pieces during the fight, in which they made free use of their lances, and of a kind of tomahawk, with a handle eight feet long, which they used on horseback.

June 18, 1876, we were turned out of our blankets at three o'clock in the morning, and sat down to eat on the ground a breakfast of hard-tack, coffee, and fried bacon. The sky was an immaculate blue, and the ground was covered with a hard frost, which made every one shiver. The animals had rested, and the wounded were reported by Surgeon Hartsuff to be doing as well "as could be expected." "Travois" were constructed of cottonwood and willow branches, held together by ropes and rawhide, and to care for each of these six men were detailed. As we were moving off, our scouts discerned three or four Sioux riding down to the battle-field, upon reaching which they dismounted, sat down, and bowed their heads; we could not tell through glasses what they were doing, but the Shoshones and Crows said that they were weeping for their dead. They were not fired upon or molested in any way. We pushed up the Rosebud, keeping mainly on its western bank, and doing our best to select a good trail along which the wounded might be dragged with least jolting. Crook wished to keep well to the south so as to get farther into the Big Horn range, and avoid much of the deep water of the streams flowing into Tongue River, which might prove too swift and dangerous for the wounded men in the "travois." In avoiding Scylla, we ran upon Charybdis: we escaped much of the deep water, although not all of it, but encountered much trouble from the countless ravines and gullies which cut the flanks of the range in every direction.

The column halted for an hour at the conical hill, crested with pine, which marks the divide between the Rosebud and the Greasy Grass,—a tributary of the Little Big Horn,—the spot where our Crow guides claimed that their tribe had whipped and almost exterminated a band of the Blackfeet Sioux. Our horses were allowed to graze until the rear-guard had caught up, with the wounded men under its care. The Crows had a scalp dance, holding aloft on poles and lances the lank, black locks of the Sioux and Cheyennes killed in the fight of the day before, and one killed that very morning. It seems that as the Crows were riding along the trail off to the right of the command, they heard some one calling, "Mini! Mini!" which is the Dakota term for water; it was a Cheyenne whose eyes had been shot out in the beginning of the battle, and who had crawled to a place of concealment in the rocks, and now hearing the Crows talk as they rode along addressed them in Sioux, thinking them to be the latter. The Crows cut him limb from limb and ripped off his scalp. The rear-guard reported having had a hard time getting along with the wounded on account of the great number of gullies already mentioned; great assistance had been rendered in this severe duty by Sergeant Warfield, Troop "F," Third Cavalry, an old Arizona veteran, as well as by Tom Moore and his band of packers. So far as scenery was concerned, the most critical would have been pleased with that section of our national domain, the elysium of the hunter, the home of the bear, the elk, deer, antelope, mountain sheep, and buffalo; the carcasses of the last-named lined the trail, and the skulls and bones whitened the hill-sides. The march of the day was a little over twenty-two miles, and ended upon one of the tributaries of the Tongue, where we bivouacked and passed the night in some discomfort on account of the excessive cold which drove us from our scanty covering shortly after midnight. The Crows left during the night, promising to resume the campaign with others of their tribe, and to meet us somewhere on the Tongue or Goose Creek.

June 19 found us back at our wagon-train, which Major Furey had converted into a fortress, placed on a tongue of land, surrounded on three sides by deep, swift-flowing water, and on the neck by a line of breastworks commanding all approaches. Ropes and chains had been stretched from wheel to wheel, so

that even if any of the enemy did succeed in slipping inside, the
stock could not be run out. Furey had not allowed his little
garrison to remain inside the intrenchments : he had insisted
upon some of them going out daily to scrutinize the country and
to hunt for fresh meat ; the carcasses of six buffaloes and three
elk attested the execution of his orders. Furey's force consisted
of no less than eighty packers and one hundred and ten teamsters, besides sick and disabled left behind. One of his assistants
was Mr. John Mott MacMahon, the same man who as a sergeant
in the Third Cavalry had been by the side of Lieutenant Cushing at the moment he was killed by the Chiricahua Apaches in
Arizona. After caring for the wounded and the animals, every
one splashed in the refreshing current; the heat of the afternoon
became almost unbearable, the thermometer indicating 103°
Fahrenheit. Lemons, limes, lime juice, and citric acid, of each
of which there was a small supply, were hunted up and used for
making a glass of lemonade for the people in the rustic hospital.

June 21, Crook sent the wounded back to Fort Fetterman,
placing them in wagons spread with fresh grass ; Major Furey
was sent back to obtain additional supplies ; the escort, consisting of one company from the Ninth and one from the Fourth
Infantry, was commanded by Colonel Chambers, with whom were
the following officers : Munson and Capron of the Ninth, Luhn
and Seton of the Fourth. Mr. MacMillan, the correspondent of
the *Inter-Ocean* of Chicago, also accompanied the party; he had
been especially energetic in obtaining all data referring to the
campaign, and had shown that he had as much pluck as any officer or soldier in the column, but his strength was not equal to
the hard marching and climbing, coupled with the violent
alternations of heat and cold, rain and shine, to which we were
subjected. The Shoshones also left for their own country, going
across the Big Horn range due west ; after having a big scalp
dance with their own people they would return ; for the same
reason, the Crows had rejoined their tribe. Five of the Shoshones remained in camp, to act in any needed capacity until the
return of their warriors. The care taken of the Shoshone
wounded pleased me very much, and I saw that the "medicine
men" knew how to make a fair article of splint from the twigs
of the willow, and that they depended upon such appliances in
cases of fracture fully as much as they did upon the singing

which took up so much of their time, and was so obnoxious to the unfortunate whites whose tents were nearest.

In going home across the mountains to the Wind River the Crows took one of their number who had been badly wounded in the thigh. Why he insisted upon going back to his own home I do not know; perhaps the sufferer really did not know himself, but disliked being separated from his comrades. A splint was adjusted to the fractured limb, and the patient was seated upon an easy cushion instead of a saddle. Everything went well until after crossing the Big Horn Mountains, when the party ran in upon a band of Sioux raiders or spies in strong force. The Crows were hailed by some of the Sioux, but managed to answer a few words in that language, and then struck out as fast as ponies would carry them to get beyond reach of their enemies. They were afraid of leaving a trail, and for that reason followed along the current of all the mountain streams, swollen at that season by rains and melting snows, fretting into foam against impeding boulders and crossed and recrossed by interlacing branches of fallen timber. Through and over or under, as the case might be, the frightened Crows made their way, indifferent to the agony of the wounded companion, for whose safety only they cared, but to whose moans they were utterly irresponsive. This story we learned upon the return of the Shoshones.

To be obliged to await the train with supplies was a serious annoyance, but nothing better could be done. We had ceded to the Sioux by the treaty of 1867 all the country from the Missouri to the Big Horn, destroying the posts which had afforded protection to the overland route into Montana, and were now feeling the loss of just such depots of supply as those posts would have been. It was patent to every one that not hundreds, as had been reported, but thousands of Sioux and Cheyennes were in hostility and absent from the agencies, and that, if the war was to be prosecuted with vigor, some depots must be established at an eligible location like the head of Tongue River, old Fort Reno, or other point in that vicinity; another in the Black Hills; and still another at some favorable point on the Yellowstone, preferably the mouth of Tongue River. Such, at least, was the recommendation made by General Crook, and posts at or near all the sites indicated were in time established and are still maintained. The merits of Tongue River and its tributaries as

great trout streams were not long without proper recognition at
the hands of our anglers.   Under the influence of the warm
weather the fish had begun to bite voraciously, in spite of the
fact that there were always squads of men bathing in the limpid
waters, or mules slaking their thirst.   The first afternoon
ninety-five were caught and brought into camp, where they were
soon broiling on the coals or frying in pans.   None of them were
large, but all were "pan" fish, delicious to the taste.   While
the sun was shining we were annoyed by swarms of green and
black flies, which disappeared with the coming of night and its
refreshingly cool breezes.

June 23, Lieutenant Schuyler, Fifth Cavalry, reported at headquarters for duty as aide-de-camp to General Crook.   He had
been four days making the trip out from Fort Fetterman, travelling with the two couriers who brought our mail.   At old Fort
Reno they had stumbled upon a war party of Sioux, but were not
discovered, and hid in the rocks until the darkness of night enabled them to resume their journey at a gallop, which never
stopped for more than forty miles.   They brought news that the
Fifth Cavalry was at Red Cloud Agency ; that five commissioners were to be appointed to confer with the Sioux ; and that
Rutherford B. Hayes, of Ohio, had been nominated by the Re-
publicans for the Presidency.   General Hayes had commanded
a brigade under General Crook in the Army of West Virginia
during the War of the Rebellion.   Crook spoke of his former
subordinate in the warmest and most affectionate manner, in-
stancing several battles in which Hayes had displayed exceptional courage, and proved himself to be, to use Crook's words,
"as brave a man as ever wore a shoulder-strap."

My note-books about this time seem to be almost the chronicle
of a sporting club, so filled are they with the numbers of trout
brought by different fishermen into camp ; all fishers did not
stop at my tent, and I do not pretend to have preserved accurate
figures, much being left unrecorded.   Mills started in with a
record of over one hundred caught by himself and two soldiers
in one short afternoon.   On the 28th of June the same party has
another record of one hundred and forty-six.   On the 29th of
same month Bubb is credited with fifty-five during the afternoon, while the total brought into camp during the 28th ran over
five hundred.   General Crook started out to catch a mess, but

met with poor luck. He saw bear tracks and followed them, bringing in a good-sized " cinnamon," so it was agreed not to refer to his small number of trout. Buffalo and elk meat were both plenty, and with the trout kept the men well fed.

The cavalry companies each morning were exercised at a walk, trot, and gallop. In the afternoon the soldiers were allowed to roam about the country in small parties, hunting and seeing what they could see. They were all the better for the exercise, and acted as so many additional videttes. The packers organized a mule race, which absorbed all interest. It was estimated by conservative judges that fully five dollars had changed hands in ten-cent bets. Up to the end of June no news of any kind, from any source excepting Crow Indians, had been received of General Terry and his command, and much comment, not unmixed with uneasiness, was occasioned thereby.

CHAPTER XIX.

KILLING DULL CARE IN CAMP—EXPLORING THE SNOW-CRESTED
BIG HORN MOUNTAINS—FINERTY KILLS HIS FIRST BUF-
FALO—THE SWIMMING POOLS—A BIG TROUT—SIBLEY'S
SCOUT—A NARROW ESCAPE—NEWS OF THE CUSTER MAS-
SACRE—THE SIOUX TRY TO BURN US OUT—THE THREE
MESSENGERS FROM TERRY—WASHAKIE DRILLS HIS SHO-
SHONES—KELLY THE COURIER STARTS TO FIND TERRY—
CROW INDIANS BEARING DESPATCHES — THE SIGN-LAN-
GUAGE—A PONY RACE—INDIAN SERENADES—HOW THE
SHOSHONES FISHED—A FIRE IN CAMP—THE UTES JOIN US.

IN the main, this absence of news from Terry was the reason
why General Crook took a small detachment with him to
the summit of the Big Horn Mountains and remained four
days. We left camp on the 1st of July, 1876, the party consisting of General Crook, Colonel Royall, Lieutenant Lemly, Major Burt, Lieutenants Carpenter, Schuyler, and Bourke, Messrs.
Wasson, Finerty, Strahorn, and Davenport, with a small train
of picked mules under Mr. Young. The climb to the summit
was effected without event worthy of note, beyond the to-be-
expected ruggedness of the trail and the beauty and grandeur
of the scenery. From the highest point gained during the
day Crook eagerly scanned the broad vista of country spread
out at our feet, reaching from the course of the Little Big Horn
on the left to the country near Pumpkin Buttes on the right.
Neither the natural vision nor the aid of powerful glasses showed
the slightest trace of a marching or a camping column ; there
was no smoke, no dust, to indicate the proximity of either Terry
or Gibbon.

Frank Gruard had made an inspection of the country to the
northwest of camp several days before to determine the truth
of reported smokes, but his trip failed to confirm the story.
The presence of Indians near camp had also been asserted, but
scouting parties had as yet done nothing beyond proving these

camp rumors to be baseless. In only one instance had there been the slightest reason for believing that hostiles had approached our position. An old man, who had been following the command for some reason never very clearly understood, had come into camp on Tongue River and stated that while out on the plain, letting his pony have a nibble of grass, and while he himself had been sleeping under a box elder, he had been awakened by the report of a gun and had seen two Indian boys scampering off to the north : he showed a bullet hole through the saddle, but the general opinion in camp was that the story had been made up out of whole cloth, because parties of men had been much farther down Tongue River that morning, scouting and hunting, without perceiving the slightest sign or trace of hostiles. Thirty miners from Montana had also come into camp from the same place, and they too had been unable to discover traces of the assailants.

The perennial character of the springs and streams watering the pasturage of the Tongue River region was shown by the great masses of snow and ice, which were slowly yielding to the assaults of the summer sun on the flanks of " Cloud Peak " and its sister promontories. Every few hundred yards gurgling rivulets and crystal brooks leaped down from the protecting shadow of pine and juniper groves and sped away to join the Tongue, which warned us of its own near presence in a cañon on the left of the trail by the murmur of its current flowing swiftly from basin to basin over a succession of tiny falls. Exuberant Nature had carpeted the knolls and dells with vernal grasses and lovely flowers ; along the brook-sides, wild rose-buds peeped ; and there were harebells, wild flax, forget-me-nots, and astragulus to dispute with their more gaudy companions—the sunflowers— possession of the soil. The silicious limestones, red clays, and sandstones of the valley were replaced by granites more or less perfectly crystallized. Much pine and fir timber was encountered, at first in small copses, then in more considerable bodies, lastly in dense forests. A very curious variety of juniper made its appearance : it was very stunted, grew prone to the ground, and until approached closely might be mistaken for a bed of moss. In the protecting solitude of these frozen peaks, lakes of melted snow were frequent ; upon their pellucid surface ducks swam gracefully, admiring their own reflection.

We did not get across the snowy range that night, but were compelled to bivouac two or three miles from it, in a sheltered nook offering fairly good grass for the mules, and any amount of fuel and water for our own use. There might be said to be an excess of timber, as for more than six miles we had crawled as best we could through a forest of tall pines and firs, uprooted by the blasts of winter. Game trails were plenty enough, but we did not see an animal of any kind ; neither could we entice the trout which were jumping to the surface of the water, to take hold of the bait offered them. General Crook returned with a black-tailed deer and the report that the range as seen from the top of one of the lofty promontories to which he had climbed appeared to be studded with lakelets similar to the ones so near our bivouac. We slashed pine branches to make an odorous and elastic mattress, cut fire-wood for the cook, and aided in the duty of preparing the supper for which impatient appetites were clamoring. We had hot strong coffee, bacon and venison sliced thin and placed in alternate layers on twigs of willow and frizzled over the embers, and bread baked in a frying-pan.

Our appetites, ordinarily good enough, had been aggravated by the climb of twelve miles in the keen mountain air, and although epicures might not envy us our food, they certainly would have sighed in vain for the pleasure with which it was devoured. After supper, each officer staked his mule in a patch of grass which was good and wholesome, although not equal to that of the lower slopes, and then we gathered around the fire for the post-prandial chat prior to seeking blankets and repose, which fortunately was not disturbed by excessive cold or the bites of mosquitoes, the twin annoyances of these great elevations. We arose early next morning to begin a march of great severity, which taxed to the utmost the strength, nervous system, and patience of riders and mules ; much fallen timber blocked the trail, the danger of passing this being increased a hundredfold by boulders of granite and pools of unknown depth ; the leaves of the pines had decayed into a pasty mass of peat, affording no foothold to the pedestrian or horseman, and added the peril of drowning in a slimy ooze to the terrors accumulated for the intimidation of the explorer penetrating these wilds.

We floundered along in the trail made by our Shoshones on

their way back to their own homes, and were the first white men, not connected with that band of Indians, who had ever ascended to this point. Immense blocks of granite, some of them hundreds of feet high, towered above us, with stunted pine clinging to the scanty soil at their bases ; above all loomed the majestic rounded cone of the Cloud Peak, a thousand feet beyond timber line. The number of springs increased so much that it seemed as if the ground were oozing water from every pore ; the soil had become a sponge, and travel was both difficult and dangerous ; on all sides were lofty banks of snow, often pinkish in tint ; the stream in the pass had diminished in breadth, but its volume was unimpaired as its velocity had trebled. At every twenty or thirty feet of horizontal distance there was a cascade of no great height, but so choked up with large fragments of granite that the current, lashed into fury, foamed like milk. The sun's rays were much obscured by the interlacing branches of the majestic spruce and fir trees shading the trail, and the rocky escarpments looming above the timber line. We could still see the little rivulet dancing along, and hear it singing its song of the icy granite peaks, the frozen lakes, and piny solitudes that had watched its birth. The "divide," we began to congratulate ourselves, could not be far off ; already the pines had begun to thin out, and the stragglers still lining the path were dwarfed and stunted. Our pretty friend, the mountain brook, like a dying swan, sang most sweetly in its last moments ; we saw it issue from icy springs above timber line, and bade it farewell to plunge and flounder across the snow-drifts lining the crest. In this last effort ourselves and animals were almost exhausted. On the "divide" was a lake, not over five hundred yards long, which supplied water to the Big Horn on the west and the Tongue on the east side of the range. Large cakes and floes of black ice, over a foot in thickness, floated on its waters. Each of these was covered deep with snow and regelated ice.

It was impossible to make camp in this place. There was no timber—nothing but rocks and ice-cold water, which chilled the hands dipped into it. Granite and granite alone could be seen in massy crags, timberless and barren of all trace of vegetation, towering into the clouds, in bold-faced ledges, the home of the mountain sheep ; and in cyclopean blocks, covering acres upon acres of surface. Continuing due west we clambered over another ridge of about the same elevation, and as deep with snow and ice, and then saw in the distance the Wind River range, one hundred and thirty miles to the west. With some difficulty a way was made down the flank of the range, through the asperous declivities of the cañon of "No Wood" Creek, and, after being sated with the monotonous beauties of precipices, milky cascades, gloomy forests, and glassy springs, the welcome command was given to bivouac.

We had climbed and slipped fifteen miles at an altitude of 12,000 feet, getting far above the timber line and into the region of perpetual snow. Still, at that elevation, a few pleasant-faced little blue and white flowers, principally forget-me-nots, kept us company to the very edge of snow-banks. I sat upon a snow-bank, and with one hand wrote my notes and with the other plucked forget-me-nots or fought off the mosquitoes. We followed down the cañon of the creek until we had reached the timber, and there, in a dense growth of spruce and fir, went into bivouac in a most charming retreat. Buffalo tracks were seen all day, the animal having crossed the range by the same trail we had used. Besides buffalo tracks we saw the trails of mountain sheep, of which General Crook and Lieutenant Schuyler killed two. The only other life was tit-larks, butterflies, grasshoppers, flies, and the mosquitoes already spoken of. The snow in one place was sixty to seventy feet deep and had not been disturbed for years, because there were five or six strata of grasshoppers frozen stiff, each representing one season. In all cases where the snow had drifted into sheltered ravines and was not exposed to direct solar action, it never melted from year's end to year's end. Our supper of mountain mutton and of sheep and elk heart boiled in salt water was eaten by the light of the fire, and was followed by a restful sleep upon couches of spruce boughs.

We returned to our main camp on the 4th of July, guided by General Crook over a new trail, which proved to be a great improvement upon the other. Mr. John F. Finerty killed his first buffalo, which appeared to be a very good specimen at the time, but after perusing the description given by Finerty in the columns of the *Times*, several weeks later, we saw that it must have been at least eleven feet high and weighed not much less than nine thousand pounds. We made chase after a herd of sixteen elk drinking at one of the lakes, but on account of the noise in getting through fallen timber were unable to approach near enough. An hour later, while I was jotting down the character of the country in my note-book, eight mountain sheep came up almost close enough to touch me, and gazed with wonder at the intruder. They were beautiful creatures in appearance : somewhat of a cross between the deer, the sheep, and the mule ; the head resembles that of the domestic sheep, surmounted by a pair of ponderous convoluted horns ; the body, in a slight degree, that of a mule, but much more graceful ; and the legs those of a deer, but somewhat more " chunky ;" the tail, short, slender, furnished with a brush at the extremity ; the hair, short and chocolate-gray in color ; the eyes rival the beauty of the topaz. Before I could grasp my carbine they had scampered around a rocky promontory, where three of them were killed : one by General Crook and two by others of the party.

Camp kept moving from creek to creek in the valley of the Tongue, always finding abundant pasturage, plenty of fuel, and an ample supply of the coldest and best water. The foot-hills of the Big Horn are the ideal camping-grounds for mounted troops ; the grass grows to such a height that it can be cut with a mowing-machine ; cattle thrive, and although the winters are severe, with proper shelter all kinds of stock should prosper. The opportunity of making a suitable cross between the acclimatized buffalo and the domestic stock has perhaps been lost, but it is not too late to discuss the advisability of introducing the Thibetan yak, a bovine accustomed to the polar rigors of the Himalayas, and which has been tamed and used either for the purposes of the dairy or for those of draught and saddle. The body of the yak is covered with a long coat of hair, which enables it to lie down in the snow-drifts without incurring any risk of catching cold. The milk of the yak is said to be remarkably rich, and the butter possesses the admirable quality of keeping fresh for a long time.

This constant moving of camp had another object : the troops were kept in practice in taking down and putting up tents ; saddling and unsaddling horses ; packing and unpacking wagons ; laying out camps, with a due regard for hygiene by building sinks in proper places ; forming promptly ; and, above all, were kept occupied. The raw recruits of the spring were insensibly converted into veterans before the close of summer. The credulity of the reader will be taxed to the utmost limit if he follow my record of the catches of trout made in all these streams. What these catches would have amounted to had there been no herds of horses and mules—we had, it must be remembered, over two thousand when the wagon-trains, pack-trains, Indian scouts, and soldiers were all assembled together—I am unable to say; but the hundreds and thousands of fine fish taken from that set of creeks by officers and soldiers, who had nothing but the rudest appliances, speaks of the wonderful resources of the country in game at that time.

The ambition of the general run of officers and men was to take from fifteen to thirty trout, enough to furnish a good meal for themselves and their messmates; but others were carried away by the desire to make a record as against that of other fishers of repute. These catches were carefully distributed throughout camp, and the enlisted men fared as well as the officers in the matter of game and everything else which the country afforded. General Crook and the battalion commanders under him were determined that there should be no waste, and insisted upon the fish being eaten at once or dried for later use. Major Dewees is credited with sixty-eight large fish caught in one afternoon, Bubb with eighty, Crook with seventy, and so on. Some of the packers having brought in reports of beautiful deep pools farther up the mountain, in which lay hidden fish far greater in size and weight than those caught closer to camp, a party was formed at headquarters to investigate and report. Our principal object was to enjoy the cool swimming pools so eloquently described by our informants; but next to that we intended trying our luck in hauling in trout of exceptional size.

The rough little bridle-path led into most romantic scenery: the grim walls of the cañon began to crowd closely upon the banks of the stream; in places there was no bank at all, and the swirling, brawling current rushed along the rocky wall, while our ponies carefully picked their way over a trail, narrow, sharp, and dangerous as the knife-edge across which true believers were to enter into Mahomet's Paradise. Before long we gained a mossy glade, hidden in the granite ramparts of the cañon, where we found a few blades of grass for the animals and shade from the too warm rays of the sun. The moss-covered banks terminated in a flat stone table, reaching well out into the current and shaded by overhanging boulders and widely-branching trees. The dark-green water in front rushed swiftly and almost noiselessly by, but not more than five or six yards below our position several sharp-toothed fragments of granite barred the progress of the current, which grew white with rage as it hissed and roared on its downward course.

We disrobed and entered the bath, greatly to the astonishment of a school of trout of all sizes which circled about and darted in and out among the rocks, trying to determine who and what we were. We were almost persuaded that we were the first white men to penetrate to that seclusion. Our bath was delightful ; everything combined to make it so—shade, cleanliness, conven-ience of access, purity and coolness of the water, and such perfect privacy that Diana herself might have chosen it for her ablu-tions ! Splash ! splash !—a sound below us ! The illusion was very strong, and for a moment we were willing to admit that the classical huntress had been disturbed at her toilet, and that we were all to share the fate of Actæon. Our apprehensions didn't last long ; we peeped through the foliage and saw that it was not Diana, but an army teamster washing a pair of unques-tionably muddy overalls. Our bath finished, we took our stand upon projecting rocks and cast bait into the stream.

We were not long in finding out the politics of the Big Horn trout ; they were McKinleyites, every one ; or, to speak more strictly, they were the forerunners of McKinleyism. We tried them with all sorts of imported and manufactured flies of gaudy tints or sombre hues—it made no difference. After suspiciously nosing them they would flap their tails, strike with the side-fins, and then, having gained a distance of ten feet, would most pro-vokingly stay there and watch us from under the shelter of slip-pery rocks. Foreign luxuries evidently had no charm for them. Next we tried them with home-made grasshoppers, caught on the banks of their native stream. The change was wonderful : in less than a second, trout darted out from all sorts of unex-pected places—from the edge of the rapids below us, from under gloomy blocks of granite, from amid the gnarly roots of almost amphibious trees. My comrades had come for an afternoon's fishing, and began, without more ado, to haul in the struggling, quivering captives. My own purpose was to catch one or two of good size, and then return to camp. A teamster, named

O'Shaughnessy, formerly of the Fourteenth Infantry, who had been brought up in the salmon districts of Ireland, was standing near me with a large mess just caught ; he handed me his willow branch, most temptingly baited with grasshoppers, at the same time telling me there was a fine big fish, "a regular buster, in the hole beyant." He had been unable to coax him out from his retreat, but thought that, if anything could tempt him, my bait would. I cautiously let down the line, taking care to keep in the deepest shadow. I did not remain long in suspense ; in an instant the big fellow came at full speed from his hiding-place, running for the bait. He was noble, heavy, and gorgeous in his dress of silver and gold and black and red. He glanced at the grasshoppers to satisfy himself they were the genuine article, and then one quick, nervous bound brought his nose to the hook and the bait into his mouth, and away he went. I gave him all the line he wanted, fearing I should lose him. His course took him close to the bank, and, as he neared the edge of the stream, I laid him, with a quick, firm jerk, sprawling on the moss. I was glad not to have had any fight with him, because he would surely have broken away amid the rocks and branches. He was pretty to look upon, weighed three pounds, and was the largest specimen reaching camp that week. He graced our dinner, served up, roasted and stuffed, in our cook Phillips's best style.

General Crook, wishing to ascertain with some definiteness the whereabouts of the Sioux, sent out during the first week of July a reconnoitring party of twenty enlisted men, commanded by Lieutenant Sibley, Second Cavalry, to escort Frank Gruard, who wished to move along the base of the mountains as far as the cañon of the Big Horn and scrutinize the country to the north and west. A larger force would be likely to embarrass the rapidity of marching with which Gruard hoped to accomplish his intention, which was that of spying as far as he could into the region where he supposed the hostiles to be ; all the party were to go as lightly equipped as possible, and to carry little else than arms and ammunition. With them went two volunteers, Mr. John F. Finerty and Mr. Jim Traynor, the latter one of the packers and an old frontiersman. Another member of the party was "Big Bat."

This little detachment had a miraculous escape from destruction : at or near the head of the Little Big Horn River, they were discovered, charged upon, and surrounded by a large body of hostile Cheyennes and Sioux, who fired a volley of not less than one hundred shots, but aimed too high and did not hit a man ; three of the horses and one of the mules were severely crippled, and the command was forced to take to the rocks and timber at the edge of the mountains, whence they escaped, leaving animals and saddles behind. The savages seemed confident of their ability to take all of them alive, which may explain in part why they succeeded in slipping away under the guidance of Frank Gruard, to whom the whole country was as familiar as a book ; they crept along under cover of high rocks until they had gained the higher slopes of the range, and then travelled without stopping for two days and nights, pursued by the baffled Indians, across steep precipices, swift torrents, and through almost impenetrable forests. When they reached camp the whole party looked more like dead men than soldiers of the army : their clothes were torn into rags, their strength completely gone, and they faint with hunger and worn out with anxiety and distress. Two of the men, who had not been long in service, went completely crazy and refused to believe that the tents which they saw were those of the command ; they persisted in thinking that they were the "tepis" of the Sioux and Cheyennes, and would not accompany Sibley across the stream, but remained hiding in the rocks until a detachment had been sent out to capture and bring them back. It should be mentioned that one of the Cheyenne chiefs, "White Antelope," was shot through the head by Frank Gruard and buried in all his fine toggery on the ground where he fell ; his body was discovered some days after by "Washakie," the head-chief of the Shoshones, who led a large force of his warriors to the spot. General Crook, in forwarding to General Sheridan Lieutenant Sibley's report of the affair, indorsed it as follows : "I take occasion to express my grateful appreciation to the guides, Frank Gruard and Baptiste Pourrier, to Messrs. Bechtel, called Traynor in my telegram, and John F. Finerty, citizen volunteers, and to the small detachment of picked men from the Second Cavalry, for their cheerful endurance of the hardships and perils such peculiarly dangerous duty of necessity involves. The coolness and judgment displayed by Lieutenant Sibley and Frank Gruard, the guide, in the conduct of this reconnaissance, made in the face of the whole force of the

enemy, are deserving of my warmest acknowledgments.   Lieutenant Sibley, although one of the youngest officers in this
department, has shown a gallantry that is an honor to himself
and the service." A very vivid and interesting description of
this perilous affair has been given by Finerty in his fascinating
volume, "War-Path and Bivouac." During the absence of the
Sibley party General Crook ascended the mountains to secure
meat for the command ; we had a sufficiency of bacon, and all
the trout the men could possibly eat, but fresh meat was not to
be had in quantity, and the amount of deer, elk, antelope, and
bear brought in by our hunters, although considerable in itself,
cut no figure when portioned out among so many hundreds of
hungry mouths.   The failure to hear from Terry or Gibbon distressed Crook a great deal more than he cared to admit ; he
feared for the worst, obliged to give ear to all the wild stories
brought in by couriers and others reaching the command from
the forts and agencies.   By getting to the summit of the high
peaks which overlooked our camps in the drainage of the Tongue,
the surrounding territory for a distance of at least one hundred
miles in every direction could be examined through glasses, and
anything unusual going on detected.   Every afternoon we were
now subjected to storms of rain and lightning, preceded by gusts
of wind.   They came with such regularity that one could almost
set his watch by them.

Major Noyes, one of our most earnest fishermen, did not return
from one of his trips, and, on account of the very severe storm
assailing us that afternoon, it was feared that some accident had
befallen him : that he had been attacked by a bear or other wild
animal, had fallen over some ledge of rocks, been carried away
in the current of the stream, or in some other manner met with
disaster.   Lieutenant Kingsbury, Second Cavalry, went out to
hunt him, accompanied by a mounted detachment and a hound.
Noyes was found fast asleep under a tree, completely exhausted
by his hard work : he was afoot and unable to reach camp with
his great haul of fish, over one hundred and ten in number; he
had played himself out, but had broken the record, and was
snoring serenely.   Mr. Stevens, chief clerk for Major Furey, the
quartermaster, was another sportsman whose chief delight in
life seemed to be in tearing the clothes off his back in efforts to
get more and bigger fish than any one else.

Word came in from General Crook to send pack mules to a locality indicated, where the carcasses of fourteen elk and other game for the command had been tied to the branches of trees. It was not until the 10th of July, 1876, that Louis Richaud and Ben Arnold rode into camp, bearing despatches from Sheridan to Crook with the details of the terrible disaster which had overwhelmed the troops commanded by General Custer; the shock was so great that men and officers could hardly speak when the tale slowly circulated from lip to lip. The same day the Sioux made their appearance, and tried to burn us out : they set fire to the grass near the infantry battalions ; and for the next two weeks paid us their respects every night in some manner, trying to stampede stock, burn grass, annoy pickets, and devil the command generally. They did not escape scot-free from these encounters, because we saw in the rocks the knife left by one wounded man, whose blood stained the soil near it; another night a pony was shot through the body and abandoned ; and on still another occasion one of their warriors, killed by a bullet through the brain, was dragged to a ledge of rocks and there hidden, to be found a week or two after by our Shoshone scouts.

The Sioux destroyed an immense area of pasturage, not less than one hundred miles each way, leaving a charred expanse of territory where had so lately been the refreshing green of dainty grass, traversed by crystal brooks ; over all that blackened surface it would have been difficult to find so much as a grasshopper ; it could be likened to nothing except Burke's description of the devastation wrought by Hyder Ali in the plains of the Carnatic. Copious rains came to our relief, and the enemy desisted ; besides destroying the pasturage, the Sioux had subjected us to the great annoyance of breathing the tiny particles of soot which filled the air and darkened the sky.

Hearing from some of our hunters that the tracks of a party—a large party—of Sioux and Cheyennes, mounted, had been seen on the path taken by Crook and his little detachment of hunters, going up into the Big Horn, Colonel Royall ordered Mills to take three companies and proceed out to the relief, if necessary, of our General and comrades. They all returned safely in the course of the afternoon, and the next day, July 11th, we were joined by a force of two hundred and thirteen Shoshones, commanded by their head-chief, "Washakie," whose resemblance in face and bearing to the eminent divine, Henry Ward Beecher, was noticeable. This party had been delayed, waiting for the Utes and Bannocks, who had sent word that they wanted to take part in the war against the Sioux; but "Washakie" at last grew tired, and started off with his own people and two of the Bannock messengers.

Of these two a story was related to the effect that, during the previous winter, they had crossed the mountains alone, and slipped into a village of Sioux, and begun to cut the fastenings of several fine ponies; the alarm was given, and the warriors began to tumble out of their beds; our Bannocks were crouching down in the shadow of one of the lodges, and in the confusion of tongues, barking of dogs, hurried questioning and answering of the Sioux, boldly entered the "tepi" just vacated by two warriors and covered themselves up with robes. The excitement quieted down after a while, and the camp was once more in slumber, the presence of the Bannocks undiscovered, and the Sioux warriors belonging to that particular lodge blissfully ignorant that they were harboring two of the most desperate villains in the whole western country. When the proper moment had come, the Bannocks quietly reached out with their keen knives, cut the throats of the squaws and babies closest to them, stalked out of the lodge, ran rapidly to where they had tied the two best ponies, mounted, and like the wind were away

Besides the warriors with "Washakie," there were two squaws, wives of two of the men wounded in the Rosebud fight, who had remained with us. As this was the last campaign in which great numbers of warriors appeared with bows, arrows, lances, and shields as well as rifles, I may say that the shields of the Shoshones, like those of the Sioux and Crows and Cheyennes, were made of the skin of the buffalo bull's neck, which is an inch in thickness. This is cut to the desired shape, and slightly larger than the required size to allow for shrinking; it is pegged down tight on the ground, and covered with a thin layer of clay upon which is heaped a bed of burning coals, which hardens the skin so that it will turn the point of a lance or a round bullet. A war-song and dance from the Shoshones ended the day.

On the 12th of July, 1876, three men, dirty, ragged, dressed in the tatters of army uniforms, rode into camp and gave their names as Evans, Stewart, and Bell, of Captain Clifford's company

of the Seventh Infantry, bearers of despatches from General
Terry to General Crook; in the dress of each was sewed a copy
of the one message which revealed the terrible catastrophe happening to the companies under General Custer.   These three modest
heroes had ridden across country in the face of unknown dangers, and had performed the duty confided to them in a manner
that challenged the admiration of every man in our camp.   I
have looked in vain through the leaves of the Army Register to
see their names inscribed on the roll of commissioned officers;
and I feel sure that ours is the only army in the world in which
such conspicuous courage, skill, and efficiency would have gone
absolutely unrecognized.

Colonel Chambers, with seven companies of infantry and a
wagon-train loaded with supplies, reached camp on the 13th.
With him came, as volunteers, Lieutenants Hayden Delaney, of
the Ninth, and Calhoun and Crittenden, of the Fourteenth Infantry, and Dr. V. T. McGillicuddy.   Personal letters received
from General Sheridan informed General Crook that General
Merritt, with ten companies of the Fifth Cavalry, had left Red
Cloud Agency with orders to report to Crook, and that as soon
after they arrived as possible, but not until then, Crook was to
start out and resume the campaign.   Courier Fairbanks brought
in despatches from Adjutant-General Robert Williams at Omaha,
Nebraska, to the effect that we should soon be joined by a detachment of Utes, who were desirous of taking part in the
movements against the Sioux, but had been prevented by their
agent.   General Williams had made a representation of all the
facts in the case to superior authority, and orders had been
received from the Department of the Interior directing their
enlistment.   Nearly fifty of the Utes did start out under Lieutenant Spencer, of the Fourth Infantry, and made a very rapid
march to overtake us, but failed to reach our wagon-train camp
until after our command had departed; and, in the opinion of
Major Furey, the risk for such a small party was too great to be
undertaken.

Camp was the scene of the greatest activity : both infantry
and cavalry kept up their exercises in the school of the soldier,
company and battalion, and in skirmishing.   Detachments of
scouts were kept constantly in advanced positions, and although
the enemy had made no attempt to do anything more than annoy

us in our strong natural intrenchments, as the camps close to the Big Horn might fairly be designated, yet it was evident that something unusual was in the wind. "Washakie" ascended to the tops of the highest hills every morning and scanned the horizon through powerful field-glasses, and would then report the results of his observations. Colonel Mills did the same thing from the peaks of the Big Horn, to some of the more accessible of which he ascended. The Shoshones were kept in the highest state of efficiency, and were exercised every morning and evening like their white brothers. At first they had made the circuit of camp unattended, and advanced five or ten miles out into the plains in the performance of their evolutions; but after the arrival of fresh troops, under Chambers, "Washakie" was afraid that some of the new-comers might not know his people and would be likely to fire upon them when they charged back to camp; so he asked General Crook to detail some of his officers to ride at the head of the column, with a view to dispelling any apprehensions the new recruits might feel. It fell to my lot to be one of the officers selected. In all the glory of war-bonnets, bright blankets, scarlet cloth, head-dresses of feathers, and gleaming rifles and lances, the Shoshones, mounted bareback on spirited ponies, moved slowly around camp, led by "Washakie," alongside of whom was borne the oriflamme of the tribe—a standard of eagle feathers attached to a lance-staff twelve feet in length. Each warrior wore in his head-dress a small piece of white drilling as a distinguishing mark to let our troops know who he was.

We moved out in column of twos; first at a fast walk, almost a trot, afterwards increasing the gait. The young warriors sat like so many statues, horse and rider moving as one. Not a word was spoken until the voices of the leaders broke out in their war-song, to which the whole column at once lent the potent aid of nearly two hundred pairs of sturdy lungs. Down the valley about three miles, and then, at a signal from "Washakie," the column turned, and at another, formed front into line and proceeded slowly for about fifty yards. "Washakie" was endeavoring to explain something to me, but the noise of the ponies' hoofs striking the burnt ground and my ignorance of his language were impediments to a full understanding of what the old gentleman was driving at. I learned afterwards that he was assuring me that I was now to see some drill such as the Shoshones alone could execute. He waved his hands ; the line spread out as skirmishers and took about two yards' interval from knee to knee. Then somebody—" Washakie " or one of his lieutenants—yelled a command in a shrill treble ; that's all I remember. The ponies broke into one frantic rush for camp, riding over sage-brush, rocks, stumps, bunches of grass, buffalo heads—it mattered not the least what, they went over it—the warriors all the while squealing, yelling, chanting their war-songs, or howling like coyotes. The ponies entered into the whole business, and needed not the heels and " quirts " which were plied against their willing flanks. In the centre of the line rode old " Washakie ; " abreast of him the eagle standard. It was an exciting and exhilarating race, and the force preserved an excellent alignment. Only one thought occupied my mind during this charge, and that thought was what fools we were not to incorporate these nomads—the finest light cavalry in the world—into our permanent military force. With five thousand such men, and our aboriginal population would readily furnish that number, we could harass and annoy any troops that might have the audacity to land on our coasts, and worry them to death.

General Crook attempted to open communication with General Terry by sending out a miner named Kelly, who was to strike for the head of the Little Big Horn, follow that down until it proved navigable, then make a raft or support for himself of cottonwood or willow saplings and float by night to the confluence of the Big Horn and the Yellowstone, and down the latter to wherever Terry's camp might be. Kelly made two attempts to start, but was each time driven or frightened back ; but the third time got off in safety and made the perilous journey, and very much in the lines laid down in his talk with Crook.

Violent storms of snow, hail, and cold rain, with tempests of wind, prevailed upon the summits of the range, which was frequently hidden from our gaze by lowering masses of inky vapor. Curious effects, not strictly meteorological, were noticed ; our camp was visited by clouds of flies from the pine forests, which deposited their eggs upon everything ; the heat of the sun was tempered by a gauze veil which inspection showed to be a myriad of grasshoppers seeking fresh fields of devastation. Possibly the burning over of hundreds of square miles of pasturage had driven them to hunt new and unharmed districts ; possibly they were driven down from the higher elevations by the rigorous cold of the storms ; possibly both causes operated. The fact was all we cared for, and we found it disagreeable enough. With these insects there was larger game : mountain sheep appeared in the lower foot-hills, and two of them were killed along our camp lines. To balk any attempt of the enemy to deprive us altogether of grass, whenever camp was moved to a new site, a detail of men was put to work to surround us with a fire-line, which would prevent the fires set by mischievous Sioux from gaining headway. In making one of these moves we found the Tongue River extremely swollen from the storms in the higher peaks, and one of the drivers, a good man but rather inexperienced, had the misfortune to lose his self-possession, and his wagon was overturned by the deep current and three of the mules drowned, the man himself being rescued by the exertions of the Shoshone scouts, who were passing at the moment.

On the 19th of July four Crow Indians rode into camp bearing despatches, the duplicates of those already received by the hands of Evans, Stewart, and Bell. General Terry, realizing the risk the latter ran, had taken the precaution to repeat his correspondence with Crook in order that the latter might surely understand the exact situation of affairs in the north. After being refreshed with sleep and a couple of good warm meals, the Crows were interrogated concerning all they knew of the position of the hostiles, their numbers, ammunition, and other points of the same kind. Squatting upon the ground, with fingers and hands deftly moving, they communicated through the " sign language " a detailed account of the advance of Terry, Gibbon, and Custer ; the march of Custer, the attack upon the village of " Crazy Horse " and " Sitting Bull," the massacre, the retreat of Reno, the investment, the arrival of fresh troops on the field, the carrying away of the wounded to the steamboats, the sorrow in the command, and many other things which would astonish persons ignorant of the scope and power of this silent vehicle for the interchange of thought.

The troops having been paid off by Major Arthur, who had come with Colonel Chambers and the wagon-train, the Shoshones each evening had pony races for some of the soldiers' money. This was the great amusement of our allies, besides gambling, fishing, drilling, and hunting. The greater the crowd assembled, the greater the pleasure they took in showing their rare skill in riding and managing their fleet little ponies. The course laid off was ordinarily one of four hundred yards. The signal given, with whip and heel each rider plied his maddened steed ; it was evident that the ponies were quite as much worked up in the matter as their riders. With one simultaneous bound the half-dozen or more contestants dart like arrow from bow ; a cloud of dust rises and screens them from vision ; it is useless to try to pierce this veil ; it is unnecessary, because within a very few seconds the quaking earth throbs responsive to many-footed blows, and, quick as lightning's flash, the mass of steaming, panting, and frenzied steeds dash past, · and the race is over. Over so far as the horses were concerned, but only begun so far as the various points of excellence of the riders and their mounts could be argued about and disputed.

This did not conclude the entertainment of each day : the Shoshones desired to add still more to the debt of gratitude we already owed them, so they held a serenade whenever the night was calm and fair. Once when the clouds had rolled by and the pale light of the moon was streaming down upon tents and pack-trains, wagons and sleeping animals, the Shoshones became especially vociferous, and I learned from the interpreter that they were singing to the moon. This was one of the most pronounced examples of moon worship coming under my observation.

The Shoshones were expert fishermen, and it was always a matter of interest to me to spend my spare moments among them, watching their way of doing things. Their war lodges were entirely unlike those of the Apaches, with which I had become familiar. The Shoshones would take half a dozen willow branches and insert them in the earth, so as to make a semi-cylindrical framework, over which would be spread a sufficiency of blankets to afford the requisite shelter. They differed also from the Apaches in being very fond of fish ; the Apaches could not be persuaded to touch anything with scales upon it, or any bird which lived upon fish ; but the Shoshones had more sense, and made the most of their opportunity to fill themselves with the delicious trout of the mountain streams. They did not bother much about hooks and lines, flies, casts, and appliances and tricks of that kind, but set to work methodically to get the biggest mess the streams would yield. They made a dam of rocks and a wattle-work of willow, through which the water could pass without much impediment, but which would retain all solids. Two or three young men would stay by this dam or framework as guards to repair accidents. The others of the party, mounting their ponies, would start down-stream to a favorable location and there enter and begin the ascent of the current, keeping their ponies in touch, lashing the surface of the stream in their front with long poles, and all the while joining in a wild medicine song. The frightened trout, having no other mode of escape, would dart up-stream only to be held in the dam, from which the Indians would calmly proceed to take them out in gunny sacks. It was not very sportsmanlike, but it was business.

I find the statement in my note-books that there must have been at least fifteen thousand trout captured in the streams upon which we had been encamped during that period of three weeks, and I am convinced that my figures are far below the truth ; the whole command was living upon trout or as much as it wanted ; when it is remembered that we had hundreds of white and red soldiers, teamsters, and packers, and that when Crook finally left this region the camp was full of trout, salt or dried in the sun or smoked, and that every man had all he could possibly eat for days and days, the enormous quantity taken must be apparent. Added to this we continued to have a considerable amount of venison, elk, and bear meat, but no buffalo had been seen for some days, probably on account of the destruction of grass. Mountain sheep and bear took its place to a certain extent.

It was the opinion and advice of Sheridan that Crook should wait for the arrival of Merritt, and that the combined force should then hunt Terry and unite with him, and punish the Sioux, rather than attempt to do anything with a force which might prove inadequate. In this view old "Washakie" fully concurred. The old chief said to Crook : "The Sioux and Cheyennes have three to your one, even now that you have been reinforced ; why not let them alone for a few days ? they cannot subsist the great numbers of warriors and men in their camp, and will have to scatter for pasturage and meat ; they'll begin to fight among

themselves about the plunder taken on the battle-field, and many
will want to slip into the agencies and rejoin their families."

But, while waiting for Merritt to come up with his ten companies of cavalry, Crook sent out two large scouting parties to
definitely determine the location and strength of the enemy.
One of these consisted entirely of Shoshones, under "Washakie;" it penetrated to the head of the Little Big Horn and
around the corner of the mountain to the cañon of the Big
Horn; the site of a great camp was found of hundreds of lodges
and thousands of ponies, but the indications were that the enemy
were getting hard pressed for food, as they had been eating their
dogs and ponies whose bones were picked up around the camp-
fires. From that point the trails showed that the enemy had
gone to the northeast towards the Powder River. The other
scouting party was led by Louis Richaud, and passed over the
Big Horn Mountains and down into the cañon of the Big Horn
River; they found where the Sioux of the big village had sent
parties up into the range to cut and trim lodge-poles in great
numbers. Richaud and his party suffered extremely from cold;
the lakes on the summit of the mountains were frozen, and on
the 1st of August they were exposed to a severe snow-storm.

Later advices from Sheridan told that the control of the Sioux
agencies had been transferred to the War Department; that Mackenzie and six companies of his regiment had been ordered to take
charge at Red Cloud and Spotted Tail, assisted by Gordon with
two companies of the Fifth Cavalry. Although showers of rain
were of almost daily occurrence, and storms of greater importance very frequent, the weather was so far advanced, and the
grass so dry and so far in seed, that there was always danger of a
conflagration from carelessness with fire.

One of the Shoshones dropped a lighted match in the dry
grass near his lodge, and in a second a rattle and crackle warned
the camp of its danger. All hands, Indian and white, near by
rushed up with blankets, blouses, switches, and branches of trees
to beat back the flames. This was a dangerous task; as, one
after another, the Shoshone frame shelters were enveloped in the
fiery embrace of the surging flames, the explosion of cartridges
and the whistling of bullets drove our men back to places of
safety. In the tall and dry grass the flames held high revel;
the whole infantry command was turned out, and bravely set to

work, and, aided by a change in the wind, secured camp from destruction. While thus engaged, they discovered a body of Indians moving down the declivity of the mountain ; they immediately sprang to arms and prepared to resist attack ; a couple of white men advanced from the Indian column and called out to the soldiers that they were a band of Utes and Shoshones from Camp Brown, coming to join General Crook.

Our men welcomed and led them into camp, where friends gave them a warm reception, which included the invariable war-dance and the evening serenade. Some of the new-comers strolled over to chat with the Shoshones who had been wounded in the Rosebud fight, and who, although horribly cut up with bullet wounds in the thigh or in the flanks, as the case was, had recovered completely under the care of their own doctors, who applied nothing but cool water as a dressing ; but I noticed that they were not all the time washing out the wounds as Americans would have done, which treatment as they think would only irritate the tender surfaces. The new-comers proved to be a band of thirty-five, and were all good men.

On the 2d of August camp was greatly excited over what was termed a game of base-ball between the officers of the infantry and cavalry ; quite a number managed to hit the ball, and one or two catches were made ; the playing was in much the same style, and of about the same comparative excellence, as the amateur theatrical exhibitions, where those who come to scoff remain to pray that they may never have to come again.

CHAPTER XX.

THE JUNCTION WITH MERRITT AND THE MARCH TO MEET TERRY
—THE COUNTRY ON FIRE—MERRITT AND HIS COMMAND—
MR. "GRAPHIC"—STANTON AND HIS "IRREGULARS"—"UTE
JOHN"—THE SITE OF THE HOSTILE CAMP—A SIOUX CEME-
TERY—MEETING TERRY'S COMMAND—FINDING TWO SKEL-
ETONS—IN THE BAD LANDS—LANCING RATTLESNAKES—
BATHING IN THE YELLOWSTONE—MACKINAW BOATS AND
"BULL" BOATS—THE REES HAVE A PONY DANCE—SOME
TERRIBLE STORMS—LIEUTENANT WILLIAM P. CLARKE.

ON the 3d of August, 1876, Crook's command marched twenty miles north-northeast to Goose Creek, where Merritt had been ordered to await its arrival. The flames of prairie fires had parched and disfigured the country. "Big Bat" took me a short cut across a petty affluent of the Goose, which had been full of running water but was now dry as a bone, choked with ashes and dust, the cottonwoods along its banks on fire, and every sign that its current had been dried up by the intense heat of the flames. In an hour or so more the pent-up waters forced a passage through the ashes, and again flowed down to mingle with the Yellowstone. The Sioux had also set fire to the timber in the Big Horn, and at night the sight was a beautiful one of the great line of the foot-hills depicted in a tracery of gold.

General Merritt received us most kindly. He was at that time a very young man, but had had great experience during the war in command of mounted troops. He was blessed with a powerful physique, and seemed to be specially well adapted to undergo any measure of fatigue and privation that might befall him. His force consisted of ten companies of the Fifth Cavalry, and he had also brought along with him seventy-six recruits for the Second and Third Regiments, and over sixty surplus horses, besides an abundance of ammunition.

The officers with General Merritt, or whose names have not

already been mentioned in these pages, were : Lieutenant-Colonel
E. A. Carr, Major John V. Upham, Lieutenant A. D. B. Smead,
A. D. King, George O. Eaton, Captain Robert H. Montgomery,
Emil Adam, Lieutenant E. L. Keyes, Captain Samuel Sumner,
Lieutenant C. P. Rodgers, Captain George F. Price, Captain
J. Scott Payne, Lieutenants A. B. Bache, William P. Hall, Cap-
tain E. M. Hayes, Lieutenant Hoel S. Bishop, Captain Sanford
C. Kellogg, Lieutenants Bernard Reilly and Robert London,
Captain Julius W. Mason, Lieutenant Charles King, Captain
Edward H. Leib, Captain William H. Powell, Captain James
Kennington, Lieutenant John Murphy, Lieutenant Charles
Lloyd, Captain Daniel W. Burke, Lieutenant F. S. Calhoun,
Captain Thomas F. Tobey, Lieutenant Frank Taylor, Lieu-
tenant Richard T. Yeatman, Lieutenants Julius H. Pardee,
Robert H. Young, Rockefeller, and Satterlle C. Plummer, with
Lieutenants W. C. Forbush as Adjutant, and Charles H. Rockwell as Quartermaster of the Fifth Cavalry, and Assistant Surgeons Grimes, Lecompt, and Surgeon B. H. Clements, who was
announced as Medical Director of the united commands by
virtue of rank. Colonel T. H. Stanton was announced as in
command of the irregulars and citizen volunteers, who in small
numbers accompanied the expedition. He was assisted by Lieutenant Robert H. Young, Fourth Infantry, a gallant and efficient soldier of great experience. At the head of the scouts
with Merritt rode William F. Cody, better known to the world
at large by his dramatic representation which has since traversed
two continents : " Buffalo Bill's Wild West Show."

Major Furey was directed to remain at this point, or in some
eligible locality close to it, and keep with him the wagon-train
and the disabled. Paymaster Arthur was to stay with him ; and
outside of that there were three casualties in the two commands : Sutorius, dismissed by sentence of general court-martial ; Wilson, resigned July 29th ; and Cain, whose mind betrayed
symptoms of unsoundness, and who was ordered to remain with
Furey, but persisted in keeping with the column until the Yellowstone had been reached. Couriers arrived with telegrams from
General Sheridan at Chicago, Williams at Omaha, and Colonel
Townsend, commanding at Fort Laramie ; all of whom had
likewise sent clippings from the latest papers, furnishing information from all points in the Indian country. From these

clippings it was learned that the stream of adventurers pouring into the Black Hills was unabated, and that at the confluence of the Deadwood and Whitewood Creeks a large town or city of no less than four thousand inhabitants had sprung up and was working the gold "placers," all the time exposed to desperate attacks from the Indians, who, according to one statement, which was afterwards shown to be perfectly true, had murdered more than eighty men in less than eight days. These men were not killed within the limits of the town, but in its environs and in the exposed "claims" out in the Hills.

Several new correspondents had attached themselves to Merritt's column; among them I recall Mills, of the New York *Times*, and Lathrop, of the *Bulletin*, of San Francisco. These, I believe, were the only real correspondents in the party, although there were others who vaunted their pretensions; one of these last, name now forgotten, claimed to have been sent out by the New York *Graphic*, a statement very few were inclined to admit. He was the greenest thing I ever saw without feathers; he had never been outside of New York before, and the way the scouts, packers, and soldiers "laid for" that man was a caution. Let the other newspaper men growl as they might about the lack of news, Mr. "Graphic," as I must call him, never had any right to complain on that score. Never was packer or scout or soldier—shall I add officer?—so weary, wet, hungry, or miserable at the end of a day's march that he couldn't devote a half-hour to the congenial task of "stuffin' the tenderfoot." The stories told of Indian atrocities to captives, especially those found with paper and lead-pencils, were enough to make the stoutest veteran's teeth chatter, and at times our newly-discovered acquisition manifested a disinclination to swallow, unstrained, the stories told him; but his murmurs of mild dissent were drowned in an inundation of "Oh, that hain't nawthin' to what I've seed 'em do." Who the poor fellow was I do not know; no one seemed to know him by any other designation than "The Tenderfoot." He had no money, he could not draw, and was dependent upon the packers and others for every meal; I must say that he never lacked food, provided he swallowed it with tales of border horrors which would cause the pages of the Boys' Own Five-Cent Novelette series to creak with terror. I never saw him smile but once, and that was under provocation sufficient to lead a corpse to laugh itself out of its shroud.

One of the biggest liars among Stanton's scouts—I do not recall whether it was "Slap-jack Billy, the Pride of the Pan-Handle," or "Pisen-weed Patsey, the Terror of the Bresh "—was devoting a half-hour of his valuable time to "gettin' in his work" on the victim, and was riding one pony and leading another, which he had tied to the tail of the first by a rope or halter. This plan worked admirably, and would have been a success to the end had not the led pony started at some Indian clothing in the trail, and jumped, and pulled the tail of the leader nearly out by the roots. The front horse wasn't going to stand any such nonsense as that ; he squealed and kicked and plunged in rage, sending his rider over his head like a rocket, and then, still attached to the other, something after the style of a Siamese twin, charged through the column of scouts, scattering them in every direction. But this paroxysm of hilarity was soon over, and the correspondent subsided into his normal condition of deep-settled melancholy. He left us when we reached the Yellowstone, and I have never blamed him.

One of the facts brought out in the telegrams received by General Crook was that eight warriors, who had left the hostiles and surrendered at Red Cloud Agency, had reported that the main body of the hostiles would turn south. Lieutenant E. B. Robertson, Ninth Infantry, found a soapstone dish on the line of march, which could have come from the Mandans only, either by trade or theft ; or, possibly, some band of Mandans, in search of buffalo, had penetrated thus far into the interior and had lost it.

In a telegram sent in to Sheridan about this date Crook said : " On the 25th or 26th, all the hostile Indians left the foot of the Big Horn Mountains, and moved back in the direction of the Rosebud Mountains, so that it is now impracticable to communicate with General Terry by courier. I am fearful that they will scatter, as there is not sufficient grass in that country to support them in such large numbers. If we meet the Indians in too strong force, I will swing around and unite with General Terry. Your management of the agencies will be a great benefit to us here."

We had one busy day ; saddles had to be exchanged or repaired, horses shod, ammunition issued, provisions packed, and all stores in excess turned into the wagon-train. The allowance of baggage was cut down to the minimum : every officer and soldier was to have the clothes on his back and no more ; one overcoat, one blanket (to be carried by the cavalry over the saddle blanket), and one India-rubber poncho or one-half of a shelter tent, was the allowance carried by General Crook, the members of his staff, and all the officers, soldiers, and packers. We had rations for fifteen days—half of bacon, sugar, coffee, and salt, and full of hard bread ; none of vinegar, soap, pepper, etc. There were two hundred and fifty rounds of ammunition to the man ; one hundred to be carried on the person, and the rest on the pack-mules, of which there were just three hundred and ninety-nine. The pack-train was in five divisions, each led by a bell-mare ; no tents allowed, excepting one for the use of the surgeons attending to critical cases. "Travois" poles were hauled along to drag wounded in case it should become necessary.

Our mess, which now numbered eleven, was, beyond dispute, the most remarkable mess the army has ever known. I challenge comparison with it from anything that has ever been seen among our officers outside of Libby or Andersonville prisons. General Crook did not allow us either knife, fork, spoon, or plate. Each member carried strapped to the pommel of his saddle a tin cup, from which at balmy morn or dewy eve, as the poets would say, he might quaff the decoction called coffee. Our kitchen utensils comprised one frying-pan, one carving-knife, one carving-fork, one large coffee pot, one large tin platter, one large and two small tin ladles or spoons, and the necessary bags for carrying sugar, coffee, bacon, and hard bread. I forgot to say that we had also one sheet-iron mess pan. General Crook had determined to make his column as mobile as a column of Indians, and he knew that example was more potent than a score of general orders.

We marched down "Prairie Dog" Creek, to its junction with Tongue River, passing through a village of prairie dogs, which village was six miles long. The mental alienation of our unfortunate friend—Captain Cain—became more and more apparent. By preference, I rode with Colonel Stanton's scouts; they called themselves the "Montana Volunteers," but why they did so I never could understand, unless it was that every other State and

Territory had repudiated them and set a price upon their heads. There was a rumor widely circulated in camp to the effect that one or two of these scouts had never been indicted for murder; it was generally suspected that Stanton himself was at the bottom of this, in his anxiety to secure a better name for his corps. There were very few of them who couldn't claim the shelter of the jails of Cheyenne, Denver, and Omaha by merely presenting themselves, and confessing certain circumstances known to the police and detectives of those thriving boroughs. Many a night Joe Wasson, Strahorn, and I sat upon our saddles, to be sure that we should have them with us at sunrise. One of the most important of these volunteers was "Ute John," a member of the tribe of the same name, who claimed to have been thoroughly civilized and Christianized, because he had once, for six months, been "dlivin' team fo' Mo'mon" in Salt Lake. "Ute John" was credited by most people with having murdered his own grand-mother and drunk her blood, but, in my opinion, the reports to his detriment were somewhat exaggerated, and he was harmless except when sober, which wasn't often, provided whiskey was handy. "John's" proudest boast was that he was a "Klischun," and he assured me that he had been three times baptized in one year by the "Mo'mon," who had made him "heap wash," and gave him "heap biled shirt," by which we understood that he had been baptized and clad in the garments of righteousness, which he sorely needed. "Ute John" had one peculiarity: he would never speak to any one but Crook himself in regard to the issues of the campaign. "Hello, Cluke," he would say, "how you gittin' on? Where you tink dem Clazy Hoss en Settin' Bull is now, Cluke?"

We had a difficult time marching down the Tongue, which had to be forded thirteen times in one day, the foot-soldiers disdaining the aid which the cavalry was ordered to extend by carrying across all who so desired. The country was found to be one gloomy desolation. We crossed the Rosebud Mountains and descended into the Rosebud Creek, where trails were found as broad and distinct as wagon-roads; the grass was picked clean, and the valley, of which I wrote so enthusiastically in the spring, was now a desert. We discovered the trap which "Crazy Horse" had set for us at the Rosebud fight on the 17th of June, and confidence in Crook was increased tenfold by the knowledge that he had outwitted the enemy on that occasion. The Sioux and Cheyennes had encamped in seven circles, covering four miles in length of the valley. The trail was from ten to twelve days old, and, in the opinion of Frank and the other guides, had been made by from ten to twenty thousand ponies.

The hills bordering the Rosebud were vertical bluffs presenting beautiful alternations of color in their stratification; there were bands of red, pink, cream, black, and purple; the different tints blending by easy gradations into a general effect pleasing to the eye. There were quantities of lignite which would be of incalculable benefit to the white settlers who might in the future flock into this region. In riding along with our Indian scouts we learned much of the secret societies among the aboriginal tribes: the "Brave Night Hearts," the "Owl Feathers," and the "Wolves and Foxes." These control the tribe, fight its battles, and determine its policy. Initiation into some one of them is essential to the young warrior's advancement. The cañon of the Rosebud would seem to have been the burying-ground of the Western Dakotas; there were dozens of graves affixed to the branches of the trees, some of them of great age, and all raided by our ruthless Shoshones and Utes, who with their lances tumbled the bones to the ground and ransacked the coverings for mementos of value, sometimes getting fine bows, at others, nickel-plated revolvers. There was one which the Shoshones were afraid to touch, and which they said was full of bad "medicine;" but "Ute John," fortified, no doubt, by the grace of his numerous Mormon baptisms, was not restrained by vain fears, and tumbled it to the ground, letting loose sixteen field mice which in some way had made their home in those sepulchral cerements.

Captain "Jack Crawford, the Poet Scout," rode into camp on the 8th of August attended by a few companions. The weather became rainy, and the trail muddy and heavy. August 11th our scouts sent in the information that a line of Indians was coming up the valley, and our men advanced as skirmishers. Soon word was received that behind the supposed enemy could be seen the white canvas covers of a long column of wagons, and we then knew that we were about to meet Terry's command. Our cavalry were ordered to halt and unsaddle to await the approach of the infantry. The Indian scouts were directed to proceed to the front and determine exactly who the strangers were. They decked themselves in all the barbaric splendors of which they were capable : war-bonnets streamed to the ground ; lances and rifles gleamed in the sun ; ponies and riders, daubed with mud, pranced out to meet our friends, as we were assured they must be.

When our Indians raised their yells and chants, the scouts at the head of the other column took fright and ran in upon the solid masses of horsemen following the main trail. These immediately deployed into line of skirmishers, behind which we saw, or thought we saw, several pieces of artillery. " Buffalo Bill," who was riding at the head of our column, waved his hat, and, putting spurs to his horse, galloped up alongside of Major Reno, of the Seventh Cavalry, who was leading Terry's advance. When the news passed down from man to man, cheers arose from the two columns ; as fast as the cheers of Terry's advance guard reached the ears of our men, they responded with heart and soul. General Crook sent Lieutenant Schuyler to extend a welcome to General Terry, and proffer to him and his officers such hospitalities as we could furnish.

Schuyler returned, leading to the tree under which Crook was seated a band of officers at whose head rode Terry himself. The meeting between the two commanders was most cordial, as was that between the subalterns, many of whom had served together during the war and in other places. We made every exertion to receive our guests with the best in our possession : messengers were despatched down to the pack-trains to borrow every knife, fork, spoon, and dish available, and they returned with about thirty of each and two great coffee-pots, which were soon humming on the fire filled to the brim with an exhilarating decoction. Phillips, the cook, was assisted on this occasion by a man whose experience had been garnered among the Nez Percés and Flat-Heads, certainly not among Caucasians, although I must admit that he worked hard and did the best he knew how. A long strip of canvas was stretched upon the ground and covered with the tin cups and cutlery. Terry and his staff seated themselves and partook of what we had to offer, which was not very much, but was given with full heart.

Terry was one of the most charming and affable of men ; his general air was that of the scholar no less than the soldier. His figure was tall and commanding ; his face gentle, yet de-

cided ; his kindly blue eyes indicated good-nature ; his complexion, bronzed by wind and rain and sun to the color of an old
sheepskin-covered Bible, gave him a decidedly martial appearance. He won his way to all hearts by unaffectedness and affa-
bility. In his manner he was the antithesis of Crook. Crook
was also simple and unaffected, but he was reticent and taciturn
to the extreme of sadness, brusque to the verge of severity. In
Terry's face I thought I could sometimes detect traces of inde-
cision ; but in Crook's countenance there was not the slightest
intimation of anything but stubbornness, rugged resolution, and
bull-dog tenacity. Of the two men Terry alone had any pretensions to scholarship, and his attainments were so great that the
whole army felt proud of him ; but Nature had been bountiful
to Crook, and as he stood there under a tree talking with Terry,
I thought that within that cleanly outlined skull, beneath that
brow, and behind those clear-glancing blue-gray eyes, there was
concealed more military sagacity, more quickness of comprehension and celerity to meet unexpected emergencies, than in any of
our then living Generals excepting Grant, of whose good qualities he constantly reminded me, or Sheridan, whose early friend
and companion he had been at West Point and in Oregon.

That evening, General Crook and his staff dined with General Terry, meeting with the latter Captains Smith and Gibbs,
Lieutenants Maguire, Walker, Thompson, Nowlan, and Mich-
aelis. From this point Terry sent his wagon-train down to the
Yellowstone, and ordered the Fifth Infantry to embark on one
of the steamboats and patrol the river, looking out for trails
of hostiles crossing or attempting to cross to the north. All the
sick and disabled were sent down with this column ; we lost Cain
and Bache and a number of enlisted men, broken down by the
exposure of the campaign. The heat in the middle of the day
had become excessive, and General Terry informed me that on
the 8th it registered in his own tent 117° Fahrenheit, and on the
7th, 110°. Much of this increase of temperature was, no doubt,
due to the heat from the pasturage destroyed by the hostiles,
which comprehended an area extending from the Yellowstone to
the Big Horn Mountains, from the Big Horn River on the west
to the Little Missouri on the east.

In two things the column from the Yellowstone was sadly
deficient : in cavalry and in rapid transportation. The Seventh

Cavalry was in need of reorganization, half of its original numbers having been killed or wounded in the affair of the Big Horn ; the pack-train, made up, as it necessarily was, of animals taken out of the traces of the heavy wagons, was the saddest burlesque in that direction which it has ever been my lot to witness—for this no blame was ascribable to Terry, who was doing the best he could with the means allowed him from Washington.   The Second Cavalry was in good shape, and so was Gibbon's column of infantry, which seemed ready to go wherever ordered and go at once.   Crook's pack-train was a marvel of system ; it maintained a discipline much severer than had been attained by any company in either column ; under the indefatigable supervision of Tom Moore, Dave Mears, and others, who had had an experience of more than a quarter of a century, our mules moved with a precision to which the worn-out comparison of "clockwork" is justly adapted.   The mules had been continuously in training since the preceding December, making long marches, carrying heavy burdens in the worst sort of weather.   Consequently, they were hardened to the hardness and toughness of wrought-iron and whalebone.   They followed the bell, and were as well trained as any soldiers in the command.   Behind them one could see the other pack-train, a string of mules, of all sizes, each led by one soldier and beaten and driven along by another—attendants often rivalling animals in dumbness—and it was hard to repress a smile except by the reflection that this was the motive power of a column supposed to be in pursuit of savages.   On the first day's march, after meeting Crook, Terry's pack-train dropped, lost, or damaged more stores than Crook's command had spoiled from the same causes from the time when the campaign commenced.

When the united columns struck the Tongue, the trail of the hostile bands had split into three : one going up stream, one down, and one across country east towards the Powder.   Crook ordered his scouts to examine in front and on flanks, and in the mean time the commands unsaddled and went into camp ; the scouts did not return until almost dark, when they brought information that the main trail had kept on in the direction of the Powder.   Colonel Royall's command found the skeletons of two mining prospectors in the bushes near the Tongue ; appearances indicated that the Sioux had captured these men and roasted them alive.   On this march we saw a large "medicine rock," in

whose crevices the Sioux had deposited various propitiatory offer-
ings, and upon whose face had been graven figures and symbols
of fanciful and grotesque outline.

In following the main trail of the enemy it seemed as if we
were on a newly cut country road ; when we reached a projecting
hill of marl and sandy clay, the lodge poles had cut into the soft
soil to such an extent that we could almost believe that we were
on the line of work just completed, with pick, spade, and shovel,
by a gang of trained laborers. Trout were becoming scarce in
this part of the Tongue, but a very delicious variety of the
"cat" was caught and added to the mess to the great delight of
the epicure members. The rain had increased in volume, and
rarely an hour now passed without its shower. One night, while
sitting by what was supposed to be our camp-fire, watching the
sputtering flames struggling to maintain life against the down-
pouring waters, I heard my name called, and as soon as I could
drag my sodden, sticky clothes through a puddle of mud I found
myself face to face with Sam Hamilton, of the Second, whom I
had not seen since we were boys together in the volunteer service
in the Stone River campaign, in 1862. It was a very melancholy
meeting, each soaked through to the skin, seated alongside of
smoking embers, and chilled to the marrow, talking of old times,
of comrades dead, and wondering who next was to be called.

The Indian trail led down the Tongue for some miles before it
turned east up the " Four Horn " Creek, where we followed it,
being rewarded with an abundance of very fine grama, called by
our scouts the " Two-Day " grass, because a bellyful of it
would enable a tired horse to travel for two days more. An
Indian puppy was found abandoned by its red-skinned owners,
and was adopted by one of the infantry soldiers, who carried it on
his shoulders. Part of this time we were in " Bad Lands," infested with rattlesnakes in great numbers, which our Shoshones
lanced with great glee. It was very interesting to watch them,
and see how they avoided being bitten : three or four would ride
up within easy distance of the doomed reptile and distract its
attention by threatening passes with their lances ; the crotalus
would throw itself into a coil in half a second, and stay there,
tongue darting in and out, head revolving from side to side,
leaden eyes scintillating with the glare of the diamond, ready to
strike venomous fangs into any one coming within reach. The

Shoshone boys would drive their lances into the coil from three or four different directions, exclaiming at the same time: "Gott tammee you! Gott tammee you!" which was all the English they had been able to master.

We struck the Powder and followed it down to its junction with the Yellowstone, where we were to replenish our supplies from Terry's steamboats. The Powder contrasted unfavorably with the Tongue: the latter was about one hundred and fifty feet wide, four feet deep, swift current, and cold water, and, except in the Bad Lands near its mouth, clear and sweet, and not perceptibly alkaline. The Powder was the opposite in every feature: its water, turbid and milky; current, slow; bottom, muddy and frequently miry, whereas that of the Tongue was nearly always hard-pan. The water of the Powder was alkaline and not always palatable, and the fords rarely good and often dangerous. The Yellowstone was a delightful stream: its width was not over two hundred and fifty yards, but its depth was considerable, its bed constant, and channel undeviating. The current flows with so little noise that an unsuspecting person would have no idea of its velocity; but steamboats could rarely stem it, and bathers venturing far from the banks were swept off their feet. The depth was never less than five feet in the main channel during time of high water. The banks were thickly grassed and covered with cottonwood and other timber in heavy copses.

Crook's forces encamped on the western bank of the Powder; the supplies we had looked for were not on hand in sufficient quantity, and Lieutenant Bubb, our commissary, reported that he was afraid that we were going to be grievously disappointed in that regard. General Terry sent steamers up and down the Yellowstone to gather up all stores from depots, and also from points where they had been unloaded on account of shallow water. Crook's men spent a great deal of the time bathing in the Yellowstone and washing their clothes, following the example set by the General himself: each man waded out into the channel clad in his undergarments and allowed the current to soak them thoroughly, and he would then stand in the sunlight until dried. Each had but the suit on his back, and this was all the cleaning or change they had for sixty days. The Utes and Shoshones became very discontented, and "Washakie" had several interviews with Crook, in which he plainly told the latter that his people would not remain longer with Terry's column, because of the inefficiency of its transportation ; with such mules nothing could be done ; the infantry was all right, and so was part of the cavalry, but the pack-train was no good, and was simply impeding progress.   The steamer "Far West," Captain Grant Marsh, was sent up the river to the mouth of the Rosebud to bring down all the supplies to be found in the depot at that point, but returned with very little for so many mouths as we now had—about four thousand all told.

A great many fine agates were found in the Yellowstone near the Powder, and so common were they that nearly all provided themselves with souvenirs from that source.   Colonel Burt was sent up the river to try to induce the Crows to send some of their warriors to take the places soon to be vacated by the Shoshones, as Crook foresaw that without native scouts the expedition might as well be abandoned.   Burt was unsuccessful in his mission, and all our scouts left with the exception of the much-disparaged "Ute John," who expressed his determination to stick it out to the last.

Mackinaw boats, manned by adventurous traders from Montana, had descended the river loaded with all kinds of knick-knacks for the use of the soldiers ; these were retailed at enormous prices, but eagerly bought by men who had no other means of getting rid of their money.   Besides the "Mackinaw," which was made of rough timber framework, the waters of the Yellowstone and the Missouri were crossed by the "bull-boat," which bore a close resemblance to the basket "coracle" of the west coast of Ireland, and, like it, was a framework of willow or some kind of basketry covered with the skins of the buffalo, or other bovine ; in these frail hemispherical barks squaws would paddle themselves and baggage and pappooses across the swift-running current and gain the opposite bank in safety.

At the mouth of Powder there was a sutler's store packed from morning till night with a crowd of expectant purchasers. To go in there was all one's life was worth : one moment a soldier stepped on one of your feet, and the next some two-hundred-pound packer favored the other side in the same manner. A disagreeable sand-storm drove Colonel Stanton and myself to the shelter of the lunette constructed by Lieutenant William P. Clarke, Second Cavalry, who had descended the Yellowstone from Fort Ellis with a piece of artillery.   Here we lunched with Clarke and Colonel Carr, of the Fifth Cavalry, stormbound like ourselves.   The Ree scouts attached to Terry's column favored our Utes and Shoshones with a "pony" dance after nightfall. The performers were almost naked, and, with their ponies, be-daubed and painted from head to foot.   They advanced in a regular line, which was not broken for any purpose, going over every obstruction, even trampling down the rude structures of cottonwood branches erected by the Utes and Shoshones for protection from the elements.   As soon as they had come within a few yards of the camp-fires of the Shoshones, the latter, with the Utes, joined the Rees in their chant and also jumped upon their ponies, which staggered for some minutes around camp under their double and even treble load, until, thank Heaven ! the affair ended.   Although I had what might be called a "dead-head" view of the dance, I did not enjoy it at all, and was not sorry when the Rees said that they would have to go back to their own camp.

There was not very much to eat down on the Yellowstone, and one could count on his fingers the "square" meals in that lovely valley.   Conspicuous among them should be the feast of hot bacon and beans, to which Tom Moore invited Hartsuff, Stanton, Bubb, Wasson, Strahorn, Schuyler, and myself long after the camp was wrapped in slumber.   The beans were cooked to a turn ; there was plenty of hard-tack and coffee, with a small quantity of sugar ; each knew the other, there was much to talk about, and in the light and genial warmth of the fire, with stomachs filled, we passed a delightful time until morning had almost dawned.

On the 20th of August, our Utes and Shoshones left, and word was also received from the Crows that they were afraid to let any of the young men leave their own country while such num-bers of the Sioux and Cheyennes were in hostility, and so close to them.   General Crook had a flag prepared for his head-quarters after the style prevailing in Terry's column, which served the excellent purpose of directing orderlies and officers promptly to the battalion or other command to which a message was to be delivered.   This standard, for the construction of which we were indebted to the industry of Randall and Schuyler, was rather primitive in design and general make-up.   It was a guidon, of two horizontal bands, white above, red beneath, with a blue star in the centre.   The white was from a crash towel contributed by Colonel Stanton, the red came from a flannel undershirt belonging to Schuyler, and an old blouse which Randall was about to throw away furnished the star.   Tom Moore had a "travois" pole shaved down for a staff, the ferrule and tip of which were made of metallic cartridges.

Supper had just been finished that day when we were exposed to as miserable a storm as ever drowned the spirit and enthusiasm out of any set of mortals.   It didn't come on suddenly, but with slowness and deliberation almost premeditated.   For more than an hour fleecy clouds skirmished in the sky, wheeling and circling lazily until re-enforced from the west, and then moving boldly forward and hanging over camp in dense, black, sullen masses.   All bestirred themselves to make such preparations as they could to withstand the siege : willow twigs and grasses were cut in quantities, and to these were added sage-brush and greasewood.   Wood was stacked up for the fire, so that at the earliest moment possible after the cessation of the storm it could be rekindled and afford some chance of warming ourselves and drying clothing.   With the twigs and sage-brush we built up beds in the best-drained nooks and corners, placed our saddles and bridles at our heads, and carbines and cartridges at our sides to keep them dry.   As a last protection, a couple of lariats were tied together, one end of the rope fastened to a picket pin in the ground, the other to the limb of the withered cottonwood alongside of which headquarters had been established ; over this were stretched a couple of blankets from the pack-train, and we had done our best.   There was nothing else to do but grin and bear all that was to happen.   The storm-king had waited patiently for the completion of these meagre preparations, and now, with a loud, ear-piercing crash of thunder, and a hissing flash of white lightning, gave the signal to the elements to begin the attack.   We cowered helplessly under the shock, sensible that human strength was insignificant in comparison with the power of the blast which roared and yelled and shrieked about us.

For hours the rain poured down—either as heavy drops which stung by their momentum ; as little pellets which drizzled through canvas and blankets, chilling our blood as they soaked into clothing ; or alternating with hail which in great, globular crystals, crackled against the miserable shelter, whitened the ground, and froze the air. The reverberation of the thunder was incessant; one shock had barely begun to echo around the sky, when peal after peal, each stronger, louder, and more terrifying than its predecessors, blotted from our minds the sounds and flashes which had awakened our first astonishment, and made us forget in new frights our old alarms. The lightning darted from zenith to horizon, appeared in all quarters, played around all objects. In its glare the smallest bushes, stones, and shrubs stood out as plainly as under the noon sun of a bright summer's day; when it subsided, our spirits were oppressed with the weight of darkness. No stringing together of words can complete a description of what we saw, suffered, and feared during that awful tempest. The stoutest hearts, the oldest soldiers, quailed.

The last growl of thunder was heard, the last flash of lightning seen, between two and three in the morning, and then we turned out from our wretched, water-soaked couches, and gathering around the lakelet in whose midst our fire had been, tried by the smoke of sodden chips and twigs to warm our benumbed limbs and dry our saturated clothing. Not until the dawn of day did we feel the circulation quicken and our spirits revive. A comparison of opinion developed a coincidence of sentiment. Everybody agreed that while perhaps this was not the worst storm he had ever known, the circumstances of our complete exposure to its force had made it about the very worst any of the command had ever experienced. There was scarcely a day from that on for nearly a month that my note-books do not contain references to storms, some of them fully as severe as the one described in the above lines; the exposure began to tell upon officers, men, and animals, and I think the statement will be accepted without challenge that no one who followed Crook during those terrible days was benefited in any way.

I made out a rough list of the officers present on this expedition, and another of those who have died, been killed, died of wounds, or been retired for one reason or another, and I find that the first list had one hundred and sixteen names and the second sixty-nine; so it can be seen that of the officers who were considered to be physically able to enter upon that campaign in the early summer months of 1876, over fifty per cent. are not now answering to roll-call on the active list, after about sixteen

years' interval. The bad weather had the good effects of bringing to the surface all the dormant geniality of Colonel Evans's
disposition : he was the Mark Tapley of the column ; the harder
it rained, the louder he laughed ; the bright shafts of lightning
revealed nothing more inspiriting than our worthy friend's smile
of serene contentment. In Colonel Evans's opinion, which he
was not at all diffident about expressing, the time had come for
the young men of the command to see what real service was
like.   " There had been entirely too much of this playing
soldier, sir ; what had been done by soldiers who were soldiers,
sir, before the war, sir, had never been properly appreciated, sir,
and never would be until these young men got a small taste of it
themselves, sir."

General Merritt's division of the command was provided with
a signal apparatus, and the flags were of great use in conveying
messages to camp from the outlying pickets, and thus saving the
wear and tear of horse-flesh ; but in this dark and rainy season
the system was a failure, and many thought that it would have
been well to introduce a code of signals by whistles, but it was
not possible to do so under our circumstances.

The " Far West " had made several trips to the depot at the
mouth of the Rosebud, and had brought down a supply of shoes,
which was almost sufficient for our infantry battalions, but there
was little of anything else, and Bubb, our commissary, was unable
to obtain more than eleven pounds of tobacco for the entire force.

We were now laboring under the serious disadvantage of
having no native scouts, and were obliged to start out without
further delay, if anything was to be done with the trail of the
Sioux, which had been left several marches up the Powder, before we started down to the Yellowstone to get supplies.   Crook
had sent out Frank Gruard, " Big Bat," and a small party to
learn all that could be learned of that trail, which was found
striking east and south.   Terry's scouts had gone to the north
of the Yellowstone to hunt for the signs of bands passing across
the Missouri.   The report came in that they had found some in
that direction, and the two columns separated, Terry going in one
direction, and Crook keeping his course and following the large
trail, which he shrewdly surmised would lead over towards the
Black Hills, where the savages would find easy victims in the
settlers pouring into the newly discovered mining claims.

Captain Cain, Captain Burrowes, and Lieutenant Eaton, the latter broken down with chills and fever as well a pistol wound in the hand, were ordered on board the transports, taking with them twenty-one men of the command pronounced unfit for field service. One of these enlisted men—Eshleman, Ninth Infantry —was violently insane. Our mess gained a new member, Lieutenant William P. Clarke, Second Cavalry, ordered to report to General Crook for duty as aide-de-camp. He was a brave, bright, companionable gentleman, always ready in an emergency, and had he lived would, beyond a doubt, have attained, with opportunity, a distinguished place among the soldiers of our country. General Terry very kindly lent General Crook five of his own small band of Ree scouts; they proved of great service while with our column.

CHAPTER XXI.

CROOK AND TERRY SEPARATE—THE PICTURESQUE LITTLE MIS-
SOURI—THE "HORSE MEAT MARCH" FROM THE HEAD OF
THE HEART RIVER TO DEADWOOD—ON THE SIOUX TRAIL
—MAKING COFFEE UNDER DIFFICULTIES—SLAUGHTERING
WORN-OUT CAVALRY HORSES FOR FOOD—THE FIGHT AT
SLIM BUTTES—LIEUTENANT VON LEUTTEWITZ LOSES A LEG
—THE DYING CHIEF, "AMERICAN HORSE," SURRENDERS—
RELICS OF THE CUSTER MASSACRE—"CRAZY HORSE" AT-
TACKS OUR LINES—SUNSHINE AND RATIONS.

ON the 23d of August we were beset by another violent storm,
worse, if such a thing were possible, than any yet experienced. All through the night we lay in from three to four
inches of water, unable to shelter ourselves against the strong
wind and pelting Niagara which inundated the country. Sleep
was out of the question, and when morning came it threw its
cold gray light upon a brigade of drowned rats, of disgusted and
grumbling soldiers. It was with difficulty we got the fires to
burn, but a cup of·strong coffee was ready in time, and with the
drinking of that the spirits revived, and with a hearty good-will
all hands pulled out from the valley of the Yellowstone, and
plodded slowly through the plastic mud which lay ankle deep
along the course of the Powder. There was a new acquisition to
the column—a fine Newfoundland dog, which attached itself
to the command, or was reported to have done so, although I
have always had doubts upon that subject. Soldiers will steal
dogs, and "Jack," as he was known to our men, may have been
an unwilling captive, for all I know to the contrary.

There was no trouble in finding the big Sioux trail, or in following it east to O'Fallon's Creek, finding plenty of water and
getting out of "the burnt district." The grass was as nutritive
as it ought to have been in Wyoming and Montana, and as it
would have been had not the red men destroyed it all. Another

trying storm soaked through clothing, and dampened the courage of our bravest. The rain which set in about four in the afternoon, just as we were making camp, suddenly changed to hail of large size, which, with the sudden fall in temperature, chilled and frightened our herds of horses and mules, and had the good effect of making them cower together in fear, instead of stampeding, as we had about concluded they would surely do. Lightning played about us with remorseless vividness, and one great bolt crashed within camp limits, setting fire to the grass on a post near the sentinel.

The 29th and 30th of August we remained in bivouac at a spring on the summit of the ridge overlooking the head waters of Cabin Creek, while our blankets and clothing were drying; and the scouts reconnoitred to the front and flanks to learn what was possible regarding the trail, which seemed much fresher, as if made only a few days previously. Hunting detachments were sent out on each flank to bring in deer, antelope and jack rabbits for the sick, of whom we now had a number suffering from neuralgia, rheumatism, malaria, and diarrhœa. Lieutenant Huntington was scarcely able to sit his horse, and Lieutenant Bache had to be hauled in a "travois."

The night of August 31, 1876, was so bitter cold that a number of General Crook's staff, commissioned and enlisted, had a narrow escape from freezing to death. In our saturated condition, with clothing scant even for summer, we were in no condition to face a sudden "norther," which blew vigorously upon all who were encamped upon the crests of the buttes but neglected those in the shelter of the ravines. The scenery in this neighborhood was entrancing. Mr. Finerty accompanied me to the summit of the bluffs, and we looked out upon a panorama grander than any that artist would be bold enough to trace upon canvas. In the western sky the waning glories of the setting sun were most dazzling. Scarlet and gold, pink and yellow—in lovely contrast or graceful harmony—were scattered with reckless prodigality from the tops of the distant hills to near the zenith, where neutral tints of gray and pale blue marked the dividing line between the gorgeousness of the vanishing sunlight and the more placid splendors of the advancing night, with its millions of stars. The broken contour of the ground, with its deeply furrowed ravines, or its rank upon rank of plateaux and ridges, resembled an angry sea whose waves had been suddenly stilled at the climax of a storm. The juiciest grama covered the pink hillocks from base to crest, but scarcely a leaf could be seen ; it was pasturage, pure and simple—the paradise of the grazier and the cowboy. We gave free rein to our fancy in anticipating the changes ten years would effect in this noble region, then the hunting ground of the savage and the lair of the wild beast.

We crossed the country to the east, going down Beaver Creek and finding indications that the hostiles knew that we were on their trail, which now showed signs of splitting ; we picked up four ponies, abandoned by the enemy, and Frank Gruard, who brought them in, was sure that we were pressing closely upon the rear of the Indians, and might soon expect a brush with them. A soldier was bitten in the thumb by a rattlesnake ; Surgeon Patzki cauterized the wound, administered ammonia, and finished up with two stiff drinks of whiskey from the slender allowance of hospital supplies. The man was saved. The trail kept trending to the south, running down towards the "Sentinel" Buttes, where our advance had a running fight with the enemy's rear-guard, killing one or two ponies.

The next point of note was the Little Missouri River, into the valley of which we descended on the 4th of September, at the place where General Stanley had entered it with the expedition to survey the line of the Northern Pacific Railroad in 1873. This is called by the Indians the "Thick Timber" Creek, a name which it abundantly deserves in comparison with the other streams flowing within one hundred miles on either side of it. We emerged from the narrow defile of Andrus' Creek, into a broad park, walled in by precipitous banks of marl, clay, and sandstone, ranging from one hundred to three hundred feet high. Down the central line of this park grew a thick grove of cottonwood, willow, and box-elder, marking the channel of the stream, which at this spot was some thirty yards wide, two to three feet deep, carrying a good volume of cold, sweet water, rather muddy in appearance. The bottom is of clay, and in places miry, and the approaches are not any too good. A small amount of work was requisite to cut them down to proper shape, but there was such a quantity of timber and brush at hand that corduroy and causeway were soon under construction. The fertility of the soil was attested by the luxuriance of the grass, the thickness of timber, the dense growth of grape-vines, wild plums, and bull berries, already ripening under the warm rays of the sun and the constant showers. Where the picket lines of Terry's cavalry had been stretched during the spring, and the horses had scattered grains of corn from their feed, a volunteer crop had sprung up, whose stalks were from ten to twelve feet high, each bearing from two to four large ears still in the milk.

Our scouts and the advance-guard of the cavalry rushed into this unexpected treasure-trove, cutting and slashing the stalks, and bearing them off in large armfuls for the feeding of our own animals. The half-ripened plums and bull berries were thoroughly boiled, and, although without sugar, proved pleasant to the taste and a valuable anti-scorbutic. Trial was also made of the common opuntia, or Indian fig, the cactus which is most frequent in that section of Dakota; the spines were burnt off, the thick skin peeled, and the inner meaty pulp fried; it is claimed as an excellent remedy for scurvy, but the taste is far from agreeable, being slimy and mucilaginous.

On the 5th of September we made a long march of thirty miles in drizzling rain and sticky mud, pushing up Davis Creek, and benefiting by the bridges which Terry's men had erected in many places where the stream had to be crossed; we reached the head of the Heart River, and passed between the Rosebud Butte on the right and the Camel's Hump on the left. Here we again ran upon the enemy's rear-guard, which seemed disposed to make a fight until our advance got up and pushed them into the bluffs, when they retreated in safety, under cover of the heavy fog which had spread over the hills all day. Of the fifteen days' rations with which we had started out from the Yellowstone, only two and a half days' rations were left. When Randall and Stanton returned from the pursuit of the enemy, the Rees, who were still with us, gave it as their opinion that the command could easily reach Fort Abraham Lincoln in four days, or five; Glendive, on the Yellowstone, in our rear, could not be much farther in a direct line; but here was a hot trail leading due south towards the Black Hills, which were filling with an unknown number of people, all of whom would be exposed to slaughter and destruction. There is one thing certain about a hot trail: you'll find Indians on it if you go far enough, and you'll find them nowhere else. Comfort and ease beckoned from

Fort Lincoln, but duty pointed to Deadwood, and straight to Deadwood Crook went. His two and a half days' rations were made to last five ; the Rees were sent in with despatches as fast as their ponies could travel to Lincoln, to inform Sheridan of our whereabouts, and to ask that supplies be hurried out from Camp Robinson to meet us. With anything like decent luck we ought to be able to force a fight and capture a village with its supplies of meat. Still, it was plain that all the heroism of our natures was to be tried in the fire before that march should be ended ; Bubb concealed seventy pounds of beans to be used for the sick and wounded in emergencies ; Surgeon Hartsuff carried in his saddle-bags two cans of jelly and half a pound of corn-starch, with the same object ; the other medical officers had each a little something of the same sort—tea, chocolate, etc. This was a decidedly gloomy outlook for a column of two thousand men in an unknown region in tempestuous weather. We had had no change of clothing for more than a month since leaving Goose Creek, and we were soaked through with rain and mud, and suffering greatly in health and spirits in consequence.

We left the Heart River in the cold, bleak mists of a cheer-less morning, which magnified into grim spectres the half-dozen cottonwoods nearest camp, which were to be imprinted upon memory with all the more vividness, because until we had struck the Belle Fourche, the type of the streams encountered in our march was the same—timberless, muddy, and sluggish. The ground was covered with grass, alternating with great patches of cactus. Villages of prairie dogs extended for leagues, and the angry squeak of the population was heard on all sides. "Jack," the noble Newfoundland dog which had been with us since we started out from the mouth of Powder, was now crazy for some fresh meat, and would charge after the prairie dogs with such impetuosity that when he attempted to seize his victim, and the loosely packed soil around the burrow had given way beneath their united weight, he would go head over heels, describing a com-plete somersault, much to his own astonishment and our amuse-ment. After turning the horses out to graze in the evening, it generally happened that camp would be visited by half a dozen jack-rabbits, driven out of their burrows by fear of the horses' hoofs. The soldiers derived great enjoyment every time one was started, and as poor pussy darted from bush to bush, doubled and twisted, bounded boldly through a line of her tormentors, or cowered trembling under some sage-brush, the pursuers, armed with nose-bags, lariats, and halters, would advance from all sides, and keep up the chase until the wretched victim was fairly run to death. There would be enough shouting, yelling, and screeching to account for the slaughter of a thousand buffaloes. We learned to judge of the results of the chase in the inverse ratio to the noise: when an especially deafening outcry was heard, the verdict would be rendered at once that an unusually pigmy rabbit had been run to cover, and that the men who had the least to do with the capture had most to do with the tumult.

The country close to the head of Heart River was strewn with banded agate, much of it very beautiful. We made our first camp thirty-five miles south of Heart River by the side of two large pools of brackish water, so full of "alkali" that neither men nor horses cared to touch it. There wasn't a stick of timber in sight as big around as one's little finger; we tried to make coffee by digging a hole in the ground upon which we set a tin cup, and then each one in the mess by turns fed the flames with wisps of such dry grass as could be found and twisted into a petty fagot. We succeeded in making the coffee, but the water in boiling threw up so much saline and sedimentary matter that the appearance was decidedly repulsive. To the North Fork of the Grand River was another thirty-five miles, made, like the march of the preceding day, in the pelting rain which had lasted all night. The country was beautifully grassed, and we saw several patches of wild onions, which we dug up and saved to boil with the horse-meat which was now appearing as our food; General Crook found half a dozen rose-bushes, which he had guarded by a sentinel for the use of the sick; Lieutenant Bubb had four or five cracker-boxes broken up and distributed to the command for fuel; it is astonishing what results can be effected with a handful of fire-wood if people will only half try. The half and third ration of hard-tack was issued to each and every officer in the headquarters mess just the same as it was issued to enlisted men; the coffee was prepared with a quarter ration, and even that had failed. Although there could not be a lovelier pasturage than that through which we were marching, yet our animals, too, began to play out, because they were carrying exhausted and half-starved men who could not sit up in the saddle, and couldn't so frequently dismount on coming to steep, slippery descents where it would have been good policy to "favor" their faithful steeds.

Lieutenant Bubb was now ordered forward to the first settlement he could find in the Black Hills—Deadwood or any other this side—and there to buy all the supplies in sight; he took fifty picked mules and packers under Tom Moore; the escort of one hundred and fifty picked men from the Third Cavalry, mounted on our strongest animals, was under command of Colonel Mills, who had with him Lieutenants Chase, Crawford, Schwatka, Von Leuttewitz, and Doctor Stevens. Two of the correspondents, Messrs. Strahorn and Davenport, went along, leaving the main column before it had reached the camp of the night. We marched comparatively little the next day, not more than twenty-four miles, going into camp in a sheltered ravine on the South Fork of the Grand River, within sight of the Slim Buttes, and in a position which supplied all the fuel needed, the first seen for more than ninety miles, but so soaked with water that all we could do with it was to raise a smoke. It rained without intermission all day and all night, but we had found wood, and our spirits rose with the discovery; then, our scouts had killed five antelope, whose flesh was distributed among the command, the sick in hospital being served first. Plums and bull berries almost ripe were appearing in plenty, and gathered in quantity to be boiled and eaten with horse-meat. Men were getting pretty well exhausted, and each mile of the march saw squads of stragglers, something which we had not seen before; the rain was so unintermittent, the mud so sticky, the air so damp, that with the absence of food and warmth, men lost courage, and not a few of the officers did the same thing. Horses had to be abandoned in great numbers, but the best of them were killed to supply meat, which with the bull berries and water had become almost our only certain food, eked out by an occasional slice of antelope or jack rabbit.

The 8th of September was General Crook's birthday; fifteen or sixteen of the officers had come to congratulate him at his fire under the cover of a projecting rock, which kept off a considerable part of the down-pour of rain; it was rather a forlorn birthday party,—nothing to eat, nothing to drink, no chance to dry clothes, and nothing for which to be thankful except that we had found wood, which was a great blessing. Sage-brush, once so despised, was now welcomed whenever it made its appearance, as it began to do from this on ; it at least supplied the means of making a small fire, and provided the one thing which under all circumstances the soldier should have, if possible. Exhausted by fatiguing marches through mud and rain, without sufficient or proper food, our soldiers reached bivouac each night, to find only a rivulet of doubtful water to quench their thirst, and then went supperless to bed.

In all the hardships, in all the privations of the humblest soldier, General Crook freely shared ; with precisely the same allowance of food and bedding, he made the weary campaign of the summer of 1876 ; criticism was silenced in the presence of a general who would reduce himself to the level of the most lowly, and even though there might be dissatisfaction and grumbling, as there always will be in so large a command, which is certain to have a percentage of the men who want to wear uniform without being soldiers, the reflective and observing saw that their sufferings were fully shared by their leader and honored him accordingly. There was no mess in the whole column which suffered as much as did that of which General Crook was a member ; for four days before any other mess had been so reduced we had been eating the meat of played-out cavalry horses, and at the date of which I am now writing all the food within reach was horse-meat, water, and enough bacon to grease the pan in which the former was to be fried. Crackers, sugar, and coffee had been exhausted, and we had no addition to our bill of fare beyond an occasional plateful of wild onions gathered alongside of the trail. An antelope had been killed by one of the orderlies attached to the headquarters, and the remains of this were hoarded with care for emergencies.

On the morning of September 9th, as we were passing a little watercourse which we were unable to determine correctly, some insisting that it was the South Fork of the Grand, others calling it the North Fork of Owl Creek—the maps were not accurate, and it was hard to say anything about that region—couriers from Mills's advance-guard came galloping to General Crook with the request that he hurry on to the aid of Mills, who had surprised and attacked an Indian village of uncertain size, estimated at twenty-five lodges, and had driven the enemy into the bluffs near him, but was able to hold his own until Crook could reach him.

The couriers added that Lieutenant Von Leuttewitz had been severely wounded in the knee, one soldier had been killed, and five wounded ; the loss of the enemy could not then be ascertained.   Crook gave orders for the cavalry to push on with all possible haste, the infantry to follow more at leisure ; but these directions did not suit the dismounted battalions at all, and they forgot all about hunger, cold, wet, and fatigue, and tramped through the mud to such good purpose that the first infantry company was overlapping the last one of the mounted troops when the cavalry entered the ravine in which Mills was awaiting them.   Then we learned that the previous evening Frank Gruard had discovered a band of ponies grazing on a hill-side and reported to Mills, who, thinking that the village was inconsiderable, thought himself strong enough to attack and carry it unaided.

He waited until the first flush of daylight, and then left his pack-train in the shelter of a convenient ravine, under command of Bubb, while he moved forward with the greater part of his command on foot in two columns, under Crawford and Von Leuttewitz respectively, intending with them to surround the lodges, while Schwatka, with a party of twenty-five mounted men, was to charge through, firing into the "tepis."   The enemy's herd stampeded through the village, awakening the inmates, and discovering the presence of our forces.   Schwatka made his charge in good style, and the other detachments moved in as directed, but the escape of nearly all the bucks and squaws could not be prevented, some taking shelter in high bluffs surrounding the village, and others running into a ravine where they still were at the moment of our arrival—eleven A.M.

The village numbered more than Mills had imagined : we counted thirty-seven lodges, not including four upon which the covers had not yet been stretched.   Several of the lodges were of unusual dimensions : one, probably that occupied by the guard called by Gruard and "Big Bat" the "Brave Night Hearts," contained thirty saddles and equipments.   Great quantities of furs—almost exclusively untanned buffalo robes, antelope, and other skins—wrapped up in bundles, and several tons of meat, dried after the Indian manner, formed the main part of the spoil, although mention should be made of the almost innumerable tin dishes, blankets, cooking utensils, boxes of caps, ammunition, saddles, horse equipments, and other supplies that would prove a serious loss to the savages rather than a gain to our-selves. Two hundred ponies—many of them fine animals—not quite one-half the herd, fell into our hands. A cavalry guidon, nearly new and torn from the staff; an army officer's overcoat; a non-commissioned officer's blouse; cavalry saddles of the McClellan model, covered with black leather after the latest pattern of the ordnance bureau; a glove marked with the name of Captain Keogh; a letter addressed to a private soldier in the Seventh Cavalry; horses branded U. S. and 7 C.—one was branded $\frac{D}{7\ C.}$: were proofs that the members of this band had taken part, and a conspicuous part, in the Custer massacre. General Crook ordered all the meat and other supplies to be taken from the village and piled up so that it could be issued or packed upon our mules. Next, he ordered the wounded to receive every care; this had already been done, as far as he was able, by Mills, who had pitched one of the captured lodges in a cool, shady spot, near the stream, and safe from the annoyance of random shots which the scattered Sioux still fired from the distant hills.

A still more important task was that of dislodging a small party who had run into a gulch fifty or sixty yards outside of the line of the lodges, from which they made it dangerous for any of Mills's command to enter the village, and had already killed several of the pack-mules whose carcasses lay among the lodges. Frank Gruard and "Big Bat" were sent forward, crawling on hands and feet from shelter to shelter, to get within easy talking distance of the defiant prisoners in the gulch, who refused to accede to any terms and determined to fight it out, confident that "Crazy Horse," to whom they had despatched runners, would soon hasten to their assistance. Lieutenant William P. Clarke was directed to take charge of a picked body of volunteers and get the Indians out of that gulch; the firing attracted a large crowd of idlers and others, who pressed so closely upon Clarke and his party as to seriously embarrass their work. Our men were so crowded that it was a wonder to me that the shots of the beleaguered did not kill them by the half-dozen; but the truth was, the Sioux did not care to waste a shot: they were busy digging rifle-pits in the soft marly soil of the ravine, which was a perfect ditch, not more than ten to fifteen feet wide, and fifteen to twenty deep, with a growth of box elder that aided in concealing their doings from

our eyes.   But, whenever a particularly good chance for doing
mischief presented itself, the rifle of the Sioux belched out its
fatal missile.   Private Kennedy, Company "C," Fifth Cavalry,
had all the calf of one leg carried away by a bullet, and at the
same time another soldier was shot through the ankle-joint.

The ground upon which Captain Munson and I were standing
suddenly gave way, and down we both went, landing in the midst
of a pile of squaws and children.   The warriors twice tried to
get aim at us, but were prevented by the crooked shape of
the ravine ; on the other side, " Big Bat " and another one
of Stanton's men, named Cary, had already secured position,
and were doing their best to induce the Indians to surrender,
crying out to them " Washte-helo " (Very good) and other expressions in Dakota, the meaning of which I did not clearly
understand.   The women and pappooses, covered with dirt and
blood, were screaming in an agony of terror ; behind and above
us were the oaths and yells of the surging soldiers ; back of the
women lay what seemed, as near as we could make out, to be
four dead bodies still weltering in their gore.   Altogether, the
scene, as far as it went, was decidedly infernal ; there was very
little to add to it, but that little was added by one of the scouts
named Buffalo White, who incautiously exposed himself to find
out what all the hubbub in the ravine meant.   Hardly had
he lifted his body before a rifle-ball pierced him through and
through.   He cried out in a way that was heart-rending :
" O, Lord ! O, Lord ! They've got me now, boys ! " and dropped
limp and lifeless to the base of the hillock upon which he had
perched himself, thirty feet into the ravine below at its deepest
point.

Encouraged by " Big Bat," the squaws and children ventured
to come up to us, and were conducted down through the winds
and turns of the ravine to where General Crook was ; he approached and addressed them pleasantly ; the women divined at
once who he was, and clung to his hand and clothing, their own
skirts clutched by the babies, who all the while wailed most dismally.   When somewhat calmed down they said that their
village belonged to the Spotted Tail Agency and was commanded
by " Roman Nose " and " American Horse," or " Iron Shield,"
the latter still in the ravine.   General Crook bade one of them
go back and say that he would treat kindly all who surrendered.

The squaw complied and returned to the edge of the ravine, there holding a parley, as the result bringing back a young warrior about twenty years old. To him General Crook repeated the assurances already given, and this time the young man went back, accompanied by "Big Bat," whose arrival unarmed convinced "American Horse" that General Crook's promises were not written in sand.

"American Horse" emerged from his rifle-pit, supported on one side by the young warrior, on the other by "Big Bat," and slowly drew near the group of officers standing alongside of General Crook ; the reception accorded the captives was gentle, and their wounded ones were made the recipients of necessary attentions. Out of this little nook twenty-eight Sioux—little and great, dead and alive—were taken ; the corpses were suffered to lie where they fell. "American Horse" had been shot through the intestines, and was biting hard upon a piece of wood to suppress any sign of pain or emotion ; the children made themselves at home around our fires, and shared with the soldiers the food now ready for the evening meal. We had a considerable quantity of dried buffalo-meat, a few buffalo-tongues, some pony-meat, and parfleche panniers filled with fresh and dried buffalo berries, wild cherries, wild plums, and other fruit—and, best find of all, a trifle of salt. One of the Sioux food preparations—dried meat, pounded up with wild plums and wild cherries—called "Toro," was very palatable and nutritious ; it is cousin-german to our own plum pudding.

These Indians had certificates of good conduct dated at Spotted Tail Agency and issued by Agent Howard. General Crook ordered that every vestige of the village and the property in it which could not be kept as serviceable to ourselves should be destroyed. The whole command ate ravenously that evening and the next morning, and we still had enough meat to load down twenty-eight of our strongest pack-mules. This will show that the official reports that fifty-five hundred pounds had been captured were entirely too conservative. I was sorry to see that the value of the wild fruit was not appreciated by some of the company commanders, who encouraged their men very little in eating it and thus lost the benefit of its anti-scorbutic qualities. All our wounded were cheerful and doing well, including Von Leuttewitz, whose leg had been amputated at the thigh.

The barking of stray puppies, the whining of children, the confused hum of the conversation going on among two thousand soldiers, officers, and packers confined within the narrow limits of the ravine, were augmented by the sharp crack of rifles and the whizzing of bullets, because "Crazy Horse," prompt in answering the summons of his distressed kinsmen, was now on the ground, and had drawn his lines around our position, which he hoped to take by assault, not dreaming that the original assailants had been re-enforced so heavily. It was a very pretty fight, what there was of it, because one could take his seat almost anywhere and see all that was going on from one end of the field to the other. "Crazy Horse" moved his men up in fine style, but seemed to think better of the scheme after the cavalry gave him a volley from their carbines; the Sioux were not left in doubt long as to what they were to do, because the infantry battalions commanded by Burt and Daniel W. Burke got after them and raced them off the field, out of range.

One of our officers whose conduct impressed me very much was Lieutenant A. B. Bache, Fifth Cavalry: he was so swollen with inflammatory rheumatism that he had been hauled for days in a "travois" behind a mule; but, hearing the roll of rifles and carbines, he insisted upon being mounted upon a horse and strapped to the saddle, that he might go out upon the skirmish line. We never had a better soldier than he, but he did not survive the hardships of that campaign. The Sioux did not care to leave the battle-field without some token of prowess, and seeing a group of ten or twelve cavalry horses which had been abandoned during the day, and were allowed to follow along at their own pace, merely to be slaughtered by Bubb for meat when it should be needed, flattered themselves that they had a grand prize within reach; a party of bold young bucks, anxious to gain a trifle of renown, stripped themselves and their ponies, and made a dash for the broken-down cast-offs; the skirmishers, by some sort of tacit consent, refrained from firing a shot, and allowed the hostiles to get right into the "bunch" and see how hopelessly they had been fooled, and then when the Sioux started to spur and gallop back to their own lines the humming of bullets apprised them that our men were having the joke all to themselves.

Just as "Crazy Horse" hauled off his forces, two soldiers bare-

footed, and in rags, walked down to our lines and entered camp ;
their horses had "played out" in the morning, and were in the
group which the Sioux had wished to capture ; the soldiers
themselves had lain down to rest in a clump of rocks and fallen
asleep to be awakened by the circus going on all around them ;
they kept well under cover, afraid as much of the projectiles of
their friends as of the fire of the savages, but were not discovered,
and now rejoined the command to be most warmly and sincerely
congratulated upon their good fortune.   It rained all night, but
we did not care much, provided as we now were with plenty of
food, plenty of fuel, and some extra bedding from the furs taken
in the lodges.   In the drizzling rain of that night the soul of
"American Horse" took flight, accompanied to the Happy Hunting Grounds by the spirit of Private Kennedy.

After breakfast the next morning General Crook sent for the
women and children, and told them that we were not making
war upon such as they, and that all those who so desired were
free to stay and rejoin their own people, but he cautioned them
to say to all their friends that the American Government was
determined to keep pegging away at all Indians in hostility until
the last had been killed or made a prisoner, and that the red
men would be following the dictates of prudence in surrendering
unconditionally instead of remaining at war, and exposing their
wives and children to accidents and dangers incidental to that
condition. The young warrior, "Charging Bear," declined to
go with the squaws, but remained with Crook and enlisted as a
scout, becoming a corporal, and rendering most efficient service
in the campaign during the following winter which resulted so
brilliantly.

"Crazy Horse" felt our lines again as we were moving off, but
was held in check by Sumner, of the Fifth, who had one or two
men slightly wounded, while five of the attacking party were seen
to fall out of their saddles.   The prisoners informed us that we
were on the main trail of the hostiles, which, although now split,
was all moving down to the south towards the agencies.   Mills,
Bubb, Schwatka, Chase, and fifty picked men of the Third
Cavalry, with a train made up of all our strong mules under
Tom Moore, with Frank Gruard as guide, were once more sent
forward to try to reach Deadwood, learn all the news possible
concerning the condition of the exposed mining hamlets near

there, and obtain all the supplies in sight. Crook was getting very anxious to reach Deadwood before "Crazy Horse" could begin the work of devilment upon which he and his bands were bent, as the squaws admitted. Bubb bore a despatch to Sheridan, narrating the events of the trip since leaving Heart River.

Knowing that we were now practically marching among hostile Sioux, who were watching our every movement, and would be ready to attack at the first sign of lack of vigilance, Crook moved the column in such a manner that it could repel an attack within thirty seconds; that is to say, there was a strong advance-guard, a rear-guard equally strong, and lines of skirmishers moving along each flank, while the wounded were placed on "travois," for the care of which Captain Andrews and his company of the Third Cavalry were especially detailed. One of the lodges was brought along from the village for the use of the sick and wounded, and afterwards given to Colonel Mills. The general character of the country between the Slim Buttes and the Belle Fourche remained much the same as that from the head of Heart River down, excepting that there was a small portion of timber, for which we were truly thankful. The captured ponies were butchered and issued as occasion required; the men becoming accustomed to the taste of the meat, which was far more juicy and tender than that of the broken-down old cavalry nags which we had been compelled to eat a few days earlier. The sight of an antelope, however, seemed to set everybody crazy, and when one was caught and killed squads of officers and men would fight for the smallest portion of flesh or entrails; I succeeded in getting one liver, which was carried in my nose-bag all day and broiled over the ashes at night, furnishing a very toothsome morsel for all the members of our mess.

While speaking upon the subject of horse-meat, let me tell one of the incidents vividly imprinted upon memory. Bubb's butcher was one of the least poetical men ever met in my journey through life; all he cared for was to know just what animals were to be slaughtered, and presto! the bloody work was done, and a carcass gleamed in the evening air. Many and many a pony had he killed, although he let it be known to a couple of the officers whom he took into his confidence that he had been raised a gentleman, and had never before slaughtered anything but cows and pigs and sheep. One evening, he killed a mare whose daughter and granddaughter were standing by her side, the daughter nursing from the mother and the granddaughter from the daughter. On another occasion he was approached by one of Stanton's scouts—I really have not preserved his name, but it was the dark Mexican who several weeks after killed, and was killed by, Carey, his best friend. After being paid off, they got into some kind of a drunken row in a gambling saloon, in Deadwood, and shot each other to death. Well, this man drew near the butcher and began making complaint that the latter, without sufficient necessity, had cut up a pony which the guide was anxious to save for his own use. The discussion lasted for several minutes and terminated without satisfaction to the scout, who then turned to mount his pony and ride away; no pony was to be seen; he certainly had ridden one down, but it had vanished into vapor; he could see the saddle and bridle upon the ground, but of the animal not a trace; while he had been arguing with the butcher, the assistants of the latter had quickly unsaddled the mount and slaughtered and divided it, and the quarters were then on their way over to one of the battalions. It was a piece of rapid work worthy of the best skill of Chicago, but it confirmed one man in a tendency to profanity and cynicism.

Our maps led us into a very serious error: from them it appeared that the South Fork of Owl Creek was not more than twenty or twenty-five miles from the Belle Fourche, towards which we were trudging so wearily, the rain still beating down without pity. The foot soldiers, eager to make the march which was to end their troubles and lead them to food and rest, were ready for the trail by three on the morning of the 12th of September, and all of them strung out before four. As soon as it was light enough we saw that a portion of the trail had set off towards the east, and Major Upham was sent with one hundred and fifty men from the Fifth Cavalry to find out all about it. It proved to be moving in the direction of Bear Lodge Butte, and the intention evidently was to annoy the settlements in the Hills; one of Upham's men went off without permission, after antelope, and was killed and cut to pieces by the prowling bands watching the column. The clouds lifted once or twice during the march of the 12th and disclosed the outline of Bear Butte, a great satisfaction to us, as it proved that we were going in the right direction for Deadwood. The country was evenly divided between cactus and grass, in patches of from one to six miles in breadth ; the mud was so tenacious that every time foot or hoof touched it there would be a great mass of "gumbo" adhering to render progress distressingly tiresome and slow. Our clothing was in rags of the flimsiest kind, shoes in patches, and the rations captured at the village exhausted. Mules and horses were black to the houghs with the accretions of a passage through slimy ooze which pulled off their shoes.

Crook's orders to the men in advance were to keep a sharp lookout for anything in the shape of timber, as the column was to halt and bivouac the moment we struck anything that would do to make a fire. On we trudged, mile succeeding mile, and still no sign of the fringe of cottonwood, willow, and elder which we had been taught to believe represented the line of the stream of which we were in search. The rain poured down, clothes dripped with moisture, horses reeled and staggered, and were one by one left to follow or remain as they pleased, while the men, all of whom were dismounted and leading their animals, fell out singly, in couples, in squads, in solid platoons. It was half-past ten o'clock that never-to-be-forgotten night, when the last foot soldier had completed his forty miles, and many did not pretend to do it before the next morning, but lay outside, in rear of the column, on the muddy ground, as insensible to danger and pain as if dead drunk.

We did not reach the Belle Fourche that night, but a tributary called Willow Creek which answered every purpose, as it had an abundance of box-elder, willow, ash, and plum bushes, which before many minutes crackled and sprang skyward in a joyous flame ; we piled high the dry wood wherever found, thinking to stimulate comrades who were weary with marching and sleeping without the cheerful consolation of a sparkling camp-fire. There wasn't a thing to eat in the whole camp but pony-meat, slices of which were sizzling upon the coals, but the poor fellows who did not get in killed their played-out horses and ate the meat raw. If any of my readers imagines that the march from the head of Heart River down to the Belle Fourche was a picnic, let him examine the roster of the command and tell off the scores and scores of men, then hearty and rugged, who now fill premature graves or drag out an existence with constitutions wrecked and enfeebled by such privations and vicissitudes.

There may still be people who give credence to the old superstitions about the relative endurance of horses of different colors, and believe that white is the weakest color. For their information I wish to say that the company of cavalry which had the smallest loss of horses during this exhausting march was the white horse troop of the Fifth, commanded by Captain Robert H. Montgomery; I cannot place my fingers upon the note referring to it, but I will state from recollection that not one of them was left behind.

On the 13th we remained in camp until noon to let men have a rest and give stragglers a chance to catch up with the command. Our cook made a most tempting ragout out of some pony-meat, a fragment of antelope liver, a couple of handfuls of wild onions, and the shin-bone of an ox killed by the Sioux or Cheyennes, and which was to us almost as interesting as the fragments of weeds to the sailors of Columbus. This had been simmering all night, and when morning came there was enough of it to supply many of our comrades with a hot platterful. At noon we crossed to the Belle Fourche, six miles to the south, the dangerous approaches of Willow Creek being corduroyed and placed in good order by a party under Lieutenant Charles King, who had been assigned by General Merritt to the work.

The Belle Fourche appealed to our fancies as in every sense deserving of its flattering title : it was not less than one hundred feet wide, three deep, with a good flow of water, and a current of something like four miles an hour. The bottom was clay and sandstone drift, and even if the water was a trifle muddy, it tasted delicious after our late tribulations. Wells dug in the banks afforded even better quality for drinking or cooking. The dark clouds still hung threateningly overhead, but what of that ? all eyes were strained in the direction of Deadwood, for word had come from Mills and Bubb that they had been successful, and that we were soon to catch a glimpse of the wagons laden with food for our starving command. A murmur rippled through camp ; in a second it had swelled into a roar, and broken into a wild cry, half yell, half cheer. Down the hill-sides as fast as brawny men could drive them ran fifty head of beef cattle, and not more than a mile in the rear wagon sheets marked out the slower-moving train with the supplies of the commissariat.

As if to manifest sympathy with our feelings, the sun unveiled himself, and for one good long hour shone down through scattering clouds—the first fair look we had had at his face for ten dreary days. Since our departure from Furey and the wagon-train, it had rained twenty-two days, most of the storms being of phenomenal severity, and it would need a very strong mind not to cherish the delusion that the elements were in league with the red men to preserve the hunting lands of their fathers from the grasp of the rapacious whites. When the supplies arrived the great aim of every one seemed to be to carry out the old command : " Eat, drink, and be merry, for to-morrow ye die." The busy hum of cheerful conversation succeeded to the querulous discontent of the past week, and laughter raised the spirits of the most tired and despondent ; we had won the race and saved the Black Hills with their thousands of unprotected citizens, four hundred of whom had been murdered since the summer began. The first preacher venturing out to Deadwood paid the penalty of his rashness with his life, and yielded his scalp to the Cheyennes. It was the most ordinary thing in the world to have it reported that one, or two, or three bodies more were to be found in such and such a gulch ; they were buried by people in no desire to remain near the scene of horror, and as the Hills were filling up with restless spirits from all corners of the world, and no one knew his neighbor, it is doubtful if all the murdered ones were ever reported to the proper authorities. When the whites succeeded in killing an Indian, which happened at extremely rare intervals, Deadwood would go crazy with delight ; the skull and scalp were paraded and sold at public auction to the highest bidder.

CHAPTER XXII.

TO AND THROUGH THE BLACK HILLS—HOW DEADWOOD LOOKED
IN 1876—THE DEADWOOD "ACADEMY OF MUSIC"—THE
SECOND WINTER CAMPAIGN—THE NAMES OF THE INDIAN
SCOUTS—WIPING OUT THE CHEYENNE VILLAGE—LIEUTEN-
ANT MCKINNEY KILLED—FOURTEEN CHEYENNE BABIES
FROZEN TO DEATH IN THEIR MOTHERS' ARMS—THE CUS-
TER MASSACRE AGAIN—THE TERRIBLE EXPERIENCE OF
RANDALL AND THE CROW SCOUTS.

THE joy of the people in the Hills knew no bounds; the towns of Deadwood, Crook City, Montana, and many others proceeded to celebrate the news of their freedom and safety by all the methods suitable to such a momentous occasion in a frontier civilization: there was much in the way of bonfires, the firing of salutes from anvils, cheering, mass-meetings, alleged music, and no small portion of hard drinking. By resolution of the Deadwood Council, a committee, consisting of the first mayor, Farnum, and councilmen Kurtz, Dawson, and Philbrick, was sent out to meet General Crook and extend to him and his officers the freedom of the city; in the same carriage with them came Mr. Wilbur Hugus, who had assisted me in burying Captain Philip Dwyer at Camp Date Creek, Arizona, four years previously. The welcome extended these representatives was none the less cordial because they had brought along with them a most acceptable present of butter, eggs, and vegetables raised in the Hills. Despatches were also received from General Sheridan, informing Crook that the understanding was that the hostiles were going to slip into the agencies, leaving out in the Big Horn country "Crazy Horse" and "Sitting Bull," with their bands, until the next spring. To prevent a recurrence of the campaign the next year, Sheridan was determined to disarm and dismount all the new arrivals, and for that purpose had stationed a strong force at each agency, but he wished Crook to move in with his command to "Red Cloud" and "Spotted Tail" and superintend the work there instead of remaining in the Hills as Crook wished to do, and continue the campaign from there with some of the towns, either Deadwood or Custer City, as might be found best adapted to the purpose, as a base. Congress had authorized the enlistment of four hundred additional Indian scouts, and had also appropriated a liberal sum for the construction of the posts on the Yellowstone. Crook was to turn over the command to Merritt, and proceed in person, as rapidly as possible, to confer with Sheridan, who was awaiting him at Fort Laramie, with a view to designating the force to occupy the site of old Fort Reno during the winter.

After enduring the hardships and discomforts of the march from the head of Heart River, the situation in the bivouac on the Whitewood, a beautiful stream flowing out of the Hills at their northern extremity, was most romantic and pleasurable. The surrounding knolls were thickly grassed; cold, clear water stood in deep pools hemmed in by thick belts of timber; and there was an abundance of juicy wild plums, grapes, and bull berries, now fully ripe, and adding a grateful finish to meals which included nearly everything that man could desire, brought down in wagons by the enterprising dealers of Deadwood, who reaped a golden harvest. We were somewhat bewildered at sitting down before a canvas upon which were to be seen warm bread baked in ovens dug in the ground, delicious coffee, to the aroma of which we had been for so long a time strangers, broiled and stewed meat, fresh eggs, pickles, preserves, and fresh vegetables. Soldiers are in one respect like children : they forget the sorrows of yesterday in the delights of to-day, and give to glad song the same voices which a few hours ago were loudest in grumbling and petty complaint. So it was with our camp : the blazing fires were surrounded by crowds of happy warriors, each rivalling the other in tales of the "times we had" in a march whose severity has never been approached by that made by any column of our army of the same size, and of which so little is known that it may truly be said that the hardest work is the soonest forgotten.

Crook bade good-by to the officers and men who had toiled along with him through the spring and summer, and then headed for the post of Fort Robinson, Nebraska, one hundred and sixty miles to the south. For one-half this distance our road followed down through the centre of the Black Hills, a most entrancing country, laid out apparently by a landscape artist; it is not so high as the Big Horn range, although Harney's and other peaks of granite project to a great elevation, their flanks dark with pine, fir, and other coniferæ; the foot-hills velvety with healthful pasturage; the narrow valleys of the innumerable petty creeks a jungle of willow, wild rose, live oak, and plum. Climbing into the mountains, one can find any amount of spruce, juniper, cedar, fir, hemlock, birch, and whitewood; there are no lakes, but the springs are legion and fill with gentle melody the romantic glens—the retreat of the timid deer.

A description of Deadwood as it appeared at that time will suffice for all the settlements of which it was the metropolis. Crook City, Montana, Hills City, Castleton, Custer City, and others through which we passed were better built than Deadwood and better situated for expansion, but Deadwood had struck it rich in its placers, and the bulk of the population took root there. Crook City received our party most hospitably, and insisted upon our sitting down to a good hot breakfast, after which we pressed on to Deadwood, twenty miles or more from our camping place on the Whitewood. The ten miles of distance from Crook City to Deadwood was lined on both sides with deep ditches and sluice-boxes, excavated to develop or work the rich gravel lying along the entire gulch. But it seemed to me that with anything like proper economy and care there was wealth enough in the forests to make the prosperity of any community, and supply not alone the towns which might spring up in the hills, but build all the houses and stables needed in the great pastures north, as far as the head of the Little Missouri. It was the 16th of September when we entered Deadwood, and although I had been through the Black Hills with the exploring expedition commanded by Colonel Dodge, the previous year, and was well acquainted with the beautiful country we were to see, I was unbalanced by the exhibition of the marvellous energy of the American people now laid before us. The town had been laid off in building lots on the 15th of May, and all supplies had to be hauled in wagons from the railroad two hundred and fifty miles away and through bodies of savages who kept up a constant series of assaults and ambuscades.

The town was situated at the junction of the Whitewood and Deadwood creeks or gulches, each of which was covered by a double line of block-houses to repel a sudden attack from the ever-to-be-dreaded enemy, the Sioux and Cheyennes, of whose cruelty and desperate hostility the mouths of the inhabitants and the columns of the two newspapers were filled. I remember one of these journals, *The Pioneer*, edited at that time by a young man named Merrick, whose life had been pleasantly divided into three equal parts—setting type, hunting for Indians, and " rasslin' " for grub—during the days when the whole community was reduced to deer-meat and anything else they could pick up. Merrick was a very bright, energetic man, and had he lived would have been a prominent citizen in the new settlements. It speaks volumes for the intelligence of the element rolling into the new El Dorado to say that the subscription lists of *The Pioneer* even then contained four hundred names.

The main street of Deadwood, twenty yards wide, was packed by a force of men, drawn from all quarters, aggregating thousands ; and the windows of both upper and lower stories of the eating-houses, saloons, hotels, and wash-houses were occupied by women of good, bad, and indifferent reputation. There were vociferous cheers, clappings of hands, wavings of handkerchiefs, shrieks from the whistles of the planing mills, reports from powder blown off in anvils, and every other manifestation of welcome known to the populations of mining towns. The almond-eyed Celestial laundrymen had absorbed the contagion of the hour, and from the doors of the " Centennial Wash-House " gazed with a complacency unusual to them upon the doings of the Western barbarians. We were assigned quarters in the best hotel of the town : "The Grand Central Hotel, Main Street, opposite Theatre, C. H. Wagner, Prop. (formerly of the Walker House and Saddle Rock Restaurant, Salt Lake), the only first-class hotel in Deadwood City, D. T."

This was a structure of wood, of two stories, the lower used for the purposes of offices, dining-room, saloon, and kitchen ; the upper was devoted to a parlor, and the rest was partitioned into bedrooms, of which I wish to note the singular feature that the partitions did not reach more than eight feet above the floor, and thus every word said in one room was common property to all along that corridor. The " Grand Central " was, as might be expected, rather crude in outline and construction, but the furniture was remarkably good, and the table decidedly better than one had a right to look for, all circumstances considered. Owing to the largeness of our party, the escort and packers were divided off between the " I. X. L." and the " Centennial" hotels, while the horses and mules found good accommodations awaiting them in Clarke's livery stable. I suppose that much of this will be Greek to the boy or girl growing up in Deadwood, who may also be surprised to hear that very many of the habitations were of canvas, others of unbarked logs, and some few "dug-outs" in the clay banks. By the law of the community, a gold placer or ledge could be followed anywhere, regardless of other property rights ; in consequence of this, the office of *The Pioneer* was on stilts, being kept in countenance by a Chinese laundryman whose establishment was in the same predicament. Miners were at work under them, and it looked as if it would be more economical to establish one's self in a balloon in the first place.

That night, after supper, the hills were red with the flare and flame of bonfires, and in front of the hotel had assembled a large crowd, eager to have a talk with General Crook ; this soon came, and the main part of the General's remarks was devoted to an expression of his desire to protect the new settlements from threatened danger, while the citizens, on their side, recited the various atrocities and perils which had combined to make the early history of the settlements, and presented a petition, signed by seven hundred and thirteen full-grown white citizens, asking for military protection. Then followed a reception in the " Deadwood Theatre and Academy of Music," built one-half of boards and the other half of canvas. After the reception, there was a performance by " Miller's Grand Combination Troupe, with the Following Array of Stars." It was the usual variety show of the mining towns and villages, but much of it was quite good ; one of the saddest interpolations was the vocalization by Miss Viola de Montmorency, the Queen of Song, prior to her departure for Europe to sing before the crowned heads. Miss Viola was all right, but her voice might have had several stitches in it, and been none the worse ; if she never comes back from the other side of the Atlantic until I send for her, she will be considerably older than she was that night when a half-drunken miner energetically insisted that she was "old enough to have another set o' teeth." We left the temple of the Muses to walk along the main street and look in upon the stores, which were filled with all articles desirable in a mining district, and many others not usual in so young a community. Clothing, heavy and light, hardware, tinware, mess-pans, camp-kettles, blankets, saddlery, harness, rifles, cartridges, wagon-grease and blasting powder, india-rubber boots and garden seeds, dried and canned fruits, sardines, and yeast powders, loaded down the shelves ; the medium of exchange was gold dust; each counter displayed a pair of delicate scales, and every miner carried a buckskin pouch containing the golden grains required for daily use.

Greenbacks were not in circulation, and already commanded a premium of five per cent. on account of their portability. Gambling hells flourished, and all kinds of games were to be found— three card monte, keno, faro, roulette, and poker. Close by these were the "hurdy-gurdies," where the music from asthmatic pianos timed the dancing of painted, padded, and leering Aspasias, too hideous to hope for a livelihood in any village less remote from civilization. We saw and met representatives of all classes of society—gamblers, chevaliers d'industrie, callow fledglings, ignorant of the world and its ways, experienced miners who had labored in other fields, men broken down in other pursuits, noble women who had braved all perils to be by their husbands' sides, smart little children, and children who were adepts in profanity and all other vices—just such a commingling as might be looked for, but we saw very little if any drinking, and the general tone of the place was one of good order and law, to which vice and immorality must bow.

We started out from Deadwood, and rode through the beautiful hills from north to south, passing along over well-constructed corduroy roads to Custer City, sixty miles to the south ; about half way we met a wagon-train of supplies, under charge of Captain Frank Guest Smith, of the Fourth Artillery, and remained a few moments to take luncheon with himself and his subordinates—Captain Cushing and Lieutenants Jones, Howe, Taylor, and Anderson, and Surgeon Price. Custer City was a melancholy example of a town with the "boom" knocked out of it ; there must have been as many as four hundred comfortable houses arranged in broad, rectilinear streets, but not quite three hundred souls remained, and all the trade of the place was dependent upon the three saw and shingle mills still running at full time. Here we found another wagon-train of provisions, under command of Captain Egan and Lieutenant Allison, of the Second Cavalry, who very kindly insisted upon exchanging their fresh horses for our tired-out steeds so as to let us go on at once on our still long ride of nearly one hundred miles south to Robinson; we travelled all night, stopping at intervals to let the horses have a bite of grass, but as Randall and Sibley were left behind with the pack-train, our reduced party kept a rapid gait along the wagon road, and arrived at the post the next morning shortly after breakfast. Near Buffalo Gap we crossed the "Amphibious" Creek, which has a double bottom, the upper one being a crust of sulphuret of lime, through which rider and horse will often break to the discomfort and danger of both; later on we traversed the "Bad Lands," in which repose the bones of countless thousands of fossilized monsters—tortoises, lizards, and others —which will yet be made to pay heavy tribute to the museums of the world. Here we met the officers of the garrison as well as the members of the commission appointed by the President to confer with the Sioux, among whom I remember Bishop Whipple, Judge Moneypenny, Judge Gaylord, and others.

This terminated the summer campaign, although, as one of the results of Crook's conference with Sheridan at Fort Laramie, the Ogallalla chiefs "Red Cloud" and "Red Leaf" were surrounded on the morning of the 23d of October, and all their guns and ponies taken from them. There were seven hundred and five ponies and fifty rifles. These bands were supposed to have been selling arms and ammunition to the part of the tribe in open hostility, and this action of the military was precipitated by "Red Cloud's" refusal to obey the orders to move his village close to the agency, so as to prevent the incoming stragglers from being confounded with those who had remained at peace. He moved his village over to the Chadron Creek, twenty-two miles away, where he was at the moment of being surrounded and arrested.

General Crook had a conference with the head men of the Ogallallas and Brulés, the Cheyennes and Arapahoes, and told them in plain language what he expected them to do. The Government of the United States was feeding them, and was entitled to loyal behavior in return, instead of which many of our citizens had been killed and the trails of the murderers ran straight for the Red Cloud Agency ; it was necessary for the chiefs to show their friendship by something more than empty words, and they would be held accountable for the good behavior of their young men. He did not wish to do harm to any one, but he had been sent out there to maintain order and he intended to do it, and if the Sioux did not see that it was to their interest to help they would soon regret their blindness.   If all the Sioux would come in and start life as stock-raisers, the trouble would end at once, but so long as any remained out, the white men would insist upon war being made, and he should expect all the chiefs there present to aid in its prosecution.

There were now fifty-three companies of soldiers at Red Cloud, and they could figure for themselves just how long they could withstand such force. " Red Cloud " had been insolent to all officers placed over him, and his sympathies with the hostiles had been open and undisguised ; therefore he had been deposed, and " Spotted Tail," who had been friendly, was to be the head chief of all the Sioux.

The assignment of the troops belonging to the summer expedition to winter quarters, and the organization from new troops of the expedition, which was to start back and resume operations in the Big Horn and Yellowstone country, occupied several weeks to the exclusion of all other business, and it was late in October before the various commands began concentrating at Fort Fetterman for the winter's work.

The wagon-train left at Powder River, or rather at Goose Creek, under Major Furey, had been ordered in by General Sheridan, and had reached Fort Laramie and been overhauled and refitted. It then returned to Fetterman to take part in the coming expedition. General Crook took a small party to the summit of the Laramie Peak, and killed and brought back sixty-four deer, four elk, four mountain sheep, and one cinnamon bear ; during the same week he had a fishing party at work on the North Platte River, and caught sixty fine pike weighing one hundred and one pounds.

Of the resulting winter campaign I do not intend to say much, having in another volume described it completely and minutely ; to that volume (" Mackenzie's Last Fight with the Cheyennes—a Winter Campaign in Wyoming") the curious reader is referred; but at the present time, as the country operated in was precisely the same as that gone over during the preceding winter and herein described—as the Indians in hostility were the same, with the same habits and peculiarities, I can condense this section to a recapitulation of the forces engaged, the fights fought, and the results thereof, as well as a notice of the invaluable services rendered by the Indian scouts, of whom Crook was now able to enlist all that he desired, the obstructive element—the Indian agent—having been displaced. Although this command met with severe weather, as its predecessor had done, yet it was so well provided and had such a competent force of Indian scouts that the work to be done by the soldiers was reduced to the zero point; had Crook's efforts to enlist some of the Indians at Red Cloud Agency not been frustrated by the agent and others in the spring, the war with the hostile Sioux and Cheyennes would have been over by the 4th of July, instead of dragging its unsatisfactory length along until the second winter and entailing untold hardships and privations upon officers and men and swelling the death roll of the settlers.

The organization with which Crook entered upon his second winter campaign was superb in equipment; nothing was lacking that money could provide or previous experience suggest. There were eleven companies of cavalry, of which only one—" K," of the Second (Egan's)—had been engaged in previous movements, but all were under excellent discipline and had seen much service in other sections.

Besides Egan's there were " H " and " K," of the Third, " B," " D," " E," " F," " I," and " M," of the Fourth, and " H " and " L," of the Fifth Cavalry. These were placed under the command of Colonel Ranald S. Mackenzie, of the Fourth Cavalry.

Colonel R. I. Dodge, Twenty-third Infantry, commanded the infantry and artillery companies, the latter serving as foot troops; his force included Batteries " C," " F," " H," and " K," of the Fourth Artillery; Companies " A," " B," " C," " F," " I," and " K," of the Ninth Infantry; " D " and " G," of the Fourteenth Infantry; and " C," " G," and " I," of the Twenty-third Infantry.

General Crook's personal staff was composed of myself as

Acting Assistant Adjutant-General ; Schuyler and Clarke, Aides-de-Camp ; Randall, Chief of Scouts ; Rockwell, of the Fifth Cavalry, as Commissary ; Surgeon Joseph R. Gibson as Chief Medical Officer.

In the list of officers starting out with this expedition are to be found the names of Major G. A. Gordon, Fifth Cavalry, and Major E. F. Townsend, Ninth Infantry, and Captain C. V. Mauck, Fourth Cavalry, and Captain J. B. Campbell, Fourth Artillery, commanding battalions ; Lieutenant Hayden Delaney, Ninth Infantry, commanding company of Indian scouts ; and the following from the various regiments, arranged without regard to rank : Wessels and Hammond ; Gerald Russell, Oscar Elting, and George A. Dodd, of the Third Cavalry ; James Egan and James Allison, of the Second Cavalry ; John M. Hamilton, E. W. Ward and E. P. Andrus, Alfred B. Taylor and H. W. Wheeler, of the Fifth Cavalry ; J. H. Dorst, H. W. Lawton, C. Mauck, J. W. Martin, John Lee, C. M. Callahan, S. A. Mason, H. H. Bellas, Wirt Davis, F. L. Shoemaker, J. Wesley Rosenquest, W. C. Hemphill, J. A. McKinney, H. G. Otis, of the Fourth Cavalry ; Cushing, Taylor, Bloom, Jones, Campbell, Cummins, Crozier, Frank G. Smith, Harry R. Anderson, Greenough, Howe, French, of the Fourth Artillery ; Jordan, MacCaleb, Devin, Morris C. Foot, Pease, Baldwin, Rockefeller, Jesse M. Lee, Bowman, of the Ninth Infantry ; Vanderslice, Austin, Krause, Hasson, Kimball, of the Fourteenth Infantry ; Pollock, Hay, Claggett, Edward B. Pratt, Wheaton, William L. Clarke, Hoffman, Heyl, of the Twenty-third Infantry ; and Surgeons Gibson, Price, Wood, Pettys, Owsley, and La Garde.

Mackenzie's column numbered twenty-eight 'officers and seven hundred and ninety men ; Dodge's, thirty-three officers and six hundred and forty-six enlisted men. There were one hundred and fifty-five Arapahoes, Cheyennes, and Sioux ; ninety-one Shoshones, fifteen Bannocks, one hundred Pawnees, one Ute, and one Nez Percé, attached as scouts ; and four interpreters.

The supplies were carried on four hundred pack-mules, attended by sixty-five packers under men of such experience as Tom Moore, Dave Mears, Young Delaney, Patrick, and others ; one hundred and sixty-eight wagons and seven ambulances—a very imposing cavalcade. Major Frank North, assisted by his brother, Luke North, commanded the Pawnees ; they, as well as all the other scouts, rendered service of the first value, as will be seen from a glance at these pages. General Crook had succeeded in planting a detachment of infantry at old Fort Reno, which was rebuilt under the energetic administration of Major Pollock, of the Ninth, and had something in the way of supplies, shelter, and protection to offer to small parties of couriers or scouts who might run against too strong a force of the enemy. This post, incomplete as it was, proved of prime importance before the winter work was over.

We noticed one thing in the make-up of our scouting force : it was an improvement over that of the preceding summer, not in bravery or energy, but in complete familiarity with the plans and designs of the hostile Sioux and Cheyennes whom we were to hunt down. Of the Cheyennes, I am able to give the names of "Thunder Cloud," "Bird," "Blown Away," "Old Crow," "Fisher," and "Hard Robe." Among the Sioux were, in addition to the young man, "Charging Bear," who had been taken prisoner at the engagement of Slim Buttes, "Three Bears," "Pretty Voiced Bull," "Yellow Shirt," "Singing Bear," "Lone Feather," "Tall Wild Cat," "Bad Boy," "Bull," "Big Horse," "Black Mouse," "Broken Leg," a second Indian named "Charging Bear," "Crow," "Charles Richaud," "Eagle," "Eagle" (2), "Feather On The Head," "Fast Thunder," "Fast Horse," "Good Man," "Grey Eyes," "James Twist," "Kills First," "Keeps The Battle," "Kills In The Winter," "Lone Dog," "Owl Bull," "Little Warrior," "Leading Warrior," "Little Bull," "No Neck," "Poor Elk," "Rocky Bear," "Red Bear," "Red Willow," "Six Feathers," "Sitting Bear," "Scraper," "Swift Charger," "Shuts The Door," "Slow Bear," "Sorrel Horse," "Swimmer," "Tobacco," "Knife," "Thunder Shield," "Horse Comes Last," "White Face," "Walking Bull," "Waiting," "White Elk," "Yellow Bear," "Bad Moccasin," "Bear Eagle," "Yankton," "Fox Belly," "Running Over," "Red Leaf"—representing the Ogallallas, Brulés, Cut Offs, Loafers, and Sans Arcs bands.

The Arapahoes were "Sharp Nose," "Old Eagle," "Six Feathers," "Little Fox," "Shell On The Neck," "White Horse," "Wolf Moccasin," "Sleeping Wolf," "William Friday," "Red Beaver," "Driving Down Hill," "Yellow Bull," "Wild Sage," "Eagle Chief," "Sitting Bull," "Short Head," "Arrow Quiver," " Yellow Owl," " Strong Bear," " Spotted Crow," " White Bear," " Old Man," " Painted Man," " Left Hand," " Long Hair," " Ground Bear," " Walking Water," " Young Chief," " Medicine Man," " Bull Robe," " Crying Dog," " Flat Foot," " Flint Breaker," " Singing Beaver," " Fat Belly," " Crazy," " Blind Man," " Foot," " Hungry Man," " Wrinkled Forehead," " Fast Wolf," " Big Man," " White Plume," " Coal," " Sleeping Bear," " Little Owl," " Butcher," " Broken Horn," " Bear's Backbone," " Head Warrior," " Big Ridge," " Black Man," " Strong Man," " Whole Robe," " Bear Wolf."

The above will surely show that we were excellently provided with material from the agencies, which was the main point to be considered. The Pawnees were led by " Li-here-is-oo-lishar " and " U-sanky-su-cola ; " the Bannocks and Shoshones by " Tupsi-paw " and " O-ho-a-te." The chief " Washakie " was not with them this time ; he sent word that he was suffering from rheumatism and did not like to run the risks of a winter campaign, but had sent his two sons and a nephew and would come in person later on if his services were needed. These guides captured a Cheyenne boy and brought him in a prisoner to Crook, who learned from him much as to the location of the hostile villages.

In the gray twilight of a cold November morning (the 25th), Mackenzie with the cavalry and Indian scouts burst like a tornado upon the unsuspecting village of the Cheyennes at the head of Willow Creek, a tributary of the Powder, and wiped it from the face of the earth. There were two hundred and five lodges, each of which was a magazine of supplies of all kinds—buffalo and pony meat, valuable robes, ammunition, saddles, and the comforts of civilization—in very appreciable quantities. The roar of the flames exasperated the fugitive Cheyennes to frenzy ; they saw their homes disappearing in fire and smoke ; they heard the dull thump, thump, of their own medicine drum, which had fallen into the hands of our Shoshones ; and they listened to the plaintive drone of the sacred flageolets upon which the medicine men of the Pawnees were playing as they rode at the head of their people. Seven hundred and five ponies fell into our hands and were driven off the field ; as many more were killed and wounded or slaughtered by the Cheyennes the night after the battle, partly for food and partly to let their half-naked old men and women put their feet and legs in the warm entrails.   We lost one officer, Lieutenant John A. McKinney, Fourth Cavalry, and six men killed and twenty-five men wounded ; the enemy's loss was unknown ; at least thirty bodies fell into our hands, and at times the fighting had a hand-to-hand character, especially where Wirt Davis and John M. Hamilton were engaged.   The village was secured by a charge on our left in which the companies of Taylor, Hemphill, Russell, Wessells, and the Pawnees participated.   The Shoshones, under Lieutenant Schuyler and Tom Cosgrove, seized a commanding peak and rained down bullets upon the brave Cheyennes, who, after putting their women and children in the best places of safety accessible, held on to the rocks, and could not be dislodged without great loss of life.

Mackenzie sent couriers to Crook, asking him to come to his help as soon as he could with the long rifles of the infantry, to drive the enemy from their natural fortifications.   Crook and the foot troops under Dodge, Townsend, and Campbell made the wonderful march of twenty-six miles over the frozen, slippery ground in twelve hours, much of the distance by night.   But they did not reach us in time, as the excessive cold had forced the Cheyennes to withdraw from our immediate front, eleven of their little babies having frozen to death in their mothers' arms the first night and three others the second night after the fight.

The Cheyennes were spoken to by Bill Roland and Frank Gruard, but were very sullen and not inclined to talk much ; it was learned that we had struck the village of " Dull Knife," who had with him " Little Wolf," " Roman Nose," " Gray Head," " Old Bear," " Standing Elk," and " Turkey Legs."   " Dull Knife " called out to our Sioux and Cheyenne scouts : " Go home—you have no business here ; we can whip the white soldiers alone, but can't fight you too."   The other Cheyennes called out that they were going over to a big Sioux village, which they asserted to be near by, and get its assistance, and then come back and clean us out.   " You have killed and hurt a heap of our people," they said, " and you may as well stay now and kill the rest of us."   The Custer massacre was represented by a perfect array of mute testimony : gauntlets, hats, and articles of clothing marked with the names of officers and men of the ill-fated Seventh Cavalry, saddles, silk guidons, and other paraphernalia pointing the one moral, that the Cheyennes had been as foremost in the battle with Custer as they had been in the battle with Crook on the Rosebud a week earlier.

All the tribes of the plains looked up to the Cheyennes, and respected their impetuous valor ; none stood higher than they as fierce, skilful fighters ; and to think that we had broken the back of their hostility and rendered them impotent was a source of no small gratification. They sent a party of young men to follow our trail and see whither we went ; these young men crawled up close to our camp-fires and satisfied themselves that some of their own people were really enlisted to fight our battles, as Ben Roland had assured them was the case. This disconcerted them beyond measure, added to what they could see of our column of scouts from the other tribes. "Dull Knife" made his way down the Powder to where "Crazy Horse" was in camp, expecting to be received with the hospitality to which his present destitution and past services entitled him. "Crazy Horse" was indifferent to the sufferings of his allies and turned the cold shoulder upon them completely, and this so aroused their indignation that they decided to follow the example of those who had enrolled under our flag and sent in word to that effect.

At first it was not easy to credit the story that the Cheyennes were not only going to surrender, but that every last man of them would enlist as a soldier to go out and demolish "Crazy Horse ; " but the news was perfectly true, and in the last days of December and the first of January the first detachment of them arrived at Red Cloud Agency; just as fast as the condition of their ponies and wounded would admit, another detachment arrived ; and then the whole body—men, women, and children—made their appearance, and announced their desire and intention to help us whip "Crazy Horse." "Crazy Horse" happened to be related by blood or by marriage to both "Spotted Tail" and "Red Cloud," and each of these big chiefs exerted himself to save him. "Spotted Tail" sounded the Cheyennes and found that they were in earnest in the expressed purpose of aiding the Americans ; and when he counted upon his fingers the hundreds of allies who were coming in to the aid of the whites in the suppression, perhaps the extermination, of the Dakotas, who had so long lorded it over the population of the Missouri Valley, he saw that it was the part of prudence for all his people to submit to the authority of the General Government and trust to its promises.

Colonel Mason was not only a good soldier, he was a man of most excellent education, broad views and humane impulses ; he had gained a great influence over " Spotted Tail," which he used to the best advantage. He explained to his red-skinned friends that the force soon to be put in the field would embrace hundreds of the Sioux at the agencies, who were desirous of providing themselves with ponies front the herds of their relations, the Minneconjous; that every warrior of the Cheyennes had declared his intention of enlisting to fight " Crazy Horse"; that there would be, if needed, two hundred and fifty men, or even more, from the Utes, Bannocks, and Shoshones ; that over one hundred Pawnees were determined to accompany any expedition setting out ; that one hundred Winnebagoes had offered their services ; that all the able-bodied Arapahoes were enrolled, and that the Crows had sent word that two hundred of their best warriors would take part. In the early part of the winter the Crows had sent two hundred and fifty of their warriors under Major George M. Randall and the interpreter, Fox, to find and join Crook's expedition. After being subjected to indescribable privations and almost frozen to death in a fierce wind and snow storm upon the summits of the Big Horn range—from the fury of which Randall and his companions were saved by the accident of discovering a herd of buffaloes hiding from the blast in a little sag, which animals they attacked, killing a number and eating the flesh raw, as no fire could live in such a blast, and putting their feet inside the carcasses to keep from freezing stiff—the brave detachment of Crows succeeded in uniting with us on Christmas morning, 1876, in one of the most disagreeable blizzards of that trip.

Their number had been reduced below one hundred, but they were still able to aid us greatly, had not Crook deemed it best for them to return home and apprise their tribe of the complete downfall of the Cheyennes and the breaking of the backbone of hostility. There might be other fights and skirmishes in the future, but organized antagonism to the whites was shattered when the Cheyenne camp was laid low, and future military operations would be minimized into the pursuit of straggling detachments or conflicts with desperate bands which had no hope of success, but would wish to sell their lives at the highest rate possible. The best thing for the Crows and Utes and Shoshones to do would be to move into, or at least close to, the Big Horn Mountains, and from there raid upon the petty villages of the Sioux who might try to live in the seclusion of the rocks and forests. " Spotted Tail " said that " Crazy Horse " was his nephew, and he thought he could make him see the absolute inutility of further resistance by going out to have a talk with him.

Mason telegraphed all the foregoing facts to General Crook, who had been summoned to Cheyenne as a witness before a general court-martial ; Crook replied that there was no objection to the proposed mission, but that " Spotted Tail " must let " Crazy Horse " understand that he was not sent out with any overtures, and that all " Crazy Horse " could count upon was safety in his passage across the country, by setting out at once before another movement should begin.   " Spotted Tail " found " Crazy Horse " encamped near the head of the Little Powder, about midway between Cantonment Reno and the southwestern corner of the Black Hills.   He made known his errand, and had no great difficulty in making his nephew see that he had better begin his movement towards the agency without a moment's delay.   Several of " Crazy Horse's " young men came in with " Spotted Tail," who was back at Camp Robinson by the last week in January, 1877. General Crook's headquarters had been transferred to that point, and there was little to do beyond waiting for the arrival of " Crazy Horse " and other chiefs.

Of our mess and its members, as well as the people who dined or supped with us, I am sure that my readers will pardon me for saying a word.

CHAPTER XXIII.

CAMP ROBINSON was situated in the extreme northwestern
corner of the State of Nebraska, close to the line of Dakota
and that of Wyoming ; aside from being the focus of military
activity, there was little in the way of attraction ; the scenery in
the vicinity is picturesque, without any special features. There
were great numbers of Indians of the Sioux, Cheyenne, and
Arapahoe tribes, to whose ranks accessions were made daily by
those surrendering, but reference to them will be postponed for
the present. The white members of our mess were General
Crook, General Mackenzie, Colonel J. W. Mason, Lieutenant
William P. Clarke, Lieutenant Hayden Delaney, Lieutenant
Walter S. Schuyler, Major George M. Randall, and myself.
Neither Mackenzie nor Mason could, strictly speaking, be called
a member of the mess, but as they generally "dropped in," and
as a plate was regularly placed for each, there is no direct violation of the unities in including them. Randall was still full of
his recent perilous adventure with the Crows, and we often were
successful in drawing him out about his experiences in the Civil
War, in which he had borne a most gallant part and of which
he could, when disposed, relate many interesting episodes. Schuyler had made a tour through Russia and Finland, and observed
not a little of the usages and peculiarities of the people of those

countries.   Mr. Strahorn, who was often with us, had wandered about in many curious spots of our own territory, and was brimful of anecdote of quaint types of human nature encountered far away from the centres of civilization.   Crook and Mackenzie and Mason would sometimes indulge in reminiscences to which all eagerly listened, and it is easy to see that such a mess would of itself have been a place of no ordinary interest ; but for me the greatest attraction was to be found in the constant presence of distinguished Indian chiefs whose names had become part and parcel of the history of our border.   General Sheridan had paid one hurried visit and remained a day, but being better known to American readers, there is no use in speaking of him and his work during the war.

There were two cooks, Phillips and Boswell, the former of whom had shared the trials and tribulations of the terrible march down from the head of Heart River, and seemed resolved to make hay while the sun shone ; he could make anything but pie—in that he failed miserably.   I think it was Oliver Wendell Holmes who once wrote an essay to demonstrate that the isothermal line of perpetual pumpkin pie was the line of highest civilization and culture.   The converse of the proposition would seem to be equally true : pie, of any kind, cannot be made except under the most æsthetic surroundings ; amid the chilling restraints of savagery and barbarism, pie is simply an impossibility. It did not make much difference what he prepared, Boswell was sure of an appreciative discussion of its merits by a mess which was always hungry, and which always had guests who were still hungrier and still more appreciative.

Taking our aboriginal guests in order of rank, the chief, of course, was "Spotted Tail."   This is, unfortunately, not the age of monument-building in America ; if ever the day shall come when loyal and intelligent friendship for the American people shall receive due recognition, the strong, melancholy features of "Sintiega-leska," or "Spotted Tail," cast in enduring bronze, will overlook the broad area of Dakota and Nebraska, which his genius did so much to save to civilization.   In youth a warrior of distinction, in middle age a leader among his people, he became, ere time had sprinkled his locks with snow, the benefactor of two races.   A diplomatist able to hold his own with the astutest agents the Great Father could depute to confer with him, "Spotted Tail" recognized the inevitable destruction of his kinsmen if they persisted in war and turned their backs upon overtures of peace. He exerted himself, and generally with success, to obtain the best terms possible from the Government in all conferences held with its representatives, but he was equally earnest in his determination to restrain the members of his own band, and all others whom he could control, from going out upon the war-path. If any persisted in going, they went to stay ; he would not allow them to return.

There was a story current in army circles that years and years ago a young daughter of "Spotted Tail" had fallen in love with an officer just out of West Point, and had died of a broken heart. In her last hours she asked of her father the pledge that he would always remain the friend of the Americans—a pledge given with affectionate earnestness, and observed with all the fidelity of a noble nature. I have often seen the grave of this young maiden at Fort Laramie—a long pine box, resting high in air upon a scaffold adorned with the tails of the ponies upon which her gentle soul had made the lonesome journey to the Land of the Great Hereafter. I may as well tell here a romance about her poor bones, which insatiate Science did not permit to rest in peace. Long after her obsequies, when "Spotted Tail's" people had been moved eastward to the White Earth country, and while the conflict with the hostiles was at its bitterest, the garrison of Fort Laramie was sent into the field, new troops taking their places. There was a new commanding officer, a new surgeon, and a new hospital steward ; the last was young, bright, ambitious, and desirous of becoming an expert in anatomy. The Devil saw his opportunity for doing mischief ; he whispered in the young man's ear : "If you want an articulated skeleton, what's the matter with those bones ? Make your own articulated skeleton." Turn where he would, the Devil followed him ; the word "bones" sounded constantly in his ears, and, close his eyes or open them, there stood the scaffold upon which, wrapped in costly painted buffalo robes and all the gorgeous decoration of bead-work, porcupine quill, and wampum that savage affection could supply, reposed the mortal remains of the Dakota maiden. . . . A dark night, a ladder, a rope, and a bag—the bones were lying upon the steward's table, cleaned, polished, and almost adjusted, and if there was one happy man in the United States Army it was the hospital steward of Fort Laramie.

How fleeting is all human joy ! A little cloud of dust arose above the hills to the northeast in the direction of the Raw-Hide ; it grew bigger and bigger and never ceased until, in front of the commanding officer's quarters, it revealed the figures of " Spotted Tail," the head chief of the Sioux, and a dozen of his warriors. The great chief had come, he said, for the bones of his child ; he was getting old, and his heart felt cold when it turned to the loved one who slept so far from the graves of her people. The way was long, but his ponies were fresh, and to help out the ride of the morrow he would start back with the rising of the moon that night. Consternation ! Panic ! Dismay ! Use any term you please to describe the sensation when the steward confessed to the surgeon, and the surgeon to the commanding officer, the perilous predicament in which they were placed. The commanding officer was polite and diplomatic. He urged upon " Spotted Tail " that the requirements of hospitality could not permit of his withdrawal until the next day ; neither was it proper that the bones of the daughter of so distinguished a chief should be carried off in a bundle uncoffined. He would have a coffin made, and when that should be ready the remains could be placed in it without a moment's delay or a particle of trouble. Once again, a ladder, a rope, and the silence of night—and the secret of the robbery was secure. When the story reached our camp on Goose Creek, Terry's Crow Indian messengers were relating to Crook the incidents of the Custer massacre.

I thought then with horror, and I still think, what might have been the consequences had " Spotted Tail " discovered the abstraction of those bones ? Neither North nor South Dakota, Wyoming nor Montana might now be on the map, and their senators might not be known in Congress ; and, perhaps, those who so ably represent the flourishing States of Kansas, Nebraska and Colorado might have some difficulty in finding all of their constituents. The Northern Pacific Railroad might not yet have been built, and thousands who to-day own happy homes on fertile plains would still be toiling aimlessly and hopelessly in the over-populated States of the Atlantic seaboard.

We found "Spotted Tail " a man of great dignity, but at all moments easy and affable in manner ; not hard to please, sharp as a brier, and extremely witty. He understood enough English to get along at table, and we picked up enough Dakota to know that when he asked for "ahúyape," he meant bread ; "wosúnna" was butter ; "wáka-maza," corn ; that "bellô" was the name for potatoes, "tollô" for beef, "pazúta-sápa" for coffee, "witkâ" for eggs ; that white sugar became in his vocabulary "chahúmpi-ska," salt was transformed into "minni-squia"; and that our mushrooms and black pepper resolved themselves into the jaw-breaking words : "yamanuminnigawpi" and "numcatchy-num-capa," respectively. He was addicted to one habit, not strictly according to our canons, of which we never succeeded in break-ing him : if he didn't like a piece of meat, or if he had been served with a greater abundance than he needed of anything, he lifted what he didn't want back upon the platter. His conversa-tional powers were of a high order, his views carefully formed, clearly expressed. My personal relations with him were ex-tremely friendly, and I feel free to say that "Spotted Tail" was one of the great men of this country, bar none, red, white, black, or yellow. When "Crow Dog" murdered him, the Dakota nation had good reason to mourn the loss of a noble son.

"Spotted Tail" was several times accompanied by "White Thunder," a handsome chief, most favorably disposed towards the whites, and of good mental calibre, but in no sense "Spotted Tail's" equal. On other occasions we had both "Spotted Tail" and "Red Cloud" at dinner or lunch on the same day. This we tried to avoid as much as possible, as they were unfriendly to each other, and were not even on speaking terms. However, at our table, they always behaved in a gentlemanly manner, and no stranger would have suspected that anything was wrong. "Red Cloud" had shown a better disposition since the coming in of the Cheyennes, their avowed intentions having as much of an effect upon him as upon "Spotted Tail." The delegation of Ogallalla warriors had done such good work during the campaign that General Crook had allowed the members of the other bands to give to the more deserving some of the ponies taken away from them and distributed among the other divisions of the Sioux. This developed a much better feeling all around, and "Red Cloud" had asked to be enlisted as a soldier, to show that he meant well.

He had also said that "Crazy Horse" could not travel in as

fast as General Crook expected, partly on account of the soft
state of the trails induced by a heavy January thaw, and partly
because it would be necessary for him to hunt in order to get
food for his women and children. If he, "Red Cloud," were
permitted to take out enough food to support the women and
children on their way to the agency, it would deprive "Crazy
Horse" of any excuse for delay, granting that he was disposed to
be dilatory in his progress; he would go out to see the band of
"Crazy Horse," and tell them all to come in at once, and give to
all the women and children who needed it the food for their support while coming down from the Black Hills. This proposition
was approved, and "Red Cloud" started out and did good work,
to which I will allude later on.

One day when the Cheyenne chief, "Dull Knife," was at
headquarters, I invited him to stay for luncheon.

"I should be glad to do so," he replied, "but my daughters
are with me."

"Bring them in too," was the reply from others of the mess,
and "Spotted Tail," who was present, seconded our solicita-
tions; so we had the pleasure of the company, not only of old
"Dull Knife," whose life had been one of such bitterness and
sorrow, but of his three daughters as well. They were fairly
good-looking—the Cheyennes will compare favorably in appearance with any people I've seen—and were quite young; one of
nine or ten, one of twelve, and the oldest not yet twenty—a
young widow who, with the coquettishness of the sex, wore her
skirts no lower than the knees to let the world see that in her
grief for her husband, killed in our fight of November 25th, she
had gashed and cut her limbs in accordance with the severest
requirements of Cheyenne etiquette. Had she lost a child she
would have cut off one of the joints of the little finger of her
left hand.

Of the other Cheyennes, there were "Little Wolf," one of the
bravest in fights, where all were brave; and "Standing Elk,"
cool and determined in action, wise in council, polite in demeanor, reserved in speech, and adhering in dress to the porcelain
bead breastplates of the tribes of the plains. Last among this
deputation was the medicine man, "High Wolf," or "Tall
Wolf," or "Big Wolf"; he had been proud to wear, as his pet
decoration, a necklace of human fingers, which he knew had

fallen into my possession in the fight with Mackenzie. There was no affection lost between us, but he imagined that by getting upon good terms with me negotiations might be opened for a return of the ghastly relic. But I knew its value too well: there is no other in the world that I know of—that is, in any museum—although the accounts of explorations in the early days in the South Sea, among the Andamanese, and by Lewis and Clark, make mention of such things having been seen. While we were destroying the Cheyenne village, "Big Bat" found two of these necklaces, together with a buckskin bag containing twelve of the right hands of little babies of the Shoshone tribe, lately killed by the Cheyennes. The extra necklace was buried, the buckskin bag with its dreadful relics was given to our Shoshone allies, who wept and wailed over it all night, refusing to be comforted, and neglecting to assume the battle-names with which the Pawnees were signalizing their prowess. The necklace belonging to "High Wolf" contained eight fingers of Indian enemies slain by that ornament of society, and has since been deposited in the National Museum, Washington, D. C.

There was an old, broken-down electrical apparatus in the post hospital, which had long ago been condemned as unserviceable, but which we managed to repair so that it would send a pretty severe shock through the person holding the poles. The Indian boys and girls looked upon this as wonderful "medicine," and hung in groups about the headquarters, from reveille till retreat, hoping to see the machine at work—not at work upon themselves exactly, but upon some "fresh fish" which they had enticed there from among the later surrenders. Many and many a time, generally about the lunch hour, a semicircle would form outside the door, waiting for the appearance of some one connected with the headquarters, who would be promptly nudged by one of the more experienced boys, as a sign that there was fun in sight. The novice couldn't exactly comprehend what it all meant when he saw at the bottom of a pail of water a shining half-dollar which was to be his if he could only reach it while holding that innocent-looking cylinder in one hand. There was any amount of diversion for everybody; the crop of shorn lambs increased rapidly, each boy thinking that the recollection of his own sorrows could be effaced in no better way than by contemplating those of the newer arrivals; and so from guard mount to parade the wonder grew as to what was the mysterious machine which kept people from seizing the piece of silver.

We were becoming more generous, or more confident, by this time, and doubled the value of the money prize, and issued a challenge to the "medicine men" to try their powers. Several of them did so, only to be baffled and disgraced. No matter what "medicine" they made use of, no matter what "medicine song" they chanted, our "medicine song" was more potent: never were the strains of "Pat Malloy" warbled to a nobler purpose, and ere long it began to be bruited about from "tepi" to "tepi"—from "Sharp Nose's" hearth-fire to "White Thunder's," and farther down the vale to where the blue smoke from "Little Wolf's" cottonwood logs curled lazily skyward—that "Wichak-pa-yamani" ("Three Stars," the Sioux name for General Crook) had a "Mini-hoa" (Ink Man-Adjutant General) whose "medicine song" would nullify anything that Cheyenne or Arapahoe or Dakota could invent; and naturally enough, this brought "High Wolf," the great doctor of the Cheyennes, to the fore. The squaws nagged him into accepting the gauntlet thrown down so boldly. Excitement ran high when word was passed around that "High Wolf" was going to test the power of the battery. There was a most liberal attendance of spectators, and both whites and reds knew that the ordeal was to be one of exceptional importance. "High Wolf" had with him a good deal of "medicine," but he asked a few moments' delay, as he had to make some more. I watched him closely to guard against trickery, but detected nothing to cause me any apprehension : he plucked one or two lengths of grass just peeping above the ground, rolled them in the palms of his hands, and then put them into his mouth, wherein he had previously placed a small stone, glanced up at the sun, and then at the cardinal points, all the while humming, half distinctly, his "medicine song," in which two sympathizing friends were joining, and then was ready for the fray.

I was not asleep by any means, but putting in all the muscle I could command in revolving the handle of the battery, and so fully absorbed in my work, that I almost forgot to summon "Pat Malloy" to my aid. "High Wolf" took one of the poles, and of course felt no shock ; he looked first at the glittering dollar in the bottom of the bucket, and next at the extra prize—five dollars, if I remember correctly—contributed by the officers standing by ; and in another second his brawny left arm was plunged up to the elbow in the crystal fluid. Not being an adept in such matters, I am not prepared to say exactly how many hundred thousand volts he got in the back of the neck, but he certainly had a more thorough experience with electricity than any aborigine, living or dead, and, worst of all, he couldn't let go. He was strong as a mule and kicked like a Texas congressman, smashing the poor, rickety battery all to pieces, which was a sad loss to us. He was neither conquered nor humiliated, and boldly announced his readiness to repeat the trial, a proposal we could not in honor decline. The battery was patched up as well as we knew how, and we allowed him to try again ; this time, as the crafty rascal knew would be the case, the wheezy machine furnished no great current, and he fished out the dollar, although moisture gathered in beads around his neck, and his fingers were doubled upon his wrists. He got the rest of the money, according to promise, and the decision of the onlookers was that the whole business must be adjudged a "draw." "High Wolf" was a powerful "medicine man" as of yore, and he alone of all the Indians at Red Cloud could compete with the white man's "medicine box" whose wheels went whir-r-r-whir-r-r-r.

The Arapahoes were well represented. Their principal men were of fine mental calibre, and in all that galaxy of gallant soldiers, white and copper-colored, whom I met during those years, none stands out more clearly in my recollection than "Sharp Nose." He was the inspiration of the battle-field. He reminded me of a blacksmith : he struck with a sledge-hammer, but intelligently, at the right spot and right moment. He handled men with rare judgment and coolness, and was as modest as he was brave. He never spoke of his own deeds, but was an excellent talker on general topics, and could not, as a matter of course, refrain from mention, at times, of active work in which he had had a share. "Washington," his boon companion and councillor, was a handsome chief who had assumed this name in token of his desire to "walk in the new road." He had been taken on a trip East, and had been so impressed with all the wonders seen, that he devoted most of his time to missionary work among his people, telling them that they could only hope for advancement by becoming good friends of these progressive white men and adopting their ways.

"Friday Fitzpatrick" had been lost when a mere child, during a fight which arose between the Arapahoes and Blackfeet, at a time when they were both on the Cimarron, engaged in trading with the Apaches, New Mexico Pueblos, Kiowas, Utes, Paw-nees, and Comanches, some distance to the south of where the foundry and smelter chimneys of the busy city of Pueblo, Colo-rado, now blacken the air. The lost Indian boy fell into the hands of Mr. Fitzpatrick, a trader of St. Louis, who had him educated by the Jesuits, an order which had also given the rudi-ments of learning to Ouray, the head chief of the Utes. "Friday" was intelligent and shrewd, speaking English fluently, but his morals were decidedly shady. I used to talk to him by the hour, and never failed to extract pages of most interesting information concerning savage ideas, manners, and customs. He explained the Indian custom of conferring names each time a warrior had distinguished himself in battle, and gave each of the four agnomens with which he personally had been honored—the last being a title corresponding in English to "The Man Who Sits in the Corner and Keeps His Mouth Shut."

"Six Feathers," "White Horse," and "Black Coal" were also able men to whom the Arapahoes looked up; the first was as firm a friend of the whites as was "Washington"—he became General Crook's "brother"; others of our mess were equally fortunate. Being an Arapahoe's "brother" possessed many advantages—for the Arapahoe. You were expected to keep him in tobacco, something of a drain upon your pocket-book, although Indians did not smoke to such an extent as white men and very rarely used chewing-tobacco. If your newly-acquired relation won any money on a horse-race, the understanding was that he should come around to see you and divide his winnings; but all the Indian "brothers" I've ever known have bet on the wrong plug, and you have to help them through when they go broke. "White Horse" was a grim sort of a wag. One day, I had him and some others of the Arapahoes aiding me in the compilation of a vocabulary of their language, of which the English traveller, Burton, had made the groundless statement that it was so harsh, meagre, and difficult that to express their ideas the Arapahoes were compelled to stand by a camp-fire and talk the "sign language." I am in a position to say that the Arapahoe language is full of guttural sounds, and in that sense is difficult of acquisition, but it is a copious, well-constructed dialect, inferior to none of the aboriginal tongues of North America. We had been hard at work for several hours, and all were tired. " To eat," said " White Horse," " is so and so ; but to eat something good, and hot, and sweet, right now, right here in this room, is so and so and so, and you can tell your good cook to bring it." It was brought at once.

I have not introduced the lesser figures in this picture : men like " American Horse," " Young Man Afraid," " Blue Horse," " Rocky Bear," and others who have since become, and were even in those days, leaders among the Dakotas. My canvas would become too crowded. It must do to say that each of these was full of native intelligence, wise in his way, and worthy of being encouraged in his progress along the new and toilsome path of civilization. But I must make room for a few words about " Three Bears " (" Mato-yamani "), a warrior fierce in battle and humane to the vanquished. I remember his coming into my tent one dismally cold night, while we lay on the Belle Fourche, on the outskirts of the Black Hills, after wiping out " Dull Knife's " village. " Three Bears's " eyes were moist, and he shook his head mournfully as he said, " Cheyenne pappoose heap hung'y."

" Sorrel Horse " (" Shunca-luta ") was a " medicine man," a ventriloquist, and a magician. The women and children stood in awe of an uncanny wretch who boasted that, if they doubted his power, they might let him cut off a lock of their hair, and inside of three days they should die. After my electrical duel with " High Wolf," " Sorrel Horse " manifested an inclination to show me what he could do. He lay down on the floor, put the hot bowl of a pipe in his mouth, and alternately inhaled the smoke or caused it to issue from the stem. Pretty soon he went into a trance, and deep groans and grunts were emitted from the abdominal region. When he came to, he assured us that that was the voice of a spirit which he kept within him. He shuffled a pack of cards, and handing it to General Mackenzie, bade him take out any one he wanted and he would tell the name ; Mackenzie did as he desired, and " Sorrel Horse " promptly fixed his fingers in diamond-shape and called out " Squaw," for the queen of diamonds, and similarly for the seven of clubs, and others as fast as drawn. He again lay down on the floor, and opened his shirt so that his ribs were exposed ; he took a small piece of tobacco, and pretended to swallow it. To all appearances, he became deathly sick : his countenance turned of an ashen hue, perspiration stood on his brow, the same lugubrious grunts issued from his stomach and throat, and I was for a moment or two in alarm about his condition; but he soon recovered consciousness, if he had ever lost it, and triumphantly drew the moist leaf of tobacco from beneath his ribs. He had been a great traveller in his day, and there was but little of the Missouri or Yellowstone drainage that he was not familiar with. I have known him to journey afoot from Red Cloud to Spotted Tail Agency, a distance of forty-three measured miles, between two in the morning and noon of the same day, bearing despatches. The Apaches, Mojaves, and other tribes of the Southwest are far better runners than the horse Indians of the plains, but I have known few of them who could excel " Sorrel Horse " in this respect.

Nothing was to be done at this time except wait for news from " Red Cloud " and " Crazy Horse." The Cheyennes were impatient to go out to war, but it was war against " Crazy Horse " and not the white man. However, the promise had been sent by General Crook to " Crazy Horse" that if he started in good faith and kept moving straight in to the agency, he should be allowed every reasonable facility for bringing all his people without molestation. " Red Cloud " sent word regularly of the march made each day : one of the half-breeds with him, a man who prided himself upon his educational attainments, wrote the letters to Lieutenant Clarke, who, with Major Randall, was in charge of the Indian scouts. The following will serve as an example :

A Pril 16th 1877.

Sir My Dear I have met some indians on road and thare say the indians on bear lodge creek on 16th april and I thought let you know it. And I think I will let you know better after I get to the camp so I sent the young man with this letter he have been to the camp before his name is arme blown off　　　　　　　　　　　　　　　　　　　　RED CLOUD.

When " Red Cloud " and his party reached " Crazy Horse " they found the statements made by the latter Indian were strictly correct. The thousands of square miles of country burned over during the preceding season were still gaunt and bare, and " Crazy Horse " was compelled to march with his famished ponies over a region as destitute as the Sahara. The rations taken out for the women and children were well bestowed; there was no food in the village, and some of the more imprudent ate themselves sick, and I may add that one of "Crazy Horse's" men sent on in advance to Camp Robinson surfeited himself and died.

While Red Cloud was absent there were several small brushes with petty bands of prowling hostiles. Lieutenants Lemly, Cumings, and Hardie, of the Third Cavalry, did spirited work near Deadwood and Fort Fetterman respectively, and a battalion of the same regiment, under Major Vroom, was kept patrolling the eastern side of the Hills.

Time did not hang heavy upon our hands at Robinson : there were rides and walks about the post for those who took pleasure in them ; sometimes a party would go as far as Crow Butte, with its weird, romantic story of former struggles between the Absaroka and the Dakota ; sometimes into the pine-mantled bluffs overlooking the garrison, where, two years later, the brave Cheyennes, feeling that the Government had broken faith with them, were again on the war-path, fighting to the death. There were visits to the Indian villages, where the courteous welcome received from the owners of the lodges barely made amends for the vicious attacks by half-rabid curs upon the horses' heels. The prismatic splendors of the rainbow had been borrowed to give beauty to the raiment or lend dignity to the countenances of Indians of both sexes, who moved in a steady stream to the trader's store to buy all there was to sell. Many of the squaws wore bodices and skirts of the finest antelope skin, thickly incrusted with vari-colored beads or glistening with the nacreous brilliancy of the tusks of elk ; in all these glories of personal adornment they were well matched by the warriors, upon whose heads were strikingly picturesque war-bonnets with eagle feathers studding them from crown to ground. These were to be worn only on gala occasions, but each day was a festal one at that time for all these people. Almost as soon as the sun proclaimed the hour of noon groups of dancers made their way to the open ground in front of the commanding general's quarters, and there favored the whites with a never-ending series of "Omaha" dances and "Spoon" dances, "Squaw" dances and "War" dances, which were wonderfully interesting and often beautiful to look upon, but open to the objection that the unwary Caucasian who ven-

tured too near the charmed circle was in danger of being seized
by stout-armed viragoes, and compelled to prance about with
them until his comrades had contributed a ransom of two dollars.

Neither were we altogether ignorant of the strange wonders of
the "Bad Lands," which began near by, and are, or were, filled
with the skeletons of mammoth saurians and other monsters of
vanished seas. "Old Paul"—I don't think he ever had any other
name—the driver of General Mackenzie's ambulance, had much
to relate about these marvellous animal cemeteries. "Loo-o-tin-
int," he would say, "it's the dog-gonedest country I ever seed—
reg'lar bone-yard. (Waugh! Tobacco juice.) Wa'al, I got lots
o' things out thar—thighs 'n jaw-bones 'n sich—them's no account, th' groun's chock full o' *them*. (Waugh! Tobacco juice.)
But, pew-trified tar'pin 'n snappin' torkle—why, them's waller-
ble. Onct I got a bone full o' pew-trified marrer; looks like
glass; guess I'll send it to a mew-see-um." (Waugh! Tobacco
juice.)

The slopes of the hills seemed to be covered with Indian boys,
ponies, and dogs. The small boy and the big dog are two of the
principal features of every Indian village or Indian cavalcade;
to these must be added the bulbous-eyed pappoose, in its bead-
covered cradle slung to the saddle of its mother's pony, and
wrapped so tightly in folds of cloth and buckskin that its optics
stick out like door-knobs. The Indian boy is far ahead of his
white contemporary in healthy vigor and manly beauty. Looking at the subject as a boy would, I don't know of an existence
with more happiness to the square inch than that of the young
redskin from eight to twelve years old. With no one to reproach
him because face or hands are unclean, to scowl because his
scanty allowance of clothing has run to tatters, and no long-
winded lessons in geography or the Constitution of the United
States, his existence is one uninterrupted gleam of sunshine.
The Indian youngster knows every bird's nest for miles around,
every good place for bathing, every nice pile of sand or earth to
roll in. With a pony to ride—and he has a pony from the time
he is four years old; and a bow—or, better luck still, a rifle—for
shooting: he sees little in the schools of civilization to excite his
envy. On ration days, when the doomed beeves are turned over to
each band, what bliss to compare to that of charging after the
frenzied steers and shooting them down on the dead run? When

the winter sun shone brightly, these martial scions would some-times forget their dignity long enough to dismount and engage in a game of shinny with their gayly-attired sisters, who rarely failed to bring out all the muscle that was in them.

It would be impossible to give more than the vaguest shadow of the occurrences of that period without filling a volume. In-dian life was not only before us and on all sides of us, but we had also insensibly and unconsciously become part of it. Our eyes looked upon their pantomimic dances—our ears were regaled with their songs, or listened to the myths and traditions handed down from the old men. "Spotted Tail" said that he could not remember the time when the Sioux did not have horses, but he had often heard his father say that in *his* youth they still had dogs to haul their "travois," as their kinsmen, the Assiniboines, to the north still do.

"Friday" said that when he was a very small child, the Ara-pahoes still employed big dogs to haul their property, and that old women and men marched in front laden with paunches filled with water, with which to sprinkle the parched tongues of the animals every couple of hundred yards.

"Fire Crow," a Cheyenne, here interposed, and said that the Cheyennes claimed to have been the first Northern Indians to use horses, and thereupon related the following story : " A young Cheyenne maiden wandered away from home, and could not be found. Her friends followed her trail, going south until they came to the shore of a large lake into which the foot-prints led. While the Indians were bewailing the supposed sad fate of their lost relative, she suddenly returned, bringing with her a fine young stallion, the first the Cheyennes had ever seen. She told her friends that she was married to a white man living near by, and that she would go back to obtain a mare, which she did. From this pair sprung all the animals which the Cheyennes, Sioux, and Arapahoes now have."

CHAPTER XXIV.

ON the 6th of May, 1877, shortly after meridian, "Crazy Horse's" band approached the agency, descending the hills in the following order : First, Lieutenant William P. Clarke, with the agency Indians—that is, "Red Cloud" and his Indian soldiers; next, "Crazy Horse," at the head of his warriors, having abreast of him "Little Big Man," "Little Hawk," "He Dog," "Old Hawk," and "Bad Road." Stringing along behind, for a dis- tance of nearly two miles, came the old men with the women and children, lodges, ponies, dogs, and other plunder. Lieuten- ant Clarke had gone out early in the morning to a point seven or eight miles from the post to meet the incoming party. "Crazy Horse," upon learning who he was, remained silent, but was not at all ungracious or surly. He dismounted from his pony, sat down upon the ground, and said that then was the best time for smoking the pipe of peace. He then held out his left hand to Clarke, telling him : "Cola (friend), I shake with this hand because my heart is on this side ; I want this peace to last for- ever." The principal warriors were then presented, each shak- ing hands. "Crazy Horse" had given his feather bonnet and all other regalia of the war-path to "Red Cloud," his brother-in-

law, as he had no further use for them. " He Dog " took off his
own war bonnet and scalp shirt and put them upon Clarke in
sign of friendly good-will. The most perfect discipline was
maintained, and silence reigned from the head of the cavalcade
to the farthest " travois."

When the post was reached, the warriors began to intone a
peace chant, in whose refrain the squaws and older children
joined, and which lasted until a halt was ordered and the work
of turning over ponies and surrendering arms began. An enu-
meration disclosed the fact that " Crazy Horse " had with him
not quite twenty-five hundred ponies, over three hundred warriors, one hundred and forty-six lodges, with an average of almost two families in each, and between eleven hundred and
eleven hundred and fifty people all told, not counting the very
considerable number who were able to precede the main body,
on account of having fatter and stronger ponies. Lieutenant
Clarke, in firm but quiet tones, informed the new arrivals that
everything in the shape of a fire-arm must be given up, and to
insure this being done he would wait until after the squaws had
pitched their " tepis," and then make the collection in person.
One hundred and seventeen fire-arms, principally cavalry carbines and Winchesters, were found and hauled away in a cart.
" Crazy Horse " himself gave up three Winchesters, and " Little
Hawk " two. By what seemed to be a curious coincidence,
" Little Hawk " wore pendent at his neck the silver medal given
to his father at the Peace Conference on the North Platte, in
1817 ; it bore the effigy of President Monroe. Some of the other
chiefs, in surrendering, laid sticks down upon the ground, saying : " Cola, this is my gun, this little one is a pistol ; send to
my lodge and get them." Every one of these pledges was redeemed by the owner. There was no disorder and no bad feeling, which was remarkable enough, considering that so many of
" Crazy Horse's " band had never been on a reservation before.
Everything ran along as smooth as clock-work, such interpretation as was necessary being made by Frank Gruard and Billy
Hunter ; Clarke, however, needed little help, as he could converse
perfectly in the sign language. Just behind the knoll overlooking the flat upon which " Crazy Horse's " village had been
erected, every one of the Cheyenne warriors was in the saddle,
armed to the teeth, and ready to charge down upon "Crazy

Horse" and settle their score with him, at the first sign of treachery.

"Crazy Horse's" warriors were more completely disarmed than any other bands coming under my observation, not so much in the number of weapons as in the pattern and condition; to disarm Indians is always an unsatisfactory piece of business, so long as the cowboys and other lawless characters in the vicinity of the agencies are allowed to roam over the country, each one a travelling arsenal. The very same men who will kill unarmed squaws and children, as was done in January, 1891, near Pine Ridge Agency, will turn around and sell to the bucks the arms and ammunition which they require for the next war-path. At the very moment when Crook was endeavoring to deprive the surrendering hostiles of deadly weapons, Colonel Mason captured a man with a vehicle loaded with metallic cartridges, brought up from Cheyenne or Sidney, to be disposed of to the young men at Spotted Tail. As with cartridges, so with whiskey: the western country has too many reprobates who make a nefarious living by the sale of vile intoxicants to savages; this has been persistently done among the Sioux, Mojaves, Hualpais, Navajos, and Apaches, to my certain knowledge. Rarely are any of these scoundrels punished. The same class of men robbed the Indians with impunity; "Spotted Tail" lost sixty head of ponies which the Indian scouts trailed down to North Platte, where they were sold among the stock-raisers. The arrest of the thieves was confided to the then sheriff of Sidney, who, somehow, always failed to come up with them; possibly the fact that he was the head of the gang himself may have had something to do with his non-success, but that is hard to say.

"Crazy Horse" took his first supper at Red Cloud Agency with Frank Gruard, who had been his captive for a long time and had made his escape less than two years previously. Frank asked me to go over with him. When we approached the chief's "tepi," a couple of squaws were grinding coffee between two stones, and preparing something to eat. "Crazy Horse" remained seated on the ground, but when Frank called his name in Dakota, "Tashunca-uitco," at the same time adding a few words I did not understand, he looked up, arose, and gave me a hearty grasp of his hand. I saw before me a man who looked quite young, not over thirty years old, five feet eight inches high, lithe and sinewy, with a scar in the face. The expression of his countenance was one of quiet dignity, but morose, dogged, tenacious, and melancholy. He behaved with stolidity, like a man who realized he had to give in to Fate, but would do so as sullenly as possible. While talking to Frank, his countenance lit up with genuine pleasure, but to all others he was, at least in the first days of his coming upon the reservation, gloomy and reserved. All Indians gave him a high reputation for courage and generosity. In advancing upon an enemy, none of his warriors were allowed to pass him. He had made hundreds of friends by his charity towards the poor, as it was a point of honor with him never to keep anything for himself, excepting weapons of war. I never heard an Indian mention his name save in terms of respect. In the Custer massacre, the attack by Reno had at first caused a panic among women and children, and some of the warriors, who started to flee, but "Crazy Horse," throwing away his rifle, brained one of the incoming soldiers with his stone war-club and jumped upon his horse.

"Little Hawk," who appeared to rank next to "Crazy Horse" in importance, was much like his superior in size and build, but his face was more kindly in expression and he more fluent in speech; he did most of the talking. "Little Big Man" I did not like in those days; principally on account of his insolent behavior to the members of the Allison Commission at this same agency, during the summer. In appearance he was crafty, but withal a man of considerable ability and force. He and I became better friends afterwards, and exchanged presents. I hold now his beautiful calumet and a finely-beaded tobacco bag, as well as a shirt trimmed with human scalps, which was once the property of "Crazy Horse."

As it is never too soon to begin a good work, Mr. Thomas Moore, the Chief of Transportation, was busy the next morning in teaching the Sioux squaws how to make bread out of the flour issued to them, which used to be wasted, fed to their ponies, or bartered off at the trader's store.

Mingling as we were with chiefs and warriors who had been fighting the Government without intermission for more than a year, and who had played such a bloody part in the Custer tragedy, it was natural that we should seek to learn all we could to throw light upon that sombre page in our military annals. I cannot say that much information was gained not already known to the public. The Indians appeared to believe that from the moment that Custer divided his forces in presence of such overwhelming odds, the destruction of the whole or the greater part was a foregone conclusion. A picture of the battle-field was drawn by one of the Indians present in hostility, and marked by myself under his direction. In some of the villages indicated there were portions of several bands.

This is the exact language of " Horny Horse " : " Some lodges came out from Standing Rock Agency and told us the troops were coming. The troops charged on the camp before we knew they were there. The lodges were strung out about as far as from here to the Red Cloud Agency slaughter-house (about two and a half miles). I was in the council-house with a lot of the old men, when we heard shots fired from up the river. The troops first charged from up the river. We came out of the council-house and ran to our lodges.

" All the young bucks got on their horses and charged the troops. All the old bucks and squaws ran the other way. We ran the troops back. Then there was another party of troops on the other side of the river. One half of the Indians pursued the first body of troops (*i. e.*, Reno's) ; the other half went after the other body (*i. e.*, Custer's). I didn't see exactly all the fight, but by noon, all of one party (*i. e.*, Custer's) were killed, and the others driven back into a bad place. We took no prisoners. I did not go out to see the bodies, because there were two young bucks of my band killed in the fight and we had to look after them.

" We made the other party of soldiers (*i. e.*, Reno's) cross the creek and run back to where they had their pack-train. The reason we didn't kill all this (Reno's) party was because while we were fighting his party, we heard that more soldiers were coming up the river, so we had to pack up and leave. We left some good young men killed in that fight. We had a great many killed in the fight, and some others died of their wounds. I know that there were between fifty and sixty Indians killed in the fight. After the fight we went to Wolf Mountain, near the head of Goose Creek. Then we followed

Rosebud down, and then went over to Bluestone Creek. We had the fight on Rosebud first, and seven days after, this fight. When we got down to Bluestone, the band broke up."

From the bands surrendering at Red Cloud and Spotted Tail agencies, many relics of the Custer tragedy were obtained. Among other things secured was a heavy gold ring, surmounted with a bloodstone seal, engraved with a griffin, which had formerly belonged to Lieutenant Reilly of the Seventh Cavalry, who perished on that day. This interesting relic was returned to his mother in Washington.

The total number of Indians surrendering at these agencies (Red Cloud and Spotted Tail) was not quite four thousand five hundred, who made no secret of the fact that they had yielded because they saw that it was impossible to stand out against the coalition made by General Crook between the white soldiers and their own people; the terrible disaster happening to the Cheyenne village had opened their ears to the counsels of their brethren still in those agencies, and the alliance between the Cheyennes and the whites proved to them that further resistance would be useless. They surrendered, and they surrendered for good ; there has never been another battle with the tribes of the northern plains as such; work of a most arduous and perilous character has been from time to time performed, in which many officers and brave soldiers have laid down their lives at the behest of duty, but the statement here made cannot be gainsaid, and will never be questioned by the honest and truthful investigator, that the destruction of the village of "Dull Knife," and the subsequent enlistment of the whole of the northern Cheyennes as scouts in the military service, sounded the death-knell of Indian supremacy for Nebraska, Wyoming, both the Dakotas, and Montana.

Crook took up the tangled threads of Indian affairs at the agencies with his accustomed energy, intelligence, coolness, patience, and foresight gained in an experience of almost twenty-five years. The new surrenders were ignorant, timid, sullen, distrustful, suspicious, revengeful, and with the departure of the Cheyennes for the Indian Territory, which took place almost immediately after, began to reflect more upon the glories of the fight with Custer than upon the disaster of November. This was the normal state of affairs, but it was intensified by the rumors, which proved to be only too well founded, that Congress was legislating to transfer the Sioux to another locality—either to the Missouri River or the Indian Territory. A delegation was sent down to the Indian Territory to look at the land, but upon its return it reported unfavorably.

"Crazy Horse" began to cherish hopes of being able to slip out of the agency and get back into some section farther to the north, where he would have little to fear, and where he could resume the old wild life with its pleasant incidents of hunting the buffalo, the elk, and the moose, and its raids upon the horses of Montana. He found his purposes detected and baffled at every turn: his camp was filled with soldiers, in uniform or without, but each and all reporting to the military officials each and every act taking place under their observation. Even his council-lodge was no longer safe : all that was said therein was repeated by some one, and his most trusted subordinates, who had formerly been proud to obey unquestioningly every suggestion, were now cooling rapidly in their rancor towards the whites and beginning to doubt the wisdom of a resumption of the bloody path of war. The Spotted Tail Agency, to which "Crazy Horse" wished to belong, was under the supervision of an army officer—Major Jesse M. Lee, of the Ninth Infantry—whose word was iron, who never swerved from the duty he owed to these poor, misguided wretches, and who manifested the deepest and most intelligent interest in their welfare. I will not bother the reader with details as to the amount of food allowed to the Indians, but I will say that every ounce of it got to the Indian's stomach, and the Indians were sensible enough to see that justice, truth, and common honesty were not insignificant diplomatic agencies in breaking down and eradicating the race-antipathies which had been no small barrier to progress hitherto. General Crook had been specially fortunate in the selection of the officers to take charge of Indian matters, and in such men as Major Daniel W. Burke and Captain Kennington, of the Fourteenth Infantry, and Mills, of the Third Cavalry, had deputies who would carry out the new policy, which had as one of its fundamentals that the Indians must not be stolen blind. The Sioux were quick to perceive the change : less than twelve months before, they had been robbed in the most bold-faced manner, the sacks which were accepted as containing one hundred pounds of flour containing only eighty-eight. When delivery was made, the mark of the inspecting and receiving officer would be stamped upon the outer sack, and the moment his back was turned, that sack would be pulled off, and the under and unmarked one submitted for additional counting.

Those two agencies were a stench in the nostrils of decent people; the attention of honest tax-payers was first called to their disgraceful management, by Mr. Welsh, of Philadelphia, and Professor Marsh, of New Haven. After a sufficiently dignified delay, suited to the gravity of the case, a congressional committee recommended the removal of the agents, and that the contractor be proceeded against, which was done, and the contractor sentenced to two years in the penitentiary.

Two other officers of the army did good work in the first and most trying days at these agencies, and their services should not be forgotten. They were Lieutenant Morris Foote, of the Ninth, and Lieutenant A. C. Johnson, of the Fourteenth Infantry. Lieutenant William P. Clarke, who had remained in charge of the Indian scouts, kept General Crook fully posted upon all that "Crazy Horse" had in contemplation; but nothing serious occurred until the fall of the year 1877, when the Nez Percé war was at its height, and it became necessary to put every available man of the Department of the Platte at Camp Brown to intercept Chief "Joseph" in his supposed purpose of coming down from the Gray Bull Pass into the Shoshone and Bannock country, in the hope of getting aid and comfort. "Crazy Horse" had lost so many of his best arms at the surrender, and he felt that he was so closely watched, and surrounded by so many lukewarm adherents, that it would be impossible to leave the agency openly; and accordingly he asked permission to go out into the Big Horn on a hunt for buffalo, which permission was declined. He then determined to break away in the night, and by making a forced march, put a good stretch of territory between himself and troops sent in pursuit.

Including the band of "Touch the Clouds," which had surrendered at Spotted Tail Agency some time before the arrival of "Crazy Horse" at Red Cloud, and the stragglers who had preceded him into the latter agency, "Crazy Horse" reckoned on having about two thousand people to follow his fortunes to British America, or whithersoever he might conclude to go.

When his purposes became known his arrest was made neces-
sary. General Crook hurried to Red Cloud Agency, and from
there started over towards Spotted Tail Agency, intending to
have a talk with "Crazy Horse" and the other chiefs; but when
about half-way our conveyance was stopped by a Sioux runner—
"Woman's Dress"—who said that he had been sent by "Spotted
Tail" and the other Indians to warn General Crook that "Crazy
Horse" had unequivocally asserted that he would kill General
Crook in the coming council, if Crook's words did not suit him.
Crook returned to Red Cloud Agency and summoned all the
chiefs, including "Crazy Horse," to a conference; "Crazy
Horse" paid no attention to the message.

General Crook informed the Indians that they were being led
astray by "Crazy Horse's" folly, and that they must preserve
order in their own ranks and arrest "Crazy Horse." The chiefs
deliberated and said that "Crazy Horse" was such a desperate
man, it would be necessary to kill him; General Crook replied
that that would be murder, and could not be sanctioned; that
there was force enough at or near the two agencies ("Crazy
Horse" had removed from Red Cloud to Spotted Tail) to round
up not only "Crazy Horse," but his whole band, and that more
troops would be sent, if necessary; he counted upon the loyal
Indians effecting this arrest themselves, as it would prove to the
nation that they were not in sympathy with the non-progressive
element of their tribe.

General Crook had started for Camp Brown to superintend in
person the massing of the troops who were to head off Chief
"Joseph," but when Sheridan heard of the threatening look of
things at the Nebraska agencies, he telegraphed to Crook under
date of September 1, 1877 : "I think your presence more necessary
at Red Cloud Agency than at Camp Brown, and wish you to get
off (the Union Pacific Railroad train) at Sidney, and go there."
Again, under date of September 3, 1877 : "I do not like the
attitude of affairs at Red Cloud Agency, and very much doubt
the propriety of your going to Camp Brown. The surrender or
capture of 'Joseph' in that direction is but a small matter com-
pared with what might happen to the frontier from a disturbance
at Red Cloud." . . . Agent Irwin, who had assumed charge
of affairs at Red Cloud Agency, was a faithful and conscientious
representative of the Indian bureau; he did all in his power to

assist in breaking down the threatened uprising, and showed a very competent understanding of the gravity of the situation.

"Crazy Horse" broke away during the night of the 3d of September, but was unable to get away from the column in pursuit, whose work may perhaps be best described in the language of General L. P. Bradley, Ninth Infantry, commanding the district of the Black Hills, which embraced the posts of Laramie, Fetterman, Robinson, and Sheridan.

"General Crook left here on the morning of the 4th, and, under his instructions, I sent out a strong force about 9 o'clock of that date to surround 'Crazy Horse's' village, about six miles below the post. The column consisted of eight companies of the Third Cavalry, and about four hundred friendly Indians. The Indian scouts were under Lieutenant Clarke; the other Indians under chiefs 'Red Cloud,' 'Little Wound,' 'American Horse,' 'Young Man Afraid of His Horses,' 'Yellow Bear,' 'Black Coal,' 'Big Road,' 'Jumping Shield,' and 'Sharp Nose.' The cavalry were under the command of Colonel Mason, Third Cavalry. When the command reached the site of the village, they found it had broken up in the night, and most of it had disappeared. A part of the lodges returned to the agency of their own accord and joined the friendly bands, a large number were overtaken by the friendly Indians and brought back, and a few went to the Spotted Tail Agency. 'Crazy Horse' escaped alone and went to the Spotted Tail Agency, where he was arrested the same day by friendly Indians and was brought here under guard of Indians on the 5th instant. My orders from General Crook were to capture this chief, confine him, and send him under guard to Omaha. When he was put in the guard-house he suddenly drew a knife, struck at the guard, and made for the door. 'Little Big Man,' one of his own chiefs, grappled with him, and was cut in the arm by 'Crazy Horse' during the struggle. The two chiefs were surrounded by the guard, and about this time 'Crazy Horse' received a severe wound in the lower part of the abdomen, either from a knife or bayonet, the surgeons are in doubt which. He was immediately removed, and placed in charge of the surgeons, and died about midnight. His father and 'Touch the Clouds,' chief of the Sans Arcs, remained with him till he died, and when his breath ceased, the chief laid his hand on 'Crazy Horse's' breast and said: 'It is good ; he has looked for death, and it has come.' The body was delivered to his friends the morning after his death. ' Crazy Horse' and his friends were assured that no harm was intended him, and the chiefs who were with him are satisfied that none was intended ; his death resulted from his own violence. The leading men of his band, ' Big Road,' ' Jumping Shield,' and ' Little Big Man,' are satisfied that his death is the result of his own folly, and they are on friendly terms with us."

The chiefs spoken of in General Bradley's telegram as accompanying "Crazy Horse" were : "Touch the Clouds," "Swift Bear," and "High Bear." All accounts agree in stating that "Crazy Horse" suddenly drew two knives, and with one in each hand started to run amuck among the officers and soldiers. "Little Big Man," seeing what he had done, jumped upon "Crazy Horse's" back and seized his arms at the elbows, receiving two slight cuts in the wrists while holding his hands down. Here, there is a discrepancy : some say that the death wound of "Crazy Horse" was given by the sentinel at the door of the guard-house, who prodded him in the abdomen with his bayonet in return for the thrust with a knife made by "Crazy Horse"; others affirm that "Little Big Man," while holding down "Crazy Horse's" hands, deflected the latter's own poniard and inflicted the gash which resulted in death. Billy Hunter, whose statement was written out for me by Lieutenant George A. Dodd, Third Cavalry, is one of the strongest witnesses on the first side, but "Little Big Man" himself assured me at the Sun Dance in 1881 that he had unintentionally killed "Crazy Horse" with the latter's own weapon, which was shaped at the end like a bayonet (stiletto), and made the very same kind of a wound. He described how he jumped on "Crazy Horse's" back and seized his arms at the elbow, and showed how he himself had received two wounds in the left wrist ; after that, in the struggle, the stiletto of the captive was inclined in such a manner that when he still struggled he cut himself in the abdomen instead of harming the one who held him in his grasp. "Little Big Man" further assured me that at first it was thought best to let the idea prevail that a soldier had done the killing, and thus reduce the probability of any one of the dead man's relatives revenging his taking off after the manner of the aborigines. The bayonet-thrust made by the soldier was received by the door of the guard-house, where

"Little Big Man" said it could still be seen. I give both stories, although I incline strongly to believe "Little Big Man."

"Crazy Horse" was one of the great soldiers of his day and generation; he never could be the friend of the whites, because he was too bold and warlike in his nature; he had a great admiration for Crook, which was reciprocated; once he said of Crook that he was more to be feared by the Sioux than all other white men. As the grave of Custer marked high-water mark of Sioux supremacy in the trans-Missouri region, so the grave of "Crazy Horse," a plain fence of pine slabs, marked the ebb.

CHAPTER XXV.

AFTER Doctor Irwin the Indians at Red Cloud had as
agent Doctor V. T. MacGillicuddy, whose peculiar fit-
ness for the onerous and underpaid responsibilities of the position brought him deserved recognition all over the western country, as one of the most competent representatives the Indian
Bureau had ever sent beyond the Missouri. Two or three times
I looked into affairs at his agency very closely, and was surprised
both at the immense amount of supplies on hand—running above
a million pounds of flour and other parts of the ration in pro-
portion—and the perfect system with which they were distributed
and accounted for. There were then eight thousand Indians of
both sexes at the agency or on the reserve, and the basis of supplies was either Pierre, in Dakota, on the Missouri, or Sidney,
Nebraska, on the Union Pacific ; the former two hundred and
the latter one hundred and twenty-five miles distant. MacGillicuddy was kept on the go all the time from morning till night,
and managed to do the work of twenty men. His salary was
the munificent sum of twenty-two hundred and fifty dollars per
annum. I could not help saying to myself that this man was carrying upon his shoulders the weight of a force equal to one-third
the United States Army ; were he in the army, MacGillicuddy

would have been a major-general, surrounded by a high-priced staff, dividing the work and relieving him of nearly all care ; he would have had three aides-de-camp, too frequently his own relations, each getting from the Government a better salary than the agent of this great concourse of savages was receiving. MacGillicuddy was expected and required to keep his wards at peace, feed and clothe them in health, see that they received proper medical attendance while sick, encourage them in habits of industry, especially farming and cattle-raising, prepare all kinds of accounts for the information of his bureau. and in his moments of leisure instruct the aborigines in the Catechism and Testament. In this matter of Indian agents, as in all that pertains to Indian affairs, the great trouble is that the American people have so little common sense. Let the salaries paid to agents be raised to such a standard that the position will be an inducement for first-class men to consider, and there will not be so much trouble in getting an honest administration, if there should be coupled a good-conduct tenure, subject to the approval of some such organization as the Indian Rights Association. Civil Service Reform may well be introduced in the Indian service.

Of the other services rendered by General Crook while in command of the Department of the Platte there is no room to speak. Much of the highest importance and greatest interest happened under his administration, and it is needless to say that all which devolved upon him to do was done well, done quietly, done without flourish of trumpets, and without the outside world learning much about it. In the line of military operations, there was the trouble with the Cheyennes who broke out from the Indian Territory during the summer of 1878, and fought their way across three military departments to the Tongue River, where they surrendered to their old commanding officer, Lieutenant William P. Clarke, Second Cavalry. There was the nipping in the bud of the outbreak among the Shoshones and Bannocks, principally the latter, led by " Tindoy " and " Buffalo Horn," both of whom were personally well known to Crook, who used his influence with them to such advantage that they remained at peace until the aggressions of the whites became too great and drove them out upon the war-path. These Indians did not, properly speaking, belong to General Crook's department, but lived on the extreme northwestern corner of it in a chain of almost inaccessible mountains in central Idaho. There was the Ute outbreak, dating back to inadequate rations and failure to keep pledges. The Utes were not of Crook's department, but it was a battalion of the Third and Fifth Cavalry and Fourth Infantry, which moved out from Rawlins, Wyoming, under Major Thornburgh, Fourth Infantry, to save the agency and the lives of the employees; and, after poor Thornburgh had been sacrificed, it was Merritt's column which made the wonderful march of one hundred and sixty miles in two and a half days to rescue the survivors in the "rat-hole" on Milk River.

Merritt had been preceded by a company of the Ninth Cavalry, commanded by Captain Dodge and Lieutenant M. B. Hughes, who had aided the beleaguered garrison to withstand the attack of the Utes till the arrival of re-enforcements. The concentration of cars and the clearing of obstacles from the track of the Union Pacific Railroad imposed a great tax upon the shoulders of its principal officials, Mr. S. H. Clark and Mr. T. L. Kimball, but they were found equal to every demand made upon them and turned over their track to General Williams and Colonel Ludington, the two staff officers charged with aiding the Merritt expedition. In the campaign, we lost Thornburgh and Weir, killed—two noble soldiers whom the country could ill afford to lose; and had a number of men killed and wounded and several officers badly hurt—Grimes, Paddock, Payne, and Cherry.

A very singular thing occurred during the time that the troops were besieged behind their feeble rifle-pits down in the hollow. One of the first to be struck was the blacksmith of the citizen train which had moved out from Fort Fred Steele under Lieutenant Butler D. Price, Fourth Infantry; his corpse, without wasting ceremony, was rolled up in place and made to do its part in supplying protection to the soldiers; a piece of canvas was thrown over it, and in the excitement and danger the dead man was forgotten. When Merritt's column arrived on the ground, the trumpeter alongside of him was ordered to sound "Officers' Call," upon hearing which the invested troops sprang upon the earthworks and gave cheer after cheer. It may have been the noise—it may have been something else—but at any rate there was a movement at one end of the rifle-pits, and slowly and feebly from under the overlying clay and canvas, the dead man arose, shook himself, put his hand wearily to his head, and asked : " My God, what's the matter, boys ? " Then he staggered about, many of the men afraid to touch him, or even go near him, and in a few moments was dead in good earnest. The explanation made by Doctor Grimes was that, in the first place, the man had been shot through the head at the intersection or junction of the jaws just under the brain ; the shock had knocked him senseless, and the blood spurting from the ghastly wound had led the soldiers to conclude somewhat hastily that he was dead ; the slip of canvas carelessly thrown over the body had preserved it from being suffocated by the earth scraped against it ; the wound was so near the brain that it would have been impossible to avoid inflammation of the latter organ, and when this set in, the victim fell dead.

The case of the Poncas was, beyond question, the most important one occurring within General Crook's jurisdiction after the pacification of the Sioux. I do not purpose entering into all its ramifications, which would be entirely too tedious for the reader, but it may be summed up in a nutshell. The Poncas were a small band of Siouan stock, closely affiliated to the Omahas, who lived at the mouth of the Niobrara, on the Missouri River. They had a reservation which, unluckily for them, was arable and consequently coveted by the white invader. From this they were bulldozed by officials of the Government and transported to the Indian Territory, where malaria and other disorders, complicated with homesickness, depleted their numbers, and made them all anxious to return to the old land. Application for permission to do this was refused, and thereupon a portion of the band tried the experiment of going at their own expense across country, walking every foot of the way, molesting nobody, and subsisting upon charity. Not a shot was fired at any one ; not so much as a dog was stolen. The western country was at that time filled with white tramps by thousands, whose presence excited no comment ; but the spectacle of nearly two hundred Indians going along peaceably back to their old habitat to seek work and earn their own bread, was too much for the equilibrium of the authorities in Washington. One of the Indians was carrying a sack tied by a string to his neck ; it contained the bones of a beloved grandchild—not a very heinous

offence in itself, but having been committed by a man whose
skin was wrinkled and red, and whose people had for generations
been the consistent friends of the white race, it was tantamount
to felony.

To make a long story short, some people in Omaha began talking about the peculiarities presented in this case of the Omahas,
and wondering why they had been arrested by the military
authorities. Lieutenant W. L. Carpenter, Ninth Infantry, had
them under his charge at Fort Omaha, and gave them an excellent character for sobriety and good behavior of every kind.
Public sympathy became aroused; meetings were held, one of
the first, if not the first, being that in the Presbyterian Church,
conducted by the Rev. Mr. Harsha and Rev. Mr. Sherrill, and
it was determined to bring the matter before the United States
court upon a writ of habeas corpus to ascertain by what right
these people were restrained of their liberty. Competent lawyers
were enlisted, and the case was taken up by the Hon. A. J.
Poppleton and Hon. J. L. Webster, two of the most prominent
members of the bar in Nebraska. Dr. George L. Miller, in
the *Herald*, and Mr. Edward Rosewater, in the *Bee*, and such
citizens as the late Judge Savage, Bishop O'Connor, Rev. John
Williams, and Bishop Clarkson brought much influence to bear;
and by the time that Judge Dundy's court had convened the
attention of the people of the United States was to some extent
converged upon the trial, which was simply to determine the
momentous question whether or not an American Indian who
had never been upon the war-path could sever his tribal relations
and go to work for his own living. Judge Dundy's decision was
to the effect that he could ; and the path of citizenship was
opened for the Indian.

Mrs. " Bright Eyes " Tibbles, an Omaha Indian lady of excellent attainments and bright intellect, and her husband, Mr. J. H.
Tibbles, editor of the Omaha *Republican*, took up the cudgels,
and travelled through the Eastern and Middle States, addressing
large concourses in all the principal towns and cities, and awakening an intelligent and potent interest in the advancement of the
native tribes which has not yet abated. President Hayes appointed a commission, to consist of General George Crook,
General Nelson A. Miles, Messrs. Stickney and Walter Allen,
and the Rev. J. Owen Dorsey, to look into the general sub-

ject of the condition and prospects of the Poncas; and as the result of this the members of the band who had returned to the mouth of the Niobrara were permitted to remain there unmolested.

To incorporate herein an account of the explorations and hunts upon which General Crook engaged while in command of the Department of the Platte, after the Indians had been reduced to submission, would be tantamount to a description of the topography of the country west of the Missouri up to and including the head-waters of the Columbia, and north and south from the Yellowstone Park to the Grand Cañon of the Colorado, and would swell in volume until it would include a description of the methods of catching or killing every fish that swam in the streams, every bird that floated in the air, and every wild animal that made its lair or burrow within those limits. Ducks, geese, turkeys, sage hens, prairie chickens; pike, pickerel, catfish, trout, salmon-trout, and whitefish; elk, deer, moose, antelope, mountain sheep; bears, wolverines, badgers, coyotes, mountain wolves—all yielded tribute to his rod or rifle. He kept adding to his collection of stuffed birds and eggs until there was no man in the country who possessed a more intimate practical knowledge of the habits of the fauna and flora of the vast region beyond the Missouri. As he made these journeys on horse or mule back, there was no man who could pretend to compare with him in an acquaintance with the trails and topography of the country off from the lines of railroad, and only one—General Sherman—who could compare in a general knowledge of the area of the United States. Sherman, while General of the army, was a great traveller, constantly on the go, but nearly all of his trips were made by rail or in stage-coach, and but few by other methods.

In company with General Sheridan, General Sackett, and General Forsyth, General Crook travelled across the then unknown territory between the Wind River and the Big Horn to the Tongue River, then down to the Custer battle-field, and by steamer from the mouth of the Little Horn to the Yellowstone, and down the Missouri to Bismarck. In company with the Hon. Carl Schurz, then Secretary of the Interior, he explored all the Yellowstone Park, and viewed its wonders—the exquisite lake, the lofty precipices of the cañon, the placid flow of the beautiful river, and its sudden plunge over the falls into the depths below, the eruptions of the geysers, the immense mass of waters contained in the springs; the pits of boiling sulphur, the solid wall of forest of so many varieties of timber, the dainty flowers, the schools of trout, the shady nooks in the hill-sides resounding to the footfall of black-tail, elk, or bear, the lofty cones, snow-crusted, reflecting back the rays of the summer sun—all the beauties, oddities, and marvels which combine to make the National Park a fairyland to dwell forever in the dreams of those who have the good fortune to enter its precincts. With all the cañons, passes, peaks, and trails of the Wahsatch, Uintah, Medicine Bow, Laramie, and other ranges he was as familiar as with his alphabet.

He was not always so prudent as he should have been while out on these trips, and several times had very close calls for death. Once, while shooting wild geese on one of the little tributaries of the Platte, he was caught in a blizzard, and while trying to make his way back to his comrades, stepped into an air-hole, and would have been drowned had it not been for the heroic exertions of Mr. John Collins and the late Mr. A. E. Touzalin. He had more adventures than I can count, with bears of all kinds and with maddened, wounded stags. Once, while hunting in the range known as the Three Tetons, he stationed his party so as to cut off the retreat of a very large bear which had taken refuge in a tule thicket or swamp; the enraged animal rushed out on the side where Crook was, and made straight towards him, mouth wide open and eyes blazing fire ; Crook allowed Bruin to come within ten feet, and then, without the quiver of a muscle or the tremor of a nerve, fired and lodged a rifle-ball in the back of the throat, not breaking out through the skull, but shattering its base and severing the spinal cord. It was a beautiful animal, and Crook was always justifiably proud of the rug.

For eight or nine years, Mr. Webb C. Hayes, of Cleveland, Ohio, hunted with Crook, and probably knows more of his encounters with ursine monsters than any living man, not excepting Tom Moore. Mr. Hayes became a renowned bear-hunter himself, and is well known in all the mountains close to the Three Tetons. In addition to being an excellent shot, he is a graceful runner ; I remember seeing him make a half-mile dash down the side of a mountain with a bear cub at his heels, and the concurrence of opinion of all in camp was that the physical

culture of Cornell University was a great thing.   General Crook
became prominently identified with the Omaha Gun Club, which
included in its membership such crack shots as the late Major
T. T. Thornburgh (afterwards killed by the Utes), Messrs. Barri-
ger, Collins, Coffman, Parmlee, Patrick, Petty, and others.   In
all their hunts General Crook participated, as well as in the fishing expeditions organized by such inveterate anglers as T. L.
Kimball, Frank Moores and the late Judge Carter, of Wyoming,
whose home at Fort Bridger offered every comfort to his friends
that could be found in a great city.

Carter was a man of means and the most hospitable, generous
instincts.   He was never content unless his house was filled
with guests, for whom nothing was too good, provided they
humored his whimsical notion that a certain patent medicine,
called "The Balm of Life," was a panacea for every ill.
Judge Carter had entered the far western country near Fort
Bridger with the expedition sent out to Utah under General
Albert Sydney Johnston, although I am not absolutely sure
as to the exact time, and had remained and accumulated means,
principally from the increase of his herds, which might truly
have been styled the cattle upon a thousand hills.   The last
time I saw this grand-looking old patriarch was at a very
substantial breakfast, served in his own princely style, where
the venison, mountain mutton, and broiled trout would have
evoked praise from Lucullus, but after which—much as the
Egyptians introduced images of mummies at their banquets—
Ludington, Bisbee, Stanton, McEldree, and I had to face the
ordeal of being dosed with the "Balm of Life," which came
near being the Balm of Death for some of us.

In the great riots of 1877, and again in 1882, Crook's energies
were severely taxed for the protection of the Government property along the line of the Union Pacific Railroad, but he performed the duty to the satisfaction of all classes.   The handsome, stately, soldierly figure of the late General John H. King,
Colonel of the Ninth Infantry, rises up in my memory in this
connection.   He rendered most valuable and efficient service
during the periods in question.   Similarly, in running down and
scattering the robber bands of Doctor Middleton, and other
horse-thieves in the Loup country, in northwestern Nebraska, the
intelligent work performed by General Crook, Captain Munson,

and Lieutenant Capron was well understood and gratefully recognized by all who were acquainted with it.   Nebraska had reason to feel indebted for the destruction of one of the most desperate gangs, led by a leader of unusual nerve and intelligence—the celebrated "Doc." Middleton, who was wounded and captured by Deputy United States Marshal Llewellyn.

CHAPTER XXVI.

BEFORE the summer of 1882 had fairly begun, Indian affairs in Arizona had relapsed into such a deplorable condition that the President felt obliged to re-assign General Crook to the command. To the occurrences of the next four years I will devote very few paragraphs, because, although they formed an epoch of great importance in our Indo-military history and in General Crook's career, they have previously received a fair share of my attention in the volume, " An Apache Campaign," to which there is little to add. But for the sake of rounding out this narrative and supplying data to those who may not have seen the book in question, it may be stated that affairs had steadily degenerated from bad to worse, and that upon Crook's return to Prescott no military department could well have been in a more desperate plight. In one word, all the Apaches were again on the war-path or in such a sullen, distrustful state of mind that it would have been better in some sense had they all left the reservation and taken to the forests and mountains.

Crook was in the saddle in a day, and without even stopping to inquire into the details of the new command—with which, however, he was to a great extent familiar from his former experience—he left the arrangement of such matters to his Adjutant-General, Colonel James P. Martin, and started across the mountains to Camp Apache.   Not many of the Apaches were to be seen, and practically none except the very old, the very feeble, or the very young.   All the young men who could shoot were hiding in the mountains, and several sharp actions had already been had with the troops : the Third and Sixth Cavalry had had a fight with the renegades from the reservation, and had had two officers— Morgan and Converse, of the Third—severely wounded ; Captain Hentig, of the Sixth, had been killed on the Cibicu some months before ; and the prospects of peace, upon a permanent and satisfactory basis, were extremely vague and unpromising.   But there was a coincidence of sentiment among all people whose opinion was worthy of consultation, that the blame did not rest with the Indians ; curious tales were flying about from mouth to mouth, of the gross outrages perpetrated upon the men and women who were trying faithfully to abide in peace with the whites.   It was openly asserted that the Apaches were to be driven from the reservation marked out for them by Vincent Collyer and General O. O. Howard, upon which they had been living for more than eleven years.   No one had ever heard the Apaches' story, and no one seemed to care whether they had a story or not.

Crook made every preparation for a resumption of hostilities, but he sent out word to the men skulking in the hills that he was going out alone to see them and hear what they had to say, and that if no killing of white people occurred in the meantime, not a shot should be fired by the troops.   In acting as he did at this time, Crook lost a grand opportunity for gaining what is known as military glory : he could have called for additional troops and obtained them ; the papers of the country would have devoted solid columns to descriptions of skirmishes and marches and conferences, what the military commander thought and said, with perhaps a slight infiltration of what he did not think and did not say ; but, in any event, Crook would have been kept prominently before the people.   His was not, however, a nature which delighted in the brass-band-and-bugle school of military renown : he was modest and retiring, shy almost as a girl, and conscientious to a peculiar degree.   He had every confidence in his own purposes and in his own powers, and felt that if not interfered with he could settle the Apache problem at a minimum of cost.   Therefore he set out to meet the Apaches in their own haunts and learn all they had to say, and he learned much.   He took with him Mr. C. E. Cooley, formerly one of his principal scouts, who was to act as interpreter ; Al Seiber, who had seen such wonderful service in that country ; Surgeon J. O. Skinner ; and myself.   Captain Wallace, with his company of the Sixth Cavalry, remained in charge of the pack-train.

Upon the elevated plateau of broken basalt which separates the current of the White River from that of the Black there is a long line of forest, principally cedar, with no small amount of pine, and much yucca, soapweed, Spanish bayonet, and mescal. The knot-holes in the cedars seemed to turn into gleaming black eyes ; the floating black tresses of dead yucca became the snaky locks of fierce outlaws, whose lances glistened behind the shoots of mescal and amole.   Twenty-six of these warriors followed us down to our bivouac in the cañon of the "Prieto," or Black River, and there held a conference with General Crook, to whom they related their grievances.

Before starting out from Camp Apache General Crook had held a conference with such of the warriors as were still there, among whom I may mention "Pedro," "Cut-Mouth Moses," "Alchise," "Uklenni," "Eskitisesla," "Noqui-noquis," "Peltie," "Notsin," "Mosby," "Chile," "Eskiltie," and some forty others of both sexes.   "Pedro," who had always been a firm friend of the whites, was now old and decrepit, and so deaf that he had to employ an ear-trumpet.   This use of an ear-trumpet by a so-called savage Apache struck me as very ludicrous, but a week after I saw at San Carlos a young baby sucking vigorously from a rubber tube attached to a glass nursing-bottle.   The world does move.

From the journal of this conference, I will make one or two extracts as illustrative of General Crook's ideas on certain seemingly unimportant points, and as giving the way of thinking and the manner of expression of the Apaches.

GENERAL CROOK : "I want to have all that you say here go down on paper, because what goes down on paper never lies.   A man's memory may fail him, but what the paper holds will be fresh and true long after we are all dead and forgotten.   This will not bring back the dead, but what is put down on this paper to-day may help the living.   What I want to get at is all that has happened since I left here to bring about this trouble, this present condition of affairs. I want you to tell the truth without fear, and to tell it in as few words as possible, so that everybody can read it without trouble."

ALCHISE : "When you left, there were no bad Indians out. We were all content ; everything was peace. The officers you had here were all taken away, and new ones came in—a different kind. The good ones must all have been taken away and the bad ones sent in their places. We couldn't make out what they wanted ; one day they seemed to want one thing, the next day something else. Perhaps we were to blame, perhaps they were ; but, anyhow, we hadn't any confidence in them. We were planting our own corn and melons and making our own living. The agent at the San Carlos never gave us any rations, but we didn't mind that, as we were taking care of ourselves. One day the agent at the San Carlos sent up and said that we must give up our own country and our corn-patches and go down there to live, and he sent Indian soldiers to seize our women and children and drive us all down to that hot land. 'Uclenni' and I were doing all we could to help the whites, when we were both put in the guard-house. All that I have ever done has been honest ; I have always been true and obeyed orders. I made campaigns against Apache-Yumas, Apache-Tontos, Pinalenos, and all kinds of people, and even went against my own people. When the Indians broke out at the San Carlos, when Major Randall was here, I helped him to go fight them ; I have been in all the campaigns. When Major Randall was here we were all happy ; when he promised a thing he did it ; when he said a word he meant it ; but all that he did was for our own good and we believed in him and we think of him yet. Where has he gone ? Why don't he come back ? Others have come to see us since he left, but they talk to us in one way and act in another, and we can't believe what they say. They say : 'That man is bad, and *that* man is bad.' I think that the trouble is, they themselves are bad. Oh, where is my friend Randall—the captain with the big mustache which he always pulled ? Why don't he come back ? He was my brother, and I think of him all the time."

Old "Pedro" talked in much the same vein : "When you (General Crook) were here, whenever you said a thing we knew that it was true, and we kept it in our minds. When Colonel Green was here, our women and children were happy and our young people grew up contented. And I remember Brown, Randall, and the other officers who treated us kindly and were our friends. I used to be happy ; now, I am all the time thinking and crying, and I say, 'Where is old Colonel John Green, and Randall, and those other good officers, and what has become of them ? Where have they gone ? Why don't they come back ? ' And the young men all say the same thing."

" Pedro " spoke of the absurdity of arresting Indians for dancing, as had been done in the case of the " medicine man," " Bobby-doklinny "—of which he had much to say, but at this moment only his concluding remarks need be preserved : " Often when I have wanted to have a little fun, I have sent word to all the women and children and young men to come up and have a dance ; other people have done the same thing ; I have never heard that there was any harm in that ; but that campaign was made just because the Indians over on the Cibicu were dancing. When you (General Crook) were here we were all content ; but we can't understand why you went away. Why did you leave us ? Everything was all right while you were here."

A matter of great grievance with the Apaches, which they could not understand, being nothing but ignorant savages and not up to civilized ways, was why their little farms, of which I will speak before ending this volume, should be destroyed—as they were—and why their cattle and horses should be driven off by soldiers and citizens. " Severiano," the interpreter, who was a Mexican by birth, taken captive in early youth, and living among the Apaches all his life, now said : "A lot of my own cattle were taken away by soldiers and citizens." Had the Apaches had a little more sense they would have perceived that the whole scheme of Caucasian contact with the American aborigines—at least the Anglo-Saxon part of it—has been based upon that fundamental maxim of politics so beautifully and so tersely enunciated by the New York alderman—"The 'boys' are in it for the stuff." The " Tucson ring " was determined that no Apache should be put to the embarrassment of working for his own living ; once let the Apaches become self-supporting, and what would become of "the boys" ? Therefore, they must all be herded down on the malaria-reeking flats of the San Carlos, where the water is salt and the air poison, and one breathes a mixture of sand-blizzards and more flies than were ever supposed to be under the care of the great fly-god Beelzebub. The conventions entered into with General Howard and Vincent Collyer, which these Apaches had respected to the letter—nay, more, the personal assurances given by the President of the United States to old "Pedro" during a visit made by the latter to Washington—were all swept away like cobwebs, while the conspirators laughed in their sleeves, because they knew a trick or two worth all of that. They had only to report by telegraph that the Apaches were "uneasy," "refused to obey the orders of the agent," and a lot more stuff of the same kind, and the Great Father would send in ten regiments to carry out the schemes of the ring, but he would never send one honest, truthful man to inquire whether the Apaches had a story or not.

It is within the limits of possibility, that as the American Indians become better and better acquainted with the English language, and abler to lay their own side of a dispute before the American people, there may be a diminution in the number of outbreaks, scares, and misunderstandings, which have cost the taxpayers such fabulous sums, and which I trust may continue to cost just as much until the tax-payer shall take a deeper and more intelligent interest in this great question. Another fact brought out in this conference was the readiness with which agents and others incarcerated Indians in guard-houses upon charges which were baseless, or at least trivial. At other times, if the charges were grave, nothing was done to press the cases to trial, and the innocent as well as the guilty suffered by the long imprisonment, which deprived the alleged criminals of the opportunity to work for the support of their families. The report of the Federal Grand Jury of Arizona—taken from the *Star*, of Tucson, Arizona, October 24, 1882—shows up this matter far more eloquently than I am able to do, and I need not say that a frontier jury never yet has said a word in favor of a red man unless the reasons were fully patent to the ordinary comprehension.

To the Honorable Wilson Hoover, District Judge :

The greatest interest was felt in the examination into the cases of the eleven Indian prisoners brought here for trial from San Carlos. The United States District Attorney had spent much time in preparing this investigation. The Department of Justice had peremptorily ordered that these cases should be disposed of at this term of court. Agent Wilcox had notified the district attorney that he should release these Indians by October 1st if they were not brought away for trial. The official correspondence from the various departments with the district attorney included a letter from Agent Tiffany to the Interior Department, asking that these Indians be at once tried, and yet Agent Tiffany released all the guilty Indians without punishment and held in confinement these eleven men for a period of fourteen months without ever presenting a charge against them, giving them insufficient food and clothing, and permitting those whose guilt was admitted by themselves and susceptible of overwhelming proof, to stalk about unblushingly and in defiance of law. This, too, under the very shadow of his authority, and in laughing mockery of every principle of common decency, to say nothing of justice.

How any official possessing the slightest manhood could keep eleven men in confinement for fourteen months without charges or any attempt to accuse them, knowing them to be innocent, is a mystery which can only be solved by an Indian agent of the Tiffany stamp. The investigations of the Grand Jury have brought to light a course of procedure at the San Carlos Reservation, under the government of Agent Tiffany, which is a disgrace to the civilization of the age and a foul blot upon the national escutcheon. While many of the details connected with these matters are outside of our jurisdiction, we nevertheless feel it our duty, as honest American citizens, to express our utter abhorrence of the conduct of Agent Tiffany and that class of reverend peculators who have cursed Arizona as Indian officials, and who have caused more misery and loss of life than all other causes combined. We feel assured, however, that under the judicious and just management of General Crook, these evils will be abated, and we sincerely trust that he may be permitted to render the official existence of such men as Agent Tiffany, in the future, unnecessary.

The investigations of the Grand Jury also establish the fact that General Crook has the unbounded confidence of all the Indians. The Indian prisoners acknowledged this before the Grand Jury, and they expressed themselves as perfectly satisfied that he would deal justly with them all. We have made diligent inquiry into the various charges presented in regard to Indian goods and the traffic at San Carlos and elsewhere, and have acquired a vast amount of information which we think will be of benefit. For several years the people of this Territory have been gradually arriving at the conclusion that the management of the Indian reservations in Arizona was a fraud upon the Government ; that the constantly recurring outbreaks of the Indians and their consequent devastations were due to the criminal neglect or apathy of the Indian agent at San Carlos; but never until the present investigations of the Grand Jury have laid bare the infamy of Agent Tiffany could a proper idea be formed of the fraud and villany which are constantly practised in open violation of law and in defiance of public justice. Fraud, peculation, conspiracy, larceny, plots and counterplots, seem to be the rule of action upon this reservation. The Grand Jury little thought when they began this investigation that they were about to open a Pandora's box of iniquities seldom surpassed in the annals of crime.

With the immense power wielded by the Indian agent almost any crime is possible. There seems to be no check upon his conduct. In collusion with the chief clerk and storekeeper, rations can be issued *ad libitum* for which the Government must pay, while the proceeds pass into the capacious pockets of the agent. Indians are sent to work on the coal-fields, superintended by white men; all the workmen and superintendents are fed and frequently paid from the agency stores, and no return of the same is made. Government tools and wagons are used in transporting goods and working the coal-mines, in the interest of this close corporation and with the same result. All surplus supplies are used in the interest of the agent, and no return made thereof. Government contractors, in collusion with Agent Tiffany, get receipts for large amounts of supplies never furnished, and the profit is divided mutually, and a general spoliation of the United States Treasury is thus effected. While six hundred Indians are off on passes, their rations are counted and turned in to the mutual aid association, consisting of Tiffany and his associates. Every Indian child born receives rations from the moment of its advent into this vale of tears, and thus adds its mite to the Tiffany pile. In the meantime, the Indians are neglected, half-fed, discontented, and turbulent, until at last, with the vigilant eye peculiar to the savage, the Indians observe the manner in which the Government, through its agent, complies with its sacred obligations.

This was the united testimony of the Grand Jury, corroborated by white witnesses, and to these and kindred causes may be attributed the desolation and bloodshed which have dotted our plains with the graves of murdered victims.

FOREMAN OF THE GRAND JURY.

The above official report of a United States Grand Jury is about as strong a document as is usually to be found in the dusty archives of courts; to its contents it is not necessary for me to add a single syllable. I prefer to let the intelligent reader form his own conclusions, while I resume the thread of my narrative where I left off in General Crook's bivouac on the Black River.

The cañon of the Black River is deep and dark, walled in by towering precipices of basalt and lava, the latter lying in loose blocks along the trail down which the foot-sore traveller must descend, leading behind him his equally foot-sore mule. The river was deep and strong, and in the eddies and swirls amid the projecting rocks were hiding some of the rare trout of the Territory, so coy that the patience of the fisherman was exhausted before they could be induced to jump at his bait. The forbidding ruggedness of the mountain flanks was concealed by forests of pine and juniper, which extended for miles along the course of the stream. The music of our pack-train bells was answered by the silvery laughter of squaws and children, as we had with us

in this place over one hundred Apaches, many of them following
out from Camp Apache to hear the results of the conference.

The Apaches with whom General Crook talked at this place
were, in addition to "Alchise" and several others who had been
sent out from Camp Apache to notify the members of the tribe
hiding in the mountains, "Nagataha," "A-ha-ni," "Comanchi,"
"Charlie," "Nawdina," "Lonni," "Neta," "Kulo," "Kan-tzi-
chi," "Tzi-di-ku," "Klishe." The whole subject of their relations with the whites was traversed, and much information
elicited. The only facts of importance to a volume of this kind
were : the general worthlessness and rascality of the agents who
had been placed in charge of them ; the constant robbery going
on without an attempt at concealment ; the selling of supplies
and clothing intended for the Indians, to traders in the little
towns of Globe, Maxey, and Solomonville ; the destruction of the
corn and melon fields of the Apaches, who had been making
their own living, and the compelling of all who could be forced
to do so to depend upon the agent for meagre supplies ; the
arbitrary punishments inflicted without trial, or without testimony of any kind ; the cutting down of the reservation limits
without reference to the Apaches. Five times had this been
done, and much of the most valuable portion had been seques-
tered ; the copper lands on the eastern side were now occupied
by the flourishing town of Clifton, while on the western limit
Globe and MacMillin had sprung into being.

Coal had been discovered at the head of Deer Creek on the
southern extremity, and every influence possible was at work to
secure the sequestration of that part of the reservation for specu-
lators, who hoped to be able to sell out at a big profit to the
Southern Pacific Railroad Company. The Mormons had tres-
passed upon the fields already cultivated by the Apaches at
Forestdale, and the agent had approached a circle of twenty of
the chiefs and head men assembled at the San Carlos, and
offered each of them a small bag, containing one hundred dollars—Mexican—and told them that they must agree to sign a
paper, giving up all the southern part of the reservation, or
troops would be sent to kill them. A silver mine had been discovered, or was alleged to have been discovered, and the agent
and some of his pals proposed to form a stock company, and
work it off on confiding brethren in the East. In none of the

curtailments, as consummated or contemplated, had the interests
or feelings of the Indians been consulted.

The rations doled out had shrunk to a surprising degree : one
of the shoulders of the small cattle of that region was made to
do twenty people for a week ; one cup of flour was issued every
seven days to each adult.   As the Indians themselves said, they
were compelled to eat every part of the animal, intestines, hoofs,
and horns.   Spies were set upon the agency, who followed the
wagons laden with the Indian supplies to Globe and the other
towns just named, to which they travelled by night, there to unload and transfer to the men who had purchased from the agent
or his underlings.   One of the Apaches who understood English
and Spanish was deputed to speak to the agent upon the matter.   It was the experience of Oliver Twist over again when
he asked for more.   The messenger was put in the guardhouse,
where he remained for six months, and was then released without trial or knowing for what he had been imprisoned.   In
regard to the civilian agents, the Apaches said they ran from bad
to worse, being dishonest, indifferent, tyrannical, and generally
incompetent.   Of Captain Chaffee, of the Sixth Cavalry, who
had been for a while in charge at San Carlos, the Apaches spoke
in terms of respect, saying that he was very severe in his notions,
but a just and honest man, and disposed to be harsh only with
those who persisted in making, selling, or drinking the native
intoxicant, "tizwin."   The rottenness of the San Carlos Agency
extended all the way to Washington, and infolded in its meshes
officials of high rank.   It is to the lasting credit of Hon. Carl
Schurz, then Secretary of the Interior, that when he learned of
the delinquencies of certain of his subordinates, he swung his
axe without fear or favor, and the heads of the Commissioner of
Indian Affairs, the Inspector-General of the Indian Bureau, and
the agent at San Carlos fell into the basket.

At the San Carlos Agency itself, Crook met such men as
" Cha-lipun,"   " Chimahuevi-sal,"   " Navatane,"   " Nodikun,"
" Santos,"   " Skinospozi,"   " Pedilkun,"   " Binilke,"   " Captain
Chiquito,"   " Eskiminzin,"   " Huan-klishe,"   and numbers of
others ; those who had always lived in the hills near the San
Carlos were content to live in the country, but such of the num-
ber as had been pulled away from the cool climate and pure water
of the Cibicu, Carrizo, and other cañons in the vicinity of Camp

Apache, and had seen their fields of corn tramped down at the orders of the agent, were full of grievous complaint.   The Apache-Yumas and the Apaches are an entirely different people, speaking different languages and resembling each other only in the bitter hostility with which they had waged war against the whites.   The young men of the Apache-Yuma bands who attended the conferences, were in full toilet—that is, they were naked from shoulders to waist, had their faces painted with deer's blood or mescal, their heads done up in a plaster of mud three inches thick, and pendent from the cartilage of the nose wore a ring with a fragment of nacreous shell.   General Crook's own estimate of the results of these conferences, which are entirely too long to be inserted here, is expressed in the following General Orders (Number 43), issued from his headquarters at Fort Whipple on the 5th of October, 1882.

"The commanding general, after making a thorough and exhaustive examination among the Indians of the eastern and southern part of this Territory, regrets to say that he finds among them a general feeling of distrust and want of confidence in the whites, especially the soldiery ; and also that much dissatisfaction, dangerous to the peace of the country, exists among them. Officers and soldiers serving in this department are reminded that one of the fundamental principles of the military character is justice to all—Indians as well as white men—and that a disregard of this principle is likely to bring about hostilities, and cause the death of the very persons they are sent here to protect.   In all their dealings with the Indians, officers must be careful not only to observe the strictest fidelity, but to make no promises not in their power to carry out ; all grievances arising within their jurisdiction should be redressed, so that an accumulation of them may not cause an outbreak.

"Grievances, however petty, if permitted to accumulate, will be like embers that smoulder and eventually break into flame.   When officers are applied to for the employment of force against Indians, they should thoroughly satisfy themselves of the necessity for the application, and of the legality of compliance therewith, in order that they may not, through the inexperience of others, or through their own hastiness, allow the troops under them to become the instruments of oppression.   There must be no division of responsibility in this matter ; each officer will be held to a strict accountability that his actions have been fully authorized by law and justice, and that Indians evincing a desire to enter upon a career of peace shall have no cause for complaint through hasty or injudicious acts of the military."

Crook's management of the Department of Arizona was conducted on the same lines as during his previous administration : he rode on mule-back all over it, and met and understood each and

every Indian with whom he might have to deal as friend or enemy ; he reorganized his pack-trains and the Indian scouts, put
the control of military affairs at the San Carlos under charge of
Captain Emmet Crawford, Third Cavalry, a most intelligent and
conscientious officer, encouraged the Indians to prepare for planting good crops the next spring, and made ready to meet the
Chiricahuas. These Indians, for whom a reservation had been
laid out with its southern line the boundary between the United
States and the Mexican Republic, had been dealing heavily at
the ranch of Rogers and Spence, at Sulphur Springs, where they
were able to buy all the vile whiskey they needed. In a row over
the sale of liquor both Rogers and Spence were killed, and the
Apaches, fearing punishment, fled to the mountains of Mexico—
the Sierra Madre. From that on, for six long years, the history of
the Chiricahuas was one of blood : a repetition of the long series
of massacres which, under " Cocheis," they had perpetrated in
the old days.

On several occasions a number of them returned to the San
Carlos, or pretended to do so, but the recesses of the Sierra
Madre always afforded shelter to small bands of renegades of the
type of " Ka-e-tan-ne," who despised the white man as a liar and
scorned him as a foe. The unfortunate policy adopted by the
Government towards the " Warm Springs " Apaches of New
Mexico, who were closely related to the Chiricahuas, had an un-
healthy effect upon the latter and upon all the other bands. The
" Warm Springs " Apaches were peremptorily deprived of their
little fields and driven away from their crops, half-ripened, and
ordered to tramp to the San Carlos ; when the band reached
there the fighting men had disappeared, and only decrepit warriors, little boys and girls, and old women remained. " Victorio " went on the war-path with every effective man, and fairly
deluged New Mexico and Chihuahua with blood.

General Crook felt that the Chiricahua Apache problem was a
burning shame and disgrace, inasmuch as the property and lives
not only of our own citizens but of those of a friendly nation, were
constantly menaced. He had not been at San Carlos twenty-four
hours before he had a party of Apaches out in the ranges to the
south looking for trails or signs ; this little party penetrated down
into the northern end of the Sierra Madre below Camp Price, and
saw some of the Mexican irregular troops, but found no fresh

traces of the enemy. Crook insisted upon the expulsion from the reservation of all unauthorized squatters and miners, whether appearing under the guise of Mormons or as friends of the late agents, and opposed resolutely the further curtailment of the reservation or the proposition to transfer the Apaches to the Indian Territory, having in mind the contemptible failure of the attempt to evict the Cherokees from the mountains of North Carolina, where some twenty-two hundred of them still cling to the homes of their forefathers. He also insisted upon giving to the Apaches all work which could be provided for them, and in paying for the same in currency to the individual Indians without the interposition of any middlemen or contractors in any guise.

This will explain in a word why Crook was suddenly abused so roundly in the very Territory for which he had done so much. People who were not influenced by the disappointed elements enumerated, saw that General Crook's views were eminently fair and sound, based upon the most extended experience, and not the hap-hazard ideas of a theoretical soldier. To quote from the Annual Message of Governor Tritle : " The Indians know General Crook and his methods, and respect both." Had the notion ever taken root among the Apaches that they were all to be transplanted to unknown regions, the country would have had to face the most terrible and costly war in its history. Crook did not want wars—he wanted to avert them. In a letter to United States District Attorney Zabriskie, he used the following language : " I believe that it is of far greater importance to prevent outbreaks than to attempt the difficult and sometimes hopeless task of quelling them after they do occur ; this policy can only be successful when the officers of justice fearlessly perform their duty in proceeding against the villains who fatten on the supplies intended for the use of Indians willing to lead peaceful and orderly lives. Bad as Indians often are, I have never yet seen one so demoralized that he was not an example in honor and nobility to the wretches who enrich themselves by plundering him of the little our Government appropriates for him."

To prevent any of the Indians from slipping off from the agency, they were all enrolled, made to wear tags as of yore, and compelled to submit to periodical counts occurring every few days. It was found that there were then at the San Carlos

Agency eleven hundred and twenty-eight males capable of bearing arms; this did not include the bands at or near Camp Apache or the Chiricahuas. The Apaches manifested the liveliest interest in the system of trial by jury, and it was apparent that criminals stood but a small chance of escaping punishment when arraigned before their own people. While we were at San Carlos on this occasion Captain Crawford had arrested two Apaches on the charge of making "tizwin," getting drunk, and arousing camp by firing off guns late at night. The jury was impanelled, the trial began, and the room soon filled with spectators. The prisoners attempted to prove an "alibi," and introduced witnesses to swear to the shooting having been done by other parties.

"Eskiminzin" impatiently arose to his feet and interrupted the proceedings: "That man is not telling the truth."

"Tell 'Eskiminzin' to sit down and keep quiet," ordered Captain Crawford; "he must not interrupt the proceedings of the court."

A few moments after, in looking down the long list of witnesses, it was discovered that "Eskiminzin" was present as a witness, and he was called upon to testify.

"Tell the Captain," said the indignant chief, "that I have nothing to say. I do not understand these white men; they let all kinds of people talk at a trial, and would just as soon listen to the words of a liar as those of a man telling the truth. Why, when I began to tell him that So-and-so was lying, he made me sit down and keep my mouth shut, but So-and-so went on talking, and every word he said was put down on paper."

It took some time to explain to "Eskiminzin" the intricacies of our laws of evidence, and to pacify him enough to induce him to give his version of the facts.

Our quarters while at San Carlos were the adobe building erected as a "school-house," at a cost to the Government of forty thousand dollars, but occupied by the late agent as a residence. It had been erected at a net cost of something between eight and nine thousand dollars, or at least I would contract to duplicate it for that and expect to make some money in the transaction besides. The walls were covered over with charcoal scrawls of Apache gods, drawn by irreverent youngsters, and the appearance of the place did not in the remotest sense suggest the habitation of the Muses.

General Crook returned late in the fall of 1882 to his headquarters at Fort Whipple, and awaited the inevitable irruption of
the Chiricahua Apaches from their stronghold in the Sierra
Madre in Mexico. Large detachments of Indian scouts, under
competent officers, were kept patrolling the boundary in the
vicinity of Cloverdale and other exposed points, and small garrisons were in readiness to take the field from Fort Bowie and
other stations. The completion of the Southern Pacific and the
Atchison, Topeka, and Santa Fé systems, and the partial completion of the Atlantic and Pacific Railroad, had wrought certain
changes in the condition of affairs, to which reference may be
made. In a military sense they had all been a great benefit by
rendering the transportation of troops and supplies a matter of
most agreeable surprise to those who still remembered the creaking
ox-teams and prairie schooners, which formerly hauled all stores
from the banks of the distant Missouri ; in a social sense they
had been the means of introducing immigration, some of which
was none too good, as is always the case with the earlier days of
railroad construction on the frontier.

The mining towns like Tombstone, then experiencing a
"boom," had been increased by more than a fair quota of gamblers, roughs, and desperate adventurers of all classes. Cowboys
and horse thieves flooded the southeastern corner of the Territory and the southwestern corner of the next Territory—New
Mexico ; with Cloverdale, in southwestern New Mexico, as a
headquarters, they bade defiance to the law and ran things with
a high hand, and made many people sigh for the better days
when only red-skinned savages intimidated the settlements.
The town of Phœnix had arisen in the valley of the Salt River,
along the lines of prehistoric irrigating ditches, marking the
presence of considerable population, and suggesting to Judge
Hayden and others who first laid it out the propriety of bestow-
ing the name it now bears. The new population were both intelligent and enterprising : under the superintendence of the Hon.
Clark Churchill they had excavated great irrigating canals,
and begun the planting of semi-tropical fruits, which has proved
unusually remunerative, and built up the community so that it
has for years been able to care for itself against any hostile
attacks that might be threatened. Prescott, being off the direct
line of railroad (with which, however, it has since been connected

by a branch), had not responded so promptly to the new condition of affairs, but its growth had been steady, and its population
had not been burdened with the same class of loafers who for so
long a time held high carnival in Tombstone, Deming, and elsewhere. Prescott had always boasted of its intelligent, bright
family society—thoroughly American in the best sense—and the
boast was still true.

There is no point in the southwestern country so well adapted,
none that can compare with Prescott as the site of a large Indian
school ; and when the time comes, as I am certain it is to come,
when we shall recognize the absurdity of educating a few Indian
boys and then returning them back to their tribes, in which they
can exert no influence, but can excite only jealousy on account
of their superior attainments—when by a slight increase of appropriations, the whole race of Indian boys and girls could be lifted
from savagery into the path to a better life—Prescott will
become the site of such a school. It is education which is to be
the main lever in this elevation, but it is wholesale education, not
retail. This phase of the case impressed itself upon the early
settlers in Canada, who provided most liberally for the training
of, comparatively speaking, great numbers of the Algonquin youth
of both sexes. In Mexico was erected the first school for the
education of the native American—the college at Patzcuaro—
built before foot of Puritan had touched the rock of Plymouth.

Prescott possesses the advantages of being the centre of a district inhabited by numbers of tribes whose children could be
educated so near their own homes that parents would feel easier in
regard to them, and yet the youngsters would be far removed from
tribal influences and in the midst of a thoroughly progressive
American community. The climate cannot be excelled anywhere ;
the water is as good as can be found ; and the scenery—of granite
peaks, grassy meads, balmy pine forests, and placid streamlets—
cannot well be surpassed. The post of Fort Whipple could be
transferred to the Interior Department, and there would be found
ready to hand the houses for teachers, the school-rooms, dormi-
tories, refectories, blacksmith-shops, wagoners' shops, saddlers'
shops, stables, granaries, and other buildings readily adaptable to
the purposes of instruction in various handicrafts. Five hundred
children, equally divided as to sex, could be selected from the
great tribes of the Navajos, Apaches, Hualpais, Mojaves, Yu-

mas, Pimas, and Maricopas. The cost of living is very moderate, and all supplies could be brought in on the branch railroad, while the absence of excitement incident to communities established at railroad centres or on through lines will be manifest upon a moment's reflection. It would require careful, intelligent, absolutely honest administration, to make it a success ; it should be some such school as I have seen conducted by the Congregationalists and Presbyterians among the Santee Sioux, under the superintendence of Rev. Alfred Riggs, or by the Friends among the Cherokees in North Carolina, under Mr. Spray, where the children are instructed in the rudiments of Christian morality, made to understand that labor is most honorable, that the saddler, the carpenter, or blacksmith must be a gentleman and come to the supper-table with clean face and combed hair, and that the new life is in every respect the better life.

But if it is to be the fraud upon the confiding tax-payers that the schools at Fort Defiance (Navajo Agency), Zuni, San Carlos, and other places that I personally examined have been, money would be saved by not establishing it at all. The agent of the Navajos reported in 1880 that his " school" would accommodate eighty children. I should dislike to imprison eight dogs that I loved in the dingy hole that he called a "school "—but then the agent had a pull at Washington, being the brother-in-law of a " statesman,"; and I had better not say too much ; and the school-master, although an epileptic idiot, had been sent out as the representative of the family influence of another " statesman," so I will not say more about him. The Indians to be instructed in the school whose establishment is proposed at Prescott, Arizona, should be trained in the line of their " atavism," if I may borrow a word from the medical dictionary—that is, they should be trained in the line of their inherited proclivities and tendencies. Their forefathers for generations— ever since the time of the work among them of the Franciscan missionaries—have been a pastoral people, raising great flocks of sheep, clipping, carding, and spinning the wool, weaving the most beautiful of rugs and blankets and sashes, and selling them at a profit to admiring American travellers. They have been saddle-makers, basket-makers, silver-smiths, and—as in the case of the Mojaves, Pimas, and Maricopas—potters and mat-makers. In such trades, preferentially, they should be instructed, and by the introduction of a few Lamb knitting machines, they could be taught to make stockings for the Southwestern market out of the wool raised by their own families, and thus help support the institution and open a better market for the products of their own tribe. They could be taught to tan the skins of their own flocks and herds, and to make shoes and saddles of the result. But all this must be put down as "whimsical," because there is no money in it "for the boys." The great principle of American politics, regardless of party lines, is that "the boys" must be taken care of at all times and in all places.

Tucson had changed the most appreciably of any town in the Southwest ; American energy and American capital had effected a wonderful transformation : the old garrison was gone ; the railroad had arrived ; where Jack Long and his pack-train in the old times had merrily meandered, now puffed the locomotive ; Muñoz's corral had been displaced by a round-house, and Muñoz himself by a one-lunged invalid from Boston ; the Yankees had almost transformed the face of nature ; the exquisite architectural gem of San Xavier del Bac still remained, but the "Shoo Fly" restaurant had disappeared, and in its place the town boasted with very good reason of the "San Xavier" Hotel, one of the best coming within my experience as a traveller. American enterprise had moved to the front, and the Castilian with his "marromas" and "bailes" and saints' days and "funcciones" had fallen to the rear ; telephones and electric lights and Pullman cars had scared away the plodding burro and the creaking "carreta"; it was even impossible to get a meal cooked in the Mexican style of Mexican viands ; our dreams had faded ; the chariot of Cinderella had changed back into a pumpkin, and Sancho was no longer governor.

"I tell you, Cap," said my old friend, Charlie Hopkins, "them railroads's playin' hob with th' country, 'n a feller's got to hustle hisself now in Tucson to get a meal of frijoles or enchiladas ; this yere new-fangled grub doan' suit me 'n I reckon I'll pack mee grip 'n lite out fur Sonora."

Saddest of all, the old-timers were thinning out, or if not dead were living under a Pharaoh who knew not Joseph ; the Postons, Ourys, Bradys, Mansfields, Veils, Rosses, Montgomerys, Duncans, Drachmans, Handys, and others were unappreciated by the incoming tide of "tenderfeet," who knew nothing of the perils and tribulations of life in Arizona and New Mexico before Crook's genius and valor had redeemed them from the clutch of the savage. On the Colorado River Captain Jack Mellon still plied the good ship "Cocopah," and Dan O'Leary still dealt out to expectant listeners tales of the terrible days when he "fit" with Crook; within sight of the "Wickytywiz," Charlie Spencer still lived among his Hualpai kinsmen, not much the worse for the severe wounds received while a scout; the old Hellings mill on the Salt River, once the scene of open-handed hospitality to all travellers, still existed under changed ownership, and the Arnolds, Ehls, Bowers, Bangharts, and other ranchmen of northern Arizona were still in place; but the mill of Don José Peirson no longer ground its toll by the current of the San Ignacio; the Samaniegos, Suasteguis, Borquis, Ferreras, and other Spanish families had withdrawn to Sonora; and, oldest survival of all, "Uncle Lew Johnson" was living in seclusion with the family of Charlie Hopkins on the Salumay on the slopes of the Sierra Ancha. It would pay some enterprising man to go to Arizona to interview this old veteran, who first entered Arizona with the earliest band of trappers; who was one of the party led by Pauline Weaver; who knew Kit Carson intimately; who could recall the days when Taos, New Mexico, was the metropolis of fashion and commerce for the whole Southwest, and the man who had gone as far east as St. Louis was looked upon as a traveller whose recitals merited the closest attention of the whole camp.

CHAPTER XXVII.

WHEN the Chiricahuas did break through into Arizona in
the early days of March, 1883, they numbered twenty-
six, and were under the command of " Chato," a young chief of
great intelligence and especial daring. They committed great
outrages and marked their line of travel with fire and blood ; by
stealing horses from every ranch they were enabled to cover not
less than seventy-five miles a day, and by their complete familiarity with the country were able to dodge the troops and citizens
sent in pursuit. One of their number was killed in a fight at
the " Charcoal Camp," in the Whetstone Mountains, and another—" Panayotishn," called " Peaches " by the soldiers—surrendered at San Carlos and offered his services to the military to
lead them against the Chiricahuas. He was not a Chiricahua himself, but a member of the White Mountain Apaches and married
to a Chiricahua squaw, and obliged to accompany the Chiricahuas when they last left the agency.

Crook determined to take up the trail left by the Chiricahuas
and follow it back to their stronghold in the Sierra Madre, and
surprise them or their families when least expected. " Peaches "
assured him that the plan was perfectly feasible, and asked per-

mission to go with the column. By the terms of the convention then existing between Mexico and the United States, the armed forces of either country could, when in pursuit of hostile Indians, cross the frontier and continue pursuit until met by troops of the country into whose territory the trail led, though this convention applied only to desert portions of territory. Crook visited Guaymas, Hermosillo (in Sonora), and Chihuahua, the capital of the Mexican State of the same name, where he conferred with Generals Topete, Bernardo Reyes, and Carbo, of the Mexican Army, Governor Torres, of Sonora, and Mayor Zubiran, of Chihuahua, by all of whom he was received most hospitably and encouraged in his purposes.

He organized a small force of one hundred and ninety-three Apache scouts and one small company of the Sixth Cavalry, commanded by Major Chaffee and Lieutenant Frank West. The scouts were commanded by Captain Emmet Crawford, Third Cavalry ; Lieutenant Gatewood, Sixth Cavalry ; Lieutenant W. W. Forsyth, Sixth Cavalry ; Lieutenant Mackay, Third Cavalry, with Surgeon Andrews as medical officer. Crook took command in person, having with him Captain John G. Bourke, Third Cavalry, and Lieutenant G. J. Febiger, Engineer Corps, as aides-de-camp ; Archie MacIntosh and Al Seiber as chiefs of scouts ; Mickey Free, Severiano, and Sam Bowman as interpreters. The expedition was remarkably successful : under the guidance of "Peaches," "To-klanni," "Alchise," and other natives, it made its way down to the head waters of the Yaqui River, more than two hundred miles south of the international boundary, into the unknown recesses of the Sierra Madre, and there surprised and captured, after a brief but decisive fight, the stronghold of the Chiricahuas, who were almost all absent raiding upon the hapless Mexican hamlets exposed to their fury. As fast as the warriors and squaws came home, they were apprehended and put under charge of the scouts.

This was one of the boldest and most successful strokes ever achieved by an officer of the United States Army : every man, woman, and child of the Chiricahuas was returned to the San Carlos Agency and put to work. They had the usual story to tell of ill-treatment, broken pledges, starvation, and other incidentals, but the reader has perhaps had enough of that kind of narrative. The last straw which drove them out from the agency was the attempt to arrest one of their young men for some trivial offence. The Chiricahuas found no fault with the arrest in itself, but were incensed at the high-handed manner in which the chief of police had attempted to carry it out : the young buck started to run away and did not halt when summoned to do so by the chief of police, but kept on in his retreat among a crowd of children and squaws. The chief of police then fired, and, his aim not being good, killed one of the squaws ; for this he apologized, but the Chiricahuas got it into their heads that he ought not to have fired in the first place ; they dissembled their resentment for a few days until they had caught the chief of police, killed him, cut off his head, played a game of football with it, and started for the Mexican boundary in high glee.

Crook's expedition passed down through the hamlets of Huachinera, Basaraca, and Bavispe, Sonora, where occurred the terrible earthquake of the next year. Mexican eye-witnesses asserted that the two or three ranges of mountains which at that point form the Sierra Madre played hide-and-seek with each other, one range rising and the others falling. The description, which had all the stamp of truth, recalled the words of the Old Testament : " What ailed thee, O sea, that thou didst flee ? And thou, O Jordan, that thou wast turned back ? Ye mountains, that ye skipped like rams ; and ye hills, like the lambs of the flock ?"

General Crook was about this time made the target of every sort of malignant and mendacious assault by the interests which he had antagonized. The telegraph wires were loaded with false reports of outrages, attacks, and massacres which had never occurred ; these reports were scattered broadcast with the intention and in the hope that they might do him injury. Crook made no reply to these scurrilous attempts at defamation, knowing that duty well performed will in the end secure the recognition and approval of all fair-minded people, the only ones whose recognition and approval are worth having. But he did order the most complete investigation to be made of each and every report, and in each and every case the utter recklessness of the authors of these lies was made manifest. Only one example need be given—the so-called " Buckhorn Basin Massacre," in which was presented a most circumstantial and detailed narrative of the surrounding and killing by a raiding party of Apaches of a small band of miners, who were forced to seek safety in a cave from which they fought to the death. This story was investigated by Major William C. Rafferty, Sixth Cavalry, who found no massacre, no Indians, no miners, no cave, nothing but a Buckhorn basin.

There was a small set of persons who took pleasure in disseminating such rumors, the motive of some being sensationalism merely, that of others malice or a desire to induce the bringing in of more troops from whose movements and needs they might make money. Such people did not reflect, or did not care, that the last result of this conduct, if persisted in, would be to deter capital from seeking investment in a region which did not require the gilding of refined gold or the painting of the lily to make it appear the Temple of Horrors ; surely, enough blood had been shed in Arizona to make the pages of her history red for years to come, without inventing additional enormities to scare away the immigration which her mines and forests, her cattle pasturage and her fruit-bearing oases, might well attract.

It was reported that the Chiricahua prisoners had been allowed to drive across the boundary herds of cattle captured from the Mexicans ; for this there was not the slightest foundation. When the last of the Chiricahuas, the remnant of "Ju's" band, which had been living nearly two hundred miles south of "Geronimo's" people in the Sierra Madre, arrived at the international boundary, a swarm of claimants made demand for all the cattle with them. Each cow had, it would seem, not less than ten owners, and as in the Southwest the custom was to put on the brand of the purchaser as well as the vent brand of the seller, each animal down there was covered from brisket to rump with more or less plainly discernible marks of ownership. General Crook knew that there must be a considerable percentage of perjury in all this mass of affidavits, and wisely decided that the cattle should be driven up to the San Carlos Agency, and there herded under guard in the best obtainable pasturage until fat enough to be sold to the best advantage. The brand of each of the cattle, probable age, name of purchaser, amount realized, and other items of value, were preserved, and copies of them are to be seen in my note-books of that date. The moneys realized from the sale were forwarded through the official military channels to Washington, thence to be sent through the ordinary course of diplomatic correspondence to the Government of Mexico, which would naturally be more competent to determine the validity of claims and make the most sensible distribution.

There were other parties in Arizona who disgraced the Territory by proposing to murder the Apaches on the San Carlos, who had sent their sons to the front to aid the whites in the search for the hostiles and their capture or destruction. These men organized themselves into a company of military, remembered in the Territory as the "Tombstone Toughs," and marched upon the San Carlos with the loudly-heralded determination to "clean out" all in sight. They represented all the rum-poisoned bummers of the San Pedro Valley, and no community was more earnest in its appeals to them to stay in the field until the last armed foe expired than was Tombstone, the town from which they had started; never before had Tombstone enjoyed such an era of peace and quiet, and her citizens appreciated the importance of keeping the "Toughs" in the field as long as possible. The commanding officer of the "Toughs" was a much better man than the gang who staggered along on the trail behind him: he kept the best saloon in Tombstone, and was a candidate for political honors. When last I heard of him, some six years since, he was keeping a saloon in San Francisco.

All that the "Tombstone Toughs" did in the way of war was to fire upon one old Indian, a decrepit member of "Eskiminzin's" band, which had been living at peace on the lower San Pedro ever since permission had been granted them to do so by General Howard; they were supporting themselves by farming and stock-raising, and were never accused of doing harm to any one all the time they remained in that place. White settlers lived all around them with whom their relations were most friendly. The "Toughs" fired at this old man and then ran away, leaving the white women of the settlements, whose husbands were nearly all absent from home, to bear the brunt of vengeance. I have before me the extract from the *Citizen* of Tucson, which describes this flight of the valiant "Toughs": "leaving the settlers to fight it out with the Indians and suffer for the rash acts of these senseless cowards, who sought to kill a few peaceable Indians, and thereby gain a little cheap notoriety, which cannot result otherwise than disastrously to the settlers in that vicinity." "The attack of the Rangers was shameful, cowardly, and foolish. They should be taken care of at once, and punished according to the crime they have committed." It is only just that the above should be inserted as a proof that there are many intelligent, fair-minded people on the frontier, who deprecate and discountenance anything like treachery towards Indians who are peaceably disposed.

By the terms of the conference entered into between the Secretary of the Interior, the Commissioner of Indian Affairs, the Secretary of War, and Brigadier-General Crook, on the 7th of July, 1883, it was stipulated that "the Apache Indians recently captured, and all such as may hereafter be captured or may surrender, shall be kept under the control of the War Department at such points on the San Carlos Reservation as may be determined by the War Department, but not at the agency without the consent of the Indian agent—to be fed and cared for by the War Department until further orders. . . . The War Department shall be intrusted with the entire police control of all the Indians on the San Carlos Reservation. The War Department shall protect the Indian agent in the discharge of his duties as agent, which shall include the ordinary duties of an Indian agent and remain as heretofore except as to keeping peace, administering justice, and punishing refractory Indians, all of which shall be done by the War Department."

In accordance with the terms of the above conference, five hundred and twelve of the Chiricahua Apaches—being the last man, woman, and child of the entire band—were taken to the country close to Camp Apache, near the head-waters of the Turkey Creek, where, as well as on a part of the White River, they were set to work upon small farms. Peace reigned in Arizona, and for two years her record of deaths by violence, at the hands of red men at least, would compare with the best record to be shown by any State in the East; in other words, there were no such deaths and no assaults. That Apaches will work may be shown by the subjoined extracts from the official reports, beginning with that of 1883, just one year after the re-assignment of General Crook to the command : " The increase of cultivation this year over last I believe has been tenfold. The Indians during the past year have raised a large amount of barley, which they have disposed of, the largest part of it being sold to the Government for the use of the animals in the public service here. Some has been sold to the Indian trader, and quite an amount to freighters passing through between Wilcox and Globe. Their corn crop is large ; I think, after reserving what will be needed for their own consumption and seed for next year, they will have some for sale. The only market they have for their produce is from freighters, the trader, and the Q. M. Department here. They are being encouraged to store their corn away and use it for meal ; for this purpose there should be a grist-mill here and one at Fort Apache. They have cut and turned in during the year to the Q. M. Department and at the agency about four hundred tons of hay cut with knives and three hundred cords of wood, for which they have been paid a liberal price." Attached to the same report was the following : " Statement showing the amount of produce raised by the Apache Indians on the White Mountain Indian Reservation during the year 1883 : 2,625,000 lbs. of corn, 180,000 lbs. of beans, 135,000 lbs. of potatoes, 12,600 lbs. of wheat, 200,000 lbs. of barley, 100,000 pumpkins, 20,000 watermelons, 10,000 muskmelons, 10,000 cantelopes. Small patches of cabbage, onions, cucumbers, and lettuce have been raised. (Signed) EMMET CRAWFORD, *Captain Third Cavalry*, Commanding."

I have seen Indian bucks carrying on their backs great bundles of hay cut with knives, which they sold in the town of Globe to the stable owners and keepers of horses.

During that winter General Crook wrote the following letter, which expresses his views on the subject of giving the franchise to Indians ; it was dated January 5, 1885, and was addressed to Mr. Herbert Welsh, Secretary of the Indian Rights Association, Philadelphia :

"MY DEAR MR. WELSH :

"The law prohibiting the sale of liquor to Indians is practically a dead letter. Indians who so desire can to-day obtain from unprincipled whites and others all the vile whiskey for which they can pay cash, which is no more and no less than the Indian as a citizen could purchase. The proposition I make on behalf of the Indian is, that he is at this moment capable, with very little instruction, of exercising every manly right ; he doesn't need to have so much guardianship as so many people would have us believe ; what he does need is protection under the law ; the privilege of suing in the courts, which privilege must be founded upon the franchise to be of the slightest value.

"If with the new prerogatives, individual Indians continue to use alcoholic stimulants, we must expect to see them rise or fall socially as do white men under similar circumstances. For my own part, I question very much whether we should not find the Indians who would then be drunkards to be the very same ones who under present surroundings experience no difficulty whatever in gratifying this cursed appetite. The great majority of Indians are wise enough to recognize the fact that liquor is the worst foe to their advancement. Complaints have frequently been made by them to me that well-known parties had maintained this illicit traffic with members of their tribe, but no check could be imposed or punishment secured for the very good reason that Indian testimony carries no weight whatever with a white jury. Now by arming the red men with the franchise, we remove this impediment, and provide a cure for the very evil which seems to excite so much apprehension; besides this, we would open a greater field of industrial development. The majority of the Indians whom I have met are perfectly willing to work for their white neighbors, to whom they can make themselves serviceable in many offices, such as teaming, herding, chopping wood, cutting hay, and harvesting; and for such labor there is at nearly all times a corresponding demand at reasonable wages. Unfortunately, there are many unscrupulous characters to be found near all reservations who don't hesitate after employing Indians to defraud them of the full amount agreed upon. Several such instances have been brought to my notice during the present year, but there was no help for the Indian, who could not bring suit in the courts. Every such swindle is a discouragement both to the Indian most directly concerned and to a large circle of interested friends, who naturally prefer the relations of idleness to work which brings no remuneration.

" Our object should be to get as much voluntary labor from the Indian as possible. Every dollar honestly gained by hard work is so much subtracted from the hostile element and added to that which is laboring for peace and civilization. In conclusion, I wish to say that the American Indian is the intellectual peer of most, if not all, the various nationalities we have assimilated to our laws, customs, and language. He is fully able to protect himself if the ballot be given, and the courts of law not closed against him. If our aim be to remove the aborigine from a state of servile dependence, we cannot begin in a better or more practical way than by making him think well of himself, to force upon him the knowledge that he is part and parcel of the nation, clothed with all its political privileges, entitled to share in all its benefits. Our present treatment degrades him in his own eyes, by making evident the difference between his own condition and that of those about him. To sum up, my panacea for the Indian trouble is to make the Indian self-supporting, a condition which can never be attained, in my opinion, so long as the privileges which have made labor honorable, respectable, and able to defend itself, be withheld from him."

Chancellor Kent has well said that unity increases the efficiency, by increasing the responsibility, of the executive. This rule applies to every department of life. The dual administration of the Apache reservation, by the Departments of War and the Interior, did not succeed so well as was at first expected : there were constant misunderstandings, much friction, with complaints and recriminations. Captain Crawford had won in a remarkable degree the esteem and confidence of the Indians upon the reservation, who looked up to him as a faithful mentor and friend. They complained that certain cows which had been promised them were inferior in quality, old and past the age for breeding, and not equal to the number promised. This complaint was forwarded through the routine channels to Washington, and the Interior Department ordered out an inspector who reported every thing serene at the agency and on the reservation. The report did not satisfy either Indians or whites, but upon receiving the report of its inspecting officer the Interior Department requested that Captain Crawford be relieved, coupling the request with remarks which Crawford took to be a reflection upon his character; he thereupon demanded and was accorded by his military superiors a court of inquiry, which was composed of Major Biddle, Sixth Cavalry, Major Purington, Third Cavalry, Captain Dougherty, First Infantry, as members, and First Lieutenant George S. Anderson, Sixth Cavalry, as Recorder. This court, all of whose members were officers of considerable experience in the Indian country, and one of whom (Dougherty) had been in charge of one of the largest Sioux reservations in Dakota, set about its work with thoroughness, examined all witnesses and amassed a quantity of testimony in which it was shown that the Apaches had good ground of complaint both in the character and in the number of cows supplied them: they were in many cases old and unserviceable, and instead of there being one thousand, there were scarcely six hundred, the missing cattle being covered by what was termed a "due bill," made out by the contractor, agreeing to drive in the missing ones upon demand.

There was only one serious case of disturbance among the Chiricahua Apaches: the young chief "Ka-e-ten-na" became restless under the restraints of the reservation, and sighed to return to the wild freedom of the Sierra Madre. He was closely watched, and all that he did was reported to headquarters by the Indian scouts. General Crook was absent at the time, by direction of the Secretary of War, delivering the address to the graduating class at the Military Academy at West Point; but Major Barber, Adjutant-General, carried out Crook's methods, and the surly young man was arrested by his own people, tried by his own people, and sentenced to be confined in some place until he learned sense. He was sent to Alcatraz Island, in San Francisco Harbor, where he remained twelve months, the greater part of the time being allowed to see the sights of the city and to become saturated with an idea of the white man's power in numbers, wealth, machinery, and other resources. He became a great friend, and rendered great help, to General Crook later on.

Under date of January 20, 1885, General Crook wrote as follows to his military superiors :

" In the event that the views of the Indian agent are approved, I respectfully request that matters referred to in the agreement be relegated to the control of the Interior Department, and that I be relieved from all the responsibilities therein imposed."

In forwarding the above communication to Washington, General John Pope, commanding the Military Division of the Pacific, indorsed the following views :

" Respectfully forwarded to the adjutant-general of the army. It is needless to reiterate what the authorities in Washington and everybody in this region know perfectly well now. General Crook's management of these Indians has been marked by unusual and surprising success, and if matters are left in his charge a very few years longer all fears of Indian trouble in Arizona may be dismissed.

" One of the difficulties (and the principal one) he has met with is the constant discord between the civilian Indian agents and the military. It is not even hoped that a stop may be put to such controversies so long as there is a joint jurisdiction over the Arizona Indians. It is not human nature that such an anomalous relation should escape such troubles, but in view of General Crook's superior ability and experience, and the great success he has met with, I must emphatically recommend that, instead of relieving him as he suggests, the entire control of the Indians be turned over to him.

"(Signed) JOHN POPE, *Major-General.*"

For people interested in the question of Indian management and of Indian pacification, no more important document can be presented than General Crook's Annual Report for the year 1885. As this document will not be accessible to every reader, I will take the liberty of making a number of extracts from it, at the same time warning the student that nothing will compensate him for a failure to peruse the complete report.

In answer to the letter forwarded with an indorsement by Major-General Pope, given above, General Crook received a telegram dated Washington, February 14, 1885, which directed him, pending conferences between the Interior and War Departments with a view of harmonizing matters, "not to interfere with farming operations of Indians who are not considered as prisoners."

General Crook replied in these terms:

"I have the honor to say that the agreement of July 7, 1883, by which 'the War Department was intrusted with the entire police control of all the Indians on the San Carlos reservation,' was entered into upon my own expressed willingness to be personally responsible for the good conduct of all the Indians there congregated. My understanding then was, and still is, that I should put them to work and set them to raising corn instead of scalps. This right I have exercised for two years without a word of complaint from any source. During all this time not a single depredation of any kind has been committed. The whole country has looked to me individually for the preservation of order among the Apaches, and the prevention of the outrages from which the southwest frontier has suffered for so many years.

"In pursuance of this understanding, the Chiricahuas, although nominally prisoners, have been to a great extent scattered over the reservation and placed upon farms, the object being to quietly and gradually effect a tribal disintegration and lead them out from a life of vagabondage to one of peace and self-maintenance. They have ramified among the other Apaches to such an extent that it is impossible to exercise jurisdiction over them without exercising it over the others as well. At the same time trusted Indians of the peaceful bands are better enabled to keep the scattered Chiricahuas under constant surveillance, while the incentive to industry and good conduct which the material prosperity of the settled Apaches brings to the notice of the Chiricahuas is so palpable that it is hardly worth while to allude to it. As this right of control has now been withdrawn from me, I must respectfully decline to be any longer held responsible for the behavior of any of the Indians on that reservation. Further, I regret being compelled to say that in refusing to relieve me from this responsibility (as requested in my letter of January 20th), and at the same time taking from me the power by which these dangerous Indians have been controlled and managed and compelled to engage in industrial pursuits, the War Department destroys my influence and does an injustice to me and the service which I represent."

The indorsement of Major-General John Pope, the commander of the military division, was even more emphatic than the preceding one had been, but for reasons of brevity it is omitted excepting these words.

"If General Crook's authority over the Indians at San Carlos be curtailed or modified in any way, there are certain to follow very serious results, if not a renewal of Indian wars and depredations in Arizona."

These papers in due course of time were referred by the War to the Interior Department, in a communication the terminal paragraph of which reads as follows, under date of March 28, 1885 :

" I submit for your consideration whether it is not desirable and advisable in the public interests, that the entire control of these Indians be placed under the charge of General Crook, with full authority to prescribe and enforce such regulations for their management as in his judgment may be proper, independently of the duties of the civil agents, and upon this question this Department will appreciate an early expression of your views.

"(Signed) WILLIAM C. ENDICOTT, *Secretary of War.*"

One of the principal causes of trouble was the disinclination of the agent to permit the Apaches to excavate and blast an irrigating ditch, which had been levelled and staked out for them by Lieutenant Thomas Dugan, Third Cavalry, one of Captain Crawford's assistants, the others being Parker, West, and Britton Davis of the Third Cavalry, Elliott of the Fourth Cavalry, and Strother of the First Infantry. Captain Crawford, feeling that his usefulness had gone, applied to be relieved from his duties at the San Carlos and allowed to rejoin his regiment, which application was granted, and his place was taken by Captain Pierce, of the First Infantry, who was also clothed with the powers of the civil agent.

It was too late. The Chiricahuas had perceived that harmony did not exist between the officials of the Government, and they had become restless, suspicious, and desirous of resuming their old career. A small number of them determined to get back to the Sierra Madre at all hazards, but more than three-fourths concluded to remain. On the 17th of May, 1885, one hundred and twenty-four Chiricahuas, of all ages and both sexes, under the command of " Geronimo " and " Nachez," the two chiefs who had been most energetic in their farm work, broke out from the reservation, but the other three-fourths listened to the counsels of " Chato," who was unfriendly to " Geronimo " and adhered to the cause of the white man. It has never been ascertained for what special reason, real or assigned, the exodus was made. It is known that for several days and nights before leaving, " Geronimo " and " Nachez," with some of their immediate followers, had been indulging in a prolonged debauch upon the " tizwin " of the tribe, and it is supposed that fearing the punishment which was always meted out to those caught perpetuating the use of this debasing intoxicant, they in a drunken frenzy sallied out for the Sierra Madre. Lieutenant Britton Davis, Third Cavalry, under whose control the Chiricahuas were, telegraphed at once to General Crook, but the wires were working badly and the message was never delivered. Had the message reached Crook it is not likely that any trouble would have occurred, as he would have arranged the whole business in a moment. To quote his own words as given in the very report under discussion :

"It should not be expected that an Indian who has lived as a barbarian all his life will become an angel the moment he comes on a reservation and promises to behave himself, or that he has that strict sense of honor which a person should have who has had the advantage of civilization all his life, and the benefit of a moral training and character which has been transmitted to him through a long line of ancestors. It requires constant watching and knowledge of their character to keep them from going wrong. They are children in ignorance, not in innocence. I do not wish to be understood as in the least palliating their crimes, but I wish to say a word to stem the torrent of invective and abuse which has almost universally been indulged in against the whole Apache race. This is not strange on the frontier from a certain class of vampires who prey on the misfortunes of their fellow-men, and who live best and easiest in time of Indian troubles. With them peace kills the goose that lays the golden egg. Greed and avarice on the part of the whites —in other words, the almighty dollar—is at the bottom of nine-tenths of all our Indian trouble."

CHAPTER XXVIII.

TO show that Apaches will work under anything like proper encouragement, the reader has only to peruse these extracts from the annual report of Captain F. E. Pierce, who succeeded Captain Emmet Crawford :

" They have about eleven hundred acres under cultivation, and have raised about 700,000 lbs. of barley and an equal amount of corn. They have delivered to the Post Quartermaster here 60,000 lbs. of barley and 60,000 lbs. to the agency, have hauled 66,0 0 lbs. to Thomas and about 180,000 lbs. to Globe, and still have about 330,000 lbs. on hand. Since they have been hauling barley to Thomas and Globe, however, where they receive fair prices, they feel much better. It gives them an opportunity to get out and mingle with people of the world, and get an idea of the manner of transacting business and a chance to make purchases at considerably less rates than if they bought of the Indian traders at San Carlos. The people at Globe are particularly kind to them, and, so far as I can learn, deal justly with them, and the more respectable ones will not permit the unprincipled to impose upon them or maltreat them in any way. The Indians also conduct themselves properly, and all citizens with whom I have conversed speak very highly of their conduct while in Globe. About a dozen are now regularly employed there at various kinds of work ; and they are encouraged as much as possible to seek work with citizens, as they thereby learn much that will be of benefit to them in the future. Shortly after the Chiricahua outbreak, word was sent to the head of each band that General Crook wanted two hundred more scouts to take the field, and all who wished to go were invited to appear here next morning. It is difficult to say how many reported, but almost every able-bodied man came. It was difficult to tell which ones to take when all were so eager to go. But a body of as fine men was selected as could well be secured in any country. They repeatedly told me they meant fight ; that they intended to do the best they could, and reports from the field show that they have made good their promises. Sixteen hundred White Mountain Indians have been entirely self-sustaining for nearly three years."

The Indians at the White Mountains, according to the official reports, were doing remarkably well.

"At this date there have been 700,000 pounds of hay and 65,000 pounds of barley purchased by the Quartermaster. Of course, the amount of hay which will yet be furnished by them will be regulated by the amount required, which will be in all about 1,800,000 pounds. As near as I can judge, the total yield of barley will be about 80,000 pounds, or about double the quantity produced last year. If no misfortune happens the crops, the yield of corn for this year should fully reach 3,500,000 pounds, including that retained by the Indians for their own consumption and for seed.

"Cantelopes, watermelons, muskmelons, beans, and pumpkins are raised by them to a considerable extent, but only for their own consumption, there being no market for this class of produce.

"A few of the Indians—principally Chiricahuas—are delivering wood on the contract at the post of Fort Apache. I have no doubt that more would engage in it if it were not for the fact that the White Mountain Apaches have no wagons for hauling it."

It would take many more pages than I care to devote to the subject to properly describe the awful consequences of the official blunder, which in this case was certainly worse than a crime, shown in the bickerings and jealousies between the representatives of the War and Interior Departments, which culminated in the " Geronimo " outbreak of May, 1885. Those of my readers who have followed this recital need no assurances that the country was as rough as rocks and ravines, deep cañons and mountain streams, could make it ; neither do they need to be assured that the trail of the retreating Chiricahuas was reddened with the blood of the innocent and unsuspecting settlers, or that the pursuit made by the troops was energetic, untiring, and, although often baffled, finally successful. No more arduous and faithful work was ever done by any military commands than was performed by those of Emmet Crawford, Lieutenant Britton Davis, Frank L. Bennett, Lieutenant M. W. Day, Surgeon Bermingham, and Major Wirt Davis in tracking the scattered fragments of the " Geronimo " party over rocks and across country soaked with the heavy rains of summer which obliterated trails as fast as made. The work done by " Chato " and the Chiricahuas who had remained on the reservation was of an inestimable value, and was fittingly recognized by General Crook, Captain Crawford, and the other officers in command of them.

Thirty-nine white people were killed in New Mexico and thirty four in Arizona, as established in official reports ; in addition to these there were numbers of friendly Apaches killed by the rene- gades, notably in the raid made by the latter during the month of November, 1885, to the villages near Camp Apache, when they killed twelve of the friendlies and carried off six women and chil- dren captive. The White Mountain Apaches killed one of the hostile Chiricahuas and cut off his head. On the 23d of June, 1885, one of the hostile Chiricahua women was killed and fifteen women and children captured in an engagement in the Bavispe Mountains, northeast of Opata (Sonora, Mexico), by Chiricahua Apache scouts under command of Captain Crawford ; these pris- oners reported that one of their warriors had been shot through the knee-joint in this affair, but was carried off before the troops could seize him. July 29, 1885, two of the hostile Chiricahua bucks were ambushed and killed in the Hoya Mountains, Sonora, by the detachment of Apache scouts with Major Wirt Davis's com- mand. August 7, 1885, five of the hostile Chiricahuas were killed (three bucks, one squaw, and one boy fifteen years old) by the Apache scouts of Wirt Davis's command, who likewise cap- tured fifteen women and children in the same engagement (north- east of the little town of Nacori, Sonora, Mexico). On the 22d of September, 1885, the same scouts killed another Chiricahua in the mountains near Bavispe.

An ex-army-officer, writing on this subject of scouting in the southwestern country, to the *Republican*, of St. Louis, Mo., ex- pressed his opinion in these words :

"It is laid down in our army tactics (Upton's ' Cavalry Tactics,' p. 477), that twenty-five miles a day is the maximum that cavalry can stand. Bear this in mind, and also that here is an enemy with a thousand miles of hilly and sandy country to run over, and each brave provided with from three to five ponies trained like dogs. They carry almost nothing but arms and ammuni- tion ; they can live on the cactus ; they can go more than forty-eight hours without water ; they know every water-hole and every foot of ground in this vast extent of country ; they have incredible powers of endurance ; they run in small bands, scattering at the first indications of pursuit. What can the United States soldier, mounted on his heavy American horse, with the necessary forage, rations, and camp equipage, do as against this supple, untiring foe ? Nothing, absolutely nothing. It is no exaggeration to say that these fiends can travel, week in and week out, at the rate of seventy miles a day, and this over the most barren and desolate country imaginable. One week of such work will kill the average soldier and his horse; the Apache thrives on it. The frontiersman, as he now exists, is simply a fraud as an Indian-fighter. He may be good for a dash, but he lacks endurance. General Crook has pursued the only possible method of solving this problem. He has, to the extent of his forces, guarded all available passes with regulars, and he has sent Indian scouts on the trail after Indians. He has fought the devil with fire. Never in the history of this country has there been more gallant, more uncomplaining, and more efficient service than that done by our little army in the attempt to suppress this Geronimo outbreak." . . .

In the month of November additional scouts were enlisted to take the place of those whose term of six months was about to expire. It was a great time at San Carlos, and the "medicine men" were in all their glory; of course, it would never do for the scouts to start out without the customary war dance, but besides that the "medicine men" held one of their "spirit" dances to consult with the powers of the other world and learn what success was to be expected. I have several times had the good luck to be present at these "spirit dances," as well as to be with the "medicine men" while they were delivering their predictions received from the spirits, but on the present occasion there was an unusual vehemence in the singing, and an unusual vim and energy in the dancing, which would betray the interest felt in the outcome of the necromancy. A war dance, attended by more than two hundred men and women, was in full swing close to the agency buildings in the changing lights and shadows of a great fire. This enabled the "medicine men" to secure all the more privacy for their own peculiar work, of which I was an absorbed spectator. There were about an even hundred of warriors and young boys not yet full grown, who stood in a circle surrounding a huge bonfire, kept constantly replenished with fresh fagots by assiduous attendants. At one point of the circumference were planted four bunches of green willow branches, square to the cardinal points. Seated within this sacred grove, as I may venture to call it, as it represented about all the trees they could get at the San Carlos, were the members of an orchestra, the leader of which with a small curved stick beat upon the drum improvised out of an iron camp-kettle, covered with soaped

calico, and partially filled with water. The beat of this rounded
stick was a peculiar rubbing thump, the blows being sliding.
Near this principal drummer was planted a sprig of cedar. The
other musicians beat with long switches upon a thin raw-hide,
lying on the ground, just as the Sioux did at their sun dance.
There were no women present at this time. I did see three old
hags on the ground, watching the whole proceedings with curious
eyes, but they kept at a respectful distance, and were Apache-
Yumas and not Apaches.

The orchestra thumped and drummed furiously, and the leader
began to intone, in a gradually increasing loudness of voice and
with much vehemence, a "medicine" song, of which I could
distinguish enough to satisfy me that part of it was words,
which at times seemed to rudely rhyme, and the rest of it the
gibberish of "medicine" incantation which I had heard so often
while on the Sierra Madre campaign in 1883. The chorus
seconded this song with all their powers, and whenever the
refrain was chanted sang their parts with violent gesticulations.
Three dancers, in full disguise, jumped into the centre of the
great circle, running around the fire, shrieking and muttering,
encouraged by the shouts and singing of the on-lookers, and by
the drumming and incantation of the chorus which now swelled
forth at full lung-power. Each of these dancers was beautifully
decorated ; they were naked to the waist, wore kilts of fringed
buckskin, bound on with sashes, and moccasins reaching to the
knees. Their identity was concealed by head-dresses, part of
which was a mask of buckskin, which enveloped the head as well
as the face, and was secured around the neck by a "draw-string"
to prevent its slipping out of place. Above this extended to a
height of two feet a framework of slats of the amole stalk,
each differing slightly from that of the others, but giving to the
wearer an imposing, although somewhat grotesque appearance.
Each "medicine man's" back, arms, and shoulders were painted
with emblems of the lightning, arrow, snake, or other powers
appealed to by the Apaches. I succeeded in obtaining drawings
of all these, and also secured one of these head-dresses of the
"Cha-ja-la," as they are called, but a more detailed description
does not seem to be called for just now. Each of the dancers
was provided with two long wands or sticks, one in each hand,
with which they would point in every direction, principally

towards the cardinal points. When they danced, they jumped, pranced, pirouetted, and at last circled rapidly, revolving much as the dervishes are described as doing. This must have been hard work, because their bodies were soon moist with perspiration, which made them look as if they had been coated with oil.

"Klashidn," the young man who had led me down, said that the orchestra was now singing to the trees which had been planted in the ground, and I then saw that a fourth "medicine man," who acted with the air of one in authority, had taken his station within. When the dancers had become thoroughly exhausted, they would dart out of the ring and disappear in the gloom to consult with the spirits; three several times they appeared and disappeared, at each return dancing, running, and whirling about with increased energy. Having attained the degree of mental or spiritual exaltation necessary for satisfactory communion with the denizens of the other world, they remained absent for at least half an hour, the orchestra rendering a monotonous refrain, mournful as a funeral dirge. At last a thrill of expectancy ran through the throng, and I saw that they were looking anxiously for the incoming of the "medicine men." When they arrived all the orchestra stood up, their leader slightly in advance, holding a bunch of cedar in his left hand. The "medicine men" advanced in single file, the leader bending low his head, and placing both his arms about the neck of the chief in such a manner that his wands crossed, he murmured some words in his ear which seemed to be of pleasing import. Each of the others did the same thing to the chief, who took his stand first on the east, then on the south, then on the west, and lastly on the north of the little grove through which the three pranced, muttering a jumble of sounds which I cannot reproduce, but which sounded for all the world like the chant of the "Hooter" of the Zunis at their Feast of Fire. This terminated the great "medicine" ceremony of the night, and the glad shouts of the Apaches testified that the incantations of their spiritual advisers or their necromancy, whichever it was, promised a successful campaign.

Captain Crawford, whose services, both in pursuit of hostile Apaches and in efforts to benefit and civilize those who had submitted, had won for him the respect and esteem of every manly man in the army or out of it who had the honor of knowing him, met his death at or near Nacori, Sonora, Mexico, January 11, 1886, under peculiarly sad and distressing circumstances. These are narrated by General Crook in the orders announcing Crawford's death, of which the following is an extract :

"Captain Crawford, with the zeal and gallantry which had always distinguished him, volunteered for the arduous and thankless task of pursuing the renegade Chiricahua Apaches to their stronghold in the Sierra Madre, Mexico, and was assigned to the command of one of the most important of the expeditions organized for this purpose. In the face of the most discouraging obstacles, he had bravely and patiently followed in the track of the renegades, being constantly in the field from the date of the outbreak in May last to the day of his death.

"After a march of eighteen hours without halt in the roughest conceivable country, he had succeeded in discovering and surprising their rancheria in the lofty ranges near the Jarras River, Sonora. Everything belonging to the enemy fell into our hands, and the Chiricahuas, during the fight, sent in a squaw to beg for peace. All arrangements had been made for a conference next morning. Unfortunately, a body of Mexican irregular troops attacked Captain Crawford's camp at daybreak, and it was while endeavoring to save the lives of others that Crawford fell.

"His loss is irreparable. It is unnecessary to explain the important nature of the services performed by this distinguished soldier. His name has been prominently identified with most of the severest campaigns, and with many of the severest engagements with hostile Indians, since the close of the War of the Rebellion, in which also, as a mere youth, he bore a gallant part."

The irregular troops of the Mexicans were Tarahumari Indians, almost as wild as the Apaches themselves, knowing as little of morality and etiquette, the mortal enemies of the Apaches for two hundred years. While it is probable that their statement may be true, and that the killing of Crawford was unpremeditated, the indignities afterwards heaped upon Lieutenant Maus, who succeeded Crawford in command, and who went over to visit the Mexican commander, did not manifest a very friendly spirit. The Government of Mexico was in as desperate straits as our own in regard to the subjugation of the Chiricahua Apaches, which could never have been effected without the employment of just such wild forces as the Tarahumaris, who alone would stand up and fight with the fierce Chiricahuas, or could trail them through the mountains.

"Geronimo" sent word that he would come in and surrender at a spot he would designate. This was the "Cañon de los Embudos," in the northeast corner of Sonora, on the Arizona line. From Fort Bowie, Arizona, to the "Contrabandista" (Smuggler) Springs, in Sonora, is eighty-four miles, following roads and trails ; the lofty mountain ranges are very much broken, and the country is decidedly rough except along the road. There are a number of excellent ranchos—that of the Chiricahua Cattle Company, twenty-five miles out from Bowie ; that of the same company on Whitewood Creek, where we saw droves of fat beeves lazily browsing under the shady foliage of oak trees ; and Joyce's, or Frank Leslie's, where we found Lieutenant Taylor and a small detachment of Indian scouts.

The next morning at an early hour we started and drove first to the camp of Captain Allan Smith, Fourth Cavalry, with whom were Lieutenant Erwin and Surgeon Fisher. Captain Smith was living in an adobe hut, upon whose fireplace he had drawn and painted, with no unskilled hand, pictures, grave and comic, which imparted an air of civilization to his otherwise uncouth surrounding. Mr. Thomas Moore had preceded General Crook with a pack-train, and with him were "Alchise," "Ka-e-tenna," a couple of old Chiricahua squaws sent down with all the latest gossip from the women prisoners at Bowie, Antonio Besias and Montoya (the interpreters), and Mr. Strauss, Mayor of Tucson. All these moved forward towards the "Contrabandista" Springs. At the last moment of our stay a photographer, named Fly, from Tombstone, asked permission for himself and his assistant—Mr. Chase—to follow along in the wake of the column ; and still another addition, and a very welcome one, was made in the person of José Maria, another Spanish-Apache interpreter, for whom General Crook had sent on account of his perfect familiarity with the language of the Chiricahuas.

San Bernardino Springs lie twelve miles from Silver Springs, and had been occupied by a cattleman named Slaughter, since General Crook had made his expedition into the Sierra Madre. Here I saw a dozen or more quite large mortars of granite, of aboriginal manufacture, used for mashing acorns and other edible nuts; the same kind of household implements are or were to be found in the Green Valley in the northern part of Arizona, and were also used for this same purpose. We left the wheeled conveyances and mounted mules saddled and in waiting, and rode over to the "Contrabandista," three miles across the boundary. Before going to bed that night, General Crook showed "Ka-e-

ten-na" a letter which he had received from Lorenzo Bonito, an
Apache pupil in the Carlisle School. "Ka-e-ten-na" had received
one himself, and held it out in the light of the fire, mumbling
something which the other Apaches fancied was reading, and at
which they marvelled greatly ; but not content with this proof of
travelled culture, "Ka-e-ten-na" took a piece of paper from me,
wrote upon it in carefully constructed school-boy capitals, and
then handed it back to me to read aloud. I repressed my hilarity
and read slowly and solemnly: "MY WIFE HIM NAME KOW-
TENNAYS WIFE." "ONE YEAR HAB TREE HUN-
NERD SIXY-FIBE DAY." "Ka-e-ten-na" bore himself with
the dignity and complacency of a Boston Brahmin ; the envy
of his comrades was ill-concealed and their surprise undisguised.
It wasn't in writing alone that "Ka-e-ten-na" was changed, but
in everything : he had become a white man, and was an apostle
of peace, and an imitation of the methods which had made the
whites own such a "rancheria" as San Francisco.

The next morning we struck out southeast across a country
full of little hills of drift and conglomerate, passing the cañons
of the Guadalupe and the Bonito, the former dry, the latter
flowing water. A drove of the wild hogs (peccaries or musk
hogs, called "jabali" by the Mexicans) ran across our path ;
instantly the scouts took after them at a full run, "Ka-e-ten-na"
shooting one through the head while his horse was going at full
speed, and the others securing four or five more ; they were not
eaten. Approaching the Cañon de los Embudos, our scouts sent
up a signal smoke to warn their comrades that they were coming.
The eyes of the Apaches are extremely sharp, and "Alchise,"
"Mike," "Ka-e-ten-na," and others had seen and recognized a
party of horsemen advancing towards us for a mile at least
before Strauss or I could detect anything coming out of the
hills : they were four of our people on horseback riding to meet
us. They conducted us to Maus's camp in the Cañon de los
Embudos, in a strong position, on a low mesa overlooking the
water, and with plenty of fine grass and fuel at hand. The surrounding country was volcanic, covered with boulders of basalt,
and the vegetation was the Spanish bayonet, yucca, and other
thorny plants.

The rancheria of the hostile Chiricahuas was in a lava bed,
on top of a small conical hill surrounded by steep ravines,

not five hundred yards in direct line from Maus, but having between the two positions two or three steep and rugged gulches which served as scarps and counter-scarps. The whole ravine was romantically beautiful: shading the rippling water were smooth, white-trunked, long, and slender sycamores, dark gnarly ash, rough-barked cottonwoods, pliant willows, briery buckthorn, and much of the more tropical vegetation already enumerated. After General Crook had lunched, "Geronimo" and most of the Chiricahua warriors approached our camp; not all came in at once; only a few, and these not all armed. The others were here, there, and everywhere, but all on the *qui vive*, apprehensive of treachery, and ready to meet it. Not more than half a dozen would enter camp at the same time. "Geronimo" said that he was anxious for a talk, which soon took place in the shade of large cottonwood and sycamore trees. Those present were General Crook, Dr. Davis, Mr. Moore, Mr. Strauss, Lieutenants Maus, Shipp, and Faison; Captain Roberts and his young son Charlie, a bright lad of ten; Mr. Daily and Mr. Carlisle, of the pack-trains; Mr. Fly, the photographer, and his assistant, Mr. Chase; packers Shaw and Foster; a little boy, named Howell, who had followed us over from the San Bernardino ranch, thirty miles; and "Antonio Besias," "Montoya," "Concepcion," "José Maria," "Alchise," "Ka-e-ten-na," "Mike," and others as interpreters.

I made a verbatim record of the conference, but will condense it as much as possible, there being the usual amount of repetition, compliment, and talking at cross-purposes incident to all similar meetings. "Geronimo" began a long disquisition upon the causes which induced the outbreak from Camp Apache: he blamed "Chato," "Mickey Free," and Lieutenant Britton Davis, who, he charged, were unfriendly to him; he was told by an Indian named "Nodiskay" and by the wife of "Mangas" that the white people were going to send for him, arrest and kill him; he had been praying to the Dawn (Tapida) and the Darkness, to the Sun (Chigo-na-ay) and the Sky (Yandestan), and to Assunutlije to help him and put a stop to those bad stories that people were telling about him and which they had put in the papers. (The old chief was here apparently alluding to the demand made by certain of the southwestern journals, at the time of his surrender to Crook in 1883, that he should be hanged.)

"I don't want that any more; when a man tries to do right, such stories ought not to be put in the newspapers. What is the matter that you [General Crook] don't speak to me? It would be better if you would speak to me and look with a pleasant face; it would make better feeling; I would be glad if you did. I'd be better satisfied if you would talk to me once in a while. Why don't you look at me and smile at me? I am the same man; I have the same feet, legs, and hands, and the Sun looks down on me a complete man; I wish you would look and smile at me. The Sun, the Darkness, the Winds, are all listening to what we now say. To prove to you that I am now telling you the truth, remember I sent you word that I would come from a place far away to speak to you here, and you see me now. Some have come on horseback and some on foot; if I were thinking bad or if I had done bad, I would never have come here. If it had been my fault would I have come so far to talk with you?" He then expressed his delight at seeing "Ka-e-ten-na" once more: he had lost all hope of ever having that pleasure; that was one reason why he had left Camp Apache.

GENERAL CROOK: "I have heard what you have said. It seems very strange that more than forty men should be afraid of three; but if you left the reservation for that reason, why did you kill innocent people, sneaking all over the country to do it? What did those innocent people do to you that you should kill them, steal their horses, and slip around in the rocks like coyotes? What had that to do with killing innocent people? There is not a week passes that you don't hear foolish stories in your own camp; but you are no child—you don't have to believe them. You promised me in the Sierra Madre that *that* peace should last, but you have lied about it. When a man has lied to me once, I want some better proof than his own word before I can believe him again. Your story about being afraid of arrest is all bosh; there were no orders to arrest you. You sent up some of your people to kill 'Chato' and Lieutenant Davis, and then you started the story that they had killed them, and thus you got a great many of your people to go out. Everything that you did on the reservation is known; there is no use for you to try to talk nonsense. I am no child. You must make up your minds whether you will stay out on the war-path or surrender unconditionally. If you stay out I'll keep after you and kill the last one if it takes fifty years. You are making a great fuss about seeing 'Ka-e-ten-na'; over a year ago, I asked you if you wanted me to bring 'Ka-e-ten-na' back, but you said 'no.' It's a good thing for you, 'Geronimo,' that we didn't bring 'Ka-e-ten-na' back, because 'Ka-e-ten-na' has more sense now than all the rest of the Chiricahuas put together. You told me the same sort of a story in the Sierra Madre, but you lied. What evidence have I of your sincerity? How do I know whether or not you are lying to me? Have I ever lied to you? I have said all I have to say; you had better think it over to-night and let me know in the morning."

During this conference "Geronimo" appeared nervous and agitated; perspiration, in great beads, rolled down his temples and over his hands; and he clutched from time to time at a buckskin thong which he held tightly in one hand. Mr. Fly, the photographer, saw his opportunity, and improved it fully: he took "shots" at "Geronimo" and the rest of the group, and with a "nerve" that would have reflected undying glory on a Chicago drummer, coolly asked "Geronimo" and the warriors with him to change positions, and turn their heads or faces, to improve the negative. None of them seemed to mind him in the least except "Chihuahua," who kept dodging behind a tree, but was at last caught by the dropping of the slide. Twenty-four warriors listened to the conference or loitered within ear-shot; they were loaded down with metallic ammunition, some of it reloading and some not. Every man and boy in the band wore two cartridge-belts. The youngsters had on brand-new shirts, such as are made and sold in Mexico, of German cotton, and nearly all—young or old—wore new parti-colored blankets, of same manufacture, showing that since the destruction of the village by Crawford, in January, they had refitted themselves either by plunder or purchase.

Mr. Strauss, Mr. Carlisle, "José Maria," and I were awakened at an early hour in the morning (March 26, 1886), and walked over to the rancheria of the Chiricahuas. "Geronimo" was already up and engaged in an earnest conversation with "Ka-e-ten-na" and nearly all his warriors. We moved from one "jacal" to another, all being constructed alike of the stalks of the Spanish bayonet and mescal and amole, covered with shreds of blanket, canvas, and other textiles. The "daggers" of the Spanish bayonet and mescal were arranged around each "jacal" to form an impregnable little citadel. There were not more than twelve or fifteen of these in the " rancheria," which was situated upon the apex of an extinct crater, the lava blocks being utilized as breastworks, while the deep seams in the contour of the hill were so many fosses, to be crossed only after rueful slaughter of assailants. A full brigade could not drive out that little garrison, provided its ammunition and repeating rifles held out. They were finely armed with Winchesters and Springfield breechloading carbines, with any quantity of metallic cartridges.

Physically, the Chiricahuas were in magnificent condition : every muscle was perfect in development and hard as adamant, and one of the young men in a party playing monte was as finely muscled as a Greek statue. A group of little boys were romping freely and carelessly together ; one of them seemed to be of Irish and Mexican lineage. After some persuasion he told Strauss and myself that his name was Santiago Mackin, captured at Mimbres, New Mexico ; he seemed to be kindly treated by his young companions, and thère was no interference with our talk, but he was disinclined to say much and was no doubt thoroughly scared. Beyoud showing by the intelligent glance of his eyes that he fully comprehended all that was said to him in both Spanish and English, he took no further notice of us. He was about ten years old, slim, straight, and sinewy, blue-gray eyes, badly freckled, light eyebrows and lashes, much tanned and blistered by the sun, and wore an old and once-white handkerchief on his head which covered it so tightly that the hair could not be seen. He was afterwards returned to his relations in New Mexico.

One of the Chiricahuas had a silver watch which he called "Chi-go-na-ay " (Sun), an evidence that he had a good idea of its purpose. Nearly every one wore " medicine " of some kind : either little buckskin bags of the Hoddentin of the Tule, the feathers of the red-bird or of the woodpecker, the head of a quail, the claws of a prairie dog, or silver crescents ; " medicine " cords—" Izze-kloth "—were also worn. I stopped alongside of a young Tubal Cain and watched him hammering a Mexican dollar between two stones, and when he had reduced it to the proper fineness he began to stamp and incise ornamentation upon it with a sharp-pointed knife and a stone for a hammer. Nearly all the little girls advanced to the edge of our camp and gazed in mute admiration upon Charlie Roberts, evincing their good opinion in such an unmistakable manner that the young gentleman at once became the guy of the packers. "Geronimo" and his warriors remained up in their village all day, debating the idea of an un-conditional surrender.

The next morning (March 27th) "Chihuahua" sent a secret message to General Crook, to say that he was certain all the Chiri-cahuas would soon come in and surrender ; but whether they did or not, he would surrender his own band at noon and come down into our camp. "Ka-e-ten-na" and "Alchise" had been busy at work among the hostiles, dividing their councils, exciting their hopes, and enhancing their fears ; could General Crook have promised them immunity for the past, they would have come down the previous evening, when "Chihuahua" had first sent word of his intention to give up without condition, but General Crook did not care to have "Chihuahua" leave the hostiles at once ; he thought he could be more useful by remaining in the village for a day or two as a leaven to foment distrust of "Geronimo" and start a disintegration and demoralization of the band. "Ka-e-ten-na" told General Crook that all the previous night "Geronimo" kept his warriors ready for any act of treachery on our part, and that during the talk of the 25th they were prepared to shoot the moment an attempt should be made to seize their leaders. It was scarcely noon when "Geronimo," "Chihuahua," "Nachita'," "Kutli," and one other buck came in and said they wanted to talk. "Nané" toddled after them, but he was so old and feeble that we did not count him. Our people gathered under the sycamores in the ravine, while "Geronimo" seated himself under a mulberry, both he and "Kutli" having their faces blackened with pounded galena. "Chihuahua" spoke as follows : "I am very glad to see you, General Crook, and have this talk with you. It is as you say : we are always in danger out here. I hope that from this on we may live better with our fami-lies, and not do any more harm to anybody. I am anxious to behave. I think that the Sun is looking down upon me, and the Earth is listening. I am thinking better. It seems to me that I have seen the one who makes the rain and sends the winds, or he must have sent you to this place. I surrender myself to you, because I be-lieve in you and you do not deceive us. You must be our God ; I am satisfied with all that you do. You must be the one who makes the green pastures, who sends the rain, who commands the winds. You must be the one who sends the fresh fruits that come on the trees every year. There are many men in the world who are big chiefs and command many people, but you, I think, are the greatest of them all. I want you to be a father to me and treat me as your son. I want you to have pity on me. There is no doubt that all you do is right, because all you say is true. I trust in all you say ; you do not deceive ; all the things you tell us are facts. I am now in your hands. I place myself at your disposition to dispose of as you please. I shake your hand. I want to come right into your camp with my family and stay with you. I don't want to stay away at a distance. I want to be right where you are. I have roamed these mountains from water to water. Never have I found the place where I could see my father or mother until to-day. I see you, my father. I surrender to you now, and I don't want any more bad feeling or bad talk. I am going over to stay with you in your camp.

"Whenever a man raises anything, even a dog, he thinks well of it, and tries to raise it up, and treats it well. So I want you to feel towards me, and be good to me, and don't let people say bad things about me. Now I surrender to you and go with you. When we are travelling together on the road or anywhere else, I hope you'll talk to me once in a while. I think a great deal of ' Alchise ' and ' Ka-e-ten-na ' ; they think a great deal of me. I hope some day to be all the same as their brother. [Shakes hands.] How long will it be before I can live with these friends ? "

Despatches were sent ahead to Bowie to inform General Sheridan of the conference and its results ; the Chiricahuas had considered three propositions : one, their own, that they be allowed to return to the reservation unharmed ; the second, from General Crook, that they be placed in confinement for a term of years at a distance from the Agency, and that, if their families so desired, they be permitted to accompany them, leaving "Nané," who was old and superannuated, at Camp Apache ; or, that they return to the war-path and fight it out. "Mangas," with thirteen of the Chiricahuas, six of them warriors, was not with "Geronimo," having left him some months previously and never reunited with him. He (General Crook) asked that instructions be sent him with as little delay as possible.

CHAPTER XXIX.

"ALCHISE" and "Ka-e-ten-na" came and awakened General Crook before it was yet daylight of March 28th and informed him that "Nachita," one of the Chiricahua chiefs, was so drunk he couldn't stand up and was lying prone on the ground; other Chiricahuas were also drunk, but none so drunk as "Nachita." Whiskey had been sold them by a rascal named Tribollet who lived on the San Bernardino ranch on the Mexican side of the line, about four hundred yards from the boundary. These Indians asked permission to take a squad of their soldiers and guard Tribollet and his men to keep them from selling any more of the soul-destroying stuff to the Chiricahuas. A beautiful commentary upon the civilization of the white man! When we reached Cajon Bonito, the woods and grass were on fire; four or five Chiricahua mules, already saddled, were wandering about without riders. Pretty soon we came upon "Geronimo," "Kuthli," and three other Chiricahua warriors riding on two mules, all drunk as lords. It seemed to me a great shame that armies could not carry with them an atmosphere of military law which would have justified the hanging of the wretch Tribollet as a foe to human society. Upon arriving at San Bernardino Springs, Mr. Frank Leslie informed me that he had seen this man Tribollet sell thirty dollars' worth of mescal in less than one hour—all to Chiricahuas—and upon being remonstrated with, the wretch boasted that he could have sold one hundred dollars' worth that day at ten dollars a gallon in silver. That night, during a drizzling rain, a part of the Chiricahuas—those who had been drinking Tribollet's whiskey—stole out from Maus's camp and betook themselves again to the mountains, frightened, as was afterward learned, by the lies told them by Tribollet and the men at his ranch. Two of the warriors upon sobering up returned voluntarily, and there is no doubt at all that, had General Crook not been relieved from the command of the Department of Arizona, he could have sent out runners from among their own people and brought back the last one without a shot being fired. Before being stampeded by the lies and vile whiskey of wicked men whose only mode of livelihood was from the vices, weaknesses, or perils of the human race, all the Chiricahuas—drunk or sober—were in the best of humor and were quietly herding their ponies just outside of Maus's camp.

"Chihuahua," and the eighty others who remained with Maus, reached Fort Bowie on the second day of April, 1886, under command of Lieutenant Faison, Lieutenant Maus having started in pursuit of "Geronimo," and followed him for a long distance, but unsuccessfully. As "Chihuahua" and his people were coming into Bowie, the remains of the gallant Captain Emmet Crawford were *en route* to the railroad station to be transported to Nebraska for interment. Every honor was shown them which could indicate the loving tenderness of comrades who had known Crawford in life, and could not forget his valor, nobleness, and high-minded character. General Crook, Colonel Beaumont, Lieutenant Neal, and all other officers present at the post attended in a body. Two companies of the First Infantry, commanded, respectively, by Captain Markland and Lieutenant Benjamin, formed the escort for one-half the distance—seven miles; they then turned over the casket to the care of two companies of the Eighth Infantry, commanded by Captain Savage and Lieutenant Smiley. The detachment of Apache scouts, commanded by Lieutenant Macdonald, Fourth Cavalry, was drawn up in line at the station to serve as a guard of honor; and standing in a group, with uncovered heads, were the officers and soldiers of the Eighth Infantry, Second and Fourth Cavalry, there on duty—Whitney, Porter, Surgeon R. H. White, Ames, Betts, Worth, Hubert, and many others.

Having been detailed, in company with Captain Charles Morton, Third Cavalry, to conduct the remains to the city of Kearney, Nebraska, and there see to their interment, my official relations with the Department of Arizona terminated. I will insert, from the published official correspondence of General Crook, a few extracts to throw a light upon the history of the Chiricahuas. Lieutenant Macdonald informed me, while at Bowie, that the "medicine men" present with his Indian scouts had been dancing and talking with the spirits, who had responded that "Geronimo" would surely return, as he had been stampeded while drunk, and by bad white men. Under date of March 30, 1886, General Sheridan telegraphed to Crook:

"You are confidentially informed that your telegram of March 29th is received. The President cannot assent to the surrender of the hostiles on the terms of their imprisonment East for two years, with the understanding of their return to the reservation. He instructs you to enter again into negotiations on the terms of their unconditional surrender, only sparing their lives. In the meantime, and on the receipt of this order, you are directed to take every precaution against the escape of the hostiles, which must not be allowed under any circumstances. You must make at once such disposition of your troops as will insure against further hostilities, by completing the destruction of the hostiles, unless these terms are acceded to."

General Crook's reply to the Lieutenant-General read as follows:

"There can be no doubt that the scouts were thoroughly loyal, and would have prevented the hostiles leaving had it been possible. When they left their camp with our scouts, they scattered over the country so as to make surprise impossible, and they selected their camp with this in view, nor would they all remain in camp at one time. They kept more or less full of mescal. To enable you to clearly understand the situation, it should be remembered that the hostiles had an agreement with Lieutenant Maus that they were to be met by me twenty-five miles below the line, and that no regular troops were to be present. While I was very averse to such an arrangement, I had to abide by it as it had already been entered into. We found them in a camp on a rocky hill about five hundred yards from Lieutenant Maus, in such a position that a thousand men could not have surrounded them with any possibility of capturing them. They were able, upon the approach of any enemy being signalled, to scatter and escape through dozens of ravines and cañons which would shelter them from pursuit until they reached the higher ranges in the vicinity. They were armed to the teeth, having the most improved arms and all the ammunition they could carry. Lieutenant Maus with Apache scouts was camped at the nearest point the hostiles would agree to his approaching. Even had I been disposed to betray the confidence they placed in me it would have been simply an impossibility to get white troops to that point either by day or by night without their knowledge, and had I attempted to do this the whole band would have stampeded back to the mountains. So suspicious were they that never more than from five to eight of the men came into our camp at one time, and to have attempted the arrest of those would have stampeded the others to the mountains."

General Crook also telegraphed that "to inform the Indians that the terms on which they surrendered are disapproved would, in my judgment, not only make it impossible for me to negotiate with them, but result in their scattering to the mountains, and I can't at present see any way to prevent it."

Sheridan replied :

"I do not see what you can now do except to concentrate your troops at the best points and give protection to the people. Geronimo will undoubtedly enter upon other raids of murder and robbery, and as the offensive campaign against him with scouts has failed, would it not be best to take up the defensive, and give protection to the business interests of Arizona and New Mexico ?"

Crook's next despatch to Sheridan said :

"It has been my aim throughout present operations to afford the greatest amount of protection to life and property interests, and troops have been stationed accordingly. Troops cannot protect property beyond a radius of one half mile from camp. If offensive operations against the Indians are not resumed, they may remain quietly in the mountains for an indefinite time without crossing the line, and yet their very presence there will be a constant menace, and require the troops in this department to be at all times in position to repel sudden raids ; and so long as any remain out they will form a nucleus for disaffected Indians from the different agencies in Arizona and New Mexico to join. That the operations of the scouts in Mexico have not proved so successful as was hoped is due to the enormous difficulties they have been compelled to encounter, from the nature of the Indians they have been hunting, and the character of the country in which they have operated, and of which persons not thoroughly conversant with the character of both can have no conception. I believe that the plan upon which I have conducted operations is the one most likely to prove successful in the end. It may be, however, that I am too much wedded to my own views in this matter, and as I have spent nearly eight years of the hardest work of my life in this department, I respectfully request that I may now be relieved from its command."

General Crook had carefully considered the telegrams from his superiors in Washington, and was unable to see how he could allow Indians, or anybody else, to enter his camp under assurances of personal safety, and at the same time "take every precaution against escape." Unless he treacherously murdered them in cold blood, he was unable to see a way out of the dilemma; and Crook was not the man to lie to any one or deal treacherously by him. If there was one point in his character which shone more resplendent than any other, it was his absolute integrity in his dealings with representatives of inferior races: he was not content with telling the truth, he was careful to see that the interpretation had been so made that the Indians understood every word and grasped every idea; and all his remarks were put down in black and white, which, to quote his own words, "would not lie, and would last long after the conferees had been dead and buried."

The whole subject of the concluding hours of the campaign against the Chiricahuas, after Crook had been relieved from command, has been fully covered by documents accessible to all students, among which may well be mentioned: Senate Documents, No. 117; General Crook's "Resumé of Operations against Apache Indians from 1882 to 1886"; the report made by Mr. Herbert Welsh, Secretary of the Indian Rights Association, of his visit to the Apache prisoners confined at Fort Marion, St. Augustine, Florida; the reports made to General Sheridan by General R. B. Ayres, commanding the military post of St. Francis Barracks (St. Augustine, Florida); the telegrams between the War Department and Brigadier-General D. S. Stanley, commanding the Department of Texas, concerning his interview with "Geronimo" and other prisoners, etc.

It may be laid down in one paragraph that the Chiricahua fugitives were followed into the Sierra Madre by two Chiricahua Apaches, sent from Fort Apache, named "Ki-e-ta" and "Martinez," who were assisted by Lieutenant Gatewood, of the Sixth Cavalry, and Mr. George Wrattan, as interpreter. Not all the band surrendered; there are several still in the Sierra Madre who, as late as the past month of January (1891), have been killing in both Sonora and Arizona. But those that did listen to the emissaries were led to believe that they were to see their wives and families within five days; they were instead hurried off to Florida and immured in the dungeons of old Fort Pickens, Pensacola, Florida, and never saw their families until the indignant remonstrances of Mr. Herbert Welsh caused an investigation to be made of the exact terms upon which they had surrendered, and to have their wives sent to join them. For "Geronimo" and those with him any punishment that could be inflicted without incurring the imputation of treachery would not be too severe ; but the incarceration of "Chato" and the three-fourths of the band who had remained faithful for three years and had rendered such signal service in the pursuit of the renegades, can never meet with the approval of honorable soldiers and gentlemen.

Not a single Chiricahua had been killed, captured, or wounded throughout the entire campaign—with two exceptions—unless by Chiricahua-Apache scouts who, like "Chato," had kept the pledges given to General Crook in the Sierra Madre in 1883. The exceptions were: one killed by the White Mountain Apaches near Fort Apache, and one killed by a white man in northern Mexico. Yet every one of those faithful scouts—especially the two, "Kieta" and "Martinez," who had at imminent personal peril gone into the Sierra Madre to hunt up "Geronimo" and induce him to surrender—were transplanted to Florida and there subjected to the same punishment as had been meted out to "Geronimo." And with them were sent men like "Goth-kli" and "Toklanni," who were not Chiricahuas at all, but had only lately married wives of that band, who had never been on the war-path in any capacity except as soldiers of the Government, and had devoted years to its service. There is no more disgraceful page in the history of our relations with the American Indians than that which conceals the treachery visited upon the Chiricahuas who remained faithful in their allegiance to our people. An examination of the documents cited will show that I have used extremely mild language in alluding to this affair.

CHAPTER XXX.

THE last years of General Crook's eventful career were spent
in Omaha, Nebraska, as Commanding General of the Department of the Platte, and, after being promoted to the rank of
Major-General by President Cleveland, in Chicago, Illinois, as
Commanding General of the Military Division of the Missouri.
During that time he averted the hostilities with the Utes of Colorado, for which the cowboys of the western section of that State
were clamoring, and satisfied the Indians that our people were
not all unjust, rapacious, and mendacious. As a member of the
Sioux Commission to negotiate for the cession of lands occupied
by the Sioux in excess of their actual needs, he—in conjunction
with his associates : ex-Governor Charles Foster, of Ohio, and
Hon. William Warner, of Missouri—effected the relinquishment
of eleven millions of acres, an area equal to one-third of the
State of Pennsylvania.

The failure of Congress to ratify some of the provisions of this
conference and to make the appropriations needed to carry them
into effect, has been alleged among the numerous causes of the
recent Sioux outbreak. In this connection the words of the
Sioux chief " Red Cloud," as spoken to the Catholic missionary
—Father Craft—are worthy of remembrance : "Then General
Crook came ; he, at least, had never lied to us. His words gave
the people hope. He died. Their hope died again. Despair
came again." General Crook also exerted all the influence he
could bring to bear to induce a rectification of the wrong inflicted

upon the faithful Chiricahua Apaches, in confounding them in
the same punishment meted out to those who had followed
" Geronimo " back to the war-path. He manifested all through
his life the liveliest interest in the preservation of the larger
game of the Rocky Mountain country, and, if I mistake not, had
some instrumentality, through his old friend Judge Carey, of
Cheyenne, now United States Senator, in bringing about the
game laws adopted by the present State of Wyoming.

General Crook's death occurred at the Grand Pacific Hotel, his
residence in Chicago, on the 21st of March, 1890 ; the cause of
his death, according to Surgeon McClellan, his attending physician, was heart failure or some other form of heart disease ; the
real cause was the wear and tear of a naturally powerful constitution, brought on by the severe mental and physical strain of
incessant work under the most trying circumstances.

It would be unjust to select for insertion here any of the
thousands of telegrams, letters, resolutions of condolence, and
other expressions of profound sympathy received by Mrs. Crook
from old comrades and friends of her illustrious husband in all
sections of our country : besides the official tribute from the
War Department, there were eloquent manifestations from such
associations as the Alumni of the Military Academy, the Military
Order of the Loyal Legion, the Sons of the American Revolution,
the Pioneers of Arizona, the citizens of Omaha, Nebraska, Prescott, Arizona, Chicago, Illinois, Dayton, Ohio, and other places
in which he had served during the thirty-eight years of his connection with the regular army, and feeling expressions uttered in
the United States Senate by Manderson and Paddock of Nebraska,
Gorman of Maryland, and Mitchell of Oregon ; and a kind tribute
from the lips of Governor James E. Boyd of Nebraska. When
the news of Crook's death reached the Apache Reservation, the
members of the tribe who had been his scouts during so many
years were stupefied : those near Camp Apache sat down in a
great circle, let down their hair, bent their heads forward on
their bosoms, and wept and wailed like children. Probably no
city in the country could better appreciate the importance of
Crook's military work against the savages than Omaha, which
through the suppression of hostilities by General Crook had
bounded from the dimensions of a straggling town to those of a
metropolis of 150,000 people. The resolutions adopted in con-

vention represent the opinions of a committee composed of the oldest citizens of that community—men who knew and respected Crook in life and revered him in death.   Among these were to be seen the names of old settlers of the stamp of the Wakeleys, Paxtons, Pritchetts, Doanes, Millers, Cowins, Clarkes, Markels, Wymans, Horbachs, Hanscoms, Collins, Lakes, Millards, Popple-tons, Caldwells, Broatches, Mauls, Murphys, Rustins, Woods, Davis, Laceys, Turners, Ogdens, Moores, Cushings, Kitchens, Kimballs, Yates, Wallaces, Richardsons, McShanes, and Kountzes —men perfectly familiar with all the intricacies of the problem which Crook had to solve and the masterly manner in which he had solved it.

As a mark of respect to the memory of his former friend and commander, General John R. Brooke, commanding the Depart-ment of the Platte, has protected and fed in honorable retire-ment the aged mule, "Apache," which for so many years had borne General Crook in all his campaigns, from British America to Mexico.

Could old "Apache" but talk or write, he might relate ad-ventures and perils to which the happy and prosperous dwell-ers in the now peaceful Great West would listen with joy and delight.

General Crook had not yet attained great age, being scarcely sixty-one years old when the final summons came, but he had gained more than a complement of laurels, and may therefore be said to have died in the fulness of years.   He was born at Dayton, Ohio, on the 23d day of September, 1829; graduated from the United States Military Academy in the class of 1852; was immediately assigned to the Fourth Infantry; was engaged with-out cessation in service against hostile Indians, in the present States of Oregon and Washington, until the outbreak of the Rebellion, and was once wounded by an arrow which was never extracted.   His first assignment during the War of the Rebellion was to the colonelcy of the Thirty-sixth Ohio, which he drilled to such a condition of efficiency that the other regiments in the same division nick named it the "Thirty-sixth Regulars."   Be-fore the war ended he had risen to the rank of brigadier and of major-general of volunteers, and was wounded in the battle of Lewisburgh, West Virginia.

He commanded the Army of West Virginia, and later on was

assigned to the command of cavalry under Lieutenant-General P. H. Sheridan. His services during the war were of the most gallant and important nature, not at all inferior to his campaigns against the western tribes, but it was of the latter only that this treatise was intended to speak and to these it has been restricted.

The funeral services were held at the Grand Pacific Hotel, where the remains had lain in state. The Rev. Dr. MacPherson conducted the services, assisted by Doctors Clinton Locke, Fallows, Thomas, and Swing. The honorary pall-bearers were Colonel James F. Wade, Fifth Cavalry, Colonel Thaddeus H. Stanton, Pay Department, John Collins, Omaha, General W. Sooy Smith, Potter Palmer, ex-President R. B. Hayes, Marshall Field, W. C. De Grannis, Wirt Dexter, Colonel J. B. Sexton, Judge R. S. Tuthill, Mayor D. C. Cregier, John B. Drake, General M. R. Morgan, General Robert Williams, P. E. Studebaker, J. Frank Lawrence, George Dunlap, Judge W. Q. Gresham, John B. Carson, General W. E. Strong, John M. Clark, W. Penn Nixon, H. J. MacFarland, and C. D. Roys. The casket was escorted to the Baltimore & Ohio Railroad Depot by a brigade of the Illinois National Guard, commanded by Brigadier-General Fitzsimmons and by the members of the Illinois Club in a body.

The interment, which took place at Oakland, Maryland, March 24, 1891, was at first intended to be strictly private, but thousands of people had gathered from the surrounding country, and each train added to the throng which blocked the streets and lanes of the little town.

Among those who stood about the bereaved wife, who had so devotedly followed the fortunes of her illustrious husband, were her sister, Mrs. Reed, Colonel Corbin, Colonel Heyl, Colonel Stanton, Major Randall, Major Roberts, Lieutenant Kennon, Mr. John S. Collins, Mr. and Mrs. W. J. Hancock, Mr. Webb C. Hayes, Andrew Peisen, who had been the General's faithful servant for a quarter of a century, and Dr. E. H. Bartlett, who had been present at the wedding of General and Mrs. Crook.

One of the General's brothers—Walter Crook, of Dayton, Ohio —came on with the funeral train from Chicago, but another brother was unable to leave Chicago on account of a sudden fit of illness.

Three of the soldiers of the Confederacy who had formed part of the detachment—of which Mrs. Crook's own brother, James Daily, was another—that had captured General Crook during the closing years of the Civil War and sent him down to Libby prison, requested permission to attend the funeral services as a mark of respect for their late foe. While the Rev. Dr. Moffatt was reciting prayer, two of them whispered their names, May and Johnson, but the third I could not learn at the moment. I have since heard it was Ira Mason.

Among those who attended from Washington were General Samuel Breck, Captain George S. Anderson, Captain Schofield, Hon. George W. Dorsey, M. C. from Nebraska, Hon. Nathan Goff, ex-Secretary of the Navy, and Hon. William McKinley, M. C. from Ohio, who during the Civil War had served as one of General Crook's confidential staff officers, and who through life had been his earnest admirer and stanch friend.

As the earth closed over the remains of a man whom I had known and loved for many years, and of whose distinguished services I had intimate personal knowledge, the thought flitted through my mind that there lay an exemplification of the restless energy·of the American people. Ohio had given him birth, the banks of the Hudson had heard his recitations as a cadet, Oregon, Washington, California, and Nevada witnessed his first feats of arms, West Virginia welcomed him as the intelligent and energetic leader of the army which bore her name, and Idaho, Arizona, New Mexico, Montana, both Dakotas, Nebraska, Wyoming, Colorado, and Utah owed him a debt of gratitude for his operations against the hostile tribes which infested their borders and rendered life and property insecure.

No man could attempt to write a fair description of General Crook's great services and his noble traits of character unless he set out to prepare a sketch of the history of the progress of civilization west of the Missouri. I have here done nothing but lay before the reader an outline, and a very meagre outline, of all he had to oppose, and all he achieved, feeling a natural distrust of my own powers, and yet knowing of no one whose association with my great chief had been so intimate during so many years as mine had been.

Crook's modesty was so great, and his aversion to pomp and

circumstance so painfully prominent a feature of his character and disposition, that much which has been here related would never be known from other sources.

Shakespeare's lines have been present in my mind :

> " Men's evil manners live in brass ; their virtues
> We write in water."

On the 11th of November, 1890, General Crook's body was transferred to Arlington Cemetery, Virginia, opposite Washington, those present being Major-General Schofield, commanding the army, and his aide, Lieutenant Andrews, Colonel H. C. Corbin, Lieutenant Kennon, Colonel T. H. Stanton, Captain John G. Bourke, Mr. Webb C. Hayes, and Mr. George H. Harries.

The escort consisted of two companies of cavalry, commanded by Major Carpenter, Captain George S. Anderson, Captain Parker, and Lieutenant Baird.